THE ACKERMAN C

CHAMPAGNE
Charles Heidsieck
Reims France

Champagne!

The very word is redolent of elegance and excitement, of sophistication and grandeur. It conjures up pictures of triumph and victory, a job well done. Champagne is synonymous with romantic love and, above all, happiness. Champagne, as Madame de Pompadour said, "is the only wine that leaves a woman beautiful after drinking it!"

To close your eyes and think of champagne, is to hear the gentle pop of the cork and then to see fine bubbles shooting upwards in the glass through pale, gold liquid. Sparkling, clear as crystal. Then the first sip. The tingling of the taste buds, the involuntary smile as the magic begins to work. Perchance to dream! However rich the imagination, it cannot touch the reality of savouring any of the four wonderful styles of champagne made by Charles Heidsieck today – Brut Réserve, Brut Vintage, Rosé Vintage and Blanc des Millénaires.

The present house of Champagne Charles Heidsieck owes much to one of its more colourful owners, Charles Camille Heidsieck (1822-1893). Charles Camille was charming as he was bold, reckless as he was entrepreneurial. He was also blessed with more than his share of good luck. His father Charles-Henri travelled all over Russia, even as far as the Volga, selling his champagnes. But when Charles Camille inherited the business, he recognised the potential of both the British and American markets. To this end, he made a number of trips across the Atlantic in the 1850's where the Americans lionized him and his fine champagne. His exploits and debonair manner possibly inspired George Leybourne to write and sing his famous Victorian music hall song, 'Champagne Charlie'. The Americans took as much champagne as Charles Heidsieck could supply – he sold 75,000 bottles a year in New Orleans alone – and the success of his champagne house was assured.

At the outbreak of the American Civil War, Charles Camille's spell of good fortune ran out. In 1862, he travelled to America to protect his stocks and his markets only to be caught up in the war. Working his passage as a barman on a paddle steamer from Alabama to New Orleans, he carried a letter from the French Consul offering French government assistance to clothe the Confederate army. By the time he reached New Orleans, the town had fallen to the Yankees and Charles Camille was arrested as a spy when the letter was discovered in his baggage. It took four months to extricate him from Fort Jackson prison.

Bad luck dogged him further. Charles Camille invested monies from sales of his wine in two ships laden with cheap cotton. On their way to France, they were taken by the navy of the North and destroyed. On top of that, his agent, David Bayaud, went bankrupt, owing him a fortune. Charles Camille returned home to France and near ruin. But luck had not deserted him for long. Thomas Bayaud (David's brother) had prospered in property speculation in Denver. He had always admired the dash and brio of Charles Camille, and mindful of his brother's debts, made him his sole heir.

But the success of the Champagne Charles Heidsieck marque could not be sustained purely on Charles Camille's charm and salesmanship. He made fine champagne; he was innovative and foresighted. He could see that he had to keep improving his wine stocks, and to keep back a portion of the better vintages to guarantee quality in the future. With the catastrophic dangers of hand-blown bottles exploding (the cellarmen all had to work in iron masks), he brought in factory-made bottles with a greater tolerance.

Today, one hundred years later, the legacy of Charles Camille Heidsieck where an individual is responsible for the 'grande marque', has been inherited by their cellarmaster, Daniel Thibault. The new owners of Champagne Charles Heidsieck, the Rémy-Cointreau group, simply told him to 'make the blend you always wanted to make' for their new Brut Réserve.

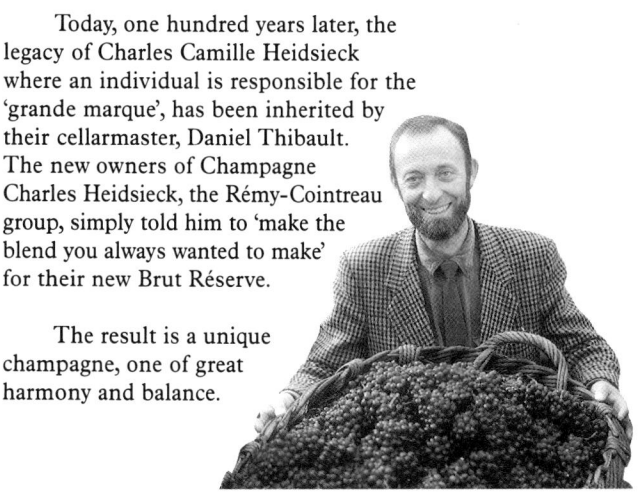

The result is a unique champagne, one of great harmony and balance.

To achieve this, Daniel Thibault draws on at least 105 differing 'crus' of Chardonnay (25 per cent), and equal Pinot Noir and Pinot Meunier. The grapes are harvested, always by hand, at least 100 days after flowering and pressed with the greatest care. At Charles Heidsieck, unlike many other champagne houses and – some would say – against commercial wisdom, only the 'cuvée', or first pressing, is used to ensure the outstanding quality of the champagne. The final 'assemblage' is drawn from over 300 elements including a large percentage of mature, reserve wines. To guarantee the consistent quality of Brut Réserve, these reserve stocks of outstanding vintage wines are being built up and aged longer.

After the blending, the actual 'champagne process' begins. A little sugar and yeast is added to the wine which is placed 'sur lattes', wooden slats used to separate the bottles during fermentation. The wine is stored in chalk caves and left, in the case of Brut Réserve, to age for more than three years. Then comes the 'remuage', still performed by hand, where each bottle is gently rotated over several weeks so that the deposit of yeast comes to the neck.

The bottle is then opened, the 'offending' yeast removed, and then topped up with a little more sugar and mature wine. A characteristic of Charles Heidsieck is to leave the champagne for at least six months to recover fully before it can be labelled and sold.

Champagne Charles Heidsieck is indeed fortunate to have such exceptional cellars. They were originally dug out as chalk mines by the Romans. Two thousand years later, legend has it that a ploughman discovered them when the ground gave way and he fell in. It was to his great cost – the caves are 30 metres deep. It is the longer ageing in these cellars, where the temperature remains a constant 9.2 degrees centigrade, that produces the fine, persistent bubbles so characteristic of the Brut Réserve. To the eye, it is pale gold in colour; on the nose, it is the delicate floral aroma of the Chardonnay that comes through; on closer contact, it is the ripe, fruity overtones of the Pinot Noir. The lasting impression is one of vanilla. The wine evenly coats the palate, leaving a full, rounded impression. There is a bounteous feeling of beautifully ripe fruit, where the flavour seems to linger forever.

Daniel Thibault's culinary comment on the champagne he has created is that it is the perfect accompaniment with all types of cuisine but "ideal with regional and home cooking, especially traditional recipes and meat casseroles such as navarin d'agneau".

In the Champagne region, a vintage year is declared only when the wines of that year are judged by the expert cellarmaster to be of truly exceptional quality.

The current vintage year is 1985. That year, the vines suffered from a series of hard frosts which considerably reduced the yield. However, the sun and fine weather in September enhanced the grapes so what was lost in quantity was rewarded by quality. The blend is 70 per cent Pinot Noir, 30 per cent Chardonnay with just a hint of Pinot Meunier. Champagne Charles Heidsieck Brut Vintage 1985 has been described as "a delicate and well-balanced vintage, that will keep well owing to its complex variety of aromas". This wine has a rich blend of aromas. The nose begins floral with a touch of hawthorn, that becomes fruitier with a discreet, but resolute, hint of ripe citrus. On the palate, it is intriguing. Distinctive from the outset, persistent and complex, it develops into ripe citrus fruits before maturing into fresh figs, candied quince and vanilla. This extraordinary variety of elaborate aromas of rare fruit sets the character of the vintage.

On the complementary cuisine to serve with the Brut Vintage 1985, Daniel Thibault believes it "enhances haute cuisine over an intimate dinner. Its strength of flavour complements sauce-based dishes and regional cheeses".

It has to be a very special year for the Pinot Noir grape for Champagne Charles Heidsieck to produce a Rosé Vintage and 1985 was such a year. Between 10 per cent and 15 per cent red wine from the Champagne region has been added to the blend to make the Rosé Vintage. The result is an exceptional and unique young wine, offering a velvety fresh sensation. To the eye, this lovely wine is reminiscent of wild rose petals. Lightly coloured, the wine sparkles, and is teeming with tiny bubbles. To the nose, it offers a marvellously refined bouquet with a subtle touch of ripened fruit and spices, vanilla and cinnamon. This evolves to the scent of currants and quince jelly, that, with a woody aroma, produces such an evocative bouquet. At first impression, the 1985 vintage is a young, yet an incredibly smooth wine. The red wine content produces the fruity flavours, which, when combined with the delicate, flowery taste of wisteria, produces a velvety yet fresh sensation. Such a taste strongly suggests that this wine would benefit from being allowed to mature.

The Rosé Vintage "accompanies grilled meats", says Daniel Thibault, "but especially complements cream-based desserts, pastries and seasonal fruit gratin and coulis".

Another fine wine to be produced by Champagne Charles Heidsieck only in exceptional years is their Blanc des Millénaires. This wine is made entirely from the white Champagne vine, the Chardonnay grape. Only the fruit from the best vineyards of the Côte des Blancs (Oger, Mesnil, Vertus, Cramant and Avise) was used in the 1983 vintage, the most recent year in which it was made. An additional feature of this exceptional Blanc de Blancs is that it has been aged longer in the cellars. It is appropriate that this fine wine should be called 'Blanc des Millénaires' having spent so long in the Gallo-Roman chalk cellars which are themselves double 'millénaires', ie. 2000 years old.

In the glass, the Blanc des Millénaires is pale golden in colour with intriguing green glints and an abundance of fine bubbles. On the nose, it has a spring freshness about it, one of undergrowth, violets and dewy moss, that precedes a nutty fragrance. This is followed by a stronger, toasted aroma, the essences of gingerbread, honey and even quince jelly. On the palate, it is fresh, smooth and velvety, with an initial hint of the vine itself. That is then enhanced by a more woody sensation, with the flavours of peel, almonds and chestnuts, and rounded off by more mature tastes of autumn fruits and of candied citrus peel.

Champagne Charles Heidsieck Blanc des Millénaires is a truly sophisticated wine - elegant and subtle. It is easily recognised as a great wine by amateur and connoisseur alike. Like the expansive qualities of this wine, so, according to Daniel Thibault, is the complementary cuisine. It should be "enjoyed with fresh truffles or foie gras - the wine also brings out the delicate flavours of fish and succulent white meats".

Champagne Charles Heidsieck has always been a 'grande marque' with a high reputation for making a wine that is unique and totally consistent. Their champagne has inspired loyalty for decades. When Chancellor Bismark dined with Kaiser Wilhelm II at Potsdam, the Kaiser served Sekt, a German sparkling wine. Bismark tasted it, winced and put down his glass. Pressed by the Kaiser, Bismark admitted that he could not drink it. When the Kaiser explained that he had served Sekt, rather than the Chancellor's beloved Champagne Charles Heidsieck, as a patriotic gesture, Bismark replied simply, "Your Majesty, I am extremely sorry, my patriotism stops short of my stomach!" Champagne Charles Heidsieck still enjoys the accolades of the discerning who recognise fine wines.

Today, Charles Heidsieck is one of the most important of the champagne houses, and its limited production ensures that its stringent ethics of quality are enviably fulfilled. Its cellars are opulent, holding almost four years' sales of reserve wines. They are only content to guarantee the best quality. That way, they can assure that every bottle they produce is nothing less than an experience of pure joy. To open any of these exceptional wines from Champagne Charles Heidsieck is a celebration in itself!

Charles Heidsieck
CHAMPAGNE

Nicholas Courtney is a writer and broadcaster whose own travels to many corners of the world have inspired much of his writing. In 1992, both he and his wife, Vanessa, circumnavigated the world 'In the Footsteps of Champagne Charlie', recreating the intrepid spirit of adventure which immortalised Charles Camille Heidsieck as an illustrious traveller, philanthropist and entrepreneur.

Introduction by ROY ACKERMAN

The recession has continued to bite and many establishments have fallen by the wayside. However, we are going to concentrate on the success stories and some of the new, sometimes brave ventures that look set to succeed, and take into account the more wide-ranging effect has been the increased demand by the customer for value for money.

There is still – and probably always will be – a market for the top of the range restaurants, as there will always be business to discuss and celebrations to be marked, for instance Michel Roux at the Waterside Inn, which now has its own elegant private dining and meeting room as well as 6 luxury bedrooms; and Nico Ladenis's latest venture, Nico at Ninety (Park Lane), which has cost much money. But overall the trend is more towards the good value place offering lots of options.

Where to go if within a group if some of you are ravenous and some just going along for the company and one course with a glass of wine? A brasserie with no fixed minimum charge. Where to go if you really want to celebrate with lots of friends but you all have mortgages to consider? A basic bistro offering a good fixed price menu with no hidden surprises.

That's the essence for today's streetwise customer – the freedom to have exactly what you want, when you want it, at a reasonable price. More and more establishments are extending their opening hours and deregulating their menus – the true brasserie tradition is at long last making its presence felt in Britain. At the same time, it's possible at such places still to get just a cup of coffee at 6 o'clock in the evening, while at the same time it's also possible to get an early supper, pre-theatre or cinema.

Another popular trend these days, especially in London, is the rise of better food in pubs. Quite often this can be set apart from the main drinking area, such as First Floor in Portobello, Harvey's Café in Fulham; or more integrated as at the Eagle in Farringdon Street. Around the country, the separated style is not so frequent, such as Jeremy's at the King's Head, or an all-time favourite of mine, Poppies at the Roebuck. Another trend, and one which I touched on in last year's introduction, is the rise of eating together as a family. It's slow progress but we are getting there, and I hope that eating together, whether at home or out at restaurants, will be an increasingly popular pastime.

Diversification is the name of the game for some restaurateurs. Sometimes, small cafés have sprung up in response to delicatessen customers wanting somewhere to taste the goods on offer and maybe have a cup of coffee as well. The other side of that particular coin is epitomised by Sally Clarke, who opened her shop, & Clarke's, next door to her Kensington restaurant to satisfy those customers who were primarily attracted by her stunning array of home-made breads. Now the bread factory (for such it has become) has moved away from the Kensington location and supplies not only Sally's restaurant and shop, but several other food outlets, both shops and restaurants, in the capital. The shop sells other delicatessen items – and still manages tables at the back for those who want a cup of coffee with delicious croissants, brioches and pastries. There are all manner of preserves, wines and confections to delight the eye and the palate. Justin de Blank, of course, was probably the progenitor of this trend, and you can still buy ingredients at his Elizabeth Street shop, as well as eat in his restaurants within, for instance, the General Trading Company. No mention in this group would be complete, however, without the St Quentin group – the shop and restaurant outlets around Knightsbridge/Brompton Road are always packed. And finally, a newcomer. At the Neal Street Restaurant, or rather next door to it, Antonio Carluccio has opened Carluccio's, where you can purchase virtually the entire menu for a dinner party at home, especially if you and your guests are mushroom-lovers. Mention of the Neal Street Restaurant brings to mind Sir Terence Conran, of course, and his new venture, Le Pont de la Tour hard by the south of Tower Bridge in some of the new dockland development. Styled 'gastrodome', the enterprise includes restaurant, bar, bakery and shops all under one roof. Let's hope it does for food and eating out what his original Habitat concept did for home furnishings.

So to sum up, while some are indeed suffering, other restaurants continue to prosper and expand. The market in my opinion is firmly in the 'go where you're known and looked after syndrome', the bistro and brasserie mood – Soho Soho, Bistrot 190, dell'Ugo, Stephen Bull Bistro – and the good local restaurant level, such as Sonny's or L'Accento. The success of the Café Flo chain and the Café Rouge/Café Pelican group speaks for itself. The top end of the range of establishments documents the well-deserved success of places like Langan's, Kensington Place, The Ivy, Le Caprice, Bibendum, and outside London McCoy's at Staddle Bridge and the Seafood Restaurant in Padstow – they all have something special to offer.

The Four-Leaf Clover

The four-leaf clover has been chosen because it is a symbol of luck and also a rare find. There is always a degree of luck involved when good ambience, excellent food, wine and service and the response of the customer combine to make a perfect occasion. A White Clover means that in my opinion, this is a very special place for many reasons, and made for a memorable experience. A Black Clover represents excellence in all aspects of food, service and decor, and these are the very best in Great Britain and the Republic of Ireland.

With new clovers for this year marked [N], The Ackerman Charles Heidsieck Guide Clover Leaf Awards for 1993 are given to:

LONDON

Alastair Little	♣
L'Arlequin	♣
Bibendum	♣
The Capital Hotel	♣
Le Caprice	✿
Claridge's	✿
Clarke's	✿
The Connaught Hotel	♣
dell'Ugo [N]	✿
The Dorchester	✿
Four Seasons Restaurant	✿
Le Gavroche	♣
The Gay Hussar	✿
Greenhouse [N]	✿
The Halkin [N]	✿
Harvey's	♣
Hilaire	✿
L'Incontro	✿
The Ivy [N]	✿
Kalamaras	✿
Kensington Place	✿
The Lanesborough [N]	✿
Langan's Brasserie	♣
Leith's [N]	✿
Le Meridien (Oak Room)	✿
Mirabelle [N]	✿
Mosimann's	♣
Nico at Ninety [N]	♣
Le Pont de la Tour [N]	✿
The Ritz Hotel	✿
River Café	✿
Les Saveurs [N]	✿
The Savoy	♣
Le Soufflé Restaurant	✿
The Square [N]	✿
Stephen Bull	✿
Le Suquet [N]	✿
La Tante Claire	♣
Turner's	✿

ENGLAND (outside London)

Amberley, Amberley Castle	✿
Aston Clinton, Bell [N]	✿
Aylesbury, Hartwell House	✿
Baslow, Fischer's	✿
Bath, Bath Spa Hotel	✿
Bilbrough, Bilborough Manor	✿
Birmingham, Swallow Hotel	✿
Bradford, Restaurant Nineteen	✿
Bray-on-Thames, Waterside Inn	♣
Brockenhurst, Le Poussin	✿
Bury, Normandie Hotel	✿
Chagford, Gidleigh Park	♣
Cheltenham, Redmond's	✿
Cheltenham, Epicurean	✿
Claygate, Les Alouettes	✿
Colerne, Lucknam Park	✿
Corse Lawn, Corse Lawn House	✿
Dartmouth, The Carved Angel	♣
Dedham, Le Talbooth	✿

East Grinstead, Gravetye Manor ♣
Faversham, Read's 🎋
Gillingham, Stock Hill House 🎋
Goring-on-Thames, Leathern Bottel 🎋
Grasmere, Michael's Nook 🎋
Great Milton, Le Manoir aux Quat'Saisons ♣
Grimston, Congham Hall [N] 🎋
Gulworthy, Horn of Plenty [N] 🎋
Haslemere, Morel's 🎋
Hastings, Rösers 🎋
Herstmonceux, Sundial 🎋
Hetton, Angel Inn 🎋
Hintlesham, Hintlesham Hall [N] 🎋
Ledbury, Hope End 🎋
Longridge, Heathcote's [N] 🎋
Lymington, Gordleton Mill [N] 🎋
Malvern, Croque-en-Bouche 🎋
Moulsford-on-Thames, Beetle & Wedge 🎋
New Milton, Chewton Glen ♣
Newcastle, 21 Queen Street 🎋
Northleach, Old Woolhouse ♣
Norwich, Adlard's 🎋
Oakham, Hambleton Hall ♣
Padstow, Seafood Restaurant ♣
Plymouth, Chez Nous 🎋
Pool-in-Wharfedale, Pool Court 🎋
Pulborough, Stane Street Hollow 🎋
Ridgeway, Old Vicarage 🎋
Romsey, Old Manor House 🎋
Shinfield, L'Ortolan ♣
South Molton, Whitechapel Manor 🎋
Speen, The Old Plow at Speen 🎋
Staddle Bridge, McCoy's ♣
Stapleford, Stapleford Park 🎋
Ston Easton, Ston Easton Park 🎋
Storrington, Manleys 🎋
Stroud, Oakes 🎋
Taplow, Cliveden 🎋
Taunton, The Castle Hotel 🎋
Thornbury, Thornbury Castle 🎋
Ullswater, Sharrow Bay ♣
Warminster, Bishopstrow House 🎋
Waterhouses, Old Beams 🎋
Windermere, Miller Howe 🎋
Windermere, Roger's Restaurant 🎋
Woburn, Paris House 🎋
Worcester, Brown's 🎋
York, Melton's 🎋
York, Middlethorpe Hall 🎋

SCOTLAND

Aberfeldy, Farleyer House 🎋
Edinburgh, Martin's 🎋
Fort William, Inverlochy Castle 🎋
Glasgow, One Devonshire Gardens 🎋
Gullane, La Potinière 🎋
Kingussie, The Cross 🎋
Linlithgow, Champanay Inn 🎋
Peat Inn, Peat Inn ♣
Ullapool, Altnaharrie Inn ♣

WALES

Abergavenny, Walnut Tree ♣
Llandudno, Bodysgallen Hall 🎋

NORTHERN IRELAND

Belfast, Roscoff 🎋
Portrush, Ramore 🎋

REPUBLIC OF IRELAND

Dublin, Patrick Guilbaud 🎋
Kenmare, Park Hotel 🎋
Shanagarry, Ballymaloe House ♣

How to Use this Guide

Main Reviews
This year we have repeated the successful formula from last year. The main reviews are set out very simply: London is arranged alphabetically by establishment name. Reviews in England, Scotland, Wales, Northern Ireland and the Republic of Ireland are arranged alphabetically by location, then by establishment name.

Some reviews are longer than others. The length of a review does not necessarily indicate the relative importance of an establishment – some have been covered more fully in previous editions of the Guide, which are available from Leading Guides.

I have used a small team of reviewers who have worked with me for some years and whose judgement I trust, and who understand what I am seeking in standards of cuisine, atmosphere and service.

Clover Award Winners
Most of our Clover Award winners are featured in a special colour section, from page 209. There is a cross-reference to the page where the review can be found.

Special Features
Since this year we are highlighting bistros, brasseries and similar establishments, our first photo-feature in this edition is an illustrative journey around some of my favourites. These can be found from page 17. Secondly, we feature in colour from page 561, Nico Ladenis Kew venture in Park Lane.

Listings
Where we are unsure about an establishment, or have visited it only once, or where there has been a change of some significance since our last visit, we list it without a full review. These listings appear at their correct geographical point amidst the main reviews.

Vital Statistics
These have been compiled from information supplied to us by the establishments themselves, in response to our questionnaires. They have been checked and we have done our best to ensure that all information contained in this book is accurate. However, it is perfectly feasible that a restaurant or hotel may choose to change its last order times, or the days of the week that it is closed. Similarly, an owner, manager or chef may well move on. Even the style of food might be changed. We assume that in most cases you will book before going to a restaurant or hotel, and if you feel that any detail is especially important, we suggest you check it at the time of booking. When we have quoted particular dishes in a review, we cannot guarantee that they will be available on your visit – this is obviously true if you visit in a different season. In most cases, menus will be more comprehensive than the extracts we have chosen.

Price
The price shown is the average cost of dinner for two people, without wine but including coffee, service and VAT. Where possible, we have quoted a set price dinner menu, which in some cases might be four or even five or more courses; otherwise the figure relates to a typical three-course meal.

Vests
As before, I have used the 'vested interest' symbol to indicate restaurants in which I have a personal investment.

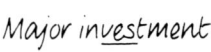

Cercle des Ambassadeurs
The symbol indicates that an establishment is host to a member of the cercle. A full list can be found on page 560.

Al San Vincenzo, W2 (see page 67)

L'Altro, W11 (see page 69)

20 THE ACKERMAN CHARLES HEIDSIECK GUIDE 1993

Above: *Arts Theatre Café, WC2 (see page 73)*

Opposite: *Blueprint Café, SE1 (see page 83)*

BISTROS AND BRASSERIES 21

BISTROS AND BRASSERIES

Blueprint Café, SE1 (see page 83)

La Brasserie, SW3 (see page 86)

BISTROS AND BRASSERIES 25

Brasserie du Marché aux Puces, W10 (see page 86)

Brasserie du Marché aux Puces, W10 (see page 86)

Café des Amis du Vin, WC2 (see page 89)

Café Delancey, WC1 (see page 89)

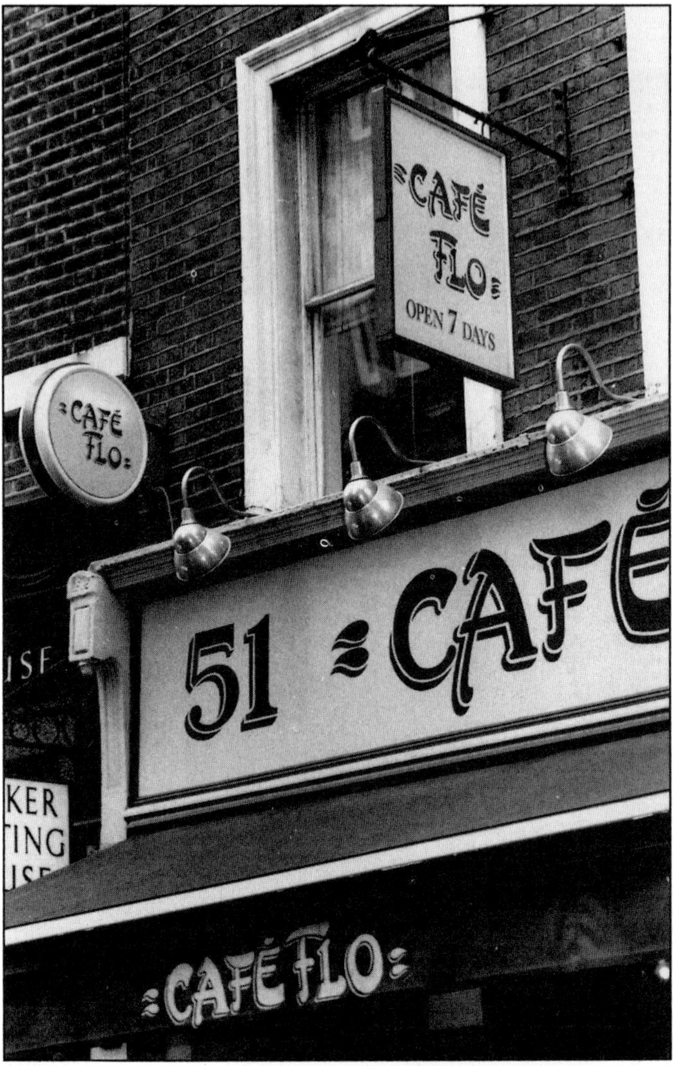
CAFÉ FLO
OPEN 7 DAYS
CAFÉ FLO
51 CAFÉ
CAFÉ FLO

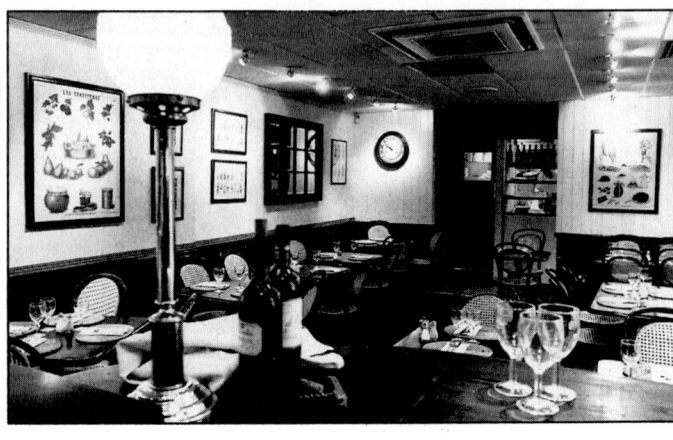

BISTROS AND BRASSERIES 33

Café Flo, WC2
(see page 91)

Café Pelican, WC2 (see page 92)

BISTROS AND BRASSERIES

Camden Brasserie, NW1 (see page 93)

BISTROS AND BRASSERIES 39

Canal Brasserie, W10 (see page 93)

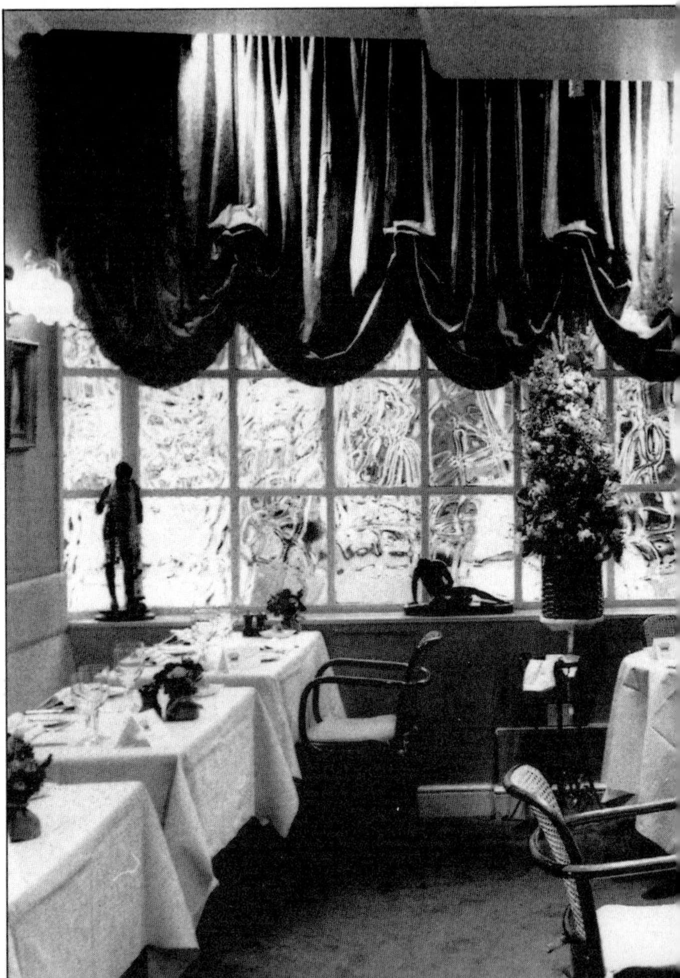

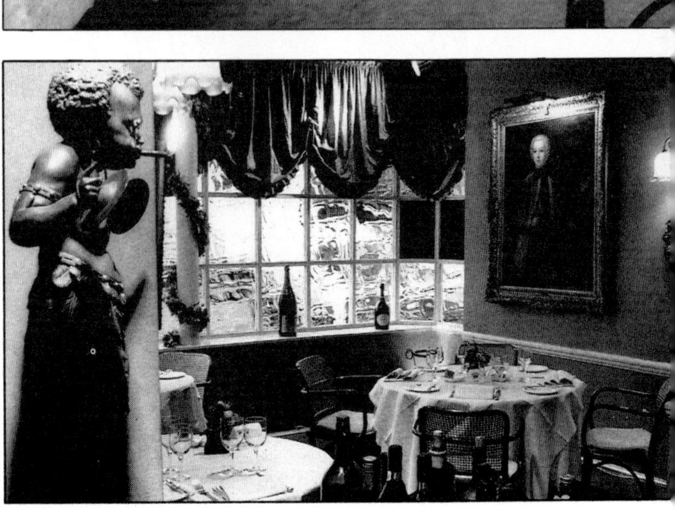

BISTROS AND BRASSERIES 41

*Chez Moi, W11
(see page 102)*

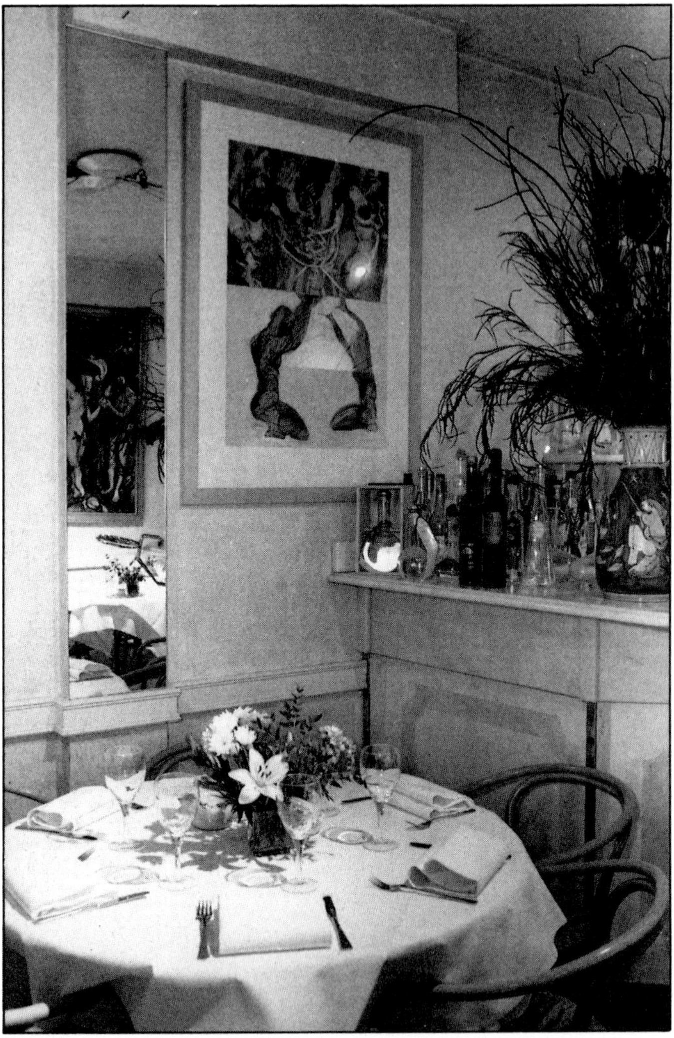

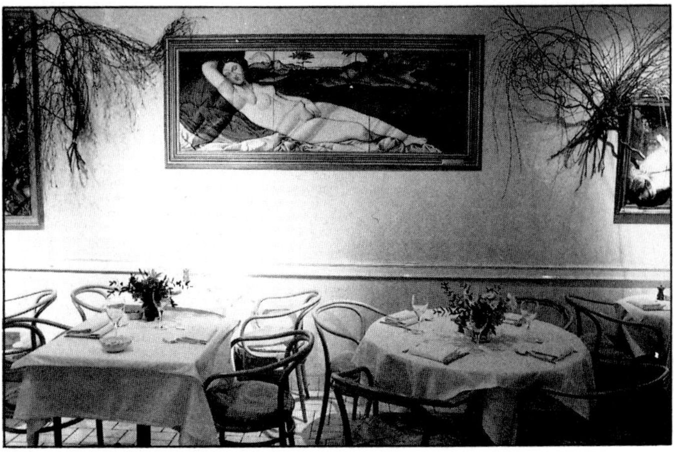

Cibo, W14 (see page 107)

44 THE ACKERMAN CHARLES HEIDSIECK GUIDE 1993

BISTROS AND BRASSERIES **45**

Opposite: *Corney & Barrow, Moorgate EC2 (see page 112)*
This page: *Corney & Barrow, Old Broad Street, EC2 (see page 112)*

Deals West, W1 (see page 114)

BISTROS AND BRASSERIES 47

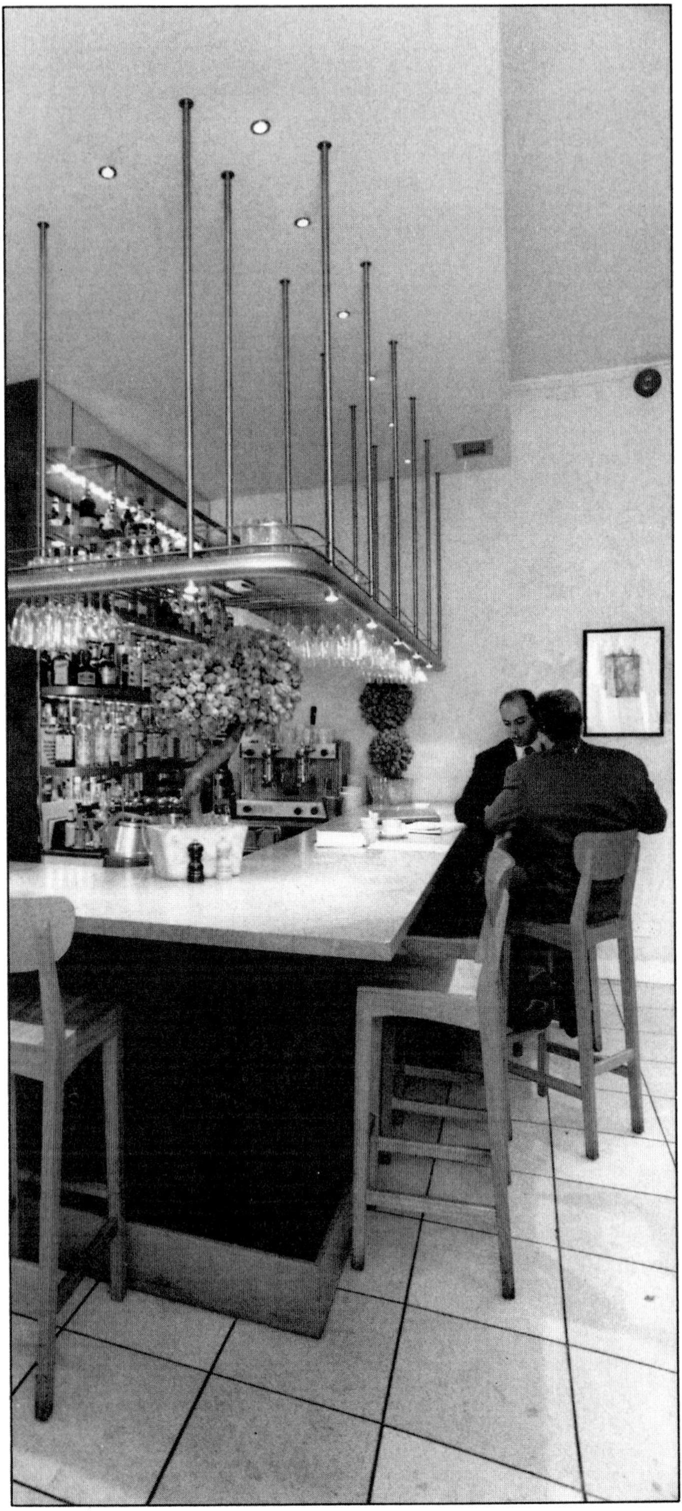

Est, W1 (see page 122)

First Floor, W11 (see page 123)

BISTROS AND BRASSERIES 51

PORTOBELLO
ART FESTIVAL
5-8 APRIL 1990
ZARZUELA
SADLERS WELLS
BROWN STUDY
Edward II

Angel City

BISTROS AND BRASSERIES 53

Meson Doña Ana, W11 (see page 156)

Milburns, W1 (see page 157)

BISTROS AND BRASSERIES 55

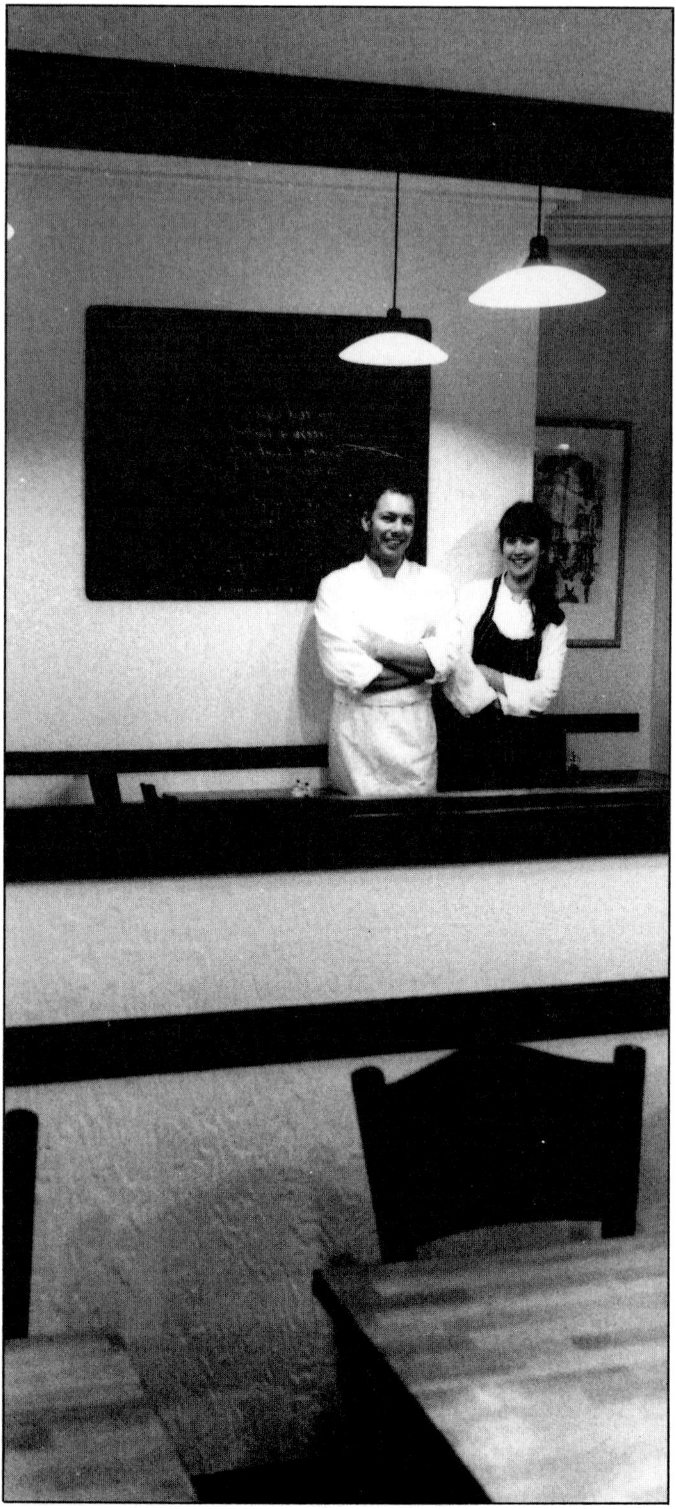

BISTROS AND BRASSERIES 57

Museum Street Café, .WC1 (see page 162)

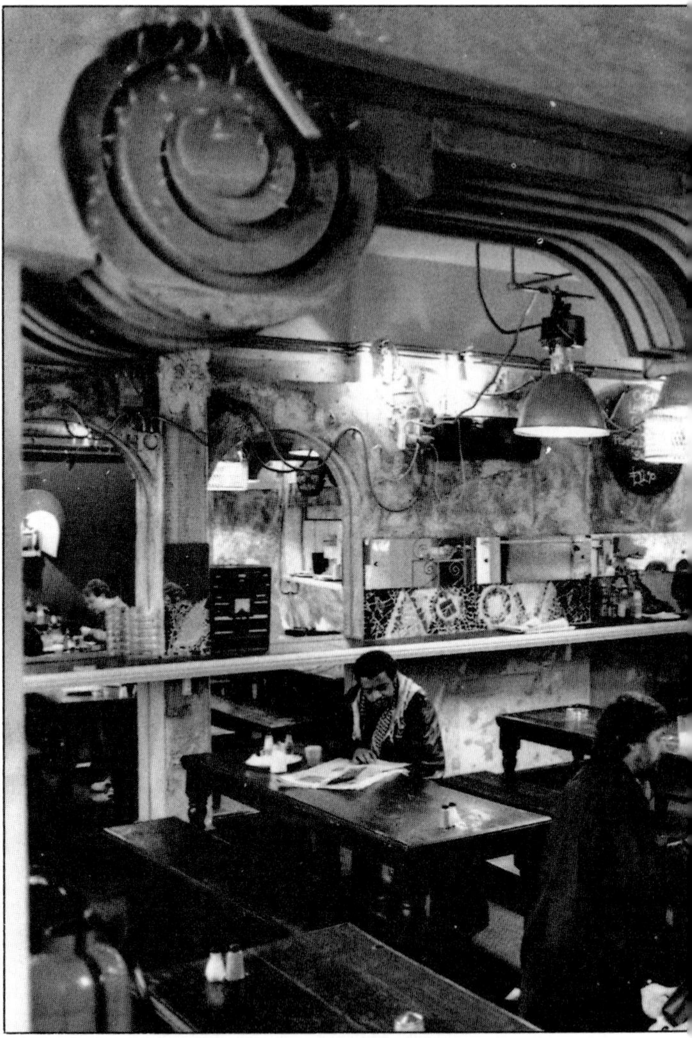

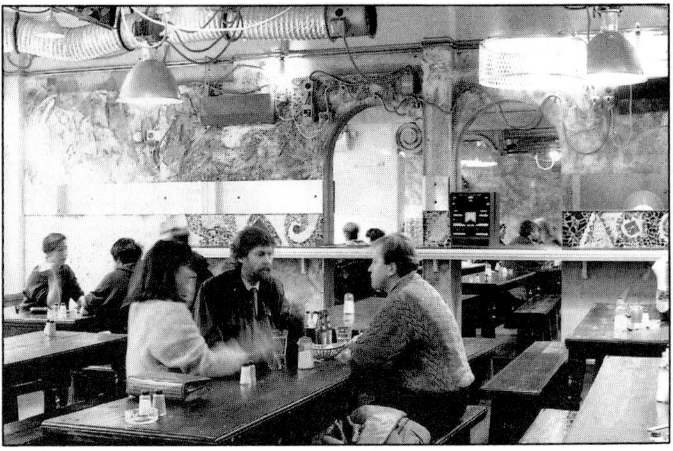

Portobello Dining Rooms, W11 (see page 174)

Serpentine Restaurant, W2 (see page 187)

BISTROS AND BRASSERIES 61

Soho Soho, W1 (see page 192)

BISTROS AND BRASSERIES **63**

*Sonny's, SW13
(see page 192))*

London Establishment Reviews

ABBEY COURT   W2
20 Pembridge Gardens, W2 4DU
Telephone: 071-221 7518
Fax: 071-792 0858
One of the first no-restaurant hotels in London.

L'ACCENTO ITALIANO   W2

16 Garway Road, W2 4NH
Telephone: 071-243 2201   £50
Open: lunch Mon-Fri, dinner Mon-Sat
Meals served: lunch 12.30-2.30, dinner 6.30-11.30

It is imperative to book at this restaurant near Westbourne Grove which has been busy ever since opening in late 1991. A fresh rustic interior with wooden tables sets the tone for fine Italian cooking by Andrea Beltrami, whose 2-course set menu represents very good value. The undeniable effort made in the kitchen is matched by enthusiastic, professional service. Tempting new dishes include garlic bread fritters with courgettes and goat's cheese and a gratin of spinach noodles with artichokes and ham. Rival pasta dishes include risotto with black cuttlefish sauce, polenta with gorgonzola or spinach and ricotta gnocchetti with pesto. Main courses range from salmon gratin with fennel and tomatoes to char-grilled sausage and borlotti beans or pan-fried calves' liver with balsamic vinegar sauce. The cold main dishes are perfect for summer and, to date, have included spiced cold roasted veal with potatoes and tomato and cold poached breast of chicken with salsa verde. For pudding, simple tastes might go for mixed berries in Marsala or vin santo with cantucci but chilled ricotta pudding with white and dark chocolate or deep-fried dumplings with vanilla ice-cream have magnetic appeal. The spare, mainly Italian wine list is well-matched to Andrea Beltrami's robust regional cooking.

ADAM'S CAFÉ	W12
77 Askew Road, W12	
Telephone: 081-743 0572	£30
Open: lunch + dinner Mon-Sat (closed Bank Holidays)	
Meals served: 7.15-6.30 (Sat 8-2), 7.30-10.30	
Neighbourhood place, trad English café by day, Tunisian restaurant by night.	

AL BUSTAN	SW1
27 Motcomb Street, SW1X 8JU	
Telephone: 071-235 8277	£60
Open: all day daily	
Meals served: 12-11pm (Sun 12-10)	
Delicious Lebanese food in light and airy surroundings.	

AL SAN VINCENZO — W2

30 Connaught Street, W2 2AS
Telephone: 071-262 9623 — **£60**
Open: lunch Mon-Fri, dinner Mon-Sat (closed Bank Holidays, 2 wks Xmas)
Meals served: lunch 12.30-2.30, dinner 7-10.30

A restaurant 'swap' with the Prince of India has meant Al San Vincenzo moving from its former location in Cheam to these small, more stylish premises in Connaught Street. There are 22 covers at present on the ground floor but this will increase to 38 with the opening of the basement in time for 1993. The room, with its terracotta pots and wooden shutters, is simple while the menu is striking for its bold invention. Flavours are robust and finely balanced with modish ingredients such as salt cod, sun-dried tomatoes, pine nuts and balsamic vinegar used liberally but intelligently. Orecchiette with rocket and pancetta was a favourite of mine in Cheam but pasta has now been outlawed, with the menu screaming 'I want to be taken seriously'. And it is. Other past masterpieces have included a casserole of mussels and cuttlefish, pigeon with fresh broad beans, sautéed onions and pancetta and, happily, the new restaurant has lost none of its fine idiosyncracies in the translation. The desserts include a fig and mascarpone pudding worth driving miles for and, for purists, a plate of mango served with dolcelatte. The excellent bread is baked on the premises. A passion for drinks makes for a fascinating list: the house aperitif is extra dry vermouth on the rocks with a dash of cassis and there is a wide range of Italian bitters (among them Cynar, distilled from artichokes) and the non-alcoholic Bitter San Pellegrino. Lemon vodka is listed beside a lemon aperitif from Amalfi. and there is an impressive range of pudding wines and grappas that kick like a mule, especially when taken as chasers to the powerful espresso. *See also page 17 – our Bistros and Brasseries Section.*

Alastair Little   W1

49 Frith Street, W1 5TE
Telephone: 071-734 5183
Open: lunch Mon-Fri, dinner Mon-Sat (closed Bank Holidays,
   1 wk Xmas/New Year)
Meals served: lunch 12-3, dinner 6-11.30

♣
£75

The matt black chairs and tables which once suggested chic '80s understatement now have a more lived-in feel in this small, rather stark restaurant. Now in his 40s, Alastair can no longer be considered one of our gastronomic enfants terribles but he is still producing some of the most exciting food in town, consistently surprising and delighting his regular customers with bold new interpretations, influences and enthusiasms. Curt menu descriptions promise little but the dishes deliver like no courier ever could. A gastronomic magpie, Alastair is particularly fond of oriental flavours, although his sure handling of classic French techniques shines in dishes like his impeccably sauced criscrisp-roasted breast of chicken swatched in cèpes or morels according to the season. Elsewhere he will tinker with a classic, as in his tournedos with a goat's cheese polenta crouton and rich parsley salad. A lighter touch is apparent in chilled pea soup with sour cream, mint and croutons or an immaculate terrine of skate and potato, speckled with savoury gems (chopped gherkin, hard-boiled egg and Dijon mustard) and served with French beans and a salsa verde spangled with mostarda di Cremona. Simple things are done to perfection: Alastair's vitello tonnato or risotto nero are near faultless and he will invest a fortune in Spanish charcuterie (from soundly reared beasts) to serve with cornichons. The small basement bar sports an identical menu but snacking – on one course or even a shared starter – is welcome and actively encouraged. Service is always young, informal and on the ball. Recession has compelled Alastair to drop his no-credit-cards policy and to introduce a set lunch at £18 for 3 courses. *See also page 209 – our Clover Award section.*

Alba	EC1

107 Whitecross Street, EC1Y 8JD
Telephone: 071-588 1798 £50
Open: lunch + dinner Mon-Fri (closed Bank Holidays, 2 wks Xmas)
Meals served: lunch 12-3, dinner 7-11

Named after the town at the heart of Piedmontese wine country, Alba is a highly evolved trattoria with northern Italian aspirations. Its cool, modern interior, all pink and grey with surprisingly comfortable spindly black armchairs and occcasional piped opera, has more atmosphere when full but there is ample compensation in the warm welcome extended by the charming and enthusiastic owners. Traditional dishes – minestrone, lasagne, calves' liver with butter and sage – rub shoulders with agnolotti served in an superior brodo or Italian pepper sausages with borlotti beans and polenta. Charcuterie is excellent: carne all'Albese is carpaccio with truffle oil, an ingredient liberally used throughout the repertoire. A walnut sauce worked better with panzerotti than with trout. Ingredients are fresh and of high quality and are mostly well-cooked and accurately seasoned. When in season, there is an abundance of porcini and truffles on the specials board: these are expensive but worth the investment and prices are clearly marked. A risotto with shaved white truffle was superb. Puddings are served from the trolley and there is good cappuccino with biscotti. The entirely Italian wine list, covering all the regions and sensibly priced, includes a great dessert wine called Muffato. Alba's function is primarily that of a user-friendly neighbourhood restaurant in something of a gastronomic wasteland, but is also an invaluable address for anyone who frequents the Barbican.

Alistair Greig's Grill	W1

26 Bruton Place, W1X 7AA
Telephone: 071-629 5613 £75
Open: lunch Mon-Fri, dinner Mon-Sat (closed Bank Holidays, Xmas/New Year)
Meals served: lunch 12.30-2.30, dinner 6.30-11
Kathy White is still at the helm here. Traditional British food, charcoal grills a speciality.

L'Altro   W11

210 Kensington Park Road, W11
Telephone: 071-792 1066   **£65**
Open: lunch Tue-Sun, dinner Tue-Sat
Meals served: lunch 12-2 (Sun 12.30-3), dinner 7-11 (Fri+Sat 7-11.30)

A rampant, neo-medieval Italian interior at the inelegant end of KPR is the backdrop to the predominantly piscine menu at L'Altro – quite literally 'the other' restaurant owned by Gino Taddei, who burst onto the nuova cucina scene with the ever-popular Cibo. The trompe l'oeil whimsy may be too hot for some to handle but it appeals to a young, style-conscious clientele who home in on healthy, lightly-sauced dishes abuzz with fresh herbs, served on colourful Tuscan crockery. Restraint is the keynote: oysters are simply prepared with spinach and lemon while moist jumbo scallops are grilled on skewers and served on a mound of rocket. L'Altro is, if anything, even pricier than its stablemate Cibo – although portions are enormous. Mimsy fillets are taboo: seabass is steamed or baked and served whole, ditto lobster, the great bargain of the menu, often served with linguini. Black tagliolini partners spider crab, red mullet is served with black cuttlefish risotto and, on an ever-changing menu you might find baked mackerel, its crisp skin spiked with rosemary, langoustines wrapped in Parma ham with courgette strips, a colourful seafood risotto or casseroles of eel or octopus in red wine – all intensely pure and dramatic. Wild seasonal mushrooms mushroom here, there and everywhere. Tables are densely crammed – which is surprising, given the price which at least includes a well-dressed salad. Service is from a young team who are genuinely well-informed and enthusiastic about both the food and the interesting, Italian wine list.
See also page 18 – our Bistros and Brasseries Section.

Anna's Place	N1

90 Mildmay Park, Newington Green, N1 4PR
Telephone: 071-249 9379 £45
Open: lunch + dinner Tue-Sat (closed 2 wks Xmas, 2 wks Easter, 2 wks Aug)
Meals served: lunch 12.15-2.15, dinner 7.15-10.45

It seems that every time you decide to venture to the the hinterlands of Islington to visit the inimitable Anna's Place, everybody else has had the same idea before you. If you haven't booked, you'll be lucky even to get a seat at the bar. The exuberant Anna Hegarty, whose presence ensures wondrous service, has been running her one-of-a-kind 'place' since 1979 (when she was arguably the country's first purveyor of gravadlax) and it's a thriving informal restaurant whose animated clientele has grown by word of mouth over the years. Relics from the building's former life as a tobacconist's shop add to the atmosphere while the big red Aga behind the bar is used for warming both bread and customers or for mulling wine. Given Anna's Scandinavian background, it is no great surprise that fish features strongly on the hearty menu, which changes frequently. Sill tallrik (two kinds of soused Swedish herring) and gravadlax are billed as starters and might be followed by sautéed monkfish, haddock or a dish of steamed fillets of brill wrapped around gingered nuggets of salmon. Lax pudding puts in an occasional appearance and consists of layers of salted fish, waxy potatoes and cream – catch it if you can. Popular meat dishes include lamkot i dill sas (a Swedish hotpot of lamb and vegetables) and biff Strindberg (marinated beef named, one assumes, in honour of the playwright). Puddings include apple cake with vanilla cream, svenska wafflor and choklad tarta which of course translate as Swedish waffles and chocolate tart. Take sufficient cash or a cheque book as credit cards are taboo. Choose your wine from the short, reasonably priced, globetrotting list, Swedish beer or drink the cardiac-arresting Aarlberg Akvavit.

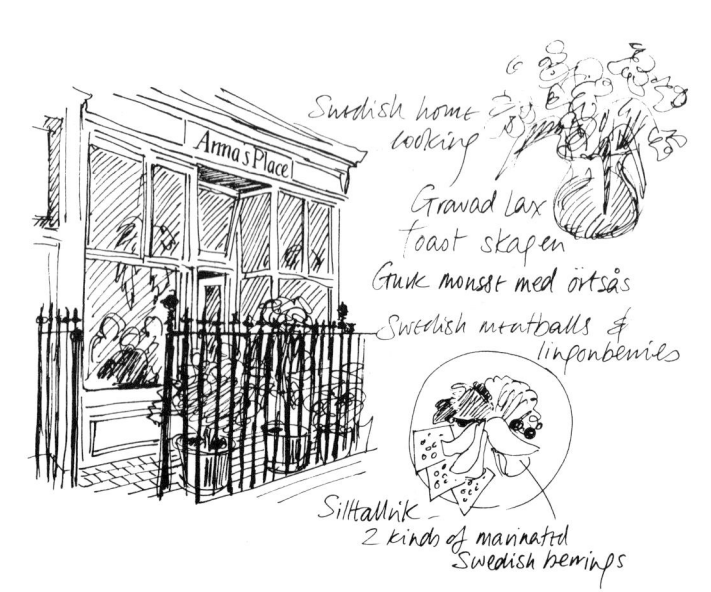

THE ARGYLL SW3

316 King's Road, SW3
Telephone: 071-352 0025
Open: lunch Tue-Sat, dinner Mon-Sat (closed Bank Holidays)
Meals served: lunch 12-2.30, dinner 7-15.15

£65

[handwritten annotation: already established locally – its reputation is set to grow!]

The minimal adornment of this large airy room, with its stripped wide-planked floors and nude white walls, has attracted mixed reactions. However, the use of pure white napery and exceedingly comfortable leather-upholstered high-backed chairs eschews '80s-style severity. That the restaurant is a welcome newcomer to Chelsea is beyond dispute. Since his days at Harvey's (whence the tagliatelle of oysters!) chef-proprietor Anand Sastry has moved deeper into the 'terroir' although a tendency towards fancy things is not entirely eliminated so you will find a mousse (or mousseline) of chicken or fish listed alongside the more wintry goose liver with braised beans and lentils. Pressed ratatouille with fennel is a sound interpretation of a classic theme and the lamb with garlic and mashed potato is similarly simple but brilliantly rendered. Fish is often treated in a similar way to, say, lamb – hence the cod roasted with a brioche herb crust and pommes boulangères, while other winners have included the pot-roasted poussin with lardons, morels and roast potatoes or pan-fried duck with lentils. The restaurant is capably run by co-patron Christian Arden, his style being more relaxed here than at Sutherland's – but then the Argyll is possibly less star-struck. Staff are young, English, chatty and eager to please. There is a choice of 3 good English cheeses and a short pudding list which might include, for instance, caramel soufflé with caramel ice-cream or a terrine of orange, strawberries and passion-fruit. The short, concise wine list is sensibly-priced.

L'ARLEQUIN — SW8

123 Queenstown Road, SW8 3RH
Telephone: 071-622 0555
Fax: 071-498 7015
Open: lunch + dinner Mon-Fri (closed Bank Holidays, 1 wk Xmas)
Meals served: lunch 12.30-2, dinner 7-10

£95

Christian Delteil's French cooking – rooted, like its creator, in the southwest – is impeccable, standing comparison with some of the best in this country and abroad. Dishes such as the bourgeois classic petit chou farci à l'ancienne (outstanding) and a persillé of ris de veau and lobster among the starters and chartreuse de grouse and aiguillette de canard en deux services as main dishes suggest the level of his accomplishment. Lighter starters include a gazpacho with caviar or escabèche of mackerel and astonishing sleight of hand with pasta makes for great ravioli of leek with asparagus tips, tagliatelle with a surfeit of cèpes or pistou de laperaux aux pâtes fraîches. Spices are used for subtle enhancement as in a dish of pigeon with apples and cinnamon. Soufflés are a speciality and bear out the theory that only a very fine chef is capable of attaining Christian's consistency in such complex and precise dishes as these. They are rivalled by lovely sorbets and ice creams and by a flawless example of the ubiquitous nougat glacé. The wine list, starting at well under £15 and climbing sharply into the vintages, is entirely in keeping with the class of the establishment but manages to include bottles that are easily affordable, although this is in any case no place to come if you're having problems with the mortgage repayments. The simple – some say plain – and restful pistachio decor is lit up by the charming Geneviève Delteil's front of house and some extremely knowledgeable young staff. *See also page 210 – our Clover Award section.*

L'ARTISTE ASSOIFFÉ — W11

122 Kensington Park Road, W11 2EP
Telephone: 071-727 4714
Open: dinner daily (closed Xmas, Easter)
Meals served: dinner 7.30-11
Friendly local French restaurant.

£45

Arts Theatre Café   WC2

6 Great Newport Street, WC2
Telephone: 071-497 8014   £**30**
Open: all day Mon-Fri (closed Bank Holidays, 1 wk Xmas/New Year)
Meals served: 12-10

One of the less visible spots in town – down a flight of red steps beneath the Arts Theatre itself – the centrally-located Café (a self-deprecating name belying its culinary aspirations) is simply furnished with whitewashed walls, black chairs and tables brightened with fresh flowers. Especially popular with students, theatregoers and luvvies alike, this is a place to search out for its lively atmosphere and food which is quality Mediterranean at remarkably low prices. Two people can dine here for the price of a West End theatre ticket. The menu changes daily and the specials make for an epic blackboard read where antipasti misti and leek, onion and tomato soup might appear among the curtain raisers, with broccoli and pancetta tart or grilled swordfish steaks with a Sicilian sauce of oil and lemon taking centre stage. Rabbit with rosemary is served on polenta croutons with a rich sauce and braised cabbage. For dessert, try the poached plums with honey and rosemary or the equally herbaceous elderflower and borage sorbet. The 3-course menu at £10.50 is great value, especially given the good country breads and quite a comprehensive, fairly-priced wine list. More places like this would be welcome – encore! *See also page 20 – our Bistros and Brasseries Section.*

The Athenaeum   W1

116 Piccadilly, W1V 0BJ
Telephone: 071-499 3464
Fax: 071-493 1860   £**70**
Open: lunch Sun-Fri, dinner daily
Meals served: lunch 12-2.30 (Sun 11.30-1.30), dinner 6-10.30

A peaceful, luxurious and smoothly run hotel whose 31 apartments (in the adjoining Edwardian townhouse) offer all the advantages of the 112 bedrooms plus the advantages and discretion of a private, intimate pied à terre. The hotel is tastefully appointed throughout (marble bathrooms are particularly fine) and boasts irreproachably unobtrusive service. The restaurant is an attractive setting for some well-executed dishes, composed with a lighter touch of late in keeping with culinary trends. The menu, with its vibrant Dufy-esque cover illustration, retains asparagus hollandaise, lobster (salad or Thermidor), sole meunière and chateaubriand for two alongside the newer salad of quail's eggs with pine kernels and walnut oil, brill baked in a herb crust with a herby shallot sauce, or grilled lamb's kidneys with rösti and Madeira sauce. Pre-theatre dinner available. The Windsor Lounge is a clubby bar listing no fewer than 50 single malts and, helpfully, serving light dishes from noon to midnight including omelette Arnold Bennett, chopped steak with fries, BLT and croque monsieur plus afternoon teas.

Au Bois St Jean	NW8
122 St John's Wood High Street, NW8 7SG	
Telephone: 071-722 0400	£50
Open: lunch + dinner daily (closed 25+26 Dec)	
Meals served: lunch 12-2.30, dinner 7-10.30 (bistro 6-10.30)	
Traditional and modern French cooking, long established local restaurant.	

Au Bon Accueil	SW3
19 Elystan Street, SW3 3NT	
Telephone: 071-589 3718	£35
Open: lunch Mon-Fri, dinner Mon-Sat (closed Bank Holidays)	
Meals served: lunch 12.30-2.30, dinner 7-11.30	
Reliable French food tempered somewhat to traditional English tastes, loyal patronage by the green welly and Range Rover brigade. Long-serving staff extend a warm welcome to regulars.	

Au Jardin des Gourmets — W1

5 Greek Street, W1V 5LA
Telephone: 071-437 1816 £65
Fax: 071-437 0043
Open: lunch Mon-Fri, dinner Mon-Sat (closed Bank Holidays)
Meals served: lunch 12.15-2.30, dinner 6.15-11.15

A great favourite of media stars and Soho Faces over its 60-odd years, Au Jardin was undergoing something of a culinary change as we went to press, the intention being to lift the cuisine to match the extensive renovations that have been carried out. Wines are helpfully suggested but there is a massive and impressive selection besides – as indeed befits one of the finest cellars in the restaurant industry, personally selected by proprietor Joseph Berkmann. The bordeaux and burgundy sections are particularly fine but there is strength too among Champagnes and new world wines, especially Californian. There are some lovely private dining suites.

L'Aventure   NW8

3 Blenheim Terrace, NW8 0EH
Telephone: 071-624 6232

favourite local

£55

Open: lunch Sun-Fri, dinner daily (closed Bank Holidays, 1 wk Xmas, 4 days Easter)
Meals served: lunch 12.30-2.30, dinner 7.30-11 (Sun 7.30-10)

Catherine Parisot's long-established French neighbourhood restaurant retains its following both in the evening and for Sunday lunches. It is particularly delightful during the summer months, when both lunch and dinner are served al fresco on the pretty pavement terrace.

Menus change daily, offering a short, innovative selection of warm salads, classic and modern main courses and good puddings: a warm confit of duck with lentils, char-grilled tuna, roast guineafowl with honey and cabbage, pink rack of lamb and pear tarte tatin or île flottante are typical.

Bacco   NW7

30 Old Brompton Road, SW7 3DL
Telephone:; 071-589 4142
Fax: 071-835 2145

£45

Open: lunch Mon-Fri, dinner daily (closed Bank Holidays except Good Friday)
Meals served: lunch 12-3, dinner 6-11.30

A breezy terracotta-toned basement houses this young Italian restaurant in South Kensington. There are simple – as well as exotic – pastas for die-hards, bruschetta or lamb cutlets with diced tomato and artichoke for new wave surfers. Smoked mozzarella, grilled over radicchio and prosciutto, is an unusual starter. The kitchen excels at risotti, particularly the seafood varieties which might include, for instance, pumpkin and scallops or asparagus and langoustine, moist and bursting with flavour.

Bahn Thai   W1

21a Frith Street, W1V 5TS
Telephone: 071-437 8504

£65

Open: lunch + dinner daily (closed some Bank Holidays)
Meals served: lunch 12-2.45 (Sun 12.30-2.30), dinner 6-11.15 (Sun 6.30-10.30)

One of the earliest and remaining one of the best Thai restaurants. Fish and shellfish are their strength, decor and service come second.

Basil Street Hotel   SW3

Basil Street, SW3 1AH
Telephone: 071-581 3311
Fax: 071-581 3693   £70
Open: lunch Sun-Fri, dinner daily
Meals served: lunch 12.30-2.30, dinner 6.30-10 (Sat+Sun 6.30-9.30)

A Knightsbridge location for this 102-bedroomed hotel translates into instant access to all the major shopping areas, museums, theatres and more that London has to offer. Privately owned, the hotel is small enough to maintain a friendly rapport with guests and overall standards of service and comfort are extremely high. The style is primarily Edwardian, with parquet floors, oriental rugs, chintz and palms. The bedrooms are well-proportioned and well-kept with gleaming bathrooms and gentle colour schemes. Food in the dining room is reliably consistent, comfortably traditional and soundly cooked, usually with a roast as the centre piece and also featuring good terrines of fish or game, noisettes of lamb, calves' liver and favourite puddings like sherry trifle and apple flan. The ungreedy list has been carefully selected and includes some excellent clarets and Beaujolais.

Belvedere in Holland Park   W8

off Abbotsbury Road, W8 6LU
Telephone: 071-602 1238   £50
Open: lunch daily, dinner Mon-Sat (closed 3 days Xmas)
Meals served: lunch 12-3, dinner 7-11

Originally the summer ballroom of Holland House, The Belvedere is one of the finest spots in London for sunny summer dining, although it appeals in winter too. The setting is unbeatable and you can even park easily! There is seating for 20 on the terrace overlooking the park, while the interior – a tall, spacious room with twin mezzanine areas – is an exercise in cool, contemporary thinking – gleaming and bright with inlaid wooden tables, vibrant paintings and neat graphics. Dishes are listed in minute type down the left-hand side of the forward-thinking menu where old-fashioned dishes are taboo: even the simpler, more accessible dishes are highly modern. Naturally, the char-grill gets top billing in the kitchen, leaving its mark on asparagus served with a balsamic dressing and pecorino, the leeks and oyster mushrooms served with grilled sea bream or the rump steak partnered by salsa verde and vegetable tempura. Other seductive starters have included a warm salad of rocket and roast tomatoes with seared squid or the ever-popular lobster ravioli in dark chicken broth, garnished with deep-fried vegetables. Calves' liver is given a herb and shallot crust and served with creamed potatoes and thyme jus, while pan-fried salmon is presented on fish pasta with creamed cucumber and dill. The warm tartlet of caramelised onions, feta and sun-dried tomatoes, imported from the now-defunct Tall Orders by chef Mark Emberton's predecessor Jeremy Strode, has become a sitting tenant on the menu. Puddings might include a pear bordelaise with poire William ice-cream and a tuile of exotic fruits with champagne ice cream. The wine list is unexpectedly Francophile but is intelligently conceived at reasonable prices.

The Berkeley SW1

Wilton Place, SW1X 7RL
Telephone: 071-235 6000
Fax: 071-235 4330 £75
Open: lunch + dinner Sun-Fri
Meals served: lunch 12.30-2.30 (Sun 12.45-2.15), dinner 6.30-10.45 (Sun 7-10.15)

The Berkeley, being a modern hotel, is the least picturesque of all those in the Savoy Group but it has a dedicated following who appreciate the Minema (its 68-seater in-house cinema), health club – with adjoining hair and beauty salon – and rooftop swimming pool (with a sliding cover for fine weather) and perhaps most of all its close proximity to Park Lane, Hyde Park and Knightsbridge shopping. The 100 stylish bedrooms and 27 suites (including the Wellington with its beautiful tiled conservatory) are all furnished and equipped with the utmost care: marble-floored bathrooms, power showers to impress even the most exacting American guest and of course bathrobes come as standard. The hotel fakes a history with its open fire in the lobby and some choice antiques while, elsewhere, you will find Lutyens' oak panelling on the walls. Many of these features were transposed from the original Berkeley in Piccadilly which moved to Knightsbridge 20 years ago. A quiet, ongoing programme of refurbishment keeps everything looking fresh and in tip-top condition. The bar and lounge make a useful meeting place and the new Café Minema is a welcome innovation, competing with the likes of Joe's in Harvey Nichols and the Cafe Montpeliano for the attention of young ladies who lunch and jetlagged guests searching for an informal salad. The main restaurant is traditional in every sense, from the tailcoated, wing-collared staff to the French repertoire of luxurious, classically-sauced dishes such as lobster soufflé, seabass with vermouth and spinach, roast pheasant for 2, or a casserole of wild boar with orange. There is a good selection of simple grills, cold platters and classic vegetables, ordered à la carte. Cheeses and savouries follow puddings from the trolley. Extensive wine list.

Berkshire Hotel W1

350 Oxford Street, W1N 0BY
Telephone: 071-629 7474 £70
Fax: 071-629 8156
Open: lunch Sun-Fri, dinner daily (closed 25 Dec-2 Jan)
Meals served: lunch 12.30-2.30, dinner 6-10.30 (Sun 6.30-10.30)

Oxford Street and Bond Street shopping lies at your feet when you stay at The Berkshire. The 147 bedrooms have a surprisingly homely feel, reflecting the aim of the hotel to create a country house atmosphere in central London. Thirty are specifically designated non-smoking rooms and the suites have whirlpool baths. The chintzy drawing room and cosy Ascots restaurant and bar continue the country house theme, a favourite of the Edwardian Hotels group. There is some competent cooking if you stick to the simple dishes on the menu such as game pâtés, consommés and soups such as green pea with smoked bacon or fish dishes such as braised salmon with sorrel, watercress and lemon butter. There are considered vegetarian dishes and a sensible calorie-counted menu.

| **BERTORELLI'S** | **WC2** |

44a Floral Street, WC2E 9DA
Telephone: 071-836 3969   *– one to look out for*   £55
Open: lunch and dinner Mon-Sat
Meals served: lunch 12-3, dinner 5.45-11.30

Maddalena Bonino has resurfaced in the new look Bertorelli's, formerly in Charlotte Street. Her arrival heralded a change of menu style to modern Italian, as seen in baked courgettes stuffed with ricotta, sundried tomato and fresh oregano, grilled lamb cutlets with a purée of whitebeans flavoured with rosemary and garlic, steamed spinach with oil and lemon. Concise, well-priced Italian wine list.

| **BIBENDUM** | **SW3** |

Michelin House, 81 Fulham Road, SW3 6RD
Telephone: 071-581 5817   ♣
Fax: 071-623 7925   £100
Open: lunch + dinner daily (closed 4 days Xmas, Easter Monday)
Meals served: lunch 12.30-2.30 (Sat+Sun 12.30-3), dinner 7-11.30 (Sun 7-10.30)

The Michelin building's spectacular architecture and Sir Terence's imaginative restoration of the interior are a fitting tribute to Simon's cuisine grandmère – a misleading term, unless his granny really was a genius and came from the South of France. It is difficult to choose from a menu dominated by starters, among them deep-fried goujons of sole with Thai dipping sauce, grilled rock oysters with curry spices and spring onions, ballotine of fresh foie gras or artichokes Barigoule with aïoli. Among fish there is everything from deep-fried lemon sole with chips and tartare sauce to poached turbot with buttered cucumber and dill with caviar or grilled lobster with lime, ginger and coriander butter. Poached salt breast of duck with Italian sausage and broad beans, roast quails with lemon, parsley and garlic, grilled rabbit with mustard sauce are just a few successful meat courses. Hopkinson has a deep love of offal with tête de veau, sauce ravigote a perennial favourite. Desserts, coffee and truffles deal the final blow but are unmissable, especially the chocolate pithiviers and fruit tarts (apple, plum, cherry and almond, prune and armagnac). Superlative cheeses come from Neal's Yard and Philippe Olivier. Generally, the quality of the food, though high, is subordinated to the larger 'experience'. Irresistible and inimitable, Bibendum is expensive unless you pay attention. The set lunch is £24 for 2 courses but with aperitifs, wine, pudding and service can climb to £100. But it's usually worth it for the experience of dining in one of London's finest and chic-est restaurants. *See also page 211 – our Clover Award section.*

Bibendum Oyster Bar SW3

Michelin House, 81 Fulham Road, SW3 6RD
Telephone: 071-589 1480
Fax: 071-823 7925 £45
Open: all day Mon-Sat, lunch + dinner Sun
Meals served: 12-10.30, lunch Sun 12-2, dinner Sun 7-10.30

The smart Oyster Bar, beneath Bibendum and adjoining the magnetic Conran Shop, is open all day and, although it takes its oysters very seriously indeed, serves other (cold) things besides, notably plateaux de fruits de mer for 2, clams, langoustines, lobster mayonnaise, gravadlax, crab mayonnaise and smoked salmon. Determined carnivores and vegetarians can choose gazpacho, Caesar salad, vitello tonnato, smoked duck salad or cold rare roast beef. Its status as a popular socioholic's rendezvous point is reflected in the extensive selection of champagnes on a good wine list. You can also buy seafood to take away from the stall outside, which is a hassle-free alternative to Harrod's.

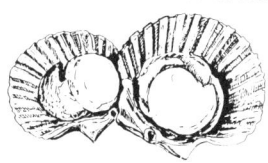

Billboard Café NW6

222 Kilburn High Road, NW6 4JP
Telephone: 071-328 1374 £35
Open: lunch Sat+Sun, dinner Mon-Sat (closed Bank Holidays)
Meals served: lunch 12-3, dinner 6.30-12.45

Cut to a fashionable Kilburn restaurant with dark Venetian blinds and neon sign outside. The dark blue and grey interior, punctuated by the occasional soft light, create the feeling that you've stumbled backstage on a movie set. The menu lists some interesting and imaginative dishes, mainly Italian-influenced with the odd oriental touch, where presentation plays second fiddle to flavour. Rainbow trout, for instance, is steamed and served in a tamarind sauce of perfect sharpness with stir-fried vegetables. The individual flavours of the vegetables – mange-tout, red peppers, mushrooms, carrots, spinach, scallions and red onions – are crisply identifiable and the glorious technicolour of the dishes more than compensates for the overly subdued lighting.

BISTROT 190	SW7

The Gore Hotel, 189 Queen's Gate, SW7 5EU
Telephone: 071-581 5666 (bistro) 071-584 6601 (hotel) £45
Open: all day daily
Meals served: 7am-12.30am (Sun 7am-11.30pm)

Bistrot 190 opened a year after 190 Queen's Gate in a move that pinpointed eating trends in the recessionary '90s. Although Antony Worrall Thompson is now based at the newer dell'Ugo, he is still creative chef/director of this phenomenally successful pair of restaurants where Chris Miller is head chef. The feisty bistro draws on big flavours to assemble a menu that will span continents and their cuisines for influences while concentrating mainly on Western Europe. Portions are enormous: a tall rösti pancake topped with grilled goat's cheese and served with salad is big enough for a main course at lunch. Lamb shank with flageolet beans, char-grilled chicken with parmesan courgettes, steak frites or squid and chips are just a few of the proper main courses. Marinated olives and fine beurre échiré accompany the country breads presented in a rustic basket for which there is a separate charge. A bottle of extra virgin olive oil sits on each table, although most dishes are correctly oiled. This large, square, high-ceilinged room has a light, countrified feel with its bunches of dried flowers and herbs, bottled fruit and pickles, wooden floors and gilded mirrors. The Bistrot shares the busy bar next door at 190 Queen's Gate with the new seafood bistro downstairs. An interesting wine policy in both places allows you to drink reasonably-priced wines by the pichet or choose from a changing list.

The Gore is a 58-bedroomed, attractively decorated hotel with a distinct style of its own that incorporates many Victorian elements. There are oriental rugs, potted palms and gilded mirrors, antique furniture and lovely prints.

Blakes Hotel — SW7

33 Roland Gardens, SW7 3PF
Telephone: 071-370 6701
Fax: 071-373 0442 £120
Open: lunch + dinner daily (closed 25+26 Dec)
Meals served: lunch 12.30-2.30, dinner 7.30-11.30

London's first designer hotel boasts 52 visually arresting rooms (of which 12 are suites), each with a bespoke interior by couturier-proprietor Lady Weinberg (alias actress Anouska Hempel) and many incorporating hi-tech CD and video systems. The hotel is fabulously well-dressed throughout, with dramatic use of blocked colour, although the public spaces are small. Downstairs, head chef David Wilson produces equally chic dishes to complement the sleek, black-lacquered, mirrored dining room with its Eastern accents. Blakes was London's original eclectic restaurant and the style still prevails. There is Szechwan crispy duck or rack of English lamb, inkfish risotto or chicken tikka with chilli raita. Salads include cucumber and dill or gruyère and endive. An almost excessively glamorous clientele sashays through the restaurant at lunch and dinner – usually spending foreign money, although home-grown devotees will be pleased to hear that prices have recently dropped (the duck dish from £29.75 to £19.75!) and prices are now high rather than airborne. This is true of the shortish, all-French wine list as well as the food. There is also a welcome 3-course set lunch at £25.00, from which a typical choice might consist of salmon tartare with coriander vinaigrette followed by lava-seared calves' liver with mustard sauce and iced chocolate and almond pudding to finish. Soufflés, from Swiss to winter berry, are a speciality. Drinks prices are still high but you pay for the view. Blakes is also a great place for sophisticated, healthy business breakfasts: don't miss the waffles or the power blini which comes with a breathtaking £30 supplement. There is a 24-hour room service menu (for people who would rather stay in their antique beds all day) which includes bayonne ham with figs, Andalusian langoustine salad and pastrami on rye.

Bloom's — NW11

130 Golders Green Road, NW11 8HB £40
Telephone: 081-455 1338
Open: all day Sun-Thurs, lunch Fri, dinner Sat (closed Good Friday, Xmas, Jewish Holidays)
Meals served: 11.30-11 (Fri 11.30-sunset, Sat sunset-3am)
Kosher restaurant, eternally popular.

BLOOM'S   E1

90 Whitechapel High Street, E1 7RA
Telephone: 071-247 6001   £40
Open: all day, Sun-Fri (closed Xmas, Jewish holidays)
Meals served: 11.30-9.30 (Fri 11.30-sunset)

Together with its Golder's Green branch, this is London's favourite Jewish restaurant, its reputation sustained by formidable helpings of good kosher food overseen by a rabbi and a religious supervisor. Salt beef is the top-selling item and the great Jewish dishes are listed alongside it, from Frankfurters to the more rarefied calves' foot jelly. Borschtes, chopped liver, latkes, tzimmas (dumplings), cold fried plaice or haddock and kishka are all expertly cooked and can be enjoyed either as a snack at the lively bar or in the large, smoothly run dining room. Sweet and sour cabbage is listed among the à la carte vegetables. Colourful service is from an efficient team of waiters who seem excessively thrilled to see you empty your plate and can be rather hostile if you don't. Brick Lane market and the excellent Whitechapel Art Gallery are close by. The wine list includes a house Israeli Cabernet Sauvignon.

BLUE ELEPHANT   SW6

4-6 Fulham Broadway, SW6 1AA
Telephone: 071-385 6595   £60
Fax: 071-386 7665
Open: lunch Sun-Fri, dinner daily (closed 25-27 Dec, 1 Jan)
Meals served: lunch 12-2.30, dinner 7-12.30 (Sun 7-10.30)

Astonishing decor, practically a complete Thai village with huts, streams, jungles and bridges. Flamboyant food and friendly service.

Blueprint Café — SE1

Design Museum, Shad Thames, Butlers Wharf, SE1 2YD
Telephone: 071-378 7031 £55
Open: lunch daily, dinner Mon-Sat (closed Bank Holidays)
Meals served: lunch 12-3, dinner 7-11

Part of Conran's ambitious scheme which also houses the Design Museum below and Le Pont de la Tour (q.v.) next door, the Blueprint offers sleek, informal dining in the Cal-Ital mode. Quality and consistency of food obviously depends on the chef in residence at the time: unfortunately chefs tend to treat the Blueprint as something of a training ground and then disappear. This is a shame as the location is quite special, with striking architecture, simple decor and big panoramic vistas of the Thames and Tower Bridge. A large terrace running the length of the restaurant is one of the better spots in London for dining al fresco on a sunny afternoon. From a short, daily-changing menu you might choose calves' liver with caramelised onions and pommes allumettes or steamed turbot with spinach and tomatoes – a dish which characterises the Blueprint's tendency towards low-fat creations. Pasta dishes are imaginative and beautifully cooked. Seasoning is invariably spot-on. A concise wine list, not unreasonably priced, is predominantly French in origin but with plenty from the New World and a decent choice of dessert wines. Attentive service from a young, stylish staff team. *See also page 21 – our Bistros and Brasseries Section.*

Bombay Brasserie — SW7

Courtfield Close, Courtfield Road, SW7 4UH
Telephone: 071-370 4040 £60
Fax: 071-835 1669
Open: lunch + dinner daily (closed 26+27 Dec)
Meals served: lunch 12.30-3, dinner 7.30-12 (Sun 7.30-11.30)

One of London's finest Indian restaurants, serving superior examples of subcontinental regional cuisines. The range and scale of the menu is impressive and defies Indian food-lovers not to discover a new dish. Fish chutneywali, ragara pattice, chicken tikka achari are among the starters, while regional mains include Tandoori prawns makhan palak and the Parsi dish lamb baffat. The Goan speciality chicken xakuti is not for the faint-hearted, though gentled with coconut. Lemon flavoured, pilau or plain basmati rice, breads including mint paratha, raitas and chutneys are all as they should be. An incomparably grand interior - complete with lavish Raj pictures, pastel paintwork, ceiling fans and exotic furnishings – makes this the most handsome Indian in town but on summer days you should try for a table in the lush, densely vegetated Conservatory, whose atmosphere, like the tempting sorbets, helps to cool the palate. The food, incidentally, is said to be overly hot for some tastes – but not mine! Service is exceptionally courteous, intelligent and swift. Tables are well-spaced and there is an excellent value serve-yourself buffet at lunchtime. Alternatives to the short wine list include a good range of fruit juices -including pear and cherry – or Cobra beer.

BOULESTIN	WC2

Garden Entrance, 1a Henrietta Street, WC2E 8PS
Telephone: 071-836 7061
Fax: 071-836 1283

still a 'grand' dining room

£95

Open: lunch Mon-Fri, dinner Mon-Sat (closed Bank Holidays, 1 wk Xmas, 3 wks Aug)
Meals served: lunch 12-2.30, dinner 7.30-11.15

Always one of London's most popular and most boisterous chefs, Kevin Kennedy ensures that Boulestin remains one of London's classiest French restaurants, having been founded in the '20s by Marcel Boulestin who was to become the world's first TV chef! A recent set-price menu began with a terrine of raw and smoked salmon with wild mushrooms, followed by roast Gressingham duck, the legs fashioned into a smoked sausage and served with Puy lentils. A pineapple and mango soufflé, chosen in preference to a gateau of hazelnuts, yoghurt and mango (rolled in praline and served with a caramel sauce), nearly finished me off. Of its type, the set menu represents excellent value for money whereas, dining from the carte – which reveals even greater skill and imagination on Kennedy's part – might cost you big money... One of London's most opulent dining-rooms, despite a basement location, Boulestin also boasts an award-winning wine cellar with serious mark-ups. Service is exceptionally attentive and knowledgeable, particularly on the wine side. Some of the power-based clientele occasionally complain about the proximity of neighbouring tables but it never seems to stop them from coming back!

Sumptuous warm decor terracotta & golds marble columns & chandeliers

The entrance facing the market piazza

BOULESTIN
restaurant français

Boyd's   W8

135 Kensington Church Street, W8 7LP
Telephone: 071-727 5452
Fax: 071-221 0615   **£60**
Open: lunch + dinner daily (closed 1 wk Xmas)
Meals served: lunch 12.30-2.30, dinner 7-11

Holding its own with rival establishments in the area, Boyd's is now open 7 days and, with its green-stained tabletops and stripped floors, has acquired a more casual air of late. The food still sparkles: tagliatelle with smoked salmon, pine nuts, lemon and shaved parmesan, salad of smoked goose and mango with a mild curry vinaigrette and grilled turbot with peppers, basil and olive oil give some idea of the range. For simplicity with style, try the grilled brill with basil butter, for imaginative invention the honey-roasted quail stuffed with spinach, bacon and pine-nuts and sitting on a Chardonnay sauce. The raised conservatory area at the back is a lovely spot for sunny lunches. Never pass up an opportunity to meet Boyd Gilmour himself: a former percussionist turned self-taught chef (with a little help from Kevin Kennedy of Boulestin), this is one charming Irishman whose company – as well as menu and varied wine list – is good value. The radiant Sharyn continues to manage the restaurant with great style.

The Brackenbury   W6

129-131 Brackenbury Road, W6   *– good local*
Telephone: 081-748 0107   **£35**
Open: lunch Tue-Fri + Sun, dinner Tue-Sat (closed Xmas, Easter)
Meals served: lunch 12.30-2.45, dinner 7-10.45

A rustic-looking restaurant in an up-and-coming area (christened Brackenbury Village by keen estate agents) serving food that's already made it. Locals love the utilitarian decor – its school benches and densely-crammed tables for 65 implying that capital is ploughed into food not frills – but customers come from farther afield too. Chef Adam Robinson has worked with the best, as his cooking reveals and is another self-proclaimed magpie in the kitchen. The results are impressive – imaginative canapés, grilled leeks vinaigrette, mussel and fennel soup, potato pancake with salmon roe and crème fraîche, Dover sole with a minted herb crust and beef stew with carrots and horseradish dumplings stand out – and prices remain staggeringly low, ensuring capacity audiences through lunch and 2 precisely-timed dinner sittings. He is adept at maximising the versatility of low-cost ingredients such as pigeon, rabbit or hake, which he might serve with lentils or with pesto mash and spinach. Unusual European cheeses are a welcome surprise and there are good ice-creams served with poached fruit. It is worth noting that the Adam and Katie Robinson have 2 small offspring themselves so the Brackenbury is baby- and children-friendly: breastfeeding at table is OK and high chairs are provided on request.

LE BRACONNIER — SW14

467 Upper Richmond Road West, SW14 7PU
Telephone: 081-878 2853 £45
Open: lunch Sun in winter, dinner daily (closed Bank Holidays, 5 days Xmas)
Meals served: lunch 12.30-2.30, dinner 7-11

Tucked away in East Sheen, this little restaurant is a cut above its local competitors, offering some excellent dishes from an interesting and entirely French repertoire by Terence Speers. Recession has forced prices down and 2 appealing set menus co-exist: the permanent one consists of bourgeois classics, the other changes monthly, travelling around the French regions. Onion soup, cassoulet with duck and ham, rabbit with prunes, apple and prune ice-cream are usually very well executed. A wine list towards the top end is intelligently selected and features some great digestifs.

LA BRASSERIE — SW3

272 Brompton Road, SW3 2AW
Telephone: 071-581 3089 £45
Fax: 071-823 8553
Open: all day, daily (closed 25+26 Dec)
Meals served: 8am-11.30pm (Sun 10am-11pm)

La Brasserie is exactly what you'd expect it to be – an authentically-styled room in the Parisian tradition open all day from first thing Monday to last thing Sunday night. It's some consolation for living on this island with its antiquated licensing laws and attitudes to eating and drinking out. Start the day with fried eggs or coffee and croissants, or drop in mid-morning for a cafe crème and a look through the papers. Lunch might be a full-blown 3-course affair, an omelette or just a casual assiette de fromages and a glass or 2 of red wine followed by some profiteroles au chocolat. A la carte, choose from grilled poussin, steak with shallots, andouillette with a crisp green salad or skate with black butter. Plats du jour can include oxtail or boeuf en daube and French fries are ubiquitous. Wine-wise, something from the selection of French country wines is preferable to the house carafes. *See also page 24 – our Bistros and Brasseries Section.*

BRASSERIE DU MARCHÉ AUX PUCES — W10

349 Portobello Road, W10 5SA
Telephone: 081-968 5828 £40
Open: lunch Sun, all day Tue-Sat
Meals served: 10am-11pm (Sun 11-4)

The street corner location and pavement dining lend an air of Gallic authenticity but the menu is somewhat more adventurous, with owner/chef Noel Ashbourne drawing on the local colour and multi-ethnicity of Portobello for inspiration. Croissants and coffee are served until midday, whereafter the menu goes pretty wild. A salad of kohlrabi with sweet potato and ginger, red snapper Caribbean style with cho cho and aubergine pancakes with tomato and cinnamon coulis convey the general wackiness but are usually well-handled. *See also page 25 – our Bistros and Brasseries Section.*

Brown's Hotel — W1

Albermarle Street, W1A 4SW
Telephone: 071-493 6020
Fax: 071-493 9381
Open: lunch + dinner daily
Meals served: 12-2.30, dinner 6.30-10 (Sat+Sun 6-9)

— an £8m. refit has been completed here, as of Oct '92

£80

A spot of tea and tiffin between 3pm and 6pm is the thing here at Brown's Hotel where Rudyard Kipling was an honoured guest – and very formal it is too. Popular with American tourists in search of Victorian values, this historic establishment flies the flag with pride, presenting old-fashioned cucumber and related sandwiches in a classically formal setting. Alternatively there is the rare option of High Tea, served between 4.15 and 4.45 pm in the restaurant and comprising the sweeter elements from the regular afternoon tea plus fishcakes, ham with chutney and a bubble and squeak confection or the mysterious 'high tea griddle'. Lunch and dinner are equally in the traditional vein, the English daily specials from the trolley being particular favourites; these include fish pie, pot-roasted duck and roast beef with all the trimmings on Sunday. Standards of furnishing and upkeep are high throughout the many public and private rooms and the 133 bedrooms. Service is always kindly and attentive.

Bubb's — EC1

329 Central Markets, EC1A 9NB
Telephone: 071-236 2435
Open: lunch Mon-Fri (closed Bank Holidays, 2 wks Xmas, 2 wks Aug)
Meals served: lunch 12-2.30

£65

This is a dinky and consistently good French restaurant in Smithfield with 2 floors linked by a spiral wrought-iron staircase. The lace curtains and well-worn chairs contribute to the overall impression of a popular restaurant in a French market town. Seasonal specialities and daily fish dishes aside, nothing much changes from one month to the next, including the male-dominated clientele. Warming favourites include gratinated onion or provençale fish soup and snails, which feature among starters alongside salads of shrimp or duck breast. Ancient tradition informs main courses like beef fillet with wild mushrooms, duck au poivre, veal with mustard, lemon sole with saffron sauce or skate with black butter, all of which are prepared with confident expertise. Classic puddings include mont blanc and crème brûlée. The wines are very generously-priced and efficient service is led by Madame Bubb herself. Be sure to book as this is one of the area's worst-kept secrets!

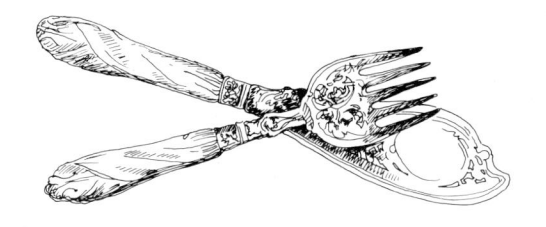

LE CADRE   N8

10 Priory Road, Crouch End, N8 7RD   *good local place.*
Telephone: 081-348 0606   £60
Open: lunch Mon-Fri, dinner Mon-Sat (closed Bank Holidays, 2 wks Aug/Sep)
Meals served: lunch 12-2.30, dinner 7-10.30

Simon Mills, based at this adventurous restaurant in Crouch End, is turning out some outstanding French dishes which deserve to be taken seriously. Fixed price menus are not unreasonably priced, nor is the comprehensive French wine list where cognac, calvados and armagnac are well-represented. Dishes straddle the ancient and modern traditions: smoked eel with hot potato salad might precede fillet of pork with sage and choucroûte or red mullet with tapenade and a warm herb vinaigrette served with a gratin dauphinois. Sautéed calves' liver with Dijon mustard sauce and pommes boulangères was superb, as was the roast saddle of rabbit with red wine. Among puddings, there is a fine apple tart with calvados sabayon or a millefeuille of caramelised pear. French cheeses are served with good raisin bread. There are occasional gourmet evenings, focussing on particular regions with well-researched menus and, in summer, there is seating on the large pavement area at the front. Several notches up from a bistro, Le Cadre is a unique and laudable venture in this gastronomically bypassed part of the world.

CAFÉ ANJOU   N13
394 Green Lanes, N13
Telephone: 081-886 7267   £5
Open: lunch + dinner Tue-Sun (closed 25+26 Dec, 1 Jan)
Meals served: lunch 12-3 (Sun 12-3.30), dinner 7-11 (Sun 7-10.30)
Informal restaurant specialising in regional French food.

CAFÉ DELANCEY   NW1

3 Delancey Street, NW1 7NN
Telephone: 071-387 1985
Fax: 071-383 5314   £4
Open: all day daily (closed Bank Holidays)
Meals served: 8am-midnight

A café, a bar, a brasserie, the original Café Delancey is open all hours giving its loyal customers exactly what they want, while not sticking to rigid gallic repertoire. Croque monsieur and steak sandwiches are well made and swiftly-served, while the menu also has a good selection of soups, salads and grills. There must be Swiss blood running in Delancey's veins: roesti (sic), as opposed to chips, come with everything, including chicken, rack of lamb, chargrilled steak, calves' liver with bacon and onions, smoked sausage with red cabbage, fried eggs and even the vegetable platter! Popular for Sunday brunch, newspapers are provided – which is then worked off with a hearty hike around the market stalls. Marble-topped tables and densely planted window boxes contribute to the lively and informal atmosphere. There is a short wine list although many prefer to consume quantities of cider or citron pressé.

Café Delancey   WC1

32 Proctor Street, Red Lion Square, WC1
Telephone: 071-242 6691
Fax: 071-383 5314   **£40**
Open: all day daily (closed Bank Holidays)
Meals served: 8am-11.30pm

The formula that made the original Café Delancey a success in Camden Town works equally well in Holborn. There is no minimum charge and a flexible continental menu is on offer all day long, providing serving all things to all people, from late breakfast to late supper. This is a proper café and might even be called a brasserie. Newspapers are provided and nobody will prevent you from poring over them for hours while consuming only a cappuccino or two. The menu lists warm goat's cheese salad with a honey vinaigrette, smoked trout with horseradish sauce and calves' liver with bacon, onions and rösti alongside other straightforward dishes which are just the ticket for lunch or dinner. En route to the bookshop or enjoying a meal with friends, Café Delancey is a useful address. It is quieter in the evenings than its northern counterpart and attracts a more touristy crowd. *See also page 30 – our Bistros and Brasseries Section.*

Café des Amis du Vin   WC2
11-14 Hanover Place, WC2
Telephone: 071-379 3444   £65
Open: lunch + dinner Mon-Sat (closed 1 wk Xmas)
Meals served: lunch 12-3, dinner 7-11.30
Popular Covent Garden venue. French food and wine. *See also p 28, our Bistros & Brasseries Section.*

CAFÉ DU MARCHÉ — EC1

22 Charterhouse Square, Charterhouse Mews, EC1M 6AH
Telephone: 071-608 1609
Open: lunch Mon-Fri, dinner Mon-Sat (closed Bank Holidays)
Meals served: lunch 12-2, dinner 6-10

– great local restaurant
£50

A rustic barn-like structure in a cobbled mews off this smart City square, the Café du Marché would be a real find if it weren't for the fact that the rest of the world seems to have found it before you! Walls of exposed brick, stripped wooden floors, an abundance of beams (especially in the upstairs grenier, an apposite name) and simple wicker furniture dispel any awareness of dining in a converted meat warehouse. Comfortably settled in this pared down, spacious room, you choose from an almost exclusively gutsy bourgeois menu on which English salt beef or gratin of polenta, mozzarellla and tomatoes stand out simply because their faces don't really fit. Warm sausage or wild mushroom salad, boudin blanc with a Bordelaise sauce, civet of hare with cassis and beetroot and chateaubriand, all from the handwritten set menu, ring more true and are followed by good, no-nonsense puddings among which crème caramel shines brightest. The casual, atmospheric 'attic' is open for lunch only and offers a simpler menu, consisting mainly of grills. Meat is of high quality, as one would expect and even demand from the Smithfield location! The short, pleasing wine list is exclusively French with two qualities of house red and white – ordinaire and superieur.

– cluttered fun interior of Café du Marché

Café Fish   SW1

39 Panton Street SW1   **£50**
Telephone: 071-930 3999
Open: lunch Mon-Fri, dinner Mon-Sat (closed 25 + 26 Dec, 1 Jan)
Meals served: lunch 12-3, dinner 5.45-11.30

The menu consists of a comprehensive range of fresh fish simply – some say blandly – prepared. No starters, but a pleasing appetiser of baguette and creamy smoked salmon pâté is presented automatically. Brochette de poissons, goujons de plie and oyster platters are typical choices. The place mats, giving the French and English names for almost every fish that swims in the sea, are invaluable and worth remembering for future reference. There is a fair selection of wines on a straightforward, inexpensive list. Beneath the big, bustling restaurant is a Francoholic basement wine bar serving a good range of sensibly priced drinks (most people drink Kir or French wines) and light dishes. Ideal for pre-or-post-theatre snacking.

Café Flo   NW3

205 Haverstock Hill, NW3 4QY
Telephone: 071-435 6744   **£35**
Open: all day daily (closed 4 days Xmas)
Meals served: 10am-11pm (Sun 10am-10.30pm)

This was the very first Café Flo and the one from which the spores for this ever-mushrooming group spread. Located bang next door to the Screen on the Hill and always crowded this, like the other Flos, offers soundly cooked, affordable bistro classics and a few innovations besides. The starters and puddings tend to outshine the main courses which are nonethless perfectly acceptable. The wine list is imaginative, drawing heavily on the New World and is not greedily marked-up. A young, bustling atmosphere prevails among both customers and staff. The coffee is excellent.

Café Flo   WC2

51 St Martins Lane, WC2N 4EA
Telephone: 071-836 8289   **£35**
Open: all day daily (closed Bank Holidays, 5 days Xmas)
Meals served: 10am-midnight, Sun 10-11.30pm

Russel and Juliette Joffe have hit the jackpot with their inexpensive chain of café-bistros in strategic spots around London. The cooking usually scores more hits than misses and is always terrific value. Seasonal bourgeois favourites such as pot-au-feu, steak frites, soupe à l'oignon, saucisses de Toulouse are competently cooked and there are assiettes of crudités, charcuteries or cheeses available for finger-foodies. Café Flo has picked up on the French 'formule' idea, offering rapid-service menus of restricted choice for White Rabbits with pressing schedules and slim wallets. Ideally located for dining either side of the theatre, cinema or opera (the Coliseum is next door), Flo also has bright service and inexpensive wines on its side. *See also page 32 – our Bistros and Brasseries Section.*

Café Pelican	WC2

45 St Martin's Lane, WC2N 4EJ
Telephone: 071-379 0309
Fax: 071-379 0782 £50
Open: all day daily (closed 24-26 Dec)
Meals served: noon-2am (closed 5-5.30pm only)

This long 100-seater brasserie, decorated in a low-key '30s style, has a welcoming bar at the front which is a great drop-in point for drinks, breakfast or snacks, especially the sandwiches (hot and cold). It is always a pleasure to find a West End bolthole which opens late and imposes no minimum charge. Perch on a high stool or sit at one of the small, marble-topped tables and wade through the morning papers. In summer, there is ample pavement seating out front. The menu throughout is very similar in style to those in Café Rouge chain (to which the Pelican is related) and, in the restaurant, it is usually best to stick to simple, classic dishes such as soups, steaks, salads or even rabbit or guineafowl rillettes with white wine and parsley. Roast monkfish with parsley and garlic butter worked better than the same fish done with a red wine sauce. Main courses come with an unlimited supply of warm baguette. There is limited choice for vegetarians if they have an aversion to filo or puff pastry, though a dish of infant veg pickled in vinegar, tarragon and shallots was good and tasty. The puddings are a highlight and can include caramel ice-cream with hazelnut sauce or nougat glacé with apricot purée. Set meals are usually good value and service charming. There is a short wine list and a very good selection of coffees and teas. *See also page 34 – our Bistros and Brasseries Section.*

Café Royal Grill Room	W1

68 Regent Street, W1R 6EL
Telephone: 071-439 6320 £80
Fax: 071-439 7672
Open: lunch Mon-Fri, dinner Mon-Sat (closed Bank Holidays)
Meals served: lunch 12.30-3, dinner 6-11
Luxurious surroundings, classic cooking by Herbert Berger, who is now Head Chef here.

Camden Brasserie — NW1

216 Camden High Street, NW1 8QR
Telephone: 071-482 2114 £45
Open: lunch + dinner daily (closed 24-26 + 31 Dec)
Meals served: lunch 12-3 (Sun 12.30-3.30), dinner 6.30-11.30 (Sun 5-10.30)

An overnight success when it opened some 10 years ago, this budget-conscious brasserie is even busier in these recessionary times. The unfussy surroundings are brightened with greenery and some jolly Mexican ceramics, not to mention the lively local clientele. Straightforward food concentrates on decent meat and fish, char-grilled to order. Good salads, great chips served in wooden bowls and hearty puddings make this a safe bet. Take your own relishes and hot sauces though, as only ketchup or mayonnaise are available. Conveniently located for Camden's numerous markets, cinemas and shops. Brief but satisfactory wine list. *See also page 36 – our Bistros and Brasseries Section.*

Canal Brasserie — W10

Canalot Studios, 222 Kensal Road, W10 5BN
Telephone: 081-960 2732 £45
Open lunch + dinner Mon-Fri (closed Bank Holidays)
Meals served: lunch 12-3.30, dinner 7.00-11 (bar open all day from 9am for snacks)

Converted from a Victorian chocolate factory in Kensal Docks which overlooks the Grand Union Canal through porthole windows, this modern brasserie occasionally opens on Saturday nights but usually only for private parties. Its spacious interior, with walls washed in gentle earthy shades, is the perfect setting for some eyecatching sculpture and temporary exhibitions by talented and worthy European artists. With its breezy glass-covered atrium, music in the evenings and children's menus the sparky Canal Brasserie is a very welcome newcomer on the North Kensington restaurant scene. The abbreviated, well-priced, broad-based menu can include dishes such as marinated baby squid on couscous, minted lamb salad or country sausage with lentils & salsa verde and there are always a couple of imaginative vegetarian dishes. Puddings are typified by a tangy citrus steamed pudding with toasted almonds or iced blueberry mousse, crème anglaise. *See also page 38 – our Bistros and Brasseries Section.*

CANNIZARO HOUSE	SW19

West Side, Wimbledon Common, SW19 4UF
Telephone: 081-879 1464 £75
Fax: 081-879 7338
Open: lunch + dinner daily
Meals served: lunch 12-2.30, dinner 7-10.30

This magnificent and unique Georgian hotel styles itself 'London's first country house hotel' and, in doing so, pitches itself predominantly at the conference trade: obviously Londoners looking for a country hotel will venture farther afield, while visitors from the provinces invariably want to be in the West End. Nonetheless, Cannizarro is a visual delight, with its endless sweeping lawns, ornamental lake and sunken gardens. There are 46 bedrooms and suites, all lavishly decorated and some with 4-poster beds. Rooms in the new wing are not as spacious as those in the main house. The public rooms are grand and vast, especially the drawing room with its ornate fireplace, and throughout the hotel you will find beautifully-draped curtains, fine repro furniture and good paintings. Cannizaro House is of course at its most glamorous and useful during Championship Fortnight when it offers well-planned packages including transport to and from the tournament. Keen players have complimentary temporary membership of the David Lloyd Sports Centre which is close at hand. A limousine service is usually available and is useful when travelling to or from either of London's airports, both of which are easily accessible from Wimbledon. In the lovely 60-seater restaurant, classic dishes of smoked salmon, duck and wild mushroom terrine, mulligatawny, fresh tuna niçoise, Dover sole and rack of lamb or chateaubriand for two are preferable to some of the more wayward nouvelle combinations. French classics such as tournedos of venison, oeufs en cocotte, oysters, galantine of duck with Cumberland sauce, darne of salmon, lemon sole or scampi provencale are listed separately. Puddings can be overwrought but don't be misled by some tortured descriptions of basically sound dishes.

The Capital   SW3

22-24 Basil Street, SW3 1AT
Telephone: 071-589 5171
Fax: 071-225 0011
Open: lunch + dinner daily
Meals served: lunch 12-2.30, dinner 7-11

£100

This exquisite townhouse hotel, partly designed by Nina Campbell and managed with flair by Jonathan Orr-Ewing, is the flagship of hotelier and restaurateur David Levin's estimable empire. There is even private garaging. Tucked away behind Harrods and built (not that you would ever guess) in 1971, it is a deceptively large establishment with some 48 rooms and 8 suites, some of which are beautifully styled using soft furnishings by Ralph Lauren. All, however, are luxuriously decorated with good oil paintings, expensive fabrics and lovely cream marble bathrooms boasting power showers, big mirrors and high-quality toiletries. Bespoke mahogany furniture was commissioned for The Capital by Margaret Levin, who plays an active part in the interior design of all the Levin concerns and supervises the hotel's glorious floral arrangements. Delightfully extravagant attention to detail includes the strewing of rugs on the bedroom sofas and the provision of an umbrella in each room. I am reliably informed that the ladies' room is one of the most alluring in London – all reds and pinks with deep copper basins! An intimate cocktail bar adjoins the elegant, high-ceilinged restaurant which, despite its size (only 35 covers) is one of Nina Campbell's more grandiose and carefully balanced projects. Chef Philip Britten purveys some of the finest set menus in town, especially at lunch, which attracts a regular business clientele and is astonishingly good value. There are two 6-course dinner menus, one of which is meat-free, as well as the à la carte. Although Britten's style is rooted in French traditions, his menus are always written in English, retaining French terminology where appropriate. The dishes are labour intensive and have admirable depth: among my favourites are crab and ginger ravioli with beurre blanc or haddock and asparagus risotto among starters, lamb cutlets with braised kohlrabi, pot roast of chicken with olives, tomatoes and confit potato or poêlé of rabbit, truffle, leek and carrots among the main courses. The use of good seasonal produce is maximised: broad beans are one of my favourite ingredients and here they are served in a salad of warm Parma ham or made into a velouté flavoured with savory. Soups are a particular strength, another favourite being red mullet soup with croûtons and crème fraîche. Both grilled pavé of beef and pot-roasted pheasant get a gutsy cèpes sauce. Britten is especially ingenious when it comes to transposing ingredients to create new classic puddings: a warm cheesecake with strawberry custard neatly twists the theme, while an orange soufflé is served with curaçao sorbet. Soufflés are excellent: prune and armagnac, pineapple, pistachio or blueberry are some that I have encountered over the years, while a caramelised pear mousse cleverly juxtaposes contrasting textures. Extensive, top of the market wine list. *See also page 212 – our Clover Award section.*

Le Caprice — SW1

Arlington House, Arlington Street, SW1A 1RT
Telephone: 071-629 2239
Fax: 071-493 9040
Open: lunch + dinner daily (closed dinner 24 Dec-lunch 2 Jan)
Meals served: lunch 12-3 (Sun 12-3.30), dinner 6-12

£65

Christopher Corbin and Jeremy King's restaurant is still *the* watering hole for the social and showbiz glitterati, despite the fact that they now have The Ivy as well. It is often said that there are no bad tables at the Caprice, which is lucky as you will probably spend most of your time with one eye on your fellow diners. It's that sort of place. Chef Mark Hix is responsible for a menu where French and Italian derivations sit happily alongside New Yorky brasserie classics and reworkings of English favourites. Lunch or dinner might consist of a Caesar salad followed by that perennial favourite, grilled poussin with sweetcorn fritters, or alternatively of chilled beetroot and horseradish soup and grilled turbot with seared scallions. On a dark day or in a dark mood, you might go for risotto nero followed by griddled scallops with cavalo nero to co-ordinate with the monochrome interior punctuated by Bailey's dramatic black and white portraits. The design, thought by some to be slightly dated, is kept gleaming and does nothing to deter a fiercely loyal clientele. Catch the Sunday brunch if you can: you can't go wrong with a pitcher of Bloody Mary, a bagel with lox and cream cheese, a dish of corned beef hash with fried egg and an Everest of newspapers. There is a concise, serious wine list with bottles from France, Italy, Spain, Australia, New Zealand and California including a couple of interesting magnums. Service, led by Jesus Adorno, is delightful. For more informal dining or swift snacks – a rabbit salad with artichokes and asparagus, say – perch at the long glossy bar and clock the revolving door.

Le Carapace — SW1
30 Winchester Street, SW1V 4NE
Telephone: 071-828 3366
Open: lunch Sun, dinner daily (closed 26+27 Dec)
Meals served: lunch 12.30-3, dinner 7-10.30
Set menus for six courses of modern regional French food. Friendly, local restaurant.

£55

Caravan Serai — W1
50 Paddington Street, W1M 3RQ
Telephone: 071-935 1208
Open: lunch Mon-Sat, dinner daily (closed 25+26 Dec)
Meals served: lunch 12-3, dinner 6-11 (Sun 6-10.30)
Afghan food, resembling Nepalese in its spicing and the first course dumplings. Middle Eastern in its reliance on flat breads.

£40

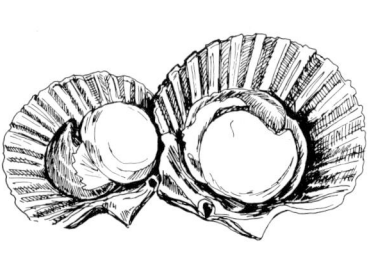

CARRARO'S SW8

32 Queenstown Road, SW8 3RX
Telephone: 071-720 5986 £50
Open: lunch Tue-Fri + Sun, dinner Tue-Sat (closed 25+26 Dec)
Meals served: lunch 12-2.30 (Sun 12-3), dinner 7-11 (Sat 7-11.30)

One of the more elegant south-of-the-river establishments, with subtly frescoed walls lending authenticity to the design, Gianfranco Carraro's restaurant serves serious regional food with a particular emphasis on the Veneto. The conspicuous nature of the live music – you might catch an opera night or a pianist banging out show tunes – can therefore be misleading. Wild boar, fungi and vialone nanno rice are flown in from Italy and the risotti – which on a recent visit combined leeks and mushrooms – are consequently among the best to be found in London. Tender cuttlefish is served in ink with grilled polenta which is also served as an accompaniment to a dish of salt cod cooked in olive oil and milk with anchovies and capers. This is clearly an unusual and imaginative menu: wild boar ham is partnered by cranberry sauce, San Daniele ham by fresh papaya. Carraro's signature dish is arguably the intriguingly successful ravioli of mascarpone and beetroot tossed in butter and and poppy seeds, though it is rivalled by those fabulous risotti, which might contain leeks and wild mushrooms or a good selection of seafood. The Venetian fritto misto is plentiful, the batter light and crunchy. Scampi are grilled and flamed in grappa while venison is cooked in a barolo sauce and garnished with walnuts and pine kernels. The kitchen knows when and where to elaborate: a classic dish like osso bucco alla milanese is allowed to speak for itself. An admirable wine list changes seasonally with the menu. Sunday lunch is a buffet of hot and cold Italian specialities, offering excellent value with children dining for half-price.

CASA COMINETTI	SE6

129 Rushey Green, SE6 4AA
Telephone: 081-697 2311   £40
Open: lunch Mon-Fri, dinner Mon-Sat (closed 25+26 Dec)
Meals served: lunch 12-2.30, dinner 6.30-11

An air of antiquity pervades this long-established local Italian restaurant – changes afoot as we went to press.

CASALE FRANCO	N1

134 Upper Street, N1 1PQ
Telephone: 071-226 8994   £45
Open: lunch Fri-Sun, dinner Tue-Sun (closed Bank Holidays, 2 wks Aug, 2 wks Dec)
Meals served: lunch 12.30-2.30, dinner 6.30-11.30

A designer-on-a-shoestring Italian restaurant that has already rocketed to fame as one of those places to be seen queuing outside (bookings are taken only at lunch). The minimalist conversion of a former garage makes for a constructivist interior with highly visible piping, raw brick walls, a chandelier wrought from copper wiring and naked bulbs and, by way of compensation, some rather good paintings. Upstairs is a barn-style attic room seating 50 which you can examine on your way to the loo. Prices are kept relatively low through a rapid turnover of tables so service needs to be swift and efficient. It usually is, often with a little brusqueness thrown in for good measure. It improves dramatically when the owners' children are working the floor. The simple menu is nonetheless more ambitious than most, including squid in its ink served with spaghetti or polenta. Specialities include spicy sausage (again served with polenta), cuttlefish in wine, lobster with tagliolini and granchio (crab) al casale. The 14 varieties of bubbling cartwheel pizza (served in the evening only) are excellent but, despite their size, you now have to order another dish as well if you dine between about 8.00-10.00pm. There is an exclusively Italian wine list with labels printed alongside. Always packed and noisy, this is by far by best Italian restaurant for miles around. Arrive early or late to avoid an unacceptably long wait or if you are reluctant to share a table.

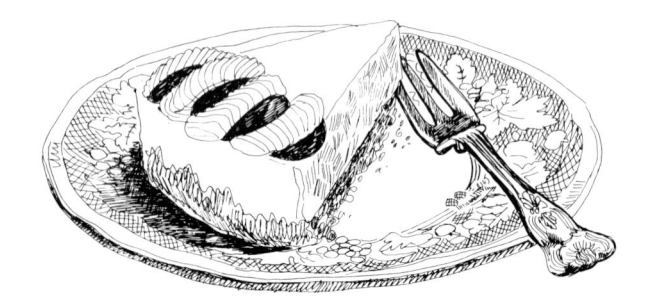

Chapter 11	SW10

47 Hollywood Road, SW10
Telephone: 071-351 1683 £40
Open: lunch + dinner Mon-Sat (closed some Bank Holidays, 3 days Xmas)
Meals served: lunch 12-3, dinner 6.45-12

This pretty, popular restaurant takes the favourite dishes of its Sloaney clientele and reassembles them on a single menu dominated by robust flavours. The appealing range of English, French, Mediterranean and Oriental dishes is mirrored in the devout eclecticism of the globetrotting wine-list. The menu lists salmon tartare with chive blinis, carpaccio and bruschetta as starters with main courses to suit most, if not all, tastes. Try the risotto with grilled vegetables, Thai chicken curry, ribeye with bearnaise and fries, chargrilled lemon and pepper chicken with citrus salad or calves' liver with crispy bacon and mash. The ultimate Franglais dish must be Chapter 11's Toulouse sausages with bubble and squeak – but it works!

Charlotte's Place	W5

16 St Matthew's Road, W5 3JT
Telephone: 081-567 7541 £45
Open: lunch Tue-Fri, dinner Tue-Sat (closed Bank Holidays, 1 wk Xmas/New Year)
Meals served: lunch 12.30-2, dinner 7.30-10

Tucked away beside Ealing Common, the unpretentious English cuisine at this predominantly pink, family-run restaurant is a notch above most home cooking. From the extensive menu you might choose a ramekin of haddock smokie, snails with garlic and parsley butter or seafood crêpe to start. Main courses range from thinly-sliced, pink-roasted duck breast with Cumberland sauce through Beef Wellington to calves' liver with sage. There is a concise, predominantly European wine list, sensibly-priced.

Chelsea Hotel   SW1

17 -25 Sloane Street, SW1X 9NU
Telephone: 071-235 4377   £65
Fax: 071-235 3705
Open: lunch + dinner daily
Meals served: lunch 12-2.30, dinner 6.30-10.30

Restored in 1990 (sadly losing the pool) and superbly located halfway down Sloane Street in the midst of the best designer stores, the Chelsea Hotel is stunningly attired. Chairs designed by Philippe Starck punctuate strikingly contemporary decor with especially bold use of colour throughout. There is an abundance of marble, glass and chrome, softened by vast and exotic flower arrangements. The lounge uses pastels to pleasing effect notably in the squidgy sofas. A visually arresting chrome/glass spiral staircase in the atrium diverts your gaze from the vertical bank of 4 TV screens. Individually-styled bedrooms play down the hyper-modernity of the public areas and have traditional comforts such as trouser press, hairdryer, air-conditioning, double-glazing. One floor has an emphatic no-smoking policy. Bathrooms are on the small side but are quite well-equipped. The bar and restaurant area has black marble floors and and a hi-tech spiral staircase. Neil Whiteford is responsible for the neat restaurant menu, priced like a brasserie, which changes every fortnight. On it you might find ballotine of duck with dried fruit chutney or warm fillet of red mullet with saffron oil and tapenade croûtes as well as classics such as French onion soup, asparagus or Parma ham with melon. Main courses take in simple grills and roast pork Normandy-style with gratin dauphinois plus the more imaginative poached fillet of brill with braised young lettuce and grain mustard sauce, grilled lamb cutlets with celeriac rösti or pan-fried calves' liver with Madeira-soaked grapes and linguini. For pudding, try the orange and raspberry parfait or the summer pudding with vanilla custard. When the bar is closed (3-5.30pm) drinks and tea are served in the lounge where interesting sandwiches on a variety of breads and other snacks are also served 24 hours a day.

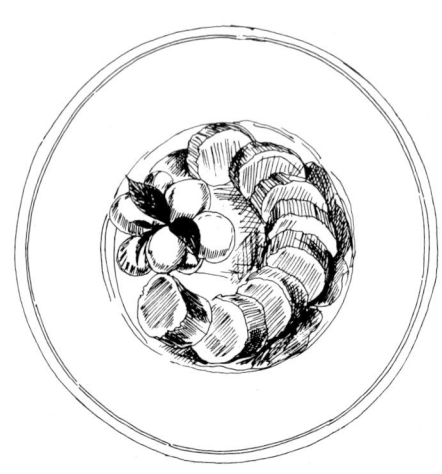

CHESTERFIELD HOTEL — W1

35 Charles Street, W1X 8LX
Telephone: 071-491 2622 £70
Open: lunch + dinner daily
Meals served: lunch 12.30-2, dinner 6.30-10.30 (Sun 7-10)

Entering the elegant foyer with its black and white marble-tiled floor reminds you that this plush Mayfair hotel was formerly the residence of the eponymous fourth earl. The bar has a refreshingly sombre English feel with its traditional decor, although The Terrace, conversely, is a light, modern, densely vegetated conservatory where you can take late breakfast or a snack aswell as lunch or dinner. Sturdy good taste prevails throughout with chandeliers, wood panelling, oil paintings, leather armchairs and Chesterfields much in evidence. Bedrooms have bold fabrics and darkwood furnishings. Charming staff and service.

CHEZ LILINE — N4

101 Stroud Green Road, N4 3PX
Telephone: 071-263 6550 £60
Open: lunch + dinner daily (closed Bank Holidays)
Meals served: lunch 12.30-3, dinner 6.30-11

This family-run Mauritian fish restaurant – the sister, or even mother to the newer La Gaulette (q.v.) – is neither sumptuous nor slick but rarely disappoints. The atmosphere is one of a brightly-lit French provincial cafe with poster-clad walls and lino floors complemented by friendly service. Portions are more then generous and those on a budget may find it cheaper to share a selection of starters although there is a minimum charge per person of around £10. The Mauritian-ness of the place comes through in the choice of tropical fish which usually include parrotfish, capitaine, bourgois, vacqua and red snapper as well as salmon or calamari and shellfish such as lobster, langoustines, prawns, mussels and scallops. Ingredients are cooked in the French/Mauritian style, with a preponderance of garlic, ginger, chilli and hot mustard sauces as well as tomato-based sauces or aïoli. For example, moules are served marinières or mauricienne (with tomato, herbs and chilli). Lobster takes the latter sauce, is stir-fried with ginger and chilli or is grilled with herbs and garlic – like the calamari. Simpler choices include oysters, seafood platters, fish soup, crab claws with aïoli. There are a number of creamy sauces, served for example with a concoction of lobster, prawn and salmon. Vegetarians will love the platter of pickled baby vegetables in a hot mustard sauce. Main dishes are accompanied by plain Basmati rice and salad and for pudding there is ice cream or a selection of tropical fruit. The house wine from Mauritius is retained on a sound, regularly updated list.

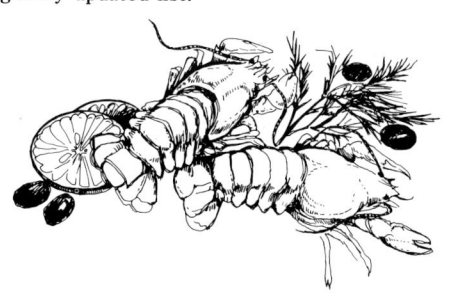

Chez Moi   W11

1 Addison Avenue, W11 4QS
Telephone: 071-603 8267   £65
Open: lunch Mon-Fri, dinner Mon-Sat (closed Bank Holidays, 1 wk Xmas)
Meals served: lunch 12.30-2, dinner 7-11

The bronze cigar-smoking cherub looks increasingly like a dissipated Peter Pan (who was, after all, a local) while Chez Moi itself seems destined to remain in Never Never Land, refusing to outgrow its fast and loose '60s childhood when the money flowed like vin de table and the red, mirrored interior was considered daring. Its clientele may now have gained in years and wrinkles but return time and again, prompted by nostalgia and a quest for new tastes. Accordingly, the menu lists Chez Moi Traditionnel to the left and Quelque Chose de Différent to the right. Recently among the 'something different's have been tortellini of pigeon to start, with a magret of Barbary duck as a main course. Greens including spinach, courgettes and French beans are done to perfection. Blithely indifferent to the harsh reality of the '90s, Chez Moi seems to have discovered the secret of eternal youth! *See also page 40 – our Bistros and Brasseries Section.*

Chinon	W14

25 Richmond Way, W14 0AS
Telephone: 071-602 5968 £65
Open: lunch Tue-Fri, dinner Tue-Sat (closed some Bank Holidays)
Meals served: lunch 12-2, dinner 7-10.30 (Fri+Sat 7-11)

The romantic, candlelit setting with its dark tented ceiling may not be to everyone's tastes but it suits me and the food is something to be reckoned with. Barbara Dean and Jonathan Hayes take pride in their work and have made Chinon rather more than just an intimate neighbourhood restaurant and a place worthy of a detour. There are good paintings and comfortable chairs and the food takes as its starting point good, fresh produce, imaginatively prepared. Presentation and flavour are paramount and the generous portions encourage you to feel well-fed as well as impressed. There is usually a crabmeat dish of the day: other fishy successes have included roast squid stuffed with pesto and a fine elaboration on the theme of a shellfish pilaff. Osso bucco is cooked with provençale herbs and served with saffron tagliatelle, a neat and delicious variation on the classic accompaniment of risotto milanese. Scallops are a definite speciality and I have yet to encounter a scallop dish here that did not work – a recent assemblage roasted them oriental-style with garlic, spring onions and ginger and served with mangetout. A stunning palette of puddings includes around 7 mini-masterpieces, while unusual cheeses are served with stunning fruit bowl. An ambitious wine list, whose contents are almost entirely French, includes some useful half bottles. You will probably need to book to beat the crush from the Beeb.

Christian's	W4

Station Parade, Burlington Lane, W4 3HD
Telephone: 081-995 0382 £55
Open: lunch Sun, dinner Mon-Sat (closed Bank Holidays)
Meals served: lunch 12.30-3, dinner 7.30-10

This very personal 10-year-old restaurant specialises in accurate French cooking by its chef/patron. The kitchen is on full view and soufflés, quenelles of salmon with hollandaise or chicken with garlic and herb sauce are typical offerings. A gutsy game terrine is served with orange pickles and an elegant mixed leaf salad. There are ample portions of vegetables and the potato dishes are unbeatable. The pudding choice is short but sound: fruit tarts and chocolate soufflé are excellent. Vegetarians are catered to with flair and imagination. There are a few tables outside in the summer.

CHRISTOPHER'S	WC2

18 Wellington Street WC2
Telephone: 071-240 4222 £65
Open: lunch Mon-Fri, dinner Mon-Sat (closed Bank Holidays)
Meals served: lunch 12-3, dinner 6-11.30

Since opening in late 1991, Christopher's, originally conceived as a highly-evolved lobster and steakhouse, has rapidly established itself as one of the most fashionable restaurants in town. The interior is a stagey interpretation of a modern palazzo: ascend the long, sweeping stone staircase with its camply-muralled dome and piped opera and enter the large, noisy frescoed dining-room dimly lit by tarantuloid steel chandeliers. The clientele is predominantly business-oriented at lunch, rowdier and sassier in the evening with a mixed crowd of socialites, celebrities, opera-goers, stargazers and wannabees. The staff are young and the place is packed every lunch and dinner. Christopher's is resolute in its steadfast adherence to a roster of plain, nothing-can-go-wrong American dishes on its main menu, although daily Californian and regional specials give chef Adrian Searing greater creative scope. This philosophy makes for a clean menu where regional and esoteric American classics such as carpetbag steak (a good fillet stuffed with oysters), midwestern meatloaf and New England boiled dinner rub shoulders with Caesar salad, clam chowder, crab cakes with red pepper mayo, oyster panroast or lobster Newburg. A very good chopped steak (offered with or without the bun) features on a lengthy list of simple grills where other highlights include Scottish or Maine lobster, the rack of lamb, the veal chop and the New York strip steak. Portions are ample and minimal saucing is supplemented by your choice from the tray of relishes and hot sauce. Searing has been allowed 2 highly successful innovations among starters: the chunky lobster coleslaw, rolled sushi-style in blanched Savoy cabbage leaves is one, the densely-flavoured smoked tomato soup another. Ideally, this should be accompanied by the winning bread, a chewy-crusted sesame and raisin number. Talked-about vegetables, ordered à la carte, include wondrous creamed spinach, deep-fried 'tobacco' onions, sweet potato hash and broccoli with garlic, black olives and chilli. The fries are skinny and crisp. Cakey puddings and pies are on the hefty side: alternatively, try some Häagen-Dazs ice-cream (frozen yoghurt if you're feeling virtuous) or one of the fruit sorbets. The well-travelled wine list features lots of good French wines as well as bottles from the New World. Downstairs is a lofty New York-style bar serving proper classic cocktails and a short day-long menu of starters, salads and sandwiches.

Chutney Mary SW10

535 King's Road, SW10 0SZ
Telephone: 071-351 3113 **£50**
Open: lunch + dinner daily (closed Sun for bar food)
Meals served: lunch 12.30-2.30 (Sun 12.30-3.30), dinner 7-11.30 (Sun 7-10)

Chutney Mary was the nickname for an Indian woman who affected English manners and dress and the term is highly apposite in describing this mould-breaking Anglo-Indian themed restaurant. The Verandah Bar at the entrance, furnished in the colonial style with wicker seating, serves Indian bar snacks (bhajis, samosas, Raj cottage pie and other starters from the main menu) alongside bottled lagers (including imported colonial beers). Wines have been selected for their ability to withstand buffeting by a wide range of spices. The dining area consists of 3 rooms downstairs, of which the Conservatory is the most spectacular, with its jungle greenery and comfortable banquettes. The menu grows in the evening although there is a good selection of regional (including vegetarian) dishes at lunch too, all served on rather dramatic china. Superb curried crab cakes come with salad and home-made pickles while the salmon and chutney kitchri is a generous, spicy variation on the traditional kedgeree. Noodles Mandalay incorporate shredded chicken in a mild coconut sauce. If you have a taste for hellfire, try the very hot green chicken curry from Goa, artistically presented with pyramids of aromatic steamed rice. An unusual side order of walnuts in yoghurt cools the palate and contrasts nicely with crispy, deep-fried okra. The less exotic dishes include Bombay bangers and devilled steak. Interesting rice accompaniments include yakhni pulao (rice cooked with lamb marrow) and lemon rice with cashewnuts. One bonus of this Anglo-Indian style is the freedom to experiment with puddings and the spicy hill station bread and butter pudding, crammed with almonds, cashews and pistachio nuts is exemplary. The Sunday buffet is excellent value and children are actively welcomed.

Ciao SW6

222 Munster Road, SW6 6AY
Telephone: 071-381 6137 £40
Fax: 071-386 0378
Open: lunch + dinner daily (closed 3 days Xmas, Sun before Bank Holiday Mon)
Meals served: lunch 12-3.30, dinner 6-11 (Sun 6-10.30)
Sister to Gavin's and the Depot, popular local restaurant.

| **Cibo** | **W14** |

3 Russell Gardens, W14 8EZ
Telephone: 071-371 6271 £70
Open: lunch daily, dinner Mon-Sat (closed Bank Holidays)
Meals served: lunch 12-2.30, dinner 7-11

In the vanguard of new-wave Italian cuisine when it opened a few years ago in far-from-fashionable North Kensington, Cibo now seems less than revolutionary compared with some of the newer places. It has nonetheless retained its fashionable status and loyal following, continuing to serve visually arresting modern Italian food on vibrant Tuscan pottery. Baby artichokes are a favourite ingredient, served sliced with a char-grilled flank steak or as a garnish for a dish of pappardelle with a light artichoke sauce. Another, more dramatic, pappardelle dish has the pasta blackened with squid ink and sauced with lobster. Gigantic grilled scampi are split in half and anointed with olive oil and fresh herbs; grilled squid is spiked with chilli. Charred lamb cutlets come with a light tomato sauce, goat's cheese and sautéed potatoes. Save space for a zabaglione with forest fruits: the dessert list is otherwise limited although tiramisu and ice-creams are good. A welcome range of grappas lends interest to the Italian wine list. Bold modern paintings contribute further to an altogether exuberant atmosphere. Good service from young staff who evidently know and enjoy what they're doing. *See also page 42 – our Bistros and Brasseries Section.*

| **Circle East** | **SE1** |

The Circle, Queen Elizabeth Street, SE1
Telephone: 071-403 9996 £45
Open: lunch Sun-Fri, dinner daily (closed Bank Holidays)
Meals served: lunch 12-2.30, dinner 6.30-10.30
New oriental restaurant in dockland setting.

CLARIDGE'S	W1

Brook Street, W1A 9JQ
Telephone: 071-629 8860
Fax: 071-499 2210
Open: lunch + dinner daily
Meals served: lunch 12.30-3, dinner 7-1

£95

The hotel has enjoyed Royal connections since its birth some 150 years ago: there is even an alcove table in the restaurant known as The Royal Box. Britannia still rules the waves at Claridge's: there is a distinctly clubby feel about the hotel, mainly because so many of the older guests are regulars and long stays are the norm. No 2 bedrooms are alike and many are decorated in the art deco style introduced by Basil Ionides in 1926 when he designed the black and white marble-tiled entrance hall with its Jazz Age themes and the stunning peach-toned Restaurant. Claridge's has, however, bowed to progress and now offers all the modern facilities befitting an internationally envied hotel. Dining at Claridge's is a primarily 2-tiered event, in more ways than one. The formal Restaurant offers a wide-ranging menu that incorporates grills, classic dishes, modern dishes plus roasts and puddings traditionally-served from trolleys. Marjan Leznik's highly-developed cuisine is available for those desirous of it and menus are market-led. Alongside 5 traditional soups you will find starters such as red mullet fillets with olive oil and sweet peppers, carpaccio of vegetables with oriental dressing or tortellini of scallops and crab with lemon thyme butter sauce, all of which strike a distinctly modern note. Your luxurious main course might be a turbot soufflé with oysters, a medley of calves' brain, kidney and sweetbread, grilled guineafowl with truffled potato or a fricassée of oysters, mussels and crayfish in a magical saffron broth or even a dish of spiced venison in game and bitter chocolate sauce. A parmesan soufflé is a nice alternative to the cheeses and puddings. The staff are highly trained and the waiters – who are really more like butlers – have astonishing memories. There is no bar but drinks are taken in the foyer to the traditional strains of the Hungarian quartet. The pink and green reading room is one of the tip-top places in London to take afternoon tea: while you're there, try to peek into the magnificent Wedgewood drawing room – one of 5 private dining rooms, all lavishly appointed. The Causerie sounds French but is in fact distinctly Scandinavian in flavour. At weekday lunch there is a smörgasbord and while not compulsory (there is an alternative menu) this is what most people tend to eat. The price, rather quaintly, depends on your choice of first drink. To order tomato soup and lamb cutlets is rather to miss – or ignore – the point. You are expected to have two stabs at the central smörgasbord (2-tiered) from which you help yourself. There are two tiers, one with lots of cold fishy things, the other with meat and hot dishes. Good international puddings and huge pots of coffee precede akvavit or flavoured schnapps distilled from grain or potatoes, taken with a lager chaser. Pre-theatre and supper menus are reasonably priced: simple home-style dishes feature strongly, among them a fricassée of lamb with dumplings or a sauté of chicken with lentils and wines by the glass are recommended to match each one.

CLARIDGE'S

Clarke's   W8

124 Kensington Church Street, W8 4BH
Telephone: 071-221 9225
Fax: 071-229 4564

£70

Open: lunch + dinner Mon-Fri (closed Bank Holidays, 1 wk Xmas, 4 days Easter, 2 wks Aug)
Meals served: lunch 12.30-2, dinner 7-10

In an age when the consumer dictates, Sally Clarke succeeds by remaining resolutely dictatorial and retaining her streamlined, modern no-choice menus. At dinner you pay your money and you hold your breath – but with this fine a chef in the kitchen the odds are definitely stacked in your favour. Some of the finest home-baked breads in town (also on sale in Sally's shop next door) set the tone for a healthy repertoire where salads, grilled meat or fish, marinades and vegetables prevail. Thinly sliced smoked salmon and raw wild salmon might be served with lemon as a starter, followed by a a char-grilled guineafowl with summer vegetables, lentils and prosciutto. Bread and butter pudding is made from brioche or panettone. Lunch is exceptionally good value and offers a limited choice. Predominantly good Californian wines complement the food perfectly. Don't miss the shop on your way out.
See also page 214 – our Clover Award section.

Coffee Gallery   WC1

23 Museum Street, WC1
Telephone: 071-436 0455

£25

Open: all day daily
Meals served: 8.30am-5.30pm (Sat 10-5.30, Sun 12-6.30)
Anglo-Italian café, unlicensed, very popular especially at lunchtimes.

THE CONNAUGHT	W1

Carlos Place, W1Y 6AL
Telephone: 071-499 7070
Open: lunch + dinner daily
Meals served: lunch 12.30-2, dinner 6.30-10.30

£100

The Connaught is one of London's – and indeed the world's – most deeply respected hotels among trade and public alike. Run in a supremely discreet, very English manner by Paolo Zago, it is the hotel to which the Establishment returns time and time again. That is why it is not a household name in the same way as, say, the Savoy (a sister establishment) or the Ritz. No brochure exists and the fax number is ex-directory. Every last detail of a guest's stay is kept on file but the fact that the staff, who have rarely been faulted during the hotel's 150-year history, have near-photographic memories impresses still further. Walk into the Connaught five years after your last visit and they will greet you by name. Bedrooms radiate understated luxury with rich brocades and fine antiques and fresh flowers. The venerable restaurant, ruled with an iron rod by chef de cuisine Michel Bourdin, offers an exemplary classic menu featuring traditional British cuisine incomparably well-cooked plus fine French dishes too. The setting is entirely grand and old-fashioned with an abundance of highly polished oak panelling, serious linen, expensive cutlery and crystal. There are recessed mirrors and an ornate plasterwork ceiling. To start, there might be foie gras with cubes of port jelly and black truffle, jellied lobster or kipper pâté. Your meal is priced according to the choice of main course and there is a fixed lunch special for each day – Irish stew on Tuesday, oxtail on Friday. Lancashire hotpot includes oysters and the roasts, such as duck with peaches, are carved from silver-domed trolleys. Among the vegetables are salsify with lardons or celeriac purée. Puddings from the trolley include rice pudding, pear crumble with vanilla custard, bread and butter pudding or even a millefeuille of wild strawberries. Alternatively, go for a savoury such as mushrooms on toast or devilled sardines. The Connaught being in a time-warp that only adds to its elegance and grandeur, dishes tend to have delightfully complicated, old-fashioned franglais names like 'crème brûlée d'un soir' or the quaint 'petits légumes frou frou'. Elsewhere the showy Franglais menu name-drops like mad and is great fun to read – spot the oysters Christian Dior, consommé Cole Porter or oeuf en gelée Stendhal. Service, from a beautifully turned-out, tailcoated team is notoriously wonderful, gliding around with faultless attention to detail. The Connaught is an especially fine place to dine during the game season. The Grill Room, open during the week only and equally grown-up, has a not dissimilar à la carte menu. Similar selection of grills is also available in the Restaurant. The French, German and Italian wine list is expensive and includes no fewer than 17 champagnes. Smoking is forbidden in both Restaurant and Grill. *See also page 216 – our Clover Award section.*

Hotel Conrad — SW10

Chelsea Harbour, SW10 0XG
Telephone: 071-823 3000
Fax: 071-351 6525 £80
Open: lunch + dinner daily
Meals served: lunch 12-3 (Sun brunch 12-3.30), dinner 7-10.30

Australia, Belgium, Canada, the French West Indies, Hong Kong, Ireland, Mexico, Monaco, Turkey – each has its own Conrad Hotel, which gives an idea of the global scale on which this massive operation in Chelsea Harbour has been conceived. A monument to hotel-keeping in the '90s, the Conrad excels in terms of capacity, design, furnishing, facilities, views and service. The interior design is by David Hicks, who has created a streamlined hotel remeniscent of an art deco cruiseship. Standards are of the highest order throughout with staff attentive and helpful. In the Compass restaurant, the dishes are printed over maps of the world to reflect Andrew Bennett's globe-trotting menu. Mediterranean fish soup rubs shoulders with fresh asparagus Flemish-style or marinated duck with leeks and ginger. There is also a Häagen-Dazs ice cream parlour which is especially popular at lunch. With Marco Pierre White and Michael Caine about to open their Canteen opposite, perhaps Chelsea Harbour will finally attract the gastronomic attention it deserves.

Cork & Bottle — WC2

44-46 Cranbourn Street, WC2H 7AN
Telephone: 071-734 7807 £50
Open: all day daily
Meals served: 11-10.30 (Sun 12-10.30)
Popular wine bar with good list.

Corney & Barrow	EC2

118 Moorgate, EC2M 6UR
Telephone: 071-628 2898 £60
Fax: 071-382 9371
Open: lunch Mon-Fri (closed Bank Holidays)
Meals served: lunch 11.30-3

Push-button waiter service and banks of VDU's make this a New York-style office away from office for City slickers, styled in red and black with mirrors galore and a striking steel staircase. Alongside the champagne bar and wine shop is a restaurant where Robin Stewart's menu is not dissimilar in style and layout to that at Cannon Street. Starters are straightforward and might include smoked salmon served with lemon and capers or a soup or carrot and spring herbs. Main courses straddle the traditional and Mediterranean modes: fillet steak with Madeira and truffle sauce might be listed beside a paella with chicken and mussels or grilled tuna steak with garlic and fresh herbs. Puddings remain comforting and traditional, with the option of a colourful platter of sliced fresh fruit. Predictably strong wine list. *See also page 44 – our Bistros and Brasseries section.*

Corney & Barrow	EC2

109 Old Broad Street, EC2N 1AP
Telephone: 071-638 9308 £60
Open: lunch Mon-Fri (closed Bank Holidays)
Meals served: lunch 11.30-3

This is the most old-fangled of the 3 restaurants, with polished service and elegant, clubby decor in muted dark greens with a single vast floral arrangement. A copy of the Financial Times is complimentary. The cooking is safe but modern, featuring dishes like pan-fried scallops with creamed leeks or skate vinaigrette with greens. Terrine of Mediterranean vegetables and red mullet strikes a distinctly modern note. Main courses are more traditional, among them braised oxtail with vegetables, grilled lamb's kidney with breadcrumbs and anchovy butter or guineafowl wrapped in a vine leaf and served with foie gras and grapes. A good choice of puddings includes rhubarb upside down tart, rice pudding or blueberry ice-cream. A wide range of teas and tisanes is listed alongside coffees that include a particularly potent ristretto. *See also page 45 – our Bistros and Brasseries Section.*

CORNEY & BARROW — EC4

44 Cannon Street, EC4N 6JJ
Telephone: 071-248 1700 £60
Open: lunch Mon-Fri (closed Bank Holidays)
Meals served: lunch 12-3

A similar formula to Moorgate but with a predominantly art deco interior featuring lavish use of glass, chrome and pastel tones. Gazpacho or gravadlax might be followed by fillet of beef with a Stilton crust, spicy chicken breast with a cucumber chilli salad or grilled sailfish with fresh herbs. Among the one-course meals there might be a giant mixed salad topped with honey-roasted duck. Fine service, excellent wines and financial gadgetry are the same as at the sister establishments. If you are pressed for time, you are guaranteed service within one hour.

Despite being based on a common formula, each of the three Corney & Barrow restaurants, run by the respected wine merchants of the same name, has its own very particular decorative style and individual atmosphere. Generous concessions are always made to healthy eating (low-fat, lightly-sauced dishes are asterisked on the menu) and there are always vegetarian options. The Cannon Street and Moorgate branches also offer one-course meals at £7.50: the rib steak grill is a popular fixture but alternatives include giant toad-in-the-hole with onion gravy, leek and potato frittata or spicy fishcakes with sweetcorn and chilli tomato sauce and curly fries. Concise but formidable wine lists feature especially wonderful clarets and burgundies, including plenty at the top end of the price range for celebrating that special deal!

LA CROISETTE — SW10

168 Ifield Road, SW10 9AF
Telephone: 071-373 3694 £65
Open: lunch Sun, dinner Tue-Sun
Meals served: lunch 1-2.30, dinner 7-11.30

Pierre Martin's successful fishy formula is repeated at this traditional restaurant where the set price buys you a kir, amuse-gueules, 2 fish courses, cheese, salad, pudding and coffee. Good value and terrific quality. Alternatives to the famous and largely irresistible plateau de fruits de mer include skate with black butter, John Dory with vermouth or salmon with leaks. Scallops, lobster and mussels are offered in a variety of styles – saffron and curry sauces are just 2 of several accompaniments for scallops for example – and there are a few meat dishes too. This is one of the few restaurants where you will still find frogs' legs on the menu, cooked here in the provençale style. Speak French to the waiters if you can: you will find that service improves dramatically! The good selection of rosé wines is a welcome feature on a short but serviceable list.

CROWTHERS	SW14

481 Upper Richmond Road West, SW14 7PU
Telephone: 081-876 6372 £60
Open: lunch Tue-Fri, dinner Mon-Sat (closed Bank Holidays)
Meals served: lunch 12-2, dinner 7-10.45

Run by two couples – the men cook, the women run front of house – Crowthers offers a set menu plus dishes of the day. The regular local audience come to applaud accomplished cooking, especially puds. Lovely baked goat's cheese in toasted sesame seeds on garlic crouton, roast lamb comes with a garlic and thyme sauce or herb-encrusted with redcurrant and rosemary sauce. They also find time to run an outside catering company called Top Table.

CZECH CLUB	NW6

74 West End Lane, NW6
Telephone: 071-372 5251 £30
Open: lunch Sat, Sun + Bank Holiday Mon, dinner daily
Meals served: lunch 12-3, dinner 6-10
Substantial Eastern European fare, very reasonable prices.

DANIELI	W4

142 Chiswick High Road, W4
Telephone: 081-994 2628 £45
Open: lunch Mon-Fri, dinner Mon-Sat (closed Bank Holidays)
Meals served: lunch 12-2.30, dinner 7-10
Friendly local Italian restaurant.

DAN'S	SW3

119 Sydney Street, SW3 6NR
Telephone: 071-352 2718 £65
Fax: 071-352 3265
Open: lunch Mon-Fri, dinner Mon-Sat (closed Bank Holidays, 1 wk Xmas)
Meals served: lunch 12.30-2.30, dinner 7-10.45 (Sat 7-10.30)

The food at this chummy local restaurant has improved under the influence of new chef Xavier Goffroy. Recent successes have included a salad of king prawns on shredded sweet-sour cabbage and another of goat's cheese, followed by crispy roast duck with Chinese spices. Puddings are on the hefty side, among them a caramelised lemon tart and a chocolate truffle cake with coffee bean sauce. Dan's is a good venue for private parties, especially the conservatory which seats 35. The garden makes it especially popular in the summer.

DAPHNE	NW1

83 Bayham Street, NW1
Telephone: 071-267 7322 £40
Open: lunch + dinner Mon-Sat (closed 25 Dec, 1 Jan)
Meals served: lunch 12-2.30, dinner 6-11.30
Friendly local Greek restaurant.

DEALS WEST RESTAURANT DINER	W1

14/16 Fouberts Place, W1
Telephone: 071-287 1001 £50
Open: all day daily
Meals served: 12-11.30 (Fri+Sat 12noon-12.30am, Sun 12-10.00)
Another branch of Eddie Lim, Lord Lichfield and Viscount Linley's popular Chelsea diner. *See also page 46 – our Bistro's & Brasseries section.*

DELL'ARTE SW1
116 Knightsbridge, SW1X 7PJ
Telephone: 071-823 9983
Open: lunch + dinner Mon-Sat (closed Bank Holidays)
Meals served: lunch 12-4 (Sat 12-3), dinner 7-11
Modern Italian restaurant near Harrods.

£50

DELL'UGO W1

Telephone: 071 734 8300
Open: lunch + dinner daily
Meals served:
Ground Floor Café: 11-12.30
First Floor: lunch 11.30-3, dinner 5.30-11.30
Second Floor: lunch 12.30-3, dinner 7.30-11.30

£40
£55

As well as remaining creative chef/director of 190 Queen's Gate, ebullient überchef Antony Worrall Thompson now presides over this jam-packed 3-floor eaterie, serving consistently inventive food to a media-dominated clientele who appreciate the generosity of portions and pricing alike. The lively ground-floor bar, which opens onto the street in fine weather, serves a menu of 'consequential nibbles' including root vegetables crisps plus bread-based snacks such as bruschetta, crostini and panino which also appear on the menu upstairs, among them a thoroughly grown-up sandwich of smoked salmon, cream cheese, crispy bacon and mango chutney. Upstairs are 2 dining rooms, one colourful and noisy with no bookings accepted, the other more subdued and clubby where reservations are taken. Here, Worrall Thompson goes around the world in 80 dishes, throwing fistfuls of fresh herbs at every idea encountered along the way. So sprawling and comprehensive is the menu that you may find it difficult to choose between seared peppered tuna sashimi with spicy lentil salad, wild mushroom risotto, steamed mussels, clams and greens with lentil and coriander broth or duck foie gras with lumpy mash and crispy onions. Among the pasta dishes is taglierini with grilled squid, olive oil, garlic, chilli and parsley; among the salads one of greens, gorgonzola, parmesan croutons and mollet egg. Many dishes are offered either as a starter or as a main course (with adjusted prices), although only a massive appetite would order baked oxtail with macaroni cheese and garlic chives as an appetiser! Recognising the fact that many people are floored by *two* of his vast courses, Worrall Thompson has a section specifically entitled 'One Pot Dining' which includes big snacks such as chopped tuna steak on niçoise salad, paillard of salmon with baked rice polenta and wilted greens or chicken baked with tomato and ginger, served with chili noodles and spicy aubergine. Puddings such as Granny Smith tart with cinnamon ice-cream are closely rivalled by near-irresistible cheese assemblages such as grappa red bliss potatoes with melted taleggio or poached red wine pears with creamy gorgonzola. There are 2 wine lists, one price-banded and coming from a different (credited) supplier every couple of months. House wines by the pichet or bottle are very good. In a typically witty touch by AWT, 'hippy teas' are listed alongside the usual choice of coffees.

DEPOT	SW14

Tideway Yard, Mortlake High Street, SW14 8SN
Telephone: 081-878 9462 £35
Fax: 081-392 1361
Open: lunch + dinner daily (closed 25+26 Dec)
Meals served: lunch 12-3, dinner 6-11 (Sun 7-10.30), open all day from 11am for snacks

Brasserie formula in a riverside location with good, well-flavoured straightforward food. The Depot is usually packed all year round, though business rockets in summer when there is al fresco seating for 20. Menus change regularly but, as at the other restaurants in this small chain of which this is the original, fresh home-made pastas are the speciality, often with unusual sauces. There are plenty of other options including lemon sole meunière, prawn stir-fry, tarragon lamb cutlets or gratinated stuffed pepper for vegetarians. Nice touches among side-orders include French beans with toasted almonds or cheese and ham crostini. It is worth noting that sandwiches, cakes and other light snacks are served all day. The wine list which appears on the back of the menu has some exceptionally good wines at user-friendly prices.

DON PEPE	NW8

99 Frampton Street, NW8 8NA
Telephone: 071-262 3834 £50
Open: lunch daily, dinner Mon-Sat (closed 24+25 Dec)
Meals served: lunch 12-3, dinner 7-1

Don Pepe was here long before tapas bars started popping up like campianones and is certain to outlive them by many years. The bigger your group the more you get to taste. Clams, meatballs, anchovies, squid rings, Spanish sausage, tortilla, patatas bravas. Also more substantial dishes including paella. The wine list boasts of a 'Spain just waiting to be tasted'. Only fools would not rush in.

THE DORCHESTER — W1

Park Lane, W1A 2HJ
Telephone: 071-629 8888
Fax: 071-409 0114
Grill: £110
Open: lunch + dinner daily
Meals served: lunch 12.30-2.30, dinner 6-11 (Sun 7-10.30)
Oriental Room: £110
Open: lunch Mon-Fri, dinner Mon-Sat
Meals served: lunch 12-2.30, dinner 7-11
Terrace Restaurant: £110
Open: dinner Tue-Sat (closed Bank Holidays)
Meals served: dinner 7-1

The lavish refurbishment of the Dorchester was a massive enterprise that has paid off. Guests rarely leave unimpressed and the hotel looks certain to regain and retain its status as a benchmark for the industry well into the next century. Public areas, bedrooms and suites are all gleaming and thoroughly up-to-date and a new, darkly chic nightclub designed by Nicky Haslam is to be found in the basement. The Oriental restaurant is perhaps the most successful element in the new-look Dorchester and is certainly among the top 3 Chinese restaurants in London. Sesame prawns with lemon sauce, stir-fried scallops with spicy chilli sauce and stir-fried strips of beef and asparagus in a yam basket are all successful and original innovations and the dipping sauces are all excellent. Irresistible favourites are here too, including Peking duck, Cantonese medallions of beef and braised superior shark's fin with brown sauce. Chef Simon Yung's cooking is spot-on, smooth-running service is faultless and the set lunch is incomparable value at £20. There are a number of delightful private dining rooms. The format in the Grill Room, lavishly Moorish in appearance, continues unchanged – Great British classics are the main attraction. The traditional menu celebrates the best domestic produce, with Morecambe Bay potted shrimps, Cornish dressed crab, Glamorgan sausages, skate with capers and brown butter, shepherd's pie or braised oxtail with vegetables. There is a lunch special each day of the week (boiled silverside with caraway dumplings on Mondays, for example) and a straightforward selection of grills including turbot or lobster. Among the marginally more exotic offerings are stuffed herrings rolled in bacon with cider sauce or pan-fried south-coast scallops on courgettes with rose petal vinaigrette. This is one of the few restaurants in London to offer pickled walnuts à la carte, best enjoyed with the fine cheeses. In the glittering Terrace restaurant, executive chef Willi Elsener and premier sous-chef Roger Narbett ensure that standards are as high as ever, while several menus make the choice even harder. Les Trouvailles du Marché comes as a 3- or 6-course version, there is a menu leger and also a formidable carte. Try the gratin of sweetbreads with asparagus and truffles or the pot-au-feu of chicken and beef with marrow. Pigeon is served as a duet, the breast sautéed and the leg presented en croûte with a sauce of wild mushrooms and asparagus tips. A terrine of blue cheese with poached pear is offered as an alternative to the cheese trolley. First among puddings is the chocolate millefeuille, closely followed by the orange tart with almond ice cream. Thoroughly professional service makes a visit to the Dorchester an experience you will want to repeat.

La Dordogne	**W4**

5 Devonshire Road, W4 2EU
Telephone: 081-747 1836 **£50**
Fax: 081-994 9144
Open: lunch Mon-Fri, dinner daily (closed Bank Holidays)
Meals served: lunch 12-2.30, dinner 7-11

This is a fine local restaurant comprising 3 cosy rooms and specialising, as the name suggests, in predominantly French cuisine but with an emphasis on lighter saucing. It also functions as an oyster bar serving natives from Cork and rock oysters from Brittany and Cork plus moules marinières. On the menu proper are pheasant terrine, marinated salmon with lime, steamed fresh fish with saffron sauce, medallions of monkfish with Meaux mustard sauce and sliced fillet of lamb with honey and mint, best accompanied by the good gratin dauphinois. Lobster is cooked in a variety of ways: it is served cold with mayonnaise in summer, poached in sweet Jurançon wine in winter. Fine puds include a warm crêpe with prunes and rum ice-cream and a gratin of apples with caramel sauce. The crème brûlée and chocolate marquise are less ambitious but equally good. An exclusively French regional wine list is well-balanced and very generously priced.

Downtown Sulemans	**SE1**

1 Cathedral Street, SE1
Telephone: 071-407 0337 £40
Open: lunch + dinner Mon-Fri
Meals served: lunch 12-2.45, dinner 7-10.30
International menu served in Southwark.

Dragon Inn	**W1**

12 Gerrard Street, W1Z 7LJ
Telephone: 071-494 0870 £25
Open: lunch + dinner daily (Closed 8pm 24-26 Dec)
Meals served: 12-11.30 (dim sum 12-4.45)
London's best dim sum. Excellent, authentically earthy Cantonese cooking. Try the tripe dishes or the pig's trotter with braised noodles. Service variable.

Dragon's Nest	**W1**

58 Shaftesbury Avenue, W1V 7DE
Telephone: 071-437 3119 £40
Open: lunch + dinner daily (closed 24+25 Dec)
Meals served: lunch 12-2.45, dinner 5-11.15 (Sat 12-11.15, Sun 12-10.45)
London's only Chinese restaurant specialising in Taiwanese cooking rather than the usual Cantonese. Ask the staff's help in ordering unfamiliar dishes and Taiwanese dumplings and breads.

Dukes Hotel   SW1

35 St James's Place, SW1A 1NY
Telephone: 071-491 4840
Fax: 071-493 1264   £90
Open: lunch Sun-Fri, dinner daily
Meals served: lunch 12.30-2, dinner 6-10 (Sun 7-10)

26 suites as well as 36 bedrooms are now available at this handsome hotel which won one of the Best Bloomin' Hotel awards in the *London in Bloom* competition. Former sous-chef Steve Robinson is now at the helm but there have been few changes in terms of either style or content to the menu which offers a well-balanced selection of competently-cooked dishes with an English bias. There is a good wine list in the middle price range.

The Eagle   EC1

159 Farringdon Road, EC1R 3AL
Telephone: 071-837 1353   £30
Open: lunch + dinner Mon-Fri (closed Bank Holidays, 3 wks Xmas)
Meals served: lunch 12.30-2.30, dinner 6.30-10.30

The yuppies of yesteryear are fast being replaced by a new breed of trendy, price-aware foodniks, all of whom seem to be flocking to The Eagle – which still takes no bookings. To all intents and purposes, this is a pub which serves the kind of dishes you would expect to find in a contemporary pseudo-Mediterranean restaurant. Scallops are sautéed with bacon, green peppers, oregano and chilli and served with a salad of watercress, fennel and green beans. Char-grilled bluefish comes with grilled Mediterranean veg, caldeira a moda de guincho is a stew of squid, swordfish, hake and prawns. Pushy flavours and bumper portions. Owners Michael Belben and David Eyre have created a popular and successful enterprise by eliminating any precious trimmings from their operation and keeping costs down. Good selection of beers and wines. Upstairs is a first floor art gallery available for private exhibitions.

ELEVEN PARK WALK SW10

11 Park Walk, SW10 0AJ
Telephone: 071-352 3449   £60
Fax: 071-351 6576
Open: lunch daily, dinner Mon-Sat (closed Bank Holidays)
Meals served: lunch 12.30-3, dinner 7-12

A rather swish and spacious Italian restaurant in the Roman trattoria style, Eleven Park Walk is extremely well-run and offers fine cooking with some contemporary touches. White tiles, mirrors and foliage create a fresh, lively atmosphere in which the smart set order their seafood salad, crudités with bagna cauda, wild boar bresaola or goose carpaccio with rocket in between table-hops. Pastas are well-made, especially the seafood varieties such as rigatoni with crab or lobster served on spaghetti or occasionally risotto, while among the heartier dishes is a good bollito misto with salsa verde. There is also an unusual dish of cod with paprika which comes off despite all expectations. This chic yet unpretentious restaurant is popular with society names whom you will often find crammed 10 to a table.

ENGLISH GARDEN SW3

10 Lincoln Street, SW3 2TS
Telephone: 071-584 7272   £70
Fax: 071-581 2848
Open: lunch + dinner daily (closed 25+26 Dec)
Meals served: lunch 12.30-2.30 (Sun 12.30-2), dinner 7.30-11.30 (Sun 7.30-10.30)

Try for a window table, bathed in a rosy glow created by the curtains, tablecloths and carpet. Popular with the smart Chelsea crowd. 18th-century English dishes are updated to suit 20th-century palates and clearly please. Gutsier than most dishes are the hare terrine with pickled cherry chutney, home-made sausages with blackcurrant relish. Feminine-sounding puddings include maids of honour with vanilla sauce, and hot blackberry and pear charlotte.

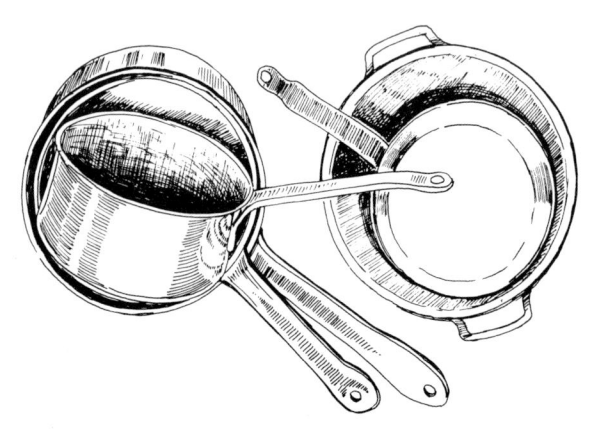

English House SW3

3 Milner Street, SW3 2QA
Telephone: 071-584 3002
Fax: 071-581 2848

£75

Open: lunch + dinner daily (closed 25+26 Dec)
Meals served: lunch 12.30-2.30, dinner 7.30-11.30 (Sun 7.30-10.30)

The chintzy, Victorian surroundings epitomise le style anglais which tourists swoon over. Thoroughly English tastes among Andrew Bailey's starters include hot herb soup with Stilton cheese straws or artichoke heart with Cornish crabmeat. He strikes a modern note with crab cakes and mustard mayonnaise or oak-smoked saddle of hare with plum preserve. Main courses fly the flag with baby lamb Wellington with prune forcemeat, grilled calves' liver with devilled kidneys or fillet of beef with grated horseradish pancake and port sauce. Prices are not unreasonable and there is a pleasing selection of wines.

Enoteca SW15

28 Putney High Street, SW15 1SQ
Telephone: 081-785 4449

£40

Open: lunch + dinner Mon-Sat (closed Bank Holidays, 1 wk Xmas)
Meals served: lunch 12.30-3, dinner 7-11.30

One of a string of restaurants on the High Street, Enoteca tends to attract thirtysomething professionals and is a useful find in Putney. Discreet background music blends nicely with the buzz of diners. Lovely service inspired by friendly owners has nice twists: if you order a glass of wine the bottle is opened at your table. Food is flavoursome trattoria fare with a regional slant: try orecchiette with broccoli or rack of lamb with grilled zucchini. There are good chargrilled vegetables with high-quality olive oil. Home-made puddings and good coffee.

Equities London EC2

1 Finsbury Avenue, EC2M 2PA
Telephone: 071-247 1051

£65

Open: lunch Mon-Fri (closed Bank Holidays)
Meals served: lunch 11.15-3

Simple setting, well-drilled staff, spot-on Franglais food and comprehensive wine list at this busy City restaurant.

Est   W1

54 Frith Street, W1V 5TE
Telephone: 071-437 0666
Open: all day Mon-Fri, dinner Sat (closed Bank Holidays)
Meals served: 12-11, dinner Sat 6-11.30

£40

1990s Scandinavian interior by owner Mogens Tholstrup in which Soho's mixed-media crowd feel utterly at home. The food has a healthy, Californian feel and includes dishes like grilled lamb marinated in olive oil and rosemary, calves' liver with fresh sage or grilled seafood salad. The daily specials might include gnocchi with gorgonzola or crostini of wild mushrooms. Grown-up sandwiches and snacks are available at the bar which occupies most of this small space and may leave diners feeling a little cramped. Luckily, eavesdropping is the whole point of the place. *See also page 48 – our Bistros and Brasseries Section.*

L'Estaminet   WC2
14 Garrick Street, WC2
Telephone: 071-379 1432
Open: lunch + dinner Mon-Sat
Meals served: lunch 12-2.30, dinner 6.30-11.30
Popular French venue in Covent Garden's scene.

£50

La Famiglia   SW10

7 Langton Street, SW10
Telephone: 071-351 0761 Fax 071-351 2409
Open: lunch + dinner daily (closed Bank Holidays)
Meals served: lunch 12-2.45, dinner 7-11.45

£65

A noisy, breezy, family-run (as you would expect from the name) Italian restaurant that makes occasional forays into modish Tuscan cuisine, La Famiglia always seems bright and modern in spite of a certain predictability where the menu is concerned. It is an immensely popular place among Chelsea residents, especially in summer when you can dine on the vast terrace which seats 125 under a cool awning. Inside, there are white walls with vibrant paintings, including one of The Family itself. Cheese features prominently among the best starters, from which you might choose prosciutto with hot smoked cheese, rigatoni with gorgonzola or lovely agnolotti in a creamy sauce. Alternatively, try the sliced smoked tuna. One favourite main course that is retained throughout the seasons is pollo al mattone – chicken cooked on a brick. The menu warns that it is 'rather burned on the outside and it is – but none the worse for that and it comes with a powerful mustard sauce. Wild boar sausages are served with chicken and bread tossed in olive oil – this is apparently a traditional Sunday dish in Chiantishire. Lighter main dishes include grilled mackerel with rosemary and mint, baby squid with a chilli-fired tomato and garlic sauce, sea bream baked with fennel and Sambuca or chicken breast and scallops in a white wine sauce. The well-priced wine list features plenty of bottles from Tuscany to comfort customers who are pining for their summer retreat.

LONDON 123

The Fenja — SW3
69 Cadogan Gardens, SW3 2RB
Telephone: 071-589 7333
Fax: 071-581 4958

Victorian house converted into a smart, comfortable hotel. Residents enjoy access to Cadogan Gardens. Thirteen bedrooms, no restaurant.

La Fin de la Chasse — London N16
176 Stoke Newington Church Street, N16 0JL
Telephone: 071-254 5975
Open: dinner Tue-Sat (closed Bank Holidays, 2 wks Xmas, 2 wks Sep)
Meals served: dinner 7-10.30

£55

Classic French food with modern affectations. Always packed so book.

First Floor — W11
186 Portobello Road, W11 1LA
Telephone: 071-243 0072
Fax: 071-221 8387
Open: lunch + dinner daily (closed 25+26 Dec)
Meals served: lunch 12.30-3.30 (Sun 11.30-3.30), dinner 7.30-11.30

£45

Seemingly recession-proof, First Floor was fashionable from the second it opened and people first started to traverse the interior gravel path to the staircase. First Floor has become something of a misnomer for a restaurant that has expanded both upwards and downwards to cope with the sheer volume of its clientele. The original first floor room might have been a drawing room in a previous existence, with its large bay windows and 19th-century cornicing and plaster mouldings. They are not seeking ordered perfection here at this vibrant, busy restaurant. Food is trendy Californian/Italian-influenced: dishes such as bruschetta of roast peppers, mozzarella and aubergine, or salad of rocket, mange tout, goat's cheese, olives and tomatoes are followed by main courses that have included herb pancakes filled with mushrooms a la grecque or leg of lamb on tomato and herb couscous. Medium choice wine list. *See also page 50 – our Bistros and Brasseries Section.*

Florians — N8
4 Topsfield Parade, Middle Lane, N8 8RP
Telephone: 081-348 8348
Open: lunch + dinner daily (closed Bank Holidays)
Meals served: lunch 12-3 (Sat+Sun 12-4), dinner 7-11 (Sat 7-10.30) (wine bar 12-11)

£45

New modern Italian restaurant in Muswell Hill.

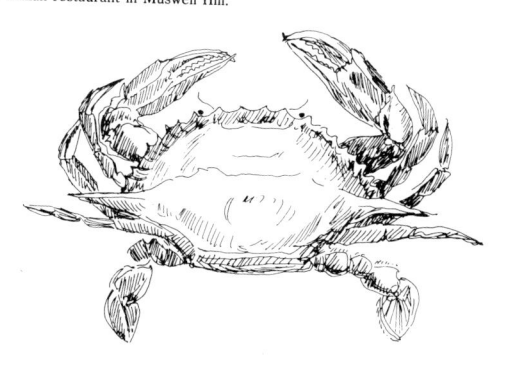

| **FREDERICK'S** | **N1** |

Camden Passage, N1 8EG — *good local restaurant*
Telephone: 071-359 2888
Fax: 071-359 5173   **£65**
Open: lunch + dinner Mon-Sat (closed Bank Holidays)
Meals served: lunch 12-2.30, dinner 6-11.30

Indefatigable oenophile Louis Segal likes to spring-clean his menu the way some people do their houses. So, although this is a restaurant that depends largely on repeat business from loyal regulars, you will rarely find the same thing on offer twice. If a dish appeals, catch it while you can. Outstanding meals in the past have commenced with creamy crab soup with cognac or tagliatelle with Parma ham followed by wild rabbit with red wine, bacon and mushrooms or rack of lamb with port, tomato, basil and pine nuts. Carefully themed events add spice: Normandy fortnight not only featured the food (lots of apples, calvados and cream of course) and wines of the region but competitions too. There is a large leafy conservatory at the back of the restaurant which can be hired for private functions. Mr Segal's award-winning wine list occupies much time and effort, philanthropically listing some quality bottles at giveaway prices.

| **FUNG SHING** | **WC2** |

15 Lisle Street, WC2
Telephone: 071-437 1539   **£40**
Open: lunch + dinner daily (closed 24-26 Dec)
Meals served: 12-11.30
The favourite amongst many of London's Chinese population. Consistently excellent Cantonese cuisine and friendly staff. Order barbecue beef, a hot-pot dish and any of the special dishes on the menu.

| **LA GAULETTE** | **W1** |

53 Cleveland Street, W1P 5PQ
Telephone: 071-580 7608   **£60**
Open: lunch Sun-Fri, dinner Mon-Sat (closed Bank Holidays)
Meals served: lunch 12-3, dinner 6.30-11.30

A younger – and arguably more talented – sister to Chez Liline (*q.v.*), La Gaulette has head chef Sylvain Ho Wing serving up Mauritian cuisine, predominantly seafood-based and blending Chinese, Indian, Creole and French influences to striking effect. Parrot fish comes with an onion sauce, crayfish tails with ginger and spring onion and red snapper is served au poivre.

| **GAVIN'S** | **London SW15** |

5 Lacy Road, SW15 1HN
Telephone: 081-785 9151
Fax: 081-788 1703   **£40**
Open: lunch + dinner daily (closed 24-27 Dec, Sun before Bank Holiday Mon)
Meals served: lunch 12-3, dinner 6.30-11
Another of Mark Milton's nice little earners, this time in Putney. Well deserving of its success which is founded on great pastas with imaginative home-made sauces.

Le Gavroche — W1

Restaurant: 43 Upper Brook Street, W1Y 1PF
Telephone: 071-408 0881   *Fax:* 071-409 0939
Open: lunch + dinner Mon-Fri (closed Bank Holidays, 23 Dec-2 Jan)
Meals served: lunch 12-2, dinner 7-11
Apartments: 47 Park Street, W1Y 4EB
Telephone: 071-491 7282   *Fax:* 071-491 7281

£150

Dining in the elegant, plush rooms of Le Gavroche, you are struck by the unfussy, unpretentious nature of its menu. The Rouxs' creations are informed by such integral commonsense and restraint that each one seems like an ancient rather than a modern classic. Where ancient recipes *are* used, they are given that little twist that transforms a good dish into a great one. The carte is serious and weighty, its dishes listed so tersely that the elaborate compositions – artful but without frills – that arrive at table are a delightful surprise. The few old-fangled dishes of the sort you might expect to find expect to find at, say, The Connaught – watercress soup, soufflé suissesse or ballotine of foie gras à l'ancienne for example – are beautifully handled but the really stunning dishes are their own. From the regular carte you might choose a ragoût of langoustines with vermicelli or a nage of scallops and star anise followed by free-range sautéed chicken en cocotte with lentils and thyme or lamb cutlets with tarragon vinegar. Day-to-day running of the kitchens is in the hands of Albert Roux's son Michel, whose daily specials can include a delectably-perfumed blanquette of lobster with baby vegetables and basil, a millefeuille of John Dory fillets with a vermouth sabayon or fillet of veal with fèves and tarragon cream. Desserts come from a roster of classics which include a raspberry soufflé, sablé of strawberries, warm fruit tarts on a thin pastry crust and a terrine of orange and pineapple. There is an assiette du chef and another of chocolate desserts for those whose appetites or curiosity are limitless. The dapper Silvano Giraldin, widely acknowledged to be among the most accomplished maîtres d'hôtel in England, is responsible for excellent service from a massive team. The wines come from a serious list which sprawls across the French regions and is definitely in the top bracket.

52 suites with integral kitchens are available at the luxurious 47 Park Street. They feature spacious, sunny sitting rooms and fine individually-tailored decorative schemes overseen by Albert Roux's wife Monique. *See also page 217 – our Clover Award section.*

Gavver's — SW1

61 Lower Sloane Street, SW1W 8DH
Telephone: 071-730 5983 £65
Open: lunch Mon-Fri, dinner Mon-Sat (closed Bank Holidays)
Meals served: lunch 12-2.30, dinner 7-11

The more modest face of the Roux Brothers' empire, Gavvers is used as a testing ground for new dishes and newly-graduated Roux-trained chefs who are about to be unleashed on the world in grander surroundings. Experimental has a different meaning chez Roux – dishes tend to be simpler and prices are kept low. If you strike it very lucky, Gavvers might possibly give you a fleeting impression of what it is like to dine at Le Gavroche or the Waterside but don't bank on it. Menus are more ambitious in the evening, when osso bucco is served with tagliatelle or pan-fried red mullet with artichoke and barigoule sauce. Starters such as a millefeuille of trout and spinach or terrine of duck studded with pistachios follow a kir which is included in the set price. At lunch, you might choose a nage of mackerel with leeks, a sauté of lemon chicken with pasta or a simple lasagne. The room decorated in shades of green is comfortable, while service from young, well-informed staff is helpful and attentive. The short French wine list is well-chosen. A good place to go after seeing a play at The Royal Court.

Gay Hussar — W1

2 Greek Street, W1V 6NB
Telephone: 071-437 0973 £50
Open: lunch + dinner Mon-Sat (closed Bank Holidays)
Meals served: lunch 12.30-2.30, dinner 5.30-11

Nothing changes at this well-loved Soho eaterie where a masculine, clubby atmosphere prevails. The tasty Hungarian food still comes piled mountain-high on the plate and the plush interior with red banquettes and oak panelling is all the better for being a little flaky round the edges. The epic dinner menu is abbreviated for lunch, though specialities such as pressed boar's head, cold pike with beetroot sauce and cucumber or the legendary wild cherry soup are always available. Among the truly hearty dishes with big, chunky flavours are roast duck with red cabbage, Hungarian potatoes and apple sauce, Transylvanian stuffed cabbage and the smoked goose with scholet (pungent smoked beans). As chef Laszlo Holecz is fond of telling people, this is a million times better than anything you will eat in Hungary itself. The cheerful, solicitous staff will urge you to contravene conventional thinking on healthy eating and order a pudding. Listen to them. The sweet cheese pancakes, the idiosyncratic walnut soufflé and, above all, the poppy seed strudel are not to be missed. The wine list starts off in France, moving onto some interesting Hungarian bottles and 7 tokajis as well as three Bulgarian wines. *See also page 218 – our Clover Award section.*

GEALE'S — W8

2 Farmer Street, W8 7SN
Telephone: 071-727 7969
Fax: 071-229 8632 £40
Open: lunch + dinner Tue-Sat (closed Bank Holidays + following Tue, 2 wks Xmas, 1 wk Easter, 2 wks Aug)
Meals served: lunch 12-3, dinner 6-11

The cult fish and chip shop of West London, Geale's is something of a monument to this great British tradition. The fish is fried in beef dripping and the chips in vegetable flat – you can try it at home but it won't be the same. Wooden chairs and tables with checked cloths appeal to a clientele that crosses all age barriers but is predominantly middle-aged Kensington professionals. More expensive than most but better.

GILBERT'S — SW7

2 Exhibition Road, SW7 2HF
Telephone: 071-589 8947 £55
Open: lunch Mon-Fri, dinner Mon-Sat (closed Xmas/New Year, 3 wks Aug)
Meals served: lunch 12.30-2, dinner 7-10.15

Friendly neighbourhood restaurant keen to win a following from beyond the immediate area. Chef/partner Julia Chalkey's menu is certainly one way to keep 'em coming. Gutsy, peasant-style dishes like oxtail daube, osso buco with gremolata, ragoût of beef with prunes and cinnamon and rabbit with mustard sauce typify the repertoire. In addition the starters from the set menu at lunch or dinner might yield fennel and potato soup, baked red pepper with brandade, venison terrine with home-made chutney or tagliatelle with walnut sauce. Delicious fudge is served with coffee.

GLAISTER'S — SW10
4 Hollywood Road, SW10 9HW
Telephone: 071-352 0352 £45
Open: lunch+dinner daily (closed Bank Holidays, 2 wks Xmas)
Meals served: lunch 12.30-4.30, dinner 7-11.45 (Sun 7-10.30)
Glaisterburgers, beef stroganoff with rice and good vegetarian dishes at this popular Chelsea haunt.

GOPAL'S OF SOHO — W1
12 Bateman Street, W1V 5TD
Telephone: 071-434 0840 £35
Open: lunch + dinner daily (closed 25+26 Dec)
Meals served: lunch 12-3, dinner 6-11.30 (Sun 6-11)
Indian owner-chef with a CV that includes the Red Fort and Lal Qila. Soft pink surroundings. Dum (hot-pot) cooking is a strength.

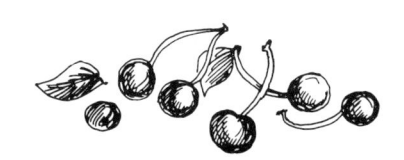

The Goring — SW1

17 Beeston Place, Grosvenor Gardens, SW1W 0JW
Telephone: 071-834 8211
Fax: 071-834 4393
Open: lunch Sun-Fri, dinner daily
Meals served: lunch 12.30-2.30, dinner 6-10

£70

One of last family owned hotels in London and proudly maintaining traditions set by previous generations of Gorings. A firm favourite for British and overseas visitors. Given its proximity to Buckingham Palace you are likely to see a number of morning suits and top hats. The restaurant offers some traditional fare and is especially good value at lunchtime. The loyal and long-serving staff make a great effort to look after customers, whether regulars or newcomers. And, just in case you didn't know, this was the first hotel in the world to offer en-suite bathroom facilities!

Grafton Français — SW4

45 Old Town, Clapham Common, SW4 0JL
Telephone: 071-627 1048
Open: lunch Sun-Fri, dinner Tue-Sat (closed Bank Holidays, 3 wks Aug, 1 wk Xmas)
Meals served: lunch 12.30-3 (Sun 12-3), dinner 7.30-11.30
French cooking, unpretentious surroundings. Good value lunches.

£60

Grahame's Seafare — W1

38 Poland Street, W1V 3DA
Telephone: 071-437 3788
Open: lunch + dinner Mon-Sat (closed Bank Holidays, Jewish New Year)
Meals served: lunch 12-2.45, dinner 5.30-9 (Fri+Sat 5.30-8)

£35

A fish-dominated kosher reataurant in rather spartan surroundings, Grahame's will cook the fish any way you like it. Deep-fried – in a matzo meal batter – is a welcome change from that offered at the local chippy. Potato latkes are a perennial favourite: mashed potato and sautéed onion rolled into little balls and fried. Service is charming.

Gran Paradiso — SW1

52 Wilton Road, SW1
Telephone: 071-828 5818
Open: lunch Mon-Fri, dinner Mon-Sat (closed Bank Holidays)
Meals served: lunch 12.15-2.15, dinner 6-11
Pimlico trattoria, favourite of Sir Roy Strong.

£50

Green Cottage — NW3

9 New College Parade, Finchley Road, NW3 5EP
Telephone: 071-722 5305
Open: lunch + dinner daily (25+26 Dec)
Meals served: 12-11
Inexpensive neighbourhood Cantonese restaurant with Chinatown quality cooking. Excellent roast duck and pork, and one-dish meals and vegetarian dishes. Free tea.

£30

Greenhouse — W1

27a Hays Mews, W1X 7RJ
Telephone: 071-499 3331
Open: lunch Sun-Fri, dinner Mon-Sat (closed Bank Holidays)
Meals served: lunch 12-2.30 (Sun 12-3), dinner 7-11

£70

Installed in 1990 at David Levin's rejuvenated Mayfair restaurant, the impish Gary Rhodes has, deservedly, won much of the credit for the revival of interest in British cuisine. European influences, principally French or Italian, are detectable more among starters than main courses, where Rhodes scores plenty of Brit hits. Traditional dishes such as faggots in gravy, braised oxtails or the mutating dish of boiled bacon (which might be served with pearl barley, split peas or root vegetables and mash) have attracted rave reviews together with updated favourites and clever innovations. Pulses, like potatoes, are intelligently used, as in the grilled herring on braised lentils with mustard sauce. The marvellous smoked haddock fillet topped with Welsh rarebit and served on a chive-speckled tomato salad has become something of a signature dish and, though listed as a starter, is hefty enough to serve as a main course. Ditto the hearty salad of black pudding, sautéed potatoes, poached egg and bacon or the soused mackerel fillet on a warm potato salad. A wonderful dessert list is pretty heavyweight, featuring a steamed ginger pudding with raisins or apple fritters with apricot purée and vanilla ice-cream. Sunday lunch, at £17.50 for three courses, is superbly balanced, features one of the finest Yorkshire puddings in town and pulls a well-heeled, younger crowd. The wine list has been criticised for its brevity but, by comprising the History of Wine's Greatest Hits at inoffensive prices, tends not to displease! Decoratively speaking, the restaurant lives up to its name: there is a conservatory-style reception area complete with garden benches and natural light floods through the windows which run the length of the restaurant on both sides. Flowers, both dried and real, are everywhere and horticultural paintings and prints continue the theme.

Green's — SW1

Marsham Court, Marsham Street, SW1P 4LA
Telephone: 071-834 9552
Fax: 071-233 6047
Open: lunch Mon-Fri, dinner daily (closed Bank Holidays, Xmas)
Meals served: lunch 12.30-3, dinner 6-11 (Sun 6.30-10.30)

£60

Order! Order! Within range of the division bell, political opinions can be forgotten for an hour or two as both sides of the house sit down at adjacent tables. Green's in Marsham Court draws a loyal ministerial following as for many years did Lockett's, the previous incumbent on the site. There are few surprises on the menu: Beth Coventry's food is likely to comfort even the most marginal seat-holder. Lamb cutlets are well-prepared, there is a generous lobster or crab salad with fresh mayonnaise for daintier appetites and daily specials include shepherd's pie on Mondays. Any younger faces amongst the diners may well be Westminster schoolboys out on a treat.

Green's Restaurant & Oyster Bar   SW1

36 Duke Street, St James's, SW1Y 6DF
Telephone: 071-930 4566
Fax: 071-930 1383   **£65**
Open: lunch daily, dinner Mon-Sat (closed 25+26 Dec, 1 Jan)
Meals served: lunch 11.30-3 (Sun 12-3.30), dinner 5.30-11

One of those oak-panelled bastions of Old England where public schoolboys who never quite weaned themselves off nursery food take their more sophisticated partners before nearby Annabel's or Tramp. Hence the juxtaposition of delicate dishes with more robust items. Porkinson's famous bangers and mash, omelette Arnold Bennett, boiled beef with carrots and dumplings sit happily alongside the special seafood platter, roast quail and smoked duck breast for more delicate palates. However, this is one of London's better – though expensive – English restaurants and the oyster bar serves several varieties as well as a range of shellfish. Champagne is the thing to drink here but the wines are well-chosen.

Grill St Quentin   SW3

3 Yeoman's Row, SW3 2AL
Telephone: 071-581 8377
Fax: 071-584 6064   **£50**
Open: all day Mon-Sat (closed 1 wk Xmas)
Meals served: 12-12

The très Parisien Grill St Quentin is a vast Coupole-style basement decorated with lots of gleaming brass and powder-blue paint. Grills are superb – steaks, lamb chops, fish and more, all done to perfection – and oysters are a new speciality. There are choucroute, foie gras, salads, a limited range of vegetables and great frites. A boisterous Gallic atmosphere lends the final authentic touches. Excellent set lunch at £9.50 or £12.50 for 2 or 3 courses.

GRITTI — WC2

11 Upper St Martin's Lane, WC2
Telephone: 071-836 5121 — £50
Open: lunch + dinner Mon-Sat (closed Bank Holidays)
Meals served: lunch 12-2.30, dinner 6-11.30
Fashionable modern Italian restaurant, useful pre- and post-theatre.

GROSVENOR HOUSE — W1

90 Park Lane, W1A 3AA
Telephone: 071-499 6363
Fax: 071-493 3341 — £125
Open: lunch Mon-Fri, dinner Mon-Sat (closed Bank Holidays)
Meals served: lunch 12.30-2.30, dinner 7.30-10.45

The Grosvenor House, always the flagship of the Forte empire, has just completed a £10m programme of renovation leaving it equipped for the next century with superlative business facilities, lavish interiors and well-marshalled service. The public areas look elegant in the contemporary style without going over the top. Rich primary colours have been used throughout the Park Terrace lounge, lobby and newly-created panelled library, predominantly reds, greens and blues with clever juxtaposition of textiles. The newest and finest rooms and suites are on the 6th and 7th floors: book the Sovereign Club package and a chauffeured Rolls Royce awaits you at the airport while your suite has VCR and CD player. A notch down is the Crown Club where suites have self-contained lounges and boardroom. The banqueting facilities of the Great Room and Ballroom have been strategically separated from guest and public dining areas, with all of the latter reborn. Just opened is the spectacular 120-seater Pavilion, offering breakfast, lunch and dinner in a splendid colonial-style setting with timber floors and cherry-wood mouldings. Although the buffet breakfast has disappeared, genuine attempts have been made to accelerate the service of both cooked and continental versions. At lunch and dinner, cooking by Sean Davies' open-face kitchen is in strictly contemporary style with a definite English bias: there is stuffed braised oxtail, Lancashire hotpot, lamb cobbler, bangers and mash, black pudding with baked onions and apple and smoked haddock pie on the menu as well as the more globetrotting spiced cardamom chicken with basmati or red mullet with virgin olive oil and basil. The casual and inexpensive Italian restaurant Pasta Vino has been refitted in gentle earth tones with emerald glass cover plates and a new pasta-based menu which makes concessions to fashionability with bruschetta, crostini and rocket salad with balsamico. To complete the transformation of the hotel, Forte have just played their trump card by attracting the sometimes irascible but always brilliant Nico Ladenis to move his operation into the space next door that was formerly Ninety Park Lane (see separate entry, Nico at Ninety). Undoubtedly the most important first-division restaurant opening of the '90s, this move is bound to place the Grosvenor House among the leading gastronomic destination hotels in the world and its transformation has provided a fitting setting for the maestro. *See pages 573 – 576 our Special Feature.*

GUERNICA — W1

3a Foley Street, W1P 7LA
Telephone: 071-580 0623 — £40
Open: lunch + dinner Mon-Sat (closed Bank Holidays, 2 wks Aug)
Meals served: lunch 12.30-2.45, dinner 7-10.45
Spanish/Basque restaurant offering good value for money.

The Halcyon   W11

81 Holland Park, W11 3RZ
Telephone: 071-727 7288   £80
Fax: 071-229 8516
Open: lunch + dinner daily
Meals served: lunch 12-2.30, dinner 7-11

Two converted townhouses restored to their Belle Epoque grandeur house 44 bedrooms and suites, each individually decorated with great flair, many featuring Jacuzzis, four-posters and private terraces. Some, like the tent-effect Arabian Room with its desert murals, are more OTT than others. The hotel is a popular London hide-out for movie and popstars and the needs of a laid-back showbiz clientele are reflected in a restaurant menu that caters equally well for local businessmen, especially at breakfast which is always packed. Brasserie classics such as Caesar salad, eggs benedict or steak & chips sit happily alongside more clever inventions – tataki of beef, stuffed vine leaves with prosciutto, fritto misto, crispy duck breast with fennel and ginger and fishcakes (the garnish, currently sorrel and harissa, changes with each new menu) are typical. Puddings include a honey mousse with baked tamarillo or hazelnut parfait with spiced apricots and The Halcyon Basket contains a bewildering array of nuts and exotic fruits. A twin-choice express lunch menu is priced at £12.00 or 15.00 for 2 or 3 courses including coffee and petit fours and might consist of chilled aubergine soup followed by roast leg of duck with pesto and iced chocolate parfait. There is a separate menu in the small, elegant bar which has good club sandwiches and BLTs plus snacks such as prawn satay, blinis with smoked salmon and caviar and imaginative salads. Rice crackers and earth chips made from celeriac, beetroot and sweet potato are served with drinks. After concerts, the bar often rocks on until late with impromptu recitals by musical guests. A place to know about in the summer when there is seating for 30 on a pretty secluded terrace.

HALKIN HOTEL — SW1

5 Halkin Street, SW1X 7DJ
Telephone: 071-333 1000
Fax: 071-333 1100
Open: lunch + dinner Mon-Sat
Meals served: lunch 12.30-2.30, dinner 7.30-11

£100

A super-sleek new addition to the hotel scene, The Halkin has been created by top Italian style gurus including Giorgio Armani who is responsible for the uniforms. A lavish use of marble in tones of peach and beige combined with matt black and burr elm surfaces fuses '80s and '90s styles but remains strictly minimalist. Most clients are either Japanese or Americans of the type who detest chintz and live in lofts. The rooms, all decorated in black, white and beige, are deeply computer-literate and have stunning marble bathrooms. Attempts have been made in recent months to gentle the appearance of the ground-floor restaurant, where there have been dramatic changes since opening. Following the defection of chef Paul Gayler, Gualtiero Marchesi - a very big cheese in Milan - was brought in as consultant chef. His menu is perhaps more in keeping with the low-key opulence of the place and includes a risotto milanese radiant with saffron - perfetto - and topped with gleaming gold leaf. Some dishes - the sirloin with red wine sauce and potato gratin, for example, or the navarin of lamb with broad beans and peas - sound distinctly French: elsewhere, there is wild boar bresaola with artichokes, rocket and parmesan, ravioli of broccoli and clams, a giant open raviolo with scallop, red mullet with tomato and basil or baked veal kidney with potato 'tortino'. More familiar-sounding are the classic vitello tonnato and the veal cutlet in breadcrumbs. Puddings are more 'international' in scope: try the iced tiramisu soufflé - a nice twist on a now inevitable theme. Wines are mainly Italian with a few French bottles and an extensive list of champagnes at the top end.

HAMPSHIRE HOTEL — WC2

31 Leicester Square, WC2 7LH
Telephone: 071-839 9399
Fax: 071-930 8122
Open: lunch + dinner daily
Meals served: lunch 12.30-3.30, dinner 5.30-11

£85

Amidst the cinemas, traffic and bright lights of Leicester Square, the Hampshire Hotel, part of the well-run Edwardian group, is a pocket of tranquillity. The 124 bedrooms include 36 sumptuous suites, all with excellent facilities and furnishings. The grandly-swagged Celebrities restaurant offers some accomplished cooking from Colin Button whose predilection is for rustic cuisine, especially expertly-prepared offal and rich sauces. Presentation, even of traditional English dishes such as boiled slipper of bacon with pease pudding, dumplings and parsley sauce, is skilful. Powerful flavours dominate dishes such as braised monkfish with bacon, mushrooms, onions and red wine veal sauce, a cassoulet of duck, pork, lamb and sausage casserole with white beans or marinated skirt of beef with anchovy sauce. To finish, try the dish of seasonal fruits with sorbets and a warm sabayon. Oscar's brasserie and bar is more suitable for lighter lunches or suppers.

HARVEYS — SW17

2 Bellevue Road, SW17 7EG
Telephone: 081-672 0114
Open: lunch Tue-Sun, dinner Tue-Sat (closed Bank Holidays,
  2 wks Xmas, 2 wks Aug/Sep)
Meals served: lunch 12.30-2.15, dinner 7.30-11.15

£100

It seems that every piece written about Harveys quotes the Wilde maxim that appears on the menu: it reads 'To get into society nowadays one has either to feed people, amuse people or shock people' and it appears that Marco Pierre White has taken it to heart by ensuring that he does all three. Half an hour on *Desert Island Discs* and a second, much-publicised marriage have certainly helped to render him fit for public consumption and, while some believe that a spell on a remote atoll would do him a power of good, most would lament the loss to the restaurant industry. Love him or loathe him, he is undoubtedly a remarkable, self-assured young chef who seems unlikely ever to run out of steam. He is driven by extraordinary creative impulses. and his cooking is at once authoritative and original, his presentation always superbly confident and artistic. To pick out dishes from the menu, on which he has stamped an indelible maker's mark, is to deny its precise balance. Pastas are always exquisite, from the now-legendary tagliatelle of oysters with caviar to the ravioli of lobster with celeriac hearts. The gélée of skate and langoustine with gazpacho sauce or escabèche of red mullet with saffron have been refined and perfected and rate alongside the braised pig's trotter or the seabass with caviar as key dishes. The roast saddle of rabbit with endive, langoustine and basil jus has all the component flavours finely balanced, as does the fillet of beef with shallots, marrowbone and red wine fumet. The set lunch, though simpler, can reach undreamed-of heights: it might consist of baked sea scallops with cinnamon and lemon followed by roast veal with tagliatelle of carrots and creamed parsley and a tarte bordelaise. The tarte tatin learnt from Albert Roux is now unsurpassable, the fruit melting yet firm with just the right degree of caramelisation. Choose if you can between the feuillantine of raspberries, the sablé of strawberries, the crackling pyramid and the soufflés of chocolate with chocolate sauce or prune and armagnac. The sprawling wine list has many serious, even grand bottles (reflecting the increasingly glitzy nature of the clientele) but there are some affordable wines as well. To have the good fortune to dine at Harveys is the perfect type of perfect pleasure: it leaves you satisfied yet wanting more. Marco gives an Oscar-winning performance.

HARVEYS CAFÉ · SW10

The Black Bull, 588 Fulham Road, SW10 9UU — *good local restaurant*
Telephone: 071-352 0625
Open: lunch Tue-Sun, dinner Tue-Sat (closed Bank Holidays, 1 wks Xmas, Aug)
Meals served: lunch 12-3, dinner 7.30-11

£45

Harvey Smallbrook is typical of the new restaurateur: a man who loves playing the host and sets up a small enterprise offering a primarily Mediterranean menu at studiously low prices. Harveys Café is based above the Black Bull pub and its playschool interior – lots of pine and turquoise paint – has clearly been put together on a shoestring, although its naïveté is redeemed by a changing exhibition of modern paintings. The menu shows a thorough understanding of what the Fulham customers are after: red pepper or crab and saffron soup, terrine of pork and veal with red onion marmalade or bruschetta with aubergine compote strike an up-to-date note among starters and precede salmon fishcakes with anchovy sauce, marinated roast quail with bulgar wheat and harissa, Turkish lamb and bean stew or marinated grilled chicken with chutney and raita. Simpler items include grilled sardines, baby leeks vinaigrette and grilled red mullet. Young families are warmly welcomed and there is a lively community feel to the place. A short wine list includes all the fashionable pre-requisites and my guess is that most people go for one of the sensibly priced New World chardonnays.

HILAIRE   SW7

68 Old Brompton Road, SW7 3LQ
Telephone: 071-584 8993
Open: lunch Mon-Fri, dinner Mon-Sat (closed Bank Holidays,
    1 wk Xmas, 1 wk Easter, 2 wks Aug)
Meals served: lunch 12.30-2.30, dinner 7-11.30

£80

Hilaire has changed little in appearance over the years but chef Bryan Webb has made a big impression since his management buyout. An introvert who prefers to remain behind the scenes, Bryan's talents put him among the top chefs in London. His most idiosyncratic touch is to refer constantly to his Welsh roots, serving laverbread in a multitude of guises alongside Glamorgan sausages, Welsh lamb wherever possible and fine Welsh cheeses. Menus change frequently as he is constantly developing and refining even his signature dishes such as the salad of griddled scallops with salsa or the gratinated oysters with Stilton and laverbread (which sometimes appear as deep-fried oysters with laverbread, coriander and chilli dip) with the result that a favourite dish – such as the fillet of lamb with aubergine and pesto or seabass with lentils, salsa verde and extra virgin olive oil – will look and taste slightly different each time you order it. There is always at least one offal dish, which might be a sauté of veal kidney and sweetbreads or a dish of calves' brains with black butter. Simple dishes are always startling in their perfection: at no Italian restaurant will you find green gnocchi done better. Puddings are superb: highlights have included a lemon tart with a caramelized topping of thinly-sliced banana, a crackling millefeuille of orange with bitter chocolate sorbet and hot chocolate sauce, a warm gratin of berries with sorbet and a grainy chocolate pithiviers (with a nod in the direction of Bibendum, perhaps?). Service is French, charming and knowledgeable and the wine list intelligently chosen with obvious consideration for the food. *See also page 220 – our Clover Award section.*

L'HIPPOCAMPE — W1

63 Frith Street, W1V 5TA
Telephone: 071-734 4545 **£60**
Open: lunch Mon-Fri, dinner Mon-Sat (closed Bank Holidays, 1 wk Xmas)
Meals served: lunch 12-2.30, dinner 6.15-11.15

L'Hippocampe (French for seahorse) is a bold redefinition of the fish and seafood restaurant, concentrating exclusively on imaginative treatments of those raw ingredients – although plain oysters are available as a starter and fish will be served plainly cooked if the customer insists. The simpler set lunch at around £17 is great value for 3 courses but you may be swayed by Mark Williamson's more exotic offerings from the carte. Steamed oysters are served with pickled lemon, ginger and diced vegetables, buckwheat noodles with mussels and gambas in saffron sauce and lobster won tons with coriander and sesame ginger butter. Main courses similarly absorb influences from all sides: there might be blackened turbot with herb and vegetable polenta, roast zander on bacon choucroûte with red wine sauce or poached red mullet with a sesame and prawn farce and soy ginger sauce. The decor eschews poissonerie clichés, going instead for a witty, post-modernist subaqueous interior. The short French wine list is naturally chosen with the fishy menu in mind.

L'HOTEL — SW3

28 Basil Street, SW3 1AT
Telephone: 071-589 6286 **£60**
Fax: 071-225 0011
Open: all day Mon-Sat (closed 25-26 Dec)
Meals served: 10.30am-11pm

Superior bed and (continental) breakfast at David Levin's 12-bedroomed hotel. In its basement is Le Métro, a classy wine bar supervised by Philip Britten from The Capital next door. A wide range of wines is on offer here, including a good selection by the glass and there is a menu combining hearty bistro dishes with salads, snacks and the odd British intrusion like bangers and mash. A goat's cheese salad might be followed by a soundly cooked confit de canard with red cabbage, roast lamb with flageolets or flaked salmon with parsley sauce or you might just opt for a croque monsieur between bouts of shopping. Le Métro is especially popular with women who feel safe and unthreatened in this relaxed atmosphere. Newspapers are provided for your information and edification.

HUBBLE & CO	EC1
44 Charterhouse Street, EC1	
Telephone: 071-253 1612	£40
Open: all day Mon-Fri	
Meals served: 12-11	
Recent city opening, modern European-style menu.	

HYATT CARLTON TOWER — SW1

2 Cadogan Place, SW1X 9PY
Telephone: 071-235 5411
Fax: 071-235 6570
Open: lunch + dinner daily
Meals served: lunch 12.30-2.45, dinner 7-10.45 (Sun 7-10)

£75

Last year, Executive Chef Bernard Gaume celebrated his 40 years in the trade with a special dinner held in his honour at The Chelsea Room. It was a fitting tribute to his skills which have played an important role in establishing the Hyatt Carlton Tower as one of London's top hotels. Recently, his most outstanding creations have included crab soup with saffron and garlic mayonnaise, a lasagne of celeriac and lobster with coriander and tomato sauce and turbot with saffron sauce, asparagus and morels. There is an out-of-the-ordinary list of luxurious grills which include veal, langoustine and lobster and, for the indecisive, a dish comprising two fillets of beef, one with a bordelaise sauce, the other sauced with shallots. The extensive wine list and diligent service are entirely appropriate to the elegant surroundings.

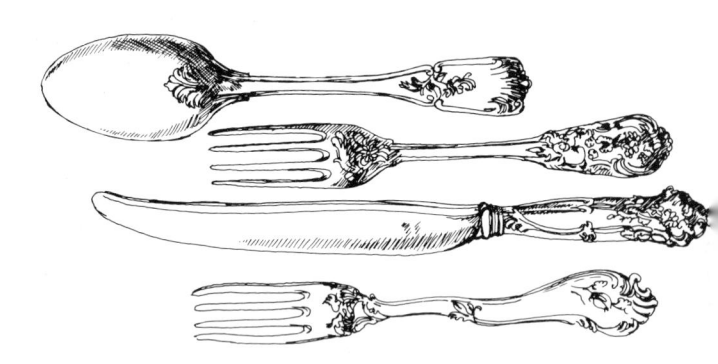

Hyde Park Hotel   SW1

66 Knightsbridge, SW1Y 7LA
Telephone: 071-235 2000   £75
Fax: 071-235 4552
Park Room: lunch + dinner daily
Meals served: lunch 12.30-2.30, dinner 7-11
Cavalry Grill: lunch + dinner Mon-Fri
Meals served: lunch 12.30-2.30, dinner 6.00-11.00pm

The Hyde Park Hotel, with distinctly Italian verve by Paolo Biscioni, is fast approaching its centenary. Floor by floor, the entire hotel has been refurbished and updated during the last few years and is now winning international awards for excellence. The Royal Suite has been home-from-home to numerous heads of state and, perhaps as famously, Pavarotti and Madonna. The function rooms are decorated in the grand style with unique views of Hyde Park. The Hyde Park has distanced itself from traditional hotel catering by providing two distinctly upmarket restaurants of radically different styles, neither of them especially cheap, both supervised by energetic young Frenchman Jerome Dutois. Entering the hotel's gleaming marble halls on noisy Knightsbridge and arriving at the Park Room with its uninterrupted green vistas is rather like walking through a wardrobe and discovering Narnia on the other side. Similarly, Fabrizio Caddei's Italian/Mediterranean menu comes as a delightful surprise to anyone who was expecting something a little more corporate. The cooking is delicate and refined, with the emphasis on healthy eating. Sauces for meat and fish are light, made with olive oil and fresh herbs as in a dish of red mullet with broad beans and mint or fillet of sea bass with braised endives and vinegar sauce. Pastas can include translucent ravioli filled with aubergine and mozzarella. There is a set lunch with plenty of choice or you might prefer to help yourself from a variety of antipasti (plenty of grilled vegetables here) at a set price of around £12. The Park Room is also one of London's most popular venues for tea: bookings are advisable if you prefer not to queue. In complete contrast, the Cavalry Grill, consisting of a pair of oak-panelled, clubby rooms, is a cross between The Connaught and Greens: very traditional, very English and a great favourite with American guests. A menu which looks deceptively modern is based around dishes such as lobster salad, smoked salmon, eggs Florentine, grilled Dover sole, steak and kidney pudding, fish pie or bangers and mash. Roast rib of beef with Yorkshire pudding is always served from one trolley and, at lunch only, a roast of the day which, according to the season might be a rack of lamb or pork, duck or even goose from the other. Smooth, traditional service is from teams of young staff led by charming and long-serving old-timers. Sound wine lists lean towards the top end in terms of price.

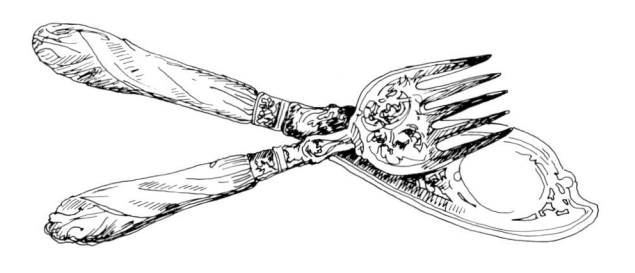

| L'INCONTRO | SW1 |

87 Pimlico Road, SW1 8PH
Telephone: 071-730 3663
Fax: 071-730 5062
Open: lunch Mon-Sat, dinner daily (closed Bank Holidays)
Meals served: lunch 12.30-2.30, dinner 7-11.30 (Sun 7-10.30)

£85

It goes without saying, really, that this is a very fine place in which to eat. Yes, it's fashionable and yes, it's right in line with the current vogue for modern Italian cooking but there is a traditional quality and consistency to the food which places it firmly amongst London's top establishments. Dishes such as gamberoni minuzzo and tagliolini al grancho as starters and fegato alla griglia and coda di rospaol forna as main courses give a foretaste of what you'll find on the menu. However Gino Santin's book *La Cucina Veneziana* will do justice to the repertoire far better than I can hope to do in such a short space. The Milan sister establishment Santini plays to packed houses in Milan and plans are afoot to expand into Brussels and Barcelona too. Incontrovertibly one of the best Italians! *See also page 222 – our Clover Award section.*

| INN ON THE PARK HOTEL | W1 |

Hamilton Place, Park Lane, W1A 1AZ
Telephone: 071-499 0888
Fax: 071-493 1895
Open: lunch + dinner daily
Meals served: lunch 12.30-3, dinner 7-11

[Now renamed 'Four Seasons Hotel']

£95

This international hotel, with its comfortable rooms and luxury facilities, is run with great charm and panache by Ramon Pajares. Since his arrival at the Four Seasons restaurant a few years ago, Bruno Loubet has quietly revolutionised its menu. Trained by Raymond Blanc, Bruno shares his imagination and creativity, creating for example signature dishes of 'ravioli' made from translucent discs of blanched turnip filled with wild mushrooms and herbs or a warm fillet of salmon smoked to order and served on a bed of mashed potato with crispy potato garnish and veal jus. Cuisine du Terroir is his theme, although health is important with low-fat dishes asterisked on the menu. He will push a classic to its logical limit, as in a dish of roast wild duck with quinces and mandarin sauce, and handles rustic offal dishes and Mediterraneana with equal dexterity, as his dishes of calves' brains braised oxtail with prunes and vinegar or a risotto of squid, saffron, tomato and basil amply demonstrate. The hotel's cellars are renowned and the wine list is a masterpiece of epic proportions with prices to match. Suggestions – on both food and wine – are always apposite. The room, though grand, is at odds with the food but one visit will nonetheless inspire you to pore over Bruno's book, *Cuisine Courante* which, like Raymond Blanc's *Cooking for Friends*, is all about cooking spectacular yet simple things at home.

LONDON **141**

Inter-continental Hotel   W1

1 Hamilton Place, Hyde Park Corner, W1V 1QY
Telephone: 071-409 3131
Fax: 071-409 7460   **£100**
Open: lunch Sun-Fri, dinner daily (closed 26 Dec, Good Friday)
Meals served: lunch 12.30-3 (Sun Brunch 12-3), dinner 7-10.30 (Sat 7-11.15)

The appointment of a full-time Japanese chef to cater for the needs of a high proportion of the hotel guests indicates the level of customer care at The Inter-Continental. The bar and Le Soufflé restaurant have recently been renovated and look in tip-top condition. In addition, a new Italian restaurant and Hamilton's nightclub have been installed on the seventh floor. The 467 bedrooms are well-equipped and admirably quiet with mostly new bathrooms. Certainly nobody can accuse this hotel of allowing standards to slip! Chef Peter Kromberg's elegant restaurant remains a great attraction and an integral factor of the hotel's success. The signature soufflés remain outstanding and imaginative examples of the versatility of the basic recipe – recent examples among starters include asparagus and smoked salmon soufflé with keta caviar and chive butter sauce or broccoli soufflé in a filo shell with tomato and chive salad while a grain mustard soufflé tops sautéed lamb fillets. However the soufflé really comes into its own among puddings where it takes centre stage with confections such as rich curd cheese soufflé with marinated berries in rum or chocolate and candied kumquat soufflé with a light whipped cream. Healthy eating has become a preoccupation of The Inter-Continental in recent years, with a Slim and Trim breakfast on offer beside the traditional English, Continental and Japanese options. Peter Kromberg picks up on the trend by offering some imaginative healthy dishes, among them red mullet fillet with thinly sliced, oven-baked new potatoes and salad or artichoke bottom filled with lobster mousse which is steamed and served on a bed of spinach with wild mushrooms. If you have an aversion to soufflés, try the sautéed scallops on a crisp potato base with pan-fried endive, risotto of cèpes with sautéed duck liver and port sauce or roe buck fillets with creamy game sauce, poached apple, wild cranberries, wild mushrooms and spaëtzle. There is a superb 6-course set menu at £43 which is probably the best way to discover Kromberg's immense talents. The classic wine list is best suited to the pockets of corporate raiders but there is a good selection of affordable bottles as long as you stay away from France and some excellent half-bottles for those who want to match quality with quality.

The Ivy — WC2

1 West Street, WC2H 9NE
Telephone: 071-836 4751
Fax: 071-497 3644
Open: lunch + dinner daily (closed 25+26 Dec, 1 Jan)
Meals served: lunch 12-3, dinner 5.30-12

£65

Suave setting for chic people to eat and be seen in and where gossip columnists take notes on the backs of lettuce leaves... A very theatrical place with lots of producers and luvvies. The paintings on the walls are art with a capital A, by the likes of David Hockney, Peter Blake and Jasper Johns. Chef Nigel Davis conducts the kitchen, turning out well-orchestrated dishes for diners, the majority of whom probably aren't here primarily for the food. Old favourites from sister restaurant Le Caprice are listed here too, such as the tomato and basil galette or bang bang chicken. Classic dishes such as oysters, caviar with buckwheat blinis, chateaubriand are served comme il faut, while more adventurous dishes include grilled squid served with bacon, roquette and salsa verde, steak and kidney pie with mashed swede or saddle of venison with a fig compote. Vegetables are à la carte, puddings first-class especially the blood orange and bitter chocolate sorbets. Wasn't it Andy Warhol who claimed that real style was being able to talk with your mouth full? Better start practising before you come here. The Ivy is always packed but if you can't get in any other time, try for Saturday brunch.

Jade Garden — W1
15 Wardour Street, W1V 3HA
Telephone: 071-437 5065
Open: lunch + dinner daily (closed 25+26 Dec)
Meals served: 12-11.45 (Sat 11.30-11.45, Sun 11.30-10.45)
Very good dim sum and other Cantonese dishes but service is variable.

£35

Jason Court Restaurant — W1
Jason Court, 76 Wigmore Street, W1
Telephone: 071-224 2992
Open: lunch Mon-Fri, dinner Mon-Sat (closed Bank Holidays, 2 wks Aug)
Meals served: lunch 12-2.30, dinner 7-10.30
Modern British food.

£60

JOE ALLEN   WC2

13 Exeter Street, WC2E 7DT
Telephone: 071-836 0651   **£50**
Open: all day daily (closed 24+25 Dec)
Meals served: noon-12.45 (Sun 12-11.45)

Still enormously popular so be sure to book. The style has shifted away from the East and towards the West Coast in recent years so you will find that certain Californian touches have created an unexpected rapprochement between this menu and that of sister establishment Orso. For those of you who like spicy food there is black bean soup, pan-fried baby calamari and rocket dressed with chilli oil and balsamic vinegar or grilled asparagus with soy, sesame and chilli. Favourite egg dishes, suitable either as a starter or a light main course, include eggs Benedict or cumberland sausages with eggs, though insider eaters who want to impress should order the chopped steak, an order so cool it doesn't appear on the menu. Main courses take in imaginative grills such as calves' liver with baked Swiss chard, cornfed chicken with grilled vegetables and roast potatoes or even salmon teriyaki with wilted spinach. That traditional Yankee favourite, barbecued ribs, is brought bang up to date by adding wilted greens to its accompaniment of black-eyed peas. A selection of wilt-free puddings as momma used to make 'em include blueberry streusel with vanilla sauce, pecan or banana cream pie, brownies and fine ice-creams by Hingston's. There is a dish of grapes and plums for healthy eaters. The short wine list has plenty of interesting bottles from California.

Joe's Café	SW3
126 Draycott Avenue, SW3 3AH	
Telephone: 071-225 2217	£70
Open: lunch + dinner daily (closed 25+26 Dec, 1 Jan)	
Meals served: lunch 12-3.30 (Sun 11-3.30), dinner 7.30-11.30	
Joseph Ettedgui's stylish café/restaurant near many of his shops at Brompton Cross.	

John Howard Hotel	SW7
4 Queen's Gate, SW7 5EH	
Telephone: 071-581 3011	
Fax: 071-589 8403	£65
Open: lunch + dinner daily	
Meals served: lunch 12-2.30, dinner 7-10.30	
Comfortable Kensington hotel, modern French cooking by Simon Gate.	

Julie's	W11

135 Portland Road, W11 3LX
Telephone: 071-229 8331 £60
Open: lunch Sun-Fri, dinner daily (closed Xmas, Easter)
Meals served: lunch 12.30-2.45 (Sun 12.30-3), dinner 7.30-11.15 (Sun 7.30-10.15)

Julie's celebrated its 21st birthday in 1990 and looks set to continue thriving well into the 21st Century. There are several rooms, all individually decorated (my favourite being the ruby-red Gothic room downstairs) and furnished with antiques, mirrors and eyecatching bits of junk and antiques. Dinner might open with steamed mussels with chardonnay and lemon sauce or a Boston clam chowder with garlic croûtons. Main dishes straddle the classic and modern English modes, from steak and kidney pie to Kent duck with fresh figs, raspberries and port sauce. Customers travel from far and wide for the traditional Sunday lunch at £18.50.

KALAMARAS   W2

76-78 Inverness Mews, W2 3JQ
Telephone: 071-727 9122
Open: dinner Mon-Sat (closed Bank Holidays)
Meals served: dinner 7-12

£40

If you live in the area the chances are you're already well-acquainted with Mr Stelios Platanos' excellent taverna. If not, make the trip; it's worth it. Situated at the end of a mews behind Queensway, this is arguably the most authentic Greek restaurant in London, from the food right through to the friendly, casual staff and lived-in decor. The menu is entirely in Greek (but using our own alphabet) with translations provided by the informative staff. Greek bread, not pitta, is offered and most people tend to share a tableful of starters which might include melitzanasalata – the aubergine 'salad' made from the baked, puréed vegetable mixed with garlic and olive oil, a similar dip-style mixture of yoghurt and garlic, crisp-skinned fried aubergine slices served with skordalia (a purée of garlic, breadcrumbs and olive oil), grilled squid tentacles, filo pastry triangles with cheese and saganaki, which despite being an anagram of Nagasaki is actually a dish of deliciously melting grilled Greek cheese. Good, simple main courses include grilled lamb with lemon, prawns with garlic and lemon parsley sauce or suckling pig. The repertoire takes in a wide range of unusual dishes not usually seen in London but for those wishing to stick with the familiar there is taramasalata, the Greek mixed salad with feta known as horiatiki, stuffed vine leaves, souvlakia, kalamarakia (deep-fried baby squid) and moussaka. The daily specials sometimes include kid and usually a straightforward salmon dish too. The wine list is entirely Greek, offering unresinated bottles as well as retsinas. The clientele includes a great number of Greek people, always a good sign. A cheaper unlicensed offshoot, Kalamaras Micro, is a few doors down at number 66. Kali orexi!

KASPIA   W1

18/18a Bruton Place, W1X 7AH
Telephone: 071-408 1627
Open: lunch + dinner Mon-Sat (closed Bank Holidays)
Meals served: lunch 12-2.30, dinner 7.30-11.30
Caviar restaurant and shop; also a branch in Paris.

£70

KENNY'S   SW3

2a Pond Place, SW3 6QJ
Telephone: 071-584 4555
Open: lunch + dinner daily
Meals served: lunch 12-3, dinner 6-11.30 (Sun 12-10.30, Gospel Brunch 12-4.30)
Chelsea branch of the Hampstead original (*qv*) – Cajun cooking, fun atmosphere.

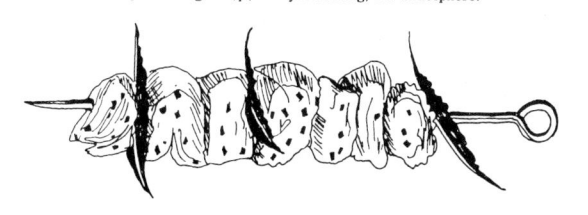

£45

| KENNY'S | NW3 |

70 Heath Street, NW3 1DN
Telephone: 071-435 6972 £45
Fax: 071-431 5694
Open: all day daily (closed 25+26 Dec)
Meals served: 11.45-11.45 (Fri+Sat 11.45-11.45, Sun 11-10.30)

Ken Miller's restaurants are now serving the best and most authentic Cajun and Creole food ever seen in Europe, thanks to the importation last year of two gen-u-ine chefs from Louisiana, Robert Greenway in the North and Sandie Brennan in the South. All the down-home greats are here – gumbo, jambalaya, spicy black bean soup, Cajun popcorn (deep-fried shrimp with dipping sauce), succotash, andouille and tasso (made in the UK to the chefs' specifications), dirty rice – and at remarkably affordable prices. Spicing is moderate but there are bottles of Louisiana sauce on the tables because some like it hot as hell. The exuberant bar staff make great cocktails but to capture the true flavour of the Deep South you should be drinking Dixie beer which is imported along with crawfish, blue soft-shell crab and catfish.

| KENSINGTON PLACE | W8 |

205 Kensington Church Street, W8 7LX
Telephone: 071-727 3184 £60
Fax: 071-229 2025
Open: lunch + dinner daily (Closed 3 days Xmas, 3 days Aug)
Meals served: lunch 12-3 (Sat+Sun 12-3.45), dinner 6.30-11.45 (Sun 6.30-10.15)

The chairs are famously uncomfortable but then, given the speed of service, you probably won't be here long enough to notice. Big, noisy, colourful, this is still one of the most consistently packed places in town and justly so. Rowley Leigh's gutsy menu features a massive list of starters, encouraging health-conscious customers to order two small courses that rarely fail to satisfy, although cassoulet of monkfish, mussels and canellini beans, spiced shoulder of lamb with couscous and harissa, grilled squid with ginger and spring onion, duck breast béarnaise, haunch of venison with pepper sauce or tournedos with morels might well divert you. Among first courses, similarly big flavours score the greatest hits, from smoked eel salad to griddled scallops with coriander and lentils and from boar's head terrine to pigeon crostini with truffle paste and rocket. Tortellini with pear and prosciutto sounds strange but tastes just fine. Vegetables are à la carte. Good puddings including chewy treacle tart and a canny wine list make it worth taking things slowly. The set lunch is fantastic value.

Lal Qila W1

117 Tottenham Court Road, W1P 9HN
Telephone: 071-387 4570 £35
Open: lunch + dinner daily (closed 25+26 Dec)
Meals served: lunch 12-3, dinner 6-11.30
Up-market Northern Indian restaurant where they would like you to start with a cocktail, but concentrate on the good tandoori and karahi dishes.

The Lanesborough SW1

1 Lanesborough Place, Hyde Park Corner, SW1X 7TA
Telephone: 071-259 5599
Fax: 071-259 5606
The Dining Room: *Open:* lunch Mon-Fri, dinner Mon-Sat
Meals served: lunch 12-2, dinner 7-10.30 £100
The Conservatory: *Open:* all day daily
Meals served 7am-11.30pm £60

Dismissed as Yankee bad taste when it first opened last Christmas, The Lanesborough has steadily built a cult following among those who realise that this really *is* how Regency palaces looked before the colours faded! With only 95 bedrooms The Lanesborough aims to provide a more intimate environment than its larger competitors while beating them on service and facilities. Rooms are equipped with a fax machine and two phone lines and regulars can keep the same direct line on each visit, giving them a sumptuous London pied à terre! Paul Gayler is in charge of two restaurants, The Dining Room and The Conservatory, which between them cater to all possible needs. The vast pastel-toned Conservatory, with chinoiserie and fountains, functions like an American hotel coffee shop, open all day from breakfast to midnight. Lunch and dinner menus are constructed with an eye to healthy eating and to feminine tastes. Although there are gutsy flavours in dishes such as minute steak served with anchovy béarnaise, onion rings and spicy fries or osso bucco of monkfish with gremolata, the many salads are particularly appealing, especially the spiced crab salad with asparagus and French beans or the fresh grilled tuna niçoise with tapenade. Paul's presentation is, as ever, faultless and he has not lost his touch with oriental spicing of which he is especially fond. Leave room for lemon tart with sour cherry syrup or cappuccino brûlée. Sunday brunch is a revelation at £21 and includes spicy crab cakes on a balsamic oriental salad, mini mixed grill with mustard butter, grilled quail and sweetcorn risotto with mushrooms and bread and butter pudding. There is also a roast for traditionalists. The Dining Room is in fact a glorious pair of interconnecting dining rooms, decorated in rich reds and pinks with definite Oriental touches. Try to bag a sofa in the first room. Simple choices include plain oysters, lobster cocktail, oak-smoked salmon with potted crab, grilled Dover sole or calves' liver and bacon but the creative dishes are the most appealing. Typical are terrine of leeks and smoked chicken, deep-fried scallops with cumin and remoulade, medallions of venison with sour cherry sauce and candied chicory or Norfolk duckling with sweet spices, turnips and radishes. Among puddings, a baked papillote of figs with cassis and almond milk ice-cream shines. Gayler was a pioneer of vegetarian haute cuisine: at The Lanesborough he does a caramelised onion and potato tart with goat's cheese and seasonal vegetables, oriental black mushroom risotto with coriander and stracci of spring vegetables with lentil Bolognese. There are comprehensive wine lists in both restaurants.

Langan's Bistro	W1

26 Devonshire Street, W1N 1RJ
Telephone: 071-935 4531 £55
Open: lunch Mon-Fri, dinner Mon-Sat (closed Bank Holidays)
Meals served: lunch 12.30-2.30, dinner 7-11.30

In an area short of this style of restaurant, it remains popular with regulars who have come to depend on a place that, while not strictly adhering to bistro prices, offers terrines maison, halibut meunière and roast rack of lamb with garlic compote as well as the more (Langan's) brasserie-style wild mushroom soup, bacon and quail's egg salad or pork fillet with raisins and cognac. Puddings include prune and armagnac tart, strawberry millefeuille or Mrs Langan's justly famous Chocolate Pudding (cheaper here than at Odin's next door). There is an abbreviated set lunch from which a typical choice might consist of an assiette of charcuterie, duck breast in red wine sauce and baked pear in filo to finish. A concise choice of wines and friendly service complete the pictures.

Langan's Brasserie	W1

Stratton Street, W1X 5FD
Telephone: 071-491 8822 £70
Open: lunch Mon-Fri, dinner Mon-Sat (closed Bank Holidays)
Meals served: lunch 12.30-3, dinner 7-11.45 (Sat 8-12.45)

Langan's was the wunderkind restaurant of the early '80s and is still at the top, serving an astonishing 500 or so meals a day, assuring customers of fresh quality produce. A vast and grand ground-floor room, hung with many well-chosen paintings, Langan's has a legendary and inimitable buzz. There is a vast menu which also incorporates the short, classy wine list. Nearly 60 dishes feature among the first and main courses alone, covering all the bases from British nursery favourites such as baked egg with cabbage and bacon hash, roast pork with sage and onion stuffing and apple sauce or black pudding with kidneys and bacon to French classics such as the famous spinach soufflé with anchovy sauce or snails in garlic butter. Puddings are among the highlights and include rice pudding, fruit crumbles or treacle tart with custard as well as clafoutis and crêpes. Vegetables – including a first-class bubble and squeak – and cheeses are à la carte. Prices remain reasonable and attract a crowd consisting of stars, tourists and many regulars who simply love the place. And yes, partner Michael Caine does eat here when he's in town. The staff have singular style – they are at once professional and down-to-earth, ensuring that dining at Langan's is always a treat. *See also page 224 – our Clover Award section.*

THE LANGHAM   W1

Portland Place, W1N 3AA
Telephone: 071-636 1000 Fax 071-323 2340   £80
Open: lunch + dinner Mon-Fri
Meals served: lunch 12.30-3, dinner 6-10.45

The lavish refurbishment of this imposing building affords some 410 tastefully-appointed bedrooms and suites and rather grand public rooms of which the lobby and the Memories of the Empire restaurant are perhaps the most impressive. Memories, as it is known, is a vast brasserie-style room with a high, trompe l'oeil painted ceiling (from which fans are suspended), wooden floors and wicker furniture. Distancing itself from its original colonial stance, the menu now blends Asian and Western cuisines where some dishes sound distinctly Californian – notably the chicken and sun-dried tomato spring roll, courgette ginger soup and the intriguing poached anise beef with vegetables. This is a result of Ken Hom's consultancy arrangement with the restaurant, whereby he puts together half a dozen or so original dishes for each new menu. The small, exclusive King's Room, elegantly decorated and suffused with light from the tall windows, offers French-based cuisine which takes genuine steps towards healthy eating. Service is as formal as the cooking: cloches are lifted to reveal langoustine and crab with rice wine and coriander dressing or fillet of red mullet with ratatouille and light basil sauce. The pièce de resistance is an intriguing poppy seed ice-cream layered with discs of caramel and served with a compote of berries. Straightforward, lighter dishes, predominantly seafood-based, are served in Tsar's, a Russian themed bar which also has a separate menu specialising in various types of caviar to suit the most extravagant connoisseur.

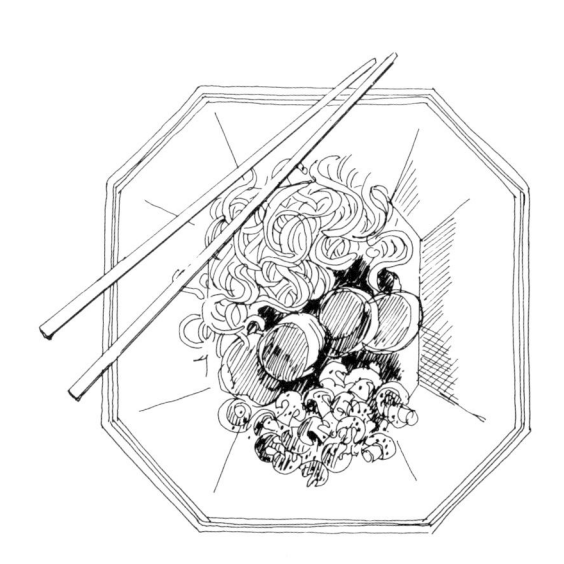

LAUNCESTON PLACE — W8

1a Launceston Place, W8 5RL
Telephone: 071-937 6912
Fax: 071-376 0581
Open: lunch Sun-Fri, dinner Mon-Sat (closed Bank Holidays)
Meals served: lunch 12.30-2.30 (Sun 12.30-3), dinner 7-11.30

— good local restaurant

£55

Recently extended, Launceston Place (under the same famous management as Kensington Place which even shares its surname) has shed its Sloaney image of late and now attracts a rather more diverse clientele, among whom its reputation for quality and value is spreading rapidly. More conservative in style than its sister establishment, there is a pleasing consistency to the cooking that makes dishes such as lamb cutlets with flageolets or duck confit with spinach a welcome safe bet. Modern British with distinct Europeanism is probably the best way to describe the food, although Sunday lunches are more traditional. There are also well-flavoured fish dishes such as brill with chervil or the more robust salmon fillet with ginger. A la carte vegetables, from the traditional gratin dauphinois, creamed leeks and roast parsnips to the more recherché baked beetroot, are excellent, as are the side salads. The pudding menu sticks to irresistible favourites: tarte tatin, steamed chocolate pudding, lemon tart, crème brûlée. An unintimidating, comfortable interior and well-chosen, mainly French, wine list complement friendly service that no longer hiccups.

LAURENT — NW2

428 Finchley Road, NW2 2HY
Telephone: 071-794 3603
Open: lunch + dinner Mon-Sat (closed Bank Holidays, 3 wks August)
Meals served: lunch 12-2, dinner 6-11
Honest local restaurant, specialising in couscous.

£35

LEITH'S   W11

92 Kensington Park Road, W11 2PN
Telephone: 071-229 4481
Open: dinner daily (closed 4 days Xmas, 2 days Aug Bank Holiday)
Meals served: 7.30-11.30

£85

In the face of some strident new competition along Kensington Park Road, this classy restaurant – a young 24-year-old – continues to hold its own, predominantly through ongoing development of its menu and an awareness of culinary trends. The lighter touch of head chef Alex Floyd is much in evidence in starters such as grilled marinated red mullet and squid with a gazpacho sauce or chicken consommé with herb quenelles, while feuilleté of rabbit with watercress, horseradish and rosemary or lasagne of cod and spinach star among main courses. Much of the produce comes from Leith's organic farm in the Cotswolds, ensuring consistent high quality as demonstrated, for instance, by braised boned poussin with spring vegetables and morels. Straightforward meaty classics for 2 to share include roast duckling or as fine a rib of beef as you will find anywhere, cooked to perfection. Prue Leith was an early champion of high-class vegetarianism and a meat-free menu – arguably the finest in London – gets equal billing on the opposite page to the carnivorous one. Typical choices might include vegetable consommé with morels, crisp potato tartlet with goat's cheese and spinach, terrine of leeks and sweet peppers with balsamic vinaigrette or mushroom ravioli with cabbage, balsamic vinegar and herb sauce. Vegans are not forgotten, either. Hors d'oeuvres, puddings and cheeses come from old-fashioned trolleys but new-fangled items include a hot banana tartlet with caramel and ginger sauce. Alternatively, try some of the excellent British cheeses. Service is smoothly professional and the classic, beautifully-conceived wine list (très français) is worth splashing out for.

LIDO   W1
41 Gerrard Street, W1V 7LP
Telephone: 071-437 4431
Open: all day daily (closed 25+26 Dec)
Meals served: 11.30am-4.30am

£40

Luxurious, spacious setting for Chinatown. Good dim sum; stay with the Cantonese dishes.

LILLY'S   W11

6 Clarendon Road, W11 3AA
Telephone: 071-727 9359
Open: lunch Mon-Fri, dinner Mon-Sat (closed Bank Holidays)
Meals served: lunch 12-2.30, dinner 7-11

£55

Roger Jones continues to serve up determinedly low-fat, low-cholesterol dishes, mostly inventive and well-cooked. Critics have claimed that portions can occasionally be on the small side but recent choices of baked red mullet provencale, casserole of pigeon breast with wild mushrooms and poached scallops with herbs have been ample. Occasional Oriental touches are welcome in a starter of sesame prawn fingers with chilli sauce and pickled vegetables or a main dish of lobster and monkfish in korma sauce. On the home front, there is shepherd's pie, grilled sirloin of Aberdeen Angus, laudable game dishes and daily chargrilled fish. British cheeses are supplied by Jeroboams (who also own the restaurant).

LINDSAY HOUSE — W1

21 Romilly Street, W1V 5TG
Telephone: 071-439 0450
Fax: 071-581 2848
Open: lunch + dinner daily (closed 25+26 Dec)
Meals served: lunch 12.30-2.30 (Sun 12-2), dinner 6-12 (Sun 7-10.30)

£70

Good theatreland venue for English cooking in a genteel period setting. Chef Dean Rodgers offers salmon and eel terrine with Sauternes jelly followed by saddle of hare with roast noodles and apple in a game sauce. Alternatively, try the grilled seafood sausage with watercress sauce, fillet of beef served with foie gras and red wine sauce. There are good puddings with savouries such as buck rarebit available as a pleasing alternative.

LONDON HILTON ON PARK LANE — W1

22 Park Lane, W1A 2HH
Telephone: 071-493 8000
Fax: 071-493 4957
Open: lunch Sun-Fri, dinner daily
Meals served: lunch 12.30-2.30, dinner 7-2 (Sun 7-1)

£100

This hotel was being refurbished as we went to press. Full Report next year.

LOU PESCADOU — SW5

241 Old Brompton Road, SW5 9HP
Telephone: 071-370 1057
Open: lunch + dinner daily (closed 25+26 Dec)
Meals served: lunch 12.30-2.30, dinner 7-12

£50

Avoid peak times as no bookings are taken and you may find yourself queueing for half an hour and tiring quickly of the decor with its heavy marine accent and catholic selection of maritime junk on the walls. Fishing nets are draped across roughcast walls, navigation lamps are used as wall lights and there is a porthole window at the front. Your order is taken by a very jolly manager and service – from waiters in matelot jumpers who seem not to understand a word of English and probably don't – is swift if occasionally haphazard. The restaurant is a fish lover's nightmare – there is simply too much to choose from! Simple favourites are expertly cooked, from moules marinières and fish soup to pan-fried mullet fillets and a petite friture of market-fresh fish. There are omelettes, pizza, pissaladière and even steak frites or beef fillet for compulsive meat-eaters. The wine list is so short that it looks as though a page is missing but is in fact perfectly adequate, listing rosé and red wines as well as white and offering three champagnes and house wine by the pichet.

LUC'S RESTAURANT & BRASSERIE — EC3

17-22 Leadenhall Market, EC3V 1LR
Telephone: 071-621 0666
Open: lunch Mon-Fri (closed Bank Holidays, 5 days Xmas)
Meals served: lunch 11.30-3

£50

Armed with a keen understanding of flexible lunch hours, Luc's has cannily positioned itself at the heart of Leadenhall Market on two floors above the related sandwich outlet below. The plats du jour are all tempting. Asparagus comes with melted lemon butter comme il faut, while veal is braised with shallots and cheese. A strawberry tart topped with whipped cream was just right.

Leadenhall market amazing Victorian ironwork painted in red, blue & cream silver 'dragons'

First floor brasserie very Gallic, great charm.

MAGNO'S BRASSERIE — WC2
65a Long Acre, WC2E 9JH
Telephone: 071-836 6077
Open: lunch Mon-Fri, dinner Mon-Sat (closed Xmas/New Year, Easter)
Meals served: lunch 12-2.30, dinner 6-11.30
Popular pre-theatre venue.

£55

MANZARA — W11
24 Pembridge Road, W11
Telephone: 071-727 3062
Open: all day Mon-Sat, daytime only Sun
Meals served: 8am-midnight but closed 5-6.30 (Sun 8-5 only)
All-Turkish restaurant, pâtisserie for breakfast, traditional favourites for lunch and dinner.

£30

Manzi's — WC2

1 Leicester Street, WC2H 7BL
Telephone: 071-734 0224
Fax: 071-437 4864
Open: lunch Mon-Sat, dinner daily (closed Xmas)
Meals served: lunch 12-2.30, dinner 5.30-11.30 (Sun 6.30-10.30)

£55

Something of an institution, Manzi's is London's most ancient seafood restaurant, decorated with fishing nets and marine-themed art nouveau tiles. Try to bag a table on the ground floor, which has the livelier atmosphere and the more interesting decor. Slap bang in the middle of theatre and cinema territory, it offers good, straightforward fish dishes that have stood the test of time and acquired a devoted following. A menu which lists potted shrimps and skate with black butter has been brought up to date lately with the inclusion of, say, grilled fresh tuna, but the old dishes are the most popular and keep pulling in the old regulars as well as newer customers proud of their discovery.

Manzi's — E14
Turnberry Quay, Pepper Street, E14 9TS
Telephone: 071-538 9615
Open: lunch + dinner Mon-Fri (closed Bank Holidays)
Meals served: lunch 12-2.30, dinner 6-11
New East End branch of the city-centre original seafood restaurant.

£45

Marine Ices — NW3
8 Haverstock Hill, NW3
Telephone: 071-485 3132
Open: lunch daily, dinner Mon-Sat, parlour open all day daily
Meals served: lunch 12-2.45, dinner 6-10.15, Sat 12-10.15; parlour 10.30am-10.45pm Mon-Sat, 11-7 Sun
One of London's most famous sources of good ice-cream to eat on site or take away. Light meals also.

£25

Martin's Bistro & Bar — NW1
239 Baker Street, NW1 6XE
Telephone: 071-935 3130
Open: lunch + dinner Mon-Fri (closed Bank Holidays)
Meals served: lunch 12-2.30, dinner 6-10.30
Martin's, once a restaurant, has restyled itself in accordance with recession-proofing trends.

£55

May Fair Inter-continental — W1

Stratton Street, W1A 2AN
Telephone: 071-629 7777
Fax: 071-629 1459
Open: lunch Mon-Fri, dinner daily (closed after lunch 25 Dec-4 Jan)
Meals served: lunch 12.30-2.30, dinner 7-11

£70

Hotelier of the Year Dagmar Woodward runs the stylish May Fair with its 322 rooms of which 65 are suites. Well-marshalled service continues throughout one of London's more quietly luxurious establishments boasting its own theatre and swimming pool. Menus in the smart restaurant might include baked fillet of sole with a minestrone sauce or loin of lamb with a panaché of beans, truffle and tarragon.

Mélange — WC2
59 Endell Street, Covent Garden, London WC2H 9AJ
Telephone: 071-240 8077
Open: lunch Mon-Fri, dinner daily (closed Bank Holidays)
Meals served: lunch 12-2.30, dinner 6-11.30
Bohemian Covent Garden restaurant, simple well cooked food.

£40

Le Meridien   W1

Piccadilly, W1V 0BH
Telephone: 071-734 8000
Fax: 071-437 3574

Oak Room: *Open:* lunch Mon-Fri, dinner Mon-Sat (closed Bank Holidays) **£100**
Meals served: lunch 12-2.30, dinner 7-10
Terrace Garden Restaurant: *Open:* all day daily   **£55**
Meals served: 7am-11.30pm

This imposing 250-roomed Mayfair hotel boasts an enviable central location on Piccadilly and high standards of decor and service throughout. The public rooms are lavishly yet unobtrusively appointed and Champney's health club in the basement is one of the most luxurious and expensive in town, although guests can of course avail themselves of its extensive facilities free of charge. The sumptuous Oak Room, ornately beflowered, is one of London's finest formal restaurants, with David Chambers offering 3 serious menus – Cuisine Traditionelle, Cuisine Creative and Le Menu Gourmand – all of which are overseen by fêted consultant chef Michel Lorain of Côtes St Jacques at Joigny. Gazpacho with warm langoustines and courgette quenelles, persillé of salmon fillet and tomato confit with herbs or marbre of goose liver with wild mushrooms or terrine of duck foie gras and baby leeks with truffle vinaigrette are suitably impressive preludes to a main course such as papillote of brill with chicory in a lemon grass and coriander sauce, roast pigeon with a potato and cabbage galette and truffle jus or roasted calves' sweetbreads on a bed of Puy lentils with celeriac and bacon. One spectacular pudding is Chambers' leaves of bitter chocolate layered with praline cream on a caramel sauce: other desserts come from the trolley. The harmonious wine list is perfectly matched to the menu. For a more casual atmosphere and simpler food, try the pretty Terrace Garden restaurant in the conservatory upstairs which gives the impression of year-round sunlight. Lunch, dinner or supper before or after the theatre might include chicken consommé scented with lemon grass, coriander and ginger, duck confit with lentils and wild mushrooms, turbot and lobster fricassée with noodles, fresh tuna with couscous and a niçoise dressing or roast lamb with ratatouille plus a wide selection of grills. For snackers or jetlagged travellers, there is an excellent choice of salads, sandwiches and wines by the glass.

MESON DOÑA ANA	W11

37 Kensington Park Road, W11 2EU
Telephone: 071-243 0666
Fax: 071-386 0337 £45
Open: lunch + dinner Mon-Fri, all day Sat+Sun (closed Bank Holidays)
Meals served: lunch 12-3, dinner 5.30-11, Sat+Sun 12-11
Similar set-up to sister, or rather brother, restaurant Meson Don Felipe. A wide variety of tapas, paella and Spanish wines remeniscent of the better bars in the mother country. *See also page 52 – our Bistros & Brasseries section.*

MESON DON FELIPE	SE1

53 The Cut, SE1 8LF
Telephone: 071-928 3237
Fax: 071-386 0337 £45
Open: lunch Mon-Fri, all day Mon-Sat (closed Bank Holidays)
Meals served: lunch 12-3, dinner 5.30-11, Sat 12-11
Ever-popular tapas establishment run by Philip and Ana Diment. Robust Spanish wines stand up well to the battery of flavours in the dishes shared by gaggles of friends and business associates.

LE MIDI	SW6

488 Fulham Road, SW6
Telephone: 071-386 0657 £50
Open: lunch Sun-Fri, dinner Mon-Sat (closed Bank Holidays)
Meals served: lunch 12-2.30 (Sun 12-3), dinner 7-10.30
Small informal restaurant, menus based around South of France cuisine.

MIJANOU — SW1

143 Ebury Street, SW1W 9QN
Telephone: 071-730 4099 **£70**
Fax: 071-823 6402
Open: lunch + dinner Mon-Fri (closed Bank Holidays, 2 wks Xmas, 1 wk Easter, 3 wks Aug)
Meals served: lunch 12.30-2, dinner 7.15-11

After quite a lengthy rebuilding period for this long-established, well-loved restaurant, Sonia Blech returned from a holiday in Bolivia with a new spring in her step and a new expansiveness in her cooking. Scallops, crab and chicory are served warm with a champagne sabayon and, in a true labour of love, large ravioli are filled with 5 different vegetable mousses and served with 2 sauces. Where ingredients are rich, there is a tendency towards lighter but powerfully-flavoured sauces, as in a tournedos marinated in Madeira and truffle oil served with mushrooms and its own jus. Quails stuffed with wild rice and foie gras come with a grainy lentil sauce. The flageolets accompanying a rack of lamb might have been cooked in yoghurt and saffron while grilled sea bass is served with wild rice and a gingered soy sauce. Puddings are strictly indulgent: choose, if you can, between a tarte tatin with cinnamon sauce, pancakes filled with pastry cream and flamed with 3 liqueurs or a chocolate mousse pudding with hazelnuts, almonds and amaretto (Sonia has a passion for nuts!). Neville Blech is responsible for an outstanding wine list, sub-divided into 20 characteristic categories such as 'big scale fruity red wines' or 'dry and pungent white wines'. Wines are suggested to match each course on the menu.

Millburns Restaurant — W1

Royal Academy of Arts, Piccadilly, W1V 0DS
Telephone: 071-287 0752
Open: lunch daily (closed 25+26 Dec, Good Friday)
Meals served: lunch 11.45-2.45

£30

Useful restaurant within the Royal Academy. *See also page 54 – our Bistros & Brasseries section.*

Mimmo d'Ischia — SW1

61 Elizabeth Street, Eaton Square, SW1
Telephone: 071-730 5406
Open: lunch + dinner Mon-Sat (closed Bank Holidays)
Meals served: lunch 12.30-2.15, dinner 7.30-11.15

£65

[handwritten annotation: long established favourite – excellent fish specials]

Tourists and Americans-in-London go a bundle on the quaint railway carriage interior and prints of quondam celebrities. The Italian cooking is appropriately old-fangled, with gnocchi, rigatoni and noodles with prosciutto among the starters and fegato Veneziana, osso bucco and lamb with rosemary and wine sauce being typical of the carni. The wine list has some excellent Italian bottles.

Mirabelle — W1

56 Curzon Street, W1
Telephone: 071-499 4636
Open: lunch Mon-Fri, dinner Mon-Sat (closed Bank Holidays)
Meals served: lunch 12-2.30, dinner 6.30-11

£120

A Japanese company now holds the purse strings at this newly reopened, once quintessentially London restaurant. Formerly one of *the* people-spotting places in town for those desirous of spying on royals, glitterati, literati and the landed gentry, the Mirabelle has now cast off its fogeyish mantle and pitched itself squarely at The New Money. Extensively revamped in an elegant, quasi-hotel style, it even houses 2 way-upmarket teppanyaki rooms, presumably for the owners to entertain their Japanese guests, where set menus start from £50 a head. In the main restaurant, with its peach colour scheme, wall lamps and arches, Michael Croft turns out some masterly dishes that have included foie gras prepared in 3 exciting ways, rabbit and basil terrine with shallots, bacon and honey-pickled vegetables or minestrone of langoustine tails with fresh pasta among starters. The modish fresh tuna niçoise makes a dashing appearance, as does a curried mussel soup with saffron and coriander. A 6-course menu surprise is on offer for special occasions or for those who wish to do justice to Croft's culinary skills. There is a list of traditional grills, roasts and simply-prepared fish dishes which might be preceded by a smartly-dressed crab or a generous lobster salad. Fine English and French cheeses are a pleasing alternative to desserts which include a superb caramelised banana tart with coconut ice. Wines from an exceptional cellar are weighted in price towards the top end of the market, which is of course entirely in keeping with the nature of the establishment.

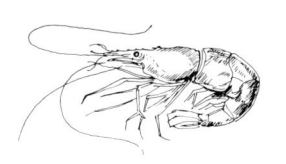

Miyama	**W1**

38 Clarges Street, W1Y 7PJ
Telephone: 071-499 2443   £70
Open: lunch Mon-Fri, dinner Mon-Sat (closed Bank Holidays, Xmas+New Year)
Meals served: lunch 12.30-2.30, dinner 6.30-10.30
West End branch of this pair of Japanese restaurants – calm, sophisticated, owner-run with two teppan-yaki bars. One of the best and one of the most beautiful . . .

Miyama	**EC4**

17 Godliman Street, EC4V 5BD
Telephone: 071-489 1937
Fax: 071-329 4225   £85
Open: lunch + dinner Mon-Fri (closed Bank Holidays)
Meals served: lunch 12-2.30, dinner 6-10
. . . and its lovely City sister.

Mon Petit Plaisir	**WC2**

21 Monmouth Street, WC2H 9DD
Telephone: 071-836 7243
Fax: 071-379 0121   £55
Open: lunch + dinner Mon-Fri (closed Bank Holidays)
Meals served: lunch 12-2.30, dinner 7-10.30
Smaller branch of Mon Plaisir and Mon Plaisir du Nord. Same theme.

Mon Plaisir   WC2

21 Monmouth Street, WC2H 9DD   *— good local restaurant*
Telephone: 071-836 7243
Fax: 071-379 0121
Open: lunch Mon-Fri, dinner Mon-Sat (closed Bank Holidays)
Meals served: lunch 12-2.15, dinner 6-11.15

50 years old this year, Mon Plaisir is a venerable and ancient traditional styled bistro, renowned throughout London for its excellent steak and chips. There are now branches in Kensington and Islington but this is the flagship and the most authentic. Old fashioned dishes such as fish soup, omelettes or the estimable coq au vin are served with correspondingly old-fashioned charm and the entrecote still comes with a red wine and mustard sauce. Vegetables are well-seasoned, notably the petits pois with butter, lettuce and crispy bacon, the excellent creamed spinach, gratin dauphinois and well-dressed green salad. There is also an awareness of contemporary tastes: grilled duck breast with béarnaise is properly seared without, properly pink within. Starters keep one eye on fashion with brioche of wild mushrooms or a warm salad of spinach and scallops dressed in walnut oil listed alongside onion soup and snails in garlic butter. Puddings include crème brûlée and moist fruit tarts, though it is difficult not to be swayed by the fine French cheeses. Always book for lunch.

Monkeys · SW3

1 Cale Street, SW3 3QT
Telephone: 071-352 4711 £55
Open: lunch + dinner Mon-Fri (closed Bank Holidays, 2 wks Easter, 3 wks Aug)
Meals served: lunch 12.30-2.30, dinner 7.30-11

If you can have a whoop of gorillas and a flange of baboons, perhaps somebody will come up with a term to describe a pack of the species known as homo sapiens gastronomicus. Here at Monkeys you can obsrve them in their natural habitat, munching their way through a menu that pitches itself firmly trans-Manche, though with plenty of game in season and roasts on Sunday. On a regular weekday, you might follow lobster and leek terrine or salad of scallops and ratatouille with paupiettes of salmon and brill with saffron sauce or roast Bresse pigeon with Muscat and grapes. A handy local restaurant to have in your neck of the urban jungle.

Mosimann's · SW1

11b West Halkin Street, SW1X 8JL
Telephone: 071-235 9625 £100
Fax: 071-245 6354
Open: lunch + dinner Mon-Sat (closed Bank Holidays)
Meals served: lunch 12-2.30, dinner 7-11

A magnificent, gently Gothicised setting in this former belfry affords Anton Mosimann a beautifully-dressed stage for his natural cuisine which has become synonymous with health, simplicity and restraint. Take cocktails on the gallery with its fine Pugin wallpaper before descending into a lush, muted dining room. The restaurant is of course run as a private dining club so unless you know a member you will have to content yourself with the cookery books and television programmes. Wonderful trio of giant ravioli filled with goat's cheese, root vegetables, carpaccio of salmon, painted onto the plate, lemon-marinated grilled chicken breast with couscous. Lunch reflects the demands of the local businessmen and is a little less genteel: in bangers and mash* and fishcakes are highlighted on the menu as house specialities. *See also page 226 – our Clover Award section.*

* but are as unlike ordinary bangers & mash as Anton's bread & butter pudding is to your mother's variety!

MOTCOMB'S	SW1

26 Motcomb Street, SW1X 8JU
Telephone: 071-235 9170 £55
Fax: 071-245 6351
Open: lunch + dinner Mon-Sat (closed Bank Holidays)
Meals served: lunch 12-3, dinner 7-11

Tables are closely packed at Philip Lawless' restaurant, situated beneath the wine bar of the same name, but air-conditioning saves the day. The walls are similarly crammed, this time with pictures, and the menu is constructed along traditional 'international' lines. To start, you might choose moules marinières or lentil and bacon soup. Swedish herring fillets with sour cream and apple and a shot of vodka, ravioli or Parma ham with sliced pickled peach demonstrate the breadth of international references and are soundly prepared. Roast crispy duckling with apple sauce and oven-baked herb-scented sea bass with olive oil and mint dressing – both cooked for 2 – are the specialities of the house and are highlights among the main courses. Others include smoked haddock with poached egg, scallops meunière, scampi provençale, tournedos Rossini and roast rack of lamb with dauphinois potatoes. When in season, grouse, partridge and pheasant are roasted for 2. There is a good wine list with plenty by the glass.

Mulligan's of Mayfair   W1

13-14 Cork Street, W1X 1PF
Telephone: 071-409 1370   £45
Open: lunch Sun-Fri, dinner Mon-Sat
Meals served: lunch 12.30-2.15 (Sun brunch 12.30-2.30), dinner 6.15-11.15

A basement restaurant beneath an Irish bar/pub in the heart of Mayfair. Mahogany panels, frosted glass and portraits of eminent Irish artists contribute to the traditional decor. In food terms, Mulligan's is quite unique and has been hailed by many critics as the Irish equivalent of The Greenhouse (*q.v.*). Home pickled crubbeens (boned, deep-fried pigs trotters), black pudding, boiled ham with parsley sauce, traditional Irish stew and a casserole of beef, Guinness and oysters take Irish cuisine to heights never dreamt of in London. There are the staples you might expect – beautifully smoked salmon and potato dishes such as champ and colcannon are perennial favourites – and some divine new dishes by chef Richard Corrigan such as curried parsnip soup or venison and red cabbage sausage with celeriac purée. Clams baked with parsley and garlic create a broth from Wonderland that ought to be labelled 'drink me'! Excellent Irish cheeses or puddings such as a good apple tart. Lovely service.

Le Muscadet   W1

25 Paddington Street, W1M 3RF
Telephone: 071-935 2883   £55
Open: lunch Mon-Fri, dinner Mon-Sat (closed Bank Holidays, 3 wks Aug)
Meals served: 12.30-2.30, dinner 7.30-10.45 (Sat 7.30-10)

This popular bistro, frequented by executives at lunch-time and by the world and his wife in the evening, offers a classic menu of French dishes so popular they might just as well be English. Alongside a starter of oeufs meurette you will find oysters, vichyssoise, asparagus hollandaise and crab bisque. Main courses include noisettes of lamb with Madeira, beef with red wine and Dover sole with Champagne sauce. There is the occasional modern touch, as in a dish of scallops with ginger and lime or roast quail stuffed with foie gras and sauced with balsamic vinegar but the reassuringly traditional repertoire prevails and that, after all, is why the customers are here. There is a concise list of French wines at good prices.

Museum Street Café	WC1

47 Museum Street, WC1A 1LY
Telephone: 071-405 3211 £45
Open: lunch + dinner Mon-Fri (closed Bank Holidays, 1 wk summer)
Meals served: lunch 12.30-2.30, dinner 7.30-9.15

Simply decorated with naive paintings, this small restaurant was a very welcome addition to Bloomsbury's gastronomic desert when it opened a couple of years ago and continues to thrive. The char-grill is the star of the short lunch and dinner menus, branding dishes that range from char-grilled guinea fowl with a pistachio and parsley purée to tuna steak with rosemary mayonnaise. There are also dishes like wild mushroom risotto and tarte tatin, all skilfully cooked using ingredients of impressive quality. The simplicity is startling, the success pleasing. Minimal interference with the true flavours of the ingredients makes for a pleasurably pared-down dining experience. The restaurant is unlicensed which allows you to bring a truly splendid bottle of wine to drink while keeping prices low. It also earns an extra brownie point for not charging corkage. Booking is essential. *See also page 56 – our Bistros and Brasseries Section.*

Nakano	SW1

11 Beauchamp Place, SW1
Telephone: 071-581 3837 £65
Fax: 071-357 7315
Open: lunch Tue-Sat, dinner Tue-Sun (closed Bank Holidays, 1 wk Aug, Xmas/New Year)
Meals served: lunch 12.30-3, dinner 6.30-11 (Sun 7-11)
Is a jaded palate your problem? Try cuttlefish marinated with its own gut and other arcane Japanese specialities at this alluring basement restaurant.

National Gallery Brasserie & Café	WC2

National Gallery, Trafalgar Square, WC2
Telephone: 071-839 3321 Brasserie: £40
Open: all day daily Café: £25
Meals served: 10-5 (Sun 12-5, Sun in Café 2-5)
Another useful resting spot after a dose of culture.

Neal Street Restaurant — WC2

26 Neal Street, WC2H 9PH
Telephone: 071-836 8368 £75
Fax: 071-497 1361
Open: lunch + dinner Mon-Sat (closed Bank Holidays, 1 wk Xmas/New Year)
Meals served: lunch 12.30-2.30, dinner 7.30-11

Another restaurant bearing the discreet signature of Sir Terence Conran, Neal Street is the stomping-ground of Britain's best-known television fungi enthusiast Antonio Carluccio, the design guru's brother-in-law. The long, well-lit room is decorated with fine modern paintings and the menu is a work of art in itself. It would be a crime to dine here and opt out of fungi-feasting altogether: look out for wild mushroom soup, pappardelle with wild fungi, tagliolini with truffle sauce among starters; pasticcio of polenta and fungi, fillet of beef with cep sauce, venison with morels and mostarda di Cremona or rabbit casserole with wild mushrooms among the mains. Seasonal specialities extend the delights still further, the ultimate treat being an impeccably-cooked risotto topped with shaved fresh white truffle at the table (one of those 'if you need to ask the price you can't afford it' dishes). If you loathe fungi you're probably at the wrong party but there are plenty of dishes even for you – black angel hair pasta with scallops or grilled lamb cutlets with minty hollandaise for instance. Interesting accompaniments include braised chicory with capers or broccoli with garlic and chilli and, to finish, cheese (presumably mascarpone) ice-cream with blueberry sauce or Barolo-poached pear with chocolate sauce. Wines cover a sensible price range with some exceptional bottles and the vin santo (served, naturally, with cantucci) is excellent. Although plenty of gastronomic 'objets trouves' are listed – dandelion tart, wild garlic soup, nettle gnocchi – never come here looking for a bargain. Carluccio's, the gleaming next-door deli run by Antonio's wife Priscilla, stocks an oustanding range of fresh and bottled fungi, fresh and dried pastas, lovely vegetables, power breads, exceptional oils and vinegars, mostardas and more. Everything is highly visible in cellophane bags and there is an irresistible Italian 'traiteur' section offering take-out salads, marinated grilled vegetables, chicken and fish dishes, giant polenta croutons, fruit tarts and more.

Neshiko	**N1**

265 Upper Street, N1 2UQ
Telephone: 071-359 9977
Open: lunch Mon-Fri, dinner Mon-Sun (closed Bank Holidays)
Meals served: lunch 12-2.30, dinner 6.30-11 (7-10.30 Sun)

£45

The Japanese owner is keen to explain the refinement of his country's cuisine to Westerners, from home cooking to elaborate banquets.

Newtons	**SW4**

73 Abbeville Road, SW4 9LA
Telephone: 081-673 0977
Open: lunch + dinner Mon-Fri, all day Sat+Sun
Meals served: lunch 12.30-2.30, dinner 7-11.30, Sat+Sun 12.30-11.30

£45

A good neighbourhood restaurant, decorated with restraint, offering something for all tastes. In other words, the menu is eclectic but deftly-prepared. Steamed chicken won ton with sweet chilli dipping sauce, satay, Thai pancake, smoked salmon blini, rabbit brioche, roast guineafowl with lemon pesto glaze and chilli potatoes, bangers and mash or fish and chips have all found their place onto menus in recent months. The 2-course set menu is very good value offering 3 choices in each section. Christopher Lee ensures that every dish is well-executed and immaculately presented. The wine list is compiled by James Rogers and reads as well as it drinks – an Italian chardonnay is described as 'bursting with youth and vigour – a toyboy of a wine!' – with some interesting little numbers available by the glass. The terrace opens in the summer for al fresco dining.

NICO AT NINETY — W1

90 Park Lane, W1A 3AA
Telephone: 071-409 1290 Fax 071-355 4877
Open: lunch Mon-Fri, dinner Mon-Sat (closed Bank Holidays, 10 days Xmas/New Year)
Meals served: lunch 12-2, dinner 7-11

£120

In an intelligent move that makes sense for all the parties concerned, Nico Ladenis moved his flagship restaurant into the Grosvenor House premises formerly known as Ninety Park Lane in August 1992. The room has brightened considerably thanks to careful tweaking of the basic design involving new upholstery, carpeting and drapes and now looks elegant and airy. Nico's 13-strong kitchen brigade, nearly all of whom are English, are performing better than ever in their new surroundings while Nico and his womenfolk (who run the front of house) are delighted with the arrangement. The food continues to astound: even the canapés, which might be a little quail's egg Benedict with truffle or a slivery croûton with mozzarella, asparagus vinaigrette and black olives, are staggering and I was impressed to discover new breads! A starter of huge grilled scallops comes with noodles and beautifully-contrasted filo purses filled with a duxelles, bronzed guinea fowl with a giant raviolo of foie gras mousse. Bresse pigeon is served on a crunchy sweetcorn pancake with garlic confit. Unambitious descriptions belie the superlative nature of puddings that include crème caramel with fresh fruit, a peach Melba and a fine apple tart with vanilla ice-cream. All are stunningly presented, and the assiette gourmande proves that it is impossible to single out a favourite as each one is a winner. The set lunch, necessarily simpler, is excellent value at £25 which includes service. At 58 (not 90!) Nico, obviously relaxed and in positive mode, is going to be a force to be reckoned with in the '90s. *See also pages 563–570 – our Special Feature.*

NICO CENTRAL — W1

35 Great Portland Street, W1N 5DD
Telephone: 071-436 8846
Open: lunch + dinner Mon-Fri (closed Bank Holidays, 10 days Xmas, 3 wks Aug)
Meals served: lunch 12-2, dinner 7-11

£150

As Nico moved to Park Lane, so these premises in Great Portland Street were transformed into a bistro-brasserie closer in style to Simply Nico. Standards remain exacting and the repertoire is perfectly contemporary with a lengthy list of starters, 2 of which would make an ample lunch. There are a number of salads, including warm potato with duck confit and mustard dressing. Heartier starters include a boudin blanc with caramelised apples and mustard sauce or a risotto of cèpes. Among main dishes you might find the strong, simple flavours of red mullet with basil-flavoured potato purée, or pot-roasted guineafowl with white coco beans. English puddings such as Bakewell tart, sherry trifle or pear crumble enjoy equal billing with crème caramel, tarte tatin and Armagnac parfait. The shortish, eclectic wine list is in the mid-price range and lists half a dozen or so good half bottles.

Nikita's	SW10

65 Ifield Road, SW10 9AU
Telephone: 071-352 6326 £55
Fax: 081-993 3680
Open: dinner Mon-Sat (closed Bank Holidays, 2 wks Aug)
Meals served: dinner 7.30-11.30

Glasnost was thriving here at Nikita's even in the darkest days of the Cold War, mainly because the party manifesto reads Let The Vodka Flow! From the witty menu, commence in traditional style with zakuski – a selection of blinis, caviar and smoked fish – then try scallops zubrovka or magret of duck flamed with pepper vodka. Caviar also adorns a steak tartare moistened with pepper vodka and an omelette of keta or sevruga with sour cream. There is raspberry and claret soup for the sweet of tooth and beef Stroganoff or chicken Kiev for tamer appetites. The pudniks (yes really) include a St Petersburg crème brûlée, gratinée Potemkin (fruit sorbet + iced vodka) and a delicious syrupy pancake filled with sweet cheese, cinnamon and sultanas. There is a list of some 17 vodkas including the Polish Zlota Woda – which has flakes of gold leaf in suspension – and chilli-fired Pertsovka.

Norma's Café	W4

183 Acton Lane, W4
Telephone: 081-994 1093 £30
Open: lunch + dinner Mon-Sat
Meals served: breakfast + lunch 7-3, dinner 6-10
Traditional café by day, Thai bistro by night. Unlicensed.

North & South	SW19

147 Arthur Road, SW19
Telephone: 081-947 8885 £30
Open: lunch Mon-Fri, dinner daily
Meals served: lunch 12-3, dinner 6-11.15
Useful local (Wimbledon) restaurant.

Now & Zen	WC2

48 Upper St Martin's Lane, WC2
Telephone: 071-497 0376 £60
Open: lunch + dinner daily (closed 25+26 Dec)
Meals served: lunch 12-3, dinner 6-11.30 (Sun 6-11)
Another of Lawrence Leung's attractive and successful Zen chain, designed by Rick Mather.

Odette's — NW1

130 Regent's Park Road, NW1 8XL — *good local restaurant*
Telephone: 071-586 5486 £55
Open: lunch Sun-Fri, dinner Mon-Sat (closed Bank Holidays, 1 wk Xmas, 2 wks Aug)
Meals served: lunch 12.30-2.30, dinner 7-11

Variety is the spice of Simone Green's delightfully cosy restaurant and maze-like structure of smaller dining rooms, each with its own distinct ambience. There is a corner somewhere in Odette's for the romantic tête-à-tête, the boisterous birthday bash or the working lunch. Although this is a mature establishment at 14, the kitchen is always up to date and chef Paul Holmes produces a menu as diverse as the restaurant's many moods and styles. There might be Japanese seafood consommé, tandoori quail or char-grilled squid on the list of starters. Main courses can include escalopes of salmon and brill, roast rump of lamb with blue puys lentils or griddled calves' liver with baby beetroot, sour cream and chives. Light dishes in the wine bar below are simpler still and might include spicy sausages, tagliatelle, hamburgers or omelettes. The wine list is wide-ranging and informative with some good half bottles. Pavement tables in summer are always an attractive proposition on fine days.

ODIN'S RESTAURANT	W1

27 Devonshire Street, W1N 1RJ — *a very special local*
Telephone: 071-935 7296   £80
Open: lunch Mon-Fri, dinner Mon-Sat (closed Bank Holidays)
Meals served: lunch 12.30-2.30, dinner 7-11.30

Crammed with paintings from end to sides, Odins is a connoisseur's delight in more ways than one. The lengthy menu (though not as long as that of sister establishment Langan's Brasserie) is more English than ever, with stewed eels and mash featuring prominently and pleasingly among a list of starters which might also include a smoked fish soufflé with dill or a bacon and potato pancake sauced with lemon cream. To follow, there is roast best end of lamb or roast duck with sage and onion stuffing and apple sauce while fish dishes include poached skate with black butter and capers, poached cod or cold salmon with mayonnaise. A dish of steamed monkfish with saffron sauce seems distinctly exotic amidst such Anglophilia! Puddings are good, gutsy classics like strawberry romanoff or date and ginger pudding with butterscotch sauce. Classy wines match the comforting interior, the subject of a careful and discreet re-decoration in 1992. A favourite with locals, studded with personalities and a contingent from the nearby BBC.

OLIVO	SW1

21 Eccleston Square, SW1W 9LX
Telephone: 071-730 2505   £55
Open: lunch Mon-Fri, dinner daily (closed Bank Holidays, 3 wks Aug/Sep)
Meals served: lunch 12-2.30, dinner 7-11
Young Italian restaurant with 46 seats. Good value set lunch, pasta made in-house, wines Italian.

190 QUEEN'S GATE	SW7

190 Queen's Gate, SW7 5EU
Telephone: 071-581 5666   **£80**
Open: lunch Sun-Fri, dinner daily (closed Bank Holidays, 10 days Xmas, 2 wks Aug)
Meals served: lunch 12-2.30, dinner 7-11.30

A new seafood bistro styled by Antony Worrall Thompson was being developed as we went to press, the decor changed in the restaurant to a lighter, more relaxed mode and the menu more attuned to the style and pricing of the '90s. *See also page 228.*

Orso   WC2

27 Wellington Street, WC2E 7DA
Telephone: 071-240 5269   £60
Fax: 071-497 2148
Open: all day daily (closed Xmas)
Meals served: 12-12

The first restaurant to use the now-ubiquitous Tuscan crockery which you can emulate by shopping at Divertimenti or Designer's Guild, Orso – a 'concept' imported from America by the creators of Joe Allen – was in the vanguard of the regional Italian movement. A vast basement space brightened with white tiles and monochrome photographs, it remains one of London's more interesting Italian restaurants, though hard to find. Mini designer-y pizzas make for an interesting first or second course. The bland but versatile soft Italian cheeses are imaginatively used in creations such as leek and ricotta ravioli with sage and butter or a risotto of radicchio and ricotta, which was among the finest I have ever tasted. Beef stew with barolo, horseradish and new potatoes, braised oxtail with Mediterranean vegetables, grilled chicken with roasted peppers. Finish with a fine pear and almond tart or sorbet with grappa. A good, concise wine selection is listed on the reverse of the menu. No credit cards means that this is a place strictly for the cash-rich.

OSTERIA ANTICA BOLOGNA	SW11

23 Northcote Road, SW11 1NG
Telephone: 071-978 4771 £40
Open: all day daily (closed Bank Holidays, 2 wks Xmas)
Meals served: 11am-11.30pm, Sat 12-11, Sun 12.30-11

This is a casual, rustic-looking restaurant with so much wood on all sides that you might be forgiven for thinking you were in a chalet. Except at the back, that is, which looks like a small, narrow conservatory (it is). Tables are densely packed so it's best to avoid intimate and private conversational matter. The Osteria prides itself on accessibility and keeping prices low: there is a £6.50 menu available until 5pm and you can compose an entire feast from 'assaggi' which translate roughly as Italian tapas. These range in price from £2 to £5 and include wine-marinated olives stuffed with peppered spinach, aubergine crostini, fried fennel in breadcrumbs, fried pumpkin squares with mint, calamari with radicchio and chilli or a torta of sardines Venetian-style. On the peasant-style menu proper, there are big pastas such as orecchiette with broccoli, garlic and chilli or a single pillow-sized raviolo filled with mushrooms and truffle. On the daily specials list there might be risotto with radicchio and asparagus or chicken in garlic sauce. A short list of à la carte vegetables and salads includes roast potatoes with garlic and lemon or sautéed leaf spinach with garlic and olive oil. Service is primarily young, Italian, female and charming. Wines are cheap and cheerfully explained – drinking by the glass is not cost-effective so go for house wines served in earthenware jugs of varying capacity (75cl costs £6.75) or something like the Bonera, a gutsy Sicilian red at £8.00.

La Paesana   W8

30 Uxbridge Street, W8 7TR
Telephone: 071-229 4332   £35
Open: lunch Mon-Fri, dinner Mon-Sat (closed Bank Holidays)
Meals served: lunch 12-2.45, dinner 6-11.45
Old favourite from the '60s, serving good range of pastas soundly cooked.

Pâtisserie Bliss   EC1

428 St John Street, EC1
Telephone: 071-837 3720   £25
Open: all day daily (closed Bank Holidays, Xmas/New Year)
Meals served: 8am-8pm (Sat+Sun 9-6)
Wonderfully authentic fruit tarts and croissants, either au naturel or stuffed with ham and cheese, are the perfect accompaniment to the strong coffee in this useful City/Islington pâtisserie.

Pelham Hotel   SW7

15 Cromwell Place, SW7 2LA
Telephone: 071-589 8288   £55
Fax: 071-589 8444
Open: lunch + dinner daily
Meals served: 12-10.30

Warm, rich colours are used throughout this beautifully-decorated 37-bedroomed hotel, especially in the rugs, tapestries and drapes. Textiles are clearly a passion of proprietors Kit and Tim Kemp and minimalists should definitely stay away. This hotel epitomises the European idea of 'le style anglais': fine antiques, including crystal chandeliers, abound and exquisite floral arrangements, many of them dried, are everywhere. The finest rooms and suites have four-posters, dressed in antique lace and piled high with pretty cushions. Mantelpieces, some surrounding open fires, are cluttered with flowers, clocks, vases and other ornaments. Such is the skill of the Kemps, however, that the rooms manage always to look tasteful and never overblown. The look remains identifiably contemporary, with modern touches such as tartan upholstery or dried flower-encrusted picture frames. The hotel's private garden across the road boasts an outdoor swimming pool which can be used by guests. A fine restaurant specialising in English themes adjoins the elegant basement bar, a popular rendezvous before social engagements in South Kensington.

Pied à Terre   W1

34 Charlotte Street, WIP 1HJ
Telephone: 071-636 1178   £80
Open: lunch Mon-Fri, dinner Mon-Sat (closed Bank Holidays, 2 wks Aug)
Richard Near and David Moore's new venture with backing from Raymond Blanc has been a new addition to the serious eating scene in London.

Pinocchio's   NW1

160 Eversholt Street, NW1 1BL
Telephone: 071-388 7482   £45
Open: lunch Mon-Fri, dinner Mon-Sat (closed Bank Holidays, 24-31 Dec)
Meals served: lunch 12-3, dinner 6.30-11
Traditional and modern Italian cooking. Especially popular at lunchtime.

Pizzeria Castello — SE1

20 Walworth Road, SE1 6SP
Telephone: 071-703 2556 £35
Open: all day Mon-Fri, dinner Sat (closed Bank Holidays, 10 days Xmas)
Meals served: 12-11 (Sat 5-11)

This large, 2-tiered functional pizza paradise lurks behind a tiny, unassuming façade at Elephant & Castle. A convenient spot for south bank theatregoers, it is usually heaving and you inevitably have to queue longer than the promised five minutes. Routine pasta dishes – lasagne, cannelloni, spaghetti in various guises – are fine but the pizzas are the outright winners with thin crisp bases and generous toppings. The names may sound familiar – margherita, napoletana, prosciutto, funghi, quattro formaggi – but the taste is quite special. Wash down with one of the cheap, sturdy wines from a short, serviceable list.

Pizzeria Condotti — W1
4 Mill Street, W1R 9TE
Telephone: 071-499 1308 £35
Open: all day Mon-Sat
Meals served: 11.30am-midnight
Useful West End pizzeria.

PJ's Bar & Grill — SW10
52 Fulham Road, SW10
Telephone: 071-589 0025 £45
Open: all day daily
Meals served: 11am-11.30pm
American-influenced bar and grill in South Kensington.

PJ's Bar & Grill — WC2
30 Wellington Street, WC2
Telephone: 071-240 7529 £40
Open: all day daily
Meals served: 11am-11.30pm
Covent Garden branch of this popular American eaterie.

Poissonnerie de l'Avenue — SW3

82 Sloane Avenue, SW3 3DZ
Telephone: 071-589 2457 £55
Open: lunch + dinner Mon-Sat (closed Bank Holidays, 10 days Xmas, 4 days Easter)
Meals served: lunch 12-3, dinner 7-12

The Poissonerie seems to have been here forever, in the capable hands of Peter Rosignoli. This restaurant has outlived many of its more modish rivals and attracts a loyal and discerning following, and the dark panelling and marine clutter make it a restaurant in the traditional style. Quality produce simply prepared is the norm, from crab salad to scallop brochette, a dozen oysters to a lobster cooked any way you like it. In the more modern vein are sole goujonettes served not with a tartare sauce but with tomato coulis and, for carnivores, a tender breast of chicken stuffed with girolles. Good French wines carefully selected to complement fish.

POLLYANNA'S — SW11

2 Battersea Rise, SW11 1ED
Telephone: 071-228 0316
Open: dinner Mon-Sat (closed 24-28 Dec, 1 Jan)
Meals served: dinner 7-12

£60

Once somewhat lacking in style, Pollyanna's has in recent years evolved into a chic and comfortable restaurant, popular with locals who rely on a roster of dishes that marry French tradition to British invention. Matt black menus list tomato consommé and fresh duck foie gras terrine among starters and roasted salmon fillet with herbs or grilled beef medallions on a red wine and shallot sauce – and you can top it with lime tart or a banoffee pie. An impressive, reasonably-priced wine list gives this place a distinct edge over much of the competition.

POMEGRANATES — SW1

94 Grosvenor Road, SW1V 3LE
Telephone: 071-828 6560
Fax: 071-828 2037
Open: lunch Mon-Fri, dinner Mon-Sat (closed 25+26 Dec)
Meals served: lunch 12.30-2.15, dinner 7.30-11.15

£65

The first in London to offer a menu of truly global inspiration when it opened some 20-odd years ago, seasoned traveller and chef/proprietor Patrick Gwynn-Jones' warm basement restaurant continues to flourish. Many of the customers are visitors to London but Pomegranates enjoys an equally strong following among the business, entertainment and catering fraternities too. Merely to pull dishes at random from the menu illustrates its range and multi-lingual dexterity: there is chicken satay, Spanish gambas with garlic, Tennessee oyster stew, steak tartare, enchiladas, West Indian curried goat with plantain, Cantonese roast duck with plum sauce and spring onion and carpetbag steak. In fact, the only cuisines conspicuous by their absence are Japanese and Italian! World cuisine also includes Britain of course, represented here by game pie, braised oxtail with mash, Gower oyster soup and Welsh salt duck with white onion sauce. Big-scale dishes for two include jambalaya or roast gigot with rosemary and garlic. The set prices at lunch and dinner include crudités with aioli and home-made bread plus vegetables or salad, though there are supplements for items like gravad lax, beef Wellington or Chateaubriand. The strong wine list is a world cruise in itself, though dominated by French bottles.

Le Pont de la Tour — SE1

Butlers Wharf Building, 36D Shad Thames, Butlers Wharf, SE1
Telephone: 071-403 8403
Open: lunch + dinner daily, Bar & Grill all day daily (closed 3 days Xmas) £75
Meals served: lunch 12-3, dinner 6-12, Bar & Grill 12-12 (Sun 12-11)   £55

Located within Conran's ambitious Gastrodome, Le Pont de la Tour takes the classical elements of Bibendum and transposes them south of the river. Still life food compositions set the mouth watering as you enter the restaurant. A long restaurant facing the river with an extensive outside eating area, Le Pont de la Tour has '30s style chairs which are comfortable whatever your girth. Tables for two are often ill-considered but here, they are angled so that both diners have a river view (although one will inevitably have to turn his or her back on the eponymous bridge) and there are even dishes prepared specifically for two: there is a perfect poulet de Bresse for two, roast pheasant with bread sauce for two, steamed sea bass for two. In addition, there are crab, lobster and aubergine salads or Arbroath smokies plus creative dishes such as an intriguing gratin dauphinois incorporating sliced scallops in camouflage. Irish chef David Burke is allowed forays into his native cuisine – champ and colcannon put in a welcome appearance – as well as that of bourgeois France, with its cassoulets or dandelion and bacon salad. The adjoining seafood bar is a more casual option, serving seafood platters and salade niçoise, for example. Drop into the bakery, delicatessen and wine merchant on the way out to assemble the ingredients to recreate your magical dinner at home. This is a true labour of love by Sir Terence: much skill and attention has gone into this enterprise, making the restaurant one of the most ambitious London has seen in many years.

Porters English Restaurant — WC2

17 Henrietta Street, WC2E 8QH
Telephone: 071-836 6466   £50
Open: all day daily (closed 25+26 Dec)
Meals served: 12-11.30, (Sun 12-10.30)

While his fellow peers tend to their crumbling piles, Lord Bradford is doing his bit for England right here. Porters dishes up bangers and mash and spotted dick as well as its self-appointed world-famous pies, from fish to game to steak and kidney. They even do faggots with onion gravy. Our glorious national pudding tradition is far from forgotten – this is the place for bread and butter pud, fruit crumble and chocolate sponge. Tiddly winks (geddit) include cocktails such as the self-effacing Lord Bradford's Nightmare and a jolly selection of wines and beers.

Portobello Dining Rooms — W11

6-8 All Saints Road, W11
Telephone: 071-243 0958   £55
Open: lunch Sat+Sun, dinner daily
Meals served: lunch 12.30-3, dinner 5.30-12.30
Another opening in the now more upmarket Portobello area, opened by the owners of First Floor. *See also page 58 – our Bistros and Brasseries section.*

Le Poulbot   EC2

45 Cheapside, EC2V 6AR
Telephone: 071-236 4379   £75
Open: lunch Mon-Fri (closed Bank Holidays)
Meals served: lunch 12-3

Tucked behind a smallish shop-front on busy Cheapside near St. Paul's, Le Poulbot is a popular and reliable venue for business lunches in the City. From omelettes and salads to steak and chips, the food in the ground floor brasserie is simply prepared, while basement restaurant offers greater elaboration. Here, the set menu might yield a terrine of duck with foie gras and pistachios, a warm salad of pigeon and artichokes or a salad of foie gras with green beans and tomato to start. Your main course might be a fillet of salmon with grilled vegetables, halibut with crab and asparagus or grilled lamb with tarragon. The high-backed banquettes lend a traditional feel to the restaurant and guard against insider eavesdropping. Good French wines are priced within the middle range. Quiet and discreet service, as you would expect from a long-serving City establishment.

Le P'tit Normand   SW18

185 Merton Road, SW18 5EF
Telephone: 081-871 0233   £40
Open: lunch Sun-Fri, dinner daily
Meals served: lunch 12-2, dinner 7-10.30 (Sun 7-10)

Friendly neighbourhood bistro, dark with beams but thoroughly clean inside. The Normandy bias makes for vast quantities of apples, calvados, butter and cream in the sauces that accompany rabbit, veal, beef and seafood. A merry atmosphere prevails, with enthusiastic service from French waitresses. The owners import their own wines from French regions, keeping prices way down. The tarte tatin and cheeseboard are good.

Le Quai St Pierre   W8

7 Stratford Road, W8 3JS
Telephone: 071-937 6388   £70
Open: lunch Tue-Sat, dinner Mon-Sat (closed 2 wks Xmas)
Meals served: lunch 12.30-2.30, dinner 7-11.30

Another of Pierre Martin's professionally-run seafood restaurants where menu, service and atmosphere are all as French as they come and where the gigantic plateaux de fruits de mers carry you across La Manche, while Kensington dims in the memory for some two or three delightful hours.

Quality Chop House   EC1

94 Farringdon Road, EC1R 3EA
Telephone: 071-837 5093   £45
Open: lunch Sun-Fri, dinner daily
Meals served: lunch 12-3 (Sun 12-3.30), dinner 6.30-12 (open from 7.30am Mon-Fri)

A restaurant that reflects the New Austerity with its uncomfy pews and table-sharing, the Chop House is Edwardian in tone and serves food from a menu wherein the 'progressive working class caterer' meets the Caprice (which is where owner Charles Fontaine learned tricks like the bang bang chicken or salmon fishcake with sorrel sauce). Warm asparagus with pecorino, artichoke vinaigrette, smoked salmon with scrambled eggs, corned beef hashcake, smoked haddock and lentil salad, Toulouse sausages with mash and gravy and roast monkfish with salsa verde have all appeared on the menu in recent months and are perfectly cooked. The chips – and chops, incidentally – are excellent. Puddings range from bread and butter to waffle with pear compote and there is a savoury of goat's cheese with olives. A short selection of wines is on offer though many go for beers or ciders instead. A combination of reliable food, good value, down-to-earth staff and relaxed atmosphere make this a winner, in tune with the times and popular with the Guardian and Independent staff who are based in the area as well as the odd gem-dealer from nearby Hatton Garden.

Quincy's   NW2

675 Finchley Road, NW2 2JP
Telephone: 071-794 8499   £50
Open: dinner Tue-Sat (closed 2 wks Sep)
Meals served: dinner 7-11

An informal, well-tended neighbourhood restaurant, Quincy's is patronised mainly by locals who appreciate the sound Franglais food and the rustic ambience created by the green frontage with its colourful windowboxes, the lace curtains, scrubbed pine tables and chairs, brass candlesticks and wooden floors. The menu changes monthly, offering a variety of dishes served in ample portions for an extremely fair set price. For starters, there might be a Stilton and walnut salad with herb dressing or soused herrings with dill cucumber, mustard and potato salad. Market-fresh fish dishes change daily while meats might include a feuilleté of braised rabbit and lentils, roast breast of goose with cranberry sauce, calves' liver with caramelised shallots, sirloin with a fumet of cèpes or corn-fed chicken with grain mustard and red wine. Great care is taken in the preparation of vegetarian dishes such as pumpkin and pistachio pie with leek and sorrel sauce, mushroom ravioli with pimento, saffron and cream or leek, onion and gruyère tart with seasonal leaves. There is a choice of French and British cheeses or, appropriately, French and British puddings – from treacle tart or fruit crumble with custard to a petit pot of chocolate injected with rum or a warm pear tart with vanilla sauce. The concise French wine list is ungreedily priced.

LONDON **177**

Rebato's — SW8
169 South Lambeth Road, SW8 1XW
Telephone: 071-735 6388
Open: lunch Mon-Fri, dinner Mon-Sat (closed Bank Holidays)
Meals served: lunch 12-2.30, dinner 7-11
Original tapas bar and restaurant – great atmosphere.

£45

Red Fort — W1
77 Dean Street, W1V 5HA
Telephone: 071-437 2525
Fax: 071-434 0721
Open: lunch + dinner daily (closed 25 Dec)
Meals served: lunch 12-3, dinner 6-11.30
Mogul Indian meat-centred cooking but with some interesting vegetable courses.

£50

Los Remos — W2
38a Southwick Street, W2 1JQ
Telephone: 071-723 5056
Open: lunch + dinner Mon-Sat
Meals served: lunch 12-3, dinner 7-12
Recently opened tapas bar.

£40

The Restaurant — SW7
Victoria & Albert Museum, SW7
Telephone: 071-581 2159
Open: all day daily
Meals served: 10-12, 12-2.45, 3-5
Simply-named, useful eating spot within one of our most famous museums.

£30

The Ritz — W1

150 Piccadilly, W1V 9DG
Telephone: 071-493 8181
Fax: 071-493 2687
Open: lunch + dinner daily
Meals served: lunch 12.30-2.30, dinner 6.30-11

[handwritten note: New chef David Nichols took over in Nov '92]

£100

Despite the fact that entrance is now from Arlington Street not Piccadilly, The Ritz has lost none of its Louis XVI-inspired grandeur and formality: the staff still wear tailcoats and female guests still wear skirts. A gradual programme of restoration of the high-ceilinged rooms has left this historic and prestigious hotel gleaming. Among the finest bedrooms are those decorated in frothy shades of oyster and pink with gilded cornicing and chandeliers. Antique furniture, fireplaces, bed linen and drapes are glorious throughout the hotel accommodation. The glittering rococo restaurant, full of marble and chandeliers and boasting a celestial painted ceiling, really is spectacular and the food, though good, is hardly the point of the exercise. During the summer, there is dining on the Terrace and Italian Garden overlooking Green Park and this is probably the prettiest spot in London for a summer lunch. There is always helpful and knowledgeable advice on your wine selection. At weekends there is dinner dancing. The Ritz is well worth visiting for the sake of this opulent room alone: those on a budget should try it for breakfast, when it buzzes with financial whispering. You still need to book a few weeks in advance for the legendary afternoon tea in the Palm Court. The Palm Court also serves light meals at lunch or dinner, comprising mainly seafood, salads and sandwiches with good wines served by the glass and hosts big band dancing from 10pm at weekends. *See also page 229 – our Clover Award section.*

RIVA	SW13

169 Church Road, SW13 9HR — *good local restaurant*
Telephone: 081-748 0434 £55
Open: lunch Sun-Fri, dinner daily (closed 25 Dec-2 Jan, 4 days Easter)
Meals served: lunch 12.15-2.30, dinner 7-11 (Sun 7-9.30)

A trendsetter which followed hot on the heels of the River Café and Cibo and boldly undercut them in price, Riva is now acclaimed by many as the finest of the 'new' Italian restaurants. A tall plain room decorated with restraint in fresco colours, Riva attracts foodies from far and wide as well as dedicated locals. The innovative menu invariably makes for an exciting dining experience and is offset by a short but thoroughly classy Italian wine list. The cooking is energetic and hearty, introducing recherché Italian ingredients and top-quality seasonal produce such as truffles or root vegetables. Green gnocchi are sauced with bitto cheese, calves' tripe is served with canellini beans and pancetta and there might be a salad of poached pike with salsa verde. A passion for potatoes is revealed in roast lamb with mash and caramelised onions or a grilled cake of thinly-sliced potato with snails, mushrooms and fennel. Duck breast mainated in balsamic vinegar and juniper berries is accompanied by roast pumpkin. Pastas include tagliatelle with beetroot and wild mushrooms or penne with pumpkin, ricotta and peperoncino. Try the warming winter stew of Savoy cabbage with spare ribs, pig's trotter and sausage or, in summer, the herby grilled calamari with celery and chilli salad. An unusual pudding list has fruit stewed in red wine with cinnamon ice cream or sweet milk gnocchi with a honey butter sauce.

River Café   W6

Thames Wharf Studios, Rainville Road, W6 9HA
Telephone: 071-381 8824   £75
Open: lunch Tue-Fri, dinner Mon-Fri (closed Bank Holidays, 10 days Xmas, 4
   days Easter)
Meals served: lunch 12.30-3, dinner 7.30-9.45

Indisputably the benchmark restaurant for new-wave Italian cooking, despite the fact that neither owners nor chefs were actually Italian, the River Café continues to dish up massive portions of decisively-flavoured rustic-looking food although prices have risen. However it is still influential and powerful, particularly for overseas visitors. Service is enhanced by the fact that all waiting staff work shifts in the kitchen to learn how dishes like veal shank with polenta, pan-roasted partridge stuffed with fresh thyme, char-grilled squid with red chilli and veal kidneys with wild mushrooms are constructed and served. For pudding there are sorbets or pear and almond tart. There are a number of tables outside during the summer. *See also page 230 – our Clover Award section.*

Rose's   NW3
515 Finchley Road, NW3
Telephone: 071-431 2199   £50
Open: lunch + dinner Mon-Sat
Meals served: lunch 12-3, dinner 6-12
Californian-style cooking in a former shop setting.

Royal Lancaster Hotel   W2
Lancaster Terrace, W2 2TY
Telephone: 071-262 6737   £60
Fax: 071-724 3191
Open: lunch Mon-Fri, dinner Mon-Sat
Meals served: lunch 12.30-2.15, dinner 6.30-10.45
Tourist and conference-based clientele. Excellent facilities in a location convenient for walks in Hyde Park as well as the shopping in Oxford Street or Knightsbridge.

RSJ	SE1

13a Coin Street, SE1 8YQ
Telephone: 071-928 4554 £50
Open: lunch Mon-Fri, dinner Mon-Sat (closed Bank Holidays)
Meals served: lunch 12-2, dinner 6-11

A place well worth knowing about if you're in the area, RSJ is a popular, stylish eaterie in Waterloo, not inconveniently located for the arts venues of the South Bank although it is also popular with local executives. A bright basement brasserie with jolly printed tablecloths has extended the premises and broadened the scope. Home-made garlic sausage is served with lentils, bubble and squeak and blackcurrant sauce, steamed mussels with curry sauce and fresh pasta. Omelette with ratatouille and spicy sausage sings with flavour. Select a straightforward pudding to finish, perhaps a lemon tart or chocolate fondant. In the restaurant proper too, reliable modern Franglais cooking is the order of the day with 2- or 3-course set menus on offer as well as the fancier à la carte. From the prix fixe, there might be a chicken and duck liver terrine with marinated veg or onion and bacon quiche to precede double lamb cutlets with ratatouille and gravy. A la carte, you might follow grilled home-made venison sausage with lentils and a cabbage and potato cake with pan-fried fillets of John Dory served with honey vinegar-marinated vegetables and tomato chilli sauce. Vegetables or salad are included in the price. To finish, choose from a gratin of berries with brioche or a hazelnut flan or try some of the well-kept cheeses. A fine and memorable wine cellar includes a famously extensive selection from the Loire. Wine tastings are held every fortnight.

RULES RESTAURANT	WC2

35 Maiden Lane, WC2E 7LB
Telephone: 071-836 5314 £55
Fax: 071-497 1081
Open: all day daily (closed 3/4 days Xmas)
Meals served: 12-12 (Sun 12-10.30)
A British original, as traditional as they come.

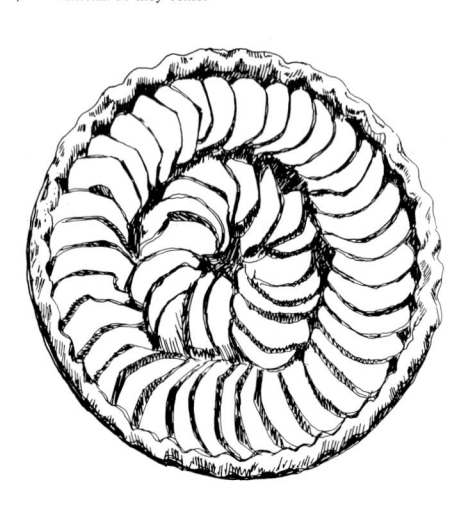

St James Court Hotel — SW1

41 Buckingham Gate, SW1E 6AF
Telephone: 071-821 1899
Fax: 071-630 7587
Open: lunch Mon-Fri, dinner Mon-Sat (closed Bank Holidays)
Meals served: lunch 12.30-2.30, dinner 7.30-10.30

£85

L'Auberge de Provence is a French restaurant supervised long-distance by Jean-André Charial of L'Oustau de Baumanière in Provence. The maroon awnings, rough plaster, cast-iron lamps and patterned carpet walls evoke a '60s interpretation of a rustic theme. Vaulted, interconnecting rooms help create a cellar-like ambience. A provençale restaurant opening in 1992 would no doubt choose heavy, peasant-style crockery: here, the exotic china gives a clue to the ambitions of the kitchen, which in London is overseen by Olivier Massart. The cooking ranges from elaborate to highly elaborate: the simple provençale techniques of the Mediterranean bandwagon have no place here. There is a good set lunch, popular with the local business community, from which you might choose steamed sea bass with aubergines, basil and olive oil. The hotel is owned by the Indian Taj group – which explains the outstanding range of vegetarian dishes in all 3 of its restaurants, L'Auberge de Provence, Inn of Happiness and the Café Mediterranée. Salads have included artichoke hearts, French and broad beans and pine nuts, while there might be ravioli of wild mushrooms in a creamy sauce or of vegetables with pistou. Wines are shipped directly from L'Oustau and standards are high.

ST QUENTIN	SW3

243 Brompton Road, SW3 2EP
Telephone: 071-581 5131 £55
Fax: 071-584 6064
Open: lunch + dinner daily
Meals served: lunch 12-3 (Sat+Sun 12-4), dinner 7-12 (Sat 6.30-11.30)

The perennially successful St Quentin, which originally styled itself as a brasserie but is now much posher than that, is a long, glittering room very much in the Parisian belle epoque style you find all along the Boulevard St Germain with lavish use of mirrors, wall-mounted chandeliers, stained glass, banquettes and brass. A long bar runs down one side. Largely French staff, smartly kitted out in black and white, provide service that is very much on the case. Richard Sawyer is now chef here, serving food that is safe with the occasional peek into the modern repertoire, attracting a smart, stylish clientèle. Starters are completely straightforward and traditional – soup, salads (frisée with lardons and croûtons), duck liver pâté, marinated salmon with a variety of garnishes and flavourings, foie gras, snails in puff with garlic and cream sauce. Fish courses are a little more contemporary and might include steamed sole lightly spiced, crisp red mullet with lobster vinaigrette or sea bass roasted in olive oil with chicory. Meats are basics like rack of lamb with fresh thyme or grilled calves liver with bacon, calves kidney with meaux sauce, fillet of beef with oxtail and savoy spuds, whole roast chicken with wild mushrooms for 2, rib of Scottish beef with tomato and béarnaise sauce. From the set menu, a venison terrine with celeriac salad might precede breast of goose with Thai herb sauce or Scotch fillet of beef with mushroom risotto. Puddings include the sublime oranges and bitter chocolate dessert, craquelin of spiced peaches with amandine ice cream, apple tart with caramel sauce. It is so easy to imagine that you are eating in France that summer pudding and bread and butter pudding are available for the homesick. Cheeses are imported via Les Specialités St Quentin, the restaurant's shop.

Sambuca — SW3

6 Symons Street, SW3
Telephone: 071-730 6571 — £50
Open: lunch + dinner Mon-Sat (closed Bank Holidays)
Meals served: lunch 12.30-2.30, dinner 7-11.30

Tucked away behind Peter Jones, Sambuca is a cosy little Italian restaurant serving a straightforward menu whose specialities include peppers roasted with garlic and olive oil, hot prawn cocktail and oven-braised lamb for two with red wine and mixed herbs. Conventional dishes include seafood salad, tuna with beans, rigatoni matriciana or steak tartare. The mainly-Italian wine list is fairly-priced.

San Frediano — SW3
62 Fulham Road, SW3 6HH
Telephone: 071-584 8375
Fax: 071-589 8860 — £50
Open: lunch + dinner Mon-Sat (closed Bank Holidays)
Meals served: lunch 12.30-2.30, dinner 7-11.30
Terrific atmosphere in this old-fashioned trattoria. Aubergine parmigiana, chicken with aubergine and mozzarella.

San Lorenzo — SW3

22 Beauchamp Place, SW3 1NL
Telephone: 071-584 1074 — £65
Open: lunch + dinner Mon-Sat (closed Bank Holidays)
Meals served: lunch 12.30-3, dinner 7.30-11.30

Food at the showbiz world's favourite restaurant takes second place after other-people-spotting. There is always at least one big table with at least one celebrity and/or member of the Royal Family. This is where Koo met Andy and is reputedly Princess Diana's favourite restaurant. Foodies loathe it but there is no denying the magic wrought by the glamorous clientele and the party atmosphere, even on a Tuesday lunchtime. Very popular with ladies-who-lunch-before-shopping and don't pay their own credit card bills. The menu – consisting largely of familiar or straightforward dishes such as penne all'arrabiata or poached sea bass anointed with oil and lemon, is given some muscle with the inclusion of bollito misto, braised oxtails or rabbit with polenta.

San Martino	SW3

103 Walton Street, SW3 2HP
Telephone: 071-589 3833 £55
Open: lunch + dinner daily (closed 10 days Xmas, 4 days Easter)
Meals served: lunch 12-3, dinner 6.30-11.30

A bright, busy and long-established trattoria, San Martino recently expanded to double its capacity. Proprietor Constanzo Martinucci grows his own herbs and vegetables to include in the splendid mixed salads dressed with balsamic vinaigrette that are a popular fixture. Although the menu is billed 'strictly Tuscan', an idiosyncratic but successful style makes for bresaola with mashed avocado or papaya with white crab meat. Interesting pasta creations include tagliatelle with hazelnuts and tarragon, while the house speciality – dating from 1971 – is spaghetti cooked in a paper bag with monkfish, clams, octopus, white wine, olive oil and lemon juice – plus 'secret ingredients'! Another perennial favourite is baby goat braised Roman style. Seasonal offerings can include Tuscan smoked ham with asparagus, stuffed calamari with wild mushroom sauce, crab-filled ravioli, vitello tonnato or lobster with wild rice. Among the original side-orders is a dish of fresh butter beans in tomato and sage sauce. Heavy silver cutlery and a massive, serious wine list with good grappas make this a proper dining experience. The otiose adjectives on the menu – superb, magnificent, delightful fantastic – add to the charm but the final judgement is made by the customers!

Sandrini	SW3

260 Brompton Road, SW3 2AS
Telephone: 071-584 1724 £55
Open: lunch + dinner daily
Meals served: lunch 12-2.30 (Sun 12-3), dinner 7-11.30

If you are in an adventurous mood, go for Piedmontese peppers, grilled radicchio with balsamic vinegar, wind-dried venison with ricotta or duck with cinnamon, balsamic vinegar and cranberries from this otherwise straightforward trattoria menu. Lovers of the ancien régime of Italian restaurants will not be disappointed: penne arrabiata, risotto marinara, pollo sorpresa and fegato alla veneziana are all here too.

Santini	SW1

29 Ebury Street, SW1W 0NZ
Telephone: 071-730 4094 Fax; 071-730 0544 £90
Open: lunch + dinner Mon-Fri (closed Bank Holidays)
Meals served: lunch 12.30-2.30, dinner 7-11.30 (Sun 7-11)

This business-oriented Venetian-style restaurant offers some elegant dishes, mostly familiar but with some inventive touches. Pasta sauced with artichokes, sea bream with olives and roast quail with herbs and polenta make a refreshing change from run-of-the-mill trattoria fare while carpaccio is served hot with rocket. Lighter dishes – a breast of chicken grilled with lemon, mustard and herbs, for instance – are plentiful and there are some fine Italian wines on an intelligent list.

SAS Portman Hotel — W1

22 Portman Square, W1H 9FL
Telephone: 071-486 5844
Fax: 071-935 0537

£70

Open: lunch Sun-Fri, dinner Mon-Sat (closed some Bank Holidays, Xmas/New Year)
Meals served: lunch 12.30-2.30 (Sun 12.30-3.30), dinner 7-11

The new ownership by Scandinavian Airlines System means that you can check in for your flight in the lobby or check into the hotel while still at the airport! A favourite with corporate high-fliers, the Portman has 272 well-designed rooms. However, consistently high standards of cooking by David Dorricott and his team continue to attract gourmets and high-lifers to this luxury hotel and Truffles restaurant superbly located in the heart of the West End. The most original and elaborate dishes are deftly handled, as in a starter of lightly-flaked salmon with coriander interlaced with crispy woven potatoes, champagne-marinated baby leeks with crisped apple layers and parsley spaetzli or tenderloin of Scottish beef layered with mousseline of celeriac and truffles on a Fleurie sauce. The simple dishes are perhaps the most modern: from these, you might select a cream of flat-leaf parsley soup, forest foie gras ravioli with wild mushrooms, carpaccio of scallops with mixed leaves, pan-fried venison medallion with mashed potato and lardons or pot-roasted partridge with braised red cabbage and garlic cloves. Both sweet trolley and cheeseboard invite indulgence. The set menus are no less imaginative or appealing. There is a live jazz brunch on Sundays when the menu includes steak and eggs with hash browns. As you would expect from a hotel restaurant of this stature, there is a comprehensive, predominantly French wine list priced with the clientele in mind. Well-drilled staff ensure that service is attentive yet unobtrusive.

Les Saveurs — W1

37a Curzon Street, W1Y 8EY
Telephone: 071-491 8919

£100

Open: lunch + dinner Mon-Fri (closed 10 days Xmas/New Year, 2 wks Aug)
Meals served: lunch 12-2.30, dinner 7-10.30

Chef Joël Antunès has trained with some of France's most highly-respected chef/patrons and his pedigree lends a restrained, serious atmosphere to this spacious basement dining-room whose stairway is approached via a lounge and hall opening onto Curzon Street. Colours are warm blonde on blonde throughout. Antunès was based for a while at Bangkok's Oriental, whence the skill with Eastern spices that pervades a dish of slivers of roast duck with fig compote and sauce of Thai spices or even the pineapple sorbet in a spicy bread pyramid. This is a formal, luxury restaurant where the menu is written in English but the techniques are entirely French, often with a southern accent. Highlights include a carpaccio of duck with pistou and artichoke chips, 'minestrone' of crayfish and white beans or a fillet of roast lamb with élan of black olives and tomato confit. Among the puddings is a cherry soup or an excellent croquant of rhubarb with praline cream. As an alternative to the good cheeses, you may like to try the niçoise terrine of goat's cheese. The set lunch is an excellent way to explore the immense talents of this fine young chef. Classic wine list priced towards the top end.

The Savoy   WC2

The Strand, WC2R 0EU
Telephone: 071-836 4343
Fax: 071-240 6040
Open: lunch + dinner daily
Meals served: lunch 12.30-2.30, dinner 7.30-11.30 (Sun 7-10.30)

♣
£85

The Savoy continues to be a living, breathing legend, developing constantly as facilities are quietly yet thoroughly updated. Art deco themes have been retained in many quarters, with pale colours and clean lines in many of the 202 high-ceilinged rooms and suites, the best of which have stunning river views and legendary '30s monochrome-tiled bathrooms with 10" showerheads that resemble a cross between a colander and a frying pan. The baths fill, jacuzzi-like, in 30 seconds. The beautiful River Restaurant boasts the finest Thames view of any restaurant in London and continues to serve food that is at once classical and inventive. Smoked eel and a poached quail's egg are set in jelly and there is a a a strong Mediteranean whiff about the tartlet of mozzarella, parmesan, tomato and basil anointed with truffle oil. More classically, a leg of rabbit has a simple apricot stuffing and there might be a classical lemon tart to finish. Maître chef Anton Edelmann oversees all food preparation throughout the hotel but it is here that his talents are allowed to shine and he has even introduced a high-class vegetarian menu. Many come here for the dancing 6 nights a week: formal evening dress is encouraged, but not imposed, at weekends. There is a good wine list chosen according to classical precepts. The Grill menu lists a variety of rather heavy French dishes alongside the simpler grills which are the things to go for. Meat is of extremely high quality and comes with fine clear gravy. Order vegetables singly rather than going for the ubiquitous selection. The wine list is impressive, not least because it is concise despite its globetrotting. 'Upstairs' is a kind of brasserie specialising in seafood and bistro dishes. Except for a pause for afternoon tea, light dishes are served all day in The Thames Foyer until midnight.

Scott's Restaurant   W1
20 Mount Street, W1Y 6HE
Telephone: 071-629 5248
Fax: 071-491 2477
Open: lunch Mon-Sat, dinner daily (closed Bank Holidays, Xmas/New Year)
Meals served: lunch 12-2.45, dinner 7-10.45 (Sun 7-10)
Traditional British fish dishes, clubby atmosphere, loyal clientele.

£85

La Sémillante — W1

3 Mill Street, W1R 9TF
Telephone: 071-499 2121 £70
Open: lunch Mon-Fri, dinner Mon-Sat (closed 2 wks Aug, 2 wks Dec/Jan)
Meals served: lunch 12.15-2.15, dinner 7.15-10.45

La Sémillante truly is a one-of-a-kind restaurant, destined to stand or fall by sheer force of style. From the ground-floor bar, descend a theatrical staircase down to the restaurant and split level bar, an extravagant use of space. The white walls are lifted by a combination of yellow and blue chairs and some iteresting pieces of furniture, though the interior was about to be remodelled as we went to press. 'Semillante' translates as libertine, and chef-proprietor Patrick Woodside takes this as a cue to plaster soft-porn photographs of naked women all over his psychedelic menu covers. Feminists beware. A disciple of Koffman and Blanc, Patrick used to be pâtissier at Harveys and shares some of Marco Pierre White's wilful unorthodoxy. There are shortish fixed menus at both lunch and dinner; neither are grabbily priced. The terse menu descriptions rely on friendly interaction between waiter and customer and make for gasps of surprise when the dish arrives. The petit pains, spiked with chives, beetroot or raisins and walnut, are exceptional and are a fitting prelude to starters such as poached foie gras in Muscadet or langoustine either wrapped in endive or roasted with baby turnips and macaroni. Escargots with a sabayon of foie gras is a clever way of making a luxury ingredient go a long way. Main courses have included navarin of lobster and basil-scented vanilla sauce, pan-fried turbot with compote of wild mushrooms or roast veal kidney with shallots and red wine. All are more elaborate than they sound and most are highly experimental. Predictably, Woodside's showmanship is at its best and strongest among puddings, although some of the descriptions on the menu are downright mystifying. What is a crystal of apples? Or a column of summer fruit? More approachable are the soufflés of white chocolate or crystallised ginger and the nougat of pear William, although even that is enigmatic. The wine list – again, adorned with readers' fantasy wives – is interesting and there is plenty at under £15.

Serpentine Restaurant — W2

Hyde Park, W2 2OH
Telephone: 071-402 1142 £65
Open: all day daily
Meals served: 10.30 am-10.30 pm
Prue Leith's popular outlet in the park, now open longer hours. *See also page 60 – our Bistros & Brasseries section.*

SHEEKEY'S RESTAURANT	WC2

28-32 St Martins Court, Leicester Square, WC2N 4AL
Telephone: 071-240 2565 £60
Fax: 071-491 2477
Open: lunch Mon-Fri, dinner Mon-Sat (closed Bank Holidays, 24 Dec-2 Jan)
Meals served: lunch 12.30-3, dinner 6-11.15

Good fish restaurant, approaching its centenary and run along traditional lines in the heart of Covent Garden. Well-located for pre- or post-show dining, its walls are, appropriately, crammed with signed photos of showbiz celebrities. The comprehensive, conventional menu lists numerous starters, among them gravadlax, whitebait, smoked eel, sardines with mustard sauce and clams with garlic butter. The great British classics are all there – grilled Dover sole, skate with black butter, smoked haddock with poached egg, fish pie, fishcakes, grilled scallops wrapped in bacon – as well as moules marinières and Sheekey's special seafood platters or, most luxurious of all, a reasonably-priced whole lobster with mixed salad. Carnivores can choose either a steak or a seasonal game dish. A la carte vegetables include mixed pulses and hash browns. There is a straightfoward dessert trolley with a good bitter chocolate mousse or, alternatively, an equally safe choice of Cheddar, Brie or Stilton. The concise wine list, sensibly listed on the right-hand side of the menu, is mainly French with the odd German, Californian (the potent Villa Zapu) and even English bottle thrown in for good measure.

SHERATON PARK TOWER	SW1

101 Knightsbridge, SW1X 7RN
Telephone: 071-235 8050 £75
Fax: 071-235 8231
Open: lunch + dinner daily
Meals served: lunch 12-3 (Sun 12-4), dinner 6.30-11

Within the striking contemporary structure that has become a landmark on the Knightsbridge skyline, you will find an air-conditioned conservatory housing a restaurant of surprising verve. Although the excellent value set lunches and cold buffets are pitched predominantly at a business clientele, the menus delight in their imagination, scope and awareness of healthy eating. The lighter dishes which spring to mind include crab and lobster ravioli with a coriander and lobster broth, steamed escalopes of lettuce-wrapped salmon with shrimps and a champagne sauce, pan-fried scallops with Indian-spiced vinaigrette and a steamed chicken breast with provencal vegetables and balsamic dressing. Modern English cooking is well-represented, with a boiled slipper of bacon with parsley sauce and chickpeas and there are equally earthy dishes of more international flavour such as rabbit ravioli with foie gras and mushrooms, boned oxtail with prunes and macaroni cheese or hare medallions on an endive and leek tart with sweet-sour sauce. Vegetarians are well-cossetted and vegetables for carnivores are also good: recent accompaniments to main courses have included an excellent gratin of swede and potato purée and another of provençale vegetables.

Signor Sassi	SW1

14 Knightsbridge Green, SW1X 7QL
Telephone: 071-584 2277 £60
Open: lunch + dinner Mon-Sat
Meals served: lunch 12-2.30 (Sat 12-2.45), dinner 7-11.30

This fashionable Italian restaurant boasts the kind of menu most restaurant-goers could by now recite in their sleep: smoked salmon, tuna with beans, seafood salad, baked stuffed aubergine, carpaccio, mozzarella 'in carrozza', minestrone, tortellini in broth or cream sauce, stracciatella, spaghetti alle vongole, deep-fried calamari, calves' liver with butter and sage to name just a few. However there are also a few unfamiliar dishes that work well: a starter of baked eggs with parma ham and tomato sauce serves equally well as a light main course while a dish of chopped veal kidney with mushrooms in white wine and garlic is somewhat heartier. A busy and popular restaurant, Signor Sassi is patronised by a regular clientèle who emjoy the friendly Italian welcome.

Simply Nico	SW1

48A Rochester Row, SW1P 1JU
Telephone: 071-630 8061 £65
Open: lunch Mon-Fri, dinner Mon-Sat (closed Bank Holidays, 10 days Xmas, 3 wks Aug)
Meals served: lunch 12-2.15, dinner 6.45-11.15

The more casual little sister of Nico Central has nonetheless been well brought up and has acquired new tastes and manners of late. Even a Caesar salad has been known to pop up on the menu, together with a risotto of smoked haddock with poached egg. The fixed price of £23 for 3 courses includes vegetables, potatoes and service. To start, eggs Benedict or a thin escalope of salmon with herb mayonnaise might appeal. They may sound pedestrian, but the Ladenis touch turns an ordinary dish into an event. Main courses include a 'pithiviers' of quail or confit of duck with herb dumplings and mustard lentils. Cheeses are, without exception, fine English specimens. English and French puddings such as Armagnac parfait with pralines or hot apple charlotte with caramel and crème anglaise carry that unmistakeable Ladenis signature and the short wine list offers some serious drinking. The house apéritif, of chilled Beaujolais and crème de mure, is wonderfully crisp and refreshing.

SIMPSON'S-IN-THE-STRAND — WC2

100 The Strand, WC2R 0EW
Telephone: 071-836 9112 £65
Fax: 071-836 1381
Open: lunch daily, dinner Mon-Sat (closed Bank Holidays)
Meals served: lunch 12-2.30, dinner 6-10.45

A bastion of male chauvinism which only admitted ladies to its vast and hallowed halls under duress, Simpson's offers the kind of conservative English menu that includes both nursery food and the odd French classic. There are fillets of smoked eel, Lancashire hotpot, boiled silverside of beef with pease pudding and beef casserole. Aylesbury duckling, like the roast beef and lamb, is served from gigantic trolleys pushed by mean knife-wielders of a certain age (whom it is considered de rigueur to tip) and can be overcooked but that, of course, is historically British. Puddings are as nanny used to make them – treacle roll, spotted dick, apple turnover. For healthy eaters and fancier palates there are salads of lobster or tomato, bacon and chicory plus quail eggs with haddock and cheese sauce or venison with red wine and cranberries. A favourite destination for tourists in search of olde England, Simpson's is not the dark, gloomy place you might imagine – in fact it is distinctly bright and airy following recent redecoration: stencilling and colourful picking-out of the trio of friezes enliven the white panelling in the South Room. However, the wine list is in the turn of the (last) century style but at turn of the (next) century prices. Provided you like your roasts, the early evening set menu, available between 6-7pm, offers the most accessible opportunity to visit this fascinating museum of English cuisine.

SIMPSON'S
IN-THE-STRAND

SINGAPORE GARDEN — NW6
83 Fairfax Road, NW6 4DY
Telephone: 071-328 5314 £40
Fax: 071-624 0656
Open: lunch + dinner daily (closed 1 wk Xmas)
Meals served: lunch 12-2.45, dinner 6-10.45 (6-11.15 Fri+Sat)
The Singapore Ambassador eats here, which should vouch for authenticity and cooking skills. Seafood dishes are the ones to go for, especially chilli crab. There is also a Chinese menu.

SNOWS ON THE GREEN — W6

166 Shepherds Bush Road, W6 7PB
Telephone: 071-603 2142

A favourite local restaurant

£55

Open: lunch Mon-Fri, dinner Mon-Sat (closed Bank Holidays, 2 wks Aug)
Meals served: lunch 12-3, dinner 7-11

Situated in Shepherd's Bush Road opposite Brook Green, this is exactly the sort of restaurant that everybody wants and needs in their neighbourhood right now. Sebastian Snow in the kitchen and his wife Melissa out front, with her team of attractive young ladies, have created a successful restaurant whose menu draws on contemporary tastes for its inspiration and has a warm, radiant, rustic look about it that belies the name. There are stripped wooden floors, wooden tables with tiled ceramic inserts, simple yet comfortable cane-backed chairs and 2-tone apricot ragged walls hung with beautiful photographs of the Ardèche taken by Chris Simpson, Melissa's brother-in-law. One features lavender fields, echoed in the little pots of lavender on each table. The flavours are robust, the preparation straightforward. Culinary influences are primarily peasant French or Italian. Alongside steak frites or bollito misto you will find char-grilled calves' liver with pumpkin, brown butter and mint, sausage, sage and bean stew or a visually arresting squid ink casserole with saffron risotto. A main course of lasagne of salmon, spinach and tomato comprising wafer-thin pasta leaves is served on a sauce that demands to be mopped up with the delicious French bread. From the 10 or so starters you might choose a confit of lamb's tongue with lentils, a warm salad of baby spinach, soft herring roe and poached egg or – more simply – brandade crostini or gnocchi with wild mushrooms and a herb sauce. Roquefort with figs is offered alongside equally seasonal puddings such as gratinated strawberries, prune and almond tart or tarte tatin. A concise and extremely reasonably-priced wine list with some interesting selections make for an enjoyable, well-rounded meal at this friendly restaurant.

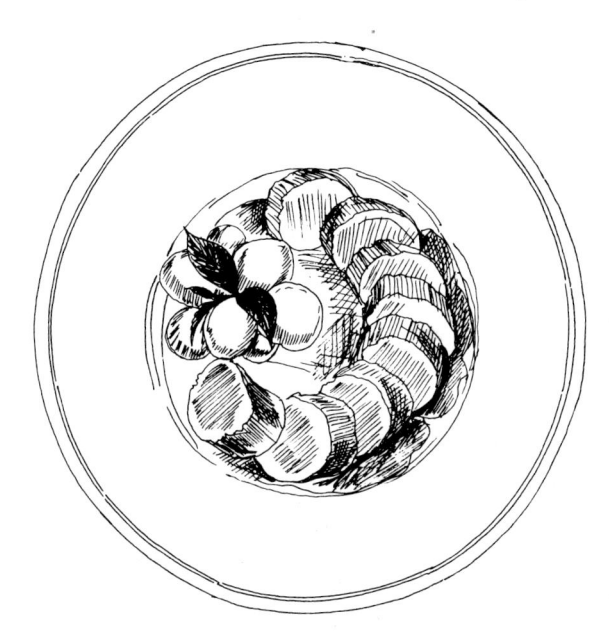

SOHO SOHO W1

11-13 Frith Street, W1
Telephone: 071-494 3491

— lively bustling place + stylish decor

£55

Open: lunch Mon-Fri, dinner Mon-Sat (closed Bank Holidays)
Meals served: lunch 12-3, dinner 6-12

Not satisfied with its first incarnation, Neville Abraham and Laurence Isaacson have transformed this restaurant and it is deservedly one of Soho's main attractions. In the first-floor restaurant, chef Tony Howarth has devised a menu of Mediterranean provenance with a strong niçois accent. From Nice comes the pissaladière, from the other end of Provence a fish soup marseillaise. There is a goat's cheese salad with tapenade, harissa-hot couscous of shrimp tails and mussels with pickled ginger and tomato sauce and the obligatory wild mushroom risotto and confit de canard. Anchovies and garlic abound, served with baked salted cod and Swiss chard or with red-wine marinated beef and mashed potato. For simpler tastes choose the grilled salmon, sirloin or fillet of beef. Daily specials can include onion soup cooked with cider or a daube of beef with orange, olives and mashed potato. The cheaper ground-floor cafe, which does not take bookings, has pavement seating in the summer and serves cheaper, snackier dishes, among them omelettes, brochettes, charcuterie and grills. There are some interesting Mediterranean wines on the well-chosen 100-strong list. A warm, friendly atmosphere prevails throughout. *See also page 62 – our Bistros and Brasseries Section.*

SONNY'S SW13

94 Church Road, SW13 0DQ
Telephone: 081-748 0393

— good local restaurant

£45

Open: lunch daily, dinner Mon-Sat (closed Bank Holidays)
Meals served: lunch 12.30-2 (Sun 12.30-3), dinner 7.30-11

A smart place for smart people – that's Sonny's. The interior is chic yet understated with cream walls, grey floor, fresh flowers, prints by hip artists and a few pieces of important art including some Stanley Spencers, a Jim Dine self-portrait and Christos' drawings for wrapping the Pont Neuf. There is no music but the atmosphere is animated with lots of talk and laughter – led and encouraged by owner Rebecca Mascarenhas. The menu offers a pleasing variety of tastes from chef Nicky Barraclough. One delightful summer dish teams pasta squares with broad beans, lettuce, mint and cream. Another meat-free delight is the baked ricotta with basil, parmesan and pine-nuts. Cold poached salmon is served with samphire and there is a hearty fillet of pork stuffed with black pudding and served with apple and onion compote. Daily fish specials maximise fresh produce and have included mahi mahi with coriander butter sauce. Throughout the menu, flavours are allowed to develop without ever becoming overpowering. Puddings are delicious. There is sunken chocolate cake with prunes and Armagnac, lemon cake with redcurrants and creme fraiche or brown sugar hazelnut meringue with summer fruits. There are hot sponge puddings in winter, home-made ices in summer. A short, reasonably-priced wine list does justice to the food. The weekday set lunch is good value. *See also page 64 – our Bistros and Brasseries Section.*

Soulard Restaurant   N1

113 Mortimer Road, N1 4JY
Telephone: 071-254 1314   **£45**
Open: lunch Tue-Fri, dinner Tue-Sat
Meals served: lunch 12-2, dinner 7-10.30

This user-friendly Islington restaurant comprises a single, compact room decorated in gentle shades of cream and green. The concise wine list with its good selection of half bottles is well-matched to the menu which is based on sound French principles, occasionally essaying a novel twist. While you study it, as a change from your usual glass of champagne try the house aperitif of red or white wine with armagnac, served with olives to nibble at. Hazelnuts add flavour and crunch to a feuillete of snails, while marinated salmon is served with blinis and herb sauce. Tagliatelle with vegetables and fresh mint is just one of the vegetarian dishes available, while for hardened carnivores there is grilled beef with roquefort sauce or duck breast with green peppercorn sauce. Your favourite French pudding is bound to appear on a list that ranges from chocolate mousse and creme brûlée to nougat glacé or poire belle Hélène.

The Square   SW1

32 King Street, St James's, SW1 6RJ
Telephone: 071-839 8787   £55
Open: lunch Mon-Fri, dinner Mon-Sat (closed most Bank Holidays)
Meals served: lunch, dinner

David Collins' anachronistic, New Yorky interior with its distinctly '70s elements – Paco Rabanne or Pierre Cardin spring to mind – is at once solid yet frivolous. One the one hand, there are comfortable cobalt-upholstered chairs, serious napery, cutlery and crystal, while on the other there are metal water-lily wall lamps, and spiral ironwork in the window. There are no such fripperies on the menu. Although modern and fashionable, it is based on multi-national common sense, with fresh ingredients, authentic flavours and good presentation, combining Mediterranean and rustic French styles to pleasing effect. More-ish warm sourdough bread is presented while you peruse a menu which, in the evening, might include a beautifully-balanced dish of smoked haddock with creamed leeks and poached gull's eggs, a carpaccio of scallops with tartare of vegetables or a salad of artichokes and shaved parmesan which sounds ordinary but tastes extraordinary. To follow, there might be caramelised calves' tongue with pot-roasted vegetables or roast seabass with red wine and olive oil mash. Certain dishes serve either as a starter or main course, among them the crisp provençale-style red mullet with herb noodles and truffle oil. The Square Meal – a simple mixed grill of either meat or fish – is a good gimmick, strictly for those who like their food very plain. And there are several. Owing to the grown-up location, the clientele is older than you might deduce from the interior, although management and staff are young. There are some truly excellent puddings, both unusual and familiar. They include an exemplary tarte tatin, something crunchy called caramel crackling, blueberry cream with caramelised wafers or roasted figs with toasted pecans and lemon fritters. From the lunchtime dishes, a typical choice might comprise warm oysters with leeks and chives or langoustine mayonnaise followed by loin of pork with buttered cabbage and grain mustard followed by a tart of caramelised banana or rhubarb, almond and cinnamon. There is one vegetarian dish per course, typically a pissaladière with sauté of wild mushrooms. It is a measure of the kitchen's confidence in its accuracy of seasoning that there is no salt and pepper on the tables and none is needed. There are some good wines at amiable prices from around the world. A fine, high-ceilinged, spacious bar downstairs continues the decorative theme and deserves to become trendy. It is one of the area's better kept secrets, well-stocked and staffed by some clever young barmen. The upmarket bar snacks tend to be starters from the menu upstairs.

Sri Siam   W1
14 Old Compton Street, W1V 5PE
Telephone: 071-434 3544   £45
Open: lunch Mon-Sat, dinner daily (closed 25+26 Dec, 1 Jan)
Meals served: lunch 12-3, dinner 6-11.15 (6-10.30 Sun)
A chef formerly at The Blue Elephant (*qv*) has at last brought success to this Soho site. Decor is as light as a butterfly. Vegetarians as well as meat-eaters are well served from the Thai menu.

The Stafford — SW1

16 St James's Place, SW1A 1NJ
Telephone: 071-493 0111
Fax: 071-493 7121
Open: lunch + dinner daily
Meals served: lunch 12.30-2.30, dinner 6-10.30 (Sun 6-9.30)

£70

The favourite London hotel with a dedicated following, The Stafford epitomises low-key style, comfort and discretion. Once a gentlemen's club, the hotel retains a hushed, male-oriented atmosphere and service is appropriately attentive and cossetting. There are some 74 well-appointed rooms which, for regulars at least, are like a home away from home. The restaurant menu is styled along traditional lines and bursts with comfort food: minestrone, eggs Benedict, lamb chops, roast chicken, steak tartare and soufflés are all competently handled, while veal with noodles and truffle sauce is one of the better 'fancy' numbers.

Stakis St Ermin's — SW1

Caxton Street, SW1H 0QW
Telephone: 071-222 7888
Fax: 071-222 6914
Open: lunch + dinner daily
Meals served: lunch 12.30-2.30, dinner 6-9.30

£65

Close to the Houses of Parliament. Unbeatable Westminster location for this swanky 290-bedroomed hotel.

STEPHEN BULL	W1

5-7 Blandford Street, W1H 3AA
Telephone: 071-486 9696   £60
Open: lunch Mon-Fri, dinner Mon-Sat (closed Bank Holidays)
Meals served: lunch 12.15-2, dinner 6.30-10.30

While the new City bistro and bar makes the headlines, this restaurant continues to trade well, providing a nearly-nude but exquisitely-lit stage for the chef/proprietor's finest culinary experiments in the imaginative modern technique. The menu is determinedly eclectic with a choice of some 9 starters and 9 main courses. Stephen Bull, advertising mogul turned chef, delivers dishes with extra clout: special memories include a twice-cooked goat's cheese soufflé, grilled seafood with gremolata and breast of duck with celeriac and endive sauerkraut. A cold salad of vegetables in tomato, caper and tarragon dressing accompanies fillets of mackerel. Puddings can be intriguing, though avocado and lime cheesecake loses out to a warm apricot tart with honey and saffron ice cream. There is a clear, balanced wine list with plenty from the New World including Elysium black muscat from California among the dessert wines. The all-white tiled interior makes this a summertime favourite – it can be seem a little chilly in winter although noisy chatter from the densely-packed tables warms up the atmosphere.

STEPHEN BULL BISTRO	EC1

71 St John STreet, EC1M 4AN
Telephone: 071-490 1750   **£50**
Open: lunch Mon-Fri, dinner Mon-Sat (closed Bank Holidays, 10 days Xmas)
Meals served: lunch 12-2.30, dinner 6-10.45

Stephen Bull's second venture near Smithfield is a stylish establishment of strategically minimal adornment (white walls, black tables) where the focus is firmly on the food. The concept and the style of cooking are very much in keeping with contemporary trends, very *now*. The buzz ingredients are all there – Mediterranean and Moroccan elements, pulses, offal, inventive use of herbs. Simple starters such as Parma ham with figs and papaya or tabbouleh with orange, pine nuts and mint are balanced by more labour-intensive items like a salad of duck confit and crispy duck skin with oranges and walnuts or a terrine of globe and Jerusalem artichokes with plum tomatoes. Main courses include skate wing with spiced lentils and yoghurt, lamb's liver with sweet-sour red cabbage and smoked bacon or tagine of lamb with apricots, almonds and white beans. Among the more inventive offal dishes is a pressed terrine of pickled lamb's tongue with caper and mustard sauce. Cheese is served with healthy oat biscuits, while self-indulgent puddings range from a chewy brown sugar meringue with hot fudge sauce to pear and almond tart or iced rhubarb parfait. Concise, reasonably-priced wine list.

Le Suquet — SW3

104 Draycott Avenue, SW3 3AE
Telephone: 071-581 1785
Open: lunch + dinner Mon-Sat
Meals served: lunch 12.30-2.30, dinner 7-11.30

£60

You can eat an indifferent starter on the beach at Cannes for the price of the 3-course 'Petite Plage' menu at Le Suquet, a popular and fashionable restaurant where standards remain high. Perhaps you miss out on the sun but if you close your eyes and inhale the French chatter and the smell of freshly grilled sardines you can almost make believe you are there. Excellent fish and seafood feature on the clean, colourful menu: langoustines, moules and coquilles St Jacques are served with a choice of traditional sauces. Gigantic plateaux de fruits de mers outshine daily specials such as filet de turbot sauce normande and feuilleté de saumon. There are meat dishes too for square pegs and a limited choice for vegetarians, notably an outstanding salad of artichoke hearts with a lovely mustardy vinaigrette. This is the sort of restaurant where you don't worry too much about the vegetables which might be a couple of tomatoes farçi or a purée of carrot – concentrate on the fish instead. The bustling, authentic atmosphere is helped along by all-French service (friendlier than ever) and vistas of the Cote d'Azur on the walls. The short wine list is a perfect partner to the menu.

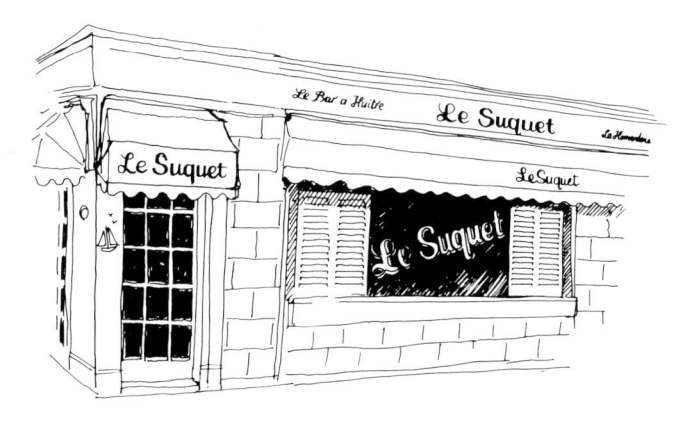

Sweetings — EC4

39 Queen Victoria Street, EC4N 4SA
Telephone: 071-248 3062
Open: lunch Mon-Fri (closed Bank Holidays, Xmas/New Year)
Meals served: lunch 12-3
City institution, seafood, nursery puddings, good wine list.

£50

Sydney Brasserie — SW11

12-14 Battersea High Street, SW11 3JB
Telephone: 071-978 5395
Fax: 071-738 1460
Open: lunch daily, dinner Mon-Sat (closed Bank Holidays)
Meals served: lunch 12-3 (Sun 12-3.30), dinner 7-11 (open all day for light meals)
English cooking, central Battersea location.

£45

Sydney Street — SW3

4 Sydney Street, SW3 6PP
Telephone: 071-352 3433 £50
Open: lunch + dinner Mon-Sat (closed 25+26 Dec, 1 Jan)
Meals served: lunch 12-3, dinner 7-11.30

A restaurant that has acquired a cult following since opening, Sydney Street proves that the Australians are now well ahead of the game when it comes to new world cuisine. On the ground floor is a trendy, laid back bar with boomerang-shaped oak counter and aboriginal-style murals in gentle, dusty shades. The point of the place, though, is down under in the basement dining room, decorated in subaqueous blues and greens with contemporary ethnic art. Food has improved dramatically since the arrival of Mary-Jane Hayward, a key player in her native Australia. Kangaroo and buffalo put in occasional appearances on a menu which might also include coral perch, barramundi, Moreton Bay bugs and other antipodean marine species. Australia's geographic definition as Pacific Rim inclines its chefs more authentically than those of, say, California, towards Orientalism: hence a starter of deep-fried crab and vermicelli balls wrapped in banana leaves sports a superbly sticky sweet red chilli sauce containing caramelised onions and Thai fish sauce. A main dish of red (giant) prawn curry with lime leaves and mangetout, served with fluffy steamed rice was as good as (if not better than) anything you will eat in Bangkok. For pure protein, try the sugar-cured salmon or tuna tartare with pickled baby vegetables. One of Mary-Jane's classier innovations is the Peara sauce served with a poached fillet of beef. Made from reduced poaching stock with bone marrow, breadcrumbs, herbs and spices, this grainy paste makes for an exhilarating new flavour and is served alongside a 'salsa' of diced beetroot and mustard seeds. Puddings include raspberry tiramisu, toffeed pear and almond tart and a superlative chewy Pavlova (billed as a tropical fruit parfait) topped with passion fruit ice cream and forest fruits. The coffee choice includes ristretto – as close as you can get to intravenous espresso! A good selection of new-world wines and young, friendly service complete this pleasing picture.

Symposio — NW1

89 Chalk Farm Road, NW1
Telephone: 071-267 6728 £35
Open: dinner Tue-Sun
Meals served: dinner 6.30-11.45 (Sun 6.30-9.45)
Greek restaurant, marbled setting, live piano music, pre-theatre menu.

Tall House Restaurant — SE1

134 Southwark Street, SE1 0SW Upstairs Restaurant: £45
Telephone: 071-401 2929 Downstairs Brasserie: £25
Open: lunch Mon-Fri
Meals served: lunch 11.45-3
Elizabeth Philip's second venture (after the Archduke Wine Bar) includes an art gallery.

Tandoori Lane — SW6

131a Munster Road, SW6 6DD
Telephone: 071-371 0440 £30
Open: lunch + dinner daily (closed 25+26 Dec)
Meals served: lunch 12-2.30, dinner 6-11.15
Hoorays shout 'Hooray!' for the Indian food here which is well above average and even the decor is somewhat out of the ordinary.

La Tante Claire — SW3

68 Royal Hospital Road, SW3 4HP
Telephone: 071-352 6045
Fax: 071-352 3257
Open: lunch + dinner Mon-Fri (closed Bank Holidays, 1 wk Xmas)
Meals served: lunch 12.30-2, dinner 7-11

£125

The Matisse on the cover, the discreet lettering, David Collins' elegant '30s-style room, the textured paper – simply ordering the food is a sensual experience here. The tireless Pierre Koffman's talent is unique, each dish a masterpiece of colour, composition and flavour. Feuilleté d'asperges, saumon fumé et oeuf de caille and bouquet de salade, émincé de volaille à l'huile de noisette are typical starters. His generous starter of fat scallops, caramelised on one side and served on a sauce based on a squid ink reduction with threads of carrot purée, is just one dish you will want to eat over and over again. Stuffed pig's trotter with morels (the original!) with fried vegetables, and roast pigeon with sweet spices, pear and spinach are typical main courses. Puddings include masterly soufflés and simple inspirations such as the croustade aux pommes. Basic ingredients are always of the highest quality. Big comfortable chairs and delightful service led by Jean-Pierre Durantet make for a truly great gastronomic experience. The set lunch at £23.50 (3 courses, coffee and friandises) is superb value and one of the very best in London. Time and again, La Tante Claire is voted the restaurateur's restaurant: visit and you will see why this is the chef/proprietor's favourite aunt. *See also page 232 – our Clover Award section.*

Thailand Restaurant — SE14

15 Lewisham Way, SE14 6PP
Telephone: 081-691 4040
Open: dinner Tue-Sat (closed Bank Holidays)
Meals served: dinner 6-10

£50

Friendly neighbourhood Thai restaurant.

Thierry's	SW3

342 King's Road, SW3 5UR
Telephone: 071-352 3365 £50
Open: lunch + dinner daily (closed Bank Holidays)
Meals served: lunch 12-2.30 (Sun 12-3), dinner 7-11 (Sun 7.30-10.30)

A local favourite with Chelsea residents, the long-established Thierry's, now capably run by Hervé Salez, offers French comfort food of the highest order. Soupe à l'oignon gratinée, feuilleté of quail's eggs, rack of lamb with braised garlic, cassoulet or grilled steak with béarnaise exemplify typical choices from the carte at this warm red-toned bistro. For purists, there are oysters with shallot vinaigrette or a plateau de fruits de mer. There is a good set lunch at just under £10 for 2 courses which might comprise moules marinières followed by skate with anchovy salsa verde, braised lamb's tongue with mashed potato or knuckle of pork with sauerkraut. Soufflés both savoury and sweet are exemplary. A good spot for a lazy dinner before, after or even without the cinema.

Thistells	SE22

65 Lordship Lane, SE22
Telephone: 081-299 1921 £50
Open: lunch Sun, dinner Mon-Sat
Meals served: lunch 12-3, dinner 7-10.30

Sami Youseff is now at Thistells, a restaurant in what looks like a converted butcher's shop. Sami being Egyptian, it follows that his menus draw on the Middle East for inspiration. Falafel with tahini sauce is a typical starter, while lamb couscous is available as a main course. House specialities are somewhat out of character, however: chicken breast sautéed with calvados, cider and apple or lamb with béarnaise sauce are just 2 examples. However the menu represents excellent value for money and, if you are dining with friends, makes for interesting conversation!

Tiramisu   NW6

327 West End Lane, NW6 1LN
Telephone: 071-433 1221   **£55**
Open: lunch Mon-Fri, dinner Mon-Sat (closed 25+26 Dec)
Meals served: lunch 12-2.30, dinner 7-11.30

A quietly modish restaurant predominantly in the new style, Tiramisu is particularly valuable in an area starved of good Italian options. Grilled oyster mushrooms with rucola and a warm salad of salt cod and kidney beans may feature among starters, while imaginative pastas include potato gnocchi with gorgonzola cream sauce, risotto with chicken liver and kidney, and canelloni of aubergine with ricotta. The fish dishes are inventive: deep-fried squid, sole and courgettes are served with an agro dolce sauce while escalopes of salmon are first steamed then sauced with balsamic vinegar and spring onions. Sautéed spinach is very good and there are specific 'cucina vegetariana' choices for non-meat-eaters. Cucina naturale is similarly highlighted for the health-conscious. After the obligatory pudding your bill can be a pleasant surprise. An intriguing Italian wine list features some unusual bottles. The restaurant is more lively in the evenings, when you will need to book.

Le Tire Bouchon   W1
6 Upper James Street, W1R 3HF
Telephone: 071-437 5348   **£40**
Open: all day Mon-Fri (closed Bank Holidays)
Meals served: 12-9.30
Simple French restaurant.

Trattoria Lucca   NW1
63 Parkway, NW1 7PP
Telephone: 071-485 6864   **£40**
Open: lunch + dinner Mon-Sat (closed Bank Holidays)
Meals served: lunch 12-3, dinner 6-10.45
Useful and popular neighbourhood restaurant, well-loved favourite Italian dishes.

La Truffe Noire   SE1

29 Tooley Street, SE1 2QF
Telephone: 071-378 0621   **£40**
Open: lunch Mon-Fri, dinner Mon-Sat (closed Bank Holidays)
Meals served: lunch 12.30-2.30, dinner 6-10.30

Situated in the Hays Galleria development this is a useful, business-oriented restaurant to know about and a welcome alternative to the more expensive Pont de La Tour. Skilled French cooking includes duck terrine with pistachio and sweet onion, squid with fresh black pasta, grilled langoustines with foie gras, potato and shiitake, pork tenderloin with cabbage and butter sauce, tournedos with marrow and red wine sauce or sweetbreads and pasta shells stewed with cèpes and truffles. There are occasional well-planned gastronomic evenings with carefully-selected wines.

Turner's	SW3

87-89 Walton Street, SW3 2HP
Telephone: 071-584 6711 £85
Fax: 071-584 9337
Open: lunch Sun-Fri, dinner daily (closed Bank Holidays, 1 wk Xmas)
Meals served: lunch 12.30-2.30, dinner 7.30-11 (Sun 7.30-10)

A compact, handsome, subtly-lit restaurant with an equally handsome menu, Turner's offers consistently inventive British food based on sound, classic principles. Elegant starters include rabbit carpaccio, shredded salmon with smoked eel vinaigrette or a salad of quail with lentils. Among main courses, try the grilled calves' kidney with sherry sauce on a bed of celeriac or the English duck breast roasted with Thai herbs. Grilled rib of beef is served with a rich bone marrow sauce, steamed brill on a bed of aubergine. While chef/proprietor Brian Turner is much in evidence on the restaurant floor, his control of the kitchen remains spot-on. *See also page 234 – our Clover Award section.*

Twenty Trinity Gardens	SW9

20 Trinity Gardens, SW9 8DP
Telephone: 071-733 8838 £40
Open: lunch Sun-Fri, dinner Mon-Sat (closed 1 wk Xmas)
Meals served: lunch 12.30-2.30 (Sun 11.30-4), dinner 7-10.30

This tastefully-appointed restaurant, situated in a Regency square behind Brixton Road, changed hands in 1992 but is still popular, especially for Sunday brunch/lunch. Original vegetarian items such as Persian broad beans on spiced rice with apricot and orange sauce or a feuilleté of field mushrooms and baby leeks in spicy sauce supplement a traditionally-based menu that includes meat and fish dishes infused with the cosmopolitan flavour of Brixton market. There is ceviche, terrine of tropical fish from Brixton Market and Cajun lamb with garlic hash browns while O'Hagan's creole jazz sausages are served with a pot of spiced black-eyed beans. More mainstream items include moules marinières, pigeon and pine-nut salad, calves' liver or roast pork. Wines are shipped in by the restaurant, making for a good selection with an appealing list of bin-ends.

Le Vagabond	SW18

11 Alma Road, SW18 1AA
Telephone: 081-870 4588 £40
Open: lunch Tue-Fri + Sun, dinner Tue-Sat (closed Bank Holidays)
Meals served: lunch 12-2 (Sun 1-3.30), dinner 7-10.30

Tucked away in a tiny Wandsworth street, this sunny little restaurant has bare boards, yellow walls hung with French cartoons, white linen and classic bistro bentwood chairs. The menu comprises variations on brasserie food based around the char-grill. There are good soups and salads followed by lamb cutlets, calves liver or salmon steak as well as pastas and vegetarian dishes. All are garnished with the traditional sauce of your choice (hollandaise, béarnaise, pepper or mustard) and either new potatoes or crisp fries. There is dining for 12 on the patio in summer.

Veronica's   W2

3 Hereford Road, W2 4AB
Telephone: 071-229 5079
Fax: 071-229 1210   £55
Open: lunch Mon-Fri, dinner Mon-Sat (closed Bank Holidays)
Meals served: lunch 12-3, dinner 7-11

This smart grey and yellow restaurant, run by the vivacious Veronica Shaw and her husband, features a menu that changes monthly and hops around British history in search of themes. One month you might find yourself in the Jazz Age, another in a medieval time warp. The well-researched menus, packed with historical explications, make for fascinating reading. Certain specials – beef, twice-roasted duck with a choice of 2 sauces, a prawn dish – are retained wherever the Tardis has landed. From the Tudor menu, the puddings were particularly appealing and included meringue with butterscotch sauce, burnt cream with oranges and Beaumes de Venise with Tudor jumbles. These might have been preceded by a hartichoak and sparagus bun then a salmagundy. The Twenties and Thirties menu was more familiar, with its mushrooms on toast, smoked haddock with poached eggs, Lancashire hotpot and traditional fish pie. As on all menus, there was a vegetarian dish, this time of lentils and rice with curried carrots. Duck with a relish of celery, apples and onions was a mite more adventurous. A lemony castle pudding vied with rice pudding in a crisp chocolate shell.

Village Taverna   SW10
196-198 Fulham Road, SW10 9TW
Telephone: 071-351 3799   £45
Open: lunch + dinner daily (4 days Xmas)
Meals served: 12 noon-1am
Favourite local Greek restaurant, especially for kieftiko.

Villandry Dining Room   W1

89 Marylebone High Street, W1M 3DE
Telephone: 071-224 3799   £45
Open: lunch Mon-Sat
Meals served: lunch 12.30-2.30 (light meals 8.30-5.30)

The moment you walk in and see the food displayed in this marvellous eat-in delicatessen you meet the wonderful cooking smells head-on. You sit and order in the back of the shop at one of the small tables – no frills but who needs them? Soups sing with flavour and there is enough in the tureen for seconds and even thirds. Salads, of which there is a delightful variety, are fresh and the cheeses in peak condition. There are pasta dishes and lovely fruity desserts. Believe it or not, you now need to book to be sure of a seat. Excellent value, although it is impossible to resist doing some luxurious shopping on the way out, be it a bar of Valrhona chocolate or a Brie, a confit de canard or some black linguini.

Wakaba   NW3
122a Finchley Road, NW3 5HT
Telephone: 071-586 7960   £55
Open: lunch + dinner Mon-Sat (closed 24-27 Dec, Good Friday, Easter Monday, 1 wk Aug)
Meals served: lunch 12-2.30, dinner 6.30-11
The architecture announces the cuisine: a pared-away look, streamlined Japanese food with some notable vegetarian options.

THE WALDORF — WC2

Aldwych, WC2B 4DD
Telephone: 071-836 2400 £95
Fax: 071-836 7244
Open: lunch Mon-Fri, dinner Mon-Sat (closed Bank Holidays, 4 wks Jul/Aug)
Meals served: lunch 12-2.30, dinner 6-10

In mid-refurbishment as we went to press, The Waldorf continues to trade as usual, boasting a location that straddles the West End and The City. Apart from thé famous thé dansant in the beautiful, spangly Palm Court Lounge every Friday, Saturday and Sunday there are also the Footlights and the oak-panelled Club bar to choose from at The Waldorf. Among the menus you will find a special pre-theatre dinner to suit most tastes. By spring '93 no fewer than 310 newly-redecorated bedrooms and 19 suites will be available.

WALTON'S — SW3

121 Walton Street, SW3 2PH
Telephone: 071-584 0204 Fax 071-581 2848 £100
Open: lunch + dinner daily (closed 25+26 Dec)
Meals served: lunch 12.30-2.30 (Sun 12.30-2), dinner 7.30-11.30 (Sun 7-10)

This smart Knightsbridge restaurant has an intimate and luxurious feel about it, with muted colours (predominantly lemon and grey), gentle lighting, botanical drawings and cushioned chairs and quilted undercloths. The menu brings new influences to bear on traditional ingredients, although it is informed by British thinking. You might find a chicken and walnut terrine with pistachio dressing on the list of starters, while a noisette of lamb served on potato and celeriac galette vies with steamed breast of guineafowl stuffed with truffle and morels on a brandy and orange sauce. Game features regularly on the menu, with a breast of pigeon in shallot and thyme sauce offered as a starter. A good choice of puddings includes fine ice creams and sorbets made on the premises. Sunday lunch combines traditional with modern: choose either roast beef with Yorkshires, game pie or red-mullet with noodles and coriander-scented sauce. In addition there are set menus at lunch and for after the theatre. Classic wine list with a couple of good half bottles.

THE WESTBURY — W1

Conduit Street, W1A 4UH
Telephone: 071-629 7755 £80
Fax: 071-495 1163
Open: lunch daily, dinner Mon-Sat
Meals served: lunch 12.30-3, dinner 6.30-11

A fine London hotel offering high quality comfort and service, this is the annual sponsor of the Westbury Cup for polo and many rooms reflect this sporting theme. Bedrooms and bathrooms are well equipped and hot food is available throughout the night. An excellent situation on the corner of Bond Street and Conduit Street makes the Westbury a good central spot for breakfast meetings in the sunny dining room.

The White Tower — W1

1 Percy Street, W1P 0ET
Telephone: 071-636 8141 £55
Open: lunch + dinner Mon-Fri (closed Bank Holidays, 1 wk Xmas, 3 wks Aug)
Meals served: lunch 12.30-2.15, dinner 6.45-10.15

Whether a French restaurant that thinks it's Greek or vice versa, The White Tower remain one of the restaurants in London that is perennially popular with politicians, minor royalty and TV execs alike. In fact the White Tower is a rather ancient and venerable establishment dating from those Dark Ages where only French would do. Hence the Greek dishes in French disguise and the bilingual menu-speak. The quaintly outmoded interior is comforting with its prints of Greek national costumes and decorative plates, not to mention pom-pom lampshades and red velvet curtains. The decor is a clue to the service to come – attentive, old-fashioned and all about charming the customer. Aubergine Imam Bayeldi and potage avgolemono are listed among hors d'oeuvres, while chop Alexis Soyer and Aylesbury duckling farci à la cypriote are examples of main dishes from the detailed menu.

Whittington's — EC4
21 College Hill, EC4 2RP
Telephone: 071-248 5855 £55
Open: lunch Mon-Fri (closed Bank Holidays)
Meals served: lunch 11.45-2.15
Modern English cooking in basement restaurant.

The Wilds — SW10

376 Fulham Road, SW10
Telephone: 071-376 5553 £55
Open: all day Mon-Sat (closed Bank Holidays)
Meals served: 12-11.30

Despite the name, the restaurant is highly civilised – though never tame. Lengths of jewel-bright plain chintz, draped like curtains onto walls where most people would hang paintings, animate the white walls while the sunken conservatory area boasts a wall glinting with distressed gold leaf. The interior may date quickly but the food continues to develop: Peter Cuff is the new chef and he prepares dishes with gusto such as Tuscan white bean soup or griddled polenta with roast vegetables and pesto to start, followed by baked salmon with caviar and dill butter sauce, pan-fried chicken with asparagus, button mushrooms and thyme or, in summer, a cold lobster with herb mayonnaise and cherry tomato salad. Hearty puds include chewy chocolate brownies with fresh berries and cream, pear tarte tatin and good home-made ice-creams and sorbets that change from one day to the next. The restaurant is owned and run by Corinne Young and Jonette Glass, a glamorous pair of South Africans – hence the preponderance of New World wines on the classy list.

WILTON'S SW1

55 Jermyn Street, SW1Y 6LX
Telephone: 071-629 9955 £80
Fax: 071-495 6233
Open: lunch Mon-Fri, dinner Mon-Sat (closed Bank Holidays)
Meals served: lunch 12.30-2.30, dinner 6.30-10.30

A pillar of the establishment-style restaurant, now owned by the Savoy Group, this is where the old boys go to network. This of course is entirely in keeping with its location: the predominantly masculine clientele and twilight interior reinforce the feeling that you are dining in one of the great gentlemen's clubs on The Mall. Game features prominently when in season but fish is the speciality here and, although treated simply, the flavours and freshness are good. Sauces are straightforward and familiar and the savouries are very good. Service is in the finest traditions. Fifty years ago, you could probably ask for it all to be put on the slate; these days you pay as you leave. You could easily find a cheaper dressed crab, lobster salad or grilled Dover sole elsewhere – but that would be to miss the point. Self-important wine list at the top end of the price range.

WODKA W8

12 St Alban's Grove, W8 5PN
Telephone: 071-937 6513 £45
Open: lunch Mon-Fri, dinner daily (closed Bank Holidays)
Meals served: lunch 12.30-2.30, dinner 7-11

As Eastern Europe becomes increasingly fashionable among the Western intelligentsia, restaurants like Wodka look likely to thrive. While in Poland they're probably craving for fast food, improbably well-heeled diners at this chic Kensington restaurant squeal in delight over solid Polish cooking such as black sausage with red cabbage and apple, rye soup, bigos (a hunter's stew) and zrarzy (beef fillet with dill, cucumber and bacon). On the other hand, rich eastern European food is the best excuse in the world for drinking too much vodka and over a dozen are represented here, including several flavoured varieties. Don't bother trying to pronounce Cytrynowka (lemon vodka), Pierprzowka or Sliwowica after the third glass: pointing a limp finger will do just as well! The Polish wine industry is far from dynamic so the wine list draws on world produce, the USA, Australia and Chile included. Predictably, the atmosphere- already relaxed – tends to grow jollier as the evening wears on.

ZEN SW3

Chelsea Cloisters, Sloane Avenue, SW3
Telephone: 071-589 1781 £60
Fax: 071-437 0641
Open: lunch + dinner daily (closed 25+26 Dec)
Meals served: lunch 12-3, dinner 6-11.30 (Sun 6-11)
The first of the Zens has an interesting and varied menu with many vegetarian dishes.

Zen Cargo — W1

3 Barrett Street, W1M 5HH
Telephone: 071-486 5269
Open: lunch + dinner daily (closed 25+26 Dec)
Meals served: lunch 12-2.30, dinner 6.30-11.30 (Sun 6.30-11)

£60

One of the more recent additions to this chain, but with a wider-reaching menu.

Zen Central — W1

20-22 Queen Street, W1
Telephone: 071-629 8103
Open: lunch + dinner daily (closed 25+26 Dec)
Meals served: lunch 12-2.30, dinner 6.30-11.30 (Sun 6.30-11)

£65

Chic, expensive Chinese restaurant with architect-designed interior. Interesting menu with classy dishes, some not often found outside Hong Kong. Salt and pepper soft shell crab, correctly made Peking duck and lobster with tangerine peel and crushed garlic are rewarding choices. Slick service.

ZeNW3 — NW3

81 Hampstead High Street, NW3 1RE
Telephone: 071-794 7863
Open: all day daily (closed Xmas)
Meals served: 12-11.30

£50

Designer Chinese in look and in the menu with light, somewhat adapted dishes. Its clients like to pose both upstairs and downstairs.

Ziani — SW3

45/47 Radnor Walk, SW3 4BT
Telephone: 071-352 2698
Open: lunch + dinner daily (closed 4 days Xmas, 4 days Easter)
Meals served: lunch 12.30-2.45 (Sun 12.30-3.15), dinner 7-11.30 (Sun 7-10.30)

£50

Not for the claustrophobic, Ziani packs in diners hungry for consistent Italian cuisine. Vibrantly decorated, this establishment is – as you will read on the elegant menu – named after an ancient Venetian dynasty and is predictably strong on seafood. The starters take in several familiar dishes plus artichoke with bagna cauda and one or two more inventive items like the smoked herring with avocado mousse. There is risi e bisi or a seafood risotto crammed with various fish. Pastas are very reliable: pansotti, for instance, are filled with cheese and spinach in a walnut cream sauce, rigatoni topped with veal sauce and there is a superb gratinati of tagliolini with prosciutto, cheese and cream. Signor Colussi knows what he's about, so follow his daily recommendations – wild mushrooms with truffles, perhaps, to start, then calves liver Venetian-style, roast quail with polenta or a mixed grill of fish. For offal-lovers, there is a fritto misto of lamb's kidney, liver, brains and sweetbreads. The curt Italian wine list gives neither vintages nor descriptions but is fairly priced.

LONDON ROUND-UP

Belgo — NW1

72 Chalk Farm Road, NW1 8AN
Telephone: 071-267 0718
Open: lunch & dinner Mon-Fri, all day Sat + Sun
Meals served: lunch 12-3, dinner 6-11.30, Sat + Sun 12-11.30

£40

Belgo is quite extraordinary, with its stone frontage barely noticeable to the casual passer-by. Walk over the gang-plank then past the open kitchen with its space-age ducting into a semi-vaulted room, which could just be a monastery refectory, with a wooden floor and tables, and chairs that look uncomfortable but are in fact the reverse. You would be hard pressed to find a larger selection of beers, ranging from blond wheat beer to a variety of fruit flavours.

Mussels are served - by the kilo - provençale or meunière, accompanied by good-sized chips, or open flat grilled, with a variety of toppings. Oysters and lobsters also feature and yes, the staff are dressed as Trappist monks and, it has been rumoured, occasionally wear their habits kilt-style! You've probably guessed by now that this is a fun place, a welcome addition to the London eating scene.

The Lexington
45 Lexington Street W1. Tel. 071 434 3401

New restaurant on the site of the former Sutherland's with a clean, distinctly New Yorky feel - chairs and banquettes, bare wooden tables. The menu, tweaked daily, borrows its philosophy partly from The Square (whence came chef Ian Loynes and owner/manager Martin Saxon), partly from modern English winners like Kensington Place.

The Criterion
224 Piccadilly, W1. Tel 071 925 0909

The neo-Byzantine Criterion is now open again, courtesy of Forte Plc & Bob Payton, and has been revitalised by some modern touches. Food is in the modish Cal-Ital style.

Rue St Jacques re-opens in Nov. 1992 following a refit.

Portobello Dining Rooms have now sadly closed.

CLOVER AWARDS 209

Alastair Little, London W1 (see page 68)

L'Arlequin, London SW8
(see page 72)

CLOVER AWARDS 211

Bibendum, London SW3 (see page 78)

The Capital Hotel, London SW3 (see page 95)

EVEN NON-VINTAGE CHAMPAGNE CHARLES HEIDSIECK CONTAINS THIS MUCH VINTAGE

Traditionally, the best champagne makers always like to include some older, reserve stocks from good years with a non-vintage, to bring the blend a much greater depth and maturity.

Champagne Charles Heidsieck is no exception. Except that, in their case, the proportion included is astoundingly generous.

Nearly 40% in fact.

Brut Réserve

Charles Heidsieck

CHAMPAGNE

FOR THE RARELY IMPRESSED

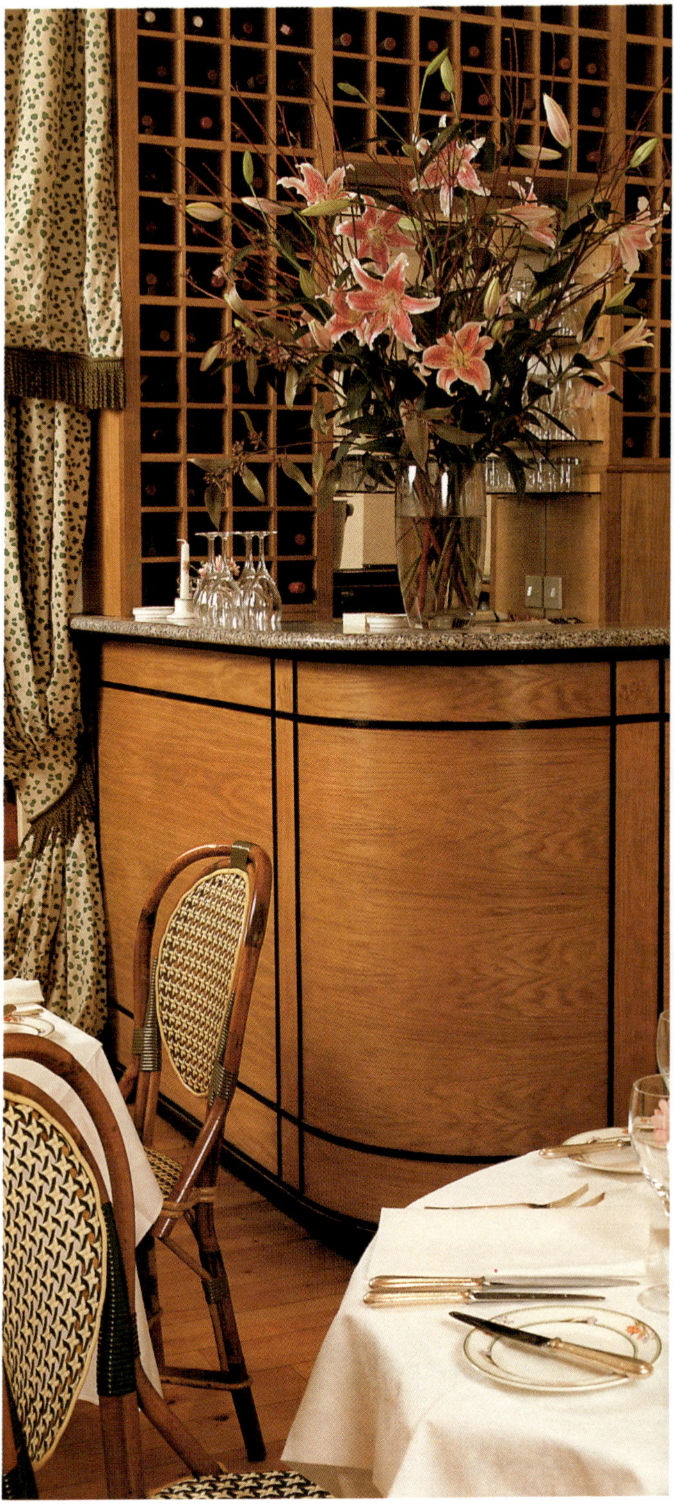

CLOVER AWARDS 215

Clarke's, London SW8 (see page 109)

CLARKE'S
open for breads, biscuits, truffles, cheeses & wines

The Connaught Hotel, London W1 (see page 110)

CLOVER AWARDS **217**

Le Gavroche, London W1 (see page 125)

218 THE ACKERMAN CHARLES HEIDSIECK GUIDE 1993

CLOVER AWARDS **219**

The Gay Hussar, London W1 (see page 126)

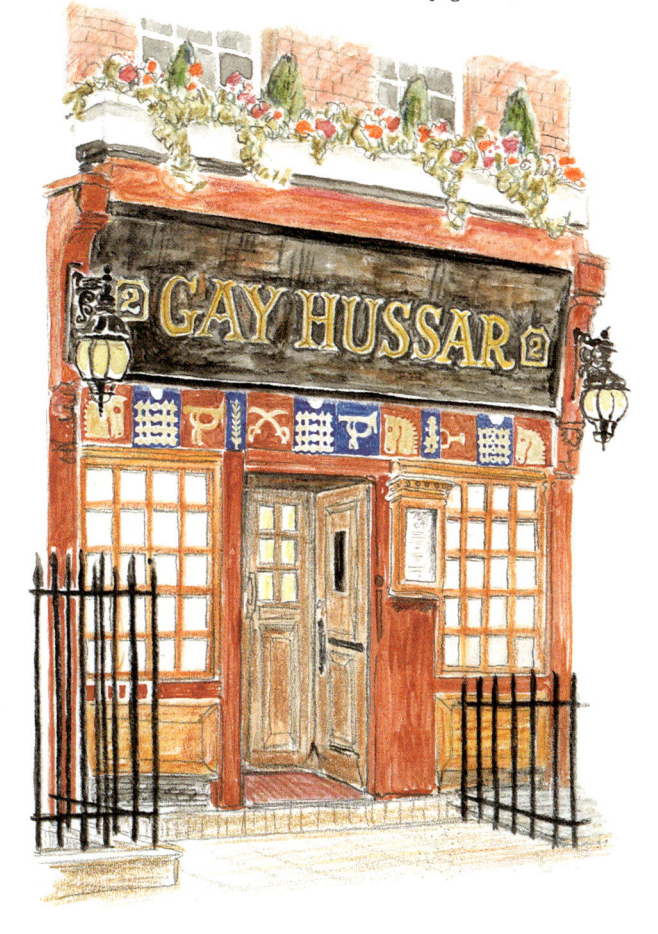

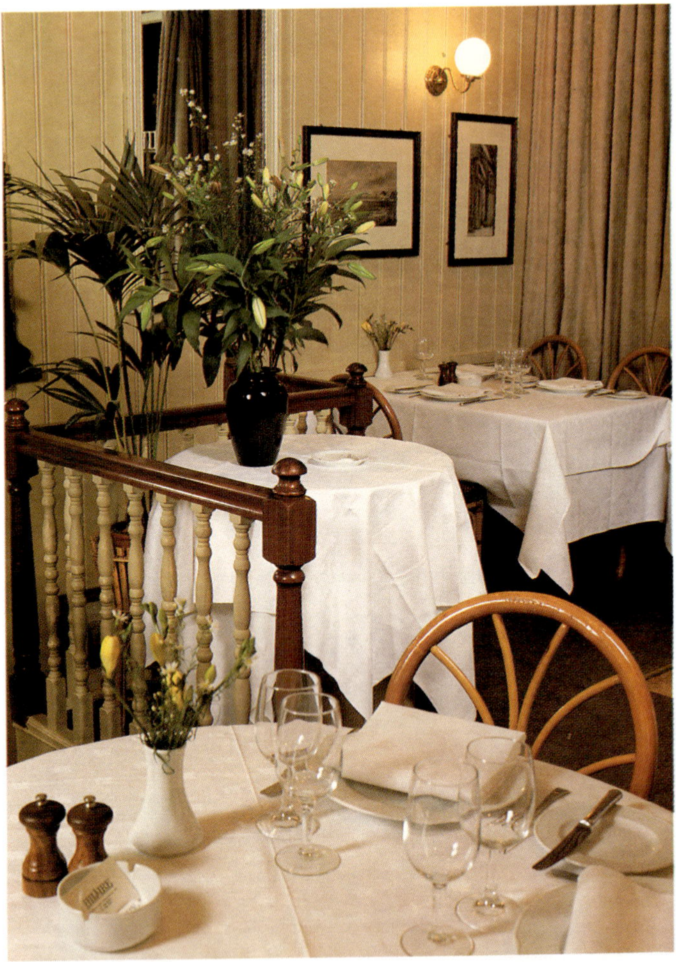

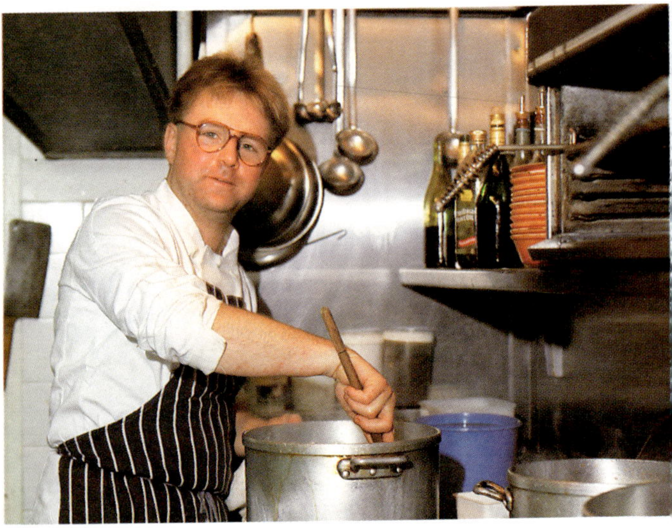

CLOVER AWARDS 221

Hilaire, London W1 (see page 136)

222 THE ACKERMAN CHARLES HEIDSIECK GUIDE 1993

L'Incontro, London W1 (see page 140)

V.S.O.P.
DE
REMY MARTIN

Fine Champagne Cognac comes exclusively from grapes grown in the two best areas of the Cognac district of France - at least 50% from the Grande Champagne and the rest from the Petite Champagne.

Rémy Martin V.S.O.P. is a blend of Fine Champagne *eaux-de-vie* aged far longer than required by law to create a Cognac of exceptional smoothness and warmth.

REMY MARTIN
FINE CHAMPAGNE COGNAC

Langan's Brasserie, London W1 (see page 148)

CLOVER AWARDS 225

Spinach soufflé

Mosimann's, London SW1 (see page 159)

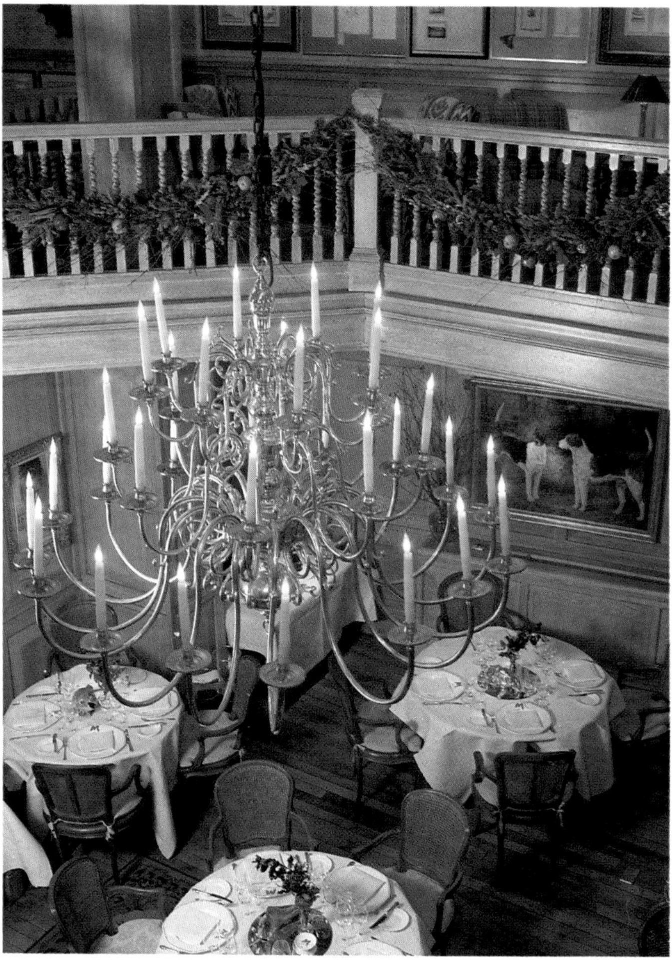

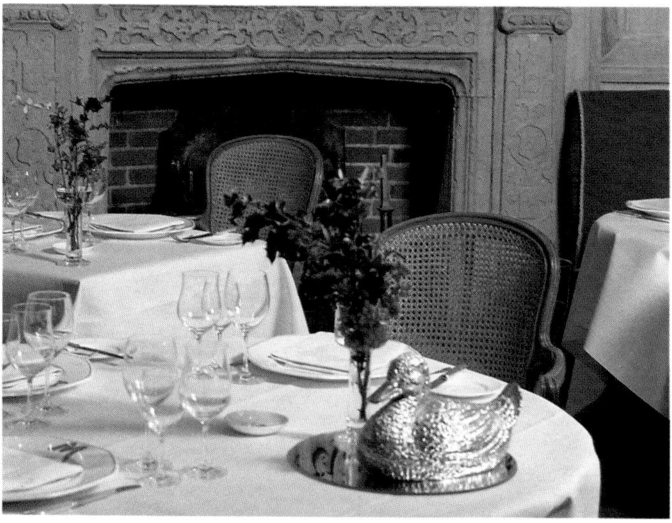

190 Queen's Gate, London SW7 (see page 168)

CLOVER AWARDS 229

The Ritz Hotel, London W1 (see page 177)

River Café, London, W6 (see page 177)

COINTREAU ON ICE...

...VOULEZ-VOUS ?

La Tante Claire, London SW3 (see page 199)

CLOVER AWARDS

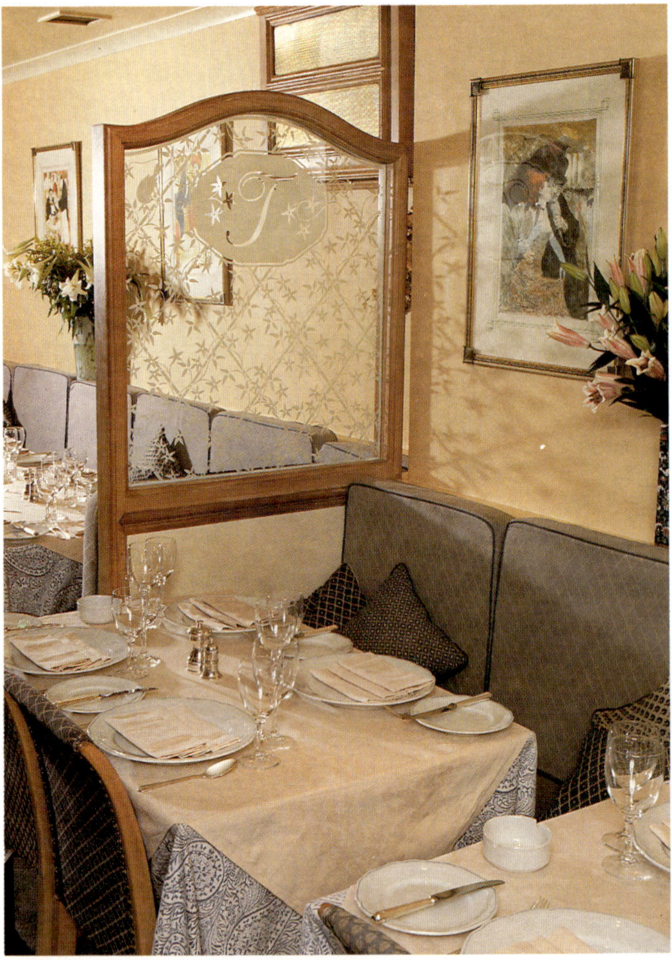

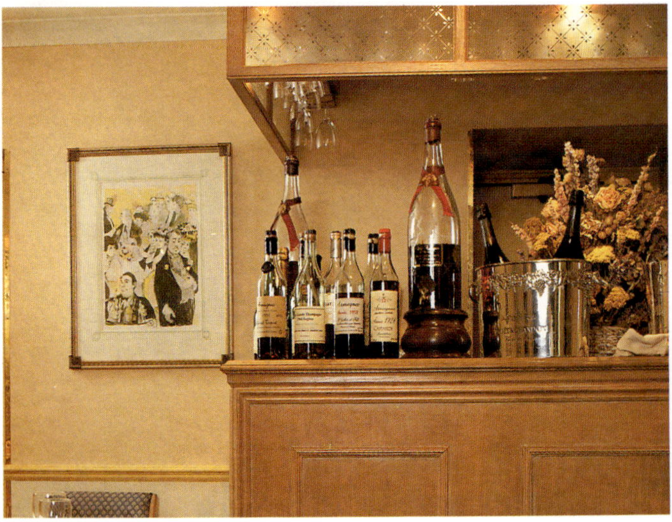

CLOVER AWARDS **235**

Turner's, London SW3
(see page 202)

Above: *Amberley Castle, Amberley (see page 291)*
Below: *Bilbrough Manor, Bilbrough (see page 303)*
Opposite: *Waterside Inn, Bray-on-Thames (see page 312)*

CLOVER AWARDS 237

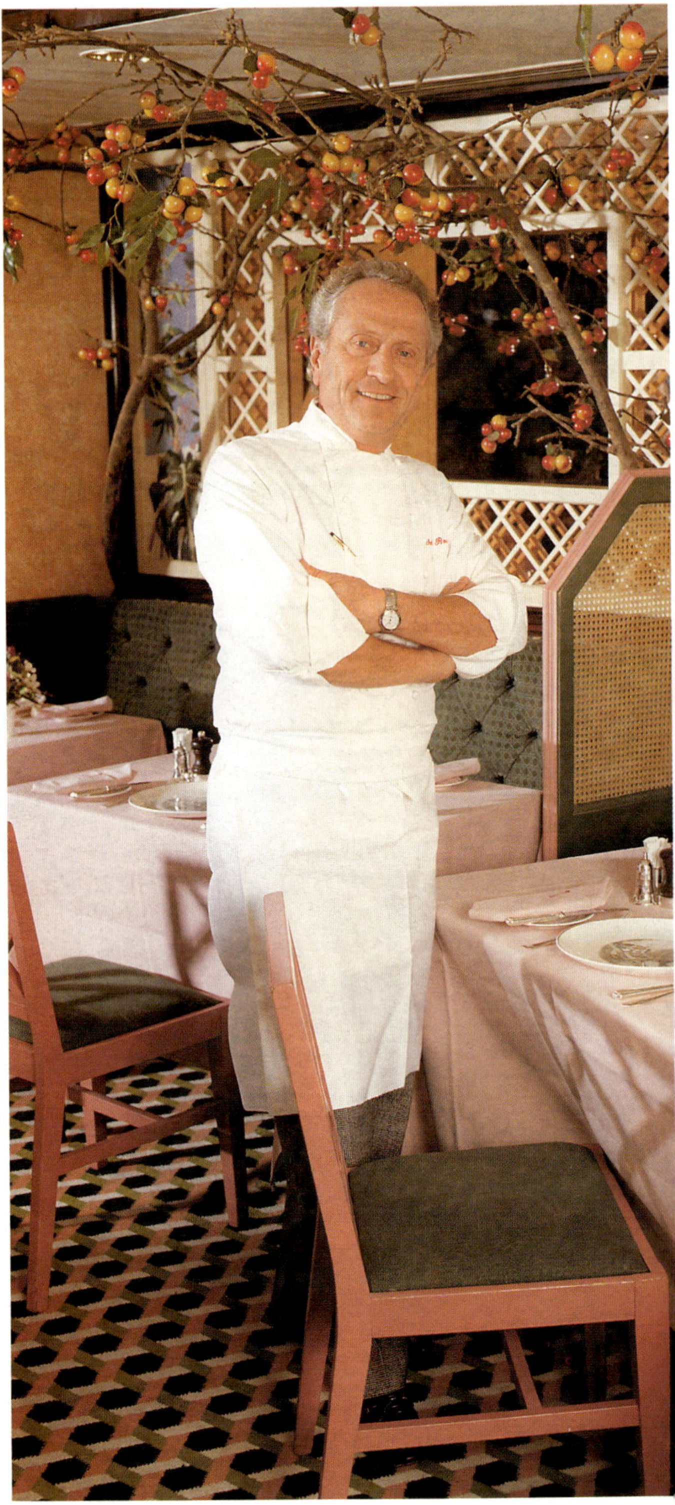

CLOVER AWARDS 239

Waterside Inn, Bray-on-Thames (see page 312)

Le Poussin, Brockenhurst (see page 319)

CLOVER AWARDS **241**

IT TAKES 105 VINEYARDS TO PRODUCE THIS BOTTLE OF CHAMPAGNE CHARLES HEIDSIECK

Every year, up to 105 carefully selected 'crus' contribute to the making of Champagne Charles Heidsieck. And in an exceptional year, a champagne will be made solely from the grapes of that year.

The declaration of a vintage year on the label – such as the excellent 1985 – is your assurance that only grapes from that year are used. A mere 105 vineyards' worth of them.

Brut Vintage 1985

Charles Heidsieck
CHAMPAGNE
FOR THE RARELY IMPRESSED

Gidleigh Park, Chagford (see page 326)

CLOVER AWARDS 243

Les Alouettes, Claygate (see page 334)

The Carved Angel, Dartmouth (see page 340)

CLOVER AWARDS 245

Above: *Le Talbooth, Dedham (see page 341)*

Below: *Congham Hall, Grimston (see page 360)*

Gravetye Manor, East Grinstead (see page 345)

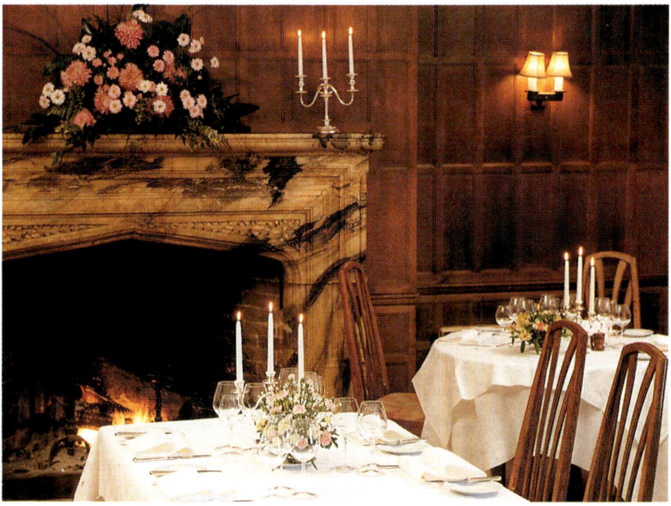

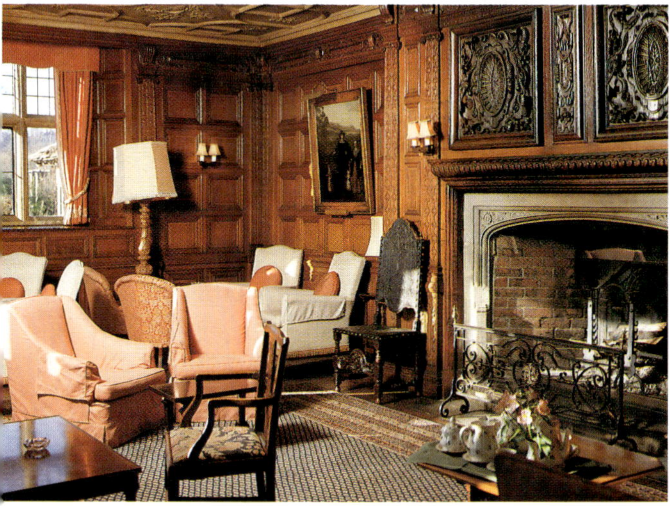

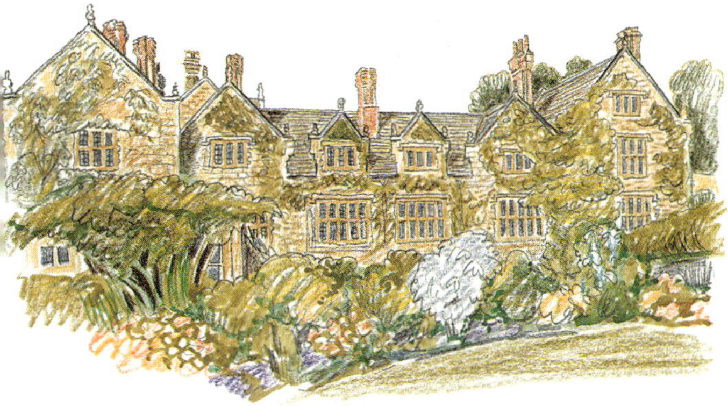

Stock Hill House, Gillingham (see page 354)

CLOVER AWARDS 249

250 THE ACKERMAN CHARLES HEIDSIECK GUIDE 1993

Michael's Nook, Grasmere (see page 356)

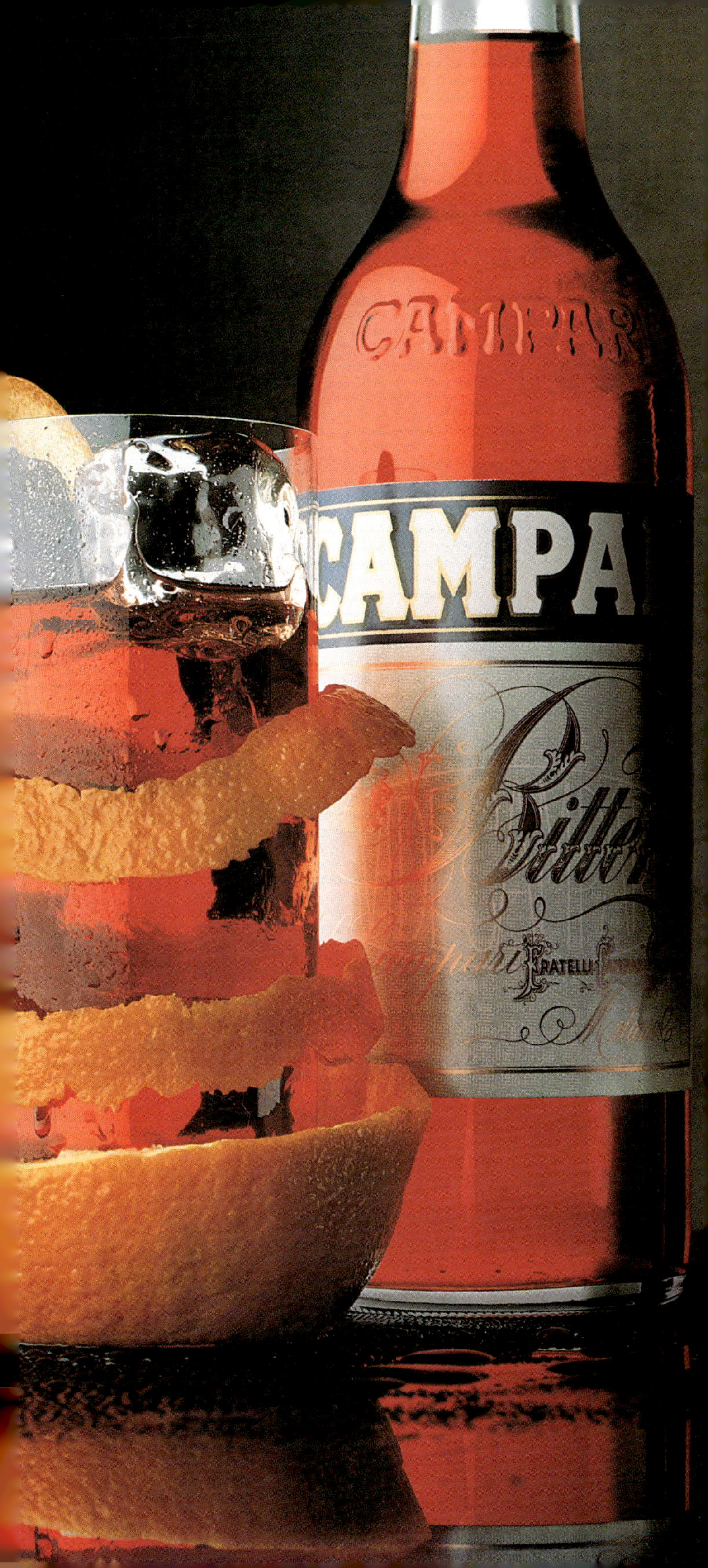
CAMPA
FRATELLI

Le Manoir aux Quat'Saisons, Great Milton (see page 359)

CLOVER AWARDS 253

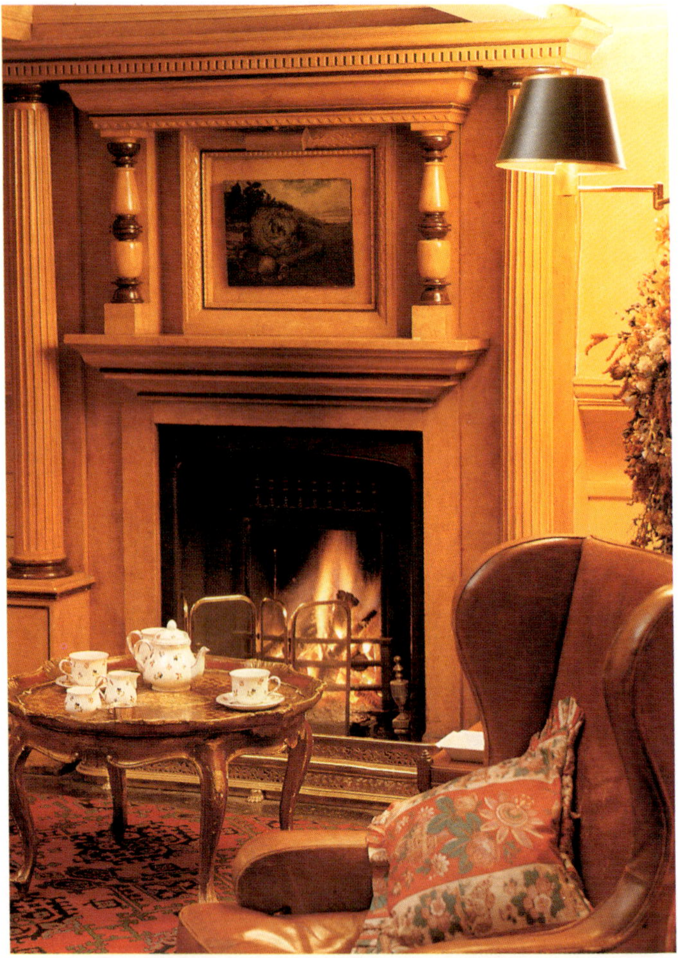

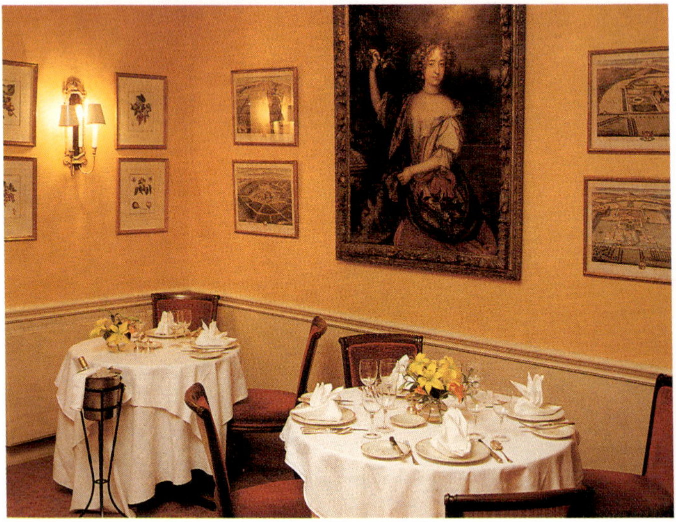

CLOVER AWARDS 255

Hambleton Hall, Hambleton (see page 405)

Sundial, Herstmonceux (see page 367)

Hope End, Ledbury (see page 382)

XO SPECIAL
DE
REMY MARTIN

Fine Champagne Cognac comes exclusively from grapes grown in the two best areas of the Cognac district of France - at least 50% from the Grande Champagne and the rest from the Petite Champagne.

Rémy Martin XO Spécial is a blend of older Fine Champagne *eaux-de-vie* characterised by subtlety, harmony and a warm lingering aftertaste.

REMY MARTIN
FINE CHAMPAGNE COGNAC

Hintlesham Hall, Hintlesham (see page 368)

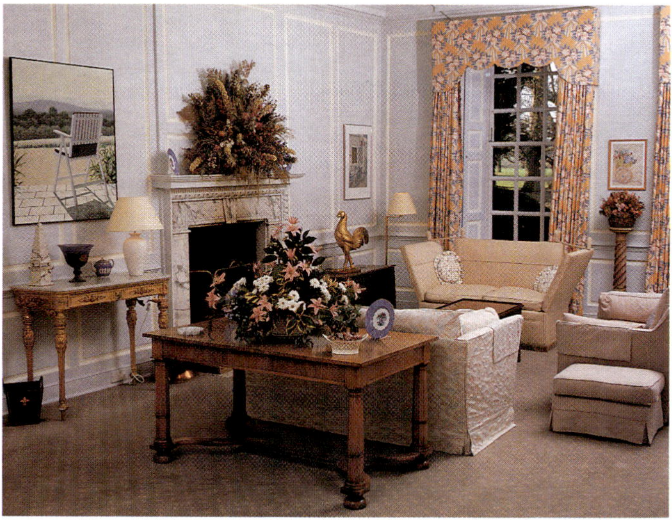

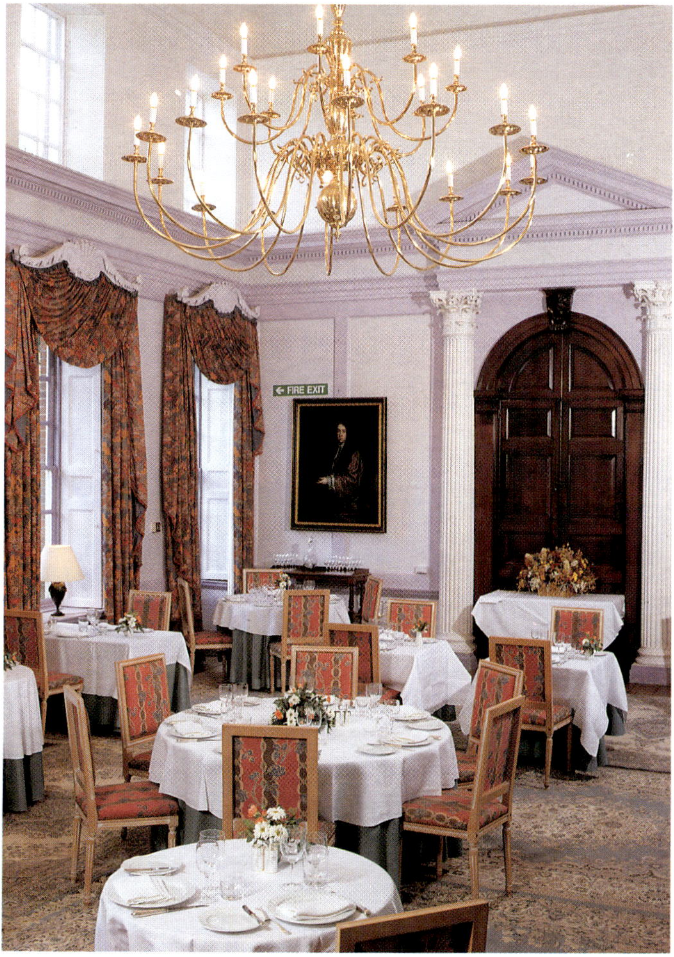
FIRE EXIT

STAPLEFORD PARK

COUNTRY HOUSE HOTEL
and Sporting Estate

Stapleford Park, Melton Mowbray (see page 430)

The Old Woolhouse, Northleach (see page 403)

Chewton Glen, New Milton (see page 400)

CLOVER AWARDS 261

Chewton Glen, New Milton (see page 400)

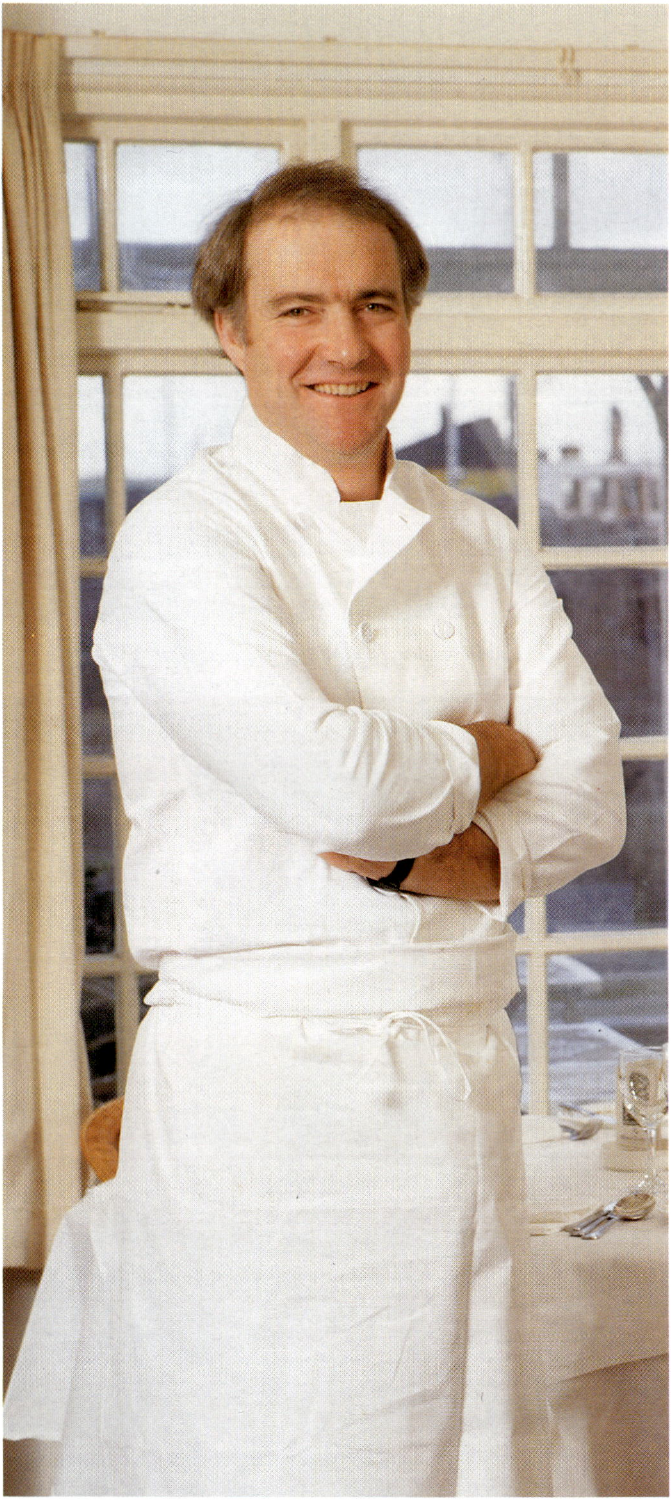

Seafood Restaurant, Padstow (see page 404)

Chez Nous, Plymouth (see page 412)

Pool Court, Pool-in-Wharfedale (see page 412)

The Faustino Guide to fine Rioja.

Faustino I, a magnificent Gran Reserva Rioja, aged in cask at least 2½ years and another 3 years in bottle. Excellent with all meat dishes as well as fish served with strong sauces.

Faustino V, an elegant Reserva Rioja aged up to 1½ years in cask and almost 2 years in bottle. Its smoothness makes it a perfect partner to pastas, red meats and any smoked meat or fish.

Faustino
FOR THOSE WHO KNOW THEIR RIOJA.

Stane Street Hollow, Pulborough (see page 415)

CLOVER AWARDS 267

The Old Manor House, Romsey (see page 418)

L'Ortolan, Shinfield (see page 425)

CLOVER AWARDS 269

McCoy's, Staddle Bridge (see page 429)

CLOVER AWARDS 271

Manley's, Storrington (see page 433)

CLOVER AWARDS 273

The Castle Hotel, Taunton (see page 441)

Thornbury Castle, Thornbury (see page 443)

Sharrow Bay, Ullswater (see page 450)

CLOVER AWARDS 275

This page and overpage: *Sharrow Bay, Ullswater (see page 450)*

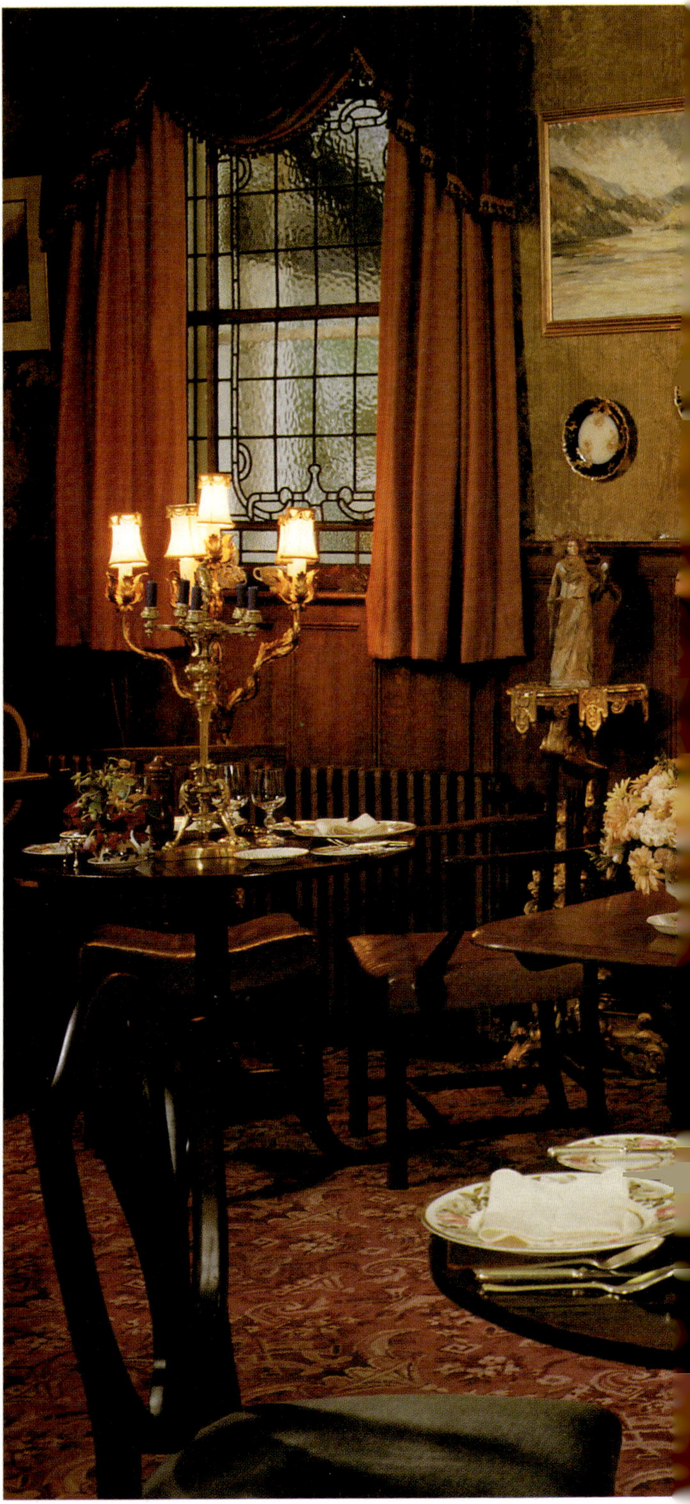

CLOVER AWARDS 277

Brown's, Worcester (see page 461)

Middlethorpe Hall, York (see page 464)

CLOVER AWARDS 279

Inverlochy Castle, Fort William (see page 483)

Champany Inn, Linlithgow (see page 492)

Peat Inn, Peat Inn (see page 495)

Ballymaloe House, Shanagarry (see page 548)

CLOVER AWARDS **281**

Walnut Tree
Inn
F. TARUSCHIO
Licensed to sell by retail Beer Wines & Spirits.
To be consumed on or off the premises.

CLOVER AWARDS **283**

Walnut Tree, Abergavenny (see page 503)

Walnut Tree, Abergavenny (see page 503)

Brut Rosé Vintage

TO PRODUCE AN OUTSTANDING CHAMPAGNE, WE ONLY EVER USE THE FIRST PRESSING

Even the strictest rules of the Champagne region allow grapes to be pressed twice, or even three times, to extract the most from the precious juices.

At Champagne Charles Heidsieck, however, we use the first and finest pressing and no other, having no desire to increase the quantity of our output at even the slightest cost to our quality. Whether the bottle in question is a Brut Réserve or a vintage such as our unique Brut Rosé Vintage.

Charles Heidsieck

CHAMPAGNE

FOR THE RARELY IMPRESSED

Altnaharrie Inn, Ullapool (see page 501)

CLOVER AWARDS **287**

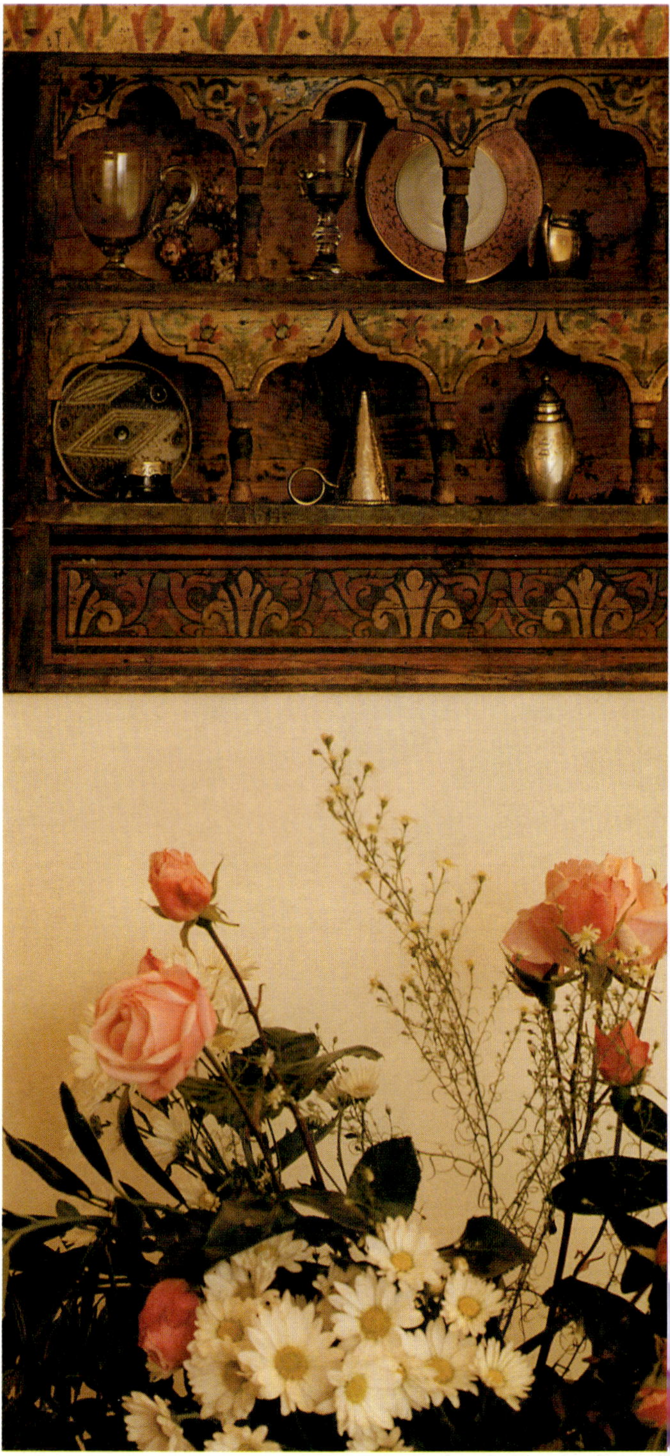

England Establishment Reviews

Abberley — Elms Hotel

Stockton Road, Abberley, Nr Worcester, Hereford & Worcester WR6 6AT
Telephone: (0299) 896666 £65
Fax: (0299) 896804
Open: lunch + dinner daily
Meals served: lunch 12.30-2, dinner 7.30-9.30

Enjoying the beauties of the Teme Valley, the Elms Hotel provides a grand and picturesque place to stay. It has 25 bedrooms located either in the main house or the adjoining Coach House and the public rooms are impeccably decorated and maintained. Surely a must if you're in this area.

Abbot's Salford — Salford Hall
Abbot's Salford, Evesham, Worcester WR11 5UT
Telephone: (0386) 871300 £60
Fax: (0386) 871301
Open: lunch + dinner daily
Meals served: lunch 12-2, dinner 7-10 (Sun 7-9)
Grade 1 listed Tudor Manor wonderfully restored. Thirty-four bedrooms.

Abingdon — Thame Lane House
Thame Lane, Culham, Abingdon, Oxfordshire OX14 3DS
Telephone: (0235) 524177 £50
Open: lunch daily, dinner Mon-Sat (closed 2 weeks Jan)
Meals served: lunch 12.30-1, dinner 7-8.30
Simple guest house with French cooking.

Alderley Edge — Alderley Edge Hotel
Macclesfield Road, Alderley Edge, Cheshire SK9 7BJ
Telephone: (0625) 583033 £65
Fax: (0625) 586343
Open: lunch + dinner daily
Meals served: lunch 12-2, dinner 7-9.30
Recently restored house set in its own grounds. Thirty-two bedrooms. Comtemporary French cooking in the restaurant.

Alderney — Inchalla Hotel
The Val, St Anne, Alderney, Channel Islands
Telephone: (0481) 823220 £35
Fax: (0481) 823551
Open: lunch Sun, dinner Mon-Sat (closed 1 wk Xmas/New Year)
Meals served: lunch 1-2, dinner 7-8.45
Small modern hotel with eleven rooms. Fresh local seafood in the restaurant.

Alderney — Nellie Gray's Restaurant
Victoria Street, St Anne, Alderney, Channel Islands
Telephone: (048 182) 3333 £50
Open: lunch + dinner Tue-Sun (closed Oct-end Mar)
Meals served: lunch 11-2, dinner 7-10
Popular local restaurant. Classic food in generous amounts.

Alnwick — John Blackmore's Restaurant
1 Dorothy Forster Court, Narrowgate, Alnwick, Northumberland NE66 1NL
Telephone: (0665) 604465 £45
Open: dinner Tue-Sat (closed Bank Holidays, Jan)
Meals served: dinner 7-9.30
A small friendly restaurant, with a warm atmosphere, in the shadow of the castle.

ALTRINCHAM	**Benedicts**

4 King's Court, Altrincham, Cheshire WA14 2RD
Telephone: 061-928 6983 £45
Open: lunch + dinner Mon-Sat
Meals served: lunch 12-3, dinner 7-10

Paul Shelton has risen to the challenge of making a go on his own of this restaurant in a small courtyard shopping area with simple furnishings. He's putting in long hours and could cause some surprises in Altrincham. Daily specials such as steamed fresh mussels with tarragon sauce and a bouillabaisse are well above expectations. The desserts also do well for the 4 o'clock crowd, who dig into their tarte au citron and iced lime torte with relish. One to keep an eye on for the future.

ALTRINCHAM	Franc's

2 Goose Green, Altrincham, Greater Manchester
Telephone: 061-941 3954 £30
Open: lunch + dinner daily
Meals served: lunch 12-3, dinner 5-11 (Sun 12-7.30)
French brasserie owned by the proprietors of Franc's in Chester.

ALTRINCHAM	**French Brasserie**

24 The Downs, Altrincham, Cheshire
Telephone: 061-928 0808 £45
Open: all day daily
Meals served: 12-11.30, Thu-Sat 12-12, Sun 12-11

As near to an authentic Paris brasserie as you'll get round these parts. The long bar, the plain tables, and the blackboards are all kind of familiar as are the dishes: coq au vin, gigot d'agneau aux haricots, boeuf au poivre. A generous glass of house wine will see you proud and a variety of desserts seem cheap and tempting. Especially busy on evenings when a band is booked in.

AMBERLEY	Amberley Castle

Amberley, Nr Arundel, West Sussex BN18 9ND
Telephone: (0798) 831992
Fax: (0798) 831998 £75
Open: lunch + dinner daily
Meals served: lunch 12-2.30, dinner 6-10

Maybe I'm a sucker for history, but I challenge anyone to enter through the portcullis archway, above which flies the flag of St George, without feeling a little flutter of good old English pride. As you sit in the Queen's Room Restaurant you feel comfortable in the knowledge that whatever happens outside you'll be safe within those great stone walls. Chef Nigel Boschetti serves up some interesting dishes. Wild boar terrine with truffle and a warm fig chutney and medallions of venison with a juniper berry sauce and a confit of turnips and chestnuts may not at first seem to be in keeping with the surroundings: Amberley Castle and Nigel Boschetti have thoroughly researched some of early English cookery books and come up with the novel idea of Castle Cuisine. Dishes based on this research are asterixed on the menu. Currently on offer are a poached loin of lamb accompanied by pearl barley and baby vegetables. From the puddings try the castle cream with seasonal berries, which is based on an original recipe, a cream cheese with herbs which forms the inspiration for the modern offering. Dining at Amberley Castle is always an experience and the staff make you feel very much at home. The castle itself has been painstakingly and carefully developed by Martin and Joy Cummings and is well worth a visit to experience in comfort a modern-day interpretation of the way our ancestors lived. *See also page 236 – our Clover Award Section.*

AMBLESIDE	Rothay Manor

Rothay Bridge, Ambleside, Cumbria LA22 0EH
Telephone: (053 94) 33605 £55
Fax: (053 94) 33607
Open: lunch + dinner daily (closed early Jan-mid Feb)
Meals served: lunch 12.30-2 (Sun 12.30-1.30, buffet only Mon-Sat), dinner 8-9

This elegant Georgian listed building, 5 minutes' walk from Lake Windermere, is a popular hotel with a loyal set of guests. Bedrooms are well equipped and in the restaurant chef Jane Binus provides good, traditional fare. Special cultural and culinary programmes are organised throughout the year.

AMBLESIDE	Sheila's Cottage

The Slack, Ambleside, Cumbria LA22 9DQ
Telephone: (053 94) 33079 £50
Open: lunch + dinner Mon-Sat (closed Jan)
Meals served: lunch 12-2.30, dinner 7-9.30 (also tea 2.30-5)

Such is the popularity of this place that Stewart and Janice Greaves have been forced to expand their operation. They now have a top floor pastry kitchen, a couple of new chefs and some additional items of the menu. Pâtisseries are still the thing – the Austrian sachertorte is scrumptious – but the lunchtime savouries hold their own as well.

AMBLESIDE	**Wateredge Hotel**

Waterhead Bay, Ambleside, Cumbria LA22 0EP
Telephone: (053 94) 32332 £55
Fax: (053 94) 32332
Open: lunch + dinner daily (closed Dec+Jan)
Meals served: lunch 12-2, dinner 7-8.30

Fresh flowers abound in this delightful originally 17th-century fisherman's cottage, now a hotel with lawns down to Lake Windermere and even a rowing boat. Ground floor suites and garden rooms all have private balconies or patio, and other rooms include a cosy beamed bar and lounges overlooking the lake. Roast sirloin of beef and guineafowl with a lemon sauce are typical of the up-to-6-course menus, and bread and preserves are made on the premises. A happy, friendly place to stay.

APPLEBY-IN-WESTMORLAND	**Tufton Arms**

Market Square, Appleby-in-Westmorland, Cumbria CA16 6XA
Telephone: (076 83) 51593 £35
Fax: (076 83) 52761
Open: lunch + dinner daily
Meals served: lunch 12-2, dinner 7.30-9.30

Plenty of period antiques and furnishings in this friendly, Victorian, family-run hotel. The bar draws local characters for a pint – or two – in the evening. The menu features lake district produce and caters for visitors and locals alike. Fishing, grouse and pheasant shooting are listed among the amenities.

APPLETHWAITE	**Underscar Manor**

Applethwaite, Keswick, Cumbria CA12 4PH
Telephone: (076 87) 75000 £60
Fax: (076 87) 74904
Open: lunch + dinner daily
Meals served: lunch 12-1.30, dinner 7-8.30

Underscar Manor is back with us and I, for one, can hardly wait to see just how impressive the place looks now that it's been restored by Derek and Pauline Harrison. We're talking big money here, and if all goes to plan it will rank as one of the best hotels around. The Harrisons have already proved their mettle at Moss Nook, while the combined talents of Robert Thornton and Stephen Yare in the kitchen will be a force to be reckoned with.

Ascot — Hyn's

4 Brockenhurst Road, Ascot, Berkshire
Telephone: (0344) 872583
Open: lunch + dinner daily (closed 25+26 Dec)
Meals served: lunch 12-2.30, dinner 6-11

£45

Popular, stylish Chinese restaurant. Elegant decor, good food.

Ascot — Royal Berkshire

London Road, Sunninghill, Ascot, Berkshire SL5 0PP
Telephone: (0344) 23322
Fax: (0344) 847280
Open: lunch + dinner daily
Meals served: lunch 12.30-2, dinner 7.30-9.30

£70

Andy Richardson is well into his stride at this stylish Hilton-owned Queen Anne mansion. His sensibly concise à la carte and set menus (including a 2-course option at lunch for those in a hurry) show invention and refinement – crab and mozzarella lasagne with a ginger and spring onion vinaigrette – venison loin with peppered noodles and mulled pear, almond and pear tart on a poire william custard. House wines and set menus offer good value. Popular with the business community who appreciate both conference and leisure facilities.

Ashbourne — Callow Hall

Mappleton Road, Ashbourne, Derbyshire DE6 2AA
Telephone: (0335) 43403
Fax: (0335) 43624
Open: lunch Tue-Sun, dinner Tue-Sat (closed 25+26 Dec, 2 wks Jan/Feb)
Meals served: lunch 12-1.15, dinner 7-9.30

£55

Proprietors of long standing, the Spencers continue to lavish care and attention (the antique filled drawing room the latest recipient) on their rambling rural retreat. Twelve bedrooms and a mile of fishing.

Ashburton — Holne Chase

Ashburton, Devon TQ13 7NS
Telephone: (036 43) 471
Fax: (036 43) 453
Open: lunch + dinner daily
Meals served: lunch 12-2, dinner 7-9

£55

Family run, friendly hotel. Local produce is the backbone of the menu.

Ashford — Eastwell Manor

Eastwell Park, Boughton Aluph, Ashford, Kent TN25 4HR
Telephone: (0233) 635751
Fax: (0233) 635530
Open: lunch + dinner daily
Meals served: lunch 12.30-2, dinner 7-9.30 (Sat 7-9.45)

£80

An impressive roll-call of royal guests lend history to this Jacobean-style manor that boasts sumptuous public rooms and 23 equally comfortable bedrooms overlooking a glorious 3,000 acre estate. Mark Clayton continues to establish his reputation in the kitchen with fixed price menus offering first rate food such as ravioli filled with goat's cheese in a fennel butter sauce, saddle of wild rabbit in puff pastry and a grain mustard sauce, coffee and whiskyparfait with a bitter chocolate sauce.

Ashford-in-the-Water — Riverside Hotel

Fennel Street, Ashford-in-the-Water, Derbyshire DE4 1QF
Telephone: (0629) 814275
Fax: (0629) 812873
Open: lunch + dinner daily
Meals served: lunch 12-1.30, dinner 7-9.30

£70

Antique furnished Georgian Manor. Imaginative cuisine served in the restaurant together with an extensive wine list.

Aspley Guise — Moore Place

The Square, Aspley Guise, Nr Woburn, Bedfordshire MK17 8DW
Telephone: (0908) 282000
Fax: (0908) 281888
Open: lunch Sun-Fri, dinner daily
Meals served: lunch 12.30-2.30, dinner 7.30-9.45

£50

Francis Moore's handsome Georgian house built in 1786, and more recent courtyard extension provide 54 comfortable bedrooms and a tented conservatory restaurant. Country Mansion Hotels are the new operators with an eye for the conference market.

Aston Clinton — Bell Inn

London Road, Aston Clinton, Buckinghamshire HP22 5HP
Telephone: (0296) 630252
Fax: (0296) 631250
Open: lunch + dinner daily
Meals served: lunch 12.30-2, dinner 7.30-9.45 (Sun 7.30-8.45)

£60

Once a pit stop for the Duke of Buckingham en route to London, this 17th-century coaching inn now houses an 'olde worlde' hotel with period pieces judiciously dotted around. Discreetly modernised and well staffed it avoids becoming merely cute. The dining room gained its reputation with a succession of ex-Connaught chefs and now scores something of a coup in this part of the world with the talented David Cavalier at the stoves. He has immediately stamped his authority on the proceedings by creating a simpler and shorter carte – carpaccio of scallops, roast guineafowl with broad beans and tomatoes, calvados soufflé – and better value set menus at lunch and dinner. Wines are selected each week with the food in mind and may be taken by the glass or the bottle. There are bedrooms in the main house and across the courtyard, with extensive banqueting facilities.

Austwick — The Traddock

Austwick, Nr Settle, North Yorkshire LA2 8BY
Telephone: (052 42) 511224
Open: all day daily
Meals served: 8am-8.30pm (closed 6pm-7.30pm only)

£35

Twelve-bedroomed Georgian hotel in the Yorkshire Dales National Park.

AVEBURY	Stones

Avebury, Nr Marlborough, Wiltshire SN8 1RF
Telephone: (067 23) 514 £30
Open: all day daily (closed mid Dec-mid Jan, also Mon-Fri Nov-mid Dec + mid Jan-Mar)
Meals served: 10-6

Seeing itself as part of a wider set of interests – both environmental and local – Stones is a restaurant with a mission. A resolutely vegetarian menu is available throughout the day offering wholesome things such as cheese scones, quiches, salads, and lip-smacking puds including their 'world-famous' date slices. Between midday and 2.30pm there is a selection of soups, savoury dishes – suitably named Megaliths – and their Mason's lunch – a choice of farmhouse cheeses with home-baked bread. You serve yourself and the bar offers some great ciders and other rural beverages. Prices are very reasonable, and it's enormously popular, especially on Sundays. If you want a foretaste, pop along to a bookshop and buy a copy of their cookbook.

AYLESBURY	Hartwell House

Oxford Road, Aylesbury, Buckinghamshire HP17 8NL
Telephone: (0296) 747444 £95
Fax: (0296) 747450
Open: lunch + dinner daily
Meals served: lunch 12.30-2, dinner 7.30-9.45

[handwritten annotation: excellent pool, tennis courts, spa bath & conference rooms + conference in thoughtfully converted coach house]

As you go up to your bedroom, pause on the staircase with its Jacobean carved figures and breathe in the history which this magnificent country house exudes. Superbly restored and furnished, it's hard to find fault. Standards in the kitchen are equally high, with Aidan McCormack performing to full potential using high-class raw materials. Fish arrives daily from around the land – Cornwall, Billingsgate and Scotland – ensuring freshness and variety. Meat is supplied by the royal estate at Highgrove. Sauces deftly complement the dishes and everything from the bread to the petits fours is made on the premises. A typical menu might include mussel and thyme soup, canon of venison roasted in juniper oil, and a hot praline soufflé baked in a pastry case. Despite the imposing surroundings, the professional staff still manage to provide friendly and helpful attention without stiffness or pomposity.

BAGSHOT	Pennyhill Park

London Road, Bagshot, Surrey GU19 5ET
Telephone: (0276) 71774 £65
Fax: (0276) 73217
Open: lunch + dinner daily
Meals served: lunch 12.30-2, dinner 7.30-10

Tennis, clay pigeon shooting, riding and golf with professional tuition are all organised here, even romantic and stress management weekends! This hotel and country club in 112 acres houses 76 attractive bedrooms, some in a converted coach house. Service and upkeep are high throughout.

BALLASALLA	La Rosette

Main Road, Ballasalla, Isle of Man
Telephone: (0624) 822940 £55
Open: lunch + dinner Mon-Sat (closed 2 wks Jan)
Meals served: lunch 12-3, dinner 7-10
Generous helpings of traditional French-style food.

BARHAM — Old Coach House

Dover Road, Barham, Nr Canterbury, Kent CT4 6SA
Telephone: (0227) 831218 £75
Open: lunch + dinner daily (but closed Sun dinner in winter)
Meals served: lunch 12-2, dinner 7-9

Bistro-style dining-room and elegant restaurant at this useful address on the A2 London to Dover road. It now has 10 bedrooms which makes it far preferable to staying in Dover or Canterbury. Friendly atmosphere – a real find.

BARNSLEY — Armstrong's

6 Shambles Street, Barnsley, South Yorkshire S70 2SQ
Telephone: (0226) 240113 £35
Open: lunch Tue-Fri, dinner Tue-Sat (closed Bank Holidays)
Meals served: lunch 12-2, dinner 7-10

Former brasserie-cum-bistro that has evolved into a restaurant of note, largely due to hard work from chef/proprietor Nick Pound. Pasta ribbons with oyster mushrooms, tomato concassée, madeira and chervil is a typical starter, with roast partridge with chestnuts and bacon as a main dish. Macon Rouge from Henri Lafarge and Penfolds Bin 389 are 2 examples from the keenly priced, well researched wine list. Good atmosphere and enjoyable food.

BARNSLEY — Restaurant Peano

102 Dodworth Road, Barnsley, South Yorkshire S70 6HL
Telephone: (0226) 244990 £50
Open: lunch Tue-Sat, dinner Mon-Sat (closed 2 wks Sep)
Meals served: lunch 12-2, dinner 7-9.30

The honeymoon period is over, but a year or so on and Michael Peano's restaurant is sustaining its initial impact in the area. His cooking is refreshingly unpretentious and thorough. Everything is made by him on the premises including the lovely bread. Home-made Jerusalem artichoke soup and baked onion served with pheasant pâté croutons are among the first courses, with lamb casserole and roast duckling in a honey and olive oil crust as main dishes. Part of Michael's ancestry can be glimpsed in the shrewd choice of Italian wines on the list. You could pay twice as much elsewhere for food not half as good as this.

BARNSTAPLE — Lynwood House

Bishop's Tawton Road, Barnstaple, Devon EX32 9DZ
Telephone: (0271) 43695 £55
Fax: (0271) 79340
Open: lunch + dinner Mon-Sat
Meals served: lunch 12-2, dinner 7-10

Mum and son Adam are in the kitchen, while dad and sons Matthew and Christian run the restaurant at this, the Roberts' family house. The seafood and organically grown vegetables are what eating here is all about and dishes such as a flimsey of fresh prawns, a plate of local mussels or a chunky home-made fish soup are super starters. Main courses might include a fillet of local turbot or the Lynwood Pot – various fish on a bed of rice in a rich white wine and cream sauce. Gourmet evenings are frequently arranged and offer the perfect opportunity to enjoy the cooking at its best. Five rooms are available and are thoughtfully equipped.

BASINGSTOKE — Audleys Wood

Alton Road, Basingstoke, Hampshire RG25 2JT
Telephone: (0256) 817555 £70
Fax: (0256) 817500
Open: lunch Sun-Fri, dinner daily (closed Bank Holidays)
Meals served: lunch 12-1.45 (Sun 12-2.15), dinner 7-9.45 (Fri+Sat 7-10.15, Sun 7-9.15)

There's not much call for Bradshaw's railway guide in these days of British Rail, but that's how Sir George Bradshaw made his pile. His house, Audleys Wood, is now a hotel with many attractive features including some fascinating examples of oak carving. The 71 bedrooms offer first class facilities and comfort. The aptly named Terence Greenhouse is chef to the restaurant set in what was the palm house and conservatory!

BASLOW — Cavendish Hotel

Baslow, Derbyshire DE4 1SP
Telephone: (0246) 582311 £60
Fax: (0246) 582312
Open: all day daily
Meals served: 11-11

Inside the 18th-century stone building the rooms are remarkably light and airy, an effect enhanced by a discreet choice of colours and materials. Views from the dining room and conservatory over the Chatsworth estate are among the pleasure you'll enjoy during your stay. A good selection on the fixed menus, with a choice of 7 starters, 6 main courses and the chef's special.

BASLOW — Fischer's Baslow Hall

Calver Road, Baslow, Derbyshire DE4 1RR
Telephone: (0246) 583259
Open: lunch Tue-Sun, dinner Mon-Sat (closed 25+26 Dec)
Meals served: lunch 12-2 (Sun 12-2.30), dinner 7-9.30 (Sat 7-10)

£70

Something special is the daily routine here at Baslow Hall. Max Fischer is firing on all cylinders in the kitchen as well as supervising his new catering enterprise on the side. Resisting the temptation to overcomplicate his cooking he serves up dishes that he can guarantee in terms of flavour, texture and consistency. Why try to be difficult for the sake of it? Thus a lunch menu might include a seafood ravioli or chef's salad with warm calves' liver among the starters, with fillet of beef maison with a herb and pepper sauce and roast saddle of spring lamb as main courses. Good selection of puds, and friendly service in the pleasant dining room. The 6 pretty country-style bedrooms allow you to enjoy your food in the evening without the prospect of the drive back home, or you could make a long weekend of it. It's well worth a visit!

BASSENTHWAITE LAKE — Armathwaite Hall

Bassenthwaite Lake, Nr Keswick, Cumbria CA12 4RE
Telephone: (076 87) 76551
Fax: (076 87) 76220
Open: lunch + dinner daily
Meals served: lunch 12.30-1.45, dinner 7.30-9.30
Set in 400 acres of deer park and woodlands the hotel makes an ideal base for the Lake District.

£70

BASSENTHWAITE LAKE — Pheasant Inn

Bassenthwaite Lake, Nr Cockermouth, Cumbria CA13 9YE
Telephone: (076 87) 76234
Open: (closed 25 Dec)
Meals served: lunch 12-1.30, dinner 7.30-8.15
Elegant dining room, good service, modern food in typical Lake District inn.

£50

BATH — Bath Spa Hotel

Sydney Road, Bath, Avon BA2 6BX
Telephone: (0225) 444424
Fax: (0225) 444006
Open: lunch + dinner daily
Meals served: lunch 12-2.30, dinner 7-10 (Sat 7-10.30)

£75

Robin Sheppard is now at the helm of Forte's quintessential hotel set in the seductive landscape of Georgian Bath. With a realistic nod to times of recession, he has lowered this exemplary operation's sights from the rarefied atmosphere of hotel elites to a more accessible but no less cosseting level. Fine furnishings and fabrics blend effortlessly with the architecture in individually-styled bedrooms and public rooms; bathrooms of mahogany and marble are beyond criticism, and the suites and leisure facilities rival the best of the rest. Attentive personal service helps make complete the deception, that it is a homely country house and not a 100-room city centre hotel.

Chef Alec Howard is making his mark with assured derivative cooking of salmon with broad beans and shallots, guineafowl with lentils, smoked bacon and parmentier vegetables, glazed Gressingham duck with apple and cider confit, but it is his cheaper mediterranean-influenced luncheon menus that are the hit. Excellent choice of wines by the glass.

BATH — Circus Restaurant

34 Brock Street, Bath, Avon BA1 2LN
Telephone: (0225) 330208   £50
Open: lunch + dinner Tue-Sat (closed 25+26 Dec, 1 Jan, Easter Monday)
Meals served: lunch 11.30-2.30, dinner 6.30-10 (Sat 6.30-11.30)

Robert Rees is now at the stoves of this city centre 'food is fun' restaurant. Dependable, familiar food with lunchtimes providing particularly good value.

BATH — Homewood Park

Hinton Charterhouse, Freshford, Bath, Avon BA3 6BB
Telephone: (0225) 723731   £75
Fax: (0225) 723820
Open: lunch + dinner daily
Meals served: lunch 12-1.45, dinner 7-9.30

An appealing, unassuming country house standing in gently rolling wooded grounds, offering 15 attractively designed and furnished bedrooms and relaxing art-filled day rooms. Fixed price 3-course dinners include a roquefort and spinach soufflé to start, roast wood pigeon or saddle of Somerset roe deer with a port and ginger sauce for main course and caramelized apples in brioche with a rum and raisin custard for pud. A small but carefully chosen wine list.

BATH	Popjoy's
Beau Nash House, Sawclose, Bath, Avon BA1 1EU
Telephone: (0225) 460494 £60
Open: lunch Tue-Fri, dinner Tue-Sat (closed Bank Holidays except 25 Dec)
Meals served: lunch 12-2, dinner 7-11
Charming Georgian house with quite formal dining room and modern food.

BATH — Priory Hotel

Weston Road, Bath, Avon BA1 2XT
Telephone: (0225) 331922 £70
Fax: (0225) 448276
Open: lunch + dinner daily
Meals served: lunch 12-2, dinner 7-9

Despite its recent setbacks, the Priory with its delightful city-fringe garden setting enchants with the style and luxury of a country gentleman's residence. Michael Collom is still at the stoves producing consistent and enjoyable food served in 3 contrastingly decorated dining rooms.

BATH — Queensberry Hotel

Russel Street Bath, Avon BA1 2QT
Telephone: (0225) 447928 £50
Fax: (0225) 446065
Open: lunch + dinner daily (closed 2 wks Xmas/New Year)
Meals served: lunch 12-2, dinner 7-10.30

Stephen and Penny Ross, having established their pedigree in the '80s at the award-winning Homewood Park, seem destined to make their mark in the '90s at their sympathetically converted terrace of John Wood-designed town houses in one of Bath's quieter streets, not far from the Upper Rooms. Twenty bedrooms are models of genteel style and comfort, some retaining their Regency ceilings. The newly opened basement Olive Tree restaurant brings Stephen back to the kitchen, together with some of his old team. Clearly influenced by recent trends, his food is more mediterranean and accessible than at Homewood.

BATH	Woods
9-13 Alfred Street, Bath, Avon BA1 2QX
Telephone: (0225) 314812 £50
Fax: (0225) 443146
Open: lunch + dinner Mon-Sat (closed 24-29 Dec)
Meals served: lunch 12-2.15, dinner 6.30-10.15 (brasserie Mon-Fri 11-11, Sat 11-3)
Popular local haunt near the centre of Bath.

BATH — Royal Crescent Hotel

16 Royal Crescent, Bath, Avon BA1 2LS
Telephone: (0225) 319090 £90
Fax: (0225) 339401
Open: lunch + dinner daily
Meals served: lunch 12.30-2, dinner 7-9.30

If you're after an address when staying in Bath it's hard to think of anywhere more illustrious than the Royal Crescent. It goes without saying that this is a first-rate establishment and in some respects holds its own with the very best in the country. The big news this year concerns the restaurant where – after much rumour and conjecture – Steven Blake has just succeeded Michael Croft in the kitchen.

BEANACRE — Beechfield House

Beanacre, Nr Melksham, Wiltshire SN12 7PU
Telephone: (0225) 703700 £50
Fax: (0225) 790118
Open: lunch + dinner daily
Meals served: lunch 12-2, dinner 7-9.30

A Wiltshire hotel which caters mostly for short weekend break customers and special occasions. Attractive gardens with many unusual trees provide a tranquil setting and pleasant views from the 24 rooms.

BEAULIEU — Montagu Arms

Beaulieu, Hampshire SO42 7ZL
Telephone: (0590) 612324 £55
Fax: (0590) 612188
Open: lunch + dinner daily
Meals served: lunch 12.30-2, dinner 7.30-9.30 (Fri+Sat 7.30-10)
Lovely New Forest setting, gardens, conservatory.

BECKINGHAM — Black Swan

Hillside, Beckingham, Lincolnshire LN5 0RF
Telephone: (0636) 626474 £50
Open: dinner Tue-Sat
Meals served: dinner 7-10

17th-century coaching inn on the banks of the River Witham. Dishes include Lincolnshire hare stew, baked pheasant breast in pastry and poached monkfish. Booking is vital.

BELTON   Belton Woods Hotel

Belton, Nr Grantham, Lincolnshire NG32 2LN
Telephone: (0476) 593200   £60
Fax: (0476) 74547
Open: lunch Sun-Fri, dinner Mon-Sat
Meals served: lunch 12.30-2.30 (Sun 12-2.30), dinner 7-10
New hotel and leisure centre in acres of grounds, good facilities for children as well.

BERWICK-ON-TWEED   Funnywayt'mekalivin

53 West Street, Berwick-on-Tweed, Northumberland TD15 1AS
Telephone: (0289) 308827   £40
Open: dinner Thu-Sat (closed 25+26 Dec, 1 Jan)
Meals served: dinner at 8
A set meal can last three hours at this unlicensed reataurant.

BIBURY   The Swan

Bibury, Gloucestershire GL7 5NW
Telephone: (0285) 740204   £45
Fax: (0285) 740473
Open: lunch + dinner daily
Meals served: lunch 12-2, dinner 7-8.30
Recently re-opened after extensive refurbishment. Lovely riverside setting, comfortable lounges.

BIGBURY-ON-SEA   Burgh Island Hotel

Burgh Island, Bigbury-on-Sea, Devon TQ7 4AU
Telephone: (0548) 810514   £70
Fax: (0548) 810243
Open: lunch + dinner daily
Meals served: lunch 12-2, dinner 7.30-9

Cast away cares as you wash up at this private island. Ideal for gregarious '30s Robinson Crusoes, this Art Deco hotel is quite special with its period furnishings and decor. Half board terms only allow exploration of new chef Adrian Parker's (ex Mosimann's and a 'stage' with Alain Senderens in Paris) expanded menu. Telephone before arrival for information on the tides and the tractor which will ferry you across.

BILBROUGH   Bilbrough Manor

Bilbrough, York, North Yorkshire YO2 3PH
Telephone: (0937) 834002
Fax: (0937) 834724
Open: lunch + dinner daily (closed 25-29 Dec)
Meals served: lunch 12-2, dinner 7-9.30 (Sun 7-9)

£70

Plans to add about 14 bedrooms at Bilbrough will I'm sure be realised in such a way so as not to spoil what's so attractive about the place – the sense of being happy in itself. It really is a lovely hotel – the oak-panelled dining room, the leaded windows, the warm colours throughout – it would be a shame to spoil it. Service is exemplary. Owners Colin and Sue Bell are there should you need anything, but it all seems to have been taken care of already! As for the food, it's in the capable hands of chef Andrew Pressley who dishes up some interesting ideas. Hot pot of Dublin Bay prawns and queen scallops and pan-fried fillet of Highland beef with a celeriac and tarragon timbale are examples from the carte. There are also vegetarian and 4-course gourmet menus and be sure to try the croustillant, a house speciality dessert. The mainly French wine list makes the occasional foray into the New World and there's also a generous selection of half bottles available. *See also page 236 – our Clover Award Section.*

BIRDLIP   Kingshead House

Birdlip, Nr Gloucester, Gloucestershire GL4 8JH
Telephone: (0452) 862299
Open: lunch Tue-Fri+Sun, dinner Tue-Sat (closed 25+26 Dec, 1 Jan)
Meals served: lunch 12.30-2.15 (Sun 12.30-2), dinner 7.30-10

£45

Chef Judy Knock draws her inspiration from 18th-century cookery books from both sides of the channel. Menus change two or three times a week and offer medaillions of pork with spinach, stilton and walnuts, and marmite des poissons à la Normande (white and shellfish in a cider, cream and saffron sauce) as typical main courses. A vegetarian option is always included. Nice views out over the fields, and one ensuite bedroom available should the carefully chosen wine list be explored too fully!

BIRMINGHAM — Chung Ying

16 Wrottesley Street, Birmingham, West Midlands B5 6RT
Telephone: 021-622 5669
Open: all day daily (closed 25 Dec)
Meals served: 12-12

£35

Original of the two Chung Ying restaurants, offering a similar menu.

BIRMINGHAM — Chung Ying Garden

17 Thorp Street, Birmingham, West Midlands B5 4AT
Telephone: 021-666 6622
Open: all day daily (closed 25 Dec)
Meals served: 12-11.30 (Sun 12-10.30)

£35

Smart, efficient restaurant offering a wide range of fim sum and other favourites, all served in generous portions.

BIRMINGHAM — Henry Wong

283 High Street, Harborne, Birmingham, West Midlands B3 1RB
Telephone: 021-427 9799
Open: lunch + dinner Mon-Sat (closed Bank Holidays, 1 wk Aug)
Meals served: lunch 12-1.45, dinner 6-11 (Fri+Sat 6-11.30)

£35

Good Cantonese restaurant at the end of the High Street.

BIRMINGHAM — Norton Place

The Patrick Collection, 180 Lifford Lane, Kings Norton, Birmingham, West Midlands B30 3NT
Telephone: 021-433-5656
Fax: 021-433-3048
Open: lunch + dinner daily
Meals served: lunch 12-2.30, dinner 7-10 (Sun 7-9)

£55

Situated within the walled gardens of the Patrick Collection – a car museum – this must rate as one of the more unusual hotel and restaurant locations in the country. This said, Norton Place offers all that you would expect of a new luxury enterprise clearly designed for the business guest and conference circuit market. Former sous chef Anthony Morgan is now the boss in the kitchen and cooks a variety of customized dishes for the executive palate. All round it's a set-up which aims to impress.

BIRMINGHAM — Sloans

27 Chad Square, Hawthorne Road, Edgbaston, Birmingham, West Midlands B15 3TQ
Telephone: 021-455 6697 £65
Fax: 021-454 4335
Open: lunch Mon-Fri, dinner Mon-Sat (closed Bank Holidays, 1wk Xmas)
Meals served: lunch 12-2, dinner 7-10

Like the shopping precinct setting there is nothing pretentious about the approach here, and novelty is scrupulously avoided. Even though Roger Narbett has moved on to fresh fields (at London's Dorchester Hotel), former sous chef Simon Booth now heads the team and if he possesses even a hint of the dedication and talent of his mentor, Birmingham will still enjoy a restaurant of the highest calibre, offering the likes of scallops marinated in lime and ginger, grilled salmon with asparagus, feves and green pea sauce, or breast of duck served with morel mushrooms, braised baby leeks and madeira sauce.

BIRMINGHAM — Swallow Hotel

12 Hagley Road, Five Ways, Birmingham, West Midlands B16 8SJ
Telephone: 021-452 1144 £65
Fax: 021-456 3442
Open: lunch Sun-Fri, dinner daily
Meals served: lunch 12.30-2.30, dinner 7.30-10.30

All too often an establishment aims to achieve distinction by associating itself with an historical figure or famous celebrity rather than establishing its own credentials in terms of excellent food and service, and yet there are exceptions, and the Sir Edward Elgar Restaurant at the Swallow Hotel is one. With a chef of Idris Caldora's calibre in the kitchen, there's no need to search for credibility – the proof is there on the plate in front of you. Dishes such as ravioli of veal sweetbreads scented with coriander and ginger and a mousse of pike on a bed of cèpes are among the starters. Main courses range from braised halibut with fennel, flavoured with pernod in a light butter sauce to fillet of beef with 5 types of onion in a Madeira sauce. Classical French cuisine, performed in the modern way, amid the most English of settings. As for the Swallow Hotel, it preserves its feel of studied opulence and ranks as a first class place in which to stay.

BISHOP'S TAWTON — Halmpstone Manor

Bishop's Tawton, Barnstaple, Devon EX32 0EA
Telephone: (0271) 830321 £55
Fax: (0271) 830826
Open: dinner daily
Meals served: dinner 7-9.30

A peaceful rural setting for this 5-bedroomed hotel run by the Stanburys. Plenty of comforts and some enjoyable food in the dining room – pheasant sausage with wild rice and mushrooms, steamed seabass with a tarragon sauce – combine with the surroundings to make this a good choice when in this part of Devon.

BLACKPOOL	September Brasserie

15-17 Queen Street, Blackpool, Lancashire FY1 1PU
Telephone: (0253) 23282 £40
Open: lunch + dinner Tue-Sat (closed 25+26 Dec, Good Friday)
Meals served: lunch 12-2.30, dinner 7-9.30

The September Brasserie is an illumination in its own right, concealed only be the unremarkable surroundings. Chef Michael Golowicz has done stints in famous restaurants, but now he's elected to do his own thing in Blackpool. Ingredients, including some wines, are as green as they come – free from chemicals, additives and colourings – and pressed into service to great effect. The stylishly hand-written rather eclectic menu includes shellfish soup with lobster ravioli and aïoli, poached turbot with lemon butter and grapefruit, even civet of kangaroo on green lentils, and shows just how seriously Michael takes his cooking. Very much a one-man band, his request for his guests' patience while awaiting their meal would be churlish to refuse. Such single-minded pursuit of quality food deserves that and more. This would be good anywhere in Britain but it's especially good in Blackpool.

BLACKWATER	Long's

Blackwater, Truro, Cornwall TR4 8HH
Telephone: (0872) 561111 £50
Open: lunch Sun, dinner Wed-Sat (closed Bank Holidays, 3/4 wks Jan/Feb)
Meals served: lunch 12.30-1.45, dinner 7.30-9.30

You'll find no half measures here. Chef Ann Long takes enormous trouble to ensure the highest possible standards in her kitchen. She is a staunch believer in the traditional ways of preparing food and turns her nose up at the current vogue for jus. Her sauces are the real thing, having been strained through a muslin cloth time after time to achieve ever greater clarity. Such painstaking work is more than justified in the final results and her restaurant deserves wider acclaim. Typical offerings include a duck parcel with spiced rice and a clear plum purée, poached escalope of salmon with creamed prawns and mushrooms, and mixed fruit crumble with vanilla custard.

BLACKWATER	Pennypots

Blackwater, Truro, Cornwall TR4 8EY
Telephone: (0209) 820347 £50
Open: dinner Tue-Sun (closed Sun in winter, 26 Dec, 1 Jan, 3 wks Winter)
Meals served: dinner 7.00-10
Probably one of the most well-established restaurants in the area. 30 seats.

Blandford Forum — La Belle Alliance

Whitecliff Mill Street, Blandford Forum, Dorset DT11 7BP
Telephone: (0258) 452842 £50
Fax: (0258) 480054
Open: dinner Tue-Sat (closed Bank Holidays, Jan)
Meals served: dinner 7-9.30 (Sat 7-10)

A restaurant with rooms run by husband and wife team Philip and Lauren Davison. Philip cooks and is keen to provide healthy dishes while still respecting the classical tradition. From the set price menu, a hot soufflé of Stilton and a salad of deep-fried celery and pine kernels might be followed by roast breast of French duck, thinly sliced and served on a bed of braised lentils. A terrine of apples with a chilled cider sauce is an attractive dessert. The newly revised wine list offers some good value drinking.

Bollington — Mauro's

88 Palmerston Street, Bollington, Nr Macclesfield, Cheshire SK10 5PW
Telephone: (0625) 573898 £50
Open: lunch + dinner Tue-Sat (closed 25+26 Dec, 3 wks Aug/Sep)
Meals served: lunch 12.15-2 (Sat 12.15-1.30), dinner 7-10, (Sat 7-10.30)

We could do with a few more places like Mauro's. Certainly going by our last visit, it looks set to prosper, with lunchtime eating at bargain prices. Select a wine from the well-chosen list and await dishes such as stracciatella alla Romana and vitello alla Milanese, which bring back happy memories of Italy – all flavour and sunshine. Gillian and Enzo Mauro's enthusiasm for their restaurant is contagious, and leaves you in ebullient mood. Molto bene!

Bollington — Randalls

22 High Street, Old Market Place, Bollington, Cheshire SK10 5PH
Telephone: (0625) 575058 £40
Open: lunch Sun, dinner Tue-Sat
Meals served: lunch 12.30-2.30, dinner 7-10 (Fri+Sat 7-10.30)
Friendly neighbourhood restaurant.

Bolton Abbey — Devonshire Arms

Bolton Abbey, Nr Skipton, North Yorkshire BD23 6AJ
Telephone: (075 671) 441 £60
Fax: (075 671) 564
Open: lunch + dinner daily
Meals served: lunch 12-2, dinner 7-10 (Sun 7-9.30)

Fine country hotel in former roadside coaching inn belonging to the Duke of Devonshire. Admire the lovely family heirlooms in the public rooms. Try to stay in one of the bedrooms in the original building itself.

Bonchurch	Winterbourne Hotel

Bonchurch, Isle of Wight PO38 1RQ
Telephone: (0983) 852535 £45
Fax: (0983) 853056
Open: dinner daily (closed mid Nov-early Mar)
Meals served: dinner 6.30-10

No doubt Dickens fans feature highly among the guests since it was here that he sought peace and seclusion while writing *David Copperfield*. He found the house the prettiest place imaginable and you can see why. Today as a hotel it retains its informal lived-in feel and the gardens are delightful throughout the seasons.

Botley	Cobbett's

15 The Square, Botley, Southampton, Hampshire SO3 2EA
Telephone: (0489) 782068 £60
Open: lunch Tue-Fri + Sun, dinner Mon-Sat (closed Bank Holidays, 2 wks summer, 2 wks winter)
Meals served: lunch 12-2, dinner 7.30-10 (Sat 7-10)

Overall there's a Tudor feel to this village restaurant with its open log fires, tapestry-like curtains and low beams. Starters include salade de pissenlits and terrine de truite fumé, while pigeon de bois aux raisins and côte de boeuf à la graine de moutarde are possible main courses. All good stuff, and the cheeses are well kept – try a selection of reblochon, chaumes and époisses. Every so often there's a gourmet evening which matches French regional specialities to the area's wines. Take your pick from Brittany, Burgundy, Bordeaux, the Loire or Provence. Everyone tries very hard to send you away happy, and as the Skipwiths write on the brochure, this is 'The restaurant where your pleasure is our challenge and reward'. This is a good local restaurant.

Boughton Monchelsea	Tanyard Hotel

Wierton Hill, Boughton Monchelsea, Nr Maidstone, Kent ME17 4JT
Telephone: (0622) 744705 £50
Open: dinner daily (closed Dec+Jan)
Meals served: dinner at 8

At the opposite end of the market to the new executive-orientated conference-leisure complexes, Jan Davies' 6-bedroomed hotel strives to retain its rough edges and creaking floorboards to make sure the human side of things isn't lost. The medieval building has lost none of its character but thankfully has enough modern contrivances to keep body and soul together! Guests are encouraged to get to know one another. Lovely surroundings.

BOURNEMOUTH — Royal Bath Hotel

Bath Road, Bournemouth, Dorset BH1 2EW
Telephone: (0202) 555555 £70
Fax: (0202) 554158
Open: lunch + dinner Mon-Fri (closed 25 Dec)
Meals served: lunch 12.30-2.15, dinner 6.30-10.15

With its imposing position overlooking its own gardens, the pier, the beach and the sea the Royal Bath makes for a pleasant stay. This large hotel boasts several reception rooms of varying sizes, plus its own swimming pool and fitness suite. Bedrooms are mostly of a good size, the best ones with a sea view carrying a supplement which is well worth paying. The bonus at the Royal Bath is the quality of the food. In a hotel dining room of this size you wouldn't normally expect to be served the choice and quality of food that is on offer here. It leaves the competition way behind. Pleasant and helpful service from a regular team with additional outside support in the season. An alternative is to eat in the smaller Oscars Restaurant, which is building up a steady clientele as a restaurant in its own right.

BOWNESS-ON-WINDERMERE — Gilpin Lodge

Crook Road, Bowness-on-Windermere, Cumbria LA23 3NE
Telephone: (053 94) 88818 £55
Fax: (053 94) 88058
Open: lunch Sun, dinner daily
Meals served: lunch 12.30-1.45, dinner 7-9

Venison pâté in a filo pastry parcel, oyster and sage soup, a brace of boned quail stuffed with asparagus mousse and a selection of desserts to finish would be a representative meal here at Gilpin Lodge, the proceedings overseen by Christian Cunliffe who cut her teeth at the restaurant in Bath, the Hole in the Wall. The good food is equalled by a high level of housekeeping in the hotel, the 9 homely bedrooms full of books and flowers, some with pine four-poster beds. Guests have free use of the leisure facilities at a nearby country club.

BOWNESS-ON-WINDERMERE — Linthwaite House

Bowness-on-Windermere, Cumbria LA23 3JA
Telephone: (053 94) 88600 £50
Fax: (053 94) 88601
Open: lunch Sun, dinner daily (closed 24-26 Dec)
Meals served: lunch 12-2, dinner 7.15-9

Owner Mike Bevans says he really doesn't mind if you want to put your feet up on the coffee table after the meal. Not that you would, I'm sure! But it just shows how strongly he feels that you should feel at home and how little he rates that over-inflated sense of importance some country houses seem to possess. Superb views are to be had from the terrace – mountaineering buffs will recognise the peaks of Skiddaw and Helvellyn – while indoors you'll find the heights of comfort and attention. Yes, you can please yourself but you're not uncared for and everyone, including the staff, seems to be having a good time. As they say in the brochure: the hotel you always promised yourself you would stay at.

BRADFIELD COMBUST	**Bradfield House**

Bradfield Combust, Nr Bury St Edmunds, Suffolk IP30 0LR
Telephone: (0284) 386301 £40
Open: lunch Sun, dinner Tue-Sat (closed 25 Dec)
Meals served: lunch 12-1.45, dinner 7-9 (Sat 7-9.30)
Roy & Sally Ghijben's perennially popular restaurant with rooms.

BRADFORD	**Restaurant 19**

Belevedere Hotel, 19 North Park Road, Heaton, Bradford, West Yorkshire BD9 4NT
Telephone: (0274) 492559 £70
Open: dinner Tue-Sat (closed 1 wk Xmas, 1 wk May, 1 wk Aug/Sep)
Meals served: dinner 7-10

When you finally draw up before it you might well think twice before entering – the Victorian building looks slightly forbidding. However a hearty welcome by Robert Barbour dispels any worries and you'll warm to the elegant restaurant right away. Chef and partner Stephen Smith supplies the food and jolly good it is too. A recent 4-course dinner offered fillet of red mullet with warm potato salad and pesto sauce as a first course, a soup of cucumber, lettuce and spring onion flavoured with lovage, followed by corn-fed poussin cooked in riesling and infused with tarragon. A chocolate amaretti pie came as dessert and coffee and petits fours brought the evening to a close. A real achievement wherever it might happen to be – here in Bradford it's nothing short of miraculous! Four comfortable bedrooms may be useful of the joys of some great wines at very reasonable prices get too much.

BRADFORD-ON-AVON	**Leigh Park Hotel**

Leigh Road West, Bradford-on-Avon, Wiltshire BA15 2RA
Telephone: (022 16) 4885 £55
Fax: (022 16) 2315
Open: lunch + dinner daily
Meals served: lunch 12-2, dinner 7-9.30
Georgian country house hotel with a restaurant which offers both traditional English andFrench cuisine.

Bradford-on-Avon — Woolley Grange

Woolley Green, Bradford-on-Avon, Wiltshire BA15 1TX
Telephone: (022 16) 4705 £65
Fax: (022 16) 4059
Open: lunch + dinner daily
Meals served: lunch 12-2.30 (Sat + Sun 12-3), dinner 7-10

There's nothing pompous or highbrow here, you can relax and be yourself and even the kids are welcome. It's the sort of place you take to immediately and want to return to another day. The Chapmans' delightful country house operation continues to defy the recession largely due to their creative flair and no-nonsense approach. Twenty rooms all contain period double beds with modest comforts and homely touches, some have gas log fires and can interconnect for family groups.

New chef Colin White is fortunate in having some superb home-grown fruit and vegetables to use in his cooking. A lighter luncheon menu is now offered in addition to the reasonably priced set menus for lunch and dinner. Griddled polenta with woodland mushrooms, salmis of pigeon with a red wine sauce and warm cherry tart with clotted cream is a typical meal. A 'customers favourites' wine list with a good selection of half bottles and some excellent producers.

Bramley — Le Berger

4a High Street, Bramley, Nr Guildford, Surrey GU5 0HB
Telephone: (0483) 894037 £60
Open: Tue-Sat (closed Bank Holidays except Easter Sunday, 2 wks Jan)
Meals served: lunch 12-2, dinner 7-9.30
Modern style food with very subtle flavours, simple and modern decor, efficient service.

BRAMPTON — Farlam Hall

Hallbankgate, Brampton, Cumbria CA8 2NG
Telephone: (069 77) 46234
Fax: (069 77) 46683
Open: dinner daily (closed 25-30 Dec, Feb)
Meals served: dinner at 8

£55

Standing in attractive grounds complete with lake about 2 miles from Brampton, this relaxing and homely country house offers tasteful Victorian-style accommodation and equally comforting cooking. There's one sitting for dinner, Barry Quinion's fixed price menu utilising local produce in dishes such as melon with West Cumberland cured ham and individual pigeon, wild mushroom and port casserole with a puff pastry lid. Excellent breakfasts. Half board terms only.

BRAY-ON-THAMES — The Waterside Inn

Ferry Road, Bray-on-Thames, Berkshire SL6 2AT
Telephone: (0628) 20691
Fax: (0628) 784710
Open: lunch Wed-Sun, dinner Tue-Sat (also Sun in summer), (closed Bank Holidays except lunch 25 Dec, Xmas-mid Feb)
Meals served: lunch 12-2 (Sun 12-3), dinner 7-10

— sparkling new decor & appointments

£130

Don't be misled by Michel's lighter, more carefree manner in his television squabbles with his brother. He's every bit as demanding in his own kitchen at the Waterside Inn as Albert is at Le Gavroche. Here at this charming restaurant on the banks of the Thames the standards are the very highest imaginable. The slightest criticism is taken to heart and corrected with unfailing charm. The Menu Exceptionnel is a fitting showcase for Michel's many talents and allows diners to sample some of the best cooking in the land. A raviole de foie gras, jus de volaille sur coulis de champignons sauvages starts the ball rolling followed by filet de Saint-Pierre sous petit paillasson de pommes de terre, sauce cidre doux. A pause is allowed to revive a palate already swooning with flavours, before noisettes d'agneau rôties à la senteur de genièvre arrive. One of those heart-rending choices follow as you decide between the delicious selection of cheeses or one of the renowned desserts by this great pâtissier. Coffee and petits fours may be taken out on the terrace. The wine list of mainly French greats is high on quality and depth. Six individually styled bedrooms prolong the pleasure further, and the private dining room means that the Waterside can now accommodate board meetings followed by lunch and dinner and an overnight stay. Having had the privilege of eating in some of the most highly-regarded restaurants in France, I have to say that Michel Roux's Waterside Inn rates with the best of them, and his national and international following is justly deserved.

See also page 237 – our Clover Award Section.

BRIDPORT — Riverside Restaurant

West Bay, Bridport, Dorset DT6 4EZ
Telephone: (0308) 22011 £35
Open: lunch daily, dinner Mon-Sat, + Sun in summer (closed Mon in winter, early Dec-early Mar)
Meals served: lunch 11.30-3 (Sat+Sun 11.30-4, earlier in winter), dinner 6.30-8.30

If you're not in a hurry and don't feel too self-important then this is the place for you. At least, that's what Arthur and Janet Watson say about their popular, bustling restaurant plus self-service café. Fish and shellfish are their strong suit, and dishes such as grilled cod steak with parsley sauce, fillet of brill, and West Bay scallops come weighing down the plates. People arrive from far and wide, families especially, and you may have to wait to take your turn. It's a very good idea to book. They have been known to extend their opening hours in high season. Customers range from local fisherman to overseas visitors, staff are young and friendly. Arthur also runs the local post office next door.

BRIDPORT — Will's

4-6 Barrack Street, Bridport, Dorset DT6 3LY
Telephone: (0308) 27517 £35
Open: dinner Tue-Sat + Mon in summer (closed Bank Holidays, 2 wks Oct/Nov)
Meals served: dinner 7-9.45 (Sat 7-10.15)
Chef/proprietor Will Longman's informal, comfortable restaurant offering seasonally-changing menus.

BRIGHTLING — Jack Fuller's

Oxley Green, Brightling, Nr Robertstbridge, East Sussex TN32 5HD
Telephone: (042 482) 212 £40
Open: lunch Tue-Sun, dinner Tue-Sat
Meals served: lunch 12-2.30, dinner 7.10

The handsomely paunched gent on the sign has clearly been indulging himself rather too often at this former pub. There's bags of choice on the menu including hearty dishes such as gammon and onion pudding, steak and kidney pie, beef stew and dumplings. Jack Fuller's puddings – should you still have room – are good old fashioned stalwarts like mother's bread pudding and sticky treacle tart. Terrific value grub.

BRIGHTON — Grand Hotel

King's Road, Brighton, East Sussex BN1 2FW
Telephone: (0273) 21188 £80
Fax: (0273) 202694
Open: lunch + dinner daily
Meals served: lunch 12-2, dinner 7-10

Much care has been taken to restore this grand 160-bedroomed hotel in its original style. Simpler choices are best from the menu in the King's Restaurant. Afternoon tea is served in the conservatory overlooking the promenade. The Grand also has its own night club andhealth spa.

BRIGHTON — Le Grandgousier

15 Western Street, Brighton, East Sussex BN1 2PG
Telephone: (0273) 772005 £30
Open: lunch Mon-Fri, dinner Mon-Sat (closed 23 Dec-3 Jan)
Meals served: lunch 12.30-2, dinner 7.30-9.30 (Sat 7.15-10.45)

Family-run French restaurant that's been going strong since 1977. The 6-course menu has a regularly-changing plat du jour or a choice of 6 main courses. The price includes a half-bottle of wine and offers excellent value in an informal bistro atmosphere. There's a short, reasonably-priced wine list.

BRIGHTON — Hayward's

51/52 North Street, Brighton, East Sussex BN1 1RH
Telephone: (0273) 24261 £35
Fax: (0273) 24228
Open: lunch Mon-Sat, dinner Tue-Sat (closed Bank Holidays, Xmas/New Year)
Meals served: lunch 12-3, dinner 6.30-10.30 (Sat 10am-11pm)
Elegant restaurant serving dishes based on English and French classics.

BRIGHTON — Hospitality Inn

Kings Road, Brighton, East Sussex BN1 2GS
Telephone: (0273) 206700 £80
Fax: (0273) 820692
Open: lunch Mon-Fri, dinner Mon-Sat (closed some Bank Holidays)
Meals served: lunch 12-2.15, dinner 7-10.15

Overlooking the sea-front, this large hotel has very modern decor and facilities that range from banqueting to a health club. The restaurant La Noblesse offers some modern interpretations of classic dishes.

BRIGHTON — Langan's Bistro

1 Paston Place, Brighton, East Sussex BN2 1HA
Telephone: (0273) 606933 £55
Open: lunch Tue-Fri, dinner Tue-Sat (closed 26 Dec, 2 wks Jan, 2 wks Aug)
Meals served: lunch 12.30-2.30, dinner 7.30-10.30

Peter Langan's name lives on here in Brighton as well as in the busy metropolis. The 'bistro' tag is a bit misleading given the quality of the food. Gratin of salmon trout and tournedos au vin rouge with a trio of chocolate for pud will do very nicely and will have many seasoned Londoners suffering a pleasant bout of déjà vu.

BRIGHTON — La Marinade

77 St George's Road, Kemp Town, Brighton, East Sussex BN2 5QT
Telephone: (0273) 600992 £45
Open: lunch Tue-Fri + Sun, dinner Tue-Sat
Meals served: lunch 12.15-2, dinner 7.15-10

M. Volant directs operations in the downstairs dining room. Very traditional French cooking using good ingredients with respect for their natural flavours. The fixed price menus make for good value eating.

BRIGHTON — Topps Hotel

17 Regency Square, Brighton, East Sussex BN1 2FG
Telephone: (0273) 729334
Fax: (0273) 203679
Open: dinner Thu-Sat + Mon-Tue (closed Jan)
Meals served: dinner 7-9.30

£45

Topps Hotel's 14 bright and airy bedrooms have a nice holiday atmosphere, are comfortably furnished and have several nice touches such as plants by the windows and good quality toiletries in the bathrooms. For the basement dining room (no longer called Bottoms), Pauline Collins' cooking combines English and French styles to good effect. Superb breakfasts served by husband Paul. Nothing is too much trouble for this friendly hotel.

BRIMFIELD — Poppies Restaurant

The Roebuck Hotel, Brimfield, Nr Ludlow, Shropshire SY8 4NE
Telephone: (058 472) 230
Open: lunch + dinner Tue-Sat (closed Xmas, 2 wks Feb, 1 wk Oct)
Meals served: lunch 12-2, dinner 7-10

— good local restaurant £60

Poppies is always a place I look forward to visiting. Chef Carole Evans is a lesson to us all and proves that culinary skill is not always something that you acquire with certificates. She's picked up what she knows along the way and thus her cooking is original and spontaneous. The main menu is supplemented by blackboard specials and might feature old fashioned steak and kidney pie or grilled salmon with a chive cream sauce. Save space for her puds, and lovers of cheese will be well satisfied with the likes of Llangloffan, Cashel Blue and Skirrid which are listed on a separate card. Around 25 half bottles are now to be found amongst the wines. If you're dining late, there is a choice of 3 comfortable bedrooms.

BRISTOL — Bistro Twenty One

21 Cotham Road South, Kingsdown, Bristol, Avon BS6 5TZ
Telephone: (0272) 421744
Open: lunch Mon-Fri, dinner Mon-Sat (closed 1 wk Xmas)
Meals served: lunch 12-2.30, dinner 6.30-11.30
Busy, popular bistro, friendly service, long menu.

£45

BRISTOL — Blue Goose

344 Gloucester Road, Bristol, Avon
Telephone: (0272) 420940
Open: dinner Mon-Sat
Meals served: dinner 6.30-11.45
Bistro setting, solid cooking.

£40

BRISTOL	Howard's

1A Avon Crescent, Bristol, Avon BS1 6XQ
Telephone: (0272) 22921 £45
Open: lunch Mon-Fri, dinner Mon-Sat (closed 25+26 Dec)
Meals served: lunch 12-2, dinner 7-11 (Sat 7-11.30)

You can kill two birds with one stone at Howard's by eating and enjoying the view of Brunel's Clifton Suspension Bridge at the same time. The seasonal à la carte is supplemented by daily specials and many come to enjoy the home-smoked dishes. A large number of business types at lunchtime give way to a youngish crowd in the evenings.

BRISTOL	Hunt's

26 Broad Street, Bristol, Avon BS1 2HG
Telephone: (0272) 265580 £50
Open: lunch Tue-Fri, dinner Tue-Sat (closed Bank Holidays, 2 wks Aug)
Meals served: lunch 12-2, dinner 7-10

The Hunt that was with Markwick, Andrew (and wife Anne) have struck out on their own and have rapidly secured a loyal following at their pleasant restaurant by St John's Arch. A sensible lunchtime fixed price menu offers a choice of aperitif as a starter, followed by perhaps fillets of red mullet en papillote with anchovy and coffee for around £12. Typical choices from the à la carte menu – moules marinières or venison and guineafowl terrine with Cumberland sauce to start, noisettes of veal fillet with wild mushrooms and Malaga or perhaps monkfish with green peppercorns and port as main course. This solo venture should allow Andy to realise fully the potential of his down-to-earth creativity.

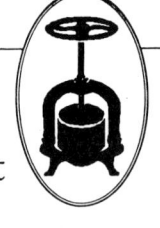

HUNT'S
Restaurant

BRISTOL	Lettonie

9 Druid Hill, Stoke Bishop, Bristol, Avon BS9 1EW
Telephone: (0272) 686456 £65
Open: lunch + dinner Tue-Sat (closed Bank Holidays, 2 wks Xmas, 4 days Easter)
Meals served: lunch 12.30-2, dinner 7-9.30

The scale and simplicity of Martin and Siân Blunos' tiny restaurant belies the finesse and attention to detail of Martin's cooking. Starters on the fixed price menu could include a clear rabbit and celery soup with potted rabbit and toasted brioche, or crab ravioli with a crab and ginger cream sauce; for main course pig's trotter stuffed with more mushrooms with a madeira sauce, or breast of guineafowl with a star anise and tarragon cream sauce, and then a choice of savouries or perhaps the intriguing apricot '5 ways', or rich chocolate marquise with poire william syrup. This is serious cooking and both the wine list and service are appropriately supportive. It falls to you to be so as well.

BRISTOL — Markwick's

43 Corn Street, Bristol, Avon BS1 1HT
Telephone: (0272) 262658 £65
Open: lunch + dinner Mon-Fri (closed Bank Holidays, 10 days Xmas, 10 days Easter, 2 wks Aug,)
Meals served: lunch 12-2, dinner 7-10

Smart, city centre eating provided by chef and owner Stephen Markwick. The restaurant is located in the old business centre of Bristol not far from the Corn Exchange with its famous nails outside. There's a lunchtime set menu for those in a hurry, while in the evening things are more relaxed. Provençale fish soup with aïoli and sauce rouille is among the starters and grilled guineafowl with apple and calvados one of several main dishes. Strong on originality and flavour, Stephen's cooking is really quite special. The wine list matches the food and includes plenty of half bottles which will fit the bill.

· *Markwicks* ·

BRISTOL — Muset

12 Clifton Road, Bristol, Avon BS8 1AF
Telephone: (0272) 732920 £45
Open: dinner Mon-Sat (closed 1 wk Xmas)
Meals served: dinner 7-10.15

They claim to be Bristol's busiest up-market bistro and, going by the number of customers on an average evening, that's probably correct. There's a maze of interconnecting rooms, exposed brickwork and arches, bentwood chairs, plastic cloths and candles – the archetypal bistro. There's a set-price 2-course menu with a modest supplement for an extra courses. Deep-sea hors d'oeuvres are served with Japanese horseradish, while a main dish of of breast of duck is roasted with garlic, pine kernels and fresh basil. Service is swift and the food adequate. They operate a bring-your-own policy for wine – and don't charge corkage – but their own list is worth a look. Clearly, it's where the Clifton set go for a night out.

BROADWAY	Collin House

Collin Lane, Broadway, Hereford & Worcester WR12 7PB
Telephone: (0386) 858354 £45
Open: lunch + dinner daily (closed 24-29 Dec)
Meals served: lunch 12-1.30, dinner 7-9

A 16th-century Cotswold stone house set amongst trees. It has loads of character and owners John and Judith Mills are intent on maintaining an easy-going, cheerful atmosphere. The candlelit, beamed restaurant is a fine setting for food which makes good use of fresh local produce. Choose from a menu where the the price of a 3-course meal is fixed by your choice of main course.

BROADWAY	Dormy House

Willersey Hill, Broadway, Worcester WR12 7LF
Telephone: (0386) 852711
Fax: (0386) 858636 £70
Open: lunch Sun-Fri, dinner daily (closed 3 days Xmas)
Meals served: lunch 12.30-2 (Sun 12.30-2.30), dinner 7.30-9.30 (Fri+Sat 7-9.30, Sun 7.30-9)
Converted 17th-century farmhouse with 49 bedrooms.

BROADWAY	Hunters Lodge

High Street, Broadway, Hereford & Worcester WR12 7DT
Telephone: (0386) 853247 £50
Open: lunch Tue-Sun, dinner Tue-Sat (closed 2 wks Feb, 2 wks Aug)
Meals served: lunch 12.30-2, dinner 7.30-10

If you like your food with the minimum amount of fuss and bother, then Hunters Lodge is a place to bear in mind. Chef Kurt Friedli's menus do the business with no unnecessary frills. Cheese and soufflé fritters come as a lunchtime starter, with poached salmon and hollandaise sauce as a main dish. There is a refreshing number of half bottles on the predominantly French list. The friendly dining room offers a warm welcome and helpful service. Plenty of repeat business from a loyal following – always a good sign.

BROADWAY	Lygon Arms

High Street, Broadway, Hereford & Worcester WR12 7DU
Telephone: (0386) 852255 £75
Fax: (0386) 858611
Open: lunch + dinner daily
Meals served: lunch 12.30-2, dinner 7.30-9.15

First mentioned in parish registers before Shakespeare was even a twinkle in his mother's eye, the Lygon Arms continues to uphold the very finest standards of English inn-keeping hospitality. It has, however, moved with the times – while retaining all its old world charm – and offers complete conference facilities and an up-to-date leisure centre. Chef Clive Howe keeps a firm grip on the kitchen and his dishes are showing an ever increasing awareness of healthy eating. The Great Hall provides a splendid dining room.

| **BROCKENHURST** | **Le Poussin** |

The Courtyard, 49-55 Brookley Road, Brockenhurst, Hampshire SO42 7RB
Telephone: (0590) 23063 **£75**
Fax: (0590) 22912
Open: lunch Tue-Sun, dinner Tue-Sat (closed 2 wks Jan)
Meals served: lunch 12-2, dinner 7-10.30

A smaller restaurant, cheaper prices, but definitely no cuts in standards. There are some real delights in store for you here at Le Poussin. The menu comes printed on the stylish headed paper and offers dishes such as tagliatelle with asparagus and lobster as a starter with rare fillet of beef with pleurottes as a main course. Mouthwatering desserts are followed by petits fours and coffee. Some very superior bottles are numbered on the wine list, but some good value drinking is also to be had by the glass. Many will be pleased to note Le Poussin is a no smoking restaurant. The move (from just around the corner) has clearly done wonders for Alex Aitken's business – long may he continue to prosper! *See also page 240 – our Clover Award Section.*

| **BROCKENHURST** | **Rhinefield House** |

Rhinefield Road, Brockenhurst, Hampshire SO42 7QB
Telephone: (0590) 22922 £55
Fax: (0590) 22800
Open: lunch Sun-Fri, dinner daily
Meals served: lunch 12.30-2, dinner 7.30-10
Traditional style Victorian country house in the New Forest with thirty-two bedrooms.

| **BROMSGROVE** | **Grafton Manor** |

Grafton Lane, Bromsgrove, Hereford & Worcester B61 7HA
Telephone: (0527) 579007 **£65**
Fax: (0527) 575221
Open: lunch Sun-Fri, dinner daily
Meals served: lunch 12.30-1.45, dinner 7.30-9 (Sat 7.30-9.30, Sun at 7.30)

A history lesson by itself, Grafton Manor has figured in many of the major events of the past and it was at a meeting here in 1615 that the Gunpowder Plot was hatched. Splendidly restored by the Morrises it boasts 2 superb rooms in the Great Parlour and the dining room, but the 9 bedrooms each have their own individual charm. In the kitchen Simon Morris and Nicola Harper have put their heads together to come up with some interesting dishes – best end of lamb is cooked with ham and spinach in olive oil and served with a thyme and béarnaise sauce, while a breast of pheasant is served on a bed of celeriac purée accompanied by pheasant pudding and a juniper berry sauce. Herbs from the ornamental garden feature strongly and contribute a taste all of their own.

BROUGHTON — Broughton Park

418 Garstang Road, Broughton, Nr Preston, Lancashire PR3 5JB
Telephone: (0772) 864087 £50
Fax: (0772) 861728
Open: lunch Sun-Fri, dinner daily
Meals served: lunch 12-2, dinner 7-10 (Sun 7-9.30)

Executive and conference-oriented hotel with extensive leisure facilities which can also be enjoyed by the private guest. The 93 bedrooms and 2 suites are carefully co-ordinated in terms of colour and furnishings, and include satellite TV. Eat in the Courtyard Restaurant which has cane chairs, lots of plants, and water bubbling up through the middle of a large circular stone, and a warm friendly welcome. Good home-made bread and appetizers are offered before the meal, at which you might start with a hot and cold salad of fresh scallops and smoked salmon, followed by a well-presented roast saddle of rabbit with smoked bacon and shallots, accompanied by truffled pasta. For dessert, try the unusual apricot and greek yoghurt terrine. Good house wines on the reasonably priced list.

BROXTED — Whitehall

Church End, Broxted, Essex CM6 2BZ
Telephone: (0279) 850603 £70
Fax: (0279) 850385
Open: lunch Sun-Fri, dinner daily (closed 26-30 Dec)
Meals served: lunch 12.30-1.30, dinner 7.30-9.30 (Sun 7.30-8.30)

From behind the Elizabethan walled garden there peers the old village church. What more could you want to enhance the atmosphere of this 15th-century manor house? Inside, the modern decor has been skilfully handled to ensure that the feel of the original building remains intact. For example, the lounge with its sophisticated pastel green walls and light grey furniture retains a timber partition.

In the kitchen new chef Paul Flavell maintains the high standard set by his predecessor. I found the wine list sensible and informative – and the home-made nibbles before the meal were a nice touch. Service throughout the hotel and restaurant is good.

BRUTON — Claire de Lune Brasserie

2-4 High Street, Bruton, Somerset BA10 0EQ
Telephone: (0749) 813395 £40
Open: lunch Sun, dinner Mon-Sat (closed 1 wk Jan, 2 wks Aug)
Meals served: lunch 12-2, dinner 7-10
Homely decor, pleasant welcome, good portions – straightforward dishes are best.

BRUTON — Truffles Restaurant

95 High Street, Bruton, Somerset BA10 0AR
Telephone: (0749) 812255 £50
Open: lunch Sun, dinner Tue-Sat (closed 26 Dec, 1 Jan, 2 wks Sept)
Meals served: lunch 12-2, dinner 7-9.30
The Bottrills' restaurant continues to offer good value for their well presented French style cuisine.

BUCKLAND — Buckland Manor

Buckland, Nr Broadway, Hereford & Worcestershire WR12 7LY
Telephone: (0386) 852626   **£70**
Fax: (0386) 853557
Open: lunch + dinner daily
Meals served: lunch 12.30-1.45, dinner 7.30-8.45

A glorious Cotswold manor house now in the capable hands of Roy and Daphne Vaughan. Their aim is to raise standards continually and they will be satisfied only when Buckland Manor stands pre-eminent in the county. Judging by present showing, they can't have far to go. Bedroom refurbishment is under way with some original fireplaces being opened up, and bathrooms are well on the way to being equally luxurious.

BURGH LE MARSH — Windmill

46 High Street, Burgh le Marsh, Lincolnshire PE24 5JT
Telephone: (0754) 810281   £35
Open: lunch Sun, dinner Tue-Sat (closed 1 wk Xmas, 1 wk Sep)
Meals served: lunch 12-1.45, dinner 7-9.15
Wholesome cooking from Tim Boskett who gets his flour from the mill next door to his restaurant.

BURY — Normandie Hotel & Restaurant

Elbut Lane, Birtle, Nr Bury, Greater Manchester BL9 6UT
Telephone: 061-764 3869   **£55**
Fax: 061-764 4866
Open: lunch Tue-Fri, dinner Mon-Sat (closed Bank Holidays, 1 wk Easter, 2 wks Xmas)
Meals served: lunch 12-2, dinner 7-9.30 (Sat 7-10)

Owners Gillian and Max Moussa have appointed Edward Denny, formerly of the Box Tree Restaurant just across the Pennines, as Executive Chef of their fine 24-bedroomed hotel, but it is still Pascal Pommier who displays an impressive range of skills as Head Chef. He cooks with assurity, his sauces are superb, and he knows exactly how to balance and complement the excellent raw materials. Chaud-froid de rougets marinés à l'huile aux herbes followed by pièce de boeuf rôti à l'echalote et porto might be chosen from the à la carte menu, with an assiette de chocolats as an excellent dessert. A command performance – and yet I sense that this man still has fully to realise his talents.

BURY ST EDMUNDS	Angel Hotel

Angel Hill, Bury St Edmunds, Suffolk IP33 1LT
Telephone: (0284) 753926 £45
Fax: (0284) 750092
Open: lunch + dinner daily
Meals served: lunch 12-2.30, dinner 7-9 (Sat 7-9.30)

Where Mr Pickwick had dinner, the virginia creeper-clad Angel Hotel has been doling out English hospitality to all and sundry for over 5 centuries. Dine in the medieval vaults or the more genteel dining room and there's a choice of 39 bedrooms and 1 suite should you want to stay. Dickens fans should try for room 15.

BURY ST EDMUNDS	Mortimer's Seafood Restaurant

31 Churchgate Street, Bury St Edmunds, Suffolk IP33 1RG
Telephone: (0284) 760623 £45
Open: lunch Mon-Fri, dinner Mon-Sat (closed Bank Holidays + following day, 2 wks Xmas, 2 wks Aug)
Meals served: lunch 12-2, dinner 7-9 (Mon 7-8.15)

BURY ST EDMUNDS	Somewhere Else

1 Langton Place, Hatter Street, Bury St Edmunds, Suffolk
Telephone: (0284) 760750 £35
Open: all day daily
Meals served: 10am-11pm (Sat 8.30am-11pm, Sun 12-11)

CALNE	Chilvester Hill House

Calne, Wiltshire SN11 0LP
Telephone: (0249) 813981 £50
Open: dinner daily
Meals served: dinner at 8 for residents only
Victorian mansion. Dinner has no choice and served in the family dining room.

CALSTOCK	Danescombe Valley Hotel

Lower Kelly, Calstock, Cornwall PL18 9RY
Telephone: (0822) 832414 £60
Open: dinner Fri-Tue (closed Nov-Easter but open Xmas)
Meals served: dinner 7.30 for 8

No television, no radio and no phone are among the facilities at this little Cornish hotel. Surely some mistake? On the contrary, without them your stay will be complete. The view of the river Tamar and the Cotehele cliffs, Anna Smith's enjoyable food – roast guineafowl with a lemon and garlic sauce, Tamar salmon roasted with spices, unpasteurised local cheeses – excellent wines, and a reassuringly informal atmosphere about the place are all you could possibly desire. A top choice in the area. Tea on the veranda remains one of life's greatest pleasures.

CAMBRIDGE — Browns

23 Trumpington Street, Cambridge, Cambridgeshire CB2 1QA
Telephone: (0223) 461655
Fax: (0223) 460426
Open: all day daily
Meals served: Mon-Sat 11am-11.30pm, Sun+Bank Holidays 12-11.30

£30

Just down the road from Pembroke and Peterhouse Colleges, Browns in Cambridge is proving to be as popular as its sister establishment in Oxford. A selection of reliable old favourites are to be had – leg of lamb, peasant's pot, steak, mushroom and Guinness pie – supplemented by the daily chef's specials. Straightforward and good value, it's the ideal place for student, parent and visitor alike.

CAMBRIDGE — Midsummer House

Midsummer Common, Cambridge, Cambridgeshire CB4 3AE
Telephone: (0223) 69299
Open: lunch Mon-Fri, dinner Mon-Sat (closed 26 Dec, 1 Jan)
Meals served: lunch 12.15-1.30, dinner 7.15-9.30

£75

A stroll across Midsummer Common and perhaps a table overlooking the Cam or in the walled garden whets the appetite for Hans Schweitzer's accomplished cooking. Charlotte of courgettes and aubergine with crottin de chavignol, pink-roasted duck with rhubarb and Gewürztraminer and the former pâtissier's definitive Black Forest gateau are typically robust offerings on his fixed-price 2- to 6-course menu. Sensible prices and some fine producers feature on the wine list.

CAMBRIDGE — Restaurant Twenty Two

22 Chesterton Road, Cambridge, Cambridgeshire CB4 3AX
Telephone: (0223) 351880
Open: dinner Tue-Sat (closed Xmas/New Year)
Meals served: dinner 7.30-9.30

£45

Short, fixed price menu which changes monthly according to seasonal produce.

CAMPSEA ASHE — Old Rectory

Campsea Ashe, Nr Woodbridge, Suffolk IP13 0PU
Telephone: (0728) 746524
Open: dinner Mon-Sat (closed Xmas/New Year, 2 wks Feb, 1 wk Nov)
Meals served: dinner 7.30-9

£45

A spinach roulade filled with smoked fish and cream cheese with a purée of red peppers, and a hot terrine of crab and lobster in beurre blanc are recent starters on Stewart Bassett's menu. Main dishes include thin slices of Barbary duck with a ginger and apricot sauce and boned leg of lamb filled with pounded bacon, garlic, parsley and crushed black peppercorns, baked in puff pastry. You can gather from the descriptions that a lot of work goes into the food and the results are worth the effort. The conservatory dining room overlooks pretty gardens and adjacent church. The wine list has plenty of half bottles, keen prices and some bin-end bargains. There are 6 bedrooms should you wish to stay.

CANTERBURY	County Hotel

High Street, Canterbury, Kent CT1 2RX
Telephone: (0227) 766266 £55
Fax: (0227) 451512
Open: lunch + dinner daily
Meals served: lunch 12.30-2.30, dinner 7-10

A clever blend of the genuinely traditional and the modern equivalent, the County Hotel provides superior accommodation in its 74 bedrooms. The size of room varies, but fabrics and furnishings are tastefully done. In Sully's Restaurant stick to the more straightforward items – lightly grilled Dover sole, roast Norfolk pigeon, for instance. By way of compensation you can afford to be more adventurous on the wine list.

CANTERBURY	George's Brasserie

71-71 Castle Street, Canterbury, Kent CT1 2QD
Telephone: (0227) 765658 £40
Open: all day Mon-Sat (closed 25 Dec, 1 Jan)
Meals served: 11-10.30
Popular brasserie in the heart of the city.

CARTMEL	Hodge Hill

Cartmel Fell, Nr Grange-over-Sands, Cumbria LA11 6NQ
Telephone: (053 95) 31480 £45
Open: lunch Sun, dinner daily
Meals served: lunch at 1, dinner 7.30 for 8
Popular local restaurant.

CARTMEL	Uplands

Haggs Lane, Cartmel, Cumbria LA11 6HD
Telephone: (053 95) 36238 £60
Open: lunch + dinner Tue-Sun (closed Jan+Feb)
Meals served: lunch 12.30 for 1, dinner 7.30 for 8

That man John Tovey has a hand in things here at Uplands as well, and needless to say this is tantamount to a royal seal of approval. That said, Tom and Diana Peter know what they're doing and the food can be relied upon for good value for money eating. Note the excellent value David Wynn wines on the carefully chosen list. The 5 comfortable bedrooms allow you to come back for more next day!

CASTLE CARY — Bond's Hotel & Restaurant

Ansford Hill, Castle Cary, Somerset BA7 7JP
Telephone: (0963) 50464 £40
Open: dinner daily (closed 1 wk Xmas)
Meals served: dinner 7-9.30

Kevin and Yvonne Bond pride themselves on avoiding the pomposity of many establishments. Their 7-bedroomed hotel allows them to do full justice to their guests' needs, and the menus can also be flexible and competitively priced. Good value all round – they justify their claims!

CASTLE COMBE — Castle Inn

Castle Combe, Nr Chippenham, Wiltshire SN14 7HN
Telephone: (0249) 782461 £55
Open: lunch Sun-Fri, dinner daily
Meals served: lunch 12-1.45, dinner 7.30-9.30
Relaxed, homely atmosphere in this eleven-bedroomed old beamed house.

CASTLE COMBE — Manor House

Castle Combe, Nr Chippenham, Wiltshire SN14 7HR
Telephone: (0249) 782206 £65
Fax: (0249) 782159
Open: lunch + dinner daily
Meals served: lunch 12.30-2, dinner 7.30-9.30 (Sat 7.30-10)

All the rooms in the main house have recently been renovated, bringing many of the original features to light. There's now a better feel to the place, although it always was attractive with its lovely garden setting in the centre of historic Castle Combe. The 36 bedrooms have character and many useful extras for good measure. In the restaurant, the food is a skilful blend of ancient and modern, showing many English favourites to best advantage – marinated chicken and rabbit bound in a delicate artichoke and saffron jelly, saddle of lamb in a potato crust on a casserole of beans and sweet garlic, and fillet of lemon sole stuffed with a shellfish mousse and mussel juices. Non-meat eaters won't be disappointed, either, as a separate menu is provided. Substantial food, substantial wine list and substantial prices. Franco Campiani MOGB runs the floor with dedication befitting this rare front-of-house award.

CHADDESLEY CORBETT — Brockencote Hall

Chaddesley Corbett, Nr Kidderminster, Hereford & Worcester DY10 4PY
Telephone: (0562) 777876 £70
Fax: (0562) 777872
Open: lunch Sun-Fri, dinner Mon-Sat (closed Bank Holidays, 2 wks Xmas/New Year)
Meals served: lunch 12.30-1.45, dinner 7.30-9.30 (Sat 7.30-10)

Didier Philipot is the latest addition to this French colony out at Chaddesley Corbett and should hopefully provide some stability and consistency at the stoves. Initial signs are good, menus are deftly constructed and sauces are a particular strong point. The hotel side of the enterprise is impeccably maintained – testimony to owners Alison and Joseph Petitjean's years spent in Switzerland. Eight pretty bedrooms look out over the landscaped gardens of this beautifully situated former beer baron's home.

CHADLINGTON	The Manor

Chadlington, Oxfordshire OX7 3LX
Telephone: (0608) 76711 £55
Open: dinner daily
Meals served: dinner 7-9

A glorious Cotswold stone manor house (once the family residence of General Rawlinson) with 7 splendid bedrooms and homely public rooms. Chris Grant prepares a fixed-price menu of reliable British favourites, David Grant presides over the service and a truly memorable wine cellar with particular depth in first-growth clarets, German late-picked rieslings and half bottles, all at unbelievably low prices.

CHAGFORD	Gidleigh Park

Chagford, Devon TQ13 8HH
Telephone: (0647) 432367 £105
Fax: (0647) 432574
Open: lunch + dinner daily
Meals served: lunch 12.30-2, dinner 7-9

Any qualms proprietor Paul Henderson might have had when he switched careers and bought the hotel must by now be laid to rest. The risk has more than paid off and Gidleigh Park is one of this country's finest exhibits, with a regular, affluent and discerning clientele. If you're not much of a walker then the miles of countryside won't hold much of an attraction and in winter the croquet lawn will be out of bounds. But so what? Many guests are content just sitting around in the public rooms in front of roaring log fires, admiring the views across the Teign valley and dreaming of the next foray into the dining room.

Chef Shaun Hill requires no introduction from me – his reputation goes before him. Gifted, intelligent, imaginative ... all are terms that are so easy to apply, but in this case so thoroughly deserved as to seem rather inadequate. In any case the food itself is what counts and you can judge for yourself. A recent speciality menu read as follows: one half ounce of Sevruga caviar on a potato galette with soured cream and chives, North Sea fish soup, saffron risotto with vegetables, roast quail with basil and olive oil mashed potato, cheese, sorbet, plate of desserts, coffee. What an elegant composition of ingredients and tastes. The wine list is extensive and superbly chosen with an admirably sensible mark up policy – an award winner in its own right. Exquisitely comfortable bedrooms are impeccably maintained and the amusing drive to the house never fails to kindle your anticipations of great things to come. *See also page 342 – our Clover Award Section.*

CHAPELTOWN	Greenhead House

84 Burncross Road, Chapeltown, Nr Sheffield, South Yorkshire S30 4SF
Telephone: (0742) 469004 £55
Open: dinner Tue-Sat (closed Bank Holidays, 2 wks Apr, 2 wks Aug)
Meals served: dinner 7.15-9

Buzzing local restaurant that draws customers from far and wide. Galantine of quail with pistachios and truffles, fillet of seabass with a fresh tomato sauce, and loin of lamb roasted with garlic and rosemary are done well with little fuss.

CHARINGWORTH — Charingworth Manor

Charingworth, Nr Chipping Camden, Gloucestershire GL55 6NS
Telephone: (038 678) 555
Fax: (038 678) 353
Open: lunch + dinner daily
Meals served: lunch 12.30-2, dinner 7.30-9.30 (Sat 7.30-10)

£70

Steeped in atmosphere, Charingworth Manor has all the charm of the old English way of life but with all the little modern necessities discreetly added. Truly glorious surroundings – a 16th-century building set in some 50 acres of grounds. A day's walking in the Cotswold countryside will whet your appetite and you'll be eager to sample Tony Robson-Burrell's cooking. Strong on fish, his sauces are an experience in themselves. Breast of cornfed chicken with a suissesse soufflé and mustard sauce is a good main course. Traditional puds include a good lemon meringue and apple Pithiviers, but if it's available try the trio of traditional British puds – bread and butter, lemon meringue and jam roly poly! An impressive wine list and relaxed but professional service in this pleasant, understated dining room. For more formal occasions, the Long Room comes into use.

CHARLBURY — The Bull at Charlbury

Sheep Street Charlbury Oxfordshire
Telephone: (0608) 811536
Open: lunch daily, dinner Mon-Sat
Meals served: lunch 12-2, dinner 7-9.30

£45

The talented Nick Gill was about to open at the Bull at Charlbury as we went to press. Nick can probably be best remembered as the chef that shaped the cuisine originally at Hambleton Hall and after working as a consultant chef at other establishments (including the Feathers at Woodstock) he is about to emerge again here in Charlbury. Knowing his prodigious talents, I am looking forward to eating there, as I am sure many of his followers will also.

CHEDINGTON	Chedington Court

Chedington, Nr Beaminster, Dorset DT8 3HY
Telephone: (0935) 891265 £60
Fax: (0935) 891442
Open: dinner daily (closed Feb)
Meals served: dinner 7-9

Remember to sign the visitors' book at some point during your stay, but other than that no-one will make any great demands upon you. Hilary and Philip Chapman are proud of the tradition of relaxed hospitality that they've built up – many guests are on their second or third visit and room keys are pretty well dispensed with. In the dining room, the spotlight is on Hilary Chapman's cooking. The fixed price, hand-written menu offers a choice of starter or fish course such as fillet of monkfish with king prawns and provençale sauce, and a main course such as roast partridge with port wine and onion sauce. A choice of home-made puds to follow and then cheese. With a reasonably priced and intelligently chosen wine list, and some of the most outstanding views over the surrounding countryside, it's no surprise that Chedington Court remains a firm favourite with those who seek good wine and food in a gentle and tranquil setting.

CHELTENHAM	Le Champignon Sauvage

24-26 Suffolk Road, Cheltenham, Gloucestershire GL50 2AQ
Telephone: (0242) 573449 £65
Open: lunch Mon-Fri, dinner Mon-Sat (closed Bank Holidays, 1 wk Xmas, 2 wks Jun)
Meals served: lunch 12.30-1.30, dinner 7.30-9.30

Despite the image of a fungus menacing one and all, David Everitt-Matthias' little restaurant is perfectly civilised and restrained within its peach and grey walls. You, on the other hand, might well be champing at the bit, eager to get your teeth into one of his accomplished dishes. A wood pigeon and black pudding tourte and wild mushroom ravioli are among typical starters, while pan-fried cod with red onions and tomato coulis, rabbit – the saddle pan-fried with marjoram and tomato, the leg braised with tapenade – come as main courses. In general it's modern French cooking with deference to new trends. A broad selection of cheeses supplied by Jacques Hennart rounds off an enjoyable meal.

CHELTENHAM — Epicurean & On The Park

Cleveland House, Evesham Road, Cheltenham, Gloucestershire
GL52 2AH
Telephone: (0242) 518898
Fax: (0242) 511526
Open: lunch Wed-Sun, dinner Tue-Sat
Meals served: lunch 12.30-2.30, dinner 7-10.15 (Fri+Sat 6-10.45)

£100

The pursuit of pleasure is a serious business, I always find, which must make me something of an Epicurean. Anyway, enough of philosophy and on with the food! Chef Patrick McDonald's restaurant is now to be found on the ground floor of On The Park. Nothing seems to have been harmed by the move since the magic remains. The special gourmet menu displays his talents to the full and the set menu selections are no less impressive. It would take several pages to do justice to food such as this, and dishes such as rabbit pie with braised vegetables, and white stew of chicken with scallops and leeks look ordinary enough in print. It's only when they come to your table and you take your first mouthful that you'll know what I'm talking about. Experiences like this don't come cheap. Look to the New World for the best value wines on the meticulously constructed list.

A listed Regency house, recently refurbished, On The Park is a fitting setting for the Epicurean. Its 8 bedrooms allow diners time to recover from their gastronomic exertions!

CHELTENHAM — Greenway

Shurdington, Cheltenham, Gloucestershire GL51 5UG
Telephone: (0242) 862352
Fax: (0242) 862780
Open: lunch Sun-Fri, dinner daily (closed Bank Holidays, 2 wks Xmas)
Meals served: lunch 12-2, dinner 7-9.30 (Sun 7-8)

£60

I've always had a soft spot for the Greenway, owing largely, I suspect, to the quiet unassuming charm and dedication of proprietor Tony Elliott who for over a decade has proven himself as one of this country's most gifted hoteliers. Perhaps it's also the creeper-covered facade, the welcoming interior, and the pretty bedrooms, whether in the main house or sympathetically converted coach house, while for many the sunken garden overlooked by the dining room is the *pièce de resistance*. A meal here on a sunny day or in the evening is something to look forward to and dishes along the lines of breast of duck on a bed of braised vegetables and pan-fried mignons of veal fillet on a bed of spinach pasta with a rhubarb sauce add to the enjoyment. The wine list makes equally enjoyable reading.

CHELTENHAM	Redmond's

Cleeve Hill, Cheltenham, Gloucestershire GL52 3PR
Telephone: (0242) 672017   £65
Open: lunch Tue-Fri + Sun, dinner Mon-Sat (closed 1 wk Jan)
Meals served: lunch 12.30-2, dinner 7.15-10

Pippa and Redmond Hayward have now dropped the 'at Malvern View,' but then it rather speaks for itself! Look out of the windows and there are the hills in their full glory. But you don't just come here for the scenery and perhaps that's what the Haywards are implying by changing the name. Redmond continues to serve up lovely food using high quality ingredients to full advantage. His sauces have become a by-word in flavour, and the dishes arrive at the table exuding freshness and delicious aromas. Try the ragoût of Cornish fish with a chive and riesling sauce or wild salmon with a herb and brioche crust – you won't be disappointed. If it's available try the hot ginger soufflé served with home-made advocaat ice-cream. Farmhouse cheeses and a reasonably priced wine list complete the picture. This hard-working team deserves support from both locals and those from farther afield – I'm looking forward to my next visit.

CHELTENHAM	Staithes

12 Suffolk Road, Cheltenham, Gloucestershire GL50 2AQ
Telephone: (0242) 260666   £60
Open: dinner Tue-Sat
Meals served: dinner 7-9.45
New incarnation on the site of the Redmonds' former restaurant. Modern cooking.

CHESTER	Chester Grosvenor

Eastgate Street, Chester, Cheshire CH1 1LT
Telephone: (0244) 324024   £100
Fax: (0244) 313246
Open: lunch Tue-Sat, dinner Mon-Sat (closed Bank Holidays)
Meals served: lunch 12-2.30, dinner 7-10.30

Historic, luxurious, distinctive – there you have it in those 3 words. Built by the Grosvenor family for the Duke of Westminster in 1866, this impressive hotel must surely be *the* place to stay when visiting Chester. Increasingly catering for an international and business clientele, the list of facilities available includes the recently refurbished Westminster banqueting and conference rooms, a sauna, solarium and gymnasium, and air conditioning and videos in the suites.

The Arkle Restaurant – named after the Duchess of Westminster's famous steeplechaser – offers modern cooking in elegant surroundings. The expensive international wine list includes a 1967 Chateau d'Yquem which will have you remortgaging your house. Maxime de ris de veau aux asperges and poêlé de pigeonneau landais au fondant de foie et crêpe de champignons are specialities of talented chef Paul Reed, with the prices written out in longhand on the menu. More modest eating is to be had in La Brasserie, with its distinctly French decor echoing various Paris brasseries. Several vegetarian options are helpfully indicated. Service throughout the restaurants and hotel is unfailingly courteous and efficient. First class.

CHESTER — Crabwall Manor

Parkgate Road, Mollington, Chester, Cheshire CH1 6NE
Telephone: (0244) 851666
Fax: (0244) 851400 £75
Open: lunch + dinner daily
Meals served: lunch 12.30-2, 7-9.45 (Sat 7-10, Sun 7-9)

Impressive without, warm and welcoming within, this well-run castellated manor house offers plush day rooms and civilised comforts in 48 spacious bedrooms. Michael Truelove's à la carte and set-price menus continue to stimulate taste buds and interest – grilled red mullet on a red pepper coulis with deep-fried coriander, roast cod with white truffle oil-flavoured potato purée, pan-fried Grand Marnier crêpe soufflé with an orange butter sauce – and put him in a class above most regional hotel dining rooms of this size.

CHESTER — Franc's

14 Cuppin Street, Chester, Cheshire CH1 2BN
Telephone: (0244) 317952 £35
Fax: (0244) 340690
Open: lunch + dinner daily (closed 1-3 Jan, 25+26 Dec)
Meals served: lunch 12-3, dinner 6-11 (Sun 6-10)

A breath of decidedly Gallic fresh air in Chester, that most English of English towns. Fight your way through the tourists and dancing Morris men in the streets to find typically robust French country cooking along the lines of coq au vin and agneau provençale. Alternatively in the evening there is La Grande Bouffe where you can eat as much as you want, mopping up your plate with hunks of fresh baguette. They say that dishes can be tailored to your tastes, but there's no provision for your clothes – after all that food you'll be wanting to let out your belt! Simple table settings, wooden tables, poster-clad walls and lots of customers give the place a friendly, vibrant feel.

CHICHESTER — Comme Ca

67 Broyle Road, Chichester, West Sussex
Telephone: (0243) 788724　　　　　　　　　　　　　　　£45
Open: lunch Tue-Sun, dinner Mon-Sat (closed Bank Holidays)
Meals served: lunch 12-2, dinner 7-10 (theatre nights 6-10.30)

New premises for Comme Ca which has moved from the centre of town out here near the Festival Theatre. Chef/patron Michel Navet serves a wide variety of orthodox French cuisine which takes in among the starters dishes such as sauté de poisson meunière and pâtes de champignons sauvages, and as main courses viande des Pyrenées and saumon à la moutarde de Pommery – a slice of salmon sautéed in butter and served with a Pommery mustard sauce. Ingredients are good and used to fine effect. Service is intelligent and polite by French waiters. Handy for a meal before or after the theatre.

CHICHESTER — Thompson's

30a Southgate, Chichester, West Sussex PO19 1DR
Telephone: (0243) 528832　　　　　　　　　　　　　　　£55
Open: lunch Tue-Sat, dinner Mon-Sat (closed Bank Holidays except Good Friday)
Meals served: lunch 12.30-2, dinner 7.30-11

Husband and wife Jonas and Elly Tester have taken over here offering familiar French and English dishes. The restaurant doubles as gallery space for a changing exhibition of paintings by local artists.

CHILGROVE — White Horse Inn

High Street, Chilgrove, Nr Chichester, West Sussex PO18 9HX
Telephone: (0243) 59219　　　　　　　　　　　　　　　£50
Fax: (0243) 59301
Open: lunch Tue-Sun, dinner Tue-Sat (closed Xmas, Feb, 1 wk Oct)
Meals served: lunch 12-1.45, dinner 7-9.30 (Sat 7-10)

Barry Phillips' wine list continues to amaze and draw customers with a nose – and a palate – for a good thing. Chef Neil Rusbridger's cooking uses excellent ingredients to great effect – lovers of offal will be in seventh heaven, though there are plenty of other choices too.

CHIPPING CAMDEN — Cotswold House

The Square, Chipping Camden, Gloucestershire GL55 6AN
Telephone: (0386) 840330　　　　　　　　　　　　　　　£55
Fax: (0386) 840310
Open: lunch Sun, dinner daily (closed 25+26 Dec)
Meals served: lunch 12.30-2, dinner 7.15-9.30

The elegant sweep of the staircase catches the eye as you enter the Greenstocks' lovingly run former wool-merchant's house. Each of the 15 bedrooms is furnished and decorated in a different style – rustic with dried flowers and wicker chairs, Edwardian with dark wood and period trimmings. A great base from which to explore this lovely part of the world.

CHIPPING CAMPDEN   Seymour House

High Street, Chipping Campden, Gloucestershire GL55 6AH
Telephone: (0386) 840429   **£45**
Fax: (0386) 840369
Open: lunch + dinner daily
Meals served: lunch 12-2.30, dinner 7.30-9.45

The High Street in Chipping Camden was for the historian G.M. Trevelyan the most beautiful village street in England. The hotel itself has a lot going for it, now in the peak of condition after a complete overhaul. The 15 bedrooms are particularly attractive with their Italianate furnishings.

CHRISTCHURCH   Splinters Restaurant
12 Church Street, Christchurch, Dorset BH23 1BW
Telephone: (0202) 483454   £45
Open: dinner Mon-Sat (closed 25+26 Dec, 1 Jan)
Meals served: dinner 6.30-10.30
French country cooking. Warm friendly atmosphere.

CLANFIELD   The Plough at Clanfield

Bourton Road, Clanfield, Oxfordshire OX8 2RB
Telephone: (036 781) 222   **£65**
Fax: (036 781) 596
Open: lunch + dinner daily
Meals served: lunch 12-2, dinner 7-10 (Sun 7-9.30)

A splendid place to come to whether for a light meal at midday or a more formal dinner in the evening. Crab and green peppercorn mousse, and baked breast of Barbary duckling with a spiced berry sauce are typical dishes and the wine list displays great depth and some hefty prices, particularly in Bordeaux. Also some cosy bedrooms, one with a 4-poster, for an overnight stop.

CLAYGATE	Les Alouettes

7 High Street, Claygate, Esher, Surrey KT10 0JW
Telephone: (0372) 464882
Fax: (0372) 65337
Open: lunch Mon-Fri, dinner Mon-Sat (closed Bank Holidays, 2 wks Jan, 2 wks Aug)
Meals served: lunch 12.15-2, dinner 7-9.30 (Sat 7-10)

£80

French cuisine of a high order at this discreet restaurant patronised by stockbrokers from the surrounding area and a smattering of local celebrities. Michel Perraud is a chef of distinction with a background embracing Troisgrois, Taillevent and, closer to home, the Waterside Inn. His seasonal carte is supplemented by market-dictated fixed-price menus, with fish a noted speciality – authentic Brittany fish soup with the usual accompaniments, an osso bucco of monkfish with mushrooms, potatoes and spring onions. Cheeses from Philippe Olivier are always in top form and prices on the almost exclusively French wine list in the top bracket. Well-deserved strong local following. *See also page 243 – our Clover Award Section.* As we went to press, Michel Perraud left and the format has changed to that of a brasserie.

CLEVEDON	Walton Park

Wellington Terrace, Clevedon, Avon BS21 7BL
Telephone: (0272) 874253
Open: dinner daily
Meals served: dinner 7-9.30
Victorian hotel overlooking the Severn estuary.

£40

CLITHEROE	Browns Bistro

10 York Street, Clitheroe, Lancashire BB7 2DL
Telephone: (0200) 26928
Open: lunch Mon-Fri, dinner Mon-Sat (closed 25+26 Dec, 1 Jan)
Meals served: lunch 12-2, dinner 7-10

£40

The tablecloths, the posters, the joie de vivre – all the ingredients of an authentice French bistro – are here, of all places, in Clitheroe. Jam-packed most days, it's worth knowing there's a bar downstairs and 20 seats for any overspill. Good value food and lots of it. Blackboard menus might include French onion soup, moules marinières, steak au poivre – that kind of thing. A respectable wine list includes some good value quaffing wines. Sit down and wait for your food, nibbling on petits pains.

CLUN — Old Post Office

9 The Square, Clun, Shropshire SY7 8JA
Telephone: (0588) 640687 £50
Open: lunch + dinner Wed-Sun (closed mid Jan-mid Mar)
Meals served: lunch 12.30-1.30, dinner 7.30-9.30 (Sun 7.30-8.30)

Try a tiered lamb's sweetbread with a whisky and rosemary sauce for a starter, followed by lamb in pastry with mint béarnaise or perhaps the fresh fish of the day. Afterwards, chocolate slab with a mango coulis seems a good way to round things off at Richard Arbuthnot's friendly restaurant. Two bedrooms are also available.

COCKERMOUTH — Quince & Medlar
13 Castlegate, Cockermouth, Cumbria CA13 9EU
Telephone: (0900) 823579 £30
Open: dinner Tue-Sun (closed Bank Holidays, 3 wks Feb, 1 wk Oct)
Meals served: dinner 7-9.30
Award-winning vegetarian restaurant.

COGGESHALL — Baumann's Brasserie
4-6 Stoneham Street, Coggeshall, Essex CO6 1TT
Telephone: (0376) 561453 £55
Open: lunch Tue-Fri + Sun, dinner Tue-Sat (closed Bank Holidays)
Meals served: lunch 12.30-2, dinner 7.30-10
Mark Baumann's popular local restaurant, informal and good value.

COGGESHALL — White Hart
Market End, Coggeshall, Essex CO6 1NH
Telephone: (0376) 561654 £50
Fax: (0376) 561789
Open: lunch daily, dinner Mon-Sat
Meals served: lunch 12-2, dinner 7.30-10
Dating from the 1400s, this eighteen-bedroomed traditional hotel is said to have two ghosts!

COLCHESTER — Stour Bay Café
39-41 High Street, Manningtree, Colchester, Essex
Telephone: (0206) 396687 £40
Open: lunch + dinner Tue-Sun (closed Bank Holidays)
Meals served: lunch 12-2.30, dinner 7-10
Popular café/restaurant

COLCHESTER — Thara's
48 St John's Street, Colchester, Essex
Telephone: (0206) 763495 £30
Open: lunch + dinner daily (closed 25 Dec)
Meals served: lunch 12.30-2.30, dinner 6-11.30 (Fri+Sat 6-12)
Good value Indian restaurant.

COLERNE	Lucknam Park

Colerne, Wiltshire SN14 8AZ
Telephone: (0225) 742777
Fax: (0225) 743536
Open: lunch + dinner daily
Meals served: lunch 12.30-2, dinner 7.30-9.30 (Sat 7.30-10)

£80

A relatively young country house hotel of honey-coloured Bath stone which has, since opening 6 years ago, established itself as one of the best. Approached via a long, straight avenue, the hotel is set in beautiful parkland with neighbouring stud farm, and large wooden-floored reception hall with rich colours and roaring fire in winter affords a warm welcome. From arrival to departure, service is impeccable throughout the hotel. The finest rooms and suites (all of which are named after flowers except for the balconied 'Juliet') are in the main house overlooking the majestic gardens, while the former courtyard buildings and cottages provide further accommodation.

This is one of the most elegantly decorated hotels in England but it always feels exceptionally comfortable and unstuffy. Peter Inston's interior schemes are graceful and often pretty without being at all twee and there is striking use of colour throughout. There are fine fabrics, well-chosen furniture – including many tasteful 4-posters – and exceptional bathrooms with good toiletries. Beside the colourful walled garden is a leisure complex where light meals are available including Sunday barbecues in the summer, but gastronomes head straight for the main restaurant where Michael Womersley offers highly-developed British cuisine in the grandly-appointed dining-room with painted ceiling and large windows overlooking the grounds.

Regional produce is used wherever possible, resulting in dishes such as grilled salmis of wood pigeon with baked aubergines and wild mushrooms, galette of Cornish crab and scallops on a bed of onions braised in cream or roast Gressingham duck filled with a confit of its legs with figs, sultanas and almonds. From the shorter lunch menu you might choose sautéed scallops with lentils and spiced coriander and mussel vinaigrette, or a warm terrine of sweetbreads and kidneys with braised shallots on a red wine sauce. Fine puddings include an iced parfait of hazelnuts and whisky, an apple meringue tart and soufflés. The classic wine list has a good selection of New World bottles as well as Mumford wine which is produced in the next village. Coffee and petits fours may be taken in the light, spacious lounge or the dimly-lit panelled library with its richly-coloured drapes.

CORFE CASTLE	Mortons House Hotel

45 East Street, Corfe Castle, Dorset BH20 5EE
Telephone: (0929) 480988　　　　　　　　　　　　　　　　　　　　£50
Fax: (0929) 480820
Open: lunch + dinner daily
Meals served: lunch 12.30-2, dinner 7.30-9

Mortons House was built in 1590 in the shape of a letter E as a tribute to Queen Elizabeth I, reflecting a time when the architectural profession and the Crown thought along the same lines! Today it stands as a 17-bedroomed hotel, thoroughly renovated but preserving many original features such as the stone fireplace in the hall. Lovely gardens.

Corse Lawn — Corse Lawn House

Corse Lawn, Nr Gloucester, Gloucestershire GL19 4LZ
Telephone: (0452) 780479
Fax: (0452) 780840
Open: lunch + dinner daily
Meals served: lunch 12-2, dinner 7-10

£75

The Hine family continues to extend a warm welcome to one and all in this Queen Anne Grade II listed building. The hotel caters for conferences and private functions as well as for individual guests. But no matter what size or importance, rest assured that they'll look after you! Baba Hine has now been joined in the kitchen by Tim Earley and between them they provide a mixture of French provincial and modern British styles. In addition, a vegetarian menu is always available with an impressive variety of choices. Try the à la carte or table d'hôte dinner menus which offer a jugged haunch of venison cooked with port and herbs, or braised oxtail in a red wine shallot and mushroom sauce. Finish with a hot butterscotch sponge pudding. A comprehensive wine list has some reasonably priced selections. There are 19 comfortably appointed bedrooms.

Corsham — Copperfields Restaurant

1 High Street, Corsham, Wiltshire SN13 0ES
Telephone: (0249) 713982
Open: dinner Tue-Sat
Meals served: dinner 7-10
English and French cooking based on traditional ideas.

£55

Corsham — Rudloe Park

Leafy Lane, Corsham, Wiltshire SN13 0PA
Telephone: (0225) 810555
Fax: (0225) 811412
Open: lunch + dinner daily
Meals served: lunch 12-2, dinner 7-10 (Sun 7-9)

£45

An 11 bedroom house with award-winning gardens notable also for Ian Overend's remarkable collection of eaux-de-vie and wines.

Cosham   Barnard's

109 High Street, Cosham, Hampshire PO6 3BB
Telephone: (0705) 370226   **£45**
Open: lunch Tue-Fri, dinner Tue-Sat (closed Bank Holidays, 1 wk Xmas, 2 wks Aug)
Meals served: lunch 12-2, dinner 7.30-9.30

In a rather dark street opposite Cosham cinema, this restaurant is rather plain from the exterior. However, what it lacks in appearances it sure makes up for in the food. Owner and chef David Barnard has talent and his cooking displays an assured mastery of the art. Terrine de pintadeau aux noix as a starter and l'entrecôte de boeuf béarnaise as a main dish can be quite an experience, with some delicious vegetables on the side. The puds are good, showing no tailing off of attention, and his wine list shows a keen eye as well. Service by Mrs Barnard in this simple 20-cover restaurant makes it a firm local favourite.

Coventry   Trinity House Hotel
28 Lower Holyhead Road, Coventry, West Midlands CV1 3AU
Telephone: (0203) 555654   £35
Open: lunch Mon-Fri, dinner daily
Meals served: lunch 12-2, dinner 7-10 (Sat 7-10.30)
Main feature at this 9-bedroomed hotel is Carl's Restaurant, chef/proprietor Carl Timmins having cut his teeth at Sloan's in Birmingham.

Cowan bridge   Cobwebs
Leck, Cowan Bridge, Nr Kirkby Lonsdale, Lancashire LA6 2H7
Telephone: (05242) 72141   £50
Open: dinner Tue-Sat (closed Jan-mid Mar)
Meals served: dinner 7.30-8
Restaurant with 5 rooms run by Paul Kelly and Yvonne Thompson.

Cranleigh   Restaurant Bonnet

High Street, Cranleigh, Surrey GU6 8AE
Telephone: (0483) 273889   **£55**
Open: lunch Tue-Fri + Sun, dinner Tue-Sat
Meals served: lunch 12-2, dinner 7-10

Located next to the Cranleigh cottage hospital, this is a pleasant, friendly restaurant in the French village mould. Lunch is a fixed price bargain with 2 or 3 courses as you wish, while dinner has a wider selection of dishes and comes at twice the price – c'est la vie! Chef Jean Pierre Bonnet's cooking is competent, and the resulting dishes are perfectly satisfying. Flan de moules aux courgettes and crème de tourteau à la badiane, ravioli au gingembre are among the first courses, while noisettes d'agneau sauce soubise, ail rôti and cuisse de canard au fumet de cèpes are possible main dishes. Desserts are nicely done and there are some reasonably priced half bottles on the wine list. One to get to know if it's in your area.

Crathorne — Crathorne Hall

Crathorne, Nr Yarm, Cleveland TS15 0AR
Telephone: (0642) 700398 — £65
Fax: (0642) 700814
Open: lunch + dinner daily
Meals served: lunch 12.30-2.30 (Sun 12.30-3), dinner 7.30-10 (Sun 7.30-9.30)
Splendid country house hotel set in fifteen acres of woodland.

Crosby-on-Eden — Crosby Lodge

High Crosby, Crosby-on-Eden, Nr Carlisle, Cumbria CA6 4QZ
Telephone: (0228) 573618 — £50
Fax: (0228) 573428
Open: lunch + dinner daily (closed 24 Dec-end Jan)
Meals served: lunch 12.15-1.30, dinner 7.30-9 (Sun 7.30-8)
Elegant country house with eleven rooms, some in the main house and others in converted stable block.

Croydon — 34 Surrey Street Restaurant

34 Surrey Street, Croydon, Surrey CR0 1RJ
Telephone: 081-686 0586 — £40
Open: lunch Mon-Fri + Sun, dinner Mon-Sat (closed Bank Holidays)
Meals served: lunch 12-3, dinner 7-9.45
Cocktail and wine bars and informal restaurant. Specialises in exotic and more familiar fish.

Cuckfield — Jeremy's at The King's Head

2 South Street, Cuckfield, West Sussex RH17 5JY
Telephone: (0444) 454006 — £45
Open: lunch + dinner Tue-Fri (closed Bank Holidays, Xmas/New Year)
Meals served: lunch 12.30-2, dinner 7.30-9.30

Apparently, many's the time George IV would call in a the King's Head on his way down to sample the delights of Brighton. Today, it houses Jeremy's rustic style restaurant which is a pretty good reason for you to stop for lunch or an evening meal. There are some fine straightforward dishes which don't pull any punches with flavour. Head and shoulders above similar establishments, this is a popular place to eat so booking is essential. There's a concise wine list, 2 bars and 9 ensuite bedrooms.

Cuckfield — Ockenden Manor

Ockenden Lane, Cuckfield, West Sussex RH17 5LD
Telephone: (0444) 416111 — £55
Fax: (0444) 415549
Open: lunch + dinner daily
Meals served: lunch 12.30-1.45 (Sun 12.30-2), dinner 7.30-9.30 (Sat 7.30-9.45)

An originally Tudor building which has been added to over the centuries, the latest being a new conservatory. Good standard of comfort in the rooms with many nice little extras. Lovely views from the rear of the hotel.

Dallington — Little Byres

Christmas Farm, Battle Road, Dallington, Heathfield, East Sussex TN21 9LE
Telephone: (042 482) 230 — £55
Open: dinner Mon-Sat
Meals served: dinner 7.30-9
Four-course, set price menu with four or five choices at each course using fresh ingredients.

DARLINGTON	Sardis

196 Northgate, Darlington, Durham DL1 1QU
Telephone: (0325) 461222 £35
Open: lunch + dinner Mon-Sat (closed Bank Holidays)
Meals served: lunch 12-2, dinner 7-10

Hip surroundings for some modish Italian food. Melanzane in carrozza – an aubergine, cheese and mozzarella dish – is among the starters, followed by braised rabbit with maize meal from the 10 or so main dishes. Special Sardinian nights sound fun, with a half bottle of wine thrown in for good measure.

DARLINGTON	Victor's Restaurant

84 Victoria Road, Darlington, Durham DL1 5JW
Telephone: (0325) 480818 £40
Open: lunch + dinner Tue-Sat (closed 1 wk Xmas)
Meals served: lunch 12-2, dinner 7-10.30

From the set price menu at dinner you might choose the timbale of white fish and prawns with dill sauce as a starter. A choice of home-made soup or a sorbet follows, before a main course of perhaps duckling with cloves and fresh peach. A selection of cheeses or desserts come next with coffee and home-made sweets to finish. Extremely popular.

DARTMOUTH	Carved Angel

2 South Embankment, Dartmouth, Devon TQ6 9BH
Telephone: (0803) 832465 £85
Open: lunch Tue-Sun, dinner Mon-Sat (closed Bank Holidays except
  Good Friday, 6 wks Jan/Feb. 1 wk Oct)
Meals served: lunch 12.30-2, dinner 7.30-9

Read any of the food and wine columns in the daily newspapers and you can't help noticing how often the name of Joyce Molyneux crops up. Her flair, and acrobatic combinations of ingredients have won her a large and devoted following. A typical menu might include stir-fried monkfish with coriander, peppers and noodles, or courgette flowers stuffed with a wonderfully light chicken mousseline as starters, with Dart salmon in pastry with currants and ginger or confit-like spiced guineafowl with curried noodles as main courses. Mouthwatering puds could be a tangy keylime pie portioned at table, or an exquisite apricot crème brûlée. The wine list makes exciting reading with carefully chosen house selections and wines of the month both being particularly good value. Impeccable standards from first to last bite. The restaurant site by the quayside remains one of the loveliest in the country. *See also page 244 – our Clover Award Section.*

DEDHAM	Fountain House & Dedham Hall

Brook Street, Dedham, Nr Colchester, Essex CO7 6AD
Telephone: (0706) 323027 £40
Open: lunch Sun, dinner Tue-Sat (closed Bank Holidays)
Meals served: lunch 12.15-3, dinner 7.30-10

I've counted no fewer than 66 items on the list – and that's just the half bottles! A good proportion are French, but there are representatives from Italy, Australia and the USA as well. Prices are extremely reasonable, and that goes for the full-size bottles also. Wendy Sarton provides some enjoyable food around which you can organise the evening's wine tasting before retiring to one of the 12 comfortable bedrooms.

DEDHAM	Le Talbooth

Gunhill, Dedham, Nr Colchester, Essex CO7 6HP
Telephone: (0206) 323150 £80
Fax: (0206) 322752
Open: lunch + dinner daily
Meals served: lunch 12-2, dinner 7-9.30

DEDHAM	Maison Talbooth

Stratford Road, Dedham, Nr Colchester, Essex CO7 6HN
Telephone: (0206) 322367
Fax: (0206) 322752

Steven Blake has now gone on to pastures new at the Royal Crescent in Bath and former head sous chef Lee Timmins has taken over the stoves. Four years with Steven and his own natural flair are already producing impressive results. Dishes such as sautéed wild rabbit, poached salmon with a tagliatelle of vegetables and gratin of fresh fruits seem set to delight customers in the years to come. The passionately compiled wine list remains a model of information and selectivity. This is a really lovely place.

Along the river and nestled in amongst the trees, Maison Talbooth continues to provide comfort and tranquillity to its fortunate guests, while Dedham Vale Hotel – the third string to the Milsoms' bow – is also just down the road. What better way to digest your evening meal than by strolling back to your room in anticipation of a nightcap before bed! *See also page 245 – our Clover Award Section.*

| DELPH | Honfleur |

Cross Keys Inn, Huddersfield Road, Delph, Greater Manchester OL3 5RQ
Telephone: (0457) 874241 £45
Open: lunch + dinner Tue-Sun
Meals served: lunch 12-2, dinner 7.30-9.30
Another lively and popular restaurant-in-a-pub, run by the Champeau family.

| DINTON | La Chouette |

Westlington Green, Dinton, Nr Aylesbury, Buckinghamshire HP17 8UW
Telephone: (0296) 747422 £60
Open: lunch Mon-Fri, dinner Mon-Sat
Meals served: lunch 12-2.15, dinner 6.30-9.15
Cosy restaurant on the village green serving French and Belgium cuisine.

DISS Weavers

Market Hill, Diss, Norfolk IP22 3JZ
Telephone: (0379) 642411 **£35**
Open: lunch Mon-Fri, dinner Tue-Sat (closed Bank Holidays, Xmas, 1 wk Aug)
Meals served: lunch 12-2, dinner 7-9.30

A town centre restaurant in a converted and extended weavers' guild chapel. Good, straightforward food such as fresh brill pan-fried in parsley butter and lemon juice or home-made steak, kidney and mushroom pie are set against a few dishes given an original twist. Useful wine list.

DORKING Partners West Street

2-4 West Street, Dorking, Surrey RH4 1BL
Telephone: (0306) 882826 **£55**
Open: lunch Tue-Fri + Sun, dinner Tue-Sat (closed Bank Holidays)
Meals served: lunch 12.30-2, dinner 7.30-9.30

Andrew Thompson and Tim McEntire's dream restaurant in a converted tea room and fish and chip shop. Their old establishment in Sutton – Partners 23 – has been renamed and reconceived as Partners Brasserie. Here in Dorking the old formula is proving successful with dishes such as home-cured beef with pink grapefruit, stuffed quails with smoked bacon and lentils and the Partners' cheese basket available on the 3-course evening menu. Several wines from the local Denbies vineyard feature on the otherwise mainly French list.

DORRINGTON	**Country Friends**

Dorrington, Nr Shrewsbury, Shropshire SY5 7JD
Telephone: (074 373) 707 £45
Open: lunch + dinner Tue-Sat (closed Bank Holidays, 1 wk Jul, 1 wk Oct)
Meals served: lunch 12-2, dinner 7-9

Rather quaint setting for a meal which might include crab ravioli served with a mild curry sauce, followed by duck breast with a corn syrup sauce and mousse of coriander and shallots. Three comfortable bedrooms.

DOUGLAS	**Boncompte's**

Admiral House, Loch Promenade, Douglas, Isle of Man
Telephone: (0624) 629551 £55
Open: lunch Mon-Fri, dinner Mon-Sat (closed 25 Dec)
Meals served: lunch 12.30-2, dinner 7.30-10
Popular local restaurant.

DOVER	**Wallett's Court**

West Cliffe, St Margaret's, Dover, Kent CT15 6EW
Telephone: (0304) 852424 £40
Open: dinner Mon-Sat (closed Xmas, 1 wk Jan, 1 wk Nov)
Meals served: dinner 7-9

The Oakleys' friendly hotel set in an Elizabethan manor house. WIth only 7 bedrooms it's a small enough operation to preserve the personal touch. Keep it in mind whether en route for the Channel ports or planning a holiday down in Kent.

DREWSTEIGNTON	**Hunts Tor House**

Drewsteignton, Devon EX6 6QW
Telephone: (0647) 21228 £40
Open: dinner daily (closed Nov-mid Mar)
Meals served: dinner at 7.30
Charming old house at the centre of a picturesque Dartmoor village.

DULVERTON	**Ashwick House**

Dulverton, Somerset TA22 9QD
Telephone: (0398) 23868 £50
Open: lunch Sun, dinner daily (closed New Year)
Meals served: lunch 12.30-1.45, dinner 7.15-8.30

It's hard to think of more beautiful surroundings than here on the top of Exmoor. Inside Ashwick House you'll notice the William Morris wallpaper – not a modern day print, it's the real thing. Richard Sherwood labours night and day to keep things ticking over smoothly, delivering the breakfast trays, shopping for produce, cooking the food, writing the menus (which come as a scroll bearing your name), and pouring the turning-in nightcaps. A Jack-Of-All-Trades – I can but admire his energy. He must look forward to his break at the New Year!

Dunbridge	Mill Arms Inn

Dunbridge, Hampshire
Telephone: (0794) 40401 £45
Open: lunch + dinner daily
Meals served: lunch 12-2 (Sun 12-2.30), dinner 7-10 (Fri+Sat 7-10.30)

You're as likely to find a Range Rover as a tractor parked outside this free house pub. The food in the restaurant is thoroughly democratic and there's something to suit all tastes. Avocado Stilton and a mushroom and bacon savoury are 2 starters with, among the main courses, traditional roast Norfolk duckling and best end of lamb with fresh herb jus. That's not forgetting the straightforward steaks also available. Blackboard specials change day by day.

Durham	Ramside Hall

Carrville, Durham, Durham DH1 1TD
Telephone: 091-386 5282
Fax: 091-386 0399 £40
Open: lunch + dinner daily
Meals served: lunch 12-2, dinner 7-9
Good quality, fresh local ingredients with good sized portions.

Easedale	Lancrigg Vegetarian Country House

Easedale, Grasmere, Cumbria LA22 9QN
Telephone: (053 94) 35317 £40
Open: dinner daily (closed 2 wks winter)
Meals served: dinner at 7
A completely vegetarian, non-smoking Lake District hotel. Ten attractive bedrooms.

East Boldon	Forsters

2 St Bedes, Station Road, East Boldon, Tyne & Wear NE36 0LE
Telephone: 091-519 0929 £55
Open: lunch Sun, dinner Tue-Sat
Meals served: lunch 12-2, dinner 7-10.30

A small and stylish restaurant with gilt-framed mirrors which make it seem larger than it is. Clever use of lighting and attractive modern art posters add to the appeal. Barry Forster's cooking can be top class and not at all what you might expect in this part of the world. As a starter, Thai prawns with ginger, spring onions and chilli oil are served on a simple white dish with no trimmings, yet the effect and the taste are stunning. A roast loin of venison as a main course is another triumph with the accompanying vegetables done to a turn. Cheeses and puds are equally fine and the service – led by Sue Forster – is judged to perfection. A positive gem of a place.

East Buckland — Lower Pitt

East Buckland, Barnstaple, Devon EX32 0TD
Telephone: (0598) 760243 **£45**
Fax: (0598) 760243
Open: dinner Tue-Sat (closed 25+26 Dec)
Meals served: dinner 7-8.30

An oriental salad with Chinese gooseberries, pineapple, marinated mushrooms and mandarin oranges is a refreshing starter on the menu, with a game casserole of pheasant, guineafowl, pigeon breast and venison among the main courses. A pavlova or a butterscotch meringue glacé will do very well for dessert. Suzanne Lyons uses local, organic produce wherever possible and many of the herbs and vegetables are home-grown and thus ensure good, natural flavours. Should you want to stay overnight, there are 3 bedrooms.

East Grinstead — Gravetye Manor

Vowels Lane, East Grinstead, West Sussex RH19 4LJ
Telephone: (0342) 810567 **£90**
Fax: (0342) 810080
Open: lunch + dinner daily (closed dinner 25 Dec)
Meals served: lunch 12.30-2, dinner 7.30-9.30 (Sun 7.30-9)

Steve Morey has taken over smoothly from Mark Raffan, making sure that Gravetye Manor remains one of the really great places to eat in this country. But it's not just a matter of his own talents – many though they are – nor the wood-panelled dining room – lovely though it is – nor the fish, meat and vegetables that are used – however excellent they may be – no, it's something else again, that special ingredient that is either there or it isn't – it's as simple as that. On the menu, the smoked salmon starter comes from the Gravetye Smoke House and you'll search hard to find any better, while the rack of lamb with a herb crust is a delight, accompanied by cocotte potatoes and a light lamb jus flavoured with rosemary. Allow time at either end of the meal to explore the delicious puddings and outstanding wine list. Proprietor Peter Herbert has been here since 1956 ensuring with unfailing courtesy and charm that standards and attention to detail remain beyond criticism. The latest improvements to his glorious Elizabethan manor include 4 immaculate new bedrooms and the exquisite gardens are now back to their full glory after damaging storms. *See also page 246 – our Clover Award Section.*

EASTBOURNE	Grand Hotel

King Edward's Parade, Eastbourne, East Sussex BN21 4EQ
Telephone: (0323) 412345 £70
Fax: (0323) 412233
Open: lunch + dinner Tue-Sat (closed Bank Holidays, 2 wks Jan, 2 wks Aug)
Meals served: lunch 12.30-2.30, dinner 7-10.30

If the sea air hasn't done the trick, then you'll certainly work up an appetite walking to the Mirabelle restaurant along corridors the size of promenades. Keith Mitchell (who as captain of the British team in the World Culinary Olympics won a gold medal for us 4 years ago in Frankfurt) oversees the whole operation, but it is his ex-sous chef, Neil Wiggins (having followed him from Horsted Place) who as head chef ensures standards are maintained with dishes well presented and flavours carefully discriminated. Red mullet ragoût with coriander and aïoli, rack of lamb with a herb and brioche crumb and rosemary sauce, and lasagne of aubergine are recent creations. The hotel offers some 60 bedrooms, including enormous rooms facing out to sea.

EASTON	Clarke's

Dereham Road, Easton, Norwich, Norfolk NR9 5AH
Telephone: (0603) 880241 £45
Open: lunch Tue-Sun, dinner Tue-Sat (closed 1 Jan)
Meals served: lunch 12-2, dinner 7-9.30

Adrian Clarke's new venture, having sold the Fox and Goose at Fressingfield (*qv*) to the Watsons, did have some initial teething problems but these have happily now been set right, and his seasonal menus offer much of interest – cream of cauliflower and calabrese soup, steak and kidney pie, home-made pavlova – all good homely stuff. His concise wine list has impeccable choices and sensible prices, particularly wines of the month.

EASTON GREY	Whatley Manor

Easton Grey, Malmesbury, Wiltshire SN16 0RB
Telephone: (0666) 822888 £65
Fax: (0666) 826120
Open: lunch + dinner daily
Meals served: lunch 12.30-1.45, dinner 7.30-9
Grade II listed building extended with great care. Modern English cooking.

EDBURTON	Tottington Manor

Edburton, Henfield, Nr Brighton, West Sussex
Telephone: (0903) 815757 £50
Open: lunch + dinner daily (closed 25+26 Dec)
Meals served: lunch 12-1.30, dinner 7-9.15
Imaginative dishes, well prepared. Eight bedrooms.

Edenbridge — Honours Mill Restaurant

87 High Street, Edenbridge, Kent TN8 5AU
Telephone: (0732) 866757 £65
Open: lunch Tue-Fri + Sun, dinner Mon-Sat (closed 12 wk Xmas)
Meals served: lunch 12.15-2, dinner 7.15-10

With already one medal winner in the family it may not be too long before the Goodhew boys strike gold at their lovely converted mill. Chef Martin Radmall produces fixed price menus (cheaper midweek) displaying a careful and sensitive touch. A roquefort soufflé to start, followed by noisettes of lamb poached in a garlic jus, then tarte tatin of pears is a typical menu.

Egham — La Bonne Franquette

5 High Street, Egham, Surrey TW20 9EA
Telephone: (0784) 439494 £80
Open: lunch Sun-Fri, dinner Mon-Sat (closed Bank Holidays)
Meals served: lunch 12-2, dinner 7-9.30

A change of ownership and proverbial lick of paint but chef David Smart and his team remain producing reliable French cooking such as game terrine with a hazelnut salad, roast tenderloin of lamb with basil, garlic and white beans and perhaps warm lemon tart to finish. The wine list leans toward the expensive end of the market.

Elcot — Elcot Park Resort Hotel

Elcot, Nr Newbury, Berkshire RG16 8NJ
Telephone: (0488) 58100 £60
Fax: (0488) 58288
Open: lunch + dinner daily
Meals served: lunch 12.30-2, dinner 7.30-9.30 (Sat 7-10)
Quality fresh produce in a traditional menu. Facilities include a new leisure centre.

Ely — Fen House Restaurant

2 Lynn Road, Littleport, Ely, Cambridgeshire CB6 1QG
Telephone: (0353) 860645 £50
Open: lunch Sun, dinner Tue-Sun (closed 25+26Dec)
Meals served: lunch 12-2, dinner 7.30-9.30
Warm, friendly restaurant.

Ely — Old Fire Engine House

25 St Mary's Street, Ely, Cambridgeshire CB7 4ER
Telephone: (0353) 662582 £40
Open: lunch daily, dinner Mon-Sat (closed Bank Holiday, 2 wks Xmas/New Year)
Meals served: lunch 12.30-2, dinner 7.30-9

A long-established favourite with no sign of any decline in its popularity. The food is your good old traditional English variety – honest soups, roasts and casseroles – and wherever possible derive from local recipes. Puds take you back to Sunday lunches as a kid and come with plenty of cream. The gallery features a monthly changing exhibition of arts and crafts.

EMSWORTH	36 On The Quay

The Quay, South Street, Emsworth, Hampshire PO10 7EG
Telephone: (0243) 375592 £65
Open: lunch Mon-Fri, dinner Mon-Sat (closed Bank Holidays, 1 wk Jan, 2 wks Sep)
Meals served: lunch 12-2, dinner 7-10

Frank Eckermann is the latest chef with the task of living up to the considerable reputation of 1989 Young Chef of the Year, Richard Wicks. He brings a lighter and less formal style to the fixed price menu at Raymond Shortland's charming quayside restaurant.

ERPINGHAM	Ark

The Street, Erpingham, Norfolk NR11 7QB
Telephone: (0263) 761535 £40
Open: lunch Sun, dinner Tue-Sat (closed part of Oct, Tue in Winter)
Meals served: lunch 12.30-2, dinner 7-9.30 (Sat 7-10) Sat)
Cottage restaurant, above average cooking, fresh local produce.

ETON	Antico

42 High Street, Eton, Berkshire SL4 6BD
Telephone: (0753) 863977 £60
Open: lunch Mon-Fri, dinner Mon-Sat (closed Bank Holidays)
Meals served: lunch 12.30-2.30, dinner 7-10.30

Having been a post office, an auction room and an inn, a restaurant is only the most recent incarnation of this 18th-century building located in Eton's High Street. Owners Ernesto Cassini and Lillo Alessi have been here 20 years and serve authentic Italian cuisine. Be warned – it's popular with the locals, so it's advisable to book.

ENGLAND **349**

| EVERSHOT | Summer Lodge |

Evershot, Dorchester, Dorset DT2 0JR
Telephone: (0935) 83424
Fax: (0935) 83005
Open: lunch + dinner daily (closed 2 wks Jan)
Meals served: lunch 12.30-1.30, dinner 7.30-9

£60

Lovers of Thomas Hardy need look no further. The village of Evershot is the 'Evershead' in the novels, with 'Kings Hintock Court' and Tess's cottage at the top of the High Street. Nigel and Margaret Corbett are the owners of this friendly establishment which maintains its intimacy by refusing large parties or conference bookings. Recent works include the bedrooms in the main building being upgraded and the dining room has been redecorated. From the kitchen, Roger Jones continues to offer sound fixed price 4-course dinners – candle-lit affairs – with unusually, soup as the second course. To start perhaps pan-fried monkfish on a tomato and ginger coulis, and saddle of venison with a candied shallot and filo parcel and juniper berry sauce for main course. For pudding try the hot caramel soufflé with prune and armagnac ice-cream if it's on that evening. Lovely wine buffs list and outstanding local cheeses. A comfortable house with plenty of places to sit and read or relax.

| EVERSLEY | New Mill Restaurant |

New Mill Road, Eversley, Hampshire RG27 0RA
Telephone: (0734) 732277
Fax: (0734) 328780
Open: lunch Mon-Fri, dinner Mon-Sat, Sun all day (Grill open lunch + dinner daily) (closed 26+27 Dec, 1 Jan)
Meals served: lunch 12-2, dinner 7-10 (Sun 12-8)

Restaurant **£60**
Grill **£40**

Turn off the A327 between Eversley and Arborfield and chug along a leafy lane to the end, where you'll find the New Mill Restaurant by the side of the river Blackwater. It's as pretty as a picture with the little bridge, water wheel and gardens and puts you in the mood for some equally appealing food. Coarse rabbit and walnut galantine with a carrot and orange salad, escalope of tuna simply grilled with a sun-dried tomato sauce, and rack of lamb with rosemary and roast garlic are typical dishes in the Riverside Restaurant, while the Mill Room Grill (situated in the oldest part of the mill) offers simpler, hearty food such as game terrine with spicy chutney, and pork and leek sausages with onion gravy and mash. An extensive wine list with unusual depth in vintage champagne.

Evesham — Riverside Hotel

The Parks, Offenham Road, Evesham, Hereford & Worcester WR11 5JP
Telephone: (0386) 446200 £50
Fax: (0386) 40021
Open: lunch Tue-Sun, dinner Tue-Sat (+ Mon in summer)
Meals served: lunch 12-2 (Sun 12-1.30), dinner 7.30-9

Not the easiest place to find, but it's worth it when you get here. The restaurant offers interesting and unpretentious fare along the lines of roast local widgeon, haunch of venison and poached salmon – prices are reasonable throughout. Furnishings and decor in the hotel are carefully co-ordinated and well maintained. Comfortable bedrooms make for a cosy night's sleep.

Exeter — St Olaves Court

Mary Arches Street, Exeter, Devon EX4 3AZ
Telephone: (0392) 217736 £50
Fax: (0392) 413054
Open: lunch Mon-Fri, dinner daily (closed Bank Holidays)
Meals served: lunch 12-2, dinner 6.30-9.30
Seventeen bedroomed hotel conveniently located close to the Cathedral.

Exeter — White Hart

South Street, Exeter, Devon EX1 1EE
Telephone: (0392) 79897 £45
Fax: (0392) 50159
Open: lunch Sun-Fri, dinner daily
Meals: lunch 12-2, dinner 7-9.30
Dating from the 15th Century, this town-centre hotel is built around a courtyard.

Eyton — Marsh Country Hotel

Eyton, Leominster, Hereford & Worcester HR6 0AG
Telephone: (0568) 613952 £50
Open: dinner daily
Meals served: dinner 7.30-9.30

Owners Martin and Jacqueline Gilleland gave up jobs in graphics and teaching home economics to devote themselves to the business of opening and running this hotel. No regrets on either side, I'm sure. This is a charming set-up with 5 cosy bedrooms and a friendly atmosphere. Jacqueline also provides some enjoyable food in the restaurant. Delightful award-winning gardens are another bonus.

FALMOUTH — Seafood Bar

Lower Quay Hill, Falmouth, Cornwall
Telephone: (0326) 315129 £35
Open: dinner Tue-Sat (closed Thu-Sat in winter, closed 10 days Xmas)
Meals served: dinner 7-11

This simple restaurant off a lane leading down to the quay draws the crowds from far and wide. An all-seafood menu save for a couple of steak dishes tagged on at the end. However you'd need your head examined eating meat here, when some of the freshest fish imaginable is there for the asking. Grilled scallops, half a dozen Helford oysters, moules marinières as starters and stir-fried squid, baked grey mullet and cod provençale for main dishes.

FARNHAM — Krug's

84 West Street, Farnham, Surrey GU9 7EN
Telephone: (0252) 723277 £45
Open: lunch Tue-Fri, dinner Tue-Sat
Meals served: lunch 12-2.30, dinner 7-11.30

Tyrolean bric-à-brac, floral curtains, and wooden tables with coarse cloths are what you will find at Gerhard Krug's Austrian restaurant. The menu draws its inspiration from the days of the Austro-Hungarian Empire – thus taking in Czechoslovak, Italian and other influences. Thankfully it avoids twee folksiness and dishes such as gulaschsuppe to start and knoblauchfilet are sturdily done. Desserts are a must – they know what torten and strudel are all about in Austria – and the various pancakes are worth investigating as well.

FAVERSHAM — Read's

Painter's Forstal, Faversham, Kent ME13 0EE
Telephone: (0795) 535344 £65
Fax: (0795) 591200
Open: lunch + dinner Tue-Sat (closed Bank Holidays, 2 wks Aug)
Meals served: lunch 12-2, dinner 7-10

Good food is good food as far as chef and patron David Pitchford is concerned. He's not one to lose sleep over the niceties of traditional or modern styles – and each to his own, say I. Whatever he wants to call his particular brand of cooking it's certainly pulling them in. Each dish runs to several lines so for reasons of space I'll just suggest tartare of fresh salmon marinated in dill, crème fraîche and lemon juice served on a cucumber salad topped with salmon caviar as a starter. Then, for a main dish, try the fillet of Wadhurst Park venison with a traditional peppered redcurrant jelly sauce accompanied by a tartlet of fresh cranberries. For desserts and cheeses you have to take pot luck on the day – they're sure to be good. The exemplary wine list includes an 'Odd and Unusual' supplement – should keep you pleasantly occupied!

Felsted — Rumbles Cottage

Braintree Road, Felsted, Essex CM6 3DJ
Telephone: (0371) 820996 £50
Open: lunch Sun, dinner Tue-Sat (closed Bank Holidays)
Meals served: lunch 12-2, dinner 7-9

Restaurant critics will be looking to their laurels here at Rumbles Cottage. Tuesdays to Thursdays chef Joy Hadley runs a 'Guinea Pig' menu after which everyone is invited to serve up their verdict – gastronome and Joe Public alike. High-faluting criticism is likely to receive short shrift since Joy believes in food being a pleasure open to all. For her, the buzz of a happy restaurant is worth all the hushed solemnity of the grander establishments. Quite right too! Tuck into dishes such as lamb pie casseroled with prunes, turmeric and cinnamon, and fillet of beef lightly pan-fried with mushrooms and grated ginger. It will be hard to find fault!

Fletching — Griffin Inn

Fletching, East Sussex TN22 3NS
Telephone: (0825) 722890 £35
Open: lunch daily, dinner Mon-Sat (closed 25 Dec)
Meals served: lunch 12-2.30, dinner 7-9.30 (Fri+Sat 7-10)
Popular local restaurant within a pub.

Flitwick — Flitwick Manor

Church Road, Flitwick, Bedfordshire MK45 1AE
Telephone: (0525) 712242 £80
Fax: (0525) 712242
Open: lunch + dinner daily
Meals served: lunch 12.30-1.45 (Sun 12-2), dinner 7-9.30 (Sun 7.30-9)

Turn off the A5120, drive up the gravel road through the lovely gardens, and you'll come to Flitwick Manor. The largely 17th-century house has undergone many changes over the years, but the 18th-century folly in the grounds remains intact. More recently, there have been changes of ownership and Somerset Moore has now moved on to Painswick. However, Flitwick Manor remains a charming and attractive establishment. There's an impressive music room with its huge mirror above the fireplace and comfortable armchairs and antiques. Three of the bedrooms have 4-poster beds, and each room has a selection of books, magazines and games and other choice little items designed to make you feel at home. The talented Ian McAndrew is now in charge of the kitchens and 1993 should see some of his culinary skills lifting the restaurant to its full potential.

| FOLKESTONE | Paul's |

2a Bouverie Road West, Folkestone, Kent CT20 2RX
Telephone: (0303) 59697 £40
Open: lunch + dinner daily (closed 25+26 Dec)
Meals served: lunch 12-2.30, dinner 7.30-9.30 (Sat 7.30-10)

Nothing too fancy, but good value eating and a friendly smile are what Paul's sets out to provide – and succeeds. The fresh ingredients are cooked with imagination and lots of cream and clearly go down well with the regulars. A haggis samosa with whisky cream is served as a starter, while a slice of monkfish is poached in cream with white burgundy, prawns and parsley. Plenty of reasonable drinking to be found on the wine list. Recent improvements include an expanded bar area and deeper pink decor.

| FOWEY | Food for Thought |

Town Quay, Fowey, Cornwall PL23 1AT
Telephone: (072 683) 2221 £55
Open: dinner Mon-Sat
Meals served: dinner 7-9.30
Prettily presented food, full of flavours served by friendly, efficient staff.

| FRAMPTON-ON-SEVERN | Saverys Restaurant |

The Green, Frampton-on-Severn, Gloucestershire GL2 7EA
Telephone: (0452) 740077 £55
Open: dinner Tue-Sat (closed Bank Holidays, 1 wk summer)
Meals served: dinner 7-9.15
John Savery's straightforward cooking in a small restaurant in a pretty village.

FRESSINGFIELD — Fox and Goose

Fressingfield, Nr Diss, Suffolk IP21 5PB
Telephone: (037 986) 247
Fax: (037 986) 8107
£65
Open: lunch + dinner Wed-Sun (closed 2 wks Xmas, 3 wks Jul)
Meals served: lunch 12-2, dinner 7-9.30

Ruth and David Watson's move from Hintlesham Hall to the Fox and Goose in Fressingfield is a sign of the times. The new emphasis is upon affordable, homely cooking, using tip-top ingredients which allow plenty of room for invention and imagination. This is food *they* like to eat themselves – and that always bodes well! There's bags of variety on the menu with several dishes available as first or second courses. Calamari and chickpea salad with garlic and lemon oil, half a roast Suffolk duck with thyme and onion stuffing, Fox and Goose sausages and mash, and seized halibut with saffron and garlic potato purée give an indication of the range. This is a very good restaurant and well worth a detour to sample the Watsons' style of hospitality and food.

GARSTANG — El Nido

Whinney Brow Lane, Forton, Garstang, Nr Preston, Lancashire PR3 0AE
Telephone: (0524) 791254
£35
Open: lunch Sun-Fri, dinner daily (closed mid-week lunches in Winter, Bank Holidays, 1 wk Jan)
Meals served: lunch 12-2, dinner 7-10.15
Spanish restaurant specialising in seafood.

GILLINGHAM — Stock Hill House

Stock Hill, Gillingham, Dorset SP8 5NR
Telephone: (0747) 823626
Fax: (0747) 825628
£60
Open: lunch Tue-Sun, dinner Tue-Sat
Meals served: lunch 12.30-1.45, dinner 7.30-8.45

Peter and Nita Hauser seem to have got it right. The war in the Gulf, increased mortgage rates and widespread recession have still not managed to halt the flow of guests to their country house hotel. Could it be their dedication, I wonder, or Peter's excellent cuisine? Probably it's combination of the two and a sure way to keep the most demanding guests satisfied and eager to return. A recent dinner in the impressive dining room listed local pike and chive quenelles on tomato cream among the starters with a cream of nettle soup with croutons to follow. Aga-roasted monkfish tail on garlic and lovage butter is accompanied by lightly cooked vegetables, while the puds include a Sachertorte from his native Austria. Lovely fresh ingredients from his own kitchen garden, straightforward treatments, and a certain 'something' supplied by Herr Hauser set meals here apart. Sound wine list at reasonable prices. Stay in one of the delightful bedrooms, now including a new suite, so that you can sample Peter's excellent breakfast! *See also page 248 – our Clover Award Section.*

Gittisham	Combe House

Gittisham, Nr Honiton, Devon EX14 0AD
Telephone: (0404) 42756 £55
Fax: (0404) 46004
Open: dinner daily (closed Sun+Mon in Jan+Feb)
Meals served: dinner 7.30-9.30

There's the feel of a private house about this Elizabethan mansion. Owners Jack and Thérèse Boswell have interests besides catering and the horse-racing photos and artworks give personality to the decoration of the hotel. The 15 bedrooms and 1 suite are tastefully furnished and well equipped. Beautiful surroundings are an added bonus.

Combe House Hotel

Glastonbury	No. 3 Restaurant & Hotel

3 Magdelene Street, Glastonbury, Somerset BA6 9EW
Telephone: (0458) 832129 £65
Open: dinner Tue-Sat (closed 25 Dec-1 Feb)
Meals served: dinner 7.30-9

A restaurant with rooms run by John and Ann Tynan. Try the liver stroganoff as a starter – a mixture of lambs' liver, mushroom and shallots cooked with garlic and a drop of sherry – with the breast of free-range chicken as a main course, taken off the bone and filled with an avocado mousse. Ann also mentions Cornish seafood as her speciality and she takes pains to ensure that the natural flavours remain intact. Vegetables are organic wherever possible and the herbs are straight from the garden. Spend a night in one of the 6 bedrooms to take advantage of what Glastonbury has to offer.

Glemsford	Barrett's Restaurant

31 Egremont Street, Glemsford, Nr Sudbury, Suffolk CO10 7SA
Telephone: (0787) 281573 £60
Open: lunch Sun, dinner Mon-Sat (closed Bank Holidays)
Meals served: lunch 12-2, dinner 7-9.30
Small local restuarant with regular customers in a small village away from the main routes.

Goathland	Mallyan Spout

Goathland, Whitby, North Yorkshire YO22 5AN
Telephone: (0947) 86206 £50
Open: lunch Sun, dinner daily
Meals served: lunch 12-2, dinner 7-8.30
Comfortable hotel with a warm and friendly atmosphere.

Golant	Cormorant Hotel

Golant, Nr Fowey, Cornwall PL23 1LL
Telephone: (0726) 833426 £55
Open: lunch + dinner daily
Meals served: lunch 12-2.30, dinner 7-9
The setting – on the riverside in a small fishing village – is a great attraction at this relaxed hotel.

GORING-ON-THAMES	The Leatherne Bottel

Riverside Inn & Restaurant, Goring-on-Thames, Berkshire RG8 0HS
Telephone: (0491) 872667
Open: lunch + dinner daily (closed 25 Dec)
Meals served: lunch 12.30-2 (Sat+Sun 12.30-2.30), dinner 9.15-9.45 (Sun 7.30-9)

£60

—some inspired & unusual cooking here

Always a pleasant place to go and eat, particularly on a balmy summer's evening when you can sit out on the terrace. The grill is the inspiration for many of the dishes – tuna marinated in coriander and olive oil with Japanese pak-choi leaves and apple mint, char-grilled salmon with lemon grass, yellow pleurotte mushrooms and ginger are fairly typical. Nothing too fussy and the service is nice and friendly. Try the home-made bread: tomato and olive oil, spinach and walnut.

GOUDHURST	Hughenden

The Plain, Goudhurst, Kent TN17 1AB
Telephone: (0580) 212065
Open: dinner Tue-Sat
Meals served: dinner 7.30-9.30
Informal, popular local restaurant run by Sarah & Michael Levett.

£55

GRASMERE	Michael's Nook

Grasmere, Nr Ambleside, Cumbria LA22 9RP
Telephone: (053 94) 35496
Fax: (053 94) 35765
Open: lunch + dinner daily
Meals served: lunch 12.30 for 1, dinner 7.30 for 8

£75

'Upon a forest side at Grasmere Vale/There dwelt a shepherd, Michael was his name'. Wordsworth's poem inspired the name of this house but even from a distance it's easy to see that this is no humble shepherd's cottage, and by the time you get inside any illusions of rustic simplicity will have been dispelled. Opened as a hotel in 1969 by Reg Gifford, Michael's Nook is a luxurious establishment with 14 fine bedrooms. The dining room is open to visitors and guests alike and offers an interesting selection of dishes from the sure hand of Kevin Mangeolles who, with more than a year under his belt, continues to build with confidence. A typical fixed-price 5-course dinner could include a warm salad of quail, foie gras and crisp potato to start, with a creamy celeriac soup with trompette de la mort mushrooms preceding pan-fried tenderloin of pork with a herb quiche and glazed apples for main course. Dessert and cheese to follow. There's a number of burgundy and bordeaux wines to investigate on the wine list, as well as an admirable choice of half bottles. *See also page 250 – our Clover Awards Section.*

GRASMERE	White Moss House

Rydal Water, Grasmere, Cumbria LA22 9SE
Telephone: (053 94) 35295 £55
Open: dinner Mon-Sat (closed Dec-Feb)
Meals served: dinner at 8

Whilst most hotels in the district are cashing in on the name of William Wordsworth, White Moss House has the distinction of actually having been *owned* by the poet. Peter Dixon follows in the English tradition of cookery with everyone sitting down at 8pm to enjoy his no-choice-until-pudding dinners. Soup to start, maybe wild mushroom, marjoram and marsala, then something fishy – a soufflé of Coniston Water char and smoked River Eden salmon – followed by a hearty roast, perhaps Westmorland beef marinated with real ale and a mustard, tarragon and red wine sauce. His desserts are still a highlight and always include a traditional pudding – huntsman's, guardsman's, Kentish well. When you're not out hiking about the countryside, the hotel is a cosy place to rest and put up your feet.

GRASMERE	Wordsworth Hotel

Grasmere, Nr Ambleside, Cumbria LA22 9SW
Telephone: (053 94) 35592 £55
Fax: (053 94) 35765
Open: lunch + dinner daily
Meals served: lunch 12.30-2, dinner 7-9 (Fri+Sat 7-9.30)

Old William didn't live here, or write his poems about the house, but he's buried in the churchyard next door instead! If you're not hiring the Coleridge Suite for a private celebration, there's the Prelude Restaurant offering, on its elongated menu, dishes using good local produce such as a mélange of woodland mushrooms and breast of Lunesdale duck filled with apricots. Excellent facilities are provided in the hotel itself.

Grayshott	Woods Place

Headley Road, Grayshott, Nr Hindhead, Surrey GU26 6LB
Telephone: (0428) 605555 £45
Open: dinner Tue-Sat (closed 1 wk Xmas)
Meals served: dinner 7-11

Eric Norrgren's friendly Scandinavian wine bar – there's an idea for you! – serves Swedish marinated herrings, Danish frikadeller and home-made doughnuts, amongst other things. His sister Anna is in charge of Anna's Place in London.

Great Dunmow	The Starr

Market Place, Great Dunmow, Essex CM6 1AX
Telephone: (0371) 874321 £70
Fax: (0371) 876337
Open: lunch Sun-Fri, dinner Mon-Sat (closed 1 wk Jan)
Meals served: lunch 12-1.30, dinner 7-9.30

English with a markedly French accent is how Mark Fisher likes to describe his highly competent cooking. Cheese and onion soup and salad of pigeon breast with pine kernels and Madeira are typical starters while fillet of brill with fennel and saffron and breast of duck with honey and figs are among the main courses. The wine list includes some astute selections and plenty of tasting notes. On Friday and Saturday nights you can benefit from special discount rates in the 8 bedrooms at this really well run hostelry.

Great Gonerby	Harry's Place

17 High Street, Great Gonerby, Grantham, Lincolnshire NG31 8JS
Telephone: (0476) 61780 £75
Open: lunch + dinner Tue-Sat (closed Bank Holidays, 1 wk Xmas)
Meals served: lunch 12-2, dinner 7-9.30

Not the cheapest place to eat, but then you're virtually paying for a private chef. This tiny little restaurant only seats 10! Harry is in charge in the kitchen while his wife Caroline serves the food. The menu is honed down to allow absolute control of the final result with a choice of 2 items for each course. Fillet of seabass with a fresh herb crust and pigeon roasted with sercial madeira, bacon and tarragon are typical main courses. Similarly restrained wine list.

GREAT MILTON Le Manoir aux Quat'Saisons

Church Road, Great Milton, Oxfordshire OX9 7PD
Telephone: (0844) 278881
Fax: (0844) 278847
Open: lunch + dinner daily
Meals served: lunch 12.15-2.15, dinner 7.15-10.15

£165

The menu is lavish, bearing a delightful framed cameo of Le Manoir standing between the gates. It unfolds to disclose a plethora of dishes each as tempting as the last. Notre Menu Gourmand is on yet another page and it reads well by itself: assiette apéritive; salade landaise; oeuf brouillé aux truffes noires du Périgord; coquilles St Jacques rôties aux topinambours, jus de dinde; sorbet au champagne: caille des dombes farcie, jus au Pineau des Charentes; les trois petits bonheurs du Manoir; and les petits fours du Manoir. As if this wasn't enough, the back of the menu lists les specialités du passé de Raymond Blanc, just to make you realise what you've missed out on! However it is a fitting tribute to the single-mindedness with which he has gone about perfecting his art. The price of a meal at Le Manoir cannot be measured in terms of sheer man hours but rather a lifetime's devotion to cooking. There's no doubt about it, Le Manoir is now in full splendour, with the grounds and herb gardens matured and the 21 rooms including those in the converted stable block well settled in. Led by Alain Desenclos the front-of-house team run the restaurant with professionalism and pride and will be only too pleased to advise you on your choice from the extensive top-end-of-the-market wine list. *See also page 252 – Our Clover Awards section.*

GREAT MISSENDEN — La Petite Auberge

107 High Street, Great Missenden, Buckinghamshire HP16 0BB
Telephone: (024 06) 5370
£55
Open: dinner Mon-Sat (closed Bank Holidays, Xmas/New Year)
Meals served: dinner 7.30-10.30
Smart local French restaurant.

GREAT YARMOUTH — Seafood Restaurant

85 North Quay, Great Yarmouth, Norfolk NR30 1JF
Telephone: (0493) 856009
£60
Open: lunch Mon-Fri, dinner Mon-Sat (closed Bank Holidays, 3 wks Xmas)
Meals served: lunch 12-1.45, dinner 7-10.30

Choose your own fish from the refrigerated display and state how you'd like it to be cooked. After that it's in the hands of the chefs, but they'll do a good job. Lobsters are available from the tank and you can have them in a variety of ways – hot with garlic butter, thermidor, mornay and so on. Mixed platters of fish and shellfish are popular and you can also choose surf and turf. The wine list is understandably strong on whites and has a fair number of half bottles.

GRIMSTON — Congham Hall

Lynn Road, Grimston, King's Lynn, Norfolk PE32 1AH
Telephone: (0485) 600250
£70
Fax: (0485) 601191
Open: lunch Sun-Fri, dinner daily (closed Bank Holiday lunches)
Meals served: lunch 12.30-2, dinner 7.30-9.30

Having had one of those horrendous journeys from London on a Friday evening – it must have happened to you at some time – I arrived an hour late at Congham Hall and half an hour past last orders. If the staff were put out, it certainly didn't show. The conservatory-style dining room has views over lawns leading to some superb trees, amongst them 140-year-old oaks. The patio area at the side is ideal for drinks or al fresco eating.

A good-sized fillet steak served with thinly sliced potatoes leafed around in pommes anna style was perfectly medium-rare, with a reduction of the juices infused with herbs. Vegetables consisted of green and yellow courgettes, broccoli and baby turnips glazed with butter. To finish there was a baked tartlet of blue cheeses with a mound of lightly dressed summer salad leaves in the centre – it tasted as good as it looked. I would have liked to have tried the ravioli of wild mushrooms flavoured with garden herbs, served on a braised rice and madeira cream sauce as a starter. Good choice of reasonably priced wines, excellent selection of herbal teas and service by a young, helpful British staff.

I didn't get to look round the gardens until the next morning, and this is when you realise the full extent of the love and hard work put in by Trevor and Christine Forecast in running Congham Hall. To me the piéce de resistance must be the magnificent herb garden which Christine will proudly show you. It's no small wonder that Murray Chapman in the kitchen brings out some exquisite flavours. Congham Hall is not in the grand style of country house hotels – it's a nicely proportioned Georgian 18th-century house where the warm welcome you receive makes it worth staying more than one night. *See also page 246 – Our Clover Awards section.*

GUERNSEY — Absolute End

St George's Esplanade, St Peter Port, Guernsey, Channel Islands
Telephone: (0481) 723822
Open: lunch + dinner Mon-Sat (closed Jan)
Meals served: lunch 12.30-2, dinner 7-10
Sea-front restaurant with the emphasis on seafood although there are meat dishes as well.

£45

GUERNSEY — La Frégate

Les Cotils, St Peter Port, Guernsey, Channel Islands
Telephone: (0481) 724624
Fax: (0481) 720443
Open: lunch + dinner daily
Meals served: lunch 12.30-1.30, dinner 7-9.30
Lovely views, traditional comfort.

£50

GUERNSEY — Louisiana

South Esplanade, St Peter Port, Guernsey, Channel Islands
Telephone: (0481) 713157
Fax: (0481) 712191
Open: lunch + dinner Wed-Mon (closed Bank Holidays)
Meals served: lunch 12-2.30, dinner 6-10.30
Smart restaurant with large windows overlooking the sea.

£40

GUERNSEY — Le Nautique

The Quay Steps, St Peter Port, Guernsey, Channel Islands
Telephone: (0481) 721714
Open: lunch + dinner Mon-Sat (closed 2 wks Jan)
Meals served: lunch 12-2, dinner 7-10
Smart, old-style restaurant, popular with locals and tourists alike. Seafood is the speciality, the style classic, the cooking accurate and full of flavour.

£45

GUERNSEY — Old Government House

Ann's Place, St Peter Port, Guernsey, Channel Islands
Telephone: (0481) 724291
Fax: (0481) 724429
Open: lunch + dinner daily
Meals served: lunch 12-2, dinner 7-9.15
Traditional service and furnishings in the original Governor's residence.

£55

GUERNSEY — St Margaret's Lodge

Forest Road, St Martin, Guernsey, Channel Islands
Telephone: (0481) 35757
Fax: (0481) 37594
Open: lunch + dinner daily
Meals served: lunch -1.45, dinner -9.30 (Sat 9.45)
Modern hotel close to airport and south coast bays.

£35

GUERNSEY — St Pierre Park Hotel

Rohais, St Peter Port, Guernsey, Channel Islands
Telephone: (0481) 728282 Fax (0481) 712041
Open: lunch Sun-Fri, dinner Mon-Sat
Meals served: lunch 12-2.30, dinner 7-10.30

£50

You can dine on filet de saumon braisé au Stilton et celeris or mignons de boeuf au porto in the Victor Hugo restaurant, or enjoy the more straightforward roasts in the Café Renoir. The hotel offers no fewer than 130 rooms and there's now the impressive Le Mirage health and leisure suite including an indoor pool. For golfers there's also a private 9-hole golf course designed by Tony Jacklin.

Guist	Tollbridge

Dereham Road, Guist, Norfolk NR20 5NU
Telephone: (036 284) 359 £50
Open: lunch Sun, dinner Mon-Sat (closed 3 wks Jan)
Meals served: lunch 12.30-1.30, dinner 7.30-9 (Sat 7-9.30)

You can hear the squabbling ducks from the terrace at this riverside restaurant. A twice-baked cheese soufflé is a tasty starter, with fish from the market or a hearty cassoulet for main course. The wine list repays a careful look and the fixed price menu format is popular, so book.

Gulworthy	Horn of Plenty

Gulworthy, Tavistock, Devon PL19 8JD
Telephone: (0822) 832528 £75
Open: lunch Tue-Sun, dinner daily (closed 25+26 Dec)
Meals served: lunch 12-2, dinner 7-9.30

This old favourite is back on song after a discordant period during the change-over in ownership. We can enjoy once more the beautiful views, well tended gardens, and charming bedrooms, safe in the knowledge of gastronomic delights to match. Elaine and Ian Gatehouse have worked wonders in a short space of time and chef Peter Gorton is delivering the goods. His home-made ravioli filled with smoked salmon in a liver and dill sauce, and the Cornish lobster and vegetable salad with asparagus in tempura are both excellent starters. Main courses include grilled turbot with tomato, peppers and saffron and a basil sauce, baked breast of duck and wild mushrooms wrapped in a cabbage leaf with a port sauce. The delicious desserts will have you craving for more. Some 160 wines on the international list, mid-price but with some handy half bottles. Welcome back to the Horn of Plenty!

Halford	Sykes House

Queen Street, Halford, Warwickshire CV36 5BT
Telephone: (0789) 740976 £65
Open: dinner daily (Sun+Tue by arrangement only)
Meals served: dinner 7.30-8.15 by reservation only
David & Peggy Cunliffe's friendly local restaurant, serving English cooking.

Hanchurch	Hanchurch Manor

Hanchurch, Nr Stoke-on-Trent, Staffordshire ST4 8JD
Telephone: (0782) 643030
Fax: (0782) 643035 £55
Open: lunch + dinner daily
Meals served: lunch 12.30-2, dinner 7.30-9.30
Lovely 12-bedroomed hotel in 9 acres of grounds.

HARROGATE	Bettys Café & Tea Rooms

1 Parliament Street, Harrogate, North Yorkshire HG1 2QU
Telephone: (0423) 502746 £35
Open: all day daily (closed 25 Dec, 1 Jan)
Meals served: 9-9

It sounds like the place in *The Last of the Summer Wine*, but it's set its sights rather higher. Here you can have the most wonderful breads and cakes which must be some of the finest in Yorkshire and are all made by hand. Children are more than welcome and can tuck into Betty's Clown with its egg hat, tomato ears and pineapple nose – just one of the items on the special kids' menu. Even a pot of tea can be made into an event, since many blends are specially selected and unobtainable elsewhere. Be warned, it's popular!

HARROGATE	Café Fleur

3 Royal Parade, Harrogate, North Yorkshire HG1 2SZ
Telephone: (0423) 503034 £40
Open: dinner daily (closed 25+26 Dec, 1 Jan)
Meals served: dinner 6-9.30

Café Fleur has blossomed right opposite the Crown Hotel. Tim and Kath Burdekin's new venture (they used to run Burdekin's, also in Harrogate) offers some good food – magret de canard sauce cassis, saumon sauce moutarde et herbes and langoustines à l'ail – in brasserie style surroundings. They throw in a half bottle of house wine on the prix fixe menu, which offers exceptional value. The small wine list spans the globe with most bottles under £15.

HARROGATE	Drum & Monkey

5 Montpellier Gardens, Harrogate, North Yorkshire HG1 2TF
Telephone: (0423) 502650 £45
Open: lunch + dinner Mon-Sat (closed Xmas/New Year)
Meals served: lunch 12-2.30, dinner 7-10.15

Not the place to come to if you're after a quiet, relaxed meal to pass the hours away. The Drum and Monkey is heaving with people – customers elbow each other in the downstairs bar and squeeze themselves around the slate-topped tables upstairs. Service is fast and furious. Seafood and more seafood is what you'll find on the menu – half a dozen oysters, hot shellfish platter, fillet of brill au safran and seafood pie give you the general idea. Freshness is guaranteed by the quick turnover. To be in with a chance of getting a table it's necessary to book for this lovely, pleasant restaurant.

Harrogate   Miller's

1 Montpelier Mews, Harrogate, North Yorkshire HG1 2TG
Telephone: (0423) 530708   £70
Open: lunch Tue-Sat, dinner Mon-Sat (closed Bank Holidays)
Meals served: lunch 12-2, dinner 7-10

Simon Gueller's streamlined operation is proving a success, which shows that every cloud has a silver lining! The revised menus are a triumph of imagination and although some of the more expensive ingredients have gone, his talent is such that you'd hardly notice. This is cooking of a high order, with beautifully crafted sauces a speciality. Try the ravioli of sweetbreads with an almond and pistachio jus followed by loin of Dutch veal with a light cream sauce of fresh thyme flowers. Finish with marquise au chocolat, coffee and petits fours.

Harvington   The Mill
Anchor Lane, Harvington, Nr Evesham, Hereford & Worcester WR11 5NR
Telephone: (0386) 870688   £50
Fax: (0386) 870688
Open: lunch + dinner daily (closed 5 days Xmas)
Meals served: lunch 12-1.45, dinner 7-8.45 (Sun 7-8.30)
Charming small hotel in idyllic surroundings by the river Avon.

Haslemere   Morel's

23 Lower Street, Haslemere, Surrey GU27 2NY
Telephone: (0428) 651462   £80
Open: lunch Tue-Fri, dinner Tue-Sat (closed Bank Holidays except Good Friday, 2 wks Feb, 2 wks Sep)
Meals served: lunch 12.30-2, dinner 7-10

Jean-Yves Morel has been doing what he does best for over 10 years here in Haslemere – French cooking of some distinction which brings smiles to the lips of his well-heeled Surrey clientele. His celebratory table d'hôte menu is still great value and shows his talents to the full, with a ballottine of duck confit with new potatoes as a starter and wild pigeon with lentils and madeira as a main course. Crème grandmère or rhubarb soufflé are 2 typical desserts but the assiette du chef from the carte is always the one to go for since it allows a taste of everything – definitely worth the supplement! Good French wine list.

Hastings   Röser's

64 Eversfield Place, St Leonards on Sea, Nr Hastings, East Sussex TN37 6DB
Telephone: (0424) 712218   £60
Open: lunch Tue-Fri, dinner Tue-Sat (closed Bank Holidays, 1 wk Jan, 1 wk Aug)
Meals served: lunch 12-2, dinner 7-10

This is not your everyday seafront restaurant, the interior belies the bland exterior, for Herr Röser has become something of an institution in this part of the world, and deservedly so. Inspiration from his homeland blends with local prime quality ingredients to great effect – hare and marjoram terrine, or genuine blinis to start, oak-smoked roast salmon with a chive and wild horseradish sauce, or wild boar chop with a lentil sauce to follow. Well-chosen New World wines supplement a list already strong on classics.

Hatfield Heath — Down Hall

Hatfield Heath, Bishop's Stortford, Hertfordshire CM22 7AS
Telephone: (0279) 731441 £55
Fax: (0279) 730416
Open: lunch + dinner daily (closed New Year)
Meals served: lunch 12-2, dinner 7-9.30

Italianate Victorian mansion with an impressive main lounge. Aimed predominantly at the business sector, it has 14 meeting rooms, 12 syndicate rooms, full leisure facilities and 2 restaurants. Superb grounds.

Haworth — Weavers

15 West Lane, Haworth, Nr Bradford, West Yorkshire BD22 8DU
Telephone: (0535) 643822 £50
Open: lunch Sun in winter, dinner Tue-Sun (closed Bank Holidays but open 25 Dec, 2 wks Xmas, 2 wks Jul)
Meals served: lunch 12-1.30, dinner 7-9.30

Eating out for the sake of eating out is how the Rushworths see their restaurant. They won't 'make a meal' of things here, just good straightforward food with no messing about. Pancakes, salads and soups get things going, and Weaver's own cow pie and a crisp roast Gressingham duck will fill you up nicely. Nanny's meringue and old school pudding with lashings of custard are there should you have space to spare. Everything is made on the premises and most of the vegetables are home grown. While you're here, you might as well make a night of it – stay in one of the 4 bedrooms and then have a look at the Brontë parsonage after breakfast.

Hayling Island — Cockle Warren Cottage

36 Seafront, Hayling Island, Hampshire PO11 9HL
Telephone: (0705) 464961 £60
Open: dinner daily for residents only
Meals served: dinner 7.30 for 8
Excellent value, set 5-course dinner.

Haytor — Bel Alp House

Haytor, Nr Bovey Tracey, Devon TQ13 9XX
Telephone: (0364) 661217 £75
Fax: (0364) 661292
Open: dinner daily (closed Dec-Feb)
Meal served: dinner 7.30-8.30
Comfortably restored house with nine bedrooms. Daily changing 5-course dinner using locally produced foods.

Helford	Riverside

Helford, Nr Helston, Cornwall TR12 6JU
Telephone: (0326) 231443 £65
Open: dinner daily (closed Nov-Feb)
Meals served: dinner 7.30-9.30

Pride of place goes to fresh local fish at the Darrells' charming cottagey restaurant with rooms – the terrace overlooking the tidal creek being a particularly lovely spot to enjoy a light breakfast. There are 2 fixed price menus for dinner, one at £18, the other £28 with perhaps a fricassée of local mussels, clams and poached oysters bound in a chive butter sauce to start, then poached fillet of brill on a beetroot butter sauce. Home-made biscuits with cheese or fruity desserts to finish. Six bedrooms make this an ideal place to stay and enjoy the beautiful setting.

Helmsley	Monet's

19 Bridge Street, Helmsley, North Yorkshire YO6 5BG
Telephone: (0439) 70618 £50
Open: lunch Tue-Sun, dinner Tue-Sat (closed Feb)
Meals served: lunch 12-2.30, dinner 7-9.30 (summer 10-5 + 7-10)
Seasonally changing menu served in a relaxed homely dining room.

Hereford	Steppes Country House Hotel

Ullingswick, Nr Hereford, Hereford & Worcester HR1 3JG
Telephone: (0432) 820424 £45
Open: dinner daily (closed 2 wks before Xmas, 2 wks after New Year)
Meals served: dinner at 7.30
Small family-run country house hotel.

Herm	The White House

Herm, Channel Islands
Telephone: (0481) 722159 £35
Fax: (0481) 710066
Open: lunch + dinner daily (closed Oct-Mar)
Meals served: lunch 12.30-1.30, dinner 7-9

The Wood family actually own this island – at least until the year 2050 – and so, in a sense, wherever you walk you're still in their back garden! The 32-bedroomed hotel is bright and comfortable and fully justifies its claims of providing peace and quiet. No cars, but a walk around the island only takes a couple of hours!

| HERNE BAY | L'Escargot |

22 High Street, Herne Bay, Kent CT6 5LH
Telephone: (0227) 373876 £35
Open: lunch + dinner daily
Meals served: lunch 12-1.30, dinner 7-9.30 (Sun only at 7)
Classic and modern dishes using fresh produce in a friendly, informal atmosphere.

| HERSHAM | La Malmaison |

17 Queens Road, Hersham, Walton-on-Thames, Surrey KT12 5ND
Telephone: (0932) 227412 £60
Open: lunch Mon-Fri, dinner Mon-Sat
Meals served: lunch 12.30-2.30, dinner 7-10
Natural flavours shine through in Jacques Troquet's classically-based French cooking. Lisa Troquet is a charming, knowledgeable hostess.

HERSTMONCEUX — Sundial Restaurant

Gardner Street, Herstmonceux, East Sussex BN27 4LA
Telephone: (0323) 832217 £65
Open: lunch Tue-Sun, dinner Tue-Sat (closed 2/3 wks Aug/Sep, Xmas-mid Jan)
Meals served: lunch 12.30-2.30, dinner 7.30-9.30 (Sat 7.30-10)

Giuseppe Bertoli's menu will keep you occupied for a while and gives weight to the term 'spoilt for choice'. On 3 pages you'll find Les Plats du Jour, Table d'Hôte du Jour, Crustacés – Hors d'Oeuvres et Entrées Chauds and Poissons – Volailles – Gibier et Viandes, and should that not be enough, there's also a Menu Surprise Gourmande. At my count that makes about 50 dishes to choose from – so take your time! In the end you'll enjoy whatever comes, champignons farçis au gruyère followed by darne de saumon aux crevettes, perhaps, or noisettes de chevreuil aux mures when in season. The house wine is reliable, but take care on the main list – it's good, but at top-of-the-range prices. This is a happy restaurant set off the main road run with care and professionalism by the Bertolis, supported by a young staff. *See also page 256 – our Clover Awards section.*

HETTON — Angel Inn

Hetton, Nr Skipton, North Yorkshire BD23 6LT
Telephone: (0756) 730263 £50
Open: lunch Sun, dinner Mon-Sat (Bar lunch + dinner daily)
Meals served: lunch 12-1.30, dinner 7-9.30 (Bar lunch 12-2, dinner 6-10)

I'm not the only one to think that Denis Watkins restaurant deserves wider critical acclaim. Many of his customers will bear me out when I say that he's set up an example for similar establishments up and down the country. The food is excellent and the service admirably efficient and friendly. Denis's 4-course menus make exciting reading and by way of example might include filet mignon of English lamb wrapped in a mousseline of duck foie gras and savoy leaves, steamed and served hot on a cream and wild mushroom sauce and fillet of monkfish wrapped in spinach and bacon, baked on fennel and carved onto a sauce beurre blanc flavoured with star anise and finished with cream. The wine list makes equally good reading. The restaurant and bar are both in an attractive, old world setting.

HEXHAM	**Black House**

Dipton Mill Road, Hexham, Northumberland NE46 1RZ
Telephone: (0434) 604744 £45
Open: dinner Tue-Sat
Meals served: dinner 7-9.30
Local restaurant with monthly-changing menus of fresh local produce.

HIGH ONGAR	**Shoes Restaurant**

The Street, High Ongar, Essex CM5 9ND
Telephone: (0277) 363350 £50
Open: lunch Sun-Fri, dinner Mon-Sat (closed Bank Holidays, 1 wk Xmas/New Year)
Meals served: lunch 12-2 (Sun 12-2.30), dinner 7-9.30
Eclectic à la carte menu which changes every six weeks. Home-made bread, pasta, sorbets and ice creams.

HINTLESHAM — Hintlesham Hall

Hintlesham, Nr Ipswich, Suffolk IP8 3NS
Telephone: (047 387) 334
Fax: (047 387) 463 £65
Open: lunch Sun-Fri, dinner daily
Meals served: lunch 12-1.45, dinner 7-9.30

I wrote in last year's guide that standards would be maintained under new ownership, and I am delighted to say that my initial impression has been more than justified. The Hall now has an 18-hole championship standard golf course which was apparently left for 2 years to mature before the opening, and a fully-equipped club-house including its own dining area, saunas, steam room and spa bath. Add to that trout fishing, tennis, clay pigeon shooting, with a swimming pool promised for 1993, and there's plenty for you to do to work off a meal at Hintlesham.

There have been some alterations inside the Hall with the dining room now transferred to the banqueting hall, the wood-panelled former dining room now the bar, and a new kitchen for Alan Ford to demonstrate his undoubted skills. Young, knowledgeable staff under the stewardship of Tim Sutherland, general manager, make for a very pleasant, relaxed stay.

There's normally a choice of 9 starters and 9 main courses, and on my last visit there I really had a problem choosing. I eventually settled for a spicy fricassée of fish served with rouille and garlic croûtes, which was nothing short of sensational, and noisettes of lamb with a dark basil and tomato sauce, the meat having a little fat left on to give that extra taste. Five different vegetables were served separately. Having tucked into a half bottle of Montrachet and further indulged in a half bottle of Gevrey Chambertin it was all I could do to nibble a piece of Milleens to finish the meal. I could have chosen from an iced raspberry parfait served in raspberry sauce, or warm filo parcels filled with banana, pear and almond cream among the choice of 6 puddings.

There are now 33 bedrooms and suites available, and I look forward to my next visit and the thrill of coming up the drive facing the magnificent 16th-century hall. For that very special occasion you can fly from central London by helicopter in 20 minutes. *See also page 258 – our Clover Awards section.*

HINTON	**Hinton Grange**

Hinton, Nr Dyrham Park, Avon SN14 8HG
Telephone: (0275) 822916 £4?
Fax: (0275) 823285
Open: dinner daily
Meals served: dinner 7-10 (Sun 7-9)
Converted farmhouse and outbuildings with informal atmosphere and friendly service.

Hoar Cross — Hoar Cross Hall

Hoar Cross, Nr Yoxall, Staffordshire
Telephone: (028 375) 671   £65
Fax: (028 375) 652
Open: lunch + dinner daily
Meals served: lunch 12-2, dinner 6-8.30
Full health spa facilities are on offer at this Grade II listed country house hotel.

Hockley Heath — Nuthurst Grange

Nuthurst Grange Lane, Hockley Heath, Warwickshire B94 5NL
Telephone: (0564) 783972   **£85**
Fax: (0564) 783919
Open: lunch Sun-Fri, dinner daily (closed 1 wk Xmas)
Meals served: lunch 12-2.30, dinner 7-9.30

The Randolphs' hotel has had the builders in this year. In the new extension there are 8 further bedrooms and a ground-floor restaurant with 2 private dining rooms. The old restaurant has been converted into a lounge but David Randolph's cooking sticks to the same formula that has made the Grange a firm favourite with the locals and travellers from further afield.

Holbeton — Alston Hall

Alston Cross, Holbeton, Plymouth, Devon PL8 1HN
Telephone: (075 530) 555   £55
Fax: (075 530) 494
Open: lunch + dinner daily
Meals served: lunch 12-2, dinner 7-9.30
Ivy-clad Edwardian mansion set in 4 acres of grounds.

Holdenby — Lynton House

The Croft, Holdenby, Nr Northampton, Northamptonshire NN6 8DJ
Telephone: (0604) 770777   £50
Open: lunch Tue-Fri, dinner Mon-Sat (closed Bank Holidays except Good Friday, 2 wks Aug)
Meals served: lunch 12.30-2.45, dinner 7.30-9.45
Former rectory, pink decor, warm Italian welcome, competent Anglo-Italian food.

Holt — Yetman's

37 Norwich Road, Holt, Norfolk NR25 6SA
Telephone: (0263) 713320   £55
Open: lunch Sat+Sun, dinner Wed-Sun
Meals served: lunch 12.30-2, dinner 7.30-9
Alison and Peter Yetman's popular restaurant uses fresh local ingredients.

Horncastle — Magpies Restaurant

73-75 East Street, Horncastle, Lincolnshire LN9 6AA
Telephone: (0507) 527004   £45
Open: lunch Tue-Sun, dinner Tue-Sat (closed Xmas, 2 wks Oct or May)
Meals served: lunch 12.30-2.30, dinner 7.30-9.30
Good food and wine at reasonable prices.

Horndon on the Hill — Hill House

High Road, Horndon on the Hill, Essex SS17 8LD
Telephone: (0375) 642463   £40
Fax: (0375) 361611
Open: lunch Tue-Fri, dinner Tue-Sat (closed Bank Holidays, 5 days Xmas)
Meals served: lunch 12.30-2, dinner 7.30-9.45
Lunch menus change daily and dinner menus fortnightly. Inventive dishes are made with top quality ingredients.

| HORTON | French Partridge |

Horton, Nr Northampton, Northamptonshire NN7 2AP
Telephone: (0604) 870033 £50
Open: dinner Tue-Sat (closed 2 wks Xmas, 2 wks Easter, 3 wks Jul/Aug)
Meals served: dinner 7.30-9

Some great quaffing is to be had from the wine list – an excellent selection and, what's more, excellent prices! Add to this the fine, predominantly French, cooking and you have a restaurant and a half. That this will be its 29th year doesn't surprise me at all. Many happy returns.

| HORTON CUM STUDLEY | Studley Priory |

Horton cum Studley, Nr Oxford, Oxon OX9 1AZ
Telephone: (086 735) 203 £60
Fax: (086 735) 613
Open: lunch + dinner daily
Meals served: lunch 12.30-1.45 (Sun 12.30-2), dinner 7.30-9.30 (Sun 7.30-9)
Elizabethan priory with a Georgian wing, nineteen bedrooms.

| HUDDERSFIELD | Paris II |

84 Fitzwilliam Street, Huddersfield, West Yorkshire HD1 5BD
Telephone: (0484) 516773 £30
Open: lunch Mon-Fri, dinner Mon-Sat
Meals served: lunch 12-2, dinner 6-10.30
Fish restaurant, good value, simple and fresh produce.

| HULL | Le Bistro |

400 Beverley Road, Hull, Humberside HU5 1LW
Telephone: (0482) 43088 £35
Open: dinner Mon-Sat (closed Xmas/New Year, 2 wks Aug)
Meals served: dinner 7-10
Small, largely vegetarian restaurant.

| HULL | Ceruttis |

10 Nelson Street, Hull, Humberside HU1 1XE
Telephone: (0482) 28501 £55
Fax: (0482) 587597
Open: lunch Mon-Fri, dinner Mon-Sat (closed Bank Holiday, 1 wk Xmas)
Meals served: lunch 12-2, dinner 7-9.30

Scampi come au gratin or bannaro (with banana and almonds), while scallops are served provençale or as a stir-fry. Dover sole Antonio, Waleska, St Brie and du Barry are all possible and many of the other fish are offered in a variety of ways. As you'll have guessed by now, this is a fish restaurant although steaks creep in at the bottom of the menu. Open since 1974, Ceruttis needs little introduction from me.

Hunstrete   Hunstrete House

Hunstrete, Chelwood, Nr Bath, Avon BS18 4NS
Telephone: (0781) 490490   **£80**
Fax: (0781) 490732
Open: lunch + dinner daily
Meals served: lunch 12.30-2.30, dinner 7.30-9.30

Worth a visit for the splendid grounds and gardens. The house itself is largely 18th Century and contains 24 well-appointed bedrooms. Other rooms are equally gracious and look out over rolling Mendip foothills.

Huntingdon   Old Bridge Hotel
1 High Street, Huntingdon, Cambridgeshire PE18 6TQ
Telephone: (0480) 52681   £55
Fax: (0480) 411017
Open: lunch + dinner daily
Meals served: lunch 12-2, dinner 7-10
18th-century house, twenty-seven bedrooms, in grounds leading to the River Ouse.

Huntsham   Huntsham Court

Huntsham, Bampton, Nr Tiverton, Devon EX16 7NA
Telephone: (039 86) 365   **£60**
Fax: (039 86) 456
Open: dinner daily
Meals served: dinner 8-10.30

Victorian bits and pieces create a bit of character and music lovers will take to the place immediately. Sit round the long dining table and get to know your fellow guests over some fine food. A bottle or two from the excellent cellar will encourage the conversation! Some bathrooms have proper tubs with feet, some bedrooms have open fires. One even has a piano. Ideal for a sybaritic weekend house-party.

Hurley   Ye Olde Bell
High Street, Hurley, Nr Maidenhead, Berkshire SL6 5LX
Telephone: (0628) 825881   £65
Fax: (0628) 825939
Open: lunch + dinner daily
Meals served: lunch 12.30-2.15, dinner 7.30-9.30 (Sun 7.30-9)
Popular since 1135, the hotel has plenty of character. Twenty-five bedrooms, some (like the dining room) overlook the gardens.

Hurstbourne Tarrant — Esseborne Manor

Hurstbourne Tarrant, Nr Andover, Hampshire SP11 0ER
Telephone: (0264) 76444 £65
Fax: (0264) 76473
Open: lunch + dinner daily
Meals served: lunch 12.30-2, dinner 7.30-9.30

You'll need to have worked up an appetite before coming to dine here. Dinner is a set price 5-course affair, 4 choices at each stage excluding the fish course. Dishes are well balanced but they're still expecting a lot of you to finish the entire menu. Overall the cooking is good and looks appealing on the plate – high points being a spiced tomato and bacon soup and a marmite of fish in saffron sauce. The hotel itself divides accommodation between the main house and the converted stable block. Whichever room you end up in, standards of furnishing and upkeep are high, and there's hours of fun in store playing with the plastic toys provided in every bathroom! A comfortable place to stay and some lovely scenery to boot.

Ilkley — Box Tree

29 Church Street, Ilkley, West Yorkshire LS29 9DR
Telephone: (0943) 608484 £60
Fax: (0943) 816793
Open: lunch Wed-Fri + Sun, dinner Wed-Sat (closed 25+26 Dec, 1 Jan)
Meals served: lunch 12.30-2 (Sun 12.30-2.30), dinner 7.30-9.45

Local hotelier Mme Avis is the new owner of this legendary restaurant and seems confident that her new young team will be up to the task of reviving its fortunes. We await with interest.

Ilkley — Rombalds Hotel
West View, Wells Road, Ilkley, West Yorkshire LS29 9JG
Telephone: (0943) 603201 £70
Fax: (0943) 816586
Open: lunch + dinner daily (closed 27-29 Dec)
Meals served: lunch 12-2 (Sun brunch 9-1.30), dinner 7-9.30 (Sun 7-8.30)
Elegant Georgian building standing at the edge of Ilkley Moor, overlooking the beautiful Wharfe Valley.

Ilkley — Sous le Nez
19-21 Church Street, Ilkley, West Yorkshire LS26 9DR
Telephone: (0943) 600566 £35
Open: lunch + dinner Mon-Sat
Meals served: lunch 12-2.30, dinner 6-10.30 (Fri+Sat 6-11)
Elegant restaurant upstairs and bistro downstairs.

Ipswich — Browns Restaurant
8 St Peters Street, Ipswich, Suffolk IP1 1XB
Telephone: (0473) 213736 £55
Open: lunch + dinner Mon-Sat (closed Bank Holidays)
Meals served: lunch 12-2, dinner 7-11
Good local restaurant.

Ipswich — Kinsella's
19 St Peters Street, Ipswich, Suffolk IP1 1XF
Telephone: (0473) 259732 £50
Open: lunch Wed-Fri (book day before), dinner Tue-Sat (closed Bank Holidays, 1 wk Xmas, 1 wk Easter)
Meals served: lunch 12-2, dinner 7-8.30
No-choice weekly changing menu. Informal atmosphere. All ingredients are free-range, organically grown.

| IPSWICH | Mortimer's on the Quay |

Wherry Quay, Ipswich, Suffolk IP4 1AS
Telephone: (0473) 230225 £40
Open: lunch Mon-Fri, dinner Mon-Sat (closed Bank Holidays + following day, 2 wks Xmas, 2 wks Aug)
Meals served: lunch 12-2, dinner 7-9 (Mon 7-8.15)
Specialising in seafood, the restaurant has a nautical theme decor and overlooks Ipswich docks.

| IPSWICH | Singing Chef |

200 St Helen's Street, Ipswich, Suffolk IP3 2RH
Telephone: (0473) 255236 £45
Open: dinner Tue-Sat (closed Bank Holidays)
Meals served: dinner 7-11
A different part of France each month is the subject of the menu whose regional French dishes are made with fresh, quality ingredients. Friendly service from the Toyes.

IXWORTH   Theobalds

68 High Street, Ixworth, Bury St Edmunds, Suffolk IP31 2HJ
Telephone: (0359) 31707 £55
Open: lunch Tue-Fri + Sun, dinner Tue-Sat (closed Bank Holidays)
Meals served: lunch 12-2, dinner 7-9.30 (Sat 7-10)

Chef Simon Theobald offers some fine food, competitively priced to encourage trade. A terrine of hare with a reducurrant sauce might precede best end of lamb with a rosemary and madeira sauce accompanied by a selection of vegetables, and there is always a vegetarian choice. Traditional puds and cheese to follow. An exciting wine list chosen with obvious passion.

JERSEY   Château la Chaire

Rozel, Jersey, Channel Islands
Telephone: (0534) 863354 £50
Fax: (0534) 865137
Open: lunch + dinner daily
Meals served: lunch 12.15-2 (Sun 12.15-2.15), dinner 7-10 (Sun + Bank Holidays 7-9.30)

An impressive looking hotel in which to stay when you're on the island. Housekeeping is first rate and the staff friendly and eager to please. The 13 bedrooms are tastefully decorated and have many thoughtful little extras. In the dining room you can enjoy some interesting food using fresh local produce to good effect.

JERSEY   Granite Corner

Rozel Harbour, Trinity, Jersey, Channel Islands
Telephone: (0534) 863590 Fax (0534) 864362 £60
Open: lunch Tue-Fri, dinner Mon-Sat
Meals served: lunch 12.30-1.30 (Sun 12.30-2), dinner 7.30-9 (Sat 7.30-9.30)

Chef Jean-Luc Robin provides some of the best eating on the island. He hails from Périgord and thus delights in serving his regional specialities. A salade de magret de canard fumé is one such starter and tournedos au foie gras et sa sauce périgueux a characteristic main dish. An attractively priced vegetarian menu is also available and might convert many – at least for the day!

JERSEY	Hotel l'Horizon

St Brelade's Bay, Jersey, Channel Islands
Telephone: (0534) 43101 £55
Fax: (0534) 46269
Open: lunch + dinner daily
Meals served: lunch 12-3, dinner 6-10.30

Sun, sand and sea are the order of the day here in St Brelade's Bay. Best of the 100+ bedrooms are those with balconies overlooking the bay and a programme of refurbishment is gradually upgrading others. A 40-ft skippered motor yacht is available for guests' use.

JERSEY	Jersey Pottery

Gorey, Jersey, Channel Islands
Telephone: (0534) 51119 £30
Open: all day Mon-Fri (closed Bank Holidays)
Meals served: 9-5.30

Seafood and more seafood is what you'll find at this highly regarded Jersey restaurant. A variety of salads is available – lobster, prawn, gambas, crab and so on – as well as hot dishes such as brill with a herb cream sauce and grilled lobster. Seafood is of the freshest quality, portions are generous, and presentation and attention to detail superb. A table displays a tempting selection of cold desserts and pastries, and the wine list is carefully chosen with an understandable bias towards whites. This impeccably-run restaurant forms part of a tourist complex containing a pottery factory and shop, and there is an attractive garden and terrace to sit in, having served yourself from the equally tempting food in the cafeteria.

JERSEY	Little Grove

Rue du Haut, St Lawrence, Jersey, Channel Islands
Telephone: (0534) 25321 £60
Fax: (0534) 25325
Open: lunch + dinner daily
Meals served: lunch 12.30-2, dinner 7.30-9.30

A country house hotel built in pink granite and characteristic of the island's architecture. The 13 bedrooms have ensuite bathrooms which are newly refurbished. The ground floor has also been completely redecorated. A friendly, welcoming place.

JERSEY — Longueville Manor

St Saviour, Jersey, Channel Islands
Telephone: (0534) 25501 £75
Fax: (0534) 31613
Open: lunch + dinner daily
Meals served: lunch 12.30-2, dinner 7.30-9.30

In terms of accommodation and service you don't do better on the island than here at Longueville Manor. Successive generations of the Lewis family have been running this hotel since 1949 and what they don't know about caring for the customer isn't worth knowing! Parts of the manor date back to the 13th Century and oak panelling and roaring fires abound. Bedrooms, some with sitting rooms, boast sumptuous drapes and furnishings and the garden and terrace by the swimming pool is an idyllic setting for afternoon tea. Two dining rooms (one non-smoking) provide an elegant setting for highly competent cooking – shellfish ragout in a lobster and basil jus, and roast partridge with apples and calvados are examples. A comprehensive cellar with best value in the New World, Alsace and Italy.

JERSEY — Old Court House Inn

St Aubin, Jersey, Channel Islands
Telephone: (0534) 46433 £35
Fax: (0534) 45103
Open: lunch + dinner daily (closed 6 wks Jan/Feb, 25+26 Dec)
Meals served: lunch 12.30-2.30, dinner 7.30-11
15th-century seaside inn – beamed cellar bar, nine pretty bedrooms, some overlooking harbour.

JERSEY — Sea Crest

Petit Port, St Brelade, Jersey, Channel Islands JE3 8HH
Telephone: (0534) 46353 £60
Open: lunch + dinner Tue-Sun (closed mid Jan-mid Feb)
Meals served: lunch 12.30-2 (Sun 12.30-3), dinner 7.30-10.15
Tradiional menu with French and Italian specialities. Seven bedrooms.

JEVINGTON	Hungry Monk Restaurant

The Street, Jevington, Nr Polegate, East Sussex BN26 5QF
Telephone: (0323) 482178　　　　　　　　　　　　　　　　£50
Open: lunch Sun, dinner daily (closed Bank Holidays, 3 days Xmas)
Meals served: lunch 12-2, dinner 7-10

It's more than 20 years since this restaurant opened and such is the quality of the food, the friendliness of the service and the general all-round consistency of the place that there seems every reason for it to continue for many years to come. Traditional English dishes are given the classical French treatment and the proof is in the pudding – so to speak!

KENDAL	Moon

129 Highgate, Kendal, Cumbria LA9 4EN
Telephone: (0539) 729254　　　　　　　　　　　　　　　　£30
Open: dinner daily (closed 25 Dec, 1 Jan)
Meals served: dinner 6-9 (Fri+Sat 6-10)

Everyone's going to the Moon these days, and who can blame them? Unpretentious surroundings, caring staff, good food and super value for money. Could you ask for anything more? Look around the walls for the menu – it'll be chalked up on blackboards. But don't take too long making your choice or someone will come along with a cloth and wipe the dish off if they've run out. Daily specials incude a vegetarian option. What a good place to come back to after a hike in the hills, ravenously hungry from all that fresh air.

Kenilworth — Restaurant Bosquet

97a Warwick Road, Kenilworth, Warwickshire CV8 1HP
Telephone: (0926) 52463 £65
Open: dinner Tue-Sat (closed 1 wk Xmas, 2 wks Aug)
Meals served: dinner 7-9.30

[handwritten: – good local restaurant.]

Perhaps this year fortune will smile favourably on Bernard Lignier and his restaurant will be given the kind of critical attention it deserves. Bernard cooks with true class doing full justice to his raw materials and their individual flavours. A light lobster and fish mousse with baby vegetables and a lobster butter sauce features among the starters, while breast of guineafowl stuffed with sweet onion, carrots and foie gras with creamed lentils and a Madeira sauce is a typical main dish. Great care and discretion is seen in his use of garnishes and accompanying trimmings, and saucing is a particular strength. Nothing fancy – it's perfectly judged each time.

Keswick — Brundholme Country House Hotel
Brundholme Road, Keswick, Cumbria CA12 4NL
Telephone: (076 87) 74495 £45
Open: dinner daily (closed 23 Dec-mid Feb)
Meals served: dinner 7.15-8.45
Fixed price menu with an entirely fish à la carte.

Kilburn — Foresters Arms Hotel
Kilburn, North Yorkshire YO6 4AH
Telephone: (034 76) 386 £35
Open: lunch + dinner daily
Meals served: lunch 12-2.30, dinner 7-9.30 (Sun 7-9)
Family cooking based on traditional English and French cooking by Andrew Cussons, former head chef at Langan's Bistro.

Kiln Pit Hill — Manor House Inn
Carterway Heads, Kiln Pit Hill, Nr Shotley Bridge, Northumberland DH8 9LX
Telephone: (0207) 55268 £45
Open: dinner Tue-Sat (closed Tue+Wed 2 Jan-31 Mar)
Meals served: dinner 7.30-10
Pub and restaurant with good value, varied menus.

Kingham — Mill House
Station Road, Kingham, Nr Chipping Norton, Oxfordshire OX7 6UH
Telephone: (0608) 658188 £60
Fax: (0608) 658492
Open: lunch + dinner daily
Meals served: lunch 12.30-2, dinner 7-9.30
Converted 17th-century flour mill now provides a charming and peaceful place to stay, right in the heart of the Cotswolds. Airy bedrooms and garden complete with trout stream.

Kings Lynn — Rococo
11 Saturday Market Place, Kings Lynn, Norfolk
Telephone: (0553) 771483 £65
*Open:*lunch Tue-Sun, dinner Mon-Sat
Meals served: lunch 12-3, dinner 7-10, light meals 10-10 in summer, coffee only 10-12 in winter
Modern French and English cooking.

KINGTON — Penrhos Court

Penrhos, Kington, Hereford & Worcester HR5 3LH
Telephone: (0544) 230720 £50
Fax: (0544) 230754
Open: lunch Sun, dinner daily (closed 25+26 Dec)
Meals served: lunch 12.30-2, dinner 7.30-9

The earliest part of Penrhos Court dates back to 1280 but it has been added to over the centuries. Martin Griffiths and Daphne Lambert lavish much care and attention on this hotel and restaurant which offers 19 bedrooms and some capable cooking.

KINTBURY — Dundas Arms

53 Station Road, Kintbury, Nr Newbury, Berkshire RG15 0UT
Telephone: (0488) 58263 £55
Fax: (0488) 58568
Open: lunch + dinner Tue-Sat (closed Bank Holidays, Xmas/New Year)
Meals served: lunch 12.30-1.30, dinner 7.30-9.15

David Dalzell-Piper is the boss now that his parents have retired. In the split-level restaurant he offers short, simply-written menus which mean what they say. If you order grilled red mullet with a citrus sauce, then that's what you'll get – he doesn't believe in elaboration or any unnecessary garnish. The results are good with textures and tastes exactly as they should be. The traditional puds are worth sampling – the bread and butter pudding is spot on. As for the wines, David is only too pleased to discuss the choices, although the house red holds its own. There are rooms at the inn also, located in the converted stable black. From them you can walk out onto the terrace and enjoy the views over the river.

KNARESBOROUGH — Four Park Place

4 Park Place, Knaresborough, North Yorkshire HG5 0ER
Telephone: (0423) 868002 Restaurant £45/Bar £25
Open: lunch daily, dinner Mon-Sat
Meals served: lunch 12.30-2.30, dinner 7.30-10
Small restaurant with great atmosphere.

KNUTSFORD — La Belle Epoque

60 King Street, Knutsford, Cheshire WA16 2DT
Telephone: (0565) 633060 *– good local restaurant* £55
Fax: (0565) 634150
Open: dinner Mon-Sat (closed Bank Holidays, 1 wk Jan)
Meals served: dinner 7.30-10

A restrained opulence hovers in the air at this remarkable art nouveau restaurant. A fresh salmon lasagne may be followed by rabbit pie with maybe a crème brûlée to finish. A fairly priced wine list, 7 comfortable bedrooms and pretty roof garden are added attractions. Knowledgeable and helpful service make the Belle Epoque a must if you are anywhere in this area.

Knutsford — Cottons Hotel

Manchester Road, Knutsford, Cheshire WA16 0SU
Telephone: (0565) 650333
Fax: (0565) 655351
Open: lunch Sun-Fri, dinner daily (closed Xmas)
Meals served: lunch 12.30-2, dinner 7.15-10 (Sun 7.15-8.45)
Hotel on a New Orleans theme.

£45

Lacock — At The Sign of The Angel

6 Church Street, Lacock, Nr Chippenham, Wiltshire SN15 2LB
Telephone: (0249) 730230
Fax: (0249) 730527
Open: lunch Tue-Fri + Sun, dinner Mon-Sat (closed 22 Dec-1 Jan)
Meals served: lunch 1-1.30, dinner 7.30-8.15

£50

If you're looking for a bit of old world charm, then this is where to come. Rooms and furnishings have an attractive 'lived in' feel and the smell of wood smoke from the fires adds the finishing touch. It's nice and reassuring to know that there's a good roast on offer in the dining room. This place blends perfectly into the beautiful and atmospheric surroundings of Lacock.

Land's End — State House

Land's End, Sennen, Cornwall TR19 7AA
Telephone: (0736) 871844
Fax: (0736) 871812
Open: lunch + dinner daily
Meals: lunch 12-2, dinner 7-9.30
Beautiful sea views, friendly staff and a peaceful atmosphere.

£50

Langar — Langar Hall

Langar, Nottinghamshire NG13 9HG
Telephone: 0949 60559
Fax: 0949 61045
Open: dinner daily (Sun residents only)
Meals served: dinner 7.30-9.30
Comfortably furnished, warm welcome and modern dishes using local and home-grown produce served in the dining room.

£50

LANGHO	Northcote Manor

Northcote Road, Langho, Nr Blackburn, Lancashire BB6 8BE
Telephone: (0254) 240555 £75
Fax: (0254) 246568
Open: lunch + dinner daily (closed 1 Jan)
Meals served: lunch 12-1.30, dinner 7-9.30 (Sat 7-10)

Once the home of a local cotton family, Northcote manor is now run as a 6-bedroomed hotel at the edge of the Ribble Valley. Partners Craig Bancroft and Nigel Haworth ensure things run well – Nigel also delivers some inventive dishes from the kitchen.

LAVENHAM	Great House

Market Place, Lavenham, Suffolk CO10 9QZ
Telephone: (0787) 247431 £50
Open: lunch Tue-Sun, dinner Tue-Sat
Meals served: lunch 12-2.30, dinner 7-9.30 (Sat 7-10.30)

Very much a restaurant with rooms reminiscent of the type you find in France. Hardly a surprise, then, to discover Monsieur Régis Crépy in charge of the kitchen and some French cuisine – très à la mode – on the menu. Filet de boeuf cru à l'huile d'olive et aux herbes is one of the starters, while magret de canard, sauce moutarde is among the main dishes. If bouillabaisse is a particular favourite of yours make this clear when you book – it's a house speciality and cooked to order. The predominantly French wine list covers the full range of prices. A lovely old house set in historic Lavenham with its wonderful buildings.

Lavenham — The Swan

High Street, Lavenham, Nr Sudbury, Suffolk CO10 9QA
Telephone: (0787) 247477 £60
Fax: (0787) 248286
Open: lunch + dinner daily
Meals served: lunch 12.30-2, dinner 7-9.30

The original 14th-century building has gradually absorbed the adjoining Elizabethan House and Wool Hall to create an atmospheric 47-bedroomed hotel with lots of appeal, operated by Forte. Service is polished throughout.

Leamington Spa — Mallory Court

Harbury Lane, Bishop's Tachbrook, Leamington Spa, Warwickshire CV33 9QB
Telephone: (0926) 330214 £95
Fax: (0926) 451714
Open: lunch + dinner daily
Meals served: lunch 12.30-2, dinner 7.30-9.45 (Sat 7.30-10, Sun 7.30-9)

Mallory Court has always strived to set the standards for other country house hotels to emulate. The kitchen has seen some comings and goings of late but co-owner Allan Holland has re-installed himself in the kitchen causing hardly a ripple on the tranquil surface of the proceedings. His team's cooking is individual and yet perfectly adjusted to the needs of the establishment – pan-fried wild salmon with asparagus, watercress and lemon butter sauce, honey-roast Gressingham duck with apple sauce and sage dumplings, iced gingerbread terrine with prunes in red wine. The staff in the dining room and the rest of the hotel remain as courteous as ever.

Leamington Spa — York House

9 York Road, Leamington Spa, Warwickshire CV31 3PR
Telephone: (0926) 424671 £35
Open: dinner daily
Meals served: dinner 6.30-8.30
Small Victorian hotel located just off the main street.

Ledbury — Grove House

Bromsberrow Heath, Ledbury, Hereford & Worcestershire HR8 1PE
Telephone: (0531) 650584 £50
Open: dinner daily for residents (closed Xmas/New Year)
Meals served: dinner at 8
Enjoy fresh garden and other local produce in the 5-course set dinners.

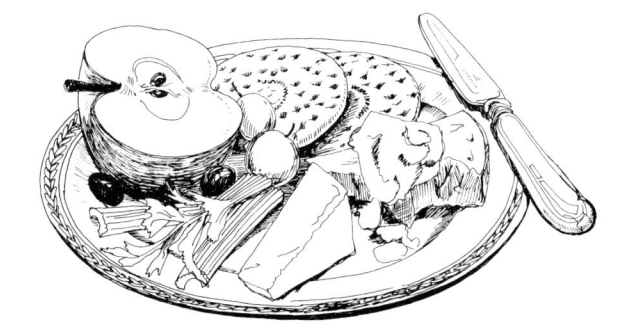

LEDBURY	Hope End

Hope End, Ledbury, Hereford & Worcester HR8 1SQ
Telephone: (0531) 3613
Fax: (0531) 5697
Open: dinner daily (Mon+Tue residents only) (closed mid Dec-mid Feb)
Meals served: dinner 7.30-8.30

£60

A less appropriate name for an establishment you'll be hard pressed to find – my hopes tend to increase as I near the Hegartys' utterly delightful country house! A stroll around gardens is now in order since the first phase of its restoration has been completed – I won't spoil the surprises which lie in store. The house itself remains pleasantly different, and Patricia's cooking is up to her usual high standards. Battling heroically with EEC regulations concerning produce, she still manages to use the best natural ingredients available to give her dishes the flavours that count. Now that she's expected to entertain her guests' palates 7 days a week, she's introduced a choice of main courses every evening, with a vegetarian option. However, considering that her casserole of duckling and turnips in white wine and baked halibut with lime and ginger hollandaise are among the options, does she really feel there's any danger of customers losing interest? Surely not! An excellent wine list too, with good value drinking from the Rhône. See also p256 – our clover Awards section.

LEEDS	42 The Calls

42 The Calls, Leeds, West Yorkshire LS2 7EW
Telephone: (0532) 440099
Fax: (0532) 344100
For restaurant details see Brasserie Forty Four.

What a shrewd move by entrepreneur Jonathan Wix. This once derelict warehouse must have been rather a long shot in 1989, but now, converted into a luxury hotel, it stands in one of the most up-and-coming areas of Leeds. Primarily aimed at executive guests it offers comfort and mod cons designed for those wanting temporary office space during their stay – there's a sensibly sized desk in each room, for example, and fax points. Obviously it's not all work and no play, and the individual CD players – with extension speakers in the bathrooms – show that it's possible to relax here as well. Food is to be obtained next door at brasserie 44 or at several other places in the vicinity that are connected to the hotel. Where it's at in Leeds!

LEEDS	Bibi's Italian Restaurant

Minerva House, 16 Greek Street, Leeds, West Yorkshire LS1 5RU
Telephone: (0532) 430905
Fax: (0532) 340844
Open: lunch + dinner Mon-Sat (closed Bank Holidays)
Meals served: lunch 12-2.15 (12-2 Sat), dinner 6-11.15
Lively Italian restaurant with a wide ranging menu.

£25

LEEDS   Brasserie Forty Four

44 The Calls, Leeds, West Yorkshire LS2 7EW
Telephone: (0532) 343232   £40
Fax: (0532) 343332
Open: lunch Mon-Fri, dinner Mon-Sat
Meals served: lunch 12-2.30, dinner 6.30-10.30

More what you'd expect in London, this brasserie must rank as a brave attempt here in Leeds. The attractively priced menu yields some nice surprises which – for the most part – work on the plate as well. Starters include an 'original' fish soup, a Chinese basket of steamed dim sum, and a terrine of foie gras and chicken livers. Main courses run to some 14 items, the 'finally famous' New York rib of beef and salmon escalope with a spinach mousse in pastry catching the eye. Traditional rhubarb crumble and brandy, almond and apricot trifle are typically tempting puds. The wine list is very reasonably priced and helpfully divided up under headings for those a little in the dark as to what to order. Go along and give it a try!

LEEDS   Bryan's of Headingley

9 Weetwood Lane, Headingley, Leeds, West Yorkshire LS16 5LT
Telephone: (0532) 785679   £25
Open: all day Mon-Sat (closed 25+26 Dec)
Meals served: 11.30-11.30 (Sun 12.30-8)

They take their fish and chips seriously up here in Leeds and places fall in and out of favour just like that. At the moment it's Bryan's that everyone seems to be going to – and with good reason. Here the fish is definitely more than the soggy lump doused in vinegar you unwrap from a sheet of yesterday's paper. The battered fish is freshly fried in dripping and is first rate. Stacks of chips and a pot of tea to wash it all down.

LEEDS   La Grillade
Wellington Street, Leeds, West Yorkshire LS1 4HJ
Telephone: (0532) 459707   £30
Fax: (0532) 426112
Open: lunch Mon-Fri, dinner Mon-Sat (closed Bank Holidays, 1 wk Xmas)
Meals served: lunch 12-2.30, dinner 7.30-11
Brasserie usefully located in the centre of town.

LEEDS   Low Hall
Calverley Lane, Horsforth, Nr Leeds, West Yorkshire LS18 4ES
Telephone: (0532) 588221   £55
Open: lunch Tue-Fri, dinner Tue-Sat (closed Bank Holidays, 1 wk Oct)
Meals served: lunch 12-2, dinner 7-10
Sixteenth-century building restored to its former grandeur, a popular business venue. Its rolling lawns are ideal for summer functions.

LEEDS   Sous le Nez en Ville
Basement, Quebec House, Quebec Street, Leeds, West Yorkshire LS1 2HA
Telephone: (0532) 440108   £45
Open: lunch Mon-Fri, dinner Mon-Sat
Meals served: lunch 12-2.30, dinner 6-10.30
Good basement bistro.

Leicester — Manor Restaurant & Hotel
The Ford, Little Glen Road, Glen Parva, Leicestershire LE2 9TL
Telephone: (0533) 477604 £35
Fax: (0533) 774976
Open: lunch daily, dinner Mon-Sat
Meals served: lunch 12-2, dinner 7-10
English and French modern cooking using the freshest ingredients available.

Leicester — Welford Place
9 Welford Place, Leicester, Leicestershire LE1 6ZH
Telephone: (0533) 470758 £45
Fax: (0533) 471843
Open: lunch + dinner daily (closed 25 Dec)
Meals served: lunch 12-3, dinner 6-11 (snacks 10.30am-11pm)
Sister establishment to Lincoln's Wig and Mitre. Popular spot for informal eating, in tune with the times.

Lenham — Chilston Park
Sandway, Lenham, Nr Maidstone, Kent ME17 2BE
Telephone: (0622) 859803 £65
Fax: (0622) 858588
Open: lunch + dinner daily
Meals served: lunch 12.30-1.45, dinner 7.30-9.30
The 17th-century house in 250 acres is a remarkable treasure trove of antiques – 200 candles light the public rooms.

Lew — Farmhouse Hotel & Restaurant
University Farm, Lew, Oxfordshire OX8 2AU
Telephone: (0993) 850297 £35
Open: dinner Mon-Sat (closed Xmas)
Meals served: dinner 7-9
Traditional English farmhouse cooking.

Lewdown — Lewtrenchard Manor
Lewtrenchard, Lewdown, Nr Okehampton, Devon EX20 4PN
Telephone: (056 683) 256 £65
Fax: (056 683) 332
Open: lunch Sun, dinner daily
Meals served: lunch 12.30-2, dinner 7.15-9.30

A medaillon of marinated monkfish steamed on samphire with a pepper sauce, and rack of lamb with a mustard and sage crust and garlic and white wine sauce are 2 of the attractive-sounding dishes on new chef Patrick Salvadori's carte. He has taken over the kitchen, having worked under James Brown last year, and will hopefully bring stability and consistency to the kitchen. Other equally sumptuous rooms with ornate plaster ceilings and rich wood panelling in this 17th-century manor house vie with 8 attractive bedrooms for comfort and civility.

Lifton — Arundell Arms
Lifton, Devon PL16 0AA
Telephone: (0566) 84666 £50
Open: lunch + dinner daily (closed 3 days Xmas)
Meals served: lunch 12.30-2, dinner 7.30-9
Popular with anglers for the twenty miles of fishing rights along the Tamar.

Lincoln — Wig & Mitre
29 Steep Hill, Lincoln, Lincolnshire LN2 1LU
Telephone: (0522) 535190 £45
Open: all day daily (closed 25 Dec)
Meals served: meals 8am-11pm
Sister establishment to Leicester's Welford Place, all-day eating available at reasonable prices.

Linton Springs — Linton Springs

Linton Springs, Nr Wetherby, West Yorkshire LS22 4AF
Telephone: (0937) 585353
Open: lunch Sun-Fri, dinner daily
Meals served: lunch 12-2.30 (Sun 12-3), dinner 7-9.30

£60

Hotel built in 1700s on the edge of the Wharfedale Valley.

Liskeard — The Well House

St Keyne, Liskeard, Cornwall PL14 4RN
Telephone: (0579) 842001
Open: lunch + dinner daily
Meals served: lunch 12.30-2, dinner 7.30-9

£65

Owner Nicholas Wainford has a 'hands-on' approach to the running of The Well House and you can be sure that everything from the gardens through to the 10 individually decorated bedrooms will be immaculately kept. In the kitchen, David Woolfall has established his patch and main dishes such as grilled red mullet with basil sauce and leeks and sauté of guineafowl with tarragon cream are certainly up to previous standards.

Little Walsingham — Old Bakehouse Restaurant

31-33 High Street, Little Walsingham, Norfolk NR22 6BZ
Telephone: (0328) 820454
Open: dinner Tue-Sat (closed 1 wk Oct, 3 wks Jan/Feb)
Meals served: dinner 7-9.30 (earlier in winter)

£45

Consistently good food, warm atmosphere and friendly staff.

Liverpool — Armadillo

20-22 Mathew Street, Liverpool, Merseyside L2 6RE
Telephone: 051-236 4123
Open: lunch + dinner Tue-Sat (closed Bank Holidays)
Meals served: lunch 12-3, dinner 6.30-10.30

£40

More upmarket than it used to be. Some good half bottles on the wine list.

Liverpool — Jenny's Seafood Restaurant

The Old Ropery, off Fenwick Street, Liverpool, Merseyside L2 7NT
Telephone: 051-236 0332
Open: lunch Mon-Fri, dinner Tue-Sat (closed Bank Holidays, 1 wk Xmas, 2 wks Aug)
Meals served: lunch 12-2.30, dinner 7-10

£35

Well established fish restaurant. Simple dishes are probably the best.

| Long Melford | Chimneys |

Hall Street, Long Melford, Sudbury, Suffolk CO10 9JR
Telephone: (0787) 79806 £60
Open: lunch daily, dinner Mon-Sat
Meals served: lunch 12-2, dinner 7-9

A well-established restaurant, recently refurbished, providing some fine, enjoyable cooking upon which you can rely. Interesting combinations of flavours with the occasional oriental touch give the dishes a lift. Some substantial wines feature on the list, including the remarkable Henschke Hill of Grace shiraz. Substantial discounts for dinner club members. Sam Chalmets' Chimneys has a well-deserved local following.

| Longhorsley | Linden Hall |

Longhorsley, Nr Morpeth, Northumberland NE65 8XF
Telephone: (0670) 516611 £50
Fax: (0670) 88544
Open: lunch + dinner daily
Meals served: lunch 12-2, dinner 7-9.45

Impressive Georgian country house with 45 bedrooms in a variety of styles. The drawing room is charmingly decorated while the dining room has sweeping views out towards the coast. The restored stable block offers 5 banqueting suites that are ideal for private functions or conferences. Plans exist to create more bedrooms and a swimming pool.

| Longridge | Heathcote's |

104-106 Higher Road, Longridge, Nr Preston, Lancashire PR3 3SY
Telephone: (0772) 784969 £70
Open: lunch Fri+Sun, dinner Tue-Sun (closed 1+2 Jan)
Meals served: lunch Sun 12-2, dinner 7-9.30

Sharrow Bay, the Connaught, Le Manoir aux Quat'Saison – chef Paul Heathcote has been there, done that. Now he's back home and doing his own thing – and very well too! There's nothing blasé about him, though, and he's only too willing to pay tribute to his teachers, Francis Coulson and Raymond Blanc especially. His cooking is modern using first-class ingredients. Speciality main courses often run to 3 lines on the menu, for instance the breast of local duckling crisply roasted and served on a potato and apple rösti, garnished with cabbage, smoked bacon and a quenelle of pea purée and accompanied with a salad made from its leg. That's quite a mouthful – in both senses of the word! Sumptuous puds are followed by an excellent selection of English regional cheeses. For this rising star, the sky's the limit.

LOUGHBOROUGH — Restaurant Roger Burdell

The Manor House, 11/12 Sparrow Hill, Loughborough, Leicestershire LE11 1BT
Telephone: (0509) 231813 £60
Open: lunch Tue-Sat, dinner Mon-Sat (closed Bank Holidays)
Meals served: lunch 12-2.30, dinner 7-10.30

Terrine of wild game as a starter, followed by an escalope of Scotch salmon with a leek and prawn mousseline baked in filo pastry as a main course, with a Normandy apple tartlet and sauce anglaise as a pud are typical of what you'll find on the menu. Roger Burdell describes his food as 'fairly robust in the modern style' and his elegant corner restaurant is one of the few havens of good food in the area.

LOUTH — Ferns

40 Northgate, Louth, Lincolnshire LN11 0LY
Telephone: (0507) 603209 £45/£25
Open: dinner Tue-Sat
Meals served: dinner 7-9.30 (preferably book by 2pm)

Book ahead to take advantage of the bargain set price menu available at Nick and Kim Thompson's restaurant. The à la carte is pricier, but also well worth a look and the wine list is notable for featuring only organic wines. Quite a find in this part of the world.

LOWER BEEDING — South Lodge

Brighton Road, Lower Beeding, West Sussex RH13 6PS
Telephone: (0403) 891711 £80
Fax: (0403) 891766
Open: lunch + dinner daily
Meals served: lunch 12-2.30, dinner 7.30-10

Once the family home to Frederick Ducane Godman, an explorer and botanist. Gardening buffs will find much to fascinate them wandering in the 90-acre grounds which boast many exotic shrubs and trees. Chef Anthony Tobin provides some good food for the dining room. Good standards of furnishing and service apply throughout the hotel.

LOWER BRAILES — Feldon House

Lower Brailes, Nr Banbury, Oxfordshire OX15 5HW
Telephone: (060 885) 580 £55
Open: lunch daily, dinner Mon-Sat (closed 2 wks autumn)
Meals served: lunch 12.30-1.30, dinner 7-8.30

Dinner party cooking for groups of a dozen or so in traditional British style.

| Lower Slaughter | Lower Slaughter Manor |

Lower Slaughter, Nr Bourton-on-the-Water, Gloucestershire GL54 2HP
Telephone: (0451) 20456   £75
Fax: (0451) 22150
Open: lunch + dinner daily
Meals served: lunch 12.30-2, dinner 7-9.30

Audrey and Peter Marks, who established a considerable reputation in the '80s when they ran Rookery Hall, tried retirement but didn't like it, and in May 1992 officially became GFPs (gluttons for punishment) and came back for more. I suppose Norman knight, Philipe de Sloitre, wasn't really responsible for the rather bloodthirsty English equivalent of his name, but here at Lower Slaughter manor everything is sweetness and light. Public rooms are decorated in delicate shades of pink and green, while the bedrooms have floral fabrics and wooden furniture – I must admit that the overall effect is quite enchanting. Serge Puyal cooks with flair and the elegant dining room does justice to his food. The structure of both menu and wine list have changed, the former now a fixed price à la carte, the latter greatly expanded with particular strengths in California, Germany and top producers in the Rhône and Burgundy.

| Ludlow | Dinham Hall |

off Market Square, Ludlow, Shropshire SY8 1EJ
Telephone: (0584) 876464   £45
Fax: (0584) 876019
Open: lunch + dinner daily
Meals served: lunch 12-2 (Sun 12-2.30) dinner 7.15-9.30 (Sun 7-9)
New owners at this late 18th-century house. Plans to expand the restaurant. Attractive setting.

| Ludlow | Feathers Hotel |

Bull Ring, Ludlow, Shropshire SY8 1AA
Telephone: (0584) 875261   £55
Fax: (0584) 876030
Open: lunch + dinner daily
Meals served: lunch 12-2, dinner 7-9

'That prodigy of timber-framed houses' according to Nikolaus Pevsner. Lovers of old English architecture won't find better that this one-time inn with its extraordinary timbered facade. The 40 bedrooms are comfortably furnished and strive to maintain the character of the building.

Lupton	Lupton Tower
Lupton, via Carnforth, Kirkby Lonsdale, Cumbria LA6 2PR	
Telephone: (053 95) 67400	£40

Open: dinner daily (closed Mon+Tue in winter if no residents, closed 3 days Xmas)
Meals served: dinner 7.30 for 8
Vegetarian hotel, 6 bedrooms.

Lymington	Gordleton Mill & Provence Restaurant

Silver Street, Hordle, Nr Lymington, Hampshire SO41 6DJ
Telephone: (0590) 682219   £80
Fax: (0590) 683073
Open: lunch Wed-Sun, dinner Wed-Sat + Mon
Meals served: lunch 12.30-2.30 (Sun 12.30-3), dinner 7.30-10 (Sat 7.30-10.30)

Enfant terrible Jean-Christophe Novelli masterminds the kitchen at Le Provence restaurant. Could he create clones of himself he'd be a happy man, since he could then control every dish from start to finish. As it is he has to dash from section to section and trust his staff to fill in the gaps. Jean-Christophe's pedigree – family chef to the Rothschilds, the Palace Court Hotel, Bournemouth, and Geddes in Southampton – is evident in his cooking. Each dish is invariably a masterpiece. A pressed terrine of lobster and young leeks with a sherry dressing, roasted red mullet flavoured with foie gras and served with a potato purée, and the now legendary assiette du boucher – an extraordinary offal-lovers' dish of pig's trotter stuffed with wild mushrooms and foie gras, poached ox-tongue, pan-fried lamb's sweetbreads and braised oxtail – all served with a potato and celeriac purée. His desserts are no less spectacular – for example the ebullient boîte surprise aux amandes. There is a terrace for pre-dinner drinks but no smoking in the restaurant. Gordleton Mill provides 7 comfortable ensuite rooms with whirlpool baths, overlooking tranquil fields or the river.

Lymington	Stanwell House
High Street, Lymington, Hampshire SO41 9AA	
Telephone: (0590) 677123	£50

Fax: (0590) 677756
Open: lunch + dinner daily
Meals served: lunch 12.30-2, dinner 7.30-9.30
Modernised hotel with Georgian exterior and pretty walled garden.

Lympstone	River House

The Strand, Lympstone, Devon EX8 5EY
Telephone: (0395) 265147   £75
Open: lunch Tue-Sun, dinner Tue-Sat (closed Bank Holidays)
Meals served: lunch 12-1.30, dinner 7-9.30

The best compliment the Wilkes family can receive from their guests is that it's just like staying with friends only without the hassle. They've built up quite a following over the 7 years and are starting to wonder if they're really running a business at all! However, there's no time for complacency, and Shirley's appearance in *The Women Chefs of Britain* has acted as a spur to further achievements. Ideas picked up on their trips abroad are often tried out in special gourmet menus which if you're lucky might coincide with your visit.

MAIDEN NEWTON — Maiden Newton House

Maiden Newton, Nr Dorchester, Dorset DT2 0AA
Telephone: (0300) 20336 £65
Fax: (0300) 21021
Open: dinner daily (closed 3 wks Dec)
Meals served: dinner at 8

Doubling as a home to Bryan and Elizabeth Ferriss and a hotel to its guests, Maiden Newton House achieves the best of both worlds. There are only 6 bedrooms, each with its own charm, and these – along with the public rooms – are carefully maintained. In the evening, you dine with your hosts (booking essential) and if there's anything you don't care for on the set menu, then they'll be happy to make adjustments. Cream of lettuce soup as a starter, breast of duckling with blackcurrant as a main course, rhubarb fool as a pud and West Country cheeses to finish is the sort of thing to look forward to. There's no need to bother about what to drink, since Bryan's already decided – 3 wines by the glass and a port or madeira at the end. Warm happy atmosphere amidst 20 tranquil acres.

MAIDEN NEWTON — Le Petit Canard

56 Dorchester Road, Maiden Newton, Dorset DT2 OBE
Telephone: (0300) 20536 £45
Open: dinner Tue-Sat
Meals served: dinner 7-9

Apparently the occasional migrant makes it to this little country restaurant, but otherwise the dining room is populated with local residents. Canadian chef Geoff Chapman cooks an intuitive blend of modern French cuisine fused with West Coast American and Chinese overtones. Quite a combination, but evidently successful. Try the stir-fried rabbit with sweet ginger, green onions and noodles, followed by char-grilled venison steak with a green peppercorn sauce and see if you agree. Concise, moderately priced wine list. Be sure to book since it's a long way to come and be disappointed.

MAIDENHEAD — Fredrick's

Shoppenhangers Road, Maidenhead, Berkshire SL6 2PZ
Telephone: (0628) 35934 £80
Fax: (0628) 771054
Open: lunch Sun-Fri, dinner daily (closed 24-30 Dec except lunch 25 Dec)
Meals served: lunch 12-2, dinner 7-9.45

Having transformed his dream into a reality, Fredrick Losel now oversees the smooth running of this classy conference-oriented hotel. The 37 bedrooms contain wood and leather furnishings making them both attractive and comfortable, and a programme of refurbishment is set to make them even more luxurious. Classic continental dishes are given modern treatments and combine quality and quantity to satisfaction. Fresh crab with langoustines and ginger might be followed by a tournedos of beef bordelaise and a choice of sweets or cheeses to finish. This is the sort of hotel restaurant you so often find on the continent, owner operated and friendly but with an eye for detail.

MALMESBURY	Old Bell Hotel
Abbey Row, Malmesbury, Wiltshire SN16 0BW	
Telephone: (0666) 822344	£35
Fax: (0666) 825145	
Open: lunch + dinner daily	
Meals served: lunch 12.30-2 (Sun 12.15-2), dinner 7-10.30 (Sun 7.30-10.30)	

Next to the Abbey, one of the chimneys dates back 800 years. The stable block has been converted more recently to give a total of thirty-six rooms.

MALVERN	Cottage in the Wood

Holywell Road, Malvern Wells, Hereford & Worcester WR14 4LG
Telephone: (0684) 573487 £55
Fax: (0684) 560662
Open: lunch + dinner daily
Meals served: lunch 12.30-2, dinner 7-9 (Sun 7-8.30)

A 20-bedroomed hotel high up on the Malvern hills with stunning views down into the Severn Valley. Accommodation is definitely cosy, but with some of the best walking in the country available, I wouldn't spend all your time indoors. Ostrich has been known to feature on the menu in the dining room, but orthodox dishes are the norm. A large wine list scans the globe with much good value drinking, especially French vins de pays.

MALVERN	Croque-en-Bouche

221 Wells Road, Malvern Wells, Hereford & Worcester WR14 4HF
Telephone: (0684) 565612 £75
Open: dinner Wed-Sat (closed Xmas/New Year)
Meals served: dinner 7.30-9.15

Be sure to arrive on time here at the Croque-en-Bouche. Robin and Marion Jones run a tight ship – she cooks while he runs front of house – and so a quarter of an hour here or there can disrupt their entire schedule. But this is a small concession to the quality of the food which you'll enjoy. Start with a soup of vegetables and salt cod in which the diced vegetables come in a broth flavoured with star anise and lemon grass, and the salt cod is spiced with coriander and ginger. Follow this with fillets of Dover sole, served on a bed of leeks with a beurre blanc with chives and shredded mangetouts. For a main course you could have a haunch of venison francatelli, the small escalopes marinated and grilled to perfection with a madeira sauce flavoured with dried porcini mushrooms. A fresh salad then arrives with light Japanese dressings before you move on to cheese and puds. The Grand Dessert is particularly tempting, allowing as it does a taste of tiramisu, tart, ginger meringue and sorbet accompanied by a glass of sweet muscat wine. Robin's wine list has established itself as one of the best around and I look forward to sampling the revised selection which includes more wines from Australia and Washington State. Once again this year, many rival establishments will be trying to keep up with the Joneses.

MANCHESTER	Gaylord

Amethyst House, Spring Gardens, Manchester, Greater Manchester M2 1EA
Telephone: 061-832 6037 £25
Open: lunch + dinner daily
Meals served: lunch 12-3, dinner 6-11.30
Good Indian cooking at reasonable prices.

MANCHESTER	Market Restaurant

104 High Street, Smithfield City Centre, Manchester, Greater Manchester M4 1HQ
Telephone: 061-834 3743 £45
Open: dinner Tue-Sat (closed 1 wk Xmas, 1 wk Easter, Aug)
Meals served: dinner 6-9.30 (Sat 7-9.30)

Quite a woman was our Elizabeth Raffald. Only 48 when she died, she nevertheless managed to give birth to 15 daughters, open 2 shops and an employment agency, compile the city's first trade directory *and* publish a cookery book. The room named in her honour at the Market Restaurant is available for private parties and also hosts the Pudding Club (see the 1990 Guide for details), which is proving very popular. Downstairs the restaurant proper continues as before and draws a wide clientele, many of whom are regulars. The menu is eclectic, presented in the modern manner. Thus Thai fish cakes, tabbouleh and patatas bravas come as starters, while lamb souvlakia, baked samosas and salmon fillet with a sorrel sauce feature as main courses. An established favourite in the area.

MANCHESTER	Moss Nook

Ringway Road, Moss Nook, Manchester, Greater Manchester M22 5NH
Telephone: 061-437 4778 £65
Open: lunch Tue-Fri, dinner Tue-Sat (closed Bank Holidays, 2 wks Xmas)
Meals served: lunch 12-1.30, dinner 7-9.30

The painting on the dessert menu looks good enough to eat with its bunches of grapes and blushing peaches. Mancunians have long loved the Harrisons' restaurant which is nearing the end of its third decade. Lace, crystal, silver plate and heavy drapes create an air of upmarket opulence. Kevin Lofthouse's food is traditional and formal.

MANCHESTER	Yang Sing

34 Princes Street, Manchester, Greater Manchester M1 4JY
Telephone: 061-236 2200 £45
Fax: 061-236 5934
Open: all day daily (closed 25 Dec)
Meals served: 12-11
Extremely popular Cantonese restaurant with extensive menu. Booking is essential.

MARKINGTON   Hob Green
Markington, Nr Harrogate, North Yorkshire HG3 3PJ
Telephone: (0432) 770031   £65
Fax: (0432) 771589
Open: lunch Sun, dinner daily
Meals served: lunch 12-1.45, dinner 7-9.30
Set in 870 acres of farm and woodland in the Yorkshire countryside, charmingly restored hotel. Constantly changing menu.

MARSTON MORTEYNE   Morteyne Manor

Woburn Road, Marston Morteyne, Bedfordshire MK43 0NG
Telephone: (0234) 767003   £80
Open: lunch + dinner daily
Meals served: lunch 12.15-2 (Sun 12.15-3), dinner 7.15-9.30 (Fri+Sat 7.15-10)

At the time of going to press, chef/proprietor Jeremy Blake O'Connor's 15th-century Tudor manor, set in lovely gardens and orchards, had been damaged by a serious fire. His considerable reputation, established at Pebbles in Aylesbury, and scrupulous seeking-out of best quality ingredients from local sources of supply will ensure highly creditable results on the plate. We wish him a speedy recovery!

MARY TAVY   The Stannary
Mary Tavy, Devon PL19 9QB
Telephone: (0822) 810897   £35
Open: dinner daily
Meals served: dinner 7-9.30
Inventive vegetarian cooking.

MASHAM   Floodlite Restaurant
Silver Street, Masham, Nr Ripon, North Yorkshire HG4 4DX
Telephone: (0765) 89000   £35
Open: lunch Fri-Sun, dinner Tue-Sun
Meals served: lunch 12-2.30, dinner 7-9.30
Carefully prepared and presented mainly classical dishes at good value prices.

MATLOCK   Riber Hall

Matlock, Derbyshire DE4 5JU
Telephone: (0629) 582795   £60
Fax: (0629) 580475
Open: lunch + dinner daily
Meals served: lunch 12-1.30, dinner 7-9.30

In this characteristic 18th-century house, old beams and 4-poster beds give the bedrooms lots of charm, while the public rooms are no less attractive. There's a good standard of up-keep and the staff maintain a happy yet efficient level of service. Food in the dining room is modern French and English with leanings towards nouvelle cuisine. Proves popular with local diners.

MAULDEN   Malletts
Silsoe Road, Maulden, Bedfordshire MK45 2AZ
Telephone: (0525) 840400   £55
Fax: (0525) 406459
Open: lunch + dinner Mon-Sat
Meals served: lunch 12-2, dinner 7-9.30 (Sat 7-10.30)
Elegant Georgian hotel in its own parkland.

| MAWNAN SMITH | Meudon Hotel |

Mawnan Smith, Nr Falmouth, Cornwall TR11 5HT
Telephone: (0326) 250541
Fax: (0326) 250543
Open: lunch + dinner daily (closed Jan+Feb)
Meals served: lunch 12-2, dinner 7.30-9
Family run hotel with private beach.

£40

MAWNAN SMITH — Nansidwell

Mawnan Smith, Nr Falmouth, Cornwall TR11 5HU
Telephone: (0326) 250340
Fax: (0326) 250440
Open: lunch + dinner (closed Jan)
Meals served: lunch 12.30-1.45, dinner 7-9 (Sun 7-8.30)

£65

A high repeat business shows that Felicity and Jamie Robertson have got the knack of keeping their customers happy at their 12-bedroomed hotel. Home-smoked meats and fish and many other home produced products guarantee some good eating. Beautiful gardens are a further bonus.

MEDMENHAM — Danesfield House

Medmenham, Marlow, Buckinghamshire SL7 3ES
Telephone: (0628) 891010
Fax: (0628) 890408
Open: lunch + dinner daily
Meals served: lunch 12-2, dinner 7-10

£70

Historical evidence indicates the Danes settled here because of the abundant supply of fish and game. More recent changes to the food supply mean there are now only 2 (there used to be 4!) restaurants to choose from – the Italian-inspired Loggia with its own speciality wine list and the more formal Oak Room with its classical fixed price menus and unusual collection of Swedish schnapps. As for the hotel itself, it's also rather an amalgam of styles – Elizabethan chimneys, square towers and Jacobean windows. Twice gutted by fire during its conversion into a hotel, the 19th-century mansion has been painstakingly restored. Set as it is on a hill between Henley and Marlow, spectacular views are to be had across the Thames Valley.

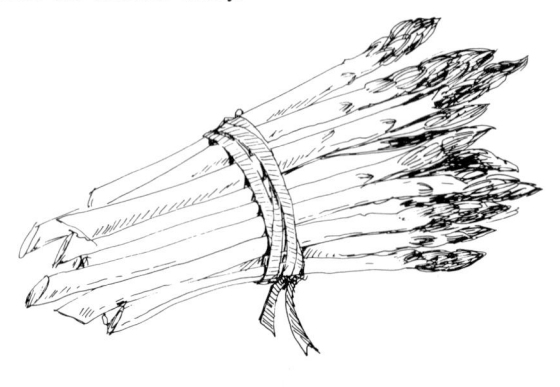

| MELBOURN | Pink Geranium |

Station Road, Melbourn, Nr Royston, Hertfordshire SG8 6DX
Telephone: (0763) 260215
Open: lunch Tue-Fri + Sun, dinner Tue-Sat
Meals served: lunch 12-2, dinner 7-10 (Sat 7-10.30)

— good local restaurant £70

The enthusiasm of owner Steven Saunders is infectious and the re-built Pink Geranium is well worth a visit with its gabled end and thatched roofs and new conservatory built onto the restaurant which now seats about 50. As you would imagine, geraniums feature strongly in the fabrics, the colourings and the landscape gardens. A mixture of antique tables and some good table settings make for a light, relaxed atmosphere. There are 2 private rooms available on the 1st floor, and make sure to book at this busy cottagey restaurant. Chef John Curtis turns out some competent food. If available, try the excellent millefeuille of gravadlax and smoked salmon – interwoven layers served with a spicy tomato vinaigrette, or perhaps the terrine of guineafowl which is studded with morels and hazelnuts served with a toasted sesame brioche. Good fish and vegetarian dishes available, or perhaps try the spring lamb roasted with thyme and served with caramelised shallots and a bordeaux and redcurrant sauce. Good homely puddings and a reasonably-priced wine list.

| MELMERBY | Village Bakery |

Melmerby, Penrith, Cumbria CA10 1HE
Telephone: (0768) 881515   £30
Open: all day daily (closed Sun in Jan+Feb, closed 25+26 Dec)
Meals served: meals 8.30-5, Sun 9.30-5 (Mon in winter 8.30-2.30)

A converted pig sty and chicken loft doesn't sound the most attractive of settings for Lis and Andrew Whitley's bakery and restaurant. In actual fact it has worked out rather well with simple dining room and conservatory extension. Breakfast, lunch and tea are all available with the rolls, bread, pies, scones and croissants coming fresh from the ovens. Healthy eating is a prime concern, the vegetables and fruit are organically grown – mostly in their own smallholding – and the wines and lagers are also organic.

| MELTON MOWBRAY | Olde Stocks Restaurant |

Grimston, Nr Melton Mowbray, Leicestershire LE14 3BZ
Telephone: (0664) 812255   £60
Open: dinner Tue-Sat (closed 2 wks Jan)
Meals served: dinner 7-10
Friendly restaurant serving a mixture of tradition and modern French and English cooking.

MIDDLE WALLOP   Fifehead Manor

Middle Wallop, Nr Stockbridge, Hampshire SO20 8EG
Telephone: (0264) 781565   **£65**
Fax: (0264) 781400
Open: lunch + dinner daily (closed 2 wks Xmas/New Year)
Meals served: lunch 12-2.30, dinner 7.30-9.30

Dating back to the 11th Century, Fifehead Manor manages to connect King Harold's mother, George Washington's father and Lady Godiva. Don't expect me to explain, ask the owner, Mrs Van Veelen, one evening during your visit. Now a hotel, it capitalises upon its medieval features while carefully combining them with more modern fixtures. The bedrooms are of generous dimensions and thoughtfully equipped. Breakfast in the morning is something to look forward to.

MIDHURST   Hindle Wakes
1 Church Hill, Midhurst, West Sussex
Telephone: 0730 813 371   £20
Open: lunch Wed-Sat, dinner Tue-Sat (closed 24-26 Dec)
Meals served: lunch 12-1.45, dinner 7-9.30
Wide ranging, good value menu specialising in game, in season.

MIDHURST   Maxine's
Elizabeth House, Red Lion Street, Midhurst, West Sussex GU29 9PB
Telephone: (0730) 816271   £40
Open: lunch Wed-Sun, dinner Wed-Sat + Mon (closed 3 wks Jan)
Meals served: lunch 12-2, dinner 7-10
Cottagey dining room in pretty half-timbered house. Classic cooking.

MILFORD-ON-SEA   Rocher's

69-71 High Street, Milford-on-Sea, Hampshire SO41 0QG
Telephone: (0590) 642340   **£45**
Open: lunch + dinner Wed-Sun (closed 2 wks Jan, 2 wks June)
Meals served: lunch 12.30-2.30, dinner 7-9

Affluent yachting types and those in the twilight years of their life with a bob or two to spare are among the clientele at this pretty little village restaurant. Chef and owner Alain Rocher works hard in tandem with his charming wife Rebecca at front of house. The food is essentially classical – terrine of pike with an asparagus dressing, roast guineafowl in a sherry vinegar sauce, nougat glacé with a passionfruit sauce. There are also fixed-price table d'hôte and lunch menus.

MINSTER LOVELL   Old Swan
Minster Lovell, Nr Witney, Oxfordshire OX8 5RN
Telephone: (0993) 774441   £45
Fax: (0993) 702002
Open: lunch + dinner daily
Meals served: lunch 12-2.30, dinner 7-10
Quintessential village setting for traditional pub with restaurant.

MONKTON COMBE   Combe Grove Manor Hotel
Brassknocker Hill, Monkton Combe, Bath BA2 7HS
Telephone: (0225) 834644   £80
Fax: (0225) 834961
Open: lunch + dinner daily
Meals served: lunch 12-2.30, dinner 7-9.30
Just outside Bath, in 68 acres of its own grounds, 41 bedroomed hotel.

Montacute — Milk House

The Borough, Montacute, Somerset TA15 6XB
Telephone: (0935) 823823 £45
Open: lunch Sun, dinner Wed-Sat
Meals served: lunch 12-2, dinner 7.30-9
Organically grown and reared produce used in good, interesting dishes.

Moreton-in-Marsh — Annie's

3 Oxford Street, Moreton-in-Marsh, Gloucestershire GL56 0LA
Telephone: (0608) 51981 £55
Open: lunch Sun, dinner Mon-Sat (closed 27 Jan-10 Feb)
Meals served: lunch 12-2, dinner 7-10

Who said that dreams never come true? For Annie's is just that for co-owner Anne Ellis. Husband David slaves away in the kitchen cooking dishes which change with the seasons, while Anne herself supervises the staff at front of house. Her enthusiasm and happiness shine through. The stylish hand-written menu includes pheasant, salmon and duck, all enhanced by innovative sauces. Good value-for-money eating, and a concise wine list.

Moreton-in-Marsh — Marsh Goose

Wish Street, Moreton-in-Marsh, Gloucestershire GL56 0AX
Telephone: (0508) 52111 £50
Open: lunch Tue-Sun, dinner Tue-Sat
Meals served: lunch 12.15-2.30, dinner 7.30-9.45

They've come and gone here, one after the other, but this one seems set to stay. I certainly hope so! The type of food varies according to whether you're having lunch or dinner. Lunch menus include hot cheese fritters with creamed onion sauce, casserole of veal with basil tomatoes and rice, braised oxtail with green peppercorns and red wine. Dinner menus, by contrast, offer a filo parcel of mushrooms, leeks and brie with creamed herb sauce; grilled monkfish tail with capers; fillet of turbot on leaf spinach garnished with prawns and shallots. Take your pick and rest assured that up-and-coming chef Sonya Kidney will more than guarantee good results.

Morpeth — Embleton Hall

Longframlington, Morpeth, Northumberland NE65 8DT
Telephone: (066 570) 249 £45
Open: lunch + dinner daily
Meals served: lunch 12-2, dinner 7-9
Warm and welcoming hotel with ten bedrooms.

Mottram St Andrew — Mottram Hall

Mottram St Andrew, Prestbury, Cheshire SK10 4QT
Telephone: (0625) 828135 £50
Fax: (0625) 829284
Open: lunch Sun-Fri, dinner daily
Meals served: lunch 12.30-2, dinner 7-9.45
Georgian mansion in 270 acres of parkland, includes a championship golf course – part of De Vere Group.

MOULSFORD-ON-THAMES	Beetle & Wedge

Moulsford-on-Thames, Oxfordshire OX10 9JF
Telephone: (0491) 651381
Fax: (0491) 651376
£65
Open: lunch + dinner daily (closed 25 Dec)
Meals served: lunch 12.30-2, dinner 7.30-10 (Restaurant & Brasserie)

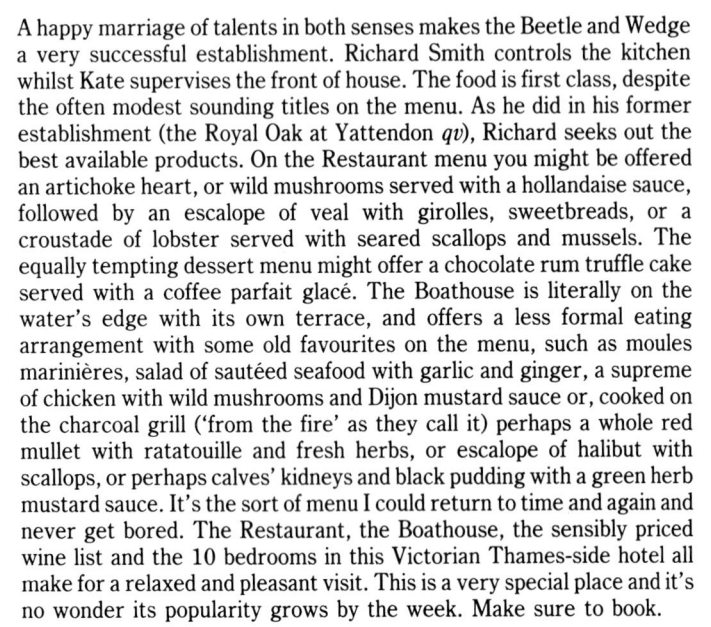

A happy marriage of talents in both senses makes the Beetle and Wedge a very successful establishment. Richard Smith controls the kitchen whilst Kate supervises the front of house. The food is first class, despite the often modest sounding titles on the menu. As he did in his former establishment (the Royal Oak at Yattendon *qv*), Richard seeks out the best available products. On the Restaurant menu you might be offered an artichoke heart, or wild mushrooms served with a hollandaise sauce, followed by an escalope of veal with girolles, sweetbreads, or a croustade of lobster served with seared scallops and mussels. The equally tempting dessert menu might offer a chocolate rum truffle cake served with a coffee parfait glacé. The Boathouse is literally on the water's edge with its own terrace, and offers a less formal eating arrangement with some old favourites on the menu, such as moules marinières, salad of sautéed seafood with garlic and ginger, a supreme of chicken with wild mushrooms and Dijon mustard sauce or, cooked on the charcoal grill ('from the fire' as they call it) perhaps a whole red mullet with ratatouille and fresh herbs, or escalope of halibut with scallops, or perhaps calves' kidneys and black pudding with a green herb mustard sauce. It's the sort of menu I could return to time and again and never get bored. The Restaurant, the Boathouse, the sensibly priced wine list and the 10 bedrooms in this Victorian Thames-side hotel all make for a relaxed and pleasant visit. This is a very special place and it's no wonder its popularity grows by the week. Make sure to book.

MOULTON	Black Bull

Moulton, Nr Richmond, North Yorkshire DL10 6QJ
Telephone: (0325) 377289
£50
Open: lunch + dinner Mon-Sat (closed 23-31 Dec)
Meals served: lunch 12-2, dinner 7-10.15

You wouldn't think it given the name, but this is one of *the* places for fish in these parts. Gleamingly fresh fish is cooked with the minimum of fuss to keep flavours absolutely intact. Dublin Bay prawns, split-grilled, pan-fried scallops on spinach, poached salmon with fresh asparagus or a simple lobster salad are all popular choices, but carnivores are not ignored – peppered fillet steak and wellington-style beef being a couple of suggestions. Quite a sound wine list, too. Eat in the converted Pulman coach or mahogany-panelled restaurant and conservatory.

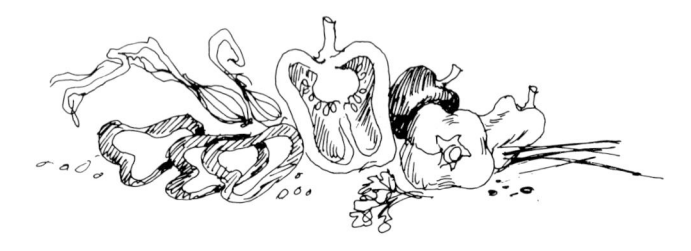

Nantwich — Rookery Hall

Worleston, Nr Nantwich, Cheshire CW5 6DQ
Telephone: (0270) 610016 £70
Fax: (0270) 626027
Open: lunch + dinner daily
Meals served: lunch 12-1.45, dinner 7-9.30 (Sat 7-10)

A rather striking building that was originally a Georgian mansion but converted into a chateau in the 1860s. The hotel has recently undergone a multi-million pound redevelopment programme and now offers 45 high-class bedrooms and extensive conference facilities. Chef Christopher Phillips has taken the period of closure as an opportunity to revamp his menus. Ravioli of seafood in a crab and caviar bisque flavoured with armagnac, pan-fried brill on an orange and saffron couscous with sorrel, saddle of venison on a celeriac galette with black pudding and apples, dark chocolate and hazelnut steamed pudding with a warm Grand Marnier sauce. An outstanding cellar with great strength in Bordeaux and Alsace.

Nayland — Martha's Vineyard

18 High Street, Nayland, Suffolk CO6 4JF
Telephone: (0206) 262888 £40
Open: dinner Tue-Sat (closed Bank Holidays, 2 wks Xmas, 4 days Easter, 2 wks summer)
Meals served: dinner 7-9 (Fri+Sat 7-9.30)
Cream-painted cottage dining room serving good food. Short interesting wine list.

New Alresford — Hunters

32 Broad Street, New Alresford, Hampshire SO24 9AQ
Telephone: (0962) 732468 £40
Open: lunch daily, dinner Mon-Sat (closed 24-27 Dec)
Meals served: lunch 12-2, dinner 7-10
Popular lunchtime business venue, friendly service.

New Milton — Chewton Glen

Christchurch Road, New Milton, Hampshire BH25 6QS
Telephone: (0425) 275341
Fax: (0425) 272310
Open: lunch + dinner daily
Meals served: lunch 12.30-2 (Sun 12.30-2.30), dinner 7.30-9.30

£95

'Quality', 'style', 'pursuit of excellence' and 'perseverance', all come to mind when seeking a suitable description for Chewton Glen. To these you would have to add dedication and an ability to pick the right team – Martin Skan has certainly done that. In each department of this fine country house he seems to have chosen the right person who shares his philosophy on aiming to be *the* hotel in the UK. Its national and international reputation has grown steadily over 25 years, and rightly so. Every year something is added to improve the hotel, but despite this, the eye is never taken off what are perhaps the most important issues – the comfort of the guests, the standard of the food, the depth of the wine cellar, and the quality of the service. The conservatory dining-room is a delight and the menu features some modern interpretations as well as classical favourites coooked by Pierre Chevillard. The wine list with its 400-odd bins is in the hands of the capable and highly acclaimed sommelier Gerard Basset, ensuring that this area is well looked-after. Add to this the new indoor pool, health club, and conference centre, and you know that Chewton Glen offers a complete break. I am certainly looking forward to spending a night there in the course of the next month or so to experience the full range of facilities on offer. On second thoughts, I think I'll make that a week! *See also p260 – our Clover Awards Section.*

Newark — Gannets Bistrot

35 Castlegate, Newark, Nottinghamshire NG24 1AZ
Telephone: (0636) 702066
Open: lunch Tue-Sat, dinner Wed-Sat (closed 1 wk Xmas)
Meals served: lunch 12-2, dinner 6.30-9.30
Catering for all tastes it has a good mix of both meat and vegetarian dishes.

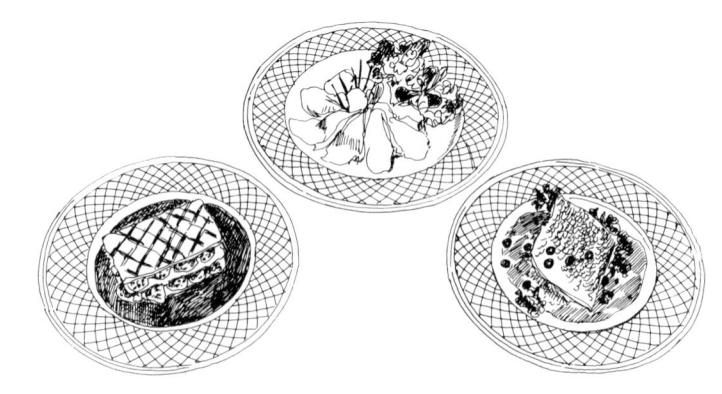

£35

Newbury — Millwaters

London Road, Newbury, Berkshire RG13 2BY
Telephone: (0635) 528838
Fax: (0635) 523406
Open: lunch + dinner daily
Meals served: lunch 12-2, dinner 7-9.30
Former miller's house set in 8 acres of award winning gardens. Wide ranging menu served in the Oasis Restaurant.

£55

NEWBURY — Regency Park Hotel

Bowling Green Road, Thatcham, Newbury, Berkshire RG13 3RP
Telephone: (0635) 871555
Fax: (0635) 871571
Open: lunch + dinner daily
Meals served: lunch 12.30-2.30, dinner 6.30-10.30 (Sun 7-9.30)
Fifty bedroomed hotel with friendly and attentive staff.

£60

NEWCASTLE-UPON-TYNE — 21 Queen Street

21 Queen Street, Princes Wharf, Quayside, Newcastle-upon-Tyne, Tyne & Wear NE1 3UG
Telephone: 091-222 0755
Fax: 091-230 5875
Open: lunch Mon-Fri, dinner Mon-Sat (closed Bank Holidays)
Meals served: lunch 12-2.30, dinner 7-10.45

£70

You'll probably find the best eating in Newcastle, and surrounding area, here at 21 Queen Street. Chef Terry Laybourne concocts some fine combinations of flavours on his menus and the very design of the menu and its colouring (modern and stylish) reflect the food that is on offer. Perhaps choose a soup of roasted yellow peppers with sage and parmesan, or langoustine raviolis served with asparagus bouillon. Excellent choice of fish dishes, or perhaps a noisette of spring lamb served with provençale vegetables flavoured with basil, or fillet of beef with wild mushrooms and baked shallots with a red wine sauce. An excellent and unusual tarte tatin of mango, served with a syrup of passionfruit and home-made mango sorbet, show the versatility of this talented chef. Polished and friendly service and a thoughtful wine list make for overall enjoyment.

NEWCASTLE-UPON-TYNE — Blackgate Restaurant

The Side, Dean Street, Newcastle-upon-Tyne, Tyne & Wear NE1 3JE
Telephone: 091-261 7356
Fax: 091-261 0926
Open: lunch Mon-Fri, dinner Tue-Sat (closed Bank Holidays)
Meals served: lunch 12-2, dinner 7-10
International cuisine with the main influences from Germany.

£50

NEWCASTLE-UPON-TYNE — Café Procope

35 The Side, Quayside, Newcastle-upon-Tyne, Tyne & Wear NE1 3JE
Telephone: 091-232 3848
Open: all day daily (closed Bank Holiday Mon)
Meals served: 10.30-10.30 (Sun 10.30-10)
Good value restaurant with a wide ranging menu.

£35

NEWCASTLE-UPON-TYNE — Courtney's Restaurant

5-7 The Side, Newcastle-upon-Tyne, Tyne & Wear NE1 3JE
Telephone: 091-232 5537
Open: lunch Mon-Fri, dinner Mon-Sat (closed Bank Holidays except Good Friday)
Meals served: lunch 12-2.30, dinner 7-10.45
Brasserie with good standards in food and service.

£40

NEWCASTLE-UPON-TYNE — Fisherman's Lodge

7 Jesmond Dene, Jesmond, Newcastle-upon-Tyne, Tyne & Wear NE7 7BQ
Telephone: 091-281 3281   **£65**
Fax: 091-281 6410
Open: lunch Mon-Fri, dinner Mon-Sat (closed Bank Holidays)
Meals served: lunch 12-2, dinner 7-11

As you'd expect, fish is what you come here for. Among the daily specialities might be pan-fried mullet with vegetables and a coriander and saffron vinaigrette as a starter, and a main dish of poached fillet of lemon sole with two sauces of white wine and langoustine garnished with lobster. Meat is also on offer and there's a separate vegetarian menu, too. Good quality wine list with some very attractive prices.

NORBITON — Graviers

9 Station Road, Norbiton, Kingston-Upon-Thames, Surrey KT2 7AA
Telephone: 081-547 1121   £60
Open: lunch Mon-Fri, dinner Mon-Sat (closed Bank Holidays, 2 wks Xmas, 2 wks Aug)
Meals served: lunch 12-2, dinner 7-10
Traditional French cooking.

NORTH HUISH — Brookdale House

North Huish, South Brent, Devon TQ10 9NR
Telephone: (0548) 82402   **£65**
Fax: (0548) 82699
Open: dinner daily (closed 3 wks Jan)
Meals served: dinner 7.15-9.15

The Trevor-Ropers continue to offer their own brand of relaxed hospitality at Brookdale and are more than happy to spend time with their guests explaining their philosophy on food or the attractions of the local area. The set menu offers some interesting choices and wherever possible they look for additive-free products and give details of their local suppliers on the menu. From a choice of 5 starters on the set menu, perhaps some local Dittisham asparagus served in a puff pastry case with hollandaise sauce, followed by a best-end of Devon lamb served with an unusual carrot and orange layered gateau and a basil sauce (from the 5 main courses on offer), all served with some excellent vegetables. Good selection of British cheeses and a choice of 5 good home-made puddings. An interesting and sometimes unusual wine list. Telephone for details of their winter breaks which allow you to experience this relaxed way of life at a very reasonable rate.

NORTHLEACH	Old Woolhouse

Market Place, Northleach, Gloucestershire GL54 3EE
Telephone: (0451) 60366 ♣
Open: dinner Tue-Sat (closed 1 wk Xmas) £70
Meals served: dinner 8.15-9.30

This remains one of my favourite places and if my reviews from year to year seem never to vary, that is because the quality of the food and the restaurant thankfully also remain the same. There are many chefs in their own establishments who envy the singlemindedness of Jacques Astic. Since the first day he opened he has concentrated on buying the best available ingredients and cooking them in a traditional French style which emphasises using the natural flavours of the product. His dishes are never fussy or oversauced. This sort of cooking withstands the whims of fashion and remains to me the essence of what food is all about. Jenny Astic will read you the menu which will consist of 4 or so starters then 4 or so main courses. These will often include 2 fish dishes and 2 meat, with game in season, and they will be offered because that is what Jacques has found available of the right quality on the day. You'll be offered a choice of 2 or 3 puddings to finish, and I guarantee all will delight. The small 4-or 5-tabled dining room is well set and cosy, and a continual stream of customers are the ones who have found this little gem and who are prepared to drive for many miles for an enjoyable evening. *See also p260 – our Clover Awards section.*

NORTHLEACH	Wickens

Market Place, Northleach, Gloucestershire GL54 3EJ
Telephone: (0451) 60421 £55
Open: lunch + dinner Tue-Sat (closed Bank Holidays)
Meals served: lunch 12.15-1.45, dinner 7.15-8.45

There's an interesting wine list including shrewd selections from Australia – the result of a visit in 1989 by Christopher and Joanna Wickens – and California, accompanied by intelligentexplanations and sensible prices. The food is expressly English including the likes of new season Cotswold lamb casseroled in cider with herb and horseradish dumplings, and roast duck with a prune and apple stuffing and port gravy. High quality raw materials are pressed into service with discipline and integrity – nothing gimmicky. Joanna's home-made puddings mean that there's always something nice to round the meal off.

NORWICH	Adlard's

79 Upper St Giles Street, Norwich, Norfolk NR2 1AB
Telephone: (0603) 633522 £60
Open: lunch Tue-Fri, dinner Tue-Sat
Meals served: lunch 12.30-1.45, dinner 7.30-9

When you're in Norwich this is *the* place to eat – there's no question about it. Something of a latecomer to the profession, David Adlard's dedication has more than made up for any lack of experience, and triumph over illness makes his achievement doubly impressive. His cooking displays intelligence and careful hours of research. First courses may include warm locally smoked salmon with chives and a tart of softly-boiled quail's egg, and seized scallops with spinach in a sauce perfumed with citrus fruits. Main dishes feature loin of venison with mushrooms, gratin dauphinois and a fricassée of seafood à la nage, with a langoustine fumet and basmati and wild rice. It's hard enough to follow these, but he manages to present some puds which steal the show – try the charlotte of coffee and praline with espresso crème anglaise. One of this country's outstanding wine lists selectively picks its way through the top domaines and producers at very realistic prices.

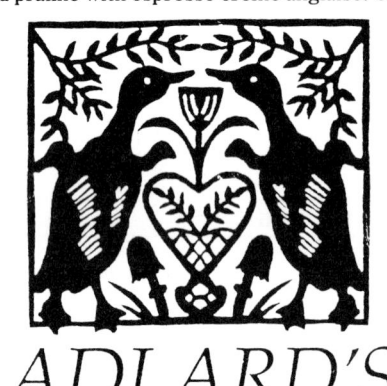

ADLARD'S

NORWICH	Greens Seafood Restaurant

82 Upper St Giles Street, Norwich, Norfolk NR13 1AQ
Telephone: (0603) 623733 £50
Open: lunch Tue-Fri, dinner Tue-Sat (closed Bank Holidays, 1 wk Xmas)
Meals served: lunch 12.15-2.15, dinner 7-10.45
Simple dishes made with fresh local fish. Well priced wines.

NORWICH	Marco's

17 Pottergate, Norwich, Norfolk NR2 1DS
Telephone: (0603) 624044 £55
Open: lunch + dinner Tue-Sat (closed Bank Holidays)
Meals served: lunch 12.30-2, dinner 7.30-10

Cooking is the reason why Marco Vessalio gets up every morning – as he says himself, 'the show must go on'. Indeed, Marco's has been going on 20+ years and continues in much the same fashion as when it started. Minestrone alla Genovese with freshly-made pesto, and fettucine laguna nera (dyed black with cuttlefish ink) are among the first courses, while steamed salmon with a spinach and mushroom stuffing or monkfish with ginger, parsley and garlic feature as main dishes. The Italian wine list is undergoing revision and will cause yet further temptation. Don't lose heart, signor!

NORWICH	St Benedict's Grill

9 St Benedicts, Norwich, Norfolk
Telephone: (0603) 765377 £35
Open: lunch+dinner Tue-Sat
Meals served: lunch 12-2, dinner 7-10.30
Popular local restaurant.

NOTTINGHAM	Loch Fyne Oyster Bar

17 King Street, Nottingham, Nottinghamshire
Telephone: (0602) 508481 £35
Open: all day Mon-Sat (closed Bank Holidays)
Meals served: 9-8
Mainly seafood served in an informal atmosphere.

NOTTINGHAM	Sonny's

3 Carlton Street, Hockley, Nottingham, Nottinghamshire NG1 1NL
Telephone: (0602) 473041 **£35**
Open: lunch + dinner Mon-Sat (closed Bank Holidays)
Meals served: lunch 12-2.30, dinner 7-10.30 (Fri + Sat 7-11)

Located on a corner, the restaurant has a smart yet informal interior. Chef Ian Broadbent's cooking is refreshingly straightforward, using the char-grill to great effect with slight Mediterranean touches. Try the grilled sardines with chilli oil and walnut to whet your appetite, followed by a fillet of lamb with sesame noodles and black beans. A sticky toffee pudding for dessert rounds things off well. Modest prices and chummy atmosphere make it a popular place. Younger sister of the Barnes, London, original.

OAKHAM	Hambleton Hall

Hambleton, Nr Oakham, Leicestershire LE15 8TH
Telephone: (0572) 756991 **£90**
Fax: (0572) 724721
Open: lunch + dinner daily
Meals served: lunch 12.15-1.45, dinner 7-9.30

'Every day is a new day, in which we have to recreate the magic' is the principle which guides Stefa and Tim Hart here at Hambleton Hall. It admirably illustrates their intentions for the hotel and explains why it has achieved such high standards of service over the years. You're hard put to find fault with this place – wherever you look everything is as it should be, and were you to want anything, then there's always someone at hand.

In the kitchen, the Harts' philosophy also holds true as far as new chef Aaron Patterson is concerned. It would be only too easy to settle back and let the elegance of the dining room and the magnificence of the views work their charm on his customers. However, his food is every bit as good as the setting and he won't accept second best. Everything on the menu carries the 'recommended' tag, but if I must single out some dishes, then why not the little salad of rabbit and wild mushrooms with a grain mustard sauce as a starter, with roast fillet of Angus beef with caramelised vegetables and a rich red wine sauce as a main course. A crunchy praline parfait with a compote of plums and citrus fruits will do nicely for dessert. The wine list is impressive and allows you to give the cooking the respect it deserves. In every category, top marks. *See also p254 – our Clover Awards section.*

OAKHAM — Whipper-In Hotel

Market Place, Oakham, Rutland, Leicestershire LE15 6DT
Telephone: (0572) 756971 **£55**
Fax: (0572) 757759
Open: lunch daily, dinner Mon-Sat
Meals served: lunch 12.30-2, dinner 7.30-9.30

A 17th-century coaching inn with a field and country feel. Now established in the area, it continues to prove popular with locals and visitors alike. Comfortable and friendly, it will keep the cold Rutland winds at bay!

OAKHILL — Oakhill House
Bath Road, Oakhill, Bath, Avon BA3 5AQ
Telephone: (0749) 840180 **£45**
Open: dinner Tue-Sat (closed Jan)
Meals served: dinner 7.30-9.30
Modern cooking largely influenced by the cuisine of the Middle East and Mediterranean.

OLD BURGHCLERE — Dew Pond

Old Burghclere, Newbury, Berkshire RG15 9LH
Telephone: (0635) 27408 **£60**
Open: lunch Tue-Fri, dinner Tue-Sat (closed 2 wks Jan, 2 wks Aug)
Meals served: lunch 12-2, dinner 7-10

At the foot of Watership Down, the Dew Pond allows lovers of Richard Adams' novel the chance to combine their tastes in literature with those in cooking. Very much a family-run set up, the restaurant occupies the entire downstairs of a 16th-century extended cottage. Menus are seasonal, as the popular winter game dishes give way to fish and fowl in the spring. Rabbit does feature among the dishes, but not, one hopes, Hazel, Bigwig et al! The excellent cheeses come all the way from Abergavenny.

ORFORD — Butley-Orford Oysterage
Market Square, Orford, Woodbridge, Suffolk IP12 2LH
Telephone: (0394)450277 **£45**
Open: lunch + dinner daily (closed dinner Sun+Mon in Oct-Mar, closed 25+26Dec)
Meals served: lunch 12-2.15, dinner 6-8.30
Go for oysters, home-smoked salmon, and a bottle of white wine; coffee-shop decor, busy on Saturdays.

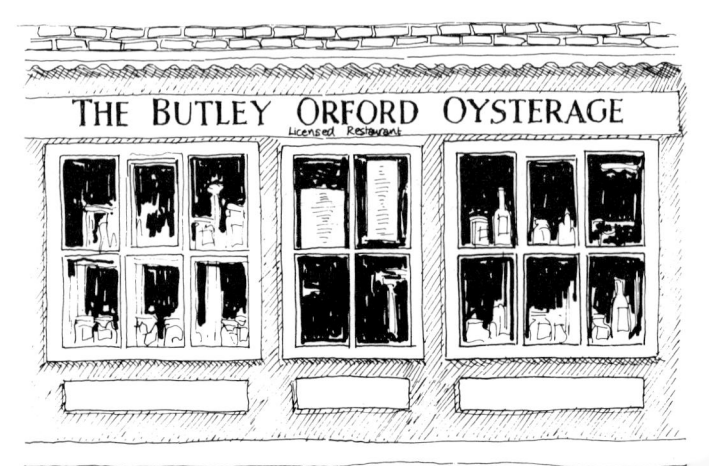

OSWESTRY	Sebastian

45 Willow Street, Oswestry, Shropshire
Telephone: (0691) 655444 £35
Open: dinner Tue-Sat
Meals served: dinner 6.30-10.30
Good quality food and friendly service.

OSWESTRY	Starlings Castle

Brony Garth, Oswestry, Shropshire SY10 7NU
Telephone: (0691) 72464 £40
Open: lunch Sun, dinner daily
Meals served: lunch 12-2.30, dinner 7-9.30 (Fri+Sat 7-10)
Small friendly and informal hotel run by Antony and Jools Pitt.

OXFORD Bath Place Hotel & Restaurant

4 & 5 Bath Place, Holywell Street, Oxford, Oxfordshire OX1 3SU
Telephone: (0865) 791812
Fax: (0865) 791834 £65
Open: lunch Tue-Sun, dinner Tue-Sat
Meals served: lunch 12-2, dinner 7-10 (Fri+Sat 7-10.30)

Tucked down a little lane off Holywell Street, it's not surprising that the Bath Place Hotel is often overlooked by visitors to Oxford. But for the discreet sign it's just another immaculately kept house – the kind of place dons tend to hide away in. Still, it's a pity that this establishment isn't better known since it offers a charming place to stay in the city and within easy walking distance of the Bodleian, the Ashmolean and the many bookshops. There are now 2 suites supplementing the 8 pristine bedrooms, and new chef Peter Cherill is manning the stoves and producing interesting dishes – roast wood pigeon with glazed onions and roast garlic in red wine and cinnamon juices, braised monkfish with haricot beans in a tomato and basil-scented olive oil – on his multiple choice fixed price menus.

OXFORD Browns

5-11 Woodstock Road, Oxford, Oxfordshire OX2 6HA
Telephone: (0865) 511995 £30
Fax: (0865) 52347
Open: all day daily
Meals served: 11am-11.30pm (Sun 12-11.30)

The first visit to Brown's remains one of the unofficial undergraduate initiation ceremonies and continues as an enjoyable ritual every so often – grants being what they are these days. Plates of spaghetti are available with a selection of sauces and garlic bread and salad on the side. Warm salads come in a variety of combinations with the dressing you prefer. Steaks and pies are served with a baked potato and perhaps a vegetable of the day. Students plus their parents figure highly among the customers during term time, but there's a good cross section of office workers and families otherwise. Undoubtedly popular and good value.

Oxford	Cherwell Boathouse

Bardwell Road, Oxford, Oxfordshire OX2 6SR
Telephone: (0865) 52746 £50
Fax: (0865) 391459
Open: lunch daily in summer, dinner Tue-Sat (closed Bank Holidays, Xmas)
Meals served: lunch 12-2, dinner 7-10 (Sat 7-10.30)

One of those Oxford Shibboleths that sort out the visitor from the resident, the Cherwell is pronounced 'Charwell' much as Magdalen is 'Maudlin'. You also have to be a bit in the know to find the restaurant as it's not that well signposted off the Banbury Road leading out of Oxford. In fact, it's part of the old boathouse from which generations of undergraduates have set off up and down the river. You can see a steady flotilla of punts pass by as you eat, your meal punctuated by the occasional burst of applause as someone falls in. The food is good on a limited choice menu and generally very reasonably priced. Try the home-made celeriac and bean soup and loin of English lamb with red wine, garlic and lime if they've come round again by the time you visit. The wine list achieved almost legendary status with great producers and vintages at unbelievably low prices.

Oxford	15 North Parade

15 North Parade Avenue, Oxford, Oxfordshire OX2 6LX
Telephone: (0865) 513773 £50
Open: lunch daily, dinner Mon-Sat (closed some Bank Holidays)
Meals served: lunch 12-2, dinner 7-10.30

Increasingly popular restaurant in a narrow side street off the banbury road leading to St Anthony's College. Chef Stanley Matthews provides some nice dishes with comforting familiarity. Thus garlic-baked mussels and calves' liver with mashed potato and onion gravy are among the options on the menu. Good char-grilled swordfish served on a bed of flageolet beans and red onions. Choose from the set menu at around £16 or from the carte. Service by well-informed young ladies. a small but nicely balanced wine list with top wines from Australia and California.

Oxford	Restaurant Elizabeth

82 St Aldate's, Oxford, Oxfordshire OX1 1RA
Telephone: (0865) 242230 £60
Open: lunch + dinner Tue-Sun (closed 24-31 Dec, Good Friday)
Meals served: lunch 12.30-2.30, dinner 6.30-11 (Sun 7-10.30)

In the city of dreaming spires things seem to progress at a slower pace than elsewhere. The Restaurant Elizabeth is a case in point, for over the 30 or so years it's been open, very little has changed. Admittedly, the dining room is smaller and the bar area has been rearranged, but in essence the clock has stood still. Chef Salvador Rodriguez delivers no surprises either from the kitchen, and regulars can no doubt recite dishes by heart. Suprême de canard à l'orange is a seasoned favourite, while saumon au vin blanc and filet de boeuf maison are no less acceptable. The wine list is equally classical with the Bordeaux region and Sauternes particularly well represented. Afterwards, a stroll in Christ Church Meadows is the perfect way to digest the meal.

OXFORD	Gee's

61a Banbury Road, Oxford, Oxfordshire OX2 6PE
Telephone: (0865) 53540 £45
Open: lunch + dinner daily (closed 25+26 Dec)
Meals served: lunch 12-2.30, dinner 7-11
Brasserie with a wide range of good value dishes set in a huge conservatory.

PADSTOW — Seafood Restaurant

Riverside, Padstow, Cornwall PL28 8BY
Telephone: (0841) 532485 £65
Fax: (0841) 533344
Open: dinner Mon-Sat (closed late Dec-early Jan)
Meals served: dinner 7-10 (Sat 7-10.30)

An exuberant harbourside restaurant with modern paintings and a light airy feel to it. Chef/patron Rick Stein reckons that 40 people is a bad night – around a 100 or so is more like it. These customers are there to enjoy the superb cooking of the freshest of ingredients. For Rick flavour is all. He cooks the simplest way possible, believing that if the fish is fresh it will look good of its own accord. Every tide brings more supplies and the constant stream of crates into the kitchen allows the time from sea to plate to be reduced to a minimum. David Pope, previously at the Well House in Liskeard, is now pastry cook here which adds another dimension to the restaurant. If you haven't been before look out for the special breaks, whereby you can stay in one of their 8 bedrooms for 2 nights with dinner, bed and breakfast for around £50 per night per person. Pick up the phone and book now. *See also p262 — our Clover Awards section.*

PAINSWICK — Painswick Hotel

Kemps Lane, Painswick, Gloucestershire GL6 6YB
Telephone: (0452) 812160 £50
Fax: (0452) 812059
Open: lunch Sun, dinner daily
Meals served: lunch 12.30-2, dinner 7-9.30 (Sun 7-8.30)

Somerset and Hélène Moore's new project, following their move from Flitwick Manor (*qv*) and already a marked improvement on what it was. The surroundings were always a strong point but now the interior is of an equal standard and all the rooms show the benefits of a complete rethink. Bedrooms, 19 in all, boast handsome mahogany furniture, some have 4-poster and canopied beds. The aptly-named Shaun Cook offers good value fixed-price menus with a special seafood menu in Spring when their seawater tank can be put to good use. Concise, impeccably chosen wine list with the definitive house selection of around 30 wines grouped by price in 3 stages, from £9.50 to £16. A delightful place to stay and eat.

PANGBOURNE	Copper Inn

Church Road, Pangbourne, Berkshire RG8 7AR
Telephone: (0734) 842244 £60
Fax: (0734) 845542
Open: lunch Sun-Fri, dinner daily
Meals served: lunch 12.30-2 (Sun 12.30-2.30), dinner 7-9.30
Large, smart public rooms with both modern and antique furnishings.

PATELEY BRIDGE	The Dusty Miller Restaurant

Low Laithe, Summerbridge, Pateley Bridge, West Yorkshire
Telephone: (0423) 780837 £55
Open: dinner Tue-Sat
Meals served: dinner 6.30-11
Good local restaurant.

PAULERSPURY	Vine House

High Street, Paulerspury, Northamptonshire NN12 7NA
Telephone: (032 733) 267 £50
Fax: (032 733) 309
Open: lunch Tue-Fri + Sun, dinner Mon-Sat
Meals served: lunch 12-2.30, dinner 7-10

Previously at Hill House in Essex, Marcus and Julie Springett are now installed here at the Vine House. The recently departed chef Jonathan Stanbury had built up quite a reputation for good food, so it remains for Marcus to maintain the high standards. However, he's got bags of energy and plenty of enthusiasm and ensures everything from breads to sweetmeats are made on the premises. His daily changing menus offer starters such as crab and smoked salmon fish cakes with lemon butter sauce, roast wild rabbit with chestnuts, cranberries and a truffle sauce for main course and perhaps British unpasteurised cheeses with home-made oatcakes or a pud to finish.

PENKRIDGE	William Harding's House

Mill Street, Penkridge, Stafford, Staffordshire ST19 5AY
Telephone: (078 571) 2955 £45
Open: lunch Sun, dinner Tue-Sat (closed Bank Holidays)
Meals served: lunch 12.30-1.45, dinner 7.30-9.30

Down in the annals as belonging to one William Harding, the house is now owned by the Bickleys and run as a cosy restaurant. Choose on the set price menu a feathered fowlie and vegetable pottage to warm you up, with perhaps rich seasonal game in suet with fine green cabbage as a main dish. The fresh produce is treated inventively and the sauces are good. Homely puddings and British regional cheeses are served from the sideboard.

Penzance — Abbey Hotel

Abbey Street, Penzance, Cornwall TR18 4AR
Telephone: (0736) 66906 £45
Fax: (0736) 51163
Open: dinner daily
Meals served: dinner 7.30-8.30

Wake up in the morning to the sound of seagulls circling above the harbour and go for a walk to taste the sea breeze before breakfast, a hearty affair in the dining room that is transformed by candlelight in the evening for cosy dinners of good quality, unfussy cooking. The fixed price 3-course menu always includes a vegetarian main course. Others could be breast of chicken filled with crab and tarragon and served with a lemon cream sauce, or grilled lemon sole with capers and beurre noisette. If you're lucky, the butterscotch pudding will be one of the desserts on offer. Seven brightly decorated bedrooms with some nice antiques for those staying over, including one with a splendid wood-panelled bathroom. A relaxed, homely place.

Petworth — Soanes

Grove Lane, Petworth, West Sussex GU28 0HY
Telephone: (0798) 43659 £65
Open: lunch Sun, dinner Wed-Sat (closed 25 Dec, 2 wks summer, 2 wks winter)
Meals served: lunch 12.30-3, dinner 7.30-11.15
Carol Godsmark cooks traditional French food, husband Derek serves short seasonal good value menus.

Pitton — Silver Plough

Pitton, Nr Salisbury, Wiltshire SP5 1DZ
Telephone: (0722) 72266 £50
Open: lunch daily, dinner Mon-Sat (closed 25 Dec, Jan+Feb)
Meals served: lunch 12-2, dinner 7-10
Above average pub food.

Plumtree — Perkins Bar Bistro

Old Railway Station, Station Road, Plumtree, Nottinghamshire NG12 5NA
Telephone: (0602) 373695 £35
Open: lunch + dinner Tue-Sat (closed 25+26 Dec, 1 Jan, Easter Monday)
Meals served: lunch 12-2, dinner 7-9.45

Back in 1982 a brasserie would have been unheard of in these parts and a restaurant would sound too stuffy, so the owners – Tony and Wendy Parkins – called it a bar bistro. Their old 1880s railway station is thronged with happy 'commuters' who enjoy the no-nonsense approach to good classically-based French bistro cooking. Typical blackboard offerings – chicken liver, port and brandy terrine, entrecôte steak béarnaise and lemon tart, with a special board offering what's good that day. Carefully chosen good value drinking on the wine list.

PLYMOUTH	Artillery Tower
Devil's Point, Durnford Street, Plymouth, Devon PL1 3QR	
Telephone: (0752) 667276	£40
Open: lunch Mon-Fri, dinner Mon-Sat	
Meals served: lunch 12-2, dinner 7-10	
Nice views over the busy harbour, humorous menu based around smuggling traditions.	

PLYMOUTH — Chez Nous

13 Frankfort Gate, Plymouth, Devon PL1 1QA
Telephone: (0752) 266793 £70
Open: lunch + dinner Tue-Sat (closed Bank Holidays, 3 wks Feb, 3 wks Sep)
Meals served: lunch 12.30-2, dinner 7-10.30

You know the kind of place you happen to find in Paris where you sit down amongst the regulars and soon you feel like you've been coming here for years? Well, that's what it's like here at Chez Nous. Jacques and Suzanne Marchal are only too happy to bring you into the conversation and Jacques almost reluctantly drags himself away to the kitchen to get on with the work! But don't get me wrong, once he's there he gets down to business and turns out some fine food that is governed scrupulously by whatever happens to be freshest and most interesting in the market that day – hence the blackboard listing specials. Typical choices from the carte could include cassolette d'escargots aux champignons, and medaillons de chevreuil poivrade, whilst the blackboard might offer coquilles St Jacques with ginger. A suitably French cellar has, typically, a sound house wine and, less typically, a good choice of halves. Gaily painted wooden chairs and walls strewn with pictures and testimonials. *See also p264 – our Clover Awards section.*

POLPERRO	Kitchen at Polperro
The Coombs, Polperro, Cornwall PL13 2RQ	
Telephone: (0503) 72780	£45
Open: dinner Wed-Mon in summer, Fri+Sat only in winter (closed 25-26 Dec)	
Meals served: dinner 7-9.30	
Interesting menus with the emphasis on fish – specials depend on the catch of the day.	

POOL-IN-WHARFEDALE — Pool Court

Pool Bank, Pool-in-Wharfedale, Otley, West Yorkshire LS21 1EH
Telephone: (0532) 842288 £65
Open: dinner Tue-Sat (closed Bank Holidays, 2 wks Xmas)
Meals served: dinner 7-9.30

Pool Court celebrated its silver anniversary last year, a testimony to the long hours and dedication of owners Michael and Hanni Gill, who are still displaying the same tireless approach that has put this restaurant with rooms up among the top establishments in the North of England and the country as a whole. Chef David Watson hails from up here and applies his instinctive Yorkshire level-headedness to the modern dishes on the menu. Ramekin of pheasant and rabbit with gingery pears and polenta, creamy parsnip soup with curried almonds, guineafowl with wild mushrooms, prune and armagnac tart with a lemon cream is a typical 4-course menu with the price of the main course denoting the total cost of the menu. Suitable suggestions from the exceptional wine list are listed at the bottom of each evening's menu. Six bedrooms are models of comfort and style and are in impeccable order. *See also p264 – our Clover Awards section.*

POOLE	Haven Hotel

Banks Road, Sandbanks, Poole, Dorset BH13 7QL
Telephone: (0202) 707333   £45
Fax: (0202) 708798
Open: lunch + dinner daily
Meals served: lunch 12.30-2, dinner 7-10
Four miles from Poole town centre, 95 bedrooms.

POOLE	Mansion House

11 Thames Street, Poole, Dorset BH15 1JN
Telephone: (0202) 685666   £55
Fax: (0202) 665709
Open: lunch Sun-Fri, dinner daily (closed 1 Jan, Easter Monday)
Meals served: lunch 12.30-2.15, dinner 7.30-10 (Sun 7.30-9)

The new general manager Jack Old has given this handsome Georgian hotel an injection of new life. Staff are busier delivering traditional service with a sense of purpose and the whole place seems brighter and airier. Twenty-eight comfortable, antique-filled bathrooms are subject to constant improvement and contain plenty of cosseting extras. In the wood-panelled restaurant there are several menus on offer depending on whether you are a member, resident, member's guest or just a visitor for the day. The dinner menu lists local mussels in a cider and cream sauce garnished with smoked bacon and mint among the starters, and a fillet of New Forest venison on a bed of creamed celeriac with blueberries as a main course. Dorset cheeses come with celery and Dorset real ale chutney. The wine list offers modest discounts for members as well as a couple of wines from Israel.

PORLOCK	Oaks Hotel

Porlock, Somerset TA24 8ES
Telephone: (0643) 862265   £35
Open: dinner daily
Meals served: dinner 7-8.30

It's a way of life for Tim and Anne Riley, the owners of this small Edwardian country house hotel. They've spent the winter refurbishing the restaurant and bedrooms and it shows in their care and concern. Anne's cooking is of equal importance and uses some fine local produce to great advantage – poached halibut steak in sauternes, grilled Exmoor venison steak with mustard sauce. New additions to the medium price bracket wine list include California and South Africa. Lots of pretty girls among the staff, who lead a happy, wonderfully chaotic style.

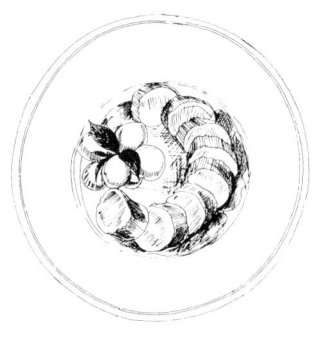

POWBURN	Breamish House

Powburn, Alnwick, Northumberland NE66 4LL
Telephone: (066 578) 266 £45
Fax: (066 578) 500
Open: lunch Sun, dinner daily (closed Jan-mid Feb)
Meals served: lunch 12.30 for 1, dinner 7.30 for 8

Originally a 17th-century farmhouse, the building was subsequently converted into a hunting lodge before being transformed into a hotel. The past year has seen extensive redecoration throughout. Eleven bedrooms available.

PUCKRUP	Puckrup Hall

Puckrup, Tewkesbury, Gloucestershire GL20 6EL
Telephone: (0684) 296200 £70
Fax: (0684) 850788
Open: lunch + dinner daily
Meals served: lunch 12.30-2, dinner 7-9.30 (Fri+Sat 7-10)

A new 18-hole golf course has just been opened as part of an ongoing programme of improvements at this elegant Regency house set in 40 acres of lawns and parkland. Bedrooms, named after each month, and suites, named and decorated to reflect the seasons, are soon to have their numbers greatly increased, and a leisure centre is also in the pipeline. Chef Geoff Balharrie continues to offer a blend of classical and modern cooking – tournedos Rossini, fillet of brill with a coriander soufflé, simply grilled fish and a couple of vegetarian options.

Pulborough — Stane Street Hollow

Codmore Hill, Pulborough, West Sussex RH20 1BG
Telephone: (0798) 872819
Open: lunch Wed-Fri, dinner Wed-Sat (closed 1 wk Xmas, 1 wk May, 2 wks Oct)
Meals served: lunch 12.30-1.15, dinner 7.30-9.15

£55

As places open and close in the blink of an eye, standards yo-yo and chefs jump on the culinary bandwagon, it's nice to know where you stand when you eat at René Kaiser's restaurant. The menus change with the seasons to allow for variety, but the quality control never wavers. Recent dishes have included champignons farcis and bresaola among the first courses, with a roasted smoked leg of duckling with a pork stuffing and a sauce of pickled cucumbers and wine as main courses. Solothurner ambassadoren teller is aptly named with its selection of beef fillet, lamb cutlet, pork fillet and lamb's kidney served on noodles with a mushroom and cream sauce – a dish like that does more for a country's image than any amount of diplomacy! René being of Swiss origin, it would be unthinkable not to sample his desserts, and on the assiette René allows you to have a bit of everything – coffee parfait, a blackberry bombe, black forest cake and apple mousse. The modestly priced wine list features 2 of his national specialities – Dole Romane and Dole Blanche du Valais – which are usually jealously guarded back home! I enjoy this friendly, low-key and honest establishment. *See also p266 – our Clover Awards section.*

Purton — Pear Tree

Church End, Purton, Nr Swindon, Wiltshire SN5 9ED
Telephone: (0793) 772100
Fax: (0793) 772369
Open: lunch Sun-Fri, dinner daily
Meals served: lunch 12-2, dinner 7-9.30

£45

Smart, comfortable public rooms with french windows on to the gardens from the lounge.

Ramsbottom — Village Restaurant

16 Market Place, Ramsbottom, Nr Bury, Greater Manchester BL0 9HT
Telephone: (0706) 825070
Open: dinner Tue-Sat (closed 1 Jan)
Meals served: dinner only at 8

£75

– good local restaurant

Chris Johnson's wine list is an education in taste. Quite how he assembles it – being an abstainer himself – baffles me! You'll find some 20 pages of first-rate drinking, reasonably priced and arranged by grape variety rather than nationality. A further innovation is a selection of 3 wines by the glass which are chosen with the menu specifically in mind. Such concern to create harmony between the wine and food is typical of the Village Restaurant.

In the kitchen, Ros Hunter cooks some truly outstanding food in a style happily referred to as 'extended dinner party'. A typical set of courses could be a selection of cured and smoked fish, scotch broth, halibut with sea urchin mousseline sauce, loin of venison with redcurrant and meaux mustard purée and mushroom dijonnaise. Then come unpasteurised cheeses. At dessert you're allowed a choice of 'sweet things' – say, crème brûlée, or meringues with lemon sauce. Some dinner party! Sheer heaven on a plate. Top quality ingredients, including a high percentage of organic produce. Set aside an evening – you'll be lucky to get away before midnight – and enjoy a meal you'll remember.

Ramsey — Harbour Bistro
5 East Street, Ramsey, Isle of Man
Telephone: (0624) 814182
Open: lunch + dinner daily (closed Xmas, Good Friday)
Meals served: lunch 12.15-2.30, dinner 6.30-10.30
Informal, maily fish restaurant which is fresh daily from the harbour.

£40

Reeth — Burgoyne Hotel
The Green, Reeth, Richmond, North Yorkshire DL11 6SN
Telephone: (0748) 84292
Open: lunch Sun, dinner daily
Meals served: lunch 12.15-2, dinner 7.30-9
Small friendly hotel on the village green.

£45

Reigate — La Barbe
71 Bell Street, Reigate, Surrey RH2 7AN
Telephone: (0737) 241966
Open: lunch Mon-Fri, dinner Mon-Sat (closed Bank Holidays except Good Friday, 25-27 Dec)
Meals served: lunch 12-2, dinner 7-10
French bistro offering modern cuisine.

£45

Remenham — The Little Angel
Remenham, Henley-on-Thames, Oxfordshire RG9 2LS
Telephone: (0491) 574165
Open: lunch + dinner daily (closed 25+26 Dec)
Meals served: lunch 12-2 (Fri+Sat 12-2.30), dinner 7-10 (Fri+Sat 7-10.30)
Popular pub and restaurant by the bridge at Henley, undergoing changes of ownership this year.

£55

Richmond — Howe Villa
Whitcliffe Mill, Richmond, North Yorkshire DL10 4TJ
Telephone: (0748) 850055
Open: dinner daily (closed Dec+Jan)
Meals served: dinner 7.30 for 8
Warm welcome, 4-course set menu. Unlicensed premises.

£40

Richmond — Kings Head
Market Place, Richmond, North Yorkshire DL10 4HS
Telephone: (0748) 850220
Fax: (0748) 850635
Open: lunch + dinner daily
Meals served: lunch 12-2 (Sun 12.30-2), dinner 7-9.15
17th-century hotel, friendly and popular with the locals.

£35

RIDGEWAY	Old Vicarage

Ridgeway Moor, Ridgeway, Nr Sheffield, Derbyshire S12 3XW
Telephone: (0742) 475814 £65
Open: lunch Sun-Fri, dinner Tue-Sat (closed Bank Holidays, 27-30 Dec)
Meals served: lunch 12.30-2.30, dinner 7-10.30

'And man hath no better thing under the sun than to eat, and to drink, and to be merry.' Thus begins the gospel according to Tessa Bramley to which I lend a willing ear – and palate! Come here to the Old Vicarage to be convered in your turn to her eclectic brand of modern cuisine. Her kitchen is thoroughly ecumenical, with a decidedly oriental twist and new lighter touch to many of the current dishes. Recommended items on the menu include beef satay, Thai-spiced fish cakes and filo packets of monkfish and lemon balm to start, a light intermediate course, then roast local duckling with cabbage, garlic and juniper, the legs made into Peking-style pancakes with hoisin sauce. I went on about her baked chocolate pudding last year – by all accounts it's still a winner – so this year let's mention the glazed lemon tart with a brandy snap basket of iced lemon parfait. Another winner. Do I hear any dissenters among the congregation? I think not. An innovation this year is a cheaper 3-course menu at £18.50, and the wine list continues to offer extraordinary depth, a veritable who's who of each region's top producers, and above all sensible prices. Son Andrew and his fiancée run the front of house with relaxed, smiling efficiency.

RIPLEY	Michel's

13 High Street, Ripley, Surrey GU23 6AQ
Telephone: (0483) 224777 £70
Open: lunch Tue-Fri + Sun, dinner Tue-Sat (closed 25+26 Dec, 1 Jan)
Meals served: lunch 12.30-1.45, dinner 7.30-9 (Sat 7-9.30)

Both setting and cooking are strong in style at this thriving Surrey restaurant. Good quality produce, assertive flavours and sound saucing typify dishes such as aubergine terrine, braised lamb shin with a vegetable ragout and herb dumping, and a soufflé of bread and butter pudding with an apricot sauce. A concise wine list with wines from Gisselbrecht, Guigal and Lafarge.

RIPPONDEN	Over the Bridge Restaurant

Millfold, Ripponden, Nr Halifax, West Yorkshire HX6 4DL
Telephone: (0422) 823722 £55
Open: dinner Mon-Sat (closed Bank Holidays)
Meals served: dinner 7-9.30

Fresh produce forms the basis of the good value menus served in this long established restaurant.

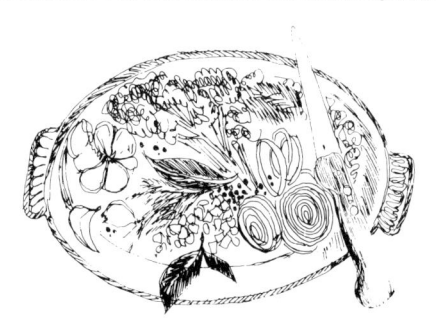

ROADE — Roadhouse

16 High Street, Roade, Northamptonshire NN7 2NW
Telephone: (0604) 863372 £55
Open: lunch Tue-Fri, dinner Tue-Sat (closed Bank Holidays, 2 wks Jul/Aug)
Meals served: lunch 12.30-1.45, dinner 7-10

Not at all the pull-in refuelling stop the name might suggest, the Roadhouse Restaurant is so comfortable you'll want to make a night of it. A shrewd balance is maintained between the ambitions of the cooking and the tastes and budgets of the clientele. The food is rich but also manages to allow flavours to come through. A fixed price lunch menu could be soup of the day followed by roast breast of pheasant with a pâté of its leg meat baked en croûte with a chocolate marquise to finish!

ROCHFORD — Hotel Renouf & Renouf's Restaurant

Bradley Way, Rochford, Essex SS4 1BU
Telephone: (0702) 541334
Fax: (0702) 549563 £55
Open: lunch Sun-Fri, dinner daily (closed 27-29 Dec)
Meals served: lunch 12-1.45, dinner 7-10
Classically based dishes with modern touches; 24 bedrooms, run by the ebullient Derek Renouf.

ROMSEY — Old Manor House

21 Palmerston Street, Romsey, Hampshire SO51 8GF
Telephone: (0794) 517353 £85
Open: lunch Tue-Sun, dinner Tue-Sat (closed 1 wk Xmas)
Meals served: lunch 12-2, dinner 7-9.30

Set in a Tudor town house, Mauro Bregoli's restaurant deserves serious consideration. His cooking is worthy of the impressive surroundings and many dishes linger in the memory. Pan-fried foie gras with a foil of sliced, buttery apple was a positive triumph, although simply enough presented. The grilled seabass fillet was another winner, arriving at the table redolent of virgin olive oil, with finely chopped peppers and black olives making a delightful complement of tastes. Finally, the apple terrine with cinnamon ice-cream and pear feuilleté was faultless in every respect. The French cheeses are outstanding as are the wines and even the petits fours deserve a mention. A reasonable priced wine list means we are talking of a good restaurant. *See also p267 – our Clover Awards section.*

ROTHERWICK — Tylney Hall

Rotherwick, Nr Hook, Hampshire RG27 9AJ
Telephone: (0256) 764881 £65
Fax: (0256) 768141
Open: lunch + dinner daily
Meals served: lunch 12.30-2, dinner 7.30-9.30

The original mansion house on this site was demolished and the present one built by Sir Lionel Phillips in 1898. A hospital during the first World War, the headquarters for the Clan Shipping Line during the second, today, it's a comfortable hotel of 91 bedrooms and some suitably baronial public rooms, ably run by manager Rita Mooney. The restaurant offers traditional dishes treated in the modern way. Stunning surroundings with gardens designed by Gertrude Jekyll.

ROWDE	**George & Dragon**

High Street, Rowde, Wiltshire SN10 2PN
Telephone: (0380) 723053 £35
Open: lunch Tue-Sun, dinner Tue-Sat (closed 25+26 Dec, 1 Jan)
Meals served: lunch 12-1.45, dinner 7-10
16th-century pub serving reasonable priced food.

RUSHLAKE GREEN	**Stone House**

Rushlake Green, Heathfield, East Sussex TN21 9QJ
Telephone: (0435) 830553 £65
Fax: (0825) 764673
Open: lunch by arrangement dinner Mon-Sat (closed Xmas-5 Jan)
Meals served: dinner 7.30-9
Menus (residents only) feature produce from the garden and local suppliers. Good French wines.

RUSPER	**Ghyll Manor**

High Street, Rusper, Nr Horsham, West Sussex RH12 4PX
Telephone: (0293) 871571 £75
Fax: (0293) 871419
Open: lunch + dinner daily
Meals served: lunch 12.30-2.30, dinner 7-10
Elizabethan manor and cottages with modern extension in 40 acres of grounds. Warm, friendly atmosphere.

RYE Landgate Bistro

5/6 Landgate, Rye, East Sussex TN31 7LH
Telephone: (0797) 222829 **£40**
Open: dinner Tue-Sat (closed Xmas, 1 wk Jun, 1 wk Oct)
Meals served: dinner 7-9.30 (Sat 7-10)

Toni Ferguson-Lee cooks every dish with her own fair hands. On the 2 occasions in the past 10 years that she's been ill, the Landgate Bistro has shut up shop. There's dedication and consistency for you! She and Nick Parkin run the kind of restaurant that *they* would most like to eat in themselves, which again guarantees good standards. Menus are seasonally based, modern and simple. Local squid braised with white wine, tomatoes and garlic, and jugged hare are typical examples. Your bill will come as a pleasant surprise since service is already included in the prices and the wine list is a model of restraint.

Rye — Mermaid Inn

Mermaid Street, Rye, East Sussex TN31 7EU
Telephone: (0797) 223065 £45
Fax: (0797) 226995
Open: lunch + dinner daily
Meals served: lunch 12.30-2.15, dinner 7.30-9.15

Once a refuge of smugglers, the Mermaid Inn now draws a more law-abiding customers with her manifold charm. Deliberately setting out to preserve its period feel, this hotel is almost a working museum of the Middle Ages. The public rooms have patterned carpets, high-backed chairs, heavy beams and pillars, and, over the fireplace, dangerously authentic spears and swords. Bedrooms, some without a right-angle in sight, have leaded windows and pleasing antiques, including a richly-carved 4-poster. A welcoming, 'olde worlde' hostel, where friendly service and open log fires make you feel safe and snug.

St Austell — Boscundle Manor

Tregrehan, St Austell, Cornwall PL25 3RL
Telephone: (072 6) 813557 £55
Fax: (0726) 814997
Open: dinner daily (closed mid Oct-Easter)
Meals served: dinner 7.30-8.30 (Sun 7.30-8)

Mary & Andrew Flint put a lot of themselves into this small hotel. So much so, in fact, that they prefer to shut down for half of the year to recharge their batteries and keep the enthusiasm going. It's a sensible idea and allows them to keep standards up to scratch. Mary's cooking uses fresh local produce to advantage in dishes such as roast duck with a cherry and brandy sauce and grilled Fowey trout with rosemary. A vegetarian alternative can be rustled up at a moment's notice. The wine list continues to be strong on clarets.

Recent improvements to the 10 bedrooms (2 in the cottage at the top of the garden and one in the Garden Room above the swimming pool) mean all doubles now have spa baths, and golf enthusiasts will appreciate the high-quality practice area newly and sympathetically created utilising the old mine workings in the wooded grounds.

ST AUSTELL — Clarets Restaurant

Trethowel House, Bodmin Road, St Austell, Cornwall PL25 5RR
Telephone: (0726) 67435 £45
Open: lunch Tue-Fri, dinner Mon-Sat (closed 25+26 Dec)
Meals served: lunch 12-2, dinner 7-10
Traditional English and French cooking.

ST MAWES — Idle Rocks Hotel

Tredenham Road, St Mawes, Cornwall TR2 5AN
Telephone: (0326) 270771 £50
Fax: (0326) 270062
Open: lunch + dinner daily (closed Jan)
Meals served: lunch 12-2.30, dinner 7-9.15

On a fine day you can spend hours happily watching the comings and goings of boats in the harbour as you sit with a drink on the terrace. Best of the bedrooms also have a sea view, those without being cheaper by way of compensation. All have benefited over the last 12 months from an extensive programme of refurbishment using colourful contemporary fabrics and some nice antique furnishings. The arrival of chef Alan Vickops from Alverton Manor, Truro, has given an added impetus to the food and he's now got a new kitchen and restaurant – the Water's Edge – in which to work. Cornish fish and shellfish feature strongly on his menus – crab and cucumber salad with a ginger dressing, Fowey sea trout plain grilled, lemon sole stuffed with a salmon and brazil nut mousse with basil cream.

SALCOMBE — Spinnakers

Fore Street, Salcombe, Devon TQ8 8JG
Telephone: (0548) 843408 £40
Open: lunch daily, dinner Mon-Sat (closed Dec+Jan)
Meals served: lunch 12-2.30, dinner 7-10

David May cooks with a sure hand while Sandra May runs the restaurant with loads of enthusiasm. For the best of the fish dishes you'll have to take your pick of the day's catch – the options are chalked up on a blackboard. Splendid views whichever way you look.

SANDIWAY — Nunsmere Hall

Tarporley Road, Sandiway, Cheshire CW8 2ES
Telephone: (0606) 889100 £75
Fax: (0606) 889055
Open: lunch + dinner daily
Meals served: lunch 12.30-2 (Sun 12-2.30), dinner 7.30-10 (Sat 7.30-10.30)

All change! For in effect Nunsmere has been transformed and doubled in size. Now Malcolm and Julie McHardy's hotel has 32 bedrooms, a fine oak-panelled cocktail bar and additional conference facilities. Standards however remain high in terms of both furnishings and decor. The restaurant has also undergone alterations and new chef Paul Kitching's fixed price daily menu might offer steamed Cornish turbot, roasted pigeon from Bresse or roast loin of Cumbrian lamb among the options. Paul's trio of oranges is his own creation and proves to be a strong favourite with the guests.

SARK — Aval du Creux

Sark, Channel Islands
Telephone: (0481) 832036 £40
Fax: (0481) 832368
Open: lunch + dinner daily (closed Oct-Apr)
Meals served: lunch 12-2, dinner 7-8

As well as running the public hotel and restaurant, the owners also cater privately for the Seigneur de Sark – so you can feel secure that everything will be of a high standard. The 12-bedroomed hotel is cosy and in the restaurant, shellfish stars on the menu.

SEAFORD — Quincy's
42 High Street, Seaford, East Sussex BN25 1PL
Telephone: (0323) 895490 £40
Open: lunch Sun, dinner Tue-Sat (closed 25+26 Dec)
Meals: lunch 12-2, dinner 7.15-10
Popular restaurant with fixed price menus offering sound, robust cooking.

SEAVIEW — Seaview Hotel
High Street, Seaview, Isle of Wight PO34 5EX
Telephone: (0983) 612711 £45
Fax: (0983) 613729
Open: lunch daily, dinner Mon-Sat (closed 25 Dec)
Meals served: lunch 12-2, dinner 7.30-9.30 (Sat at 7.15 + 9.15)
Family-run, 16-bedroomed hotel. Good seafood menus.

SETTLE — Blue Goose
Market Square, Settle, North Yorkshire BD24 9EJ
Telephone: (0729) 822901 £35
Open: lunch Tue-Sat, dinner Mon-Sat
Meals served: lunch 12-2, dinner 7-10
Small 34-seat restaurant in the centre of town.

SEVENOAKS — Royal Oak

High Street, Sevenoaks, Kent TN14 5PG
Telephone: (0732) 451109 £60
Fax: (0732) 740187
Open: lunch Sun-Fri, dinner daily
Meals served: lunch 12.30-2, dinner 7.30-10

A 39-bedroomed hotel and restaurant set in a 17th-century inn. Chef James Butterfill is the new arrival in the kitchen and already he's made an impression. His menus will suit most palates and his cooking is above average. Cream of broccoli and asparagus soup is one of the starters while fillets of salmon and halibut are served on a lemon and chive sauce as a main dish.

SHAFTESBURY — La Fleur de Lys
25 Salisbury Street, Shaftesbury, Dorset
Telephone: (0747) 53717 £40
Open: lunch Tue-Sun, dinner Mon-Sat
Meals served: lunch 12-3, dinner 7-10
Opened last year by a trio formerly at Lewtrenchard Manor.

Shanklin Old Village — The Cottage

8 Eastcliff Road, Shanklin Old Village, Isle of Wight PO37 6AA
Telephone: (0983) 862504 £45
Open: lunch Tue-Sun, dinner Tue-Sat (closed 26 Dec, 4 wks Feb/Mar, Oct)
Meals served: lunch 12-2, dinner 7.30-9.45

'The local's local' is how owners Neil Graham and Alan Priddle like to describe their little restaurant that's been going strong now for many years. This dynamic duo divide the duties between them – Neil in the kitchen, Alan in charge of the dining room. Among the dishes quenelles of sole with a lobster sauce, salmon dieppoise, and tournedos Ludgate with a port and grape sauce, and plenty of choices to be had amongst the desserts. A good old-fashioned repertoire – and why not? It's a tried and trusted formula that has withstood the test of time. Well done to the pair of them!

Sheffield — Bay Tree

119 Devonshire Street, Sheffield, South Yorkshire S3 7SB
Telephone: (0742) 759254 £25
Open: lunch Mon-Sat, dinner Thu+Fri (closed Bank Holidays)
Meals served: lunch and snacks 9.30-3 (Sat 9.30-4), dinner 6.30-9

Lovage and potato soup, fennel goulash, and seafood casserole are typical items from Brenda Tyson's repertoire at the small vegetarian and fish restaurant she runs with partner Linda Crabtree. Fresh produce and lots of it. Bring your own wine, or have a glass of freshly pressed apple juice.

Sheffield — Charnwood Hotel

10 Sharrow Lane, Sheffield, South Yorkshire S11 8AA
Telephone: (0742) 589411 Henfrey's Restaurant £60
Fax: (0742) 555107 Brasserie Leo £40
Open: Restaurant: dinner Tue-Sat, Brasserie all day daily (closed Bank Holidays)
Meals served: Restaurant: dinner 7-10, Brasserie 7am-11pm

A pleasant 21-bedroomed hotel that's benefited from a recent re-think by the owners Chris and Val King. Henfrey's Restaurant – named after John Henfrey, once the city's Master Cutler and owner of the original house – is now to be found on the first floor of the adjoining building. The decor is oddly Victorian given the modern cuisine, and chef Kevin Hensby is the new addition to the kitchen. A man with talent to spare, he established a considerable local following in Brixham, Devon, and seems set to turn some heads once he has had time to stamp his authority and style on the menus.

A further innovation here is the Brasserie Leo which can be entered either from the hotel or the entrance in London Road. Fulfilling its promise of providing true brasserie service, the hours are seven in the morning to eleven at night and you can have what you like, when you like, no matter what the time of day. Rabbit and venison pie, Leo's steak sandwich, some super puds – which would also go very nicely with a cappuccino in the morning – they all add up to a really bright idea. It'll catch on I'm sure!

| SHEFFIELD | Harley, The Restaurant & Hotel |

334 Glossop Road, Sheffield, South Yorkshire S10 2HW
Telephone: (0742) 752288 £35
Fax: (0742) 722383
Open: lunch + dinner Mon-Sat (closed Bank Holidays)
Meals served: lunch 12-2.15, dinner 7-9.30 (Sat 7.30-9.30)
Small, friendly hotel with 22 bedrooms.

| SHEPPERTON | Edwinn's Restaurant |

Church Square, Shepperton, Middlesex TW17 9JY
Telephone: (0932) 223543 £45
Open: lunch Sun-Fri, dinner Mon-Sat (closed Bank Holidays)
Meals served: lunch 12-2 (Sun 12-3), dinner 7-10.30 (Sat 6.30-10.30)
Frequently changing menu of English and French cuisine.

SHEPTON MALLET — Blostin's Restaurant

29 Waterloo Road, Shepton Mallet, Somerset BA4 5HH
Telephone: (0749) 343648 £35
Open: dinner Tue-Sat (closed 2 wks Jan, 1 wk Jun, 1 wk Nov)
Meals served: dinner 7-9.30

Another of those successful husband-and-wife teams lies behind this friendly bistro-style restaurant. Nick Reed's cooking is unfussy and flavours are given full rein. According to the time of year you might find a salad of smoked duck breast with sun-dried tomatoes and roquette salad as a starter, and as a main dish, breast of chicken with fresh asparagus and tarragon sauce. Lynne takes charge of front of house. All round, an eminently affordable and enjoyable place in which to eat.

SHERBORNE — Eastbury Hotel

Long Street, Sherborne, Dorset DT9 3BY
Telephone: (0935) 813131 £50
Fax: (0935) 817296
Open: lunch + dinner daily
Meals served: lunch 12.30-2, dinner 7.30-9.30

A friendly hotel set in a traditional town house with maintains much of its 18th-century character. The 15 bedrooms are each named after an English flower and have nicely co-ordinated furnishings. Hardy country lies around you, waiting to be explored.

The Eastbury

Shifnal — Weston Park

Weston Park, Shifnal, Shropshire TF11 8LE
Telephone: (095 276) 201 £55
Fax: (095 276) 430
Open: by arrangement
Meals served: by arrangement

The Earl of Bradford makes full use of his atmospheric 17th-century stately home with houseparty events (you need to come with 20 or so people) such as murder mystery weekends. The 20 bedrooms are furnished in keeping with the decorative splendour of the rest of the building, and the dining room overlooking Italianate gardens is the setting for perhaps terrine of pheasant followed by glazed trout with a watercress and mustard mayonnaise with a chocolate and hazelnut marquise to finish.

Shinfield — L'Ortolan

Old Vicarage, Church Lane, Shinfield, Nr Reading, Berkshire RG2 9BY
Telephone: (0734) 883783 £105
Fax: (0734) 885391
Open: lunch Tue-Sun, dinner Tue-Sat (closed 2 wks Aug, 2 wks Feb)
Meals served: lunch 12.15-2.15, dinner 7.15-10.30

John Burton-Race's pedigree speaks volumes. His cassolette d'écrivisses à la nage et crème aux fines herbes and ballotine de pied de cochon aux ris de veau sauce porto make your mouth water just reading them off the menu! Indeed, they taste as good as they sound and it is difficult to do full justice to John's culinary expertise in just a few paragraphs. To me he is one of the most talented chefs we have in Great Britain, and deserves every bit of recognition that he receives. His wife, Marie-Christine, runs front of house and ensures smooth, unobtrusive service by the young French waiters. The wine list is extensive, erring towards the extravagant, and Australasian wines offer value for money. Set in a mellow Victorian vicarage, this is without doubt one of the top restaurants in Great Britain, and deservedly so. *See also p268 – our Clover Awards section.*

Sissinghurst — Rankins

The Street, Sissinghurst, Kent TN17 2JH
Telephone: (0580) 713964 £65
Open: lunch Sun, dinner Wed-Sat (closed Bank Holidays, 1 wk Oct, 1 wk May)
Meals served: lunch 12.30-1.30, dinner 7.30-9

A rural restaurant holding out against the influx of ethnic and fast food outlets operated since 1986 by Hugh and Leonora Rankin. Typical dishes include rich crab soup garnished with spicy white crab meat as a starter, while pot-roast lamb shoulder with onion, tarragon and red wine makes a hearty main course. Finish with rhubarb and orange crumble. Nearly 20 half bottles on a concise list of around 50 wines.

SIX MILE BOTTOM	Swynford Paddocks

Six Mile Bottom, Nr Newmarket, Cambridgeshire CB8 0UE
Telephone: (063 870) 234 £65
Fax: (063 870) 283
Open: lunch Sun-Fri, dinner daily (closed Xmas-New Year)
Meals served: lunch 12.30-2, dinner 7-9.30 (Sun 7-8.30)

Warm welcome, fresh flowers and open fires in winter time are some of the ingredients that enhance the atmosphere in this traditional English country house hotel.

SOURTON	Collaven Manor

Sourton, Nr Okehampton, Devon EX20 4HH
Telephone: (083 786) 522 £50
Open: lunch + dinner daily (closed 23 Dec-7 Jan)
Meals served: lunch 12.30-2, dinner 7.30-9 (Fri+Sat 7.30-9.30)

What a homely place this is – with every year the creeper over the entrance stealing another yard on the soft grey stonework. Inside, the bedrooms are comfortable without being luxurious, but then that's part of the charm. The central heating is supplemented by crackling log fires in the winter, warming the hands and the heart. Chef Jacky Rae cooks with care and provides separate menus for the Hamilton Restaurant and the Inglenook Restaurant, one being more adventurous than the other.

SOUTH BRENT	Glazebrook House

Glazebrook, South Brent, Devon TQ10 9JE
Telephone: (0364) 73322 £50
Fax: (0364) 72350
Open: dinner daily
Meals served: dinner 7-9

Traditional English country house hotel.

SOUTH GODSTONE	La Bonne Auberge

Tilburstow Hill, South Godstone, Surrey RH9 8JY
Telephone: (0342) 893184 £75
Fax: (0342) 893435
Open: lunch Tue-Sun, dinner Tue-Sat (closed Bank Holidays)
Meals served: lunch 12-2, dinner 7-10

In the capable hands of the Jalley family since 1961, La Bonne Auberge offers enjoyable food in an attractive setting. Expectations created by the menu are for the most part justified by the results on the plate, with chef Martin Bradley's carte offering dishes such as bouillabaisse or carpaccio of beef to start, and breast of duck hot smoked to order with stuffed cabbage and a thyme jus, or pigeon breast with a sweet raspberry vinegar sauce for main course. Besides the à la carte there are also Menu Zazou and Menu Tintin, which would seem to offer good value.

South Molton — Whitechapel Manor

South Molton, Devon EX36 3EG
Telephone: (0769) 573377
Fax: (0769) 573797
Open: lunch + dinner daily
Meals served: lunch 12.30-2, dinner 7-8.45

£80

You've either got it or you haven't – and Whitechapel Manor has. From the moment you arrive and John or Patricia Shapland come out to greet you and show you up to your room, there's a sense that this is going to be a place to remember. Indeed, over the period of your stay you get to know them and their lovingly restored Elizabethan manor in its meadow and woodland setting, it becomes clear that this is a very special haven. Public rooms are beautifully furnished as are the bedrooms. Extras are standard and you won't be left wanting anything. As for the food, Thierry Leprêtre-Granet directs a skilled brigade and the cooking is first class without ever becoming self-indulgent. At dinner, starters include cream of Jerusalem artichoke with croutons, or sautéed breast of wood pigeon with a beetroot purée and deep-fried leeks. Main courses feature braised leg of hare and roasted fillet of seabass with strips of vegetables and a red wine sauce. Presentation, flavour and service all score top marks, and the excellent wines are moderately priced.

Southend-on-Sea — Slassor's

145 Eastern Esplanade, Southend-on-Sea, Essex SS1 2YD
Telephone: (0702) 614880
Open: lunch Tue-Fri, dinner Mon-Sat (closed Bank Holidays, 2 wks summer)
Meals served: lunch 12-2, dinner 7-9.30

£50

Popular, simple, family-run restaurant. Unlicensed so bring your own bottle.

Southsea — Bistro Montparnasse

103 Palmerston Road, Southsea, Hampshire PO5 3PS
Telephone: (0705) 816754
Open: dinner Tue-Sat (closed Bank Holidays, 3 wks Jan)
Meals served: dinner 7-10 (Sat 7-10.30)

£65

A restaurant which provides 3 courses of good, competently cooked food at affordable price should be treasured and adored by the local inhabitants. Soft boiled quail's eggs in a nest of leeks with a tarragon and chive beurre blanc opens the set-price menu, while pan-roast partridge arrives in its own sauce with sweet potato purée as a main dish. Lovely puds make for a resounding finale.

| SOUTHWOLD | The Crown |

90 High Street, Southwold, Suffolk IP18 6DP
Telephone: (0502) 722275 £45
Fax: (0502) 722740
Open: lunch + dinner daily (closed 1 wk Jan)
Meals served: lunch 12.30-1.45, dinner 7.30-9.30

A 12-bedroomed inn with a very popular restaurant and bar. The straightforward food puts the emphasis on local Suffolk produce and fish features strongly – fresh pasta with seafood sauce and cod and prawn bake are on the bar menu, while fillet of turbot and saffron sauce and red mullet with lime, ginger and garlic are what you'll find in the restaurant. They suggest an accompanying 3 glasses of wine, but there's loads more to choose from on the very good and reasonably priced list.

| SOUTHWOLD | The Swan |

Market Place, Southwold, Suffolk IP18 6EG
Telephone: (0502) 722186 £45
Fax: (0502) 724800
Open: lunch + dinner daily (closed dinner 3rd Sun in Jan)
Meals served: lunch 12.15-1.45 (Sun 12.15-1.30), dinner 7-9.30 (Sun 7-9)

Lovers of good beer won't mind the brewery that stands behind the hotel, safe in the knowledge that the tawny elixir is bubbling away for their benefit. The Swan is a delightful place to stay amid the pretty streets and houses of Southwold – I think the word to describe the town in 'picturesque'. The menu in the dining room features several fish dishes as you'd expect at a seaside restaurant. The cooking is competent and the wine list runs to over 100 bottles, with much to raise a smile in terms of quality and price. Service, by young helpful staff, is occasionally erratic but comes good in the end.

| SPARK BRIDGE | Bridgefield House |

Spark Bridge, Ulverston, Cumbria LA12 8DA
Telephone: (0229) 85239 £50
Fax: (0229) 85379
Open: dinner daily
Meals served: dinner 7.30 for 8

The views over Spark Bridge and the river, and old-fashioned comforts and hospitality are good reasons why people come to stay at the Glisters' modest stone-built turn-of-the-century house set in heavily wooded grounds. Rosemary Glister's cooking is another, and her food continues to achieve a nice balance between traditional dishes and modern interpretations. The 6-course menu should keep the wolf from the door, with perhaps lamb's sweetbreads and button mushrooms in a cream sauce to start, then a carrot and brown lentil soup with Cheddar bannocks, followed by chicken breast roasted in dry cider and garlic, an apple mint water ice before pudding (choice of 3) then cheese or a savoury. For those of you with kids, under-3s are free and high chairs, baby listening sets and other paraphernalia are provided at no extra cost in the 5 double rooms. Equally, the lone traveller is not penalized by room supplements and this is typical of the Glisters' fine sense of values.

Speen	The Old Plow Inn at Speen

Flowers Bottom Lane, Speen, Nr Princes Risborough Buckinghamshire HP27 0PZ
Telephone: (0494) 488300 £65
Open: lunch Tue-Fri + Sun, dinner Tue-Sat (closed Bank Holidays)
Meals served: lunch 12-2, dinner 7-9

Maxims de Paris in London and The Ritz figure in Malcolm Cowan's past appointments and thus a pronounced classical French style to his food comes as no great surprise. However, he's also travelled far afield and brought back some interesting culinary souvenirs in the shape of exotic Far Eastern dishes which crop up now and again on his menus. The Cowans' bistro-style bar operation is also going great guns with an equally adventurous approach – tuna steaks and Indian Oceam bream rubbing shoulders with Leicestershire black pudding with red cabbage, bacon and mustard sauce – and is anything but your typical bar menu, making this place well worth a visit.

Staddle Bridge	McCoy's

The Cleveland Tontine, Staddle Bridge, Nr Northallerton, North Yorkshire DL6 3JB
Telephone: (060 982) 671 £75
Open: Restaurant: dinner Mon-Sat, Bistro: lunch + dinner daily (closed Bank Holidays except Good Friday)
Meals served: Restaurant: dinner 7-10, Bistro: lunch 12-2, dinner 7-10.30

Were the Marx brothers to have run a restaurant, I suspect it may have been something like this. I wouldn't want to push the comparison between the 2 sets of brothers too far, but at least it gives a sense of the slight craziness underlying this place. In fact, you can't really compare them or their restaurant with anyone or anything – they're a law unto themselves – although one thing is for sure: the food's superb. Dishes like pork fillets, blue cheese and walnuts, beef wellington, red wine and mushroom, or monkfish, cassis and lime sauce sound straightforward but the result on the plate is anything but. Tom McCoy cooks with a sensitivity and precision that belies his uninhabited approach. Six comfortable bedrooms are suitably indulgent should the exploration of single growers on the well-researched wine list be too fruitful! *See also p270 – our Clover Awards section.*

STANDON	No. 28
28 High Street, Standon, Nr Ware, Hertfordshire SG11 1LA	
Telephone: (0920) 821055	£60
Fax: (0920) 822630	
Open: dinner Tue-Sat	
Meals served: dinner 7-9.30	

Small restaurant with short set priced menu.

STAPLECROSS	Olivers
Cripps Corner, Staplecross, Nr Robertsbridge, East Sussex TN32 5RY	
Telephone: (0580) 830387	£55
Open: lunch + dinner Wed-Sun (closed Bank Holidays, 3 wks Jan)	
Meals served: lunch 12-1.30, dinner 7-9.30 (Sun 7-9)	

Well presented dishes, modern style with oriental influences.

STAPLEFORD — Stapleford Park

Stapleford, Nr Melton Mowbray, Leicestershire LE14 2EF
Telephone: (057 284) 522
Fax: (057 284) 651
Open: lunch + dinner daily
Meals served: lunch 12-3 (Sun 12-3.30), dinner 7-10 (Sat 7-10.30, Sun 7-9.30)

£75

'There's no question of us selling, we are here for good and everything is just fine in sunny Leicestershire.' Bob Payton has in 5 years created a reputation and a market that would take more humbler hotel operators 20 years to achieve. People have questioned whether there is substance behind the hype – there's only one way to find out, go there for yourself. You won't be disappointed, either by the magnificent architecture of the stately house, the parklands designed by Capability Brown, or the magnificent and sometimes unusual interior. I suppose with a choice of 35 bedrooms, each with its individual style and designer name attached, you should opt for a different room every time you visit. It's that sort of place. One thing is for sure, the whole enterprise has style. Sometimes it is idiosyncratic, sometimes lighthearted and very often unusual but it blends together with the warmth and good nature of the proprietors and the relaxed but laid-back professionalism of the staff. It is indeed a very special and unusual country house hotel.

STOKE-BY-NAYLAND — Angel Inn

Stoke-by-Nayland, Suffolk CO6 4SA
Telephone: (0206) 263245 £45
Open: lunch Wed-Sun, dinner Tue-Sat (closed 25+26 Dec)
Meals served: lunch 12-2, dinner 6-9
Bar food and restaurant available in this popular local haunt.

STOKESLEY — Chapters

27 High Street, Stokesley, North Yorkshire TS9 5AD
Telephone: (0642) 711888 £45
Open: dinner Mon-Sat
Meals served: dinner 7-9.30 (Sat 7-10)

Imaginative cooking by chef David Brownless in bright summery surroundings. Try a baked brioche filled with fresh Scottish scallops in a chervil sauce followed by fillet of beef with a wild mushroom tartlet on a truffle sauce. Lunch in the restaurant is by arrangement only but there is a new bistro serving simpler food and excellent coffee in one of the front rooms of this former pub with 13 bedrooms.

STON EASTON — Ston Easton Park

Ston Easton, Nr Bath, Avon BA3 4DF
Telephone: (0761) 241631 £75
Fax: (0761) 241377
Open: lunch + dinner daily
Meals served: lunch 12.30-2, dinner 7.30-9.30 (Fri + Sat 7.30-10)

A splendidly imposing Palladian mansion set amidst sweeping parkland not far from Bath. Sumptuous public rooms and equally fine bedrooms envelop you in a swirl of luxury, while the dining room has always had a light conservatory feel. Mark Harrington's food, on the other hand, is serious stuff – chicken liver parfait studded with smoked foie gras and truffles, grilled salmon layered with a ragout of scallops, and I still remember one of the finest pieces of beef with a celeriac purée that I had some time ago. Simple but superb. The restored Victorian kitchen garden supplies much of the kitchen's herb and vegetable needs.

STONEHOUSE — Eastington Grange Hotel

Eastington, Stonehouse, Gloucestershire GL10 3RT
Telephone: (0453) 791511 £45
Fax: (0453) 791513
Open: lunch + dinner daily
Meals served: lunch 12-2.15, dinner 7-9.30
Thirteen bedroomed Cotswold hotel and Saddlers Restaurant.

STONEHOUSE — Stonehouse Court

Bristol Road, Stonehouse, Gloucestershire GL10 3RA
Telephone: (0453) 825155 £55
Fax: (0453) 824611
Open: lunch + dinner daily
Meals served: lunch 12.30-2, dinner 7.30-9.30

Seventeenth-century manor house with attractive gardens. The nearby canal offers charming walks and privileged angling. Bedrooms are located in the main building and in a more recent extension.

STONHAM	Mr Underhill's

Stonham, Nr Stowmarket, Suffolk IP14 5DW
Telephone: (0449) 711206 £65
Open: dinner Tue-Sat (closed Bank Holidays except 25+26 Dec)
Meals served: dinner 7.30-9

Forget Tolkien and concentrate on the food. Chris and Judy Bradley's restaurant has come through some trying times in its 11-year history and fully deserves its success. A recent holiday – the first in those 11 years! – was something of a busman's holiday for the pair. They returned with bags of ideas which they immediately decided to try out on their customers. These lucky people sampled a range of some Italian menus including traditional breads, slow-cooked lamb shanks, fillet of brill with sun-dried tomatoes and olives and lovely cheeses. Not at all an attempt to 'get with it' and serve modern Italian food – this is enthusiasm, pure and simple. They have recently restyled the evening menu which now offers 3 or 4 courses at varying set prices. Sunday lunch in their cheerfully decorated beamed restaurant remains good value. The wine list exemplifies hours of passionate research unearthing often as yet unknown tiny producers of exceptional quality, as well as good-value classic drinking. Determined to do well, Chris and Judy are to be admired and supported in this underpopulated part of the country.

STONOR	Stonor Arms

Stonor, Nr Henley-on-Thames, Oxfordshire RG9 6HE
Telephone: (0491) 63345 £70
Fax: (0491) 638863
Open: lunch Sun, dinner Mon-Sat
Meals served: lunch 12-1.45, dinner 7-9.30

Two-tier eating either at the bar – where you can have as many courses as you like – or in the restaurant with its impressive fixed price menus. Once a pub, it has now firmly established its reputation and deserves to be taken seriously. Seven bedrooms are available for accommodation.

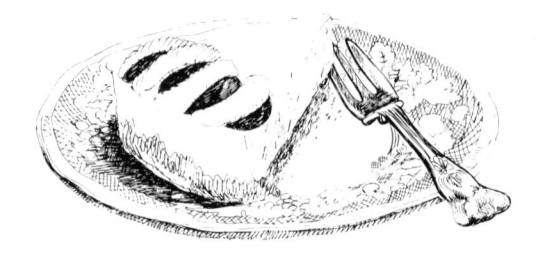

STORRINGTON   Abingworth Hall

Thakeham Road, Storrington, West Sussex RH20 3EF
Telephone: (0798) 813636   **£65**
Fax: (0798) 813914
Open: lunch + dinner daily (closed 2 wks Jan)
Meals served: lunch 12.30-1.45, dinner 7.15-9

This hotel, run by the Bulmans, is a relaxed and pleasant place to stay. The Edwardian building, set in its own grounds and boasting its own lake, has been pleasantly and carefully restored. There are 21 bedrooms. Peter Cannon in the kitchen produces some sensible menus which allow you to choose from à la carte or table d'hôte, which really gives value for money. The menu is written clearly, in English with no frills. The food echoes this philosophy and uses the best available local and national products. You can enjoy a well-presented tranche of grilled Scottish salmon served with brandy and crab sauce, or a roast best end of English lamb with rosemary and garlic. From the puddings try the unusual and very good raspberry and yoghurt ice-cream. Concise wine list with some reasonable choices.

STORRINGTON   Little Thakeham

Merrywood Lane, Storrington, West Sussex RH20 3HE
Telephone: (0903) 744416   **£80**
Fax: (0903) 745022
Open: lunch daily, dinner Mon-Sat (closed 2 wks Xmas/New Year)
Meals served: lunch 12.30-2, dinner 7.30-9

Luxury country house hotel in Grade One listed building. Architecture by Lutyens and gardens in the style of Jekyll. The surroundings are paramount!

STORRINGTON   Manley's

Manleys Hill, Storrington, West Sussex RH20 4BT
Telephone: (0903) 742331   **£70**
Open: lunch Tue-Sun, dinner Tue-Sat (closed Bank Holidays except Good Friday,
    2 wks Jan)
Meals served: lunch 12-2, dinner 7-9.30

Karl Löderer cooks some solid, reliable dishes at this cottagey restaurant with its oak beams and low ceilings and enjoys a good local following. From the lunch menu, an excellent braised knuckle of veal served with a madeira sauce and pasta, or perhaps the pan-fried medallions of venison with mushrooms, shallots and wild cherries in a rich red wine sauce, or for something lighter with an oriental flavour try the strips of sole and calamari pan-fried with spring onions and ginger and served on some stir-fried vegetables given a good tangy flavour with a lime reduction, or the unusual and tasty best-end of lamb roasted with herbs with the bone taken out, served with a pee pureé and crisply fried onions. Leave room for his excellent puddings. This restaurant serves some consistently good food and deserves their loyal following. *See also p272 – our Clover Awards section.*

STORRINGTON — Old Forge

6a Church Street, Storrington, West Sussex RH20 4LA
Telephone: (0903) 743402 £55
Open: lunch Tue-Sun, dinner Tue-Sat (closed Bank Holidays, 3 wks Oct)
Meals served: lunch 12.30-1.30, dinner 7.30-9

Clive Roberts likes to follow his nose when he cooks, exploring the possibilities of different countries' traditions so as to find something a little different for his loyal set of customers. Working through his menus you can enjoy the fruits of his research – thinly sliced seabass marinated in provençale olive oil flavoured with vanilla as a starter, with perhaps fillet of English pork with caraway and a cabbage parcel of chestnuts and bacon as a main course. Puds include his own ice-creams and sorbets, as well as a mirabelle and plum parfait and a warm panaché of fruits. A programme of food and wine evenings has recently been launched with Australia, the Middle East and Spain among the options, so you can join Clive on his travels! The short wine list is equally nomadic, including a pinot noir from Canada.

STOW BRIDGE — Swinton House
Stow Bridge, King's Lynn, Norfolk PE34 3PP
Telephone: (0366) 383151 £40
Open: lunch Sun, dinner Tue-Sat (closed 1 wk Xmas)
Meals served: lunch 12-2, dinner 7-9
Small, popular local restaurant with a welcoming and friendly atmosphere.

STOW-ON-THE-WOLD — Epicurean Bistro
1 Park Street, Stow-on-the-Wold, Gloucestershire
Telephone: (0451) 31613 £45
Open: all day Tue-Sat, lunch Sun
Meals served: 11.30-11.30 (Sun 12-3)
On the site of the Epicurean, now in Cheltenham. Accessible menus, well presented.

STOW-ON-THE-WOLD — Grapevine Hotel

Sheep Street, Stow-on-the-Wold, Gloucestershire GL54 1AU
Telephone: (0451) 30344 £50
Fax: (0451) 32278
Open: lunch + dinner daily (closed Bank Holidays, 24 Dec-10 Jan)
Meals served: lunch 12-2, dinner 7-9.30

'A little Cotswold hotel that just tries very hard', is how Sandra Elliott likes to describe her hotel and I think many of her guests would agree. Her staff show a high level of commitment and loyalty which ensures that the standards of service and upkeep are exemplary. If needed fixed price dinner menus are supplemented by marked specials and an impressive vegetarian selection. Pan-fried swordfish steak on a spinach cream, and game casserole with garlic and juniper are typical dishes. Twenty-three cosy bedrooms include some with canopies, and a 4-poster.

ENGLAND **435**

Stow-on-the-Wold — Wyck Hill House

Burford Road, Stow-on-the-Wold, Gloucestershire GL54 1HY
Telephone: (0451) 31936 £70
Fax: (0451) 32243
Open: lunch + dinner daily
Meals served: lunch 12.30-2, dinner 7.30-9.30 (Sat 7-10)

Home to the feudal lords of the Wyck Rissington, the early 18th-century house fell into disrepair during the early part of this century. Extensive repairs began in 1984 and the hotel now looks set for the next 100 years! Discreetly updated, Wyck Hill House offers a comfortable atmosphere in which to relax and admire the breathtaking surroundings from the 31 plush bedrooms boasting good quality materials and workmanship and an eye for co-ordinated design. Quiet, comfortable sitting rooms are an ideal place in which to peruse Ian Smith's tempting menus. To start, perhaps fresh Cornish crab and spinach lasagna on a 2-caviar sauce, followed by a casserole of wild rabbit with a light watercress sauce and stuffed cabbage, then a hot coconut soufflé with warm pineapple coulis to finish. Some excellent vegetarian offerings.

Stratford-upon-Avon — Billesley Manor

Billesley, Alcester, Nr Stratford-upon-Avon, Warwickshire B49 6NF
Telephone: (0789) 400888 £70
Fax: (0789) 764145
Open: lunch + dinner daily
Meals served: lunch 12.30-2, dinner 7.30-9.30

Wood-panelled rooms, splendid fireplaces and deep comfy armchairs make Billesley Manor an attractive place to stay when visiting Shakespear country. In the restaurant, as well as some enjoyable food, you can sample a taste of one of England's very own wines – the locally produced Astley Severn Vale.

Stratford-upon-Avon — Ettington Park

Alderminster, Stratford-upon-Avon, Warwickshire CV37 8BS
Telephone: (0789) 450123 £80
Fax: (0789) 450472
Open: lunch + dinner daily
Meals served: lunch 12.30-2, dinner 7-9.30 (Sat 7-10)

The conservatory, long gallery meeting room and graceful lounge are outstanding features of this grand neo-Gothic building. The 48 bedrooms have tastefully co-ordinated fabrics and furnishings maintained to high standards. An indoor pool and plenty of outdoor pursuits appeal to both midweek conference groups and the weekend break market.

STRATFORD-UPON-AVON	Falcon Hotel

Chapel Street, Stratford-upon-Avon, Warwickshire CV37 6HA
Telephone: (0789) 205777 £40
Fax: (0789) 414260
Open: lunch + dinner daily (closed Xmas)
Meals served: lunch 12.30-2, dinner 6.30-9 (Sun 7-9)
Hotel dating back to 1640, 73 bedrooms.

STRATFORD-UPON-AVON	Shakespeare Hotel

Chapel Street, Stratford-upon-Avon, Warwickshire CV37 6ER
Telephone: (0789) 294771 £60
Fax: (0789) 415111
Open: lunch + dinner daily
Meals served: lunch 12.30-2, dinner 6-10 (Sun 6-9.15)
Combines traditional charm with modern comfort and a good base for the town. Seventy rooms.

STRATFORD-UPON-AVON	Stratford House

18 Sheep Street, Stratford-upon-Avon, Warwickshire CV37 6EF
Telephone: (0789) 268288 £35
Fax: (0789) 295580
Open: lunch + dinner Tue-Sat (closed 4 days Xmas)
Meals served: lunch 12-2, dinner 7-9.45
Comfortable, friendly hotel convenient for the theatre and shops.

STRETTON — Ram Jam Inn

Great North Road, Stretton, near Oakham, Rutland, Leicestershire LE15 7QX
Telephone: (0780) 410776 **£35**
Fax: (0572) 410361
Open: all day daily (closed 25 Dec)
Meals served: meals 7.30am-11pm

Spirits droop and the palate curls up at the prospect of pulling in at a roadside café, but the Ram Jam Inn has altered that when you're passing by Stretton! A one-off, it's a pity there aren't more places following suit. Here you can pick and choose between the restaurant, snack bar, coffee bar and 'pub', confident that the food is going to be head and shoulders above what you'll find a few miles further on. Freshly made pasta comes with a choice of sauces – sautéed chicken, leeks and Pommery mustard; smoked salmon and mushrooms, bell peppers, basil and tomato sauce – and main courses include char-grilled steaks and lamb, pork and chicken treated in imaginative ways as well as daily fish dishes. The puds are satisfying numbers like blackberry and apple pie and almond tart, served with dollops of ice-cream or custard. Climb back in the car after that and you'll feel like you've had a meal; or better still stay in one of the 10 bedrooms.

Stroud — Oakes

169 Slad Road, Stroud, Gloucestershire GL5 1RG **WC**
Telephone: (0453) 759950 **£70**
Open: lunch Tue-Sun, dinner Tue-Sat (closed Bank Holidays, 4 wks Xmas, 2 wks Aug)
Meals served: lunch 12.30-1.45, dinner 7.30-9.30

Chris Oakes is now well-established in this former Cotswold school house, set back from the side of the road, and he concentrates here on the important things – good raw produce (he lists his suppliers on the menu), consistency of dishes and concentration of the natural flavours that his food produces. His menu and specialities vary with the seasons and can include some interesting dishes such as home-made venison sausage garnished with noodles and served with a juniper sauce, or roast lamb cutlets served with a casserole of beans, bacon and shallots. Simple-sounding desserts like glazed egg custard with fresh fruit salad, are under-stated but excellent in flavour and the description of his hot cinnamon soufflé which is served with a Drambuie cream, was 'simply sublime'. At around £17 the lunch menu is excellent value, and a 3-course dinner of this quality for under £35 takes some beating. If I lived in the area, there is no doubt Oakes would have a regular visitor. The simple setting of the dining-room is enhanced by warm and friendly service.

Stuckton — The Three Lions

Stuckton, Nr Fordingbridge, Hampshire SP6 2HF *—good local restaurant*
Telephone: (0425) 52489 **£65**
Open: lunch + dinner Tue-Sat (closed Bank Holidays, 10 days Xmas/New Year, Feb, 2 wks summer)
Meals served: lunch 12.15-1.30, dinner 7.15-9 (Sat 7.15-9.30)

Croûte of forest mushrooms with goat's cheese, Swedish herrings and a terrine of baby leeks with hot duck liver are among the starters, while red marlin steak with capsicum sauce, bratwurst mit sauerkraut and grilled kidneys with mustard sauce are possible main courses at this popular converted pub with a long-standing reputation for solid, no-nonsense cooking. Karl and June Wadsack have a loyal local following who appreciate being able to return to sample their favourite dishes time and again. No modern fads or fancies here! Good, sound stuff. There should be more of them.

STURMINSTER NEWTON	Plumber Manor

Hazelbury Bryan Road, Sturminster Newton, Dorset DT10 2AF
Telephone: (0258) 72507 £55
Fax: (0258) 73370
Open: dinner daily (closed Feb)
Meals served: dinner 7-9.30

Home to the Prideaux-Brunes since the 17th Century, Plumber Manor – an imposing Jacobean residence set behind sweeping lawns – retains the family tradition, with Richard in charge of the house while Brian directs operations in the kitchen. Dinner offers the choice of 2 set menus with loin of venison with a mushroom and leek timbale, lemon sole with smoked salmon and dill sauce and peppered medaillons of beef with mustard sauce being typical main courses. Main house bedrooms, some with fine antiques, are reached via a gallery hung with family portraits, whilst those in the converted stable block are more modern.

SUDBURY	Mabey's Brasserie

47 Gainsborough Street, Sudbury, Suffolk CO10 7SS
Telephone: (0787) 74298 £40
Open: lunch + dinner Tue-Sat (closed Bank Holidays)
Meals served: lunch 12-2, dinner 7-10

No 'maybes' about this one. If there's anything you're not sure about on the blackboard menu, ask the guy in the open-plan kitchen. Robert Mabey cooks, owns and – together with wife Johanna – runs this successful, cheerfully decorated brasserie that's clearly a hit among Sudbury's locals. He's worked in grander places, but for him a good working environment with happy staff and happy customers is what it's really all about. Some typical dishes – chicken and crab roulade with garlic mayonnaise, fillet of fresh salmon on wild rice with a home-grown fresh basil sauce, lemon and lime tart with home-made vanilla ice-cream – and only 3 wines on a 40-strong list are over £15! Well worth a visit.

Surbiton — Chez Max

85 Maple Road, Surbiton, Surrey KT6 4AW
Telephone: 081-399 2365 £60
Open: lunch Tue-Fri, dinner Tue-Sat (closed Bank Holidays)
Meals served: lunch 12.30-2, dinner 7.30-10

A conservatory-roofed suburban restaurant where chef-patron Max Markarian cooks familiar French classics with a sure hand and a contemporary slant. Start with a cheese soufflé with a spinach cream sauce, then perhaps breast of guineafowl with vermouth and garlic, or fillet of salmon on a sorrel sauce, and a hazelnut meringue with strawberries to follow. There's a fixed price menu for lunch and an almost exclusively French wine list with leanings to Bordeaux.

Sutton — Partners Brasserie

23 Stonecot Hill, Sutton, Surrey SM3 9HB
Telephone: 081-644 7743 £55
Open: lunch Tue-Fri + Sun, dinner Tue-Sat (closed Bank Holidays, 2 wks Aug)
Meals served: lunch 12-2, dinner 7-9.30

The partners have moved on to their new more up-market Partners West Street in Dorking (*qv*), but still have an interest in this pretty pastel green and yellow restaurant - not really a brasserie at all - located in a shopping street. The menu could include spinach and walnut flan, roast monkfish with garlic and herbs, with bread and butter pudding to finish, and generally changes monthly.

Sutton Coldfield — New Hall

Walmley Road, Sutton Coldfield, West Midlands B76 8QX
Telephone: 021-378 2442
Fax: 021-378 4637 £80
Open: lunch Sun-Fri, dinner daily
Meals served: lunch 12.30-2 (Sun 12.30-2.15), dinner 7-10 (Sun 7-9.30)

Ian and Caroline Parker lend a personal touch to this crenellated hotel with what is said to be this country's oldest moat. They're evidently eager for the place to succeed and run a tight ship. Service is impeccable and the standard of decor and furnishings is good. Glenn Purcell follows in the footsteps of Allan Garth who worked here some years ago, and, on recent form, seems to be well on the way to establishing an equally fine reputation. He balances seasoning and flavour with skill, typical dishes being a lobster, prawn and leek cannelloni, sautéed salmon with a feuilleté of queen scallops, and roast guineafowl with a sage jus. The butterscotch soufflé with orange and cinnamon ice-cream is a must. Sixty bedrooms provide good quality accommodation.

Swanage — Galley

9 High Street, Swanage, Dorset BH19 2LN
Telephone: (0929) 427299 £45
Open: dinner daily (closed Jan-Mar)
Meals served: dinner 6.30-9.30 (Sat 6.30-10)
Even though decorated with fishing nets, half the menu consists of meat dishes.

Sway	The Tower

Sway, Hampshire SO41 6DE
Telephone: (0590) 682117 £55
Fax: (0590) 683785
Open: dinner by arrangement
Meals served: book day beforehand
Unusual British folly that has been converted into a hotel with just 4 suites.

Taplow	Cliveden

Taplow, Nr Maidenhead, Buckinghamshire SL6 0JF
Telephone: (0628) 668561 £100
Fax: (0628) 661837
*Open:*lunch + dinner daily (Waldo's: dinner only)
Meals served: lunch 12.30-2, dinner 7.30-9.30

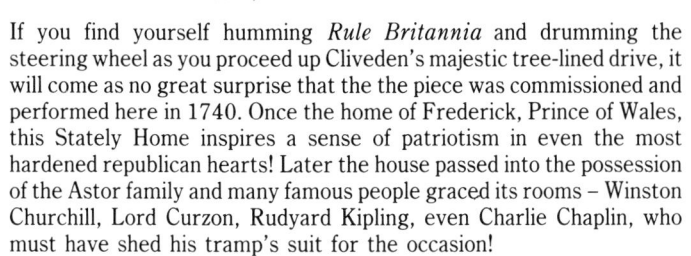

If you find yourself humming *Rule Britannia* and drumming the steering wheel as you proceed up Cliveden's majestic tree-lined drive, it will come as no great surprise that the the piece was commissioned and performed here in 1740. Once the home of Frederick, Prince of Wales, this Stately Home inspires a sense of patriotism in even the most hardened republican hearts! Later the house passed into the possession of the Astor family and many famous people graced its rooms – Winston Churchill, Lord Curzon, Rudyard Kipling, even Charlie Chaplin, who must have shed his tramp's suit for the occasion!

Today the hotel offers excellent accommodation and facilities: 31 bedrooms, all sumptuously furnished, both outdoor and indoor swimming pools, tennis and squash courts, sauna and solarium . . . the list is endless. The Terrace Dining Room serves classical British cooking with modern adaptations, while Waldo's caters unashamedly for the more discerning palate. Ron Maxfield's 4- to 6-course menu could include a warm terrine of foie gras, potato and bacon with a lentil dressing, a lasagne of lobster and langoustine with a truffle-scented dressing, squab pigeon with cured ham, sage and savoy cabbage on a marsala sauce with mixed pulses in a garlic cream, and a deep-fried ravioli of bananas and dates with an orange sauce and caramel ice-cream. The cheeseboard and wine list are outstanding, the latter now more reasonably priced. After dinner, take your coffee in the great hall. Amid such regal splendour, settle back and think of England . . .

Taunton — Castle Hotel

Castle Green, Taunton, Somerset TA1 1NF
Telephone: (0823) 272671
Fax: (0823) 336066
Open: lunch + dinner daily
Meals served: lunch 12.30-2, dinner 7.30-9

£85

Whenever an establishment is prepared to list its suppliers on the menu invariably the food's going to be good. Kit Chapman's Castle Hotel is no exception. Chef Philip Vickery's dishes are bursting with natural flavours and though many thought Gary Rhodes' departure would signal the end of an era, Philip – with a year or so under his belt and supported and encouraged by Kit – has lifted the food to new heights. The carte has been abandoned in favour of fixed price menus which, at dinner, range from £17.90 to £28.50 including all frills (canapés, petits fours etc) and a 2-course lunch can be had for as little as £13.50. It's worth driving a long way for such value.

Steamed lobster sausage with couscous and lobster caviar dressing or perhaps a salad of braised ham hocks with mustard and shallots could be followed by shoulder of lamb with thyme, garlic and locally-grown vegetables, or seared scallops with baby leeks, poached bacon and a chive butter sauce. Desserts include a rich egg custard with candied ginger and poached rhubarb. All rather interesting, I think you'll agree, and it shows what traditional British cooking can be like when treated with suitable imagination. The famous wine list continues to yield new treasures. High standards are apparent throughout the hotel which offers weekends of fine wine and music during winter and spring months, and, a nice touch, special rates for honeymooners, and parents and old boys of local schools! *See also p273 – our Clover Awards section.*

Taunton — Nightingales

Bath House Farm, Lower West Hatch, Nr Taunton, Somerset TA3 5RH
Telephone: (0823) 480392
Open: dinner Tue-Sat
Meals served: dinner 7.30-9.30
Popular local restaurant.

£45

Taunton — Porters

49 East Reach, Taunton, Somerset TA1 3EX
Telephone: (0823) 256688
Open: lunch Mon-Fri, dinner Mon-Sat (closed Bank Holidays)
Meals served: lunch 12.30-2, dinner 7.30-10
Wholesome food, wines by the glass.

£35

Teddington — Spaghetti Junction

20/22 High Street, Teddington, Middlesex TW11 8EW
Telephone: 081-977 9199
Fax: 081-977 8890
Open: lunch + dinner Tue-Sat (closed Bank Holidays, 3/4 days Xmas, Easter)
Meals served: lunch 12-2, dinner 6-11.15
Stylish Italian restaurant, good seafood and pasta.

£40

TEIGNMOUTH	Thomas Luny House

Teign Street, Teignmouth, Devon TQ14 8EG
Telephone: (0626) 772976 £35
Open: dinner daily only for residents and their guests (closed mid Dec-mid Jan)
Meals served: dinner at 7.30

Ring the door bell and wait for an answer. It's exactly as if you were calling on someone – which, in effect, you are. This is the home of Alison and John Allan and they'll welcome you in, take your bags for you, and tell you which room is yours. Dinner, for residents and their guests only, is served with everyone sat around the same table. Now that's a family atmosphere for you!

TETBURY	Calcot Manor

Tetbury, Gloucestershire GL8 8YJ
Telephone: (0666) 890391 £80
Fax: (0666) 890394
Open: lunch daily, dinner Mon-Sat
Meals served: lunch 12.30-2, dinner 7.30-9.30

A jumble of old farm buildings in rustic Cotswold stone, including a 14th-century tithe bar, form what is now Calcot Manor. The Ball family still oversee proceedings and standards are generally maintained. Enjoy croquet on the lawn or a swim before dinner, with new chef Ben Davis offering a range of menus from light lunches to a surprise 6-course dinner.

TETBURY	The Close

8 Long Street, Tetbury, Gloucestershire GL8 8AQ
Telephone: (0666) 502272 £70
Fax: (0666) 504401
Open: lunch + dinner daily (closed 1 wk Jan)
Meals served: lunch 12.30-2, dinner 7.30-10 (Sun 7.30-9.30)

This former wool merchant's house has been lovingly transformed into a stylish haven of modern comforts and period furnishings. Notable features include the original fireplaces and Adam ceilings in the dining room and the individually designed bedrooms. You'll find everything is as it should be and the efficient staff are eager to please. Former sous-chef Paul Welch provides a selection of regional dishes using excellent ingredients – individual pie of Exmoor venison with quince jelly, Dorset jugged steak scented with redcurrant and cloves – and the newly formatted wine list subdivides wines of the world by grape variety.

Thame Spread Eagle

Cornmarket, Thame, Oxfordshire OX9 2BW
Telephone: (0844) 213661 £45
Fax: (0844) 261380
Open: lunch Sun-Fri, dinner daily (closed 29+30 Dec)
Meals served: lunch 12.30-2, dinner 7-10 (Sun 7-9)

Once run by John Fothergill, aesthete and chum of Oscar Wilde, the hospitality of the Spread Eagle has been enjoyed by many eminent literary figures. Today, the bright yellow menu might recall the Yellow Book and 'Fothergill's Choice' contains delicacies to titillate even the most decadent palate. Crabe au xeres en croûte is followed by a sorbet au citron before a main dish such as medaillons de venaison des Cotswolds accompagnés de champignons huitres, une prune et une sauce de grains de moutarde. The Brideshead Wing (Evelyn Waugh was a regular visitor) has just opened and adds 11 rooms and 2 suites to the hotel's capacity.

Thornbury Thornbury Castle

Thornbury, Nr Bristol, Avon BS12 1HH
Telephone: (0454) 418511 £70
Fax: (0454) 416188
Open: lunch + dinner daily (closed 10 days Jan, Xmas for residents only)
Meals served: lunch 12-2, dinner 7-9.30 (Sun 7-9)

Thornbury Castle is one of those places I always look forward to visiting. The standards are consistently good and there are always little touches improving the facilities. This is a castle, albeit a partially ruined one, but as a castle it does not just rely on its historic setting to draw countless European and American visitors. To eat and sleep in a castle in this day and age is always a special treat and to do it in such style is all the more wonderful. You will find yourself allotted to one of the 18 bedchambers, maybe with a 4-poster to make you feel you have really stepped back into the past, with old-fashioned courtesy and service to match. Peter Brazill has taken over as head chef in 1992 and is proving more than capable of producing some interesting dishes that keep Thornbury ahead of the competition. From a 3-course set dinner with a choice of 5 starters you might find the old-fashioned fan of avocado with a variety of garnishes, but I personally would settle for the terrine of game served with a red onion and whisky marmalade, or perhaps the creamed artichoke and parsnip soup. For main courses, try a brace of quail stuffed with a walnut farce served on wild mushrooms, or a more straightforward fillet of prime Scotch Angus beef served with a pink peppercorn and cognac sauce. For pudding, if it's available, try the black cherry clafoutis, or the Thornbury Castle hot butterscotch pudding. Excellent wine list which deserves a review in itself with some good halves. There is no doubting Thornbury is a very special place and is probably the only Tudor castle in England that I know of that operates as a hotel. *See also p274 – our Clover Awards section.*

Thornton Cleveleys — Victorian House

Trunnah Road, Thornton Cleveleys, Lancashire FY5 4HF
Telephone: (0253) 860619 £50
Fax: (0253) 865350
Open: lunch Tue-Sat, dinner Mon-Sat (closed 1 wk Mar, 1 wk Nov)
Meals served: lunch 12-2, dinner 7-9.30

Four-course fixed price menus of traditional French inspiration are the order of the day here. All staff are dressed in Victorian costume, and offer friendly efficient service in the period dining room. There's a good, French wine list.

Thornton-le-Fylde — River House

Skippool Creek, Thornton-le-Fylde, Nr Blackpool, Lancashire FY5 5LF
Telephone: (0253) 883497 £65
Fax: (0253) 892083
Open: dinner Mon-Sat (closed some Bank Holidays, 2 wks Aug)
Meals served: dinner 7.30-9.30

Overlooking tidal Skippool Creek, Bill Scott's River House represents a very special and highly personal brand of hospitality. It's not particularly grand, bedrooms are quite small but very comfortable, and public rooms have a jumble of memorabilia, nice homely furniture and deep relaxing sofas, but you feel instantly welcome and part of the family, so to speak. The wine list remains as impressive as ever, and dishes such as Mrs Sykes' duck (not her only one, we hope!) with a sweet and sour sauce, loin of lamb en croûte and salmon teriaki show an equally worldly approach. If you're staying overnight, make sure you enjoy a proper Victorian shower-bath.

Thundridge — Hanbury Manor

Thundridge, Nr Ware, Hertfordshire SG12 0SD
Telephone: (0920) 487722 £90
Fax: (0920) 487692
Open: lunch daily, dinner Mon-Sat
Meals served: lunch 12-3, dinner 7-10

Set in 30 acres of parkland including an 18-hole golf course, this Jacobean style manor has been extensively restored and enlarged to create a grand 96-bedroomed hotel. For those wanting to work or work out no expense has been spared in making this hotel a first class business and conference venue. The Assembly Room, Poles Hall, the Thundridge Room, the Hawthorn and Magnolia rooms come complete with every mod con an executive could desire. For the private guest it also has lots to offer including complete health, beauty and leisure facilities. Bedrooms in stately home style contain every conceivable luxury. Chef Rory Kennedy leads the brigade in the kitchen, concocting Roux-guided dishes ranging from health-conscious snacks in the light and airy conservatory to traditional club-like food in the Vardon Grill, whilst the Zodiac Room offers fine dining and sumptuous setting.

TIVERTON	Lowman Restaurant

45 Gold Street, Tiverton, Devon EX16 6QB
Telephone: (0884) 257311 £50
Open: lunch Tue-Sun, dinner Tue-Sat (closed Xmas/New Year)
Meals served: lunch 12-2, dinner 6-9 (Fri+Sat 6-9.30)

Lamb kofta and quail's Scotch eggs with a sweet and sour sauce figure among the starters at dinner, while rack of lamb scented with orange and garlic, and venison and red wine pie are possible main courses at this cottage-style restaurant. Lunchtime eating has each dish individually priced, but in fact it works out very reasonably.

TORQUAY	Mulberry House

1 Scarborough Road, Torquay, Devon TQ2 5UJ
Telephone: (0803) 213639 £40
Open: lunch Wed-Sun, dinner Fri+Sat
Meals served: lunch 12.15-2.30, dinner 7.30-9.30
Victorian guesthoue with excellent home-cooking.

TORQUAY	Remy's

3 Croft Road, Torquay, Devon TQ2 5UN
Telephone: (0803) 292359 £50
Open: dinner Tue-Sat (closed 2 wks Xmas/New Year)
Meals served: dinner 7-9.30

Remy and Dolene Bopp aren't interested in winning awards and being fêted by the critics – keeping the place going, sending the customers away happy and paying the bills are their main concerns. Thus they provide a sensible, fixed price menu which has indeed kept their customers very content over the years, and Remy's lapin à la moutarde and cailles rôties aux raisins suit the palate and the wallet equally. Reasonably priced wine list, candlelit setting.

TORQUAY	Table Restaurant

135 Babbacombe Road, Babbacombe, Torquay, Devon TQ1 3SR
Telephone: (0803) 324292 £55
Open: dinner Tue-Sun (closed Bank Holidays, 2 wks Feb, 2 wks Sep)
Meals served: dinner 7.30-10 (Sun 7.30-9.30)

A step along the way to higher things is how Trevor Brooks and Jane Corrigan see their modest restaurant. Nevertheless, the Table will do fine for now and Trevor's cooking holds much promise for the future. A Brixham fish soup with saffron followed by pheasant with air-dried ham on lentil and pineapple chutney, or some excellent local seafood might be among the choices on the set price menu and are consistently well executed.

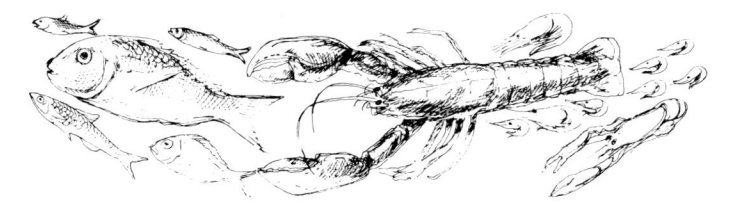

TRURO	Alverton Manor

Tregolls Road, Truro, Cornwall TR1 1XQ
Telephone: (0872) 76633 £65
Fax: (0872) 222989
Open: lunch + dinner daily
Meals served: lunch 12-1.45, dinner 7.15-9.45

Twenty-five spacious rooms with pretty fabrics; convenient location on edge of town for this former convent.

TUNBRIDGE WELLS	Cheevers

56 High Street, Tunbridge Wells, Kent TN1 1XF
Telephone: (0892) 545524 £55
Open: lunch + dinner Tue-Sat (closed Bank Holidays, 2 wks Jan)
Meals served: lunch 12.30-2 (Sat 12.30-1.45), dinner 7.30-10.30

The enterprising Tim Cheevers not only mans the stoves at the highly successful double-fronted restaurant he runs with partner Martin Miles, he also now writes and publishes the quarterly *Cheevers News* advising all his many fans of events past and plans future. His fixed price menu also reads well - mussell and fennel broth, wild salmon poached with sorrel, fillet of beef pan-fried with yoghurt and coriander, hot walnut and ginger pudding. The wine list echoes Tim's peripatetic nature.

TUNBRIDGE WELLS	Eglantine

65 High Street, Tunbridge Wells, Kent TN1 1XX
Telephone: (0892) 524957 £50
Open: lunch + dinner Tue-Sat (closed 24-28 Dec, 1 Jan)
Meals served: lunch 12.15-1.45, dinner 7.15-9.30 (Sat 7.15-10)

Chef/proprietor Susan Richardson has set her sights high – as might be expected from someone who's spent several years with the Roux brothers. Her menus are shrewdly designed with her clients' tastes and incomes in mind and also allow her to supervise every stage. Start with tomato and apple soup, then perhaps roast monkfish with a mustard and tarragon sauce, or best end of lamb with a herb crust and port sauce, with a delicious pud to finish. Cheerful service and an equally happy pastel pink and blue feel to the decor.

TUNBRIDGE WELLS Thackeray's House

85 London Road, Tunbridge Wells, Kent TN11 1EA
Telephone: (0892) 511921 £80
Open: lunch + dinner Tue-Sat (closed Bank Holidays, 1 wk Xmas)
Meals served: lunch 12.30-2.30, dinner 7-10 (Downstairs open all day, daily)

For those who found *Vanity Fair* a bit of a slog, Thackeray's House will be a more relaxed experience. Once home to the novelist, it now houses Bruce Wass's fine restaurant. Dishes such as Gressingham duck with kumquats and Chinese pepper, and noisettes of venison with pear, port and juniper on the dinner menu are done with such style as to make them rather out of the ordinary. The substantial wine list encourages experimentation - aided by some very reasonable prices and good half bottles. The self-effacing Mr Wass also operates Downstairs at Thackeray's in the bistro style.

TWICKENHAM Café Cezanne

68 Richmond Road, Twickenham, Middlesex TW1 3BE
Telephone: 081-892 3526 £45
Open: lunch Mon-Fri, dinner Mon-Sat (closed Bank Holidays)
Meals served: lunch 12.30-2, dinner 7-10.30 (Fri + Sat 7-11)

Judging by the slabs of bread, meat and onions that feature often in his paintings, the great artist might well have approved of the 'snackettes' on offer here. A baguette filled with slices of fillet steak and herb butter and Toulouse sausages with onions and mash have a peasant simplicity about them – and taste good too. Other more sophisticated dishes are also available – swordfish steak, escalope of veal with provençale ham and cheese, rack of lamb with rosemary and madeira, and crêpes or crème brûlée are suitable puds.

TWICKENHAM Hamiltons
43 Crown Road, St Margarets, Twickenham, Middlesex TW1 3EJ
Telephone: 081-892 3949 £45
Open: lunch Tue-Fri + Sun, dinner Tue-Sat (closed 1 wk New Year)
Meals served: lunch 12-2.30, dinner 7-11
Anglo French food. Live jazz on Sundays and Tuesdays.

TWICKENHAM McClements

12 The Green, Twickenham, Middlesex TW2 5AA
Telephone: 081-755 0176 £55
Open: lunch Mon-Fri, dinner Mon-Sat (closed 2 wks Xmas)
Meals served: lunch 12-2.30, dinner 7-10 (Sat 7-10.30)

A tiny restaurant squeezed into a row of houses opposite Twickenham Green is home to John McClement's cooking. The red window blinds proclaim 'French Cuisine' and that's exactly what you get. Working as a one-man team he keeps his overheads down and his canvas small, but the results are all the better for it. Grilled mullet with a tomato and basil sauce is among the starters and main dishes include a whole roast English partridge and grilled breast of duck with caramelised apple and juniper berry sauce. The delicate chocolate mousses for pud are exquisite. A meticulously judged performance which deserves a wider audience.

| UCKFIELD | Hooke Hall |

250 High Street, Uckfield, East Sussex TN22 1EN
Telephone: (0825) 761578 £50
Fax: (0825) 768025
Open: dinner daily (closed Xmas)
Meals served: dinner 7.30-9.30
The restaurant, open to non-residents on Friday and Saturday evenings, serves Juliet Percy's cordon bleu cooking.

| UCKFIELD | Horsted Place |

Little Horsted, Uckfield, East Sussex TN22 5TS
Telephone: (0825) 75581 £65
Fax: (0835) 75459
Open: lunch Sun-Fri, dinner daily (closed 10 days Jan)
Meals served: lunch 12.30-2, dinner 7.30-9.15

Built in 1850, this extremely handsome country house, once owned by Prince Philip's equerry, stands amidst well-tended gardens and fields. If Pugin's work is a favourite of yours, then Horsted Place holds even greater attractions. Although he wasn't actually the architect, he nevertheless exerted an influence over the design – seen particularly in the oak staircase. Tasteful furnishings in the 17 bedrooms and public rooms and an impressive level of service add up to a high quality establishment. Ex-Gravetye chef Allan Garth directs operations in the kitchen, his fixed price menus displaying a deft touch and sensitive use of prime produce – timbale of rabbit with a green peppercorn sauce, poached stripy seabass on a bed of spinach and basil sauce, roast saddle of lamb with minted hollandaise and asparagus. The Hon. John Sinclair (ex-Cliveden) has recently been appointed to direct the group's interests, including the new East Sussex National golf courses adjoining Horsted, whose residents enjoy half-price green fees – and the European Open is due to be held there in September 1993.

ULLSWATER Leeming House

Watermillock, Ullswater, Cumbria CA11 0JJ
Telephone: (076 84) 86622   £75
Fax: (076 84) 86443
Open: lunch + dinner daily
Meals served: lunch 12.30-1.45, dinner 7.30-8.45

Leeming House offers all the peace and seclusion a budding Wordsworth might need for inspiration, as well as facilities designed with the moneyed customer in mind, whether on holiday or on business. Super views are to be had from the little bedroom balconies and the dining room out over Lake Ullswater and to the hills on the other side. The wide-ranging menu includes traditional local dishes such as roast loin of lamb and breast of mallard duckling cooked in the modern way. Tasty bread and chutneys bring the alternative cold meat selection to life. There are some 240 bottles on the wine list which runs the full gamut of prices. Wander lonely as a cloud – but be back in time for tea!

ULLSWATER Old Church Hotel
Watermillock, Penrith, Cumbria CA11 0JN
Telephone: (076 84) 86204   £50
Fax: (076 84) 86368
Open: lunch + dinner daily (closed Dec-Feb)
Meals served: lunch 12.30-1.45, dinner 7.30-8
House guests rather than visitors is the approach given by the Whitmores. Superb views of the mountains and lake.

ULLSWATER Rampsbeck Country House Hotel
Watermillock, Ullswater, Nr Penrith, Cumbria CA11 0LP
Telephone: (076 84) 86442   £50
Open: lunch + dinner daily (closed 6 wks Jan/Feb)
Meals served: lunch 12-1.45, dinner 7-8.45
18th-century house with gardens on the shore of the lake. Friendly atmosphere, owner-run.

ULLSWATER	Sharrow Bay

Ullswater, Howtown, Nr Penrith, Cumbria CA10 2LZ
Telephone: (076 84) 86301
Fax: (076 84) 86349
Open: lunch + dinner daily (closed Dec-Feb)
Meals served: lunch 1-1.45, dinner 8-8.45

£85

Arriving at Sharrow Bay always lifts the spirits. Although in some ways this is quintessentially the much-loved and admired Lake District setting you might also be in the Swiss or Italian Alps with this mid-19th-century house surrounded by woodlands set right on the side of the lake. On my last visit to Sharrow Bay, I had not taken into account the fact that whilst many other places in the area were suffering a lack of trade at lunchtime, *this* was Sharrow Bay. The dining room was packed full to bursting with a selection of local business-men, honeymoon couples, tourists from near and far and a number of families, all intent on enjoying the 5-course lunch.

There is a choice of 10 starters – the ragôut of monkfish with fresh prawns which was served with finely chopped garlic and diced vegetables in a filo pastry tart and served on a saffron cream sauce was simply delicious! The next course, which was fixed, was a fillet of sole topped with toasted almonds with a calvados sauce accompanied by an individual suissesse cheese soufflé. Then a fresh apricot fruit sorbet, and from a choice of 9 main courses I opted for the roast leg of English lamb served with a rosemary-flavoured lamb gravy and a tartlet of onion sauce and 4 vegetables. Some of the other main course choices included honey-baked roast Lunesdale duckling and escalope of fresh salmon. From a choice of 7 cold and 2 hot desserts a must has to be the famous and *original* icky-sticky toffee pudding. With a menu like this you are simply spoilt for choice. Here diversity doesn't mean a compromise in quality. The food is rich, steadfastly traditional and there is lots of it.

The wine list probably deserves its own review and is reasonably priced with great choice. Service in the restaurant, under the capable Alan Farkins, is by helpful young men and the dining rooms themselves have a charm particular to Sharrow Bay. Start or finish with a drink on the terrace overlooking Ullswater and consider, on your next visit, which of the 28 individually-styled bedrooms, either in the main house or a little further up the road at the Bank House (which also has some superb views) you are going to book. If this review is longer than most in this book, it is perhaps to join in the celebration of Sharrow Bay's 44th season and whilst Francis Coulson and Brian Sack rightfully take pride of place, it is good to see the tribute paid to all of their staff at the top of the menu. Sharrow Bay is very different and very special. *See also p274 – our Clover Awards section.*

Ulverston — Bay Horse Inn & Bistro

Canal Foot, Ulverston, Cumbria LA12 9EL
Telephone: (0229) 53972 £45
Open: lunch Tue-Sat, dinner Mon-Sat·(closed Jan)
Meals served: lunch 12-2, dinner 7.30 for 8

Put the nosebag on here at this inn run by John Tovey and Robert Lyons. You can eat at the bar – home-made meat and potato pie, bobotie and courgettes stuffed with haggis for instance – or in the restaurant with its more sophisticated dishes. Fillets of lemon sole are filled with a fresh salmon mousse, wrapped in smoked salmon and then lightly poached and served with a reduction of stock, cream and white wine suggests the kind of level I'm talking about. The recently added New World wines on the list are all decidedly affordable and offer some interesting drinking.

Underbarrow — Tullythwaite House

Thorns Lane, Underbarrow, Kendal, Cumbria LA8 8BB
Telephone: (044 88) 397 £55
Open: lunch Sun, dinner Wed-Sat (closed Feb)
Meals served: lunch 12.30 for 1, dinner 7 for 7.30 and 7.30 for 8

Fixed price, 5-course menu, using home grown herbs and vegetables and home-made breads, biscuits and petits fours.

Upper Slaughter — Lords of the Manor

Upper Slaughter, Nr Bourton-on-the-Water, Gloucestershire GL54 2JD
Telephone: (0451) 20243 £75
Fax: (0451) 20696
Open: lunch + dinner daily
Meals served: lunch 12.30-2, dinner 7.30-9.30

Converted 17th-century rectory offering traditional country house accommodation and atmosphere. Emphasis is placed on caring for the individual guest. New chef Jenny Coaker is now established in the kitchen. Dishes are strong on flavour and presentation, a novelty being a lake in the 8-acre grounds, well stocked with brown trout allowing guests to catch their own dinner.

Uppingham — The Lake Isle

16 High Street East, Uppingham, Leicestershire LE15 9PZ
Telephone: (0572) 822951 £45
Fax: (0572) 822951
Open: lunch Tue-Sun, dinner Mon-Sat
Meals served: lunch 12.30-1.45 (Sun 12.30-2), dinner 7.30-9.30 (Sat 7-10, Sun 7.30-8.30)

One of the best selections of half bottles you'll come across on a wine list is one very good reason for coming here to David and Claire Whitfield's town centre restaurant with rooms. David cooks with flair a weekly-changing, limited choice menu which derives from the French farmhouse style. Haunch of wild boar with apple and sage sauce, steamed monkfish in chinese leaves with a mushroom and Ricard sauce, and venison and mushroom pie are typical examples. The 11 bedrooms have recently been refurbished and offer modern conveniences in cottagey decor.

| WALKINGTON | Manor House |

Northlands, Walkington, Beverley, Humberside HU17 8RT
Telephone: (0482) 881645 £75
Fax: (0482) 866501
Open: dinner Mon-Sat
Meals served: dinner 7.30-9.30
Late 19th-century manor house, impeccably maintained. Homely touches. French menu.

| WALTERSTONE | Allt Yr Ynys Hotel |

Walterstone, Hereford & Worcestershire HK2 0DU
Telephone: (0873) 890307 £45
Open: dinner daily (closed 25+26 Dec)
Meals served: dinner 7.30-9.30
Elegant country house on the banks of the River Monnow.

| WANSFORD-IN-ENGLAND | Haycock Hotel |

Wansford-in-England, Peterborough, Cambridgeshire PE8 6JA
Telephone: (0780) 782223 £50
Fax: (0780) 783031
Open: lunch + dinner daily
Meals served: lunch 12-2, dinner 7-10.15
Traditional English cooking in a traditional hotel.

WARMINSTER — Bishopstrow House

Boreham Road, Warminster, Wiltshire BA12 9HH
Telephone: (0985) 212312 £70
Fax: (0985) 216769
Open: lunch + dinner daily
Meals served: lunch 12-2, dinner 7.30-9 (Sat 7.30-9.30)

Chris Suter has already excited the food world with his finely developed sense of design and subtle flavour combinations, and continues to cook with consistency and maturity. His current menus offer a warm salad of wood pigeon and soup of mussels with John Dory and Thai herbs among the starters at dinner. Main dishes include new season's lamb with a sauce of salsa verde and pan-fried fillet of brill with tagliatelle, broad beans and fresh season's morels. The 32 bedrooms are spacious and almost decadently luxurious with sunken spa baths. Leisure facilities include indoor and outdoor swimming pools and an indoor tennis court.

WATERHOUSES — Old Beams

Leek Road, Waterhouses, Staffordshire ST10 3HW
Telephone: (0538) 308254 £60
Open: lunch Tue-Fri + Sun, dinner Tue-Sat (closed Bank Holidays, 2 wks Jan)
Meals served: lunch 12-2, dinner 7-10

Ann Wallis found the house enchanting and so she and her husband Nigel set about bringing it back to life. What better way than as a restaurant with rooms – and some rather nice cooking, too! A hot soufflé of Dublin Bay prawns and freshwater crayfish is a starter, with grilled marinated rabbit in a creamy mustard sauce among the main courses. A good choice of dessert wines by the half bottle and glass accompany rhubarb crumble or a hot tart of frangipane and pears on a raspberry coulis. There's a friendly welcome here, and 6 charming bedrooms.

WATH-IN-NIDDERDALE — Sportsman's Arms

Wath-in-Nidderdale, Pateley Bridge, Nr Harrogate, North Yorkshire HG3 5PP
Telephone: (0423) 711306 **£50**
Open: lunch Sun, dinner Mon-Sat (closed 25 Dec)
Meals served: lunch 12-2, dinner 7-9.30

A bit off the beaten track, but nevertheless a very popular place to come and eat. The combined talents of Ray Carter and Chris Williamson go together well and the kitchen's output is quite impressive. Fresh Scottish mussels are cooked in white wine with shallots, garlic, cream and a hint of curry, while best end of local lamb is roasted pink with black olives, tomato concassé, whole roast garlic and asparagus in a natural gravy. English cooking with definite Continental overtones, and a thorough commitment to simple flavours with sauces that complement, rather than obliterate, the dishes. Worth a visit.

WATLINGTON — Well House

30-40 High Street, Watlington, Oxfordshire OX9 5PY
Telephone: (049 161) 3333 **£60**
Open: lunch Tue-Fri + Sun, dinner Tue-Sat (closed most Bank Holidays except dinner 25 Dec)
Meals served: lunch 12.30-2, dinner 7-9.15 (Sat 7-9.30)

You can't help but warm to this place. It's not out to impress and the food is straightforward English and uses some interesting ingredients, while the service is attentive and friendly. You might choose from the set price menu the mushroom tartlets with béarnaise topping as a first course, to follow with boned pink trout stuffed with tomato and spinach served with either vegetables or salad, and one of the selection of puds to finish. The owners prefer to think of this place as a restaurant withrooms than a hotel proper, and as such it fits the bill well. The 11 bedrooms are comfortable and ideal for a stopover.

WELLS   Ritcher's
5 Sadler Street, Wells, Somerset BA5 2RR
Telephone: (0749) 679085   £30
Open: lunch + dinner Mon-Sat (closed Bank Holidays)
Meals served: lunch 12-2.30, dinner 7-9.30
Bistro-style food, courtyard for al fresco eating in the warm weather.

WELLS-NEXT-THE-SEA   The Moorings
6 Freeman Street, Wells-Next-The-Sea, Norfolk NR23 1BA
Telephone: (0328) 710949   £40
Open: lunch Fri-Mon, dinner daily (closed 24-26 Dec, 2 wks Dec, 2 wks Jun)
Meals served: lunch 12.30-2, dinner 7.30-9
Cooking and presentation are simple, as the restaurant itself. An interesting, good value wine list.

WEOBLEY   Jules Café
Portland Street, Weobley, Hereford & Worcester HR4 8SB
Telephone: (0544) 318206   £35
Open: lunch + dinner daily (closed some Mons in winter, 25 Dec)
Meals served: lunch 12-2, dinner 7.15-9.30
Simple ingredients, mainly organic, in well priced dishes.

WEST AUCKLAND   Old Manor House
West Auckland, Durham Dl14 9HW
Telephone: (0388) 834834   £40
Fax: (0388) 833566
Open: dinner daily (closed 24+26 Dec)
Meals served: dinner 7.30-9.30
17th-century manor house with thirty bedrooms.

WEST MERSEA   Le Champenois Restaurant
Blackwater Hotel, 20-22 Church Road, West Mersea, Essex CO5 8QH
Telephone: (0206) 383338   £50
Open: lunch Wed-Mon, dinner Mon-Sat (closed 3 wks Jan/Feb)
Meals served: 12-2 (Sun 12-2.15), dinner 7-10 (Sat 7-10.30)
Popular local haunt.

WETHERAL   Fantails
The Green, Wetheral, Nr Carlisle, Cumbria CA4 8ET
Telephone: (0228) 60239   £45
Open: lunch + dinner Mon-Sat
Meals served: lunch 12.30-2, dinner 7.30-9.30
Family-run, popular local restaurant.

WETHERSFIELD   Dicken's
The Green, Wethersfield, Nr Braintree, Essex CM7 4BS
Telephone: (0371) 850723   £60
Open: lunch Wed-Fri + Sun, dinner Wed-Sat (closed Bank Holidays, 2 wks Feb)
Meals served: lunch 12.30-2, dinner 7.30-9.30
John Dicken's (ex-Connaught and Longueville Manor) dishes are well executed with delicate flavours and simple presentation. Maria serves with charm and efficiency.

WEYMOUTH   Perry's
The Harbourside, 4 Trinity Road, Weymouth, Dorset DT4 8TJ
Telephone: (0305) 785799   £45
Open: dinner daily (closed Xmas/New Year)
Meals served: dinner 7-10.30
Friendly restaurant beside the harbour.

Whimple

Woodhayes Hotel

Whimple, Nr Exeter, Devon EX5 2TD
Telephone: (0404) 822237
Open: dinner daily
Meals served: dinner 7-9.30

£55

Indulge in a bit of the old 'upstairs-downstairs' routine her at the Rendles' hotel. They like to beaver away in the background ensuring that you, their guest, won't have to lift a finger. Katherine is in charge of the kitchen but although she provides a set menu, she's also very happy to discuss the food with you and will slip in a favourite dish if the ingredients are to hand. A typical 6-course dinner could be seafood salad, pear and watercress soup, fillets of lotte with fresh pasta, olive oil and tomatoes, rack of lamb with a garlic and herb tartlet, a choice of puds, local mature Cheddar and coffee. Very reasonably price wines.

Whitby
14 Pier Road, Whitby, North Yorkshire YO21 3PU

Magpie Café

Telephone: (0947) 602058
Open: all day daily (closed late Nov-Mar)
Meals served: 11.30-6.30

£20

Fresh fish, chips, bread and butter and tea – very popular so expect to wait and perhaps share a table.

Whitby
New Quay Road, Whitby, North Yorkshire YO21 1DH

Trenchers

Telephone: (0947) 603212
Open: all day daily (closed Xmas-mid Mar)
Meals served: 11-9

£30

Popular fish restaurant.

Whitwell-on-the-Hill
Whitwell-on-the-Hill, Nr York, North Yorkshire YO6 7JJ

Whitwell Hall

Telephone: (065 381) 551
Fax: (065 381) 554
Open: lunch + dinner daily
Meals served: lunch 12-1.45 (Sun 12.30-1.45), dinner 7.30-8.45

£45

Ivy-clad hall in 80 acres of parkland.

Wickham

Old House Hotel

The Square, Wickham, Hampshire PO17 5JG
Telephone: (0329) 833049
Fax: (0329) 833672
Open: lunch Tue-Fri, dinner Mon-Sat (closed Bank Holidays, 2 wks Xmas, 2 wks Easter, 2 wks Jul/Aug)
Meals served: lunch 12.30-1.45, dinner 7-9.45

£55

An attractive hotel set in an early 18th-century Georgian house. The rooms and furnishings are an exercise in taste and restraint. The 12 bright bedrooms are nicely laid out and include baby listening facilities. Chef Nicholas Harman's menus change weekly and offer largely French influenced cuisine – filet de boeuf au Stilton and noisettes d'agneau au Meursault are 2 typical main dishes, with tarte tatin of pears to finish.

| WILLITON | White House |

Williton, Nr Taunton, Somerset TA4 4QW
Telephone: (0984) 32306 £55
Open: dinner daily (closed Nov-May)
Meals served: dinner 7.30-8.30

It's a bit of a haul should you be coming down from London, but it's worth it when you arrive. Dick and Kay Smith are friendly people and they run their 12-bedroomed hotel much as they'd run their own house – which really it is. In the dining room, there's some good food to be had on the limited choice 5-course menus: pan-fried breast of duck, baked quail and grilled escalope of salmon are typical main dishes. The handwritten wine list is worth reading through and there's an ample selection of half bottles.

| WILMSLOW | Stanneylands |

Stanneylands Road, Wilmslow, Cheshire SK9 4EY
Telephone: (0625) 525225 £55
Fax: (0625) 537282
Open: lunch daily, dinner Mon-Sat (closed Bank Holidays)
Meals served: lunch 12.30-2, dinner 7-10

Previously the home of a Mancunian businessman, this family-owned and run hotel set in several acres of gardens is still popular with today's executives. A cosy and informal atmosphere pervades with the emphasis placed on good old traditional values. The aptly-named Steven Kitchen has been part of the team since 1984 but now has full rein as head chef, developing menus with a sound classical base and a modern signature – ballotine of guineafowl and goose liver with a quince and orange jelly, escalope of salmon baked under a citrus caramel with champagne butter sauce, breast of chicken pot-roasted with truffles and leeks.

| WINCHESTER | Lainston House |

Sparsholt, Winchester, Hampshire SO21 2LJ
Telephone: (0962) 863588 £80
Fax: (0962) 72672
Open: lunch + dinner daily
Meals served: lunch 12.30-2, dinner 7.30-10

Once in its long history used as a lunatic asylum, today the guests as Lainston House tend to come of their own volition! It's a handsome William and Mary house, the public rooms beautifully furnished and the 32 bedrooms spacious and comfortable. The grounds are impressive, too, with a 12th-century chapel and dovecote amongst their charms. A converted barn is useful for functions and seminars, and stables have recently been converted to add 6 new bedrooms.

| WINDERMERE | Miller Howe |

Rayrigg Road, Windermere, Cumbria LA23 1EY
Telephone: (053 94) 42536
Fax: (053 94) 45664
Open: dinner daily (closed early Dec-early Mar)
Meals served: dinner at 8.30 (Sat + Bank Holidays at 7 + at 9.30)

£80

Signed copies of the *Radio Times* could go on sale in the reception, which tells you quite a lot about John Tovey's cooking, reputation and Miller Howe itself - the famous name, the famous restaurant with some superb views over Lake Windermere. Ian Dutton is very much in charge of the kitchens now and turns out some consistently good food in the John Tovey style. A famous 5-course set menu with a choice of puddings still delights the faithful following. John Tovey oversees the running of the house and restaurant and this remains one of *the* places to visit in the Lake District. There are 13 comfortable bedrooms from which to base yourself and explore the surrounding countryside.

| WINDERMERE | Roger's Restaurant |

4 High Street, Windermere, Cumbria LA23 1AF
Telephone: (053 94) 44954
Open: dinner Mon-Sat (closed 1 wk Xmas)
Meals served: dinner 7-9.30

£55

'I like good quality food messed around with as little as possible', says proprietor and chef Roger Pergl-Wilson. So don't come here hungry for the latest fad as you'll go away disappointed. However, if you want well-cooked dishes along the lines of roast rack of lamb with a herb crust and madeira sauce, or roast Gressingham duck with blackcurrant sauce, then there'll be no hard feelings. Look out for his special fish night menus and French provincial nights, which visit the food and wines of specific regions. Plenty of New World, halves and good value bin ends on the wine list.

Windsor	Oakley Court

Windsor Road, Water Oakley, Nr Windsor, Berkshire SL4 5UR
Telephone: (0628) 74141 £90
Fax: (0628) 37011
Open: lunch + dinner daily
Meals served: lunch 12.30-2, dinner 7.30-10

Oakley Court has established its reputation over the years. The turreted Victorian Gothic manor house was built in 1859 and many of the original features remain, for instance the oak-panelled public rooms. Recently a separate wing has been opened, only a few yards from the main building. It contains 27 newly refurbished bedrooms, all decorated and equipped to a high standard. Situated on a beautiful stretch of the Thames, Oakley Court has its own private jetty which acts as the starting point for cruises up and down the river. And after an afternoon messing about in boats, what could be better than a meal cooked by Murdo MacSween in the elegant Oakleaf restaurant? Start with a mousseline of artichoke with forest mushrooms, then noisettes of venison with braised red cabbage and baby turnips, with an apple tart to finish. This year sees an increased choice of vegetarian dishes.

Winkleigh	Pophams Café

Castle Street, Winkleigh, Devon EX19 8HQ
Telephone: (0837) 83767 £25
Open: all day Mon-Sat
Meals served: 9-3
Small café, home-made good, excellent value.

Winteringham	Winteringham Fields

Winteringham, Humberside DN15 9PF
Telephone: (0724) 733096 £65
Fax: (0724) 733898
Open: dinner Mon-Sat (closed Bank Holidays, 2 wks Mar, 1 wk Aug)
Meals served: dinner 7-9.30

I admit that hopes for a continued gastronomic experience usually aren't high venturing out in this part of England, but there's a pleasant surprise in store here. Chef Germain Schwab has dreamed up some original combinations of flavours, seen in dishes such as savoy cabbage filled with monkfish and foie gras with a sorrel sauce or marinated casserole of goat with roasted pear, offered alongside more traditional dishes. Lovers of those rare Swiss wines will be delighted with a 1989 Pinot Noir du Valais Oeil de Perdrix or a 1989 Dole du Sion Fin Bec among the bottles listed. There are 7 bedrooms available, 3 in converted courtyard stables, and a conservatory extension to the bar/lounge area.

WITHERSLACK — Old Vicarage

Church Road, Witherslack, Cumbria LA11 6RS
Telephone: (044 852) 381 £60
Fax: (044 852) 373
Open: dinner daily
Meals served: dinner 7.30-8

An attractive Georgian country house with Victorian character. The 14 bedrooms are comfortable with some useful extras such as CD players for music lovers. Good honest English cooking comes in the form of 5 (or 6, if you have 2 puds!) course set menus with perhaps a mousse of salmon with Dover sole and dill hollandaise, then leek and rosemary soup with home-made bread, followed by roast local guineafowl with traditional trimmings, 2 dessert choices, regional cheeses and coffee with a piece of mint cake.

WIVELISCOMBE — Langley House

Langley Marsh, Wiveliscombe, Nr Taunton, Somerset TA4 2UF
Telephone: (0984) 23318 £60
Fax: (0984) 24573
Open: dinner daily (closed Feb)
Meals served: dinner 7.30-8.30 (Sat only at 8.30)

A beautifully unspoilt part of Somerset with award-winning gardens is the lovely setting for this little 8-bedroomed hotel. Owners Peter and Anne Wilson take an active hand in proceedings, and Peter also masterminds the kitchen. His cooking derives its inspiration from whatever is available that day, thus ensuring variety and fresh flavours. A recent 5-course dinner featured a warm quail breast salad, hot vichysoisse, grilled turbot with a crust of crab, pan-fried rosettes of new season Somerset lamb with an onion and cassis purée, with a choice of desserts or delicious unpasteurised Long Clawson Stilton to finish. Fine clarets on the wine list. It's also worth getting up early to do full justice to the breakfasts!

Woburn	Paris House

Woburn Park, Woburn, Bedfordshire MK17 9QP
Telephone: (0525) 290692 £70
Fax: (0525) 290471
Open: lunch Tue-Sun, dinner Tue-Sat (closed Feb)
Meals served: lunch 12-2, dinner 7-10

Peter Chandler's horse, Paris House, has recently come in a winner and his restaurant is continually up among the favourites! Peter's menus continue to evolve, featuring robust cooking accompanied by classical rich sauces – surely a reflection of his years with the Roux brothers. Sample dishes might be a tartlet of smoked chicken and black pudding with onion marmalade, or fisherman's soup for starters, followed by ragoût of pig's trotters and morels or salmon in champagne, and a hot raspberry soufflé to finish. This unusual timber-framed house set in Woburn Park itself makes an ideal setting for Peter Chandler's undoubted culinary skills.

Wolverhampton	Victoria Park

Lichfield Street, Wolverhampton, West Midlands WV1 4DB
Telephone: (0902) 29922 £40
Fax: (0902) 29923
Open: lunch Sun-Fri, dinner daily
Meals served: lunch 12-2.30, dinner 7-10

Well-turned-out hotel which has been completely transformed from the rather downmarket establishment it was before. The business clientele enjoy conference and function facilities for up to 200. Bedrooms number some 118 and standards are high throughout.

Woodbridge	Captain's Table

3 Quay Street, Woodbridge, Suffolk IP12 1BX
Telephone: (0394) 383145 £30
Open: lunch + dinner Tue-Sat
Meals served: lunch 12-2, dinner 6.30-9.30 (Sat 6.30-10)
Restaurant specialising in seafood.

Woodbridge	Wine Bar

17 Thoroughfare, Woodbridge, Suffolk IP12 1AA
Telephone: (0394) 382557 £30
Open: lunch + dinner Tue-Sat (closed 25+26 Dec)
Meals served: lunch 12-2, dinner 7-11
Favourite wine bar with the locals.

Woodstock	Bear Hotel

Park Street, Woodstock, Oxfordshire OX7 1SZ
Telephone: (0993) 811511 £55
Fax: (0993) 813380
Open: lunch + dinner daily
Meals served: lunch 12.30-2 (Sun 12.15-2.30), dinner 7-10 (Sun 7-9.30)

A hotel for the affluent visitor in the immaculately preserved village of Woodstock. This historic coaching inn with 45 bedrooms also has public rooms of great period charm, full of antiques, in the extended restaurant, roast and seafood dishes are the best.

Woodstock — Feathers Hotel

Market Street, Woodstock, Oxfordshire OX7 1SX
Telephone: (0993) 812291 £70
Fax: (0993) 813158
Open: lunch + dinner daily
Meals served: lunch 12.30-2.30, dinner 7.30-9.45

A beautifully furnished charming hotel, as is just about everything in Woodstock – even the old village stocks down the road appear delightfully quaint. Newly refurbished rooms still retain their original character but also offer modern comforts. The dining room provides some imaginative cooking which never exceeds the bounds of decorum. First courses include a salad of citrus fruits laced with pink champagne and a wild mushroom ravioli flavoured with tarragon. Among the main dishes there is roasted salmon with wild thyme and shallots. The wine list allows you to drink some classy wine by the glass.

Wootton Common — Lugleys

Staplers Road, Wootton Common, Isle of Wight PO33 4RW
Telephone: (0983) 882202 £50
Open: dinner Tue-Sat (closed 25+26 Dec)
Meals served: dinner 7-9.30 (times vary in winter)

Owner and chef Angela Hewitt runs Lugleys purely for the pleasure of it. For her, the reward is in the doing and the greatest compliment you can pay her is to return again. The simple menu offers 3 or 4 choices at each course. Seasonal dishes are specified also and subject to availability.

Worcester — Brown's

24 Quay Street, Worcester, Hereford & Worcester WR1 2JJ
Telephone: (0905) 26263 £70
Open: lunch Sun-Fri, dinner Mon-Sat (closed Bank Holidays, 1 wk Xmas)
Meals served: lunch 12.30-1.45, dinner 7.30-9.45 (Sat 7.30-10)

One day I suspect the ivy will creep all the way across the wall and then no-one will be able to see the menus and discreet plaque which reads Brown's Restaurant. However, I doubt that this place would sink into oblivion, the food's too good for that! The Tansleys have readjusted their prices of late and so lunchtime eating is proving even more of a pleasure. Boudin of rabbit with Puy lentils is a typical starter with a sirloin of beef with shallots and red wine as one of the main dishes. Yoghurt mousse with caramelised apricots will do nicely as a pud, or there is a selection of English and continental cheeses. More and more they find that they are returning to dishes that were on the menus some 20-odd years ago, which should allow many of us to indulge in a little nostalgia! The carefully converted warehouse enjoys a riverside setting. *See also p278 – our Clover Awards section.*

Wylam	Laburnum House

Main Street, Wylam, Northumberland NE41 8AJ
Telephone: (0661) 852185 **£45**
Open: dinner Tue-Sat (closed Bank Holidays except Good Friday, 2 wks Feb)
Meals served: dinner 6.30-9.30 (Sat 6.30-10)

Venison pâté with mango purée or smoked salmon to start, duck breast with plum sauce accompanied by a selection of fresh vegetables as a main course – these are typical of what's on offer on Kenn Elliott's menus. Four comfortable bedrooms are also available.

Wymondham	Number Twenty Four

24 Middleton Street, Wymondham, Norfolk
Telephone: (0953) 607750 £35
Open: lunch Mon-Sat, dinner Wed-Sat
Meals served: lunch at 1, dinner 7.30-9.30, snacks 8.30am-4.30pm
Thirty seat restaurant offering modern and classical English cuisine.

Yattendon	Royal Oak

The Square, Yattendon, Nr Newbury, Berkshire RG16 0UF
Telephone: (0635) 201325 **£75**
Fax: (0635) 201926
Open: lunch + dinner daily (closed 25 Dec)
Meals served: lunch 12.30-2, dinner 7-10

Delightful village inn with a warm welcome, the Royal Oak offers a piece of old England. As you stand in the bar with its beams and tiled floor the overwhelming impression is that time has stood still. Yet, believe it or not, behind the scenes things have been moving fast. Chef and partner Dominique Orizet continues to refine and Anglo-French menu, using only the freshest ingredients – grilled scallops and noodles with asparagus and lemon sauce, fricassée of lobster and John Dory with saffron, medaillons of venison with glazed shallots, hot blackcurrant and sloe gin pancake – and co-owner Julie Huff runs the front of house with great efficiency. They had good teachers, both having worked under the previous owners Richard and Kate Smith.

Yeovil	Little Barwick House

Barwick Village, Nr Yeovil, Somerset BA22 9TD
Telephone: (0935) 23902 **£45**
Fax: (0935) 20908
Open: dinner Mon-Sat (closed 2 wks Jan)
Meals served: dinner 7-9 (Sat 7-9.30)

Veronica and Christopher Colley are a charming couple and they'll quickly put you at your ease here in their restaurant with rooms. The food is extremely enjoyable and features game and fish. There are good puds and a smashing breakfast the next morning!

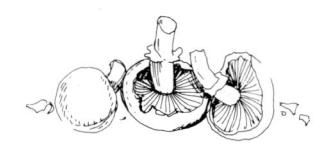

York — 19 Grape Lane

19 Grape Lane, York, North Yorkshire YO1 2HU
Telephone: (0904) 636366 £50
Open: lunch + dinner Tue-Fri (closed 3 days Xmas, 3 days New Year, 2 wks Feb, 2 wks Sep)
Meals served: lunch 12-2, dinner 7.30-10.30 (Sat 7-10.30)

Right in the centre of the city is where you'll find Gordon Alexander's restaurant. It's a place that takes itself seriously and quite rightly so. Chef Michael Fraser's cooking includes some interesting items prepared with a bit of flair. Standards on the menu are roast loin of lamb in shortcrust pastry, collops of beef and medaillons of hare with field mushrooms, but check the blackboard for daily specials. Around 20 half bottles are listed among the wines.

York — Grange Hotel

Clifton, York, North Yorkshire YO3 6AA
Telephone: (0904) 644744 £50
Fax: (0904) 612453
Open: lunch + dinner daily
Meals served: lunch 12.30-2.30, dinner 7-10

A super little hotel, restored to perfection, with the foyer and morning room being especially eye-catching. The 29 bedrooms have been thought out with care and much trouble has been taken to make them comfortable and attractive. A smart brasserie in the basement is open from 10am till late in the evening should you feel peckish outside restaurant hours. The Ivy Restaurant itself is where chef Cara Baird executes some fine dishes, treating traditional recipes in contemporary ways. A couple of years as a saucier at Le Gavroche have paid handsome dividends. Recently on her set-price dinner menu you could find a terrine of grouse with Cumberland sauce as a starter, with best end of lamb in a tomato and basil sauce as a main course. Her puds are good too – as you might have guessed!

York — Melton's

7 Scarcroft Road, York, North Yorkshire YO2 1ND
Telephone: (0904) 634341 £50
Open: lunch + dinner Tue-Sat (closed 3 wks Xmas/New Year, 1 wk Aug)
Meals served: lunch 12.30-2, dinner 7-10

Paris House and Le Poulbot feature on Michael Hjort's *cv* which means he's another chef who's spreading the Roux brothers' word up here in York. His cooking is what you'd expect after such a formation and his menus are admirably composed. From a typical menu you might decide on a shellfish consommé and continue with braised shanks of lamb with flageolet beans. Tuesdays see a special seafood feature with perhaps scallops in filo pastry with watercress sauce, whilst Thursday favours vegetarians. Flavour is what it's all about and Michael treats everything with a delicate yet assured touch. His wife Lucy is the ideal hostess, supervising the unobtrusive grey, blue and pink decorated room hung with a frequently changing gallery of artwork.

York	Middlethorpe Hall

Bishopthorpe Road, York, North Yorkshire YO2 1QB
Telephone: (0904) 641241
Fax: (0904) 620176
Open: lunch + dinner daily
Meals served: lunch 12.30-2.30, dinner 7.30-9.45

£70

A grand setting for chef Kevin Franksen's cooking. The daily changing set menu contains much of interest with starters such as a cassoulet of pheasant and duck with herb dumplings served on a lime and lentil sauce. Main dishes include collops of salmon and scallops in walnut oil and roast Yorkshire woodcock served traditionally. Sauces are well constructed, flavours are strong yet never overpowering. The à la carte menu is more conservative and offers fish dishes such as fillet of turbot or whole boned Dover sole as a main or a first course as well as a steamed venison and rabbit pudding and roast rack of lamb among the selections for meat-eaters. A vegetarian option is also provided. On the back page you'll find a variety of sweets, any one of which will fit the bill. After a treat like this it's about all you can do to climb the grand staircase and make for your room. The individually-styled bedrooms make this a favourite for business and foreign visitors and an exceptionally well cared for interior has been sympathetically designed, and decorated with some beautiful antiques. The hall, with its wonderfully elegant façade, stands in 26 acres of gardens and parkland near the racecourse. *See also p278 – our Clover Awards section.*

York	Ristorante Bari

The Shambles, York, North Yorkshire
Telephone: (0904) 633807
Open: lunch + dinner daily (closed 25+26 Dec, 1 Jan)
Meals served: lunch 10-2.30, dinner 6-11
80-seater Italian restaurant in the heart of historic York.

£25

Scotland Establishment Reviews

Aberdeen	Faraday's

2 Kirk Brae, Cults, Aberdeen, Grampian AB1 9SQ
Telephone: (0224) 819666 £45
Open: lunch Tue-Sat, dinner Mon-Sat
Meals served: lunch 12-1.30, dinner 7-9.30

Named in honour of Michael Faraday, the man who discovered electricity, this restaurant is set in a one-time generating station. The outside is unexciting, but inside it's pure Victoriana. Owner and chef John Inches' cooking is interesting as well – all the more so for being in an area where sheer quantity is the yardstick by which good food is measured. Main dishes such as a ragoût of Scots venison with glazed winter root vegetables, game pâté barquette, and spicy Turkish lamb cooked with cinnamon and fenugreek make it clear that he loves what he's doing.

Aberdeen	Silver Darling

Pocra Quay, North Pier, Aberdeen, Grampian AB2 1DQ
Telephone: (0224) 576229 £55
Open: lunch Mon-Fri, dinner daily (closed Sun Dec-Easter, 2 wks Xmas)
Meals served: lunch 12-2, dinner 7-10
French restaurant in former customs house; fish a speciality.

ABERFELDY	Farleyer House

Aberfeldy, Tayside PH15 2JE
Telephone: (0887) 20332
Fax: (0887) 29430
Open: dinner daily
Meals served: dinner 7.30-8.30 (Bistro 10-2 + 6.30-9.30)

£65

Jonathan Brown has now joined Frances Atkins in the kitchen. His previous experience at L'Ortolan stands him well with the new team.

The restaurant choice from a fixed menu might be a boudin of salmon served with a chive sauce from a choice of two starters, followed by a good home-made soup made from seasonal vegetables, then a fillet of Angus beef with excellent caramelised shallots and served with wild mushrooms in a well reduced red wine sauce, from a choice of two main courses, followed by some good local and English cheeses and a choice of three puddings. Service is friendly.

The Scottish country house with its relaxed atmosphere and well tended grounds boasts not only the Atkins Restaurant, but the addition of what they describe as a Scottish Bistro where from 20 or so dishes you might choose a venison sausage or some char-grilled fresh tuna with tomato.

There's always a warm welcome from the Atkins at Farleyer House.

ABERFOYLE	Braeval Old Mill

Braeval, By Aberfoyle, Highland FK8 3UY
Telephone: (087 72) 711
Open: lunch Sun, dinner Tue-Sat (closed Bank Holidays, 2 wks Nov)
Meals served: lunch 12-1.30, dinner 7-9.30

£70

A good solid stone mill matched by some good cooking! The style of the menu has moved from à la carte to fixed price with choice. In this way chef Nick Nairn can guarantee consistency and flavour. Watercress soup and terrine of duck with Cumberland sauce are included as starters with rump of lamb and roast fillet of beef with a confit of shallots as main courses. Extensive wine list includes a commendable selection of half bottles.

Achiltibuie — Summer Isles

Achiltibuie, by Ullapool, Highland IV26 2YG
Telephone: (085 482) 282 £60
Fax: (085 482) 251
Open: dinner daily (closed mid Oct-Easter)
Meals served: dinner at 8

As the Irvines say, 'there's a marvellous amount of nothing to do' here in Achiltibuie. They'll do their best to make sure you do lots of it in comfort and style at this 10-bedroomed hotel. As for the food, the fish and seafood is marvellously fresh and the home-made bread a meal in itself.

Alloa — Gean House

Gean Park, Tullibody Road, Alloa, Central FK10 2HS
Telephone: (0259) 219275 £70
Fax: (0259) 213827
Open: lunch + dinner daily
Meals served: lunch 12-2, dinner 7-9.30

An advertisement in the *Times* led John Taylor and Anthony Mifsud to Gean House and since then they've not looked back. Derelict for some 10 years, there was an enormous amount of work to do. However today the results more than justify their efforts and Gean House is a stunning new addition to Scotland's list of luxury hotels. Bedrooms bear names derived from the surrounding hills or the family of the original owners, the Forrester-Patons, while the crockery is decorated with a wild cherry motif since this is what 'gean' means in Scots.

In the kitchen Anthony dons the chef's toque and executes dishes following his own culinary philosophy. From a cornucopia of ingredients he aims to achieve a 'symphysis' of taste. A terrine of pigeon, hazelnut and pistachio is served with Cumberland sauce and the poached cushion of salmon is accompanied by a tarragon and leek sauce. Desserts include the more straightforward bread and butter pudding and blackcurrant delight, all this served in a walnut panelled dining room.

This is an unusual house with some beautiful furnishings and some well-chosen pieces to complement the atmosphere. They say that their guests should come here to relax and be pampered. Sounds good to me!

Alyth — Drumnacree House

St Ninians Road, Alyth, Tayside PH11 8AP
Telephone: (082 83) 2194 £45
Open: lunch Tue-Sun, dinner Tue-Sat (closed 25+26 Dec, 1+2 Jan)
Meals served: lunch 12-2, dinner 7-10

An amateur turned pro, Allan Cull has taken to the business of being a chef like the proverbial duck to water. A fillet of salmon with Glamis asparagus shows the more orthodox side of his skills, while the Cajun specialities – say a cheese, corn and aubergine casserole or a blackened herb- and spice-covered fillet of salmon – reveal that he's a dab hand with the more exotic. He is full of imagination and energy, and you can see that he's been storing up ideas all those long years!

ANSTRUTHER	Cellar

24 East Green, Anstruther, Fife KY10 3AA
Telephone: (0333) 310378 **£65**
Open: lunch Fri+Sat, dinner Mon-Sat (closed dinner Mon Oct-May, Bank Holidays, 10 days Xmas)
Meals served: lunch 12.30-1.30, dinner 7.30-9

Ask around and you'll find that more than a few people consider this to be one of *the* places to eat fish in Scotland. Superb quality specimens are beautifully cooked by chef Peter Jukes with the minimum of fuss. When you have such quality raw materials it seems a pity to dress them up too much. Thus the halibut is grilled with citrus juices and served with hollandaise sauce. Perfect! Monkfish roasted with herb and garlic butter and served with a tomato and basil sauce is another favourite from the four or five fish main courses, or you could choose the meat alternative. An excellent wine list allows for more than mere accompaniments to the food in this simple setting with a beamed ceiling and tiled floor.

APPIN	Invercreran Hotel

Appin, Glen Creran, Highland PA38 4BJ
Telephone: (063 173) 414 £50
Fax: (063 173) 532
Open: lunch + dinner daily (closed 16 Nov-28 Feb)
Meals served: lunch 12-2, dinner 7-8
Small hotel (9 bedrooms), family run.

ARISAIG	Arisaig House

Beasdale, Arisaig, Highland PH39 4NR
Telephone: (068 75) 622 **£75**
Fax: (068 75) 626
Open: lunch + dinner daily (closed mid Nov-early Mar)
Meals served: lunch 12.30-2, dinner 7.30-8.30

Stroll in the beautiful rhododendron gardens, or lounge in one of the copious armchairs in the morning or drawing rooms, or simply enjoy the privacy of your own comfortably furnished bedroom which has all you need to keep you happy. However, a trip to the dining room to sample chef Matthew Burns' cooking is one appointment you must keep. Choose from 8 starters which might include Arisaig scallops served on a tomato and ginger confit, or a salad of sea fish marinated in lime juice and fresh basil and olive oil; and from the main courses, perhaps a grilled fillet of sea bass served with crisp fried celery and leeks or a baked breast of guinea fowl served with fresh noodles and a creamed chive sauce. Good choice of puddings, including hot chocolate soufflé which is served with a pistachio ice-cream. Pleasant service in the panelled dining room of this well-run Highland hotel.

Arisaig House

AUCHTERARDER	**Gleneagles Hotel**

Auchterarder, Tayside PH3 1NF
Telephone: (0764) 62231 **£90**
Fax: (0764) 62134
Open: lunch + dinner daily
Meals served: lunch 12.30-2, dinner 7.30-10

Whether you want to shoot, ride, get trim, or simply browse round some shops, then Gleneagles is the hotel for you. Facilities, service, and accommodation make this a hard place to beat in terms of sheer comfort and all round excellence. Conversation in the bars and lounges is peppered with terms like 'five iron', 'wedge shot', 'albatross' and 'ten under par' and many of the guests seem to sport rather natty sweaters and loud check slacks. Am I imagining things, or could there be perhaps a golf course in the vicinity?

Gleneagles remains a monument to the days of the huge grand hotel where everything is available for the visitor, and in today's market where sport and leisure are becoming more of an integral part of people's lives Gleneagles offers not only golf, but also shooting, tennis, croquet, pitch and putt, bowling, indoor pool and health spa, all of top quality with the top named professionals from each sport being involved. Add to this sumptuous bedrooms and a choice of restaurants, and you can see why so many people return time and again.

AUCHTERHOUSE	**Old Mansion House**

Auchterhouse, By Dundee, Tayside DD3 0QN
Telephone: (082 626) 366 £50
Fax: (082 626) 400
Open: lunch + dinner daily (closed Xmas, 1 wk Jan)
Meals served: lunch 12-2, dinner 7-9.30 (Sun 7-9)
Baronial house, splendid views, six comfortable bedrooms, welcoming service.

AYR	**Fouters Bistro**

2a Academy Street, Ayr, Strathclyde KA7 1HS
Telephone: (0292) 261391 **£50**
Open: lunch Tue-Sat, dinner Tue-Sun (closed 25+26 Dec, 1-3 Jan)
Meals served: lunch 12-2, dinner 6.30-10.30 (Sun 7-10)

One of those easy to miss restaurants, but it's worth your while retracing your steps to find the narrow entrance way and descending stairs. Inside the flower stencilled walls are attractive and the prices even more so – the 2- or 3-course lunch menus are great value. A platter of pâtés to start, followed by the day's fish special as a main course and then one of the puds to finish. You can trust the house wines and the excellent list is more than tempting. Candles are brought out in the evening and the Brasserie menu is very popular.

Ayr	The Stables

Queens Court, 41 Sandgzte, Ayr, Strathclyde KA7 1BD
Telephone: (0292) 283704 £35
Open: all day Mon-Sat (closed 25+26 Dec, 1+2 Jan)
Meals served: 10-10 (Mon 10-5)

I won't even attempt to describe the architectural niceties of this v-shaped restaurant set in a converted stables – you'll have to wait and see for yourself. During the day there's homely food available but it's in the evening that the place really comes into its own. The kilted owner, Ed Baines, makes his appearance and is what you'd call a bit of a character. He'll go through the menu with each table in turn, transforming the most ordinary dish into an anecdote. A stockbroker by profession, his previous experience is pressed into service and given half a chance he'll convince you to order something you'd never have thought of while lamenting the unfair reputation of William McGonagall. The food – when it arrives at the table – has a lot to live up to with such a good front man. Worth trying if available are rumbledethumps (a mixture of mashed potato with cabbage and cheese grated on top), or steak and pickled walnut pie.

Ballater	Balgonie House

Braemar Place, Ballater, Grampian AB35 5RQ
Telephone: (033 97) 55482 £55
Fax: (033 97) 55482
Open: lunch + dinner daily
Meals served: lunch 12.30-2, dinner 7-9
Opened in April 1991, set in 4 acres of gardens, Scottish cuisine.

Ballater	Craigendarroch Hotel

Braemar Road, Ballater, Tayside AB3 5XA
Telephone: (033 97) 55858 £55
Fax: (033 97) 55447
Open: lunch + dinner daily (closed 5-10 Jan)
Meal served: lunch 12.30-2.30, dinner 7.30-10 (Sun 7.30-9.30)
Leisure centre and all manner of other sports facilities. Fifty bedrooms. Oaks Restaurantserves modern cooking.

Ballater	Tullich Lodge

Ballater, Grampian AB35 5SB
Telephone: (033 97) 55406 £55
Fax: (033 97) 55397
Open: lunch + dinner daily (closed Dec-Mar)
Meals served: lunch at 1, dinner 7.30-8.30

A Victorian baronial mansion overlooking the river Dee. For those unable to make it up to the third floor Tower Room there are 9 other bedrooms besides, all with furnishings in keeping with the surroundings. Some good furnishings and unusual pieces are well thought out. You can relax and turn back the pages of history in this elegant setting. Sensible, short, hand-written dinner menus are good value with 4 courses and coffee. Local fish and game feature strongly. Good breads and accompaniments.

BANCHORY — Invery House

Bridge of Feugh, Banchory, Grampian AB31 3NJ
Telephone: (033 02) 4782　　　　　　　　　　　　　　　　　　　　£75
Fax: (033 02) 4712
Open: lunch + dinner daily
Meals served: lunch 12.30-2.15, dinner 7.30-10 (Sun 7.30-9)

If the mark of good interior design is that you're not aware of it, then Invery House is a triumph of the art. Co-owner Sheila Spence is the one responsible and the results work beautifully – you feel at home the moment you walk in. Bedrooms, public rooms and dining room are all to the same high standard. As for the food this is similarly impressive, cooked by chef Clive Lamb. His menus are dedicated to the tradition of Scottish cooking and any Sassenach affections are avoided. Thus you'll find roast guinea fowl as a typical main course. The hotel's location near Aberdeen, established now as a leading oil capital, means a large proportion of guests are business-orientated and from all over Europe. But with many whisky distilleries in the vicinity I'm sure there are other ways to justify a visit! Extensive wine list.

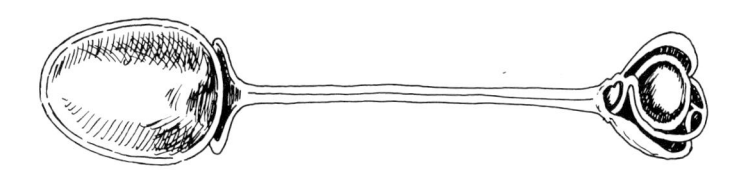

BEARSDEN — October Restaurant

128 Drymen Road, Bearsden, Glasgow, Strathclyde G61 3RB
Telephone: 041-942 7272　　　　　　　　　　　　　　　　　　　　£60
Fax: 041-942 9650
Open: lunch + dinner Mon-Sat (closed Bank Holidays, 2 wks Aug, 1 wk Easter)
Meals served: lunch 12-2, dinner 7-10

What Lettonie is to Bristol, the October Restaurant is to Glasgow. Which is to say it's a bit off the beaten track both in its location and the style of cooking. Ferrier Richardson has dreamed up an eclectic assortment of dishes assembled from his various sabbaticals but, in his own words, 'staying clear of over the top fashionable whims'! An onion and Stilton soup and Oban mussels with garlic, onions and white wine are two of the starters, with teriyaki beef with wasabi and spiced ginger livening things up a bit as a main dish. Come here at lunchtime to take advantage of the set menu – it's a snip at the price! – and a good wine list.

BLAIRGOWRIE	Kinloch House

Kinloch, by Blairgowrie, Tayside PH10 6SG
Telephone: (0250) 884237 £50
Fax: (0250) 884333
Open: lunch + dinner daily (closed 2 wks Dec)
Meals served: lunch 12.30-2, dinner 7-9.15

This mid 19th-century house was extended in 1911 and provides the perfect setting for owners David and Sarah Shentall's hospitality. The 21 bedrooms are all well furnished with 8 in the new wing. Public rooms include a delightful conservatory for after dinner coffee and drinks. Food in the restaurant is Scottish through-and-through.

BRIDGE OF ALLAN	Kipling's

Mine Road, Bridge of Allan, Central FK9 4DT
Telephone: (0786) 833617 £35
Open: lunch Tue-Sun, dinner Tue-Sat (closed Bank Holidays except Good Friday, 2 wks Aug, 1 wk Xmas)
Meals served: lunch 12.30-1.30, dinner 7-9
Popular local restaurant, daily changing menus. Chef/patron Peter Bannister.

CAIRNDOW	Loch Fyne Oyster Bar

Clachan Farm, Cairndow, Strathclyde PA26 8BH
Telephone: (049 96) 264 £35
Fax: (049 96) 234
Open: all day daily
Meals served: 9-9

If you like fish and seafood then here the world is your oyster. I doubt that I'm the first to say that, nor that I'm the last, but it just about sums up the place. Stop for a plate of these little fellows and a good glass of white wine at lunchtime in this straightforward simple roadside setting with views over the Loch.

CALLANDER	Roman Camp

off Main Street, Callander, Tayside FK17 8BG
Telephone: (0877) 30003 £75
Fax: (0877) 31533
Open: lunch + dinner daily
Meals served: lunch 12-2, dinner 7-9
Privately owned, 14-bedroomed hotel. Excellent fishing on the River Teith.

Canonbie — Riverside Inn

Canonbie, Dumfries & Galloway DG14 0UX
Telephone: (038 73) 71512 £50
Open: lunch Mon-Sat, dinner daily (closed 25+26 Dec, 1+2 Jan, 2 wks Nov, 2 wks Feb)
Meals served: lunch 12-2, dinner 7.30-8.30

A traditional country inn offering come traditional country cooking with a few pleasant surprises thrown in. Ham and spinach pastry parcels are served in a tomato sauce as a starter, while a fresh wild salmon fillet comes with a tarragon and watercress sauce. Hot apple and marmalade charlotte with cream as a pud hits just the right spot. Local, organic produce is heavily stressed, as are the award-winning cheeses. Friendly dining room and service.

This is the sort of place you would like to arrive at after a long drive but all too rarely do.

Castle Douglas — Collin House

Auchencairn, Castle Douglas, Fife DG7 1QN
Telephone: (055 664) 292 £50
Fax: (055 664) 292
Open: dinner daily (closed 3/4 wks Jan/Feb)
Meals served: dinner 7.30 for 8
Recently opened by Pam Hall and John Wood, small comfortable hotel with lovely grounds and views.

Colbost — Three Chimneys Restaurant

Colbost, By Dunvegan, Isle of Skye, Highland IV55 8ZT
Telephone: (047 081) 258 £50
Open: lunch + dinner Mon-Sat, + Sun before Bank Holidays (closed Nov-Easter)
Meals served: lunch 12.30-2, dinner 7-9

Home-made bread, including a saffron loaf offered with seafood, and good old-fashioned puds are two splendid reasons for coming here to eat. Leek roulade with pears and crowdie as a starter and wild Skye salmon with champagne sauce and strawberries as a main dish are perfect preparation for the 'sweet treats' which change daily. This old crofter's cottage with its low ceilings, near Loch Dunvegan, is one to visit on the Isle.

Contin — Coul House

Contin, By Strathpeffer, Highland IV14 9EY
Telephone: (0997) 21487 £55
Fax: (0997) 21945
Open: lunch + dinner daily
Meals served: lunch 12-2, dinner 7-9
Highland mansion house dating back to 1821 set in an extensive garden. Twenty-one bedrooms.

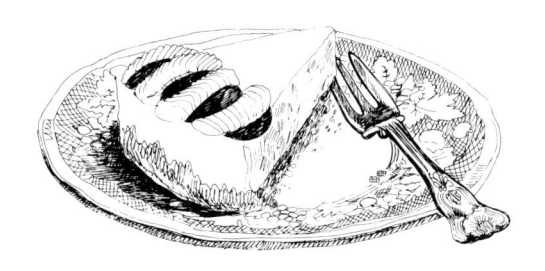

CRINAN	Crinan Hotel

Crinan, By Lochgilphead, Strathclyde PA31 8SR
Telephone: (054 683) 261 *Lock 16 Restaurant:* £75
Fax: (064 683) 292 *Westward Room:* £60
Lock 16 Restaurant:
Open: dinner Tue-Sat (closed Oct-Mar)
Meals served: dinner at 8
Westward Room:
Open: dinner daily (closed Oct-Mar)
Meals served: dinner 7-9

This hotel is right on the waterfront and has spectacular and uninterrupted views out to sea with breathtaking sunsets. The top floor houses the seafood restaurant, Lock 16, which serves the freshest of fresh fish and shellfish. The catch is landed at 4.30pm and you sit down to eat at 8.00pm – you can't say that the food's been hanging around! The disadvantage of this arrangement is that the menu is entirely dependent on the vagaries of the weather and the tide. If nothing comes in then the kitchen remains closed. However, the ground floor restaurant, the Westward Room, is an alternative and offers a wider selection of dishes – fresh asparagus hollandaise as a starter and charcoal grilled fillet of Aberdeen Angus with sautéed mushrooms were recently to be had for dinner. Nick Ryan has broughthis wine list up to scratch and it lists getting on for 150 names – that's more than you'll find in the telephone directory for Crinan!

CROMARTY	Thistles

20 Church Street, Cromarty, Highland IV11 8XA
Telephone: (038 17) 471 £50
Open: lunch Tue-Sun, dinner Tue-Sat (closed 25+26 Dec, 1+2 Jan, 1 wk Oct, 2 wks Feb)
Meals served: lunch 12-2, dinner 7.30-9

Family run and patriotically named restaurant up in Cromarty. Chef David Wilkinson was once to be found at Arisaig House but now spends his time here dashing off reliable dishes such as saddle of Scottish lamb and sole and monkfish with fennel and garlic. The menu changes frequently and vegetarians are catered for as well.

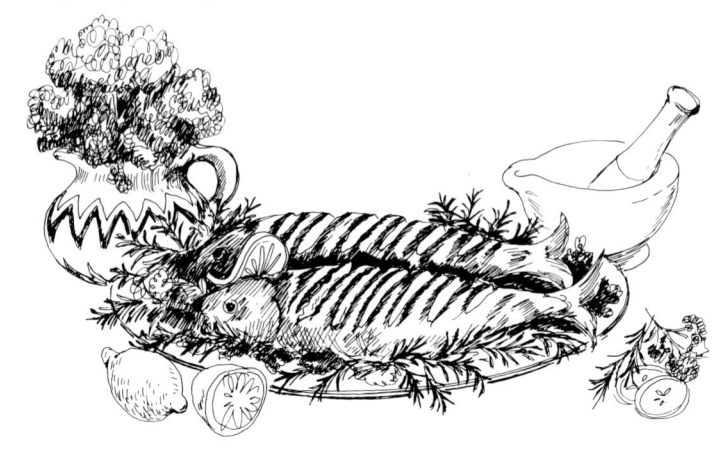

CUMBERNAULD — Westerwood Hotel

St Andrews Drive, Westerwood, Cumbernauld, Strathclyde G68 0EW
Telephone: (0236) 457171 £60
Fax: (0236) 738478
Open: lunch Mon-Fri, dinner Mon-Sat
Meals served: lunch 12-2.30, dinner 7.30-9.45

The legendary Severiano Ballesteros had a hand in the layout of the new golf course, and at the Westerwood Hotel they're intent on creating another legend. It takes time to build up a reputation and this establishment has only been open for a short time. But the signs are very favourable – a good standard of fittings and furnishings are to be noticed throughout. The Old Master's Restaurant has the old master himself – Bruce Sangster from Murrayshall (qv) – as executive chef which guarantees accomplished dishes with chef de cuisine Tom Robinson offering some excellent choices. From the 4- or 5-course menu you could have fine slices of River Tay smoked salmon served with a horseradish cream, followed by a light consommé enhanced with fine leeks and prunes, followed by a medallion of beef on a burgundy and forest mushroom sauce. Tasty puds finish things off nicely. A good opening drive – let's see how things go down the fairway!

CUPAR — Ostlers Close

25 Bonnygate, Cupar, Fife KY15 4BU
Telephone: (0334) 55574 £55
Open: lunch + dinner Tue-Sat (closed 25+26 Dec, 1+2 Jan, 1 wk Jun)
Meals served: lunch 12.15-2, dinner 7-9.30 (Sat 7-10)

An unassuming little restaurant run by Amanda and Jimmy Graham. The strong regular following creates a relaxed, convivial atmosphere in which to enjoy the food. Jimmy uses organic vegetables, free range duck and salad and herbs from his own garden. Mushrooms he might chance upon during his walks in the surrounding forests also make their way into the dishes. The wine list includes some useful half bottles. Friendly service in this simple restaurant situated in an alley off the main street.

DALGUISE	Kinnaird

Kinnaird Estate, Dalguise, By Dunkeld, Tayside PH8 0LB
Telephone: (079 682) 440 £75
Fax: (079 682) 289
Open: lunch + dinner daily (closed Feb)
Meals served: lunch 12.30-1.45, dinner 7.15-9.30

Teddy bears with 'do not disturb' badges are typical of the homely approach you'll find at Kinnaird. Mrs Constance Ward is the proud owner of this house and she welcomes you in person. There are only 8 bedrooms and 1 suite but they're splendidly furnished and give just the right 'lived in' feel with deep sofas, large armchairs, walls covered in portraits, paintings and stuffed fish. Beautifully painted panels in the dining room with beautiful views over the gardens and Tay Valley. Chef John Webber offers some fine food, taking care with ingredients to allow flavours to come through. Perhaps home-cured beef with some slivers of parmesan cheese and a little olive oil with a spicy potato salad from a choice of 5 starters (I would have liked to try them all) and a main course of breast of Gressingham duck simply roasted, slightly pink, with the legs served as confit, or a good fillet of Scotch steak cooked medium pink accompanied by some creamed celeriac, served with a reduction of red wine and port, from the choice of 5 main courses. A good selection of cheeses served from the trolley, or perhaps finish with a very good sugar-glazed pear in a case of puff pastry set on a caramel sauce. Good wine list with a selection of half bottles.

DRUMNADROCHIT	Polmaily House

Drumnadrochit, Highland IV3 6XT
Telephone: (045 62) 343 £55
Open: dinner daily (closed Nov-Easter)
Meals served: dinner 7.30-9.30

The Parsons' comfortable hotel has a private house feel to it, and maintains a very convivial atmosphere in which you know you can just relax and take things easy. The 9 bedrooms are nicely furnished. Local dishes feature on the good value menu. feel to it.

Drybridge — Old Monastery Restaurant

Drybridge, Buckie, Grampian AB56 2JB
Telephone: (0542) 32660 £50
Open: lunch + dinner Tue-Sat (closed Bank Holidays, 3 wks Jan, 2 wks Nov)
Meals served: lunch 12-1.45, dinner 7-9.30 (Sat 7-10)

The attractive dining room retains a spartan yet homely feel with the simple wooden chairs and tables, candlelight and rafters. A largely successful marriage of Scottish and French cuisine provides dishes such as medallions of venison with bramble and mead sauce, and pan-fried Aberdeen Angus steak served with sherry and mushroom sauce. Have a wander through the Monastery Garden before or after your meal. Delightful views across Spey Bay and the Moray Firth.

Dryburgh — Dryburgh Abbey

St Boswells, Dryburgh, Borders TD6 0RQ
Telephone: (0835) 22261 £50
Fax: (0835) 23945
Open: lunch + dinner daily
Meals served: lunch 12.15-2, dinner 7-8.30
Recently refurbished Victorian hotel near the Abbey, on the banks of the Tweed.

Dulnain Bridge — Auchendean Lodge

Dulnain Bridge, Grantown-on-Spey, Highland PH26 3LU
Telephone: (047 985) 347 £40
Open: dinner daily (closed 2 wks Jan)
Meals served: dinner 7.30-9

'The field of shelter' is what the name means and that's what you'll find at this converted hunting and fishing lodge. The views over the river Spey – with the Cairngorm Mountains beyond – are hard to beat and the surrounding countryside offers all manner of leisure pursuits. The hotel itself is warm and cosy with 7 well-appointed bedrooms. Period furnishings are to be found all over the house lend character and charm. Simple dishes are the best choices from the 4-course menu.

Dunblane — Cromlix House

Kinbuck, Dunblane, Central FK15 9JT
Telephone: (0786) 822125 £75
Fax: (0786) 825450
Open: lunch + dinner daily (closed Xmas)
Meals served: lunch 12.30-2, dinner 7.30-9.30 (Sun 7.30-9)

Whether you want to go tramping across the moors (this Victorian house is set in its own 5000 acre estate), salmon and sea trout fishing, or just relax before a roaring log fire with a glass of whisky (or in my case champagne) at your elbow, then Cromlix House will fit the bill. Priding itself on a tradition of country house hospitality, the hotel manages a winning combination of warmth, quality and restfulness. Quite rightly it has established itself as one of the best hotels north of the border. In the kitchen Ian Corkhill is the new chef and he takes full advantage of the readily available local produce. Thus game, fish and Cromlix's very own Jacob lamb feature strongly. So, pack your rod and reel and a copy of Robbie Burns and head for Dunblane to experience the Scottish tradition of country house hospitality.

| DUNDONNELL | Dundonnell Hotel |

Dundonnell, By Garve, Highland IV23 2QR
Telephone: (085 483) 204 £45
Fax: (085 483) 366
Open: dinner daily (closed Dec-Xmas, New Year-Easter)
Meals served: dinner 7-8.30
Splendid location, family owned and run.

| EDINBURGH | Alp-Horn |

167 Rose Street, Edinburgh, Lothian EH2 4LS
Telephone: 031-225 4787 £40
Open: lunch + dinner Mon-Sat (closed Bank Holidays, 1 wk Jan, 2 wks Jul)
Meals served: lunch 12-2, dinner 6.30-10
Down-to-earth Swiss restaurant, excellent rösti. Popular, long-running establishment.

EDINBURGH — L'Auberge

56 St Mary Street, Edinburgh, Lothian EH1 1SX
Telephone: 031-556 5888 **£55**
Open: lunch + dinner daily (closed 25+26 Dec, 2 wks Jan)
Meals served: lunch 12.15-2, dinner 6.30-9.30 (Sat 6.30-10)

The entente cordials between British and French forces in the kitchen is producing some good results. David Wencker's restaurant of some 17 years standing seems to have hit form of late. Hurry along!

EDINBURGH — Caledonian Hotel

Princes Street, Edinburgh, Lothian EH1 2AB
Telephone: 031-225 2433   *Pompadour Room:* **£90**
Fax: 031-225 6632   *Carriages Restaurant:* **£55**
Open: lunch Mon-Fri, dinner Mon-Sat
Meals served: lunch 12.30-2.30, dinner 6.30-10.30 (Sun 6.30-10)
Open: lunch + dinner daily
Meals served: lunch 12.30-2.30, dinner 6.30-10

On the site of the Old Caledonian Railway Station, the 'Caley' carries on the railway tradition in the Pullman Lounge and Platform 1 bars, as well as the Carriages Restaurant. This refurbished restaurant offers a wide selection of favourites – haggis with neaps and tatties, roast leg of lamb with rosemary and gravy, grilled whole lemon sole with a butter and chive sauce. Upstairs is the more prestigious Pompadour Restaurant where the capable chef Tony Binks is allowed full rein on the 'Legends Choice' lunch menu – a chance to sample renowned Scottish dishes. Thus pot-roast haunch of Highland venison and honey-roast Border duckling feature as main dishes. In the evening things are rather more French (with English sub-titles) and one way of trying the extensive selection is to go for the 5-course Menu Dégustation. Formal service, and wines which range in price and country of origin, the admirable list of half bottles includes some 40 items. The Caledonian is undoubtedly one of the top hotels in Edinburgh both for its cuisine and accommodation, there are 240 bedrooms.

EDINBURGH Channings Hotel
South Learmouth Gardens, Edinburgh, Lothian EH4 1EZ
Telephone: 031-315 2226
Fax: 031-332 9631   £70
Open: lunch + dinner daily
Meals served: lunch 12.30-2, dinner 6.30-9.30
48-bedroomed hotel, popular with businesspeople and tourists. Useful downstairs brasserie-cum-restaurant.

EDINBURGH Doric Tavern Wine Bar & Bistro
15 Market Street, Edinburgh, Lothian EH1 1DE
Telephone: 031-225 1084   £40
Open: lunch + dinner Mon-Sat
Meals served: lunch 12-2.30, dinner 7-10.30
Friendly bistro, popular with a cross-section of citizens.

EDINBURGH Howard Hotel
36 Great King Street, Edinburgh, Lothian EH3 6QH
Telephone: 031-557 3500   £70
Fax: 031-557 6515
Open: lunch Sun-Fri, dinner daily (closed Xmas/New Year)
Meals served: lunch 12.30-2, dinner 7.30-9.45
Up for sale at present – some of the best rooms in Edinburgh. All set to rediscover its town house character. Let's hope things are sorted out soon.

EDINBURGH Howie's Restaurant
75 St Leonard's Street, Edinburgh, Lothian
Telephone: 031-668 2917   £30
Open: lunch Wed-Fri+Sun, dinner daily (closed 25+26 Dec, 1+2 Jan)
Meals served: lunch 12-2.30, dinner 6-10.30 (later during Festival)
Friendly, informal, unlicensed bistro.

EDINBURGH Indian Cavalry Club
3 Atholl Place, Edinburgh, Lothian EH3 8HP
Telephone: 031-228 3282   £50
Open: lunch + dinner daily
Meals served: lunch 12-2.30, dinner 5.30-11.30
Staff dressed in military-style uniforms, there are some unusual dishes on the menu.

EDINBURGH Le Marché Noir
2/4 Eyre Place, Edinburgh, Lothian EH3 5EP
Telephone: 031-558 1608   £45
Open: lunch Mon-Fri, dinner daily (closed 25+26 Dec, 1+2 Jan)
Meals served: lunch 12-2, dinner 7-10
As popular as ever for its good value menu (cheaper at lunch). Simply described French dishes, great atmosphere.

EDINBURGH	Martin's

70 Rose Street, North Lane, Edinburgh, Lothian EH2 3DX
Telephone: 031-225 3106 £60
Open: lunch Tue-Fri, dinner Mon-Sat (closed 4 wks Dec/Jan, 1 wk Oct)
Meals served: lunch 12-2, dinner 7-10

One of those restaurants where the immediate surroundings belie what's to be found inside. Martin and Gay Irons will win you over the moment you walk in and take a seat in the simple dining room with its white tablecloths and pink napkins. The menus come on little cards with a cartoon at the top. Chef David Macrae has now moved on, but his number two – Forbes Scott – has ably filled his shoes and thus the cooking has been kept on an even keel.

Ingredients are excellent and virtually all the vegetables are organic. For dinner recently you could have had a warm salad of duck breast with smoked bacon and pine kernels to start, with poached fillet of sole and brill with a red pepper and basil coulis as a main dish. A nice selection of puds included apple and walnut strudel, chocolate tart and kummel parfait with strawberries. Some good half bottles on the concise wine list.

EDINBURGH	Pierre Victoire

10 Victoria Street, Edinburgh, Lothian EH1 2HE
Telephone: 031-225 1721 £40
Fax: 031-557 5216
Open: lunch + dinner Mon-Sat, + Sun in Aug (closed 25+26 Dec, 1+2 Jan)
Meals served: lunch 12-3, dinner 6-11

As of this moment in time there are three offshoots to this, the original, Pierre Victoire in Victoria Street. Chef/owner Pierre Levicky seems to have hit on a winning combination and being the right price range with his straight-down-the-line bistro food and atmosphere. Grilled mussels with garlic and pernod butter, a warm brioche with leeks, gruyère cheese and crispy bacon, rare roast rib of beef with horseradish cream to follow, or baked salmon steak from a choice of 6 starters, 6 or so main courses and desserts all at the same price. As Pierre says on his menus 'Bon Appétit'. If you like this one go and check out the others at 38 Grassmarket (also in Edinburgh), 18 Union Street in Leith and 75 Castle Street in Inverness.

EDINBURGH	Round Table

31 Jeffrey Street, Edinburgh, Lothian EH1 1DH
Telephone: 031-557 3032 £30
Open: all day Tue-Sat + daytime Mon (closed some Bank Holidays)
Meals served: 10-10 (closed 5.30-6.30), Mon 10-5.30 only
Good fish dishes.

EDINBURGH	Sheraton Hotel

1 Festival Square, Edinburgh, Lothian EH3 9SR
Telephone: 031-229 9131 £60
Fax: 031-228 4510
Open: lunch + dinner daily
Meals served: lunch 12-2, dinner 7-9
Modern hotel near Edinburgh castle, facilities on offer include a health and leisure club.

EDINBURGH — The Shore

3/4 The Shore, Leith, Edinburgh, Lothian EH6 6QW
Telephone: 031-553 5080   £45
Open: lunch + dinner daily
Meals served: lunch 12-2.30, dinner 6-10
Fish restaurant on the Leith waterfront.

EDINBURGH — Szechuan House

95 Gilmore Place, Edinburgh, Lothian EH3 9NU
Telephone: 031-229 4655   £20
Open: lunch Sat+Sun, dinner daily
Meals served: dinner 5.30-12
Friendly Szechuan restaurant striving for authenticity.

EDINBURGH — Vintners Room, The Vaults

87 Giles Street, Leith, Edinburgh, Lothian EH6 6BZ
Telephone: 031-554 6767   £55
Open: lunch + dinner Mon-Sat (closed 2 wks Xmas)
Meals served: lunch 12-2.30, dinner 7-10.30

Having only just established itself on the gastronomic map of Scotland the Vintners Rooms' fate now hangs in the balance as it is on the market this year. Devotees of Tim Cumming's food will have to wait with bated breath for the outcome. Watch this space!

ERISKA — Isle of Eriska

Eriska, Ledaig, by Oban, Strathclyde PA37 1SD
Telephone: (063 172) 371   £75
Fax: (063 172) 531
Open: dinner daily (closed Nov-Mar)
Meals served: dinner 7.30-9

It's rather an understatement to say you're getting away from it all when you come to stay at the Isle of Eriska. You can walk for hours on the island without seeing a soul, enjoying a landscape the memory of which you'll treasure for the rest of your life. Robin and Sheena Buchanan-Smith run the hotel, which is a converted baronial mansion. How it came to be built in 1884 before there was a bridge is something to ponder during your stay. Just about all the 16 bedrooms are named after the Western Isles. Very comfortable surroundings are made even more pleasant by the friendly service. In the Edwardian-style dining room you are offered 5 courses, each with alternative and normally including a roast carved at your table. As much as possible the food is home produced. This coupled with attentive hosts makes Eriska a special place to visit. Comprehensive wine list.

Fort William   Crannog Seafood Restaurant

Town Pier, Fort William, Highland PS33 7NG
Telephone: (0397) 705589   £35
Open: lunch + dinner daily (closed Tue + Wed in winter, closed Nov)
Meals served: lunch 12-2.30, dinner 6-9.30

A converted ticket office and bait store slap bang on the quay. Unfussy surroundings and service. You come here for fish and fish is what you gets! Crannog bouillabaisse, langoustines in garlic butter and pan-fried salmon are options written up on the blackboard.

Fort William   The Factor's House

Torlundy, Fort William, Highland PH33 6SN
Telephone: (0397) 705767   £45
Fax: (0397) 702953
Open: dinner Tue-Sun (closed mid Nov-mid Mar)
Meals served: dinner 7-9

Seven-bedroomed country house hotel and little sister to Inverlochy Castle (the Factor's House was originally the castle estate manager's residence). Homely and informal atmosphere with eclectic collection of ornaments dotted around. New chef Lorraine Chapman cooks old Scottish favourites at reasonable prices.

SCOTLAND

FORT WILLIAM — Inverlochy Castle

Torlundy, Fort William, Highland PH33 6SN
Telephone: (0397) 702177/8
Fax: (0397) 702953
Open: lunch + dinner daily (closed mid Nov-mid Mar)
Meals served: lunch 12.30-1.45, dinner 7.15-9.30

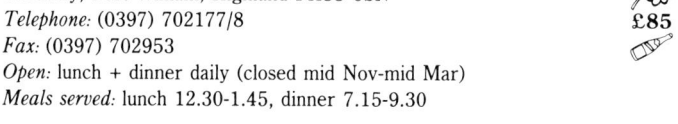

£85

Never easy to please, Queen Victoria fell in love with the West Highlands at first sight. 'I never saw a lovelier or more romantic spot' she noted in her diary. Who knows, then, what she would have made of Inverlochy Castle? For here, this 19th-century castle stands in its own 500 acres of grounds in the foothills of Ben Nevis with breath-taking views all around. If you're not already over-awed by the scenery, wait until you get inside – it's quite extraordinary. Even American visitors have been known to speak in hushed voices as they walk around for the first time! Yet manager Michael Leonard and his staff are adept at making you feel at home despite the scale and luxury of the place.

The arrival of chef David Whiffen has restored Inverlochy to its rightful gastronomic standards. Charmingly self-effacing – he claims his cooking is 'simple' – David executes dishes with aplomb and uses only the best raw materials. Fillet of sole and scallops bonne femme and noisettes of lamb Edward VII are guaranteed to please. As should be expected, the dishes follow the descriptions, for instance, Loch Linnhe prawns served with a herb-scented mayonnaise, or brawn with home-made piccalilli from the starters, or roast tail of monkfish with grain mustard, and roast loin of roe deer with roasted pears and walnuts from the main courses. Some impressive bottles on the wine list have prices to match! *See also p279 – our Clover Awards section.*

GAIRLOCH — Creag Mor

Charleston, Gairloch, Highland IV21 2AH
Telephone: (0445) 2068
Fax: (0445) 2044
Open: dinner daily
Meals served: dinner 7-10

£50

Useful hotel in the area, personally run by the Niettos. There are now 17 bedrooms.

GLAMIS — Castleton House

Eassie, By Glamis, Forfar, Tayside DD8 1SJ
Telephone: (030 784) 340
Fax: (030 784) 506
Open: lunch + dinner daily
Meals served: lunch 12-2.30, dinner 7-9.30

£50

Good food, friendly service and the surrounding moors and mountains make this an excellent holiday base.

GLASGOW — Brasserie on West Regent Street

176 West Regent Street, Glasgow, Strathclyde G2 8HF
Telephone: 041-248 3801
Open: all day Mon-Fri, lunch + dinner Sat (closed Bank Holidays)
Meals served: 12-11, lunch Sat 12-3, dinner Sat 6-12

£40

Useful post-theatre venue – very much a Scottish interpretation of a French brasserie!

Glasgow	Buttery

652 Argyle Street, Glasgow, Strathclyde G3 8UF
Telephone: 041-221 8188 **£70**
Open: lunch Mon-Fri, dinner Mon-Sat (closed Bank Holidays)
Meals served: lunch 12-2.30, dinner 7-10.30

Browse among the objets d'art before settling yourself in the dining room where you'll find plenty more to keep you interested. Chef Stephen Johnson's elegantly written menus include starters such as leaf pastry parcel with vegetables on a curried chutney cream, and venison and sweetbread terrine with port and thyme aspic. Main dishes can be a roast supreme of guinea fowl on a spicy turnip and smoked onion jus, or pan-fried skate wing in a prawn, caper and tarragon butter. A separate vegetarian menu offers several options at each course. As well as caffeine-free coffee, they also list a selection of teas and tisanes – apple and cinnamon, rose-hip and nettle among others. An established favourite in the area.

Glasgow	D'Arcy's

Basement Courtyard, Princes Square, Glasgow, Strathclyde
Telephone: 041-226 4309 **£35**
Open: all day Mon-Sat, daytime Sun (closed 25+26 Dec, 1+2 Jan)
Meals served: 9.30am-midnight, Sun 11-6
Wines by the bottle or glass, cross-indexed to match the food.

Glasgow	October Café

Princes Square, Off Buchanan Street, Glasgow, Strathclyde G1 3JN
Telephone: 041-221 0303 **£35**
Open: lunch + dinner Mon-Sat
Meals served: lunch 12-2.30, dinner 6-11

If you're one of Glasgow's 'beautiful people' then you'll know all about the October Café, in fact you might have worked here as well. Service is laid back. Current 'in' dishes are listed on the menu – grilled swordfish steak, marinated rib steak with cracked pepper and stir-fried chicken with mange tout and spring onion. Food at the bar is cheaper and quicker – BLT sandwiches and dips with fried potato skins for instance.

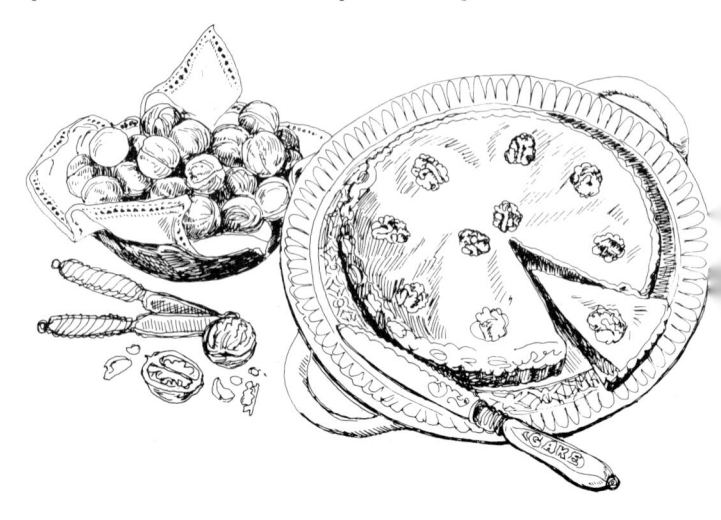

GLASGOW — One Devonshire Gardens

1 Devonshire Gardens, Glasgow, Strathclyde G12 0UX
Telephone: 041-339 2001
Fax: 041-337 1663
Open: lunch Sun-Fri, dinner daily
Meals served: lunch 12.30-2, dinner 7-10

£70

From the brochure you'll gather that the late, great Leonard Bernstein stayed here and enjoyed every bit of it. It's easy to see that the luxurious hotel would appeal to him – he could even listen to one of his recent recordings on one of the CD players installed in each of the 27 bedrooms. Hushed lighting, muted colours and perfectly tuned service are carefully orchestrated allowing you to experience the style and sumptuousness of the establishment, but also enjoy its warmth and comfort. Chef Andrew Fleming's cooking is in harmony with the elegant rooms, and roast guinea fowl, medallions of monkfish and tournedos of beef Rossini were among recent main courses at dinner. An interesting wine list includes 6 organic wines, and over 30 half bottles and show the depth of the hotel's cellar.

To quote Leonard Bernstein, 'A wonderful stay – friendly and pure theatre – truly inspirational'. I look forward to my next visit.

GLASGOW — Ristorante Caprese

217 Buchanan Street, Glasgow, Strathclyde
Telephone: 041-332 3070
Open: lunch Mon-Fri, dinner Mon-Sat (closed Bank Holidays)
Meals served: lunch 12-2.30, dinner 5.30-11

£40

This basement old-style Italian restaurant offers all the traditional Italian dishes, with a regular clientele, bustling service. Cheer yourself up on a drizzly Glasgow day with a spaghetti alle vongole, a bistecca pizzaiola and a bottle of Valpolicella!

GLASGOW — Rogano

11 Exchange Place, Glasgow, Strathclyde G1 3AN
Telephone: 041-248 4055
Fax: 041-248 2608
Open: lunch + dinner daily (closed Bank Holidays)
Meals served: lunch 12-2.30, dinner 7-11 (Sun 7-10)

£60

Virtually unchanged since 1935, Art Deco ground floor restaurant, basement café. Fish a strong point.

GLASGOW — Two Fat Ladies

88 Dumbarton Road, Glasgow, Strathclyde G11 6NX
Telephone: 041-339 1944
Open: dinner Tue-Sat (closed 2 wks Xmas/New Year)
Meals served: dinner 6.30-10.30

£50

Lots of fresh fish and vegetables are on offer here. Even the prices are expressed as .88 pence, to continue the theme!

Glasgow	Ubiquitous Chip

12 Ashton Lane, Glasgow, Strathclyde G12 8SJ
Telephone: 041-334 5007 £50
Open: lunch + dinner daily (closed Xmas/New Year)
Meals served: lunch 12-2.30, dinner 5.30-11

This Glasgow legend munches on under the steady hand of Ron Clydesdale with a growing reputation for reasonably priced wines both to enjoy here or take away from the wine shop. Eat either in the ground floor glassed-in courtyard or Upstairs at the Chip which has a cheaper but no less interesting menu. Downstairs some of the old favourites reappear and beside the venison haggis and neaps, they offer a vegetarian version or perhaps you would prefer the Loch Fyne mussels farcie. Excellent choices from main courses include Aberdeen Angus steak, a braised silverside of Scottish beef or a saddle of Ayreshire hare sprinkled with toasted pine kernels and served with a rich game sauce. Good puds and friendly service.

Gullane	Greywalls Hotel

Muirfield, Gullane, Lothian EH31 2EG
Telephone: (0620) 842144 £70
Fax: (0620) 842241
Open: lunch + dinner daily (closed Dec-Mar)
Meals served: lunch 12.30-2, dinner 7.30-9.30

The house is by Lutyens, the gardens by Gertrude Jekyll – so there's two reasons for visiting Greywalls. If you want some more, then there's its convenient location to Muirfield golf course, the homely hotel atmosphere, chef Paul Baron's cooking and, last but not least, a real eye-opener of a wine list.

Gullane	La Potinière

Main Street, Gullane, Lothian EH31 2AA
Telephone: (0620) 843214 £60
Open: lunch Sun-Tue + Thurs, dinner Fri+Sat (closed 25+26 Dec, 1+2 Jan, 1 wk
  Jun, 1 wk Oct)
Meals served: lunch at 1, dinner at 8

La Potinière is a labour of love for husband and wife team David and Hilary Brown. Profit margins aren't the raison d'être here – if they started to lose interest in what they were doing *then* the restaurant would be in trouble. Hilary's cooking never ceases to amaze, all the more since – if anything – it's getting better! David's wine list is a positive wonder including as it does nearly 400 wines and yet managing to be affordable as well. That's some achievement. Let's hope they carry on enjoying themselves!

Grippy.

ONE OF the differences between greatness and mere eccentricity, is an ability in the truly great *to draw out the genius* in another.

So it was with some smacking of the lips that we heard of a recent tasting organized by Decanter Magazine.

Three of Scotland's *MOST LAUDED* malt whiskies were to be rated in terms of 'partnership appeal' with that other great Scottish contribution to world gastronomy~ *SMOKED SPEYSIDE SALMON*.

And which one emerged with commendations such as 'a real corker...', 'full, strong, dry *grippy flavours*' and 'the perfect partner'?

Yes, you have *smoked it out*. 'I love it and would recommend it.'

The Macallan. The Malt.

| INGLISTON | Norton House |

Ingliston, Edinburgh EH28 8LX
Telephone: 031-333 1275
Fax: 031-333 5305 £60
Open: lunch + dinner daily
Meals served: lunch 12-2, dinner 7-9.30
Forty-six bedroomed Victorian mansion with a conservatory restaurant.

| INVERNESS | Bunchrew House |

Bunchrew, Inverness, Highland IV3 6TA
Telephone: (0463) 234917 £55
Fax: (0463) 710620
Open: lunch + dinner daily
Meals served: lunch 12-2, dinner 7-9

Another of those splendid Scottish houses that are dotted across the Highlands. The new bedrooms are now in operation and are receiving the finishing touches. Alan and Patsy Wilson still hold the fort and maintain the friendly atmosphere. Wonderful views are to be had of Ben Wyvis and the Black Isle.

| INVERNESS | Culloden House |

Culloden, Inverness, Highland 1VI 2NZ
Telephone: (0463) 790461 £70
Fax: (0463) 792181
Open: lunch + dinner daily
Meals served: lunch 12.30-2, dinner 7-9

This grand Georgian Mansion is rather special and the lounge and private rooms are particularly impressive. Local fish, lamb, venison and beef feature strongly on chef Michael Simpson's menus. Efficient service in the dining room and throughout the hotel is ably led by owners Ian and Marjory McKenzie. Good wine list with generous selection of half-bottles.

| INVERNESS | Dunain Park |

Inverness, Highland IV3 6JN
Telephone: (0463) 230512 £50
Fax: (0463) 224532
Open: dinner daily (closed 2 wks Feb)
Meals served: dinner 7-9

A quiet 14-bedroomed country hotel offering some ambitious cooking using local produce. The wine list is especially fine and features some 35 half bottles. Lunch is available by arrangement.

KENTALLEN OF APPIN — Ardsheal House

Kentallen of Appin, Highland PA38 4BX
Telephone: (063 174) 227   £75
Fax: (063 174) 342
Open: lunch + dinner daily (closed early Nov-wk before Easter)
Meals served: lunch 12-2, dinner at 8.15

Built in the early 1500s as a manor house of the Stewarts, the building was destroyed during the Uprisings in 1745 and rebuilt in 1760. A couple of centuries and a few additions later and Ardsheal House stands proud as a lovely country house hotel. Owners Robert and Jane Taylor are wonderful hosts and make everyone feel one of the party. Dinner is in the country house style, with introductions by Robert Taylor. The food continues to be well thought out and fits well with the style of the dining room and hotel. Magnificent views over Loch Linnhe.

KENTALLEN OF APPIN — Holly Tree
Kentallen of Appin, Argyll, Highland PA38 4BY
Telephone: (063 174) 292   £60
Fax: (063 174) 345
Open: lunch + dinner daily
Meals served: lunch 12.30-2, dinner 7.30-10
Railway station turned hotel, 11 well-equipped bedrooms.

KILCHRENAN — Ardanaiseig
Kilchrenan, By Taynuilt, Strathclyde PA35 1JG
Telephone: (086 63) 333   £75
Fax: (086 63) 222
Open: lunch + dinner daily (closed Nov-Easter)
Meals served: lunch 12-2, dinner 7.30-9
Now owned by Tom & Carmen Robbins, set amid glorious views over Loch Awe. 14 bedrooms. Beautiful rhododendron gardens.

KILCHRENAN — Taychreggan Hotel
Kilchrenan, By Taynuilt, Strathclyde PA35 1HQ
Telephone: (086 63) 211   £55
Fax: (086 63) 244
Open: lunch + dinner daily (closed Nov-Feb)
Meals served: lunch 12.15-2.15, dinner 7.30-8.45
15-bedroomed hotel, formerly a cattle drovers' inn. Views of Loch Awe.

KILDRUMMY
Kildrummy Castle

Kildrummy, Alford, Grampian AB3 8RA
Telephone: (097 55) 71288 £55
Fax: (097 55) 71345
Open: lunch + dinner daily (closed 3 wks Jan)
Meals served: lunch 12.30-1.45 (Sun 12.30-1.15), dinner 7-9

The beautifully carved staircase would be justification enough for your visit, but there's are lots more reasons besides – charming public rooms, well-equipped bedrooms and attentive staff. The gardens are also lovely throughout the year and there are the ruins of the old castle to explore.

KILFINAN
Kilfinan Hotel

Kilfinan, By Tighnabruaich, Strathclyde PA21 2AP
Telephone: (070 082) 201 £45
Fax: (070 082) 205
Open: lunch + dinner daily
Meals served: lunch 12-2, dinner 7.30-9.30
Sporting hotel, eleven bedrooms, traditional food in restaurant.

KILLIECRANKIE
Killiecrankie Hotel

Killiecrankie, By Pitlochry, Tayside PH16 5LG
Telephone: (0796) 473220 £45
Fax: (0796) 472451
Open: lunch + dinner daily (closed Jan+Feb)
Meals served: lunch 12.30-2, dinner 6.30-9.30
Superb woodland setting by the River Garry. 11 bedrooms. All the staff are dressed in tartan.

KILMORE
Glenfeochan House

Kilmore, Oban, Strathclyde PA34 4QR
Telephone: (063 177) 273 £60
Fax: (063 177) 624
Open: dinner daily (closed Nov-early Mar)
Meals served: dinner at 8

Look out to Loch Feochan from your bedroom window or wander around the 5-acre garden with its rare trees and rhododendrons. This characterful hotel built in 1875 with turrets and ornate plaster work is run with care and attention by the owners, David and Patricia Baber. In the dining room there's some traditional food, but with some imaginative tweaks from Patricia who is an ex-Cordon Bleu teacher. Delightful gardens set in 6 acres, including a Victorian walled garden. Glenfeochan House guarantees a peaceful, relaxing break.

KILMUN
Fern Grove

Kilmun, Strathclyde PA23 8SB
Telephone: (036 984) 334 £50
Open: lunch + dinner daily
Meals served: lunch 12-2.30 (Sat+Sun 12-3), dinner 7-9.30
Family-run country hotel, home-cooked fare.

KINCLAVEN BY STANLEY — Ballathie House

Kinclaven by Stanley, Tayside PH1 4QN
Telephone: (0250) 883268 £55
Fax: (0250) 883396
Open: lunch + dinner daily (closed 25+26 Dec, 3 wks Feb)
Meals served: lunch 12.15-1.45, dinner 6.45-8.30

You can eat in style here in the dining room of this Baronial style mansion overlooking the River Tay. Chef Stephen Robertson's cooking includes some pretty ambitious sounding combinations which work well, while the simpler, more straightforward dishes using fresh ingredients are my preference. The 27 attractive bedrooms and charming service make for a pleasant place to stay.

KINGUSSIE — The Cross

25 High Street, Kingussie, Highland PH21 1HX
(moves to Ardbroilach Road 1/3/93)
Telephone: (0540) 661166 £60
Open: dinner Tue-Sat (closed 3 wks May/Jun, 6 wks Nov/Dec)
Meals served: dinner 6.30-9 (Sat 6.30-9.30)

The Hadleys are moving in March 1993 to the new premises (called the Old Tweedmill) within shouting distance of their present location. This new setting has 4 acres of grounds, and alongside the restaurant runs the Gynack Burn. They are determined to keep to the same format of restaurant with rooms with the emphasis remaining firmly on the food. Gastronomically I doubt there'll be any changes and Ruth and Tony's talents in the cooking and wine departments respectively will continue to keep The Cross firmly in its place as one of Scotland's leading restaurants.

Some of Ruth's recent dishes on the set-price dinner menu (with 3 choices at each course) have included mousseline of pike served warm with a creamed prawn sauce, and following the soup perhaps half a roast wild Gressingham duck, served with a blackcurrant sauce. Good selection of cheeses and a pear and raspberry upside-down pudding to finish. Excellent wine list.

KIRKNEWTON — Dalmahoy Hotel

Kirknewton, Lothian EH27 8EB
Telephone: 031-333 1845 £65
Fax: 031-335 3203
Open: lunch Sun-Fri, dinner daily
Meals served: lunch 12-2, dinner 7-10
115 bedrooms, leisure centre, and a restaurant that overlooks the 2 golf courses.

LINLITHGOW — Champany Inn

Champany, Linlithgow, Lothian EH49 7LU
Telephone: (050 683) 4532
Open: lunch Mon-Fri, dinner Mon-Sat (closed 2 wks Xmas)
Meals served: lunch 12.30-2, dinner 7-10

£80

Not one for the vegetarians, the Champany Inn has built its reputation on charcoal-grilled Aberdeen Angus beef – possibly the best steaks you'll find in the length and breadth of this island. Salads, baked potatoes, chips and mushrooms come as accompaniments and there's also fish and lobsters to choose from. A feast's in store! The strength of this restaurant is really the quality of its produce and the character of the owners, Clive and Anne Davidson, who concentrate on giving the customers what they want – which is an excellently prepared variety of steaks ranging from rib-eye to Chateaubriand for two, or some excellent char-grilled salmon plus lobsters and crayfish from the tank. Start with some of their own smoked salmon or some Scottish Islay Oysters. The wine cellar has won almost every award going and is truly comprehensive and deserves a half-hour's read with an aperitif before you order. *See also p279 – our Clover Awards section.*

LINLITHGOW — Champany Inn Chop & Ale House

Champany, Linlithgow, Lothian EH49 7LU
Telephone: (050 683) 4532
Open: lunch + dinner daily (closed 2 wks Xmas)
Meals served: lunch 12-2 (Sat 12-2.15, Sun 12.30-2.30), dinner 6.30-10

£40

A more modest version of the Champany Inn both in terms of price and portions. However, you might still find it difficult to polish off what's on your plate. Premium quality steak and burgers hog the limelight, so to speak.

MARKINCH — Balbirnie House

16 Rothesay Mews, Markinch, By Glenrothes, Fife KY7 6NE
Telephone: (0592) 610066
Fax: (0592) 660529
Open: lunch + dinner daily
Meals served: lunch 12-2, dinner 7.30-9.30 (Sat 7.30-10)

£55

Lovely house, 18th-century classical proportions, gallery with vaulted ceiling, marble fireplaces, oil paintings, thirty bedrooms.

MARYCULTER — Maryculter House

South Deeside Road, Maryculter, Grampian AB1 0BB
Telephone: (0224) 732124
Fax: (0224) 733510
Open: lunch daily, dinner Mon-Sat
Meals served: lunch 12.30-2.30, dinner 7-9.30

£55

Traditional hospitality, not far from Aberdeen.

MELROSE — Burts Hotel

Market Square, Melrose, Borders TD6 9PN
Telephone: (089 682) 2285
Fax: (089 682) 2870
Open: lunch + dinner daily (closed 26 Dec)
Meals served: lunch 12-2, dinner 7-9.30 (Sun 7-9)

£50

Situated on the side of Melrose Market Square, run by owners Graham & Anne Henderson. 21 bedrooms.

MOFFAT — Well View Hotel

Ballplay Road, Moffat, Dumfries & Galloway DG10 9JU
Telephone: (0683) 20184
Open: lunch + dinner daily (closed 1 wk Jan, 1 wk Nov)
Meals served: lunch 12.15-1.15, dinner 6.30-8.30

£55

Good home cooking, 7 bedrooms.

MUIR-OF-ORD — Dower House

Highfield, Muir-of-Ord, Highland IV6 7XN
Telephone: (0463) 870096
Fax: (0463) 870090
Open: dinner daily (closed Xmas, 2 wks Feb, 1 wk Oct)
Meals served: dinner 7.30-8.30

£55

With only 5 bedrooms, the Dower House feels more like a private house than a hotel. Owner and chef Robyn Aitchison offers a limited choice menu in the modern British style. Thus langoustine and avocado salad precedes a cream of spinach soup, followed by fillet of venison with a piquant sauce and poached pears. A chocolate soufflé and cheeses round the dinner off nicely.

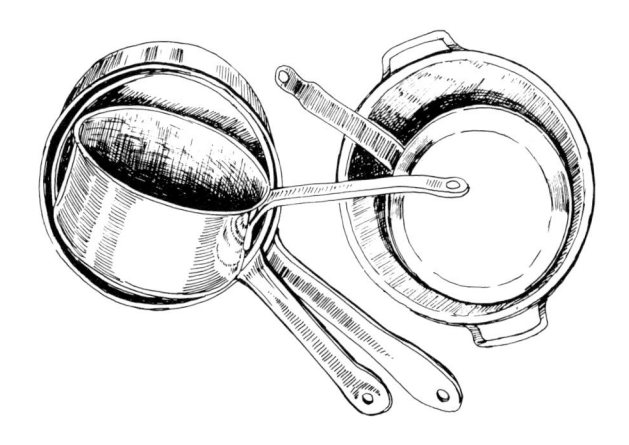

NAIRN — Clifton Hotel

Viewfield Street, Nairn, Highland IV12 4HW
Telephone: (0667) 53119 £50
Fax: (0667) 52836
Open: dinner daily (closed Nov-Mar)
Meals served: dinner 7-9.30

Ask around among the other guests and you'll no doubt find many who are coming back not just for the first time, but maybe the third or fourth. Who knows, some may even be able to tell you what the owner Mr Macintyre was like as a wee bairn in the days when his father ran the hotel! Today he's quite a character and not the least of the reasons why people come back, year in year out. The rooms have bags of personality with antiques, objets d'art, paintings and classical music wafting through and there's some good food to be had as well from the French style menu. Add to this home-made bread, marmalade and oat-cakes and a classy wine list numbering well over 300 bottles including some impressive red bordeaux. Plenty of whiskies are also there for a taste of Scotland's pride and joy. A relaxing place to stay.

NEWMILL-ON-TEVIOT — Old Forge Restaurant

Newmill-on-Teviot, Nr Hawick, Borders TD9 0JU
Telephone: (0450) 85298 £35
Open: dinner Tue-Sat (closed Bank Holidays, 2 wks May/Jun, 2 wks Nov)
Meals served: dinner 7-9.30

Booking is essential at this small restaurant run by Bill and Margaret Irving. An established favourite in the district, the food mixes some firm favourites with more adventurous combinations. Good home-made breads. The wide-ranging wine list contains some very cheap drinking. Given the size of the operation, a late arrival for an early sitting can cause havoc with the service. Be on time!

NEWTONMORE — Ard-na-Coille Hotel

Kingussie Road, Newtonmore, Highland PH20 1AY
Telephone: (0540) 673214 £50
Fax: (0540) 673453
Open: dinner daily (closed 6 wks Nov/Dec, 1 wk Apr, 1 wk Sep)
Meals served: dinner at 7.45

In Gaelic it means 'high in the woods' and certainly the air is bracing up here amongst the pine trees. Nancy Ferrier and Barry Cottam are the hard working owners and they've done much for this one-time shooting lodge with 7 bedrooms. Menus are set 5 courses which result in some good food being presented. The soup might possibly be carrot, ginger and coriander; the main courses roast guinea fowl with the legs served stuffed and the breast roasted separately with a tarragon and shallot sauce, or a char-grilled fillet of salmon with an unusual shellfish and whisky sauce. Good vegetables and an exceptionally interesting wine list make each day of your stay a pleasure. They want you to come back again – you'll want to as well!

SCOTLAND

North Berwick — Harding's Restaurant
2 Station Road, North Berwick, Lothian EH39 4AU
Telephone: (0620) 4737   £45
Open: lunch + dinner Wed-Sat (closed 1 wk Xmas, 4 wks Jan/Feb, 1 wk Oct)
Meals served: lunch 12-2, dinner 7-9
Local produce is the basis of the short lunch menu and daily set dinner menus.

North Middleton — Borthwick Castle
North Middleton, Nr Gorebridge, Lothian EN23 4QY
Telephone: (0875) 20514   £75
Fax: (0875) 21702
Open: dinner daily
Meals served: dinner 7-9
Set in a small glen just south of Edinburgh the castle dated back to 1430. Traditional Scottish cooking.

Oban — Knipoch Hotel
by Oban, Strathclyde PA34 4QT
Telephone: (085 26) 251   £70
Fax: (085 26) 249
Open: dinner daily (closed mid Nov-mid Feb)
Meals served: dinner 7.30-9
Family run hotel close by the water's edge in a wooded setting. Numerous sporting facilities can be arranged.

Onich — Allt-nan-Ros Hotel
Onich, by Fort William, Highland PH33 6RY
Telephone: (085 53) 250/210   £40
Fax: (085 53) 462
Open: lunch + dinner daily (closed early Nov-Mar)
Meals served: lunch 12.30-2, dinner 7-8.30
16-bedroomed, family run hotel situated between Glencoe and Ben Nevis.

Peat Inn — Peat Inn

Peat Inn, By Cupar, Fife KY15 5LH
Telephone: (033 484) 206   £70
Fax: (033 484) 530
Open: lunch + dinner Tue-Sat (closed 2 wks Nov, 2 wks Jan)
Meals served: lunch at 1, dinner 7-9.30

To make your stay worthwhile, book yourself into one of the 8 suites which will allow you to enjoy the full delights of the extensive wine list. David and Patricia Wilson work hard maintaining standards at this award-winning establishment, perhaps illustrated by David's comment that 'If I were to die in the next five minutes, I would go happy'. That's some claim, but reflects David's thrill in doing what he does, day in day out. Hardly surprising then, that he consistently figures as one of Scotland's top chefs. An excellent way of sampling the full range of his talents is to try the Tasting Menu, served in slightly smaller portions. It saves you the problem of choosing from the always tempting menu which includes starters such as julienne of pigeon breast which is served in a light beef broth with a range of pulses, or the excellent Peat Inn fish soup. From the 8 menu courses, roast monkfish served on a bed of onion and potato, unusually with a reduced meat sauce, or perhaps a fillet of beef grilled pink served with a cèpes sauce. I always find making a choice from the menu difficult as there are always a number of dishes I would like to try. I shall just have to book in for an extra night! *See also p279 – our Clover Awards section.*

| Peebles | Cringletie House |

Peebles, Lothian EH45 8PL
Telephone: (072 13) 233 £45
Fax: (072 13) 244
Open: lunch + dinner daily (closed Jan-mid Mar)
Meals served: lunch 1-1.45, dinner 7.30-8.30

Mid 19th-century Baronial mansion house offering 13 bedrooms with en suite bathrooms. Panelled public rooms have a sombre yet ancestral feel. In the kitchen, chef Aileen Maguire prepares wholesome home cooking using the hotel's own fruit and vegetables. A good base for those not wishing to stay in Edinburgh itself.

| Perth | Number Thirty Three |

33 George Street, Perth, Tayside PH1 5LA
Telephone: (0738) 33771 £45
Open: lunch + dinner Tue-Sat (closed 10 days Xmas/New Year)
Meals served: lunch 12.30-2.30, dinner 6.30-9.30

The Billinghursts' seafood restaurant is one to earmark for when you're in Perth. You can either eat at the Oyster Bar for some lighter meals such as deep-fried whitebait or a platter of assorted smoked and fresh fish, or in the Restaurant and perhaps try Mary's Seafood Casserole consisting of a whole range from the menu including monkfish, squid, prawns and salmon, topped with a langoustine, or grilled hake rolled in sesame seeds served with a piquant sauce. They organise special wine evenings with food to match, all reasonably priced.

Port Appin — Airds Hotel

Port Appin, Appin, Strathclyde PA38 4DF
Telephone: (063 173) 236　　　　　　　　　　　　　　　　　　　£75
Fax: (063 173) 535
Open: lunch + dinner (closed early Jan-early Mar)
Meals served: lunch 12.30-1.30, dinner 8-8.30

Much work and effort has been put into refurbishing the bedrooms, not to say a fair bit of cash. The results are worthwhile. No less rewarding is the restaurant for which as much as possible is bought locally. The set menu offers a choice of 5 starters, followed by a soup and a choice of 3 main courses then 6 puds. None of the dishes is ever over-elaborate in the presentation and the fresh fish on offer, whether as a starter or main course, is always worth a try. If it's available, choose the excellent date pudding which Betty Allen serves with a butterscotch sauce. There's a good selection of French and Scottish cheeses.

The prodigious wine list requires and repays careful study. The 8 pages of half bottles indicate the range available and both they and the 75cl bottles run from the modest to the very expensive. Just think, for the price of the '67 Premier Cru Superieur Chateau d'Yquem you could stay for 4 nights here in a single room and still have a bit left over for souvenirs!

Portpatrick — Knockinaam Lodge

Portpatrick, Nr Stranraer, Dumfries & Galloway DG9 9AD
Telephone: (077 681) 471　　　　　　　　　　　　　　　　　　£65
Fax: (077 681) 435
Open: lunch + dinner daily (closed Jan-mid Mar)
Meals served: lunch 12-2, dinner 7.30-9

Stunning views across the Irish Sea, a lovely comfortable hotel and owners who really believe in their job are reasons for making the journey to Knockinaam Lodge. This isn't forgetting chef Daniel Gamiche's contribution – thoroughly good French cooking using local fish, seafood and beef to great effect. On the 3 course menu there is a choice of 2 dishes per course. A starter of escalope de saumon poêlé à la creme d'herbes et pommes paillasson followed by filet d'agneau grillé à la goret, son jus au romarin et vinaigre, with perhaps a soufflé chaud au chocolat mi-amer, sa tuile à l'orange to finish. Extensive wine list and charming service in this elegant, crisp dining room.

QUOTHQUAN	Shieldhill

Quothquan, Biggar, Strathclyde ML12 6NA
Telephone: (0899) 20035 £60
Fax: (0899) 21092
Open: lunch + dinner daily
Meals served: lunch 12-2, dinner 7-9 (Sat 7-9.30)
Refurbished, beautiful historic country house hotel set amongst parklands and lawns.

ST ANDREWS	Lathones Manor

By Largoward, St Andrews, Fife KY9 1JE
Telephone: (0334) 84494 £50
Open: lunch + dinner daily (closed Sun+Mon Oct-Mar, closed Bank Holidays, 2 wks Jan/Feb)
Meals served: lunch 12-2, dinner 7-9.30
Hotel with old world charm – gas coal fire and easy chairs and sofas in the bar. Home-made ice creams and sorbets are a speciality.

ST ANDREWS   St Andrews Old Course Hotel

St Andrews, Fife KY16 9SP
Telephone: (0334) 74371 £55
Fax: (0344) 77668
Open: lunch + dinner daily
Meals served: lunch 12-2.30, dinner 7-10

It's just possible that the odd stray ball would make it in through one of the bedroom windows. However, it's the only thing that *would* disturb the composure of this luxurious hotel, pitched on the 17th hole of the Old Course. Golfing addicts will be in heaven with some 30 courses to choose from in the area and a team of stewards plus professionals on hand to give advice on that troublesome swing. The standards of this hotel are high, having undergone a complete face-lift a couple of year's ago. A hearty Scottish breakfast features Scottish porridge with cream or heather honey, grilled East Neuk kipper or poached Finnan haddock, Aberdeen Butterie with smoked bacon, grilled chicken, cheddar cheese, poached egg, tomato and basil hollandaise, or french toast crusted with corn and oatmeal served with maple syrup or heather honey.

Superb public rooms and bedrooms show every attention to furnishings and detail. If you visit this hotel, you will understand how a high number of international visitors make the pilgrimage here. A la carte available with a table d'hote menu which gives a choice of 4 starters, 2 soups and 4 main courses. Comprehensive wine list, not unreasonably priced for the situation and surroundings. Lavish health and fitness facilities.

Scone — Murrayshall House

Scone, Tayside PH2 7PH
Telephone: (0738) 51171 £65
Fax: (0738) 52595
Open: lunch Sun, dinner daily (closed 2 wks Jan)
Meals served: lunch 12-2, dinner 7-9.30

Executive chef Bruce Sangster is the brains behind the kitchen here and although he doesn't personally place his signature on every dish – he has other duties elsewhere – the cooking does him proud. In fact one of his team, chef de partie Nicola Robinson, won the vote for Young Scottish Chef of the Year at Queen Margaret College, Edinburgh.

The Old Masters Restaurant presents a Taste of Scotland menu. Murrayshall's Supper Menu and an à la carte. Lined up among the starters are a home-made apple soup perfumed with a little curry and a cushion of locally smoked salmon filled with their own home-reared free range eggs, served on a chive and butter sauce. Main courses might be a charcoal grilled breast of Gressingham duckling with a calvados, apple and pink peppercorn sauce, or a roast end of lamb carved and served with a cheese and onion tartlet in its own juices. Desserts finish proceedings with a flourish – an iced banana parfait centred with pear sorbet is fresh and attractively presented. Food that's more than par for the course! The Old Masters Restaurant is indeed set with some 16th- & 17th-century Dutch oil paintings. The service is professional but friendly and the hotel itself is set in 300 acres which include the golf course. 19 ensuite bedrooms all with up to date facilities and lounges and furnishings which I originally thought were on the bright side have worn well and toned down. There is no doubt that the Murrayshall is a very pleasant place to stay whether or not you are a golf enthusiast.

Sleat — Kinloch Lodge

Sleat, Isle of Skye, Highland IV43 8QY
Telephone: (047 13) 214 £70
Fax: (047 13) 277
Open: dinner daily (closed Dec-mid Mar)
Meals served: dinner 7.30-8.30

Lord and Lady Macdonald have opened their family home as a hotel to allow others the enjoyment of the house and its surroundings. The 10 bedrooms vary in size but then you'll not be wanting to spend all your days indoors! Food is under the supervision of Lady Macdonald and consists of 5 courses including soup. Starters might include devilled kidneys with garlic croûtons, or sautéed squid with tomato and black olive sauce, then the home-made soup to follow with perhaps fillet of wild salmon baked and served with hollandaise sauce, or roast duck for main courses. Good vegetables and a choice of 2 puddings, followed by cheese. Peter Macpherson, who assists Lady Macdonald in the kitchen, strives for fresh additive-free food, therefore whenever possible they use local ingredients. Wine is in the capable hands of Lord Macdonald. Fishing, shooting and stalking are available and – obviously – some great walks.

STEWARTON	Chapeltoun House

Stewarton-Irvine Road, Stewarton, Strathclyde KA3 3ED
Telephone: (0560) 82696 £65
Fax: (0560) 85100
Open: lunch + dinner daily (closed 1 wk Jan)
Meals served: lunch 12-2, dinner 7-9.15 (Sun 7-9)
Light modern dishes with some well executed combinations. Eight bedrooms.

STRACHUR	Creggans Inn

Strachur, Strathclyde PA27 8BX
Telephone: (036 986) 279 £55
Fax: (036 986) 637
Open: lunch + dinner daily
Meals served: lunch 12.15-2.15, dinner 7-9
On the edge of Loch Fyne – fine views from the lounges.

STRANRAER	North West Castle

Cairnryan Road, Stranraer, Dumfries & Galloway DG9 8EH
Telephone: (0776) 4413 £50
Fax: (0776) 2646
Open: lunch + dinner daily
Meals served: lunch 12-2, dinner 7-9.30
Aptly-named hotel (opposite the ferry port), 74 bedrooms, good leisure facilities.

STRATHTUMMEL	Port-an-Eilean Hotel

Strathtummel, By Pitlochry, Tayside PH16 5RU
Telephone: (088 24) 233 £40
Open: dinner daily (closed Nov-Apr)
Meals served: dinner 7.30-8.30
Another lochside location for a hunting lodge. Antiques, eight bedrooms.

TAYNUILT   Taynuilt Hotel

Taynuilt, Highland PA35 1JG
Telephone: (086 62) 437 £40
Open: dinner Wed-Sun
Meals served: dinner 7-9

Angie and Alistair Scott were formerly at Kilchrenan. Here, the restaurant is worth a visit with Hugh Cocker as its recently installed chef. On the small and inexpensive menu, the celery soup packs a big flavour and the accompanying home-made soda bread is delicious. A main dish of salmon is simply poached with a pungent purple basil sauce and the surrounding vegetables are fresh and well cooked. The wine list remains embryonic but it will expand with time. If the whole enterprise can be brought up to the standard of the food it will be a great success, I'm sure.

TIRORAN   Tiroran House

Tiroran, Isle of Mull, Strathclyde PA69 6ES
Telephone: (068 15) 232 £60
Fax: (068 15) 232
Open: dinner daily (closed early Oct-mid May)
Meals served: dinner at 7.45

A warm welcome awaits you from Robin and Sue Blockley in this comfortably-decorated hotel which is the Blockleys' home. A fixed main course meal with a choice of starters, served in this dinner party atmosphere. An ideal place for an away-from-it-all relaxing break. Provides everything you would expect from a Scottish sporting lodge which is set amongst beautiful scenery.

SCOTLAND

TOBERMORY | **Tobermory Hotel**
53 Main Street, Tobermory, Isle of Mull, Strathclyde PA75 6NT
Telephone: (0688) 2091
Fax: (0688) 2140 £40
Open: dinner daily
Meals served: dinner 7-8
Small, welcoming hotel with comfortable public rooms and 15 bedrooms.

TROON | **Highgrove House**
Old Loans Road, Troon, Strathclyde KA10 7HL
Telephone: (0292) 312511 £60
Open: lunch + dinner daily
Meals served: lunch 12-2.30, dinner 7-9.30
9 bedrooms, 80-seater dining room, popular with locals.

UIG | **Baile-Na-Cille**
Timsgarry, Uig, Isle of Lewis, Western Isles PA86 9JD
Telephone: (085 175) 242 £40
Open: all day daily (closed Oct-Mar)
Meals served: 9.30-5, snacks to 7.30pm
Comfortable rooms with magnificent views. Dining room is gas lit if there's a power cut.

ULLAPOOL Altnaharrie Inn

Ullapool, Highland IV26 2SS
Telephone: (085 483) 230 £100
Open: dinner daily (closed early Nov-Easter)
Meals served: dinner at 8

The Greta Garbo of gastronomy, Scandinavian chef Gunn Eriksen remains an enigma. Shunning publicity she continues to produce star quality food the likes of which it is hard to describe. Comparisons are individious – quite simply tasting is believing. There's no denying that the trip to remote Altnaharrie is a daunting prospect and not for the faint of heart. Yet the ferry journey can seem almost to be a rite of passage in preparation for the cooking. Those who have made it there return with a strange gleam in their eye having eaten (from the 6-course fixed menu) such simple-sounding dishes as layers of foie gras and asparagus with a lemon and mustard sauce, a little basil with a layer of puff pastry, or the equally simple crab in a sheet of parsleyed pasta served in a reduced sauce of vegetable juices and dry muscat. The main course might be saddle of rabbit with a rabbit and mushroom forcemeat served with 2 sauces. The dining room is a simple affair with whitewashed walls, wooden tables with Norwegian glassware and settings, and views out over the loch – this is definitely not a country house hotel – but the 250-odd-binned wine list is enough to keep most people more than happy. There are only 8 bedrooms and the waves really do lap at the edge of the garden. This is an away from it all stay but well worth the journey. As one of our reviewers said 'As we were sitting there, porpoises jumped for joy outside, and we jumped for joy quietly inside'.

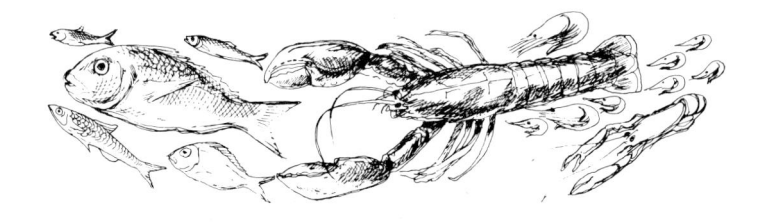

ULLAPOOL	Ceilidh Place
14 West Argyle Street, Ullapool, Highland IV26 2TY	
Telephone: (0854) 612103	£45
Fax: (0854) 612886	
Open: lunch + dinner daily (closed 2 wks Jan)	
Meals served: lunch 12-5, dinner 7-9.30	
15-bedroomed hotel, with restaurant and café.	

WHITEBRIDGE	Knockie Lodge
Whitebridge, Highland IV1 2UP	
Telephone: (045 63) 276	£55
Fax: (045 63) 389	
Open: dinner daily (closed Nov-Apr)	
Meals served: dinner 7-9.30	

The Milwards' 10-bedroomed comfortable hotel overlooking Loch Nan Lann has some spectacular views. It's a peaceful place to spend a holiday and, with numbers kept low, you'll really be made to feel at home. Fishing and stalking by arrangement. This hotel is accessible from Inverness in a short space of time. Good Scottish foods are served in unpretentious style.

Wales Establishment Reviews

ABERAERON	Hive on the Quay

Cadwgan Place, Aberaeron, Dyfed SA46 0BT
Telephone: (0545) 570445 £35
Open: lunch + dinner daily (closed Oct-Apr)
Meals served: lunch 12-2, dinner 6-9.30

Waterfront café and restaurant, bee exhibition and shop. Organic and wholemeal produce used whenever possible.

ABERCYNON — Llechwen Hall

Abercynon, Nr LLanfabon, Mid-Glamorgan CF37 4HP
Telephone: (0443) 742050 £55
Fax: (0443) 742189
Open: lunch + dinner daily
Meals served: lunch 12-2, dinner 7-10

Popular inn-cum-hotel offering 11 bedrooms and plenty of Welsh hospitality. High up on a hill, lovely views are to be had of the surrounding valleys.

ABERDOVEY	Old Coffee Shop

13 New Street, Aberdovey, Gwynedd LL35 0EH
Telephone: (0654) 767652 £30
Open: all day Tue-Sun, dinner Fri+Sat in summer
Meals served: lunch 12-3, dinner 7-9, light meals 10-5.30
Friendly unlicensed café, home-cooked food.

ABERGAVENNY — Walnut Tree Inn

Llandewi Skirrid, Abergavenny, Gwent NP7 8AW
Telephone: (0873) 852797 £55
Fax: (0873) 859764
Open: lunch + dinner Tue-Sat (closed Xmas, 2 wks Feb)
Meals served: lunch 12-3, dinner 7.15-10

This place is what its name implies, it is simply an unpretentious inn and rests solidly on the Taruschios' past and future reputation.

Italian country cooking of some distinction is what Franco Taruschio has made his living by for many years. Wild mushrooms and polenta, bresaola and a pasta e fagioli soup are among the starters, while brodetto, breast of guineafowl with spinach and raisins and an Italian seafood platter are possible main dishes. There's an oriental touch now and again – goujonettes of Dover sole with a Thai dip for instance. An ample selection of puds and his fine native wines complete the picture. All this talk of the Italiano 'new wave' in London – it was here in South Wales long ago! *See also p282 – our Clover Awards section.*

Abersoch	Porth Tocyn Hotel

Bwlchtocyn, Abersoch, Gwynedd LL53 7BU
Telephone: (075 881) 3303 £40
Fax: (075 881) 3538
Open: lunch + dinner daily (closed Nov-wk before Easter)
Meals served: lunch 12.30-2, dinner 7.30-9.30
Converted from a row of lead-mining cottages into a family-run hotel with magnificent seaviews.

Abersoch	Riverside Hotel

Abersoch, Gwynedd LL53 7HW
Telephone: (075 881) 2419 £45
Open: lunch + dinner daily (closed mid Nov-end Feb)
Meals served: lunch 12-2, dinner 7.30-9

Set between the harbour and the River Soch, this 12-bedroomed hotel is run with lots of energy by John and Wendy Bakewell. Architecturally not the most exciting of buildings, it has nevertheless built up quite a loyal following over the years – a tribute to the owners and the relaxed atmosphere they have created. A choice of 6 starters and main courses – home-made puds from the trolley and some good Welsh cheese, served in the no-frills beamed dining room.

Aberystwyth	Conrah Country Hotel

Chancery, Aberystwyth, Dyfed SY23 4DF
Telephone: (0970) 617941 £65
Fax: (0970) 624546
Open: lunch + dinner daily (closed 1 wk Xmas)
Meals served: lunch 12-2, dinner 7-9

Originally the mansion house to the Ffosrhydygaled Estate, the hotel is approached along a drive lined with rhododendrons. There are 20 pretty bedrooms located either in the main building or around the courtyard. Views are to be had across the Cader Idris mountains to the north, and the surrounding countryside of Mid-Wales is a delight.

Barry	Bunbury's

14 High Street, Barry, South Glamorgan CF6 8EA
Telephone: (0446) 732075 £40
Open: lunch + dinner Tue-Sat (closed Bank Holidays)
Meals served: lunch 10.30-2.30, dinner 7.30-10 (Sat 7.30-10.30)

A South Glamorgan 2-man band where John Gasset tinkles the ivories and Chris Hogg rattles the pans. Rather daring dishes include aubergine and walnut caviar as a starter with a roasted duck breast served with a blackcurrant and cassis sauce as a main course. Cheaper lunch-time alternatives on offer.

Beaumaris	Ye Olde Bulls Head Inn

Castle Street, Beaumaris, Anglesey, Gwynedd LL58 8AP
Telephone: (0248) 810329 £50
Fax: (0248) 811294
Open: lunch + dinner daily (closed 25+26 Dec, 1 Jan)
Meals served: lunch 12-2.30, dinner 7.30-9.30
Parts of this coaching inn date back to 1617. Fresh, local produce is served in the bar and dining room.

BUILTH WELLS   Caer Beris Manor

Builth Wells, Powys LD2 3NP
Telephone: (0982) 552601   £45
Open: lunch + dinner daily
Meals served: lunch 12.30-2.30, dinner 7.30-10
Set in 27 acres of parkland beside the River Irfon, Elizabethan-style manor with twenty-two bedrooms.

CARDIFF   Armless Dragon

97 Wyevern Road, Cathays, Cardiff, South Glamorgan CF2 4BG
Telephone: (0222) 382357   **£45**
Open: lunch Tue-Fri, dinner Tue-Sat (closed Bank Holidays except Good Friday, 24 Dec-1 Jan)
Meals served: lunch 12.30-2.15, dinner 7.30-10.30 (Sat 7.30-11)

Training in London and Geneva and a spell in the West Indies plus lots of reading have resulted in David Richards' inspired and informal establishment – particularly here in South Wales! Soused herring with wasabi and Barbados fish cakes are exotic starters, with a fish main course prepared 'orientale' in a lightly curried cream sauce with prawns, as well as more homely offerings of home-made sausages and good local fish. This team works hard and deserve the following that they have built up and the philosophy of the food can best be summed up by David Richard's comment – 'We are a part of all that we have met'.

CARDIFF   La Brasserie

60 St Mary Street, Cardiff, South Glamorgan
Telephone: (0222) 372164   £40
Open: lunch + dinner Mon-Sat (closed 25+26 Dec)
Meals served: lunch 12-2.30, dinner 7-12.15
Same owners as Champers and Le Monde, French menu and wines.

CARDIFF   Le Cassoulet

5 Romilly Crescent, Canton, Cardiff, South Glamorgan CF1 9NP
Telephone: (0222) 221905   £50
Open: lunch Tue-Fri, dinner Tue-Sat (closed 3wks Jul/Aug)
Meals served: lunch 12-2, dinner 7-10
Good value plats du jour at lunch.

CARDIFF   Champers

St Mary Street, Cardiff, South Glamorgan CF1 1FE
Telephone: (0222) 373363   £45
Open: lunch Mon-Sat, dinner daily (closed 25+26 Dec)
Meals served: lunch 12-2.30, dinner 7-12.15
Busy, straightforward wine bar and brasserie.

CARDIFF   Le Monde

60 St Mary Street, Cardiff, South Glamorgan CF1 1FE
Telephone: (0222) 387376   £40
Open: lunch + dinner Mon-Sat (closed 25+26 Dec)
Meals served: lunch 12-3, dinner 7-12.15
Third in the Cardiff chain (see above).

CARDIFF	New House Country Hotel

Thornhill, Cardiff, South Glamorgan CF4 5UA
Telephone: (0222) 520280 £55
Fax: (0222) 520324
Open: lunch + dinner daily (closed 25+26 Dec, 1 Jan)
Meals served: lunch 12-2, dinner 7-9.30
Fine old house with lovely valley views.

CARDIFF	Quayles

6/8 Romilly Crescent, Cardiff, South Glamorgan CF1 9NR
Telephone: (0222) 341264 £35
Open: lunch daily, dinner Mon-Sat (closed Bank Holidays)
Meals served: lunch 12-2.30 (Sun 11.30-4.30), dinner 7.30-10.30

The Canning family's revamped enterprise on the site of their former Gibson's restaurant. Now a brasserie, it offers a popular menu during the week but Sunday lunch is more upmarket. Good vegetarian dishes include mushroom roast with tamari sauce, vegan tortellini with sun-dried tomatoes and olives, and spinach and cheese cannelloni.

CHEPSTOW	Beckfords

15-16 Upper Church Street, Chepstow, Gwent NP6 5EX
Telephone: (029 12) 6547 £55
Open: lunch daily, dinner Mon-Sat (closed Bank Holidays)
Meals served: lunch 12-2.30 (Sun 12-4.30), dinner 7.30-10

The eccentric author and folly builder William Beckford finds a devotee in owner Jeremy Hector, and prints of Fonthill Abbey adorn the walls of the dining room. Starters include a smoked fish terrine with tomato and tarragon sauce, with roasted pheasant among the main dishes. Of the many puds, try 'pie in the sky' – a soft caramel layer with sliced bananas, walnuts and coffee- and chocolate-whipped cream topping.

COLWYN BAY	Café Nicoise

124 Abergele Road, Colwyn Bay, Clwyd LL29 7PS
Telephone: (0492) 531555 £45
Open: lunch Tue-Sat, dinner Mon-Sat (closed 1 wk Jan, 1 wk Nov)
Meals served: lunch 12-2, dinner 7-10
Friendly popular local French restaurant.

CONWY	Sychnant Pass Hotel

Sychnant Pass Road, Conwy, Gwynedd LL32 8BJ
Telephone: (0492) 596868 £35
Fax: (0492) 870009
Open: lunch + dinner daily (closed none)
Meals served: lunch 12.30-2, dinner 7-9
14-bedroomed hotel with lovely views and comfortable public rooms.

COYCHURCH	**Coed-y-Mwstwr Hotel**

Coychurch, Bridgend, Mid Glamorgan CF35 6AF
Telephone: (0656) 860621 £55
Fax: (0656) 863122
Open: lunch + dinner daily
Meals served: lunch 12-2.30, dinner 7.30-10.15 (Sat 7.30-10.30, Sun 7.30-9)
Victorian mansion hotel, lovely staircase, dinner four courses and sorbet. Good wines.

CRICKHOWELL	**Bear Hotel**

High Street, Crickhowell, Powys NP8 1BW
Telephone: (0873) 810408 £50
Fax: (0873) 811696
Open: lunch + dinner Mon-Sat
Meals served: lunch 12-2, dinner 7-9.30 (Sat 7-9.45)
Former coaching inn, low beams, farmhouse furniture, twenty-four rooms.

CRICKHOWELL	**Gliffaes Country House Hotel**

Crickhowell, Powys NP8 1RH
Telephone: (0874) 730371 £45
Fax: (0874) 730463
Open: lunch + dinner daily (closed Jan+Feb)
Meals served: lunch 1-2.30, dinner 7.30-9.30
Set in its own grounds, traditional sports facilities, comfortable public rooms.

DINAS MAWDDWY	**Old Station Coffee Shop**

Dinas Mawddwy, Gwynedd SY20 9LS
Telephone: (065 04) 338 £25
Open: all day daily (closed mid-Nov to mid-Mar)
Meals served: 9.30-5, Mar+Nov 9-4.30
Mainly vegetarian café, home-made food, very popular.

DOLGELLAU	**Dolmelynllyn Hall**

Ganllwyd, Dolgellau, Gwynedd LL40 2HP
Telephone: (034 140) 273 £45
Open: dinner daily (closed Dec-end Feb)
Meals served: dinner 7.30-8.30
Country house hotel, relaxed atmosphere, good home cooking.

DOLGELLAU	**Dylanwad Da**

2 Smithfield Street, Dolgellau, Gwynedd LL40 1BS
Telephone: (0341) 422870 £35
Open: dinner daily (Thu-Sat only in winter, closed Feb)
Meals served: dinner 7-9.30
Generous portions of simply-cooked fare, good value for money.

EAST ABERTHAW	**Blue Anchor Inn**

East Aberthaw, Nr Barry, South Glamorgan CF6 9DD
Telephone: (0446) 750329 £45
Open: lunch daily, dinner Mon-Sat (closed 26 Dec, 1 Jan)
Meals served: lunch 12-2.45, dinner 7-9.30 (Sat 7-9.45)
Restaurant within a pub serving well above-average food.

EGLWYSFACH	Ynyshir Hall

Eglwysfach, Machynlleth, Powys SY20 8TA
Telephone: (0654) 781209 £50
Open: lunch + dinner daily
Meals served: lunch 12-1.30, dinner 7-8.30

One of those hotels you hope you don't need to ask the way to – 'yes, it's in Eglwysfach near Machynlleth' – since Welsh place names rarely trip off the tongue! Once you've found it, you can relax and enjoy the Reens' comfortable Georgian house and admire Rob's paintings that adorn the walls. All the rooms have been recently refurbished and this and other improvements have rightly pushed the hotel ahead of many of its rival establishments.

EWLOE	St David's Park Hotel

St David's Park, Ewloe, Clwyd CH5 3YB
Telephone: (0244) 520800 £40
Fax: (0244) 520930
Open: lunch + dinner daily
Meals served: lunch 12.30-2, dinner 7-10
New, Georgian-style hotel designed with the company account customer in mind. Extensive leisure facilities, 121 bedrooms.

FISHGUARD	Three Main Street

3 Main Street, Fishguard, Dyfed SA65 9HG
Telephone: (0348) 874275 £35
Open: lunch daily, dinner Mon-Sat
Meals served: lunch 12-2.30, dinner 7-9.30
3 bedrooms, morning coffee, afternoon tea, lunch and dinner all available in a newly restored Georgian building.

GLANWYDDEN	Queen's Head

Glanwydden, Gwynedd LL31 9JP
Telephone: (0492) 546570 £35
Open: lunch + dinner daily
Meals served: lunch 12-2.15, dinner 6.30-9 (Sat 7-9)
Above-average food in a pub restaurant.

GOWERTON	Cefn Goleu Park

Cefn Stylle Road, Gowerton, West Glamorgan SA4 3QS
Telephone: (0792) 873099 £55
Open: lunch Sun, dinner Tue-Sat
Meals served: lunch 12.30-2, dinner 7.30-9.30

Quite an eye-opener, this one, and not at all what you might expect. Entering the Welsh manor house you are struck by the main hall with its reception desk and bar, while above there's a minstrels' gallery and high rafters. The bedrooms will also impress – they're huge and have their own dressing rooms and ornate bathrooms. Owners Claude and Emma Rossi apparently fell in love with the place at first sight and it's easy to see why. The food in the restaurant offers plenty of choice with the stuffed mussels and langoustine in garlic butter being good starters and the more straightforward poached salmon with lobster sauce and prawns a typical main course. Puds from the trolley.

HARLECH	Llew Glas

Plas-y-Goits, High Street, Harlech, Gwynedd LL46 2YA
Telephone: (0766) 780700 £30
Open: lunch + dinner daily (closed Nov-Feb except Xmas)
Meals served: lunch 10-4, dinner 7-10
Restaurant and tea room, bakery and delicatessen, run by Trevor Pharoah.

HARLECH	The Cemlyn

High Street, Harlech, Gwynedd LL46 2YA
Telephone: (0766) 780425 £50
Open: dinner daily (closed Nov-mid Mar)
Meals served: dinner 7-9 (Sat 7-9.30)

A 'Mineral Kingdom' dinner, an Italian evening, a 'Food from Burgundy' Saturday menu and an evening of Greek and Middle Eastern food are just some of the themes for Ken Goody's dinner parties here at The Cemlyn. Fine flavours from the local produce win him a wide following.

From his regular dinner menu, try dishes such as fresh salmon fish cakes from the 5 or so starters, or perhaps a fillet of free range Lleyn pork cooked in yoghurt and honey with cardamom, cinnamon and orange from the 5 main courses. Good tarte aux pommes served with Anglesey cream and a choice of Welsh cheeses.

Handwritten menus that change regularly and a reasonably priced wine list.

LAKE VYRNWY	Lake Vyrnwy Hotel

Lake Vyrnwy, (via Oswestry), Llanwyddyn, Powys SY10 0LY
Telephone: (069 173) 692 £50
Fax: (069 173) 289
Open: lunch + dinner
Meals served: lunch 12.15-1.45, dinner 7.30-9.15

Breathtaking views over the lake, hunting and fishing, and Welsh hospitality are what's on offer at this 30-bedroomed hotel with 2 additional suites. Situated on the slopes of the Berwyn Mountains, the architecture is Victorian but the interior is warm and welcoming. Extensive, reasonably priced wine list. Some competent dishes come from the kitchen including home-made venison sausages served with a red wine sauce. Good roast leg of lamb flamed with rosemary, and perhaps a hot chocolate and cointreau pud to finish.

A good base from which to explore the area.

LLANBERIS	Y Bistro

43-45 High Street, Llanberis, Gwynedd LL55 4EU
Telephone: (0286) 871278 £40
Open: dinner daily (closed Bank Holidays, Sun+Mon in winter)
Meals served: dinner 7.30-9.30 (Sat 7.30-9.45)
Nerys and Danny Roberts' friendly restaurant, local produce used whenever possible.

LLANDRILLO	Tyddyn Llan

Llandrillo, Nr Corwen, Clwyd LL21 0ST
Telephone: (049 084) 264 £55
Fax: (049 084) 264
Open: lunch + dinner daily (closed 1 wk Feb)
Meals served: lunch 12.30-2, dinner 7.30-9.30

Georgian country house set in the Vale of Edeyrnion. Owners Peter and Bridget Kindred set great store by the restaurant, for which chef David Barratt does his stuff. Pan-fried oyster mushrooms with puff pastry and escalopes of sole and salmon with leeks and cheese steamed and served with a prawn sauce show a good understanding of the raw materials and their flavours. The hotel has recently acquired rights to 4 miles of fishing on the river Dee. The 10 bedrooms have ensuite facilities and some are furnished with antiques.

LLANDUDNO	Bodysgallen Hall

Llandudno, Gwynedd LL30 1RS WC
Telephone: (0492) 584466 £55
Fax: (0492) 582519
Open: lunch + dinner daily
Meals served: lunch 12.30-2, dinner 7.30-9.45

There's not much to feel proud of in Wales these days, what with the downturn in fortunes of the Welsh rugby team. But there *is* Bodysgallen Hall, one of the finest hotels in the Principality, if not in the British Isles. The spectacular surroundings are matched by the quality of the interiors – every room exudes elegance and sophistication. As for the food, the new chef Mair Lewis cooks classic British dishes with admirable restraint taking advantage, of course, of some marvellous local produce. An extensive wine list will suit most tastes and pockets, although the 1964 Chateau Petrus might cause you to think twice!

LLANDUDNO	Richard at Lanterns

7 Church Walks, Llandudno, Gwynedd LL30 2HD
Telephone: (0492) 877924 £50
Open: dinner daily (closed Mon in winter)
Meals served: dinner 6.30-10
Restaurant and bistro run by Richard Hendey – modern British cooking.

LLANDUDNO   St Tudno Hotel

The Promenade, Llandudno, Gwynedd LL30 2LP
Telephone: (0492) 874411
Fax: (0942) 860407   £50
Open: lunch + dinner daily (closed 2 wks Dec/Jan)
Meals served: lunch 12.30-2, dinner 6.45-9.30
Seafront hotel, friendly owners, twenty-four rooms, fixed price or à la carte meals.

LLANGAMMARCH WELLS   Lake Country House

Llangammarch Wells, Powys LD4 4BS
Telephone: (059 12) 202   £60
Fax: (059 12) 457
Open: dinner daily (closed Jan)
Meals served: dinner 7-8.45

There's a glorious setting for this unusual converted late 19th-century country house hotel. The lake and acres of grounds make it a haven for anglers and bird-watchers – the rare Red Kite has been spotted here. Owners Jean-Pierre and Jan Mifsud make it their business to make you feel as comfortable as possible. The hotel was refurbished in 1992. From the menu, the simpler dishes on offer have been the ones to choose, and the copious wine list runs to some 380 bottles which includes some affordable drinking.

LLANGEFNI   Tre-Ysgawen Hall

Capel Coch, Nr Llangefni, Anglesey, Gwynedd LL77 7UR
Telephone: (0248) 750750   £55
Fax: (0248) 750035
Open: lunch + dinner daily
Meals served: lunch 12-2.30 (Sat 12.30-2.30), dinner 7.30-9.30

A late 19th-century country house which stands head and shoulders above rival establishments in the area. Transformed by the Craighead family, it now offers superior accommodation with every room displaying attention to fabric, furnishings and decoration. The Conservatory restaurant offers a variety of menus – 3-course set lunches and table d'hôte at lunchtime; table d'hôte, à la carte and menu gourmand at dinner. Chef Steven Morris achieves a good balance of modern and traditional cuisine – in other words it looks pretty but there's also enough to satisfy your appetite! Typical dishes in the evening might be a starter of home-made terrine of rabbit with crisp lettuce leaves and hot brioche toast, or light puff pastry case filled with spinach, asparagus and wild mushrooms on a truffle butter sauce. From a choice of 5 main courses, the fillet of Anglesey Beef topped with Pommery mustard soufflé with Madeira and pink peppercorn sauce, or supreme of pan-fried guineafowl served with the legs garnished with glazed baby turnips, noodles and baby leeks or a herb and cream sauce. Desserts and coffee do justice to the main meal.

LLANGYBI   Cwrt Bleddyn Hotel

Tredunnock, Nr Usk, Gwent NP5 1PG
Telephone: (0633) 49521   £50
Fax: (0633) 49220
Open: lunch + dinner daily (Sun 12.30-2.45)
Meals served: lunch 12.30-2.30, dinner 7.30-10.30 (Sun 7.30-9.30)
Thirty-six bedroomed hotel which offers good Welsh hospitality.

LLANRUG	**Seiont Manor**

Llanrug, Caernarfon, Gwynedd LL55 2AQ
Telephone: (0286) 673366 £40
Fax: (0286) 2840
Open: lunch Sun-Fri, dinner daily
Meals served: lunch 12-2, dinner 7-10

The original building has been carefully extended to bring the number of bedrooms to 28. Lots of modern comforts and facilities include spa baths in the suites and a stylish indoor swimming pool. The beautiful surrounding countryside is ideal for walkers.

LLANRWST	**Meadowsweet**

Station Road, Llanrwst, Gwynedd LL26 0DS
Telephone: (0492) 640732 £55
Open: lunch + dinner daily in summer, dinner only in winter
Meals served: lunch 12-1.30, dinner 6.30-9.30 (Sun 6.30-9)

This small hotel overlooking the Conwy valley is where owner and chef John Evans cooks some enjoyable food. You can now select a variety of dishes on the menu so long as they meet the minimum charge – and it looks to be a successful innovation. Wines remain a strong point and 5 of the 10 bedrooms have now been refurbished.

LLANSANFFRAID GLAN CONWY	**Old Rectory**

Llanrwst Road, Llansanffraid Glan Conwy, Gwynedd LL28 5LF
Telephone: (0492) 580611 £55
Fax: (0492) 584555
Open: dinner Fri-Wed (closed 7 Dec-20 Feb)
Meals served: dinner at 8

A 4-bedroomed hotel located on the beautiful Conwy Estuary. In the dining room, everyone sits at the same table for dinner unless a separate table is previously requested. Traditional Welsh cooking blends with more continental styles on the menu to pleasing effect. Perhaps fish and seafood in a herb broth accompanied by baby vegetables from the starters, and from the main courses, a roast fillet of Welsh beef served with a red wine sauce and leek pancakes, followed by a goat's cheese soufflé accompanied by a salad. Finish your meal with a choice of puds. Great pride is taken in the fact that they serve only Welsh mountain lamb and Welsh black beef. Reasonably priced wine list with good choice.

Good for booking the 4 rooms with a group of friends and making a weekend of it.

LLYSWEN	Llangoed Hall

Llyswen, Brecon, Powys LD3 0YP
Telephone: (0874) 754525 £80
Fax: (0874) 754545
Open: lunch + dinner daily
Meals served: lunch 12.15-2.30, dinner 7.15-9.30

Sir Bernard Ashley's multi-million pound enterprise has won several awards of late. As he comments, 'It has always been my ambition to find a country house hotel that would successfully recreate the atmosphere of an Edwardian house party'. He and his young team have achieved this aim. Chef Mark Salter's cooking is spot-on and the set 6-course dinner menu shows his talents to the full. Pan-fried breast of baby chicken is followed by an escalope of salmon with a warm truffle vinaigrette and steamed samphire. In this elegant dining room, an apple sorbet revives the palate and then there's char-grilled calves' liver and lamb's kidney with a purée of potatoes and a thyme sauce. For dessert there's a chocolate and rum soufflé with banana ice cream and coffee and petits fours to finish.

If you're staying in one of the beautiful bedrooms overnight, look out for the imaginative and interesting breakfast menu.

MATHRY	Ann Fitzgerald's Farmhouse Kitchen

Mabws Fawr, Mathry, Haverfordwest, Dyfed SA62 5JB
Telephone: (0348) 831347 £45
Open: lunch + dinner daily (closed lunch Xmas-Easter)
Meals served: lunch 12-2, dinner 7-9
Popular restaurant with take-away service if you phone in advance.

MISKIN	Miskin Manor

Penddylan Road, Pontyclun, Miskin, Glamorgan CF7 8ND
Telephone: (0443) 224204 £50
Fax: (0443) 237606
Open: lunch Sun-Fri, dinner daily (closed 1 wk Xmas/New Year)
Meals served: lunch 12-2, dinner 7-9.45 (Sun 7-9.30)
32-bedroomed, refurbished country hotel, comfortable public rooms, garden, woodland and leisure facilities.

MUMBLES	P.A.'s Winebar

95 Newton Road, Mumbles, West Glamorgan SA3 4BN
Telephone: (0792) 367723 £30
Open: lunch + dinner Mon-Sat (closed 3 wks Oct, 2 days Xmas)
Meals served: lunch 12-2.30, dinner 6-9.30

Paul Davies is in the kitchen and Andrew Hetherington supervises front of house – put them together and you get P.A.'s Wine Bar. The cosy interior is in shades of green, with 2 brick and stone open fireplaces (but with electric log fires!), wooden cast-iron based tables and comfortable carver's armchairs. The menu changes according to season but recently cockles, laverbread and bacon were a speciality starter, with fish fresh from Swansea market being a good main course option – steamed hake with an orange hollandaise for instance. For carnivores – try the casserole of lamb. Wines cover the entire range of prices but rest assured there's plenty of affordable drinking on offer!

NEWPORT	Celtic Manor

Coldra Woods, Newport, Gwent NP6 2YA
Telephone: (0633) 413000 £50
Fax: (0633) 412910
Open: lunch Mon-Fri, dinner Mon-Sat
Meals served: lunch 12-2.30, dinner 7-10.30

The Gateway to Wales is a true enough description for the Celtic Manor offers an ideal base from which to explore South Wales with excellent access by means of road or rail. Its estate covers 300 acres in all and there are enjoyable walks to be had in the Coldra woods. Indoors, excellent modern facilities mean you don't go without your exercise whatever the weather. The 75 bedrooms are well furnished.

NEWPORT	Cnapan Country House

East Street, Newport, Nr Fishguard, Dyfed SA42 0WF
Telephone: (0239) 820575 £40
Open: lunch + dinner Wed-Mon (closed Xmas, Feb, Tue during Mar-Oct)
Meals served: lunch 12-2 (Sun 12-2.30), dinner 7.30-8.45 (Sun 7.30-8)

The Lloyds and the Coopers run this, their family home and listed building. Five bedrooms are available, each nicely personalised with their own bits and pieces. The food also has an individual touch with a particular emphasis being given to vegetarian dishes – they're listed separately in a green folder. In addition, Judith Lloyd is happy to cater for any particular dietary needs. I notice that there's even a non-alcoholic wine available amongst the bottles - no one should feel left out!

NORTHOP	Soughton Hall

Northop, Nr Mold, Clwyd CH7 6AB
Telephone: (0352) 86811 £65
Fax: (0352) 86382
Open: lunch Sun, dinner daily (closed 2 wks Jan)
Meals served: lunch 12-2, dinner 7-9.30 (Sat 7-10, Sun 7-7.30)

In last year's Guide I don't think I gave enough credit to the grandeur and stateliness of this unusual Hall, set in some 150 acres of parkland, which manages to combine an informality and welcoming feel whilst still being impressive. The Rodenhurst family have converted with care and attention what was originally a bishop's palace dating from 1714. Thomas Leudecke in the kitchen provides some interesting dishes on either the chef's special menu, the house set menu or the à la carte. Comprehensive wine list with some reasonably-priced wines and some affordably half bottles.

Unusual and highly ornate dining room with wooden floors and formal table settings.

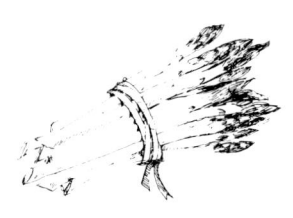

| PORTH | G & T's Village Bistro |

64 Pontypridd Road, Porth, Mid Glamorgan CF39 9NL
Telephone: (0443) 685775 £40
Fax: (0443) 687614
Open: lunch daily, dinner Mon-Sat
Meals served: lunch 12.15-2.15, dinner 7.30-9.30 (Sat 7.30-10)
French bistro with 7 rooms. Reasonably priced wine list.

| PORTHKERRY | Egerton Grey |

Porthkerry, Nr Cardiff, South Glamorgan CF6 9BZ
Telephone: (0446) 711666 £50
Fax: (0446) 711690
Open: lunch + dinner daily
Meals served: lunch 12-2, dinner 7-9.30

Catch up on your holiday reading in the library or write your postcards in the Edwardian drawing room. Alternatively you can just potter around the lovely grounds returning now and again for some enjoyable food. Rated highly in South Wales, Egerton Grey is certainly worth a visit. Ten ensuite bedrooms.

| PORTMEIRION | Hotel Portmeirion |

Portmeirion, Gwynedd LL48 6ER
Telephone: (0766) 770228 £55
Fax: (0766) 771331
Open: lunch Sun, dinner daily
Meals served: lunch 12.30-2.30, dinner 7-9.30 (Sat 7-9.45)

Sir Clough Williams-Ellis's dream village of Portmeirion is unique and really deserves a visit, whether to stay in one of the village rooms or the main hotel rooms, which have been extensively re-appointed. The unusual architecture and the views over the Traeth Bach estuary give the feeling of being a world away from reality.

The food under a new team lives up to the superb surroundings. Some sensible dishes which combine the best of British with a touch of continental/mediterranean flavours can be seen in alternatives such as pan-fried black pudding and meally pudding with plums, or fresh globe artichoke. A main course of fillet of Welsh lamb served with ratatouille and rosemary jus, or rondelles of beef and veal 'Maurice', is served with a selection of vegetables in season. 180-bin wine list with some reasonable buys. Friendly and helpful service. The hotel has a wonderfully eccentric amalgam of styles, furnishings and influences. Coming to stay here, you take your place in an illustrious line of guests including H.G. Wells, George Bernard Shaw and Noel Coward.

Pwllheli	Plas Bodegroes

Nefyn Road, Pwllheli, Gwynedd LL53 5TH
Telephone: (0758) 612363 £60
Fax: (0758) 701247
Open: dinner Tue-Sun (closed Jan+Feb)
Meals served: dinner 7-9.30 (Sun 7-9)

Chef and owner Chris Chown is another of those people who've changed direction and found where their true vocation lies. This Georgian house (set in pretty, secluded gardens) terms itself 'restaurant with rooms', which shows the emphasis that the owners put on it. Formerly an accountant, Chris threw in the daily grind of totting up figures for the risky business and long hours of catering. However, the success of Plas Bodegroes must mean that the sums are adding up well at the end of each week! Superb quality raw materials are due to Chris' tireless search for the best on offer in the area. Mention New Zealand lamb and you're likely to find yourself out on the street – he's fiercely proud of his country's produce. The food is cooked in the modern manner with little time for fussiness. Good choices on the set 5-course dinner menu might include Carmarthen ham and mushrooms and roast fillet of seabass with fennel and tarragon sauce. No less than 356 wines are there for the drinking on the list and nothing too expensive. Good selection of half bottles and a helpful mention of bin ends. Lovers of Alsation wines will be in their element.

Reynoldston	Fairyhill

Reynoldston, Gower, Swansea, West Glamorgan SA3 1BS
Telephone: (0792) 390139 £45
Fax: (0792) 391358
Open: lunch Sun, dinner daily (closed Nov-Feb)
Meals served: lunch 12.30-2.15, dinner 7.30-9
Set in twenty-four peaceful acres. 18th-century house, antique furniture.

Rossett	Llyndir Hall

Llyndir Lane, Rossett, Nr Wrexham, Clywd LL12 0AY
Telephone: (0244) 571648 £60
Fax: (0244) 571258
Open: lunch + dinner daily
Meals served: lunch 12-2, dinner 7-10
Elegant and tasteful hotel. Careful cooking; restaurant overlooks the garden.

Ruthin	Hunters

57 Well Street, Ruthin, Clywd LL15 1AF
Telephone: (082 42) 2619 £45
Open: lunch daily, dinner Mon-Sat (closed dinner 25+26 Dec)
Meals served: lunch 12-2, dinner 7.30-9.30 (Sat 7.30-10)
Elegant modern restaurant.

Swansea	Annie's

56 St Helen's Road, Swansea, West Glamorgan SA1 4BE
Telephone: (0792) 655603 £45
Open: dinner Tue-Sat (closed Bank Holidays)
Meals served: dinner 7-10 (Fri+Sat 7-10.30)
A la carte and fixed price menus served in an informal stripped pine setting. Welsh cheeses and French wines.

Swansea	La Braseria

28 Wind Street, Swansea, West Glamorgan SA1 1DZ
Telephone: (0792) 469683 £40
Open: lunch + dinner Mon-Sat
Meals served: lunch 12-2.30, dinner 7-12
Spanish sister of the French trio in Cardiff.

Swansea	Number One

1 Wind Street, Swansea, West Glamorgan SA1 1DE
Telephone: (0792) 456996 £35
Open: lunch Mon-Sat, dinner Wed-Sat (closed 25-30 Dec)
Meals served: lunch 12-2.30, dinner 7-9

Kate Taylor's solid reputation has meant a good initial reception for this, her new venture all on her own. Clientele seem to be old friends which makes for a chummy atmosphere all round. The food's good too. One to look out for in Swansea.

Talsarnau	Maes-y-Neuadd

Talsarnau, Nr Harlech, Gwynedd LL47 6YA
Telephone: (0766) 780200 £55
Fax: (0766) 780211
Open: lunch Sun, dinner daily
Meals served: lunch 12-2, dinner 7-9

Chances are 2 golden retrievers will come bounding down the little lane to meet you and follow you back to the sturdy granite and slate house. Much work has been put in, both inside and out, and to good effect. Maes-y-Neuadd now offers some splendid bedrooms and public rooms with loads of charm. Sensible 4-course menus and some reasonable prices on the wine list. Friendly service.

Tintern Abbey	Royal George

Tintern Abbey, Nr Chepstow, Gwent NP6 6SF
Telephone: (0291) 689205 £45
Fax: (0291) 689448
Open: lunch + dinner daily
Meals served: lunch 12-2, dinner 7.9.30 (Sat 7-10)
17th-century inn, 19 bedrooms.

TRELLECH	Village Green

Trellech, Nr Monmouth, Gwent NP5 4PA
Telephone: (0600) 860119 £55
Open: lunch Tue-Sun, dinner Mon-Sat including Bank Holidays (closed 10 days Jan)
Meals served: lunch 12-1.45, dinner 7-9.45 (Sat 7-10)

It's taken time to get going, but now things are starting to take off for chef-patron Bob Evans. Once a priory and then a coaching inn, his restaurant-cum-brasserie offers Gallic-Welsh food, from fisherman's pie and joint of lamb through to magret de canard with blackberry sauce and a fillet of beef with orange and green peppercorns. A reasonable wine list is sprinkled with amusing literary quips.

WELSH HOOK	Stone Hall

Welsh Hook, Wolfscastle, Nr Haverfordwest, Dyfed SA62 5NS
Telephone: (0348) 840212 £40
Fax: (0348) 840815
Open: dinner daily (closed Mon Dec-Mar, closed 2 wks Dec)
Meals served: dinner 7.30-9.30

Off the A40 between Haverfordwest and Fishguard you'll find Stone Hall near the hamlet of Welsh Hook. Set in an old Pembrokeshire manor house, the hotel has kept the slate-flagged floors and oak beams. Food in the dining room is mostly regional French cooking. Either 4-course table d'hôte or à la carte.

WHITEBROOK	Crown at Whitebrook

Whitebrook, Nr Monmouth, Gwent NP5 4TX
Telephone: (0600) 860254 £55
Open: lunch + dinner daily (residents only lunch Mon, dinner Sun)
Meals served: lunch 12-2, dinner 7-9.30
Fixed price menu, award-winning wine list and friendly and efficient service.

Northern Ireland Establishment Reviews

BELFAST — Belfast Castle
Antrim Road, Belfast, Co Antrim BT15 5GR
Telephone: (0232) 776925 — £60
Open: lunch Sun, dinner Thu-Sat (in Bistro lunch Mon-Sat, dinner daily)
Meals served: lunch 12-2.30, dinner 7.30-10, meals in Bistro 5-10
Owned and restored by Belfast City Council, 19th-century castle with a variety of dining areas and function facilities.

BELFAST — La Belle Epoque
103 Great Victoria Street, Belfast, Co Antrim BT2 7AG
Telephone: (0232) 323244 — £55
Open: dinner Mon-Sat (closed 25+26Dec)
Meals served: dinner 7-11.30
French restaurant with good modern cooking.

BELFAST — Branigans Restaurant
11a Stranmills Road, Belfast, Co Antrim BT9 5AS
Telephone: (0232) 666845 — £35
Open: lunch + dinner Mon-Sat
Meals served: lunch 12-3, dinner 7-11.45
Simple bistro-type dishes. No licence so bring your own wine.

BELFAST — Crown Liquor Saloon
46 Great Victoria Street, Belfast, Co Antrim BT2 7BA
Telephone: (0232) 249476 — £45
Open: lunch + dinner daily (closed 25 Dec)
Meals served: lunch 12-3, dinner 7-11.15
Victorian pub with no real alterations since it was built in the 1800s, infectiously happy atmosphere.

BELFAST — Dukes Hotel

65 University Street, Belfast, Co Antrim BT7 1HL
Telephone: (0232) 236666 — **£40**
Fax: (0232) 237177
Open: lunch Sun-Fri, dinner Mon-Sat
Meals served: lunch 12.30-2.30 (Sun 1.30-2.30), dinner 6.30-10.15 (Sat 6.30-10.45)

Dukes Hotel could be described as the smallest large hotel in Northern Ireland for its sense of intimacy coupled with extensive facilities. Located beside Queen's University, it is 10 minutes' walk from the centre. Closer to hand are the Botanical Gardens, the Palm House and the Ulster Museum and Art Gallery. Twenty-one bedrooms.

BELFAST	Nick's Warehouse

35-39 Hill Street, Belfast, Co Antrim BT1 2LB
Telephone: (0232) 439690 £40
Open: lunch + dinner Mon-Fri (closed Bank Holidays)
Meals served: lunch 12-3, dinner 6-9

Nick and Kathy Price run this wine bar and restaurant in a converted warehouse. Brick walls, varnished floor boards and green tables downstairs; carpets, white tablecloths and fresh flowers upstairs reflect the two-tier operation. Staff wear T-shirts and aprons. On a recent visit the menu included a tasty leek and watercress soup, fillet of salmon with herb butter sauce and, for dessert, zuccotto – a kind of summer pudding and rather a cause célèbre – or other puddings from the sideboard. Short chatty wine list with reasonable house wines.

BELFAST	Restaurant 44

44 Bedford Street, Belfast, Co Antrim BT2 7FF
Telephone: (0232) 244844 £45
Open: lunch Mon-Fri, dinner Mon-Sat (closed Bank Holidays)
Meals served: lunch 12-3, dinner 7-10.30
Friendly welcome to the intimate, candle-lit restaurant.

BELFAST	Roscoff

Lesley House, Shaftesbury Square, Belfast, Co Antrim
Telephone: (0232) 331532 £50
Open: lunch Mon-Fri, dinner Mon-Sat (closed 11+12 Jul, 26 Dec, 1 Jan)
Meals served: lunch 12.30-2, dinner 6.30-10.30

Roscoff, is *the* place to eat in town. Chef Paul Rankin's experiences in restaurants while globetrotting have certainly paid dividends, as has a couple of years with Albert Roux at Le Gavroche. Settled back in Belfast with his Canadian wife Jeanne they have established a firm reputation. Dishes are imaginative and deftly executed. The handwritten set menu offering 4 or 5 choices per course might comprise cream of fennel soup with buttery croutons followed by roast breast of pheasant with sautéed apples and a light curry cream, with hazelnut parfait with mocha sauce to finish. Fish also features since Paul sets great store by what the Irish Sea has to offer – langoustine, brill and skate. Good wine list includes some useful half bottles.

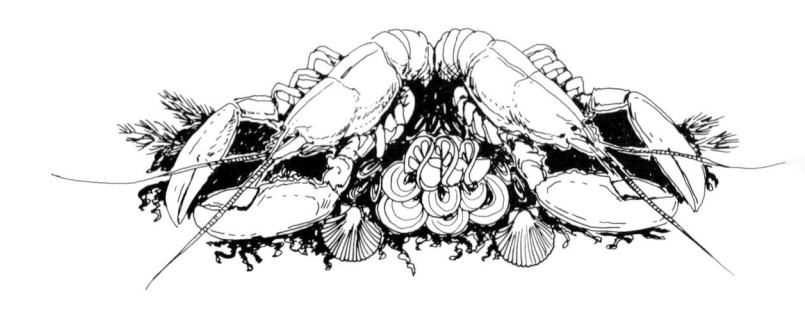

NORTHERN IRELAND

BELFAST	Strand Restaurant

12 Stranmillis Road, Belfast, Co Down BT9 5AA
Telephone: (0232) 682266 £30
Open: all day Mon-Sat, lunch + dinner Sun (closed Bank Holidays)
Meals served: Mon-Sat 12-12, lunch Sun 12-3, dinner Sun 5-10

Anne Turkington's popular restaurant that's been going strong for 10 years and spawned many imitations in the city. Drop in throughout the day for a coffee, snack or something more substantial. The food is eclectic and there's lots of it! You are encouraged to try a couple of starters at lunch time and from a choice of 15 or so there's something for everyone's taste. Main courses range from steak with a choice of parsley and garlic, blue cheese or horseradish butter to Italian-style meatballs served in a tomato and garlic sauce, with green tagliatelle. Reasonably priced food and wine list.

BELFAST	Welcome Restaurant

22 Stranmillis Road, Belfast, Co Antrim BT9 5AA
Telephone: (0232) 381359 £55
Open: lunch Mon-Fri, dinner daily (closed 24-26 Dec)
Meals served: lunch 12-1.45, dinner 5-11.30 (Sun 5-10.30)

There's a little pagoda roof over the gate and plenty of Chinese decorations inside – lanterns, dragons and screens – to set the scene. Run by the Wong family, it offers Cantonese, Pekinese and Szechuan dishes. Every year one of the chefs returns to Hong Kong to glean new ideas and add to the repertoire. Judging by the number of customers, the restaurant is indeed welcome in the area!

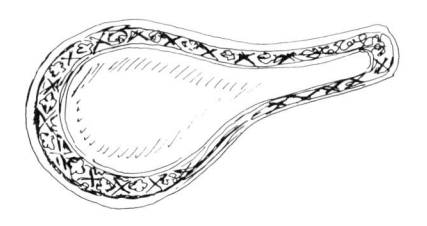

BELLANALECK	Sheelin

Bellanaleck, Co Fermanagh
Telephone: (036 582) 232 £45
Open: lunch + dinner Tue-Sun
Meals served: lunch 12.30-2.30, dinner 7-9.30
Bakery shop and restaurant, set dinners on Saturday evenings.

CRAWFORDSBURN	Old Inn

15 Main Street, Crawfordsburn, Co Down BT19 1JH
Telephone: (0247) 853255 £40
Fax: (0247) 852775
Open: lunch + dinner daily (closed 25+26 Dec)
Meals served: lunch 12.30-2.30, dinner 7-9.30 (Sun 5-7.30)

And old it certainly is with references to this hostelry going back to the year 1614. These days it's run as a cosy hotel with 32 bedrooms and company cars are now parked where the mail coaches once stood. Tourists tend to feature more during the summer months.

DUNADRY	Dunadry Inn

2 Islandreagh Drive, Dunadry, Co Antrim BT41 2HA
Telephone: (084 94) 32474 £40
Fax: (084 94) 33389
Open: lunch Sun-Fri, dinner daily (closed 24-27 Dec)
Meals served: lunch 12.30-1.45, dinner 7-9.45 (Sun 5.30-9.45)

This imaginatively converted former paper mill has 67 well equipped bedrooms with windows opening into a central courtyard. The word 'inn' is somewhat misleading as the unusual architecture and size of the main building, plus the various other buildings including separate executive suites that cover the site of the original village, make this a good-sized enterprise. The panelled restaurant overlooks Six Mile Water, and is situated over the mill stream. There is a choice of reception rooms available for meetings and conferences including the Bleach House. There are pleasant gardens and views, and a country club equipped for all health pursuits including pool and jacuzzi.

GARVAGH	Blackheath House & MacDuff's Restaurant

112 Killeague Road, Blackhill, Garvagh, Co Londonderry BT51 4HH
Telephone: (0265) 868433 £45
Open: dinner Tue-Sat (closed 25+26 Dec, 12 Jul)
Meals served: dinner 7-9.30

The Erwins' small, family-run business is set in a late 18th-century rectory, now a listed building with MacDuff's being in the former cellars of the house. Margaret's handwritten menus might include a bacon and mushroom pancake with a mushroom and cream sauce as a light starter, with a dish of venison braised in a marinade of burgundy, juniper berries and rosemary as something of a speciality main course. An apple and passionfruit glory and a selection of home-made sorbets feature among the puds. The wine list includes some very attractively priced bottles which if you wish you can choose from an original wine vault. As for the hotel, it offers 5 spacious bedrooms, an indoor swimming pool and splendid landscaped gardens.

Holywood — Culloden Hotel

142 Bangor Road, Craigavad, Holywood, Co Down BT18 0EX
Telephone: (023 17) 5223 £50
Fax: (023 17) 6777
Open: lunch Sun-Fri, dinner daily (closed 24+25 Dec)
Meals served: lunch 12.30-2.30, dinner 7-9.45 (Sun 7-8.30)

The Culloden Hotel comprises the older main building and newer extensions, set in its own lovely gardens with views over Belfast Lough – a favourite with the business community. The hotel offers numerous conference and meeting rooms and has 50 bedrooms. The more straightforward of the choices offer the best value in the main restaurant which can seat up to 150 and the hotel also boasts its own fully-equipped health and fitness club complete with pool plus its own 'Cultra Inn' within the hotels grounds.

Portaferry — Portaferry Hotel

10 The Strand, Portaferry, Co Down BT22 1PE
Telephone: (024 77) 28231 £50
Open: lunch + dinner daily (closed 25 Dec)
Meals served: lunch 12-2.30, dinner 7-9 (Sat 7-10)
Convenient for the ferry; the large menu has an emphasis on seafood.

PORTRUSH	Ramore

The Harbour, Portrush, Co Antrim BT56 8VM
Telephone: (0265) 822448
Open: dinner Tue-Sat (closed Xmas/New Year, 2 wks Feb)
Meals served: dinner 7-10

£50

Try ravioli of prawns and turbot, seafood fettucini, a mosaic of salmon and monkfish or maybe one of that day's fish specials or perhaps try a rack of lamb, roasted and served dowsed in a beurre noisette with garlic and thyme and accompanied by grilled vegetables.

From the puddings if available try the praline marquise or better still the dessert selection, the aptly named 'grand dessert'. A reasonably priced wine list, plus views from the harbourside make a visit to George McAlpin's Ramore a pleasure.

STRANGFORD	Lobster Pot

11 The Square, Strangford, Co Down BT30 7ND
Telephone: (039 686) 288
Open: lunch + dinner daily
Meals served: lunch 12-2.30, dinner 7-9.30 (Sun 7-9)
Restaurant and bar specialising in seafood.

£35

TEMPLEPATRICK	Templeton Hotel

882 Antrim Road, Templepatrick, Ballyclare, Co Antrim
Telephone: (084 94) 32984
Fax: (084 94) 33406
Restaurant:
Open: lunch + dinner daily
Meals served: lunch 12.30-1.45, dinner 7-9.45 (Sun 5.30-7.45)
Grill:
Open: lunch + dinner Mon-Sat, all day Sun
Meals served: lunch 12-2.30, dinner 5-9 (Fri+Sat 5-9.45), Sun 12-7.45

Restaurant: £35
Grill: £20

For night-time arrivals the hotel has a rather futuristic appearance with its floodlights and triangular windows. Inside you'll find an unusual juxtaposition of styles; chrome staircases, Japanese pools, Scandinavian banqueting hall and medieval motifs – 20 bedrooms at present with the mod cons you'd expect such as satellite television. Friendly Irish welcomes from the staff. Choose from the main restaurant overlooking the terrace and lawns, or the grill room.

Republic of Ireland Establishment Reviews

Adare — Adare Manor

Adare, Co Limerick
Telephone: (061) 396566
Fax: (061) 396124
Open: lunch + dinner daily
Meals served: lunch 12.30-2.30 (Sun 12.30-3), dinner 7.30-10

£80

I haven't been up there to prove it, but I'm told that the legend on the south parapet reads: 'Except the lord build the house, their labour is but lost that build it'. Since Adare Manor has survived the comings and goings of Ireland's turbulent history and today stands in gleaming condition, I can only think that the heavens shone favourably on its Gothic turrets! Inside, the bedrooms (64), public rooms and facilities are all that you'd expect from an establishment of this calibre, with many ornate ceilings, top-class furnishings, an oak stairway and a gallery (apparently the 2nd longest in Europe) which is modelled on the Palace of Versailles. Add to this a classically-inspired dining room complete with crystal chandeliers – sumptuous is the word for it.

There have been changes in the last year in both the kitchen and restaurant and there are some competent and well-chosen dishes available from either the table d'hôte or the à la carte menu. The meat dishes and grills have seen the best choice of late with good quality steaks served with béarnaise sauce and pommes frites, a breast of duck char-grilled served on a tomato-garlic sauce with olive oil, or the loin of Adare lamb. The Taste of Ireland menu is worth trying with its 5 courses plus sorbet. Sensibly-sized portions allow you to taste some interesting choices. Good choice of puddings and a comprehensive wine list.

Adare — Dunraven Arms

Adare, Co Limerick
Telephone: (061) 396209
Fax: (061) 396541
Open: lunch + dinner daily (closed 25 Dec, Good Friday)
Meals served: lunch 12.30-2 (Sun 12.30-2.15), dinner 7.30-9.30 (Sat 7.30-10)

£55

A 45-bedroomed hotel set in the beautiful village of Adare, and home of the County Limerick Hunt. There are 3 golf courses within half-an-hour of the hotel. Salmon and trout fishing plus many other outdoor pursuits in the area which the hotel will help you to arrange if required. Good meeting and conference rooms. Helpful friendly staff.

ADARE	Mustard Seed

Main Street, Adare, Co Limerick
Telephone: (061) 396451 £55
Open: dinner Tue-Sat (closed 25+26 Dec, Feb)
Meals served: dinner 7-10

Your fellow diners might be from the States or just around the corner in Adare, making for a healthy balance of foreign and local custom. The Mustard Seed has established quite a reputation for itself in the 6 years it's been running and things look rosy for the future. Chef Michael Weir's cooking is a seductive patois of the Académie Francaise and Irish blarney, as seen in one of his menus – 'A Celebration of Country Styles'. Slivers of smoked eel and pink grapefruit are served on a bed of seaweed-dressed salad, followed by a pumpkin and coconut soup. 'Pot on the stone' comes next – oxtail, beef and tongue with winter vegetables. From a recent menu came delicious wild mushroom and couscous in a filo pastry roll served with a timbale of spring onion and a five-spice sauce. Desserts might include a bittersweet heart of chocolate and honey with hazelnuts or Meg Gordan's goat's cheese with grapes.

AHAKISTA	Shiro

Ahakista, Nr Bantry, Co Cork
Telephone: (027) 67030 £65
Open: dinner daily
Meals served: dinner 7-9

Well, where are you? It's understandable to feel a little bewildered arriving at this restaurant in a village called Ahakista, to be greated by Herr Werner Pilz, knowing you're about to enjoy some Japanese food and yet – you're still in Ireland. Never mind, you'll get used to it, and Kei Pilz's exquisite paintings will help to create the mood. Not just an artist with the brush and ink, Kei is also a talented cook and her set price menu – with plenty of choice – is outstanding both in flavour and presentation. In the land where the spud was king she's finding a wider audience and has won a select band of admirers with offerings including tempura, sashimi, yakitori and teriyaki and the more unusual masu-yaki apppearing on recent set-price menus.

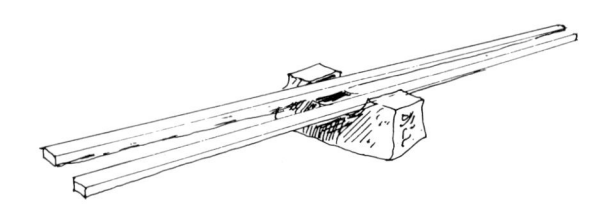

Athy — Tonlegee House

Athy, Co Kildare
Telephone: (0507) 31473
Fax: (0507) 31473
Open: lunch Sun, dinner Mon-Sat (closed 25+26 Dec, Good Friday)
Meals served: lunch 12.30-3, dinner 7-10.30

£50

Gradually this fine old house is coming back to life under the care and attention of Mark and Marjorie Molloy. They're also doing their best to ensure that their guests have an experience they'll treasure and want to come back for more. Five en suite bedrooms have been sympathetically brought up to date and 4 more are planned for the coming year. In the restaurant, Mark cooks some interesting dishes which are a cut above what's on offer elsewhere in the area. Ravioli of crab and cockles served with fennel sauce or boudin of chicken with a Pommery mustard sauce and to follow, perhaps fillets of brill with garlic potatoes and a lobster sauce.

Ballina — Mount Falcon Castle

Ballina, Co Mayo
Telephone: (096) 21172
Fax: (096) 21172
Open: dinner daily (closed Xmas, Feb+Mar)
Meals served: dinner at 8

£45

Mrs Constance Aldridge and Mount Falcon Castle are by now inseparable and guests return as much out of affection for her as for the hotel itself. Dinner is something to look forward to as you all sit around the same table and enjoy the food and conversation in equal measure. Go with friends or make some new ones during your stay.

Ballydehob — Annie's

Main Street, Ballydehob, Co Cork
Telephone: (028) 37292
Open: lunch + dinner Tue-Sat (closed 25+26 Dec, 3 wks Oct)
Meals served: lunch 12.30-2.30, dinner 6.30-9.30

£45

Small friendly restaurant. Anne Ferguson will come and take your order while you wait in the pub across the road!

| BALLYLICKEY | Ballylickey Manor House |

Ballylickey, Bantry Bay, Co Cork
Telephone: (027) 50071 £50
Fax: (027) 50124
Open: lunch + dinner daily (closed Nov-Mar, Wed to non-residents)
Meals served: lunch 12.30-2, dinner 7.30-9.30

The gardens and the view over Bantry Bay would alone justify a stay at Ballylickey. Over the years this 17th-century manor house has established a reputation for quality and comfort. You can choose between bedrooms located in the main building or in the wooden chalets set in the grounds. These are nicely furnished with fabrics and have en suite bathrooms. Rather delightfully 'Swiss Family Robinson' but with the Irish weather being what it is be prepared for a quick dash through the wind and rain to reach the dining room and banked peat fires of the lounge! The hotel has rights to private salmon and trout fishing and with 2 golf courses nearby and the wonderful coastline there's plenty to keep you amused.

| BALLYVAUGHAN | Gregans Castle |

Ballyvaughan, Co Clare
Telephone: (065) 77005 £60
Fax: (065) 77111
Open: lunch + dinner daily (closed Nov-Mar)
Meals served: lunch 12-3 (in bar), dinner 7-8.30

You're in Yeats country here at Gregans Castle and Lady Gregory's Coole Park is but a short drive from the hotel. However you don't need to resort to literature to find the inspiration for a visit – the beautiful gardens and wonderful views of the Burren mountains are there for all to see. The house itself is no less impressive. Peter Haden in the kitchen offers a 5-course set-price menu with some reasonable choices which normally include one or two good fish dishes.

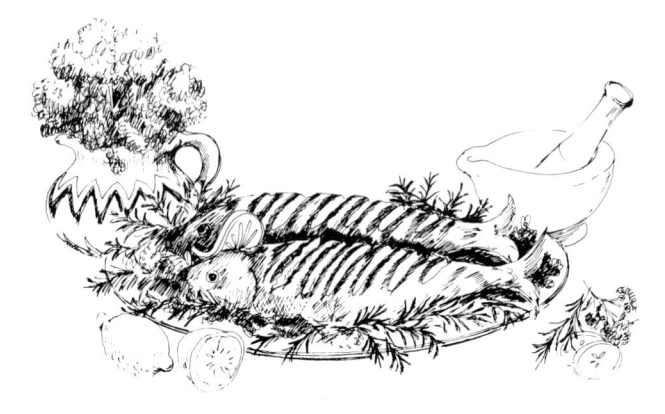

BUNRATTY	MacCloskey's

Bunratty House Mews, Bunratty, Co Clare
Telephone: (061) 364082 £60
Open: dinner Tue-Sat (closed 22 Dec-24 Jan, Good Friday)
Meals served: dinner 7-10

From the fixed-price, 5-course dinner menu you might begin with baked snails and mushrooms with a hollandaise sauce, follow with a carrot and spearmint soup, before moving on to an assiette of lamb with garlic and rosemary. A feuilleté of pear with a raspberry coulis is a good way to finish off, with coffee afterwards. Freshness, presentation and taste are the buzz words in the kitchen and carry through to the finished product. The restaurant is actually situated within the castle grounds.

CASHEL	Cashel House

Cashel, Co Galway
Telephone: (095) 31001 £60
Fax: (095) 31077
Open: lunch + dinner daily (closed 10-31 Jan)
Meals served: lunch 1-2, dinner 7.30-8.30 (Sun 7.30-9)

Every now and then you come away from a place with the satisfaction that everything is as it should be. Just such an occasion could be your departure from Cashel House. The friendly and efficient staff, the well-kept public rooms, the stylish bedrooms, the stunning gardens are all impeccable and owners Dermot and Kay McEvilly have every right to feel proud of their establishment. Standards are maintained in the restaurant, with fixed price menus using high quality local produce. Perhaps Cleggan Bay flat oysters as a starter or a home-made brioche stuffed with scallops and served with a Noilly Prat sauce. A good fish soup to follow from a choice of 2 soups, then a roast leg of Connemara lamb with rosemary or a whole poached or grilled lobster. Some good Irish cheeses, or a yellow plum tart served with cream to finish. Medium-priced wine list.

CASHEL	Cashel Palace

Main Street, Cashel, Co Tipperary
Telephone: (062) 61411 £60
Fax: (062) 61521
Open: lunch + dinner daily (closed 25+26 Dec)
Meals served: lunch 12-2.15, dinner 7.30-9.30

A 20-bedroomed hotel set in a Palladian mansion. The gardens are particularly fine with the Queen Anne Mulberry still flourishing on the lawn. You can eat in the Bishop's Buttery or the Four Seasons Restaurant.

Cashel	Chez Hans

Rockside, Cashel, Co Tipperary
Telephone: (062) 61177 £60
Open: dinner Tue-Sat (closed Bank Holidays, 3 wks Jan)
Meals served: dinner 6.30-10

The restaurant has recently undergone a face-lift and looks better for it. Hans-Peter Mattiä's cooking, however, needs no rejuvenating – it's as good as it ever was. Some superb fish and shellfish dishes are to be enjoyed here – quenelles of brill and turbot, hot buttered lobster from Kinsale, and cassoulet of fresh seafood to give but a few examples. Mainly French mid-price wine list.

Castledermot	Doyle's School House

Main Street, Castledermot, Co Kildare
Telephone: (0503) 44282 £45
Open: lunch Sun, dinner Tue-Sat (closed mid-Jan-mid Feb)
Meals served: lunch 12.30-2, dinner 6.30-10.30 (Nov-Mar 7.30-10.30)

The simple setting of the School House provides a platform for some extremely good food by chef John Doyle who cooks with sophistication traditional dishes that can be as simple as boiled ham with mild mustard sauce, steak and oyster pie. Vegetables and puds show the same care and attention. Small reasonably-priced wine list. A favourite with both locals and the many tourists who come to this area. Twelve bedrooms.

Clifden	O'Grady's

Market Street, Clifden, Co Galway
Telephone: (095) 21450 £40
Open: lunch + dinner Mon-Sat (closed 16-30 Dec, 12 Jan-12 Mar)
Meals served: lunch 12.30-2.30, dinner 6.30-10
Predominantly seafood restaurant, but also some meat dishes.

Clones	Hilton Park

Scotshouse, Clones, Co Monaghan
Telephone: (047) 56007 £55
Fax: (047) 56033
Open: to residents only (closed Oct – Apr)
Meals served: by arrangement
In the same family (the Maddens) for 250 years – full of their personal touches. Popular with sporting parties.

CONG   Ashford Castle

Cong, Co Mayo
Telephone: (092) 46003   **£80**
Fax: (092) 46260   *Connaught Room:* **£90**
Open: lunch + dinner daily
Meals served: lunch 12.45-2, dinner 7-9.30
Open: lunch + dinner daily
Meals served: lunch 1-2.30, dinner 6.30-10.30

A spectacular hotel housed in a 13th-century castle with panelled halls and some interesting mixes of antique and period pieces. Spectacular surroundings. You can even fish from the castle's own lakes and almost every other sporting activity is catered for. President Reagan stayed here during his state visit to Ireland in 1984, and one of his hero's films was shot in the Co Mayo countryside – John Wayne's *The Quiet Man*. Claiming to offer the chance of living an Irish legend, Ashford Castle is almost like a Hollywood dream come true - the place simply exudes history. Its 83 bedrooms are impeccable and have the full complement of extras. Dining is divided between the George V Room Restaurant and the Connaught Room, directed by Denis Linehan who provides cooking to a very high standard, the Connaught Room catering for a smaller, gourmet clientele. A good way of experiencing the food is to try the Taste of Ireland menu which offers some traditional and well-cooked choices. Comprehensive wine list. Quite an experience.

CORK   Arbutus Lodge

Montenotte, Cork, Co Cork
Telephone: (021) 501237   **£60**
Fax: (021) 502893
Open: lunch + dinner Mon-Sat (closed 1 wk Xmas)
Meals served: lunch 1-2, dinner 7-9.30

I rather liked Pauline Bewick's illustration on the cover of the menu – an oriental looking Irish lass sinking her teeth into a pig's trotter as she reads a slim volume of Samuel Beckett, Ireland's expatriate writer. No surprises, then, that traditional crubeens feature inside, along with Galway oysters, and West Cork asparagus as well as Gallic specialities such as cassolette of prawn tails and mouclade of mussels. The Ryan family continue to extend warm and friendly hospitality in this 20-bedroomed hotel.

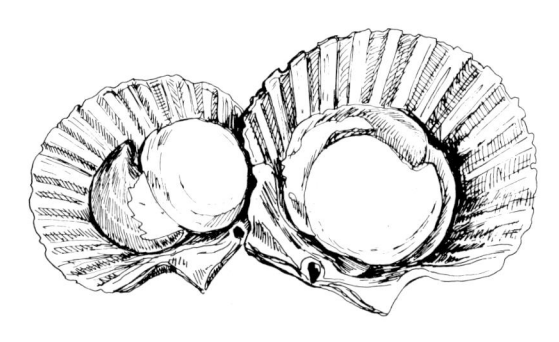

Cork — Bully's

40 Paul Street, Cork, Co Cork
Telephone: (021) 273555 £25
Open: all day daily (closed 25+26 Dec, Good Friday)
Meals served: 12-11.30

The local furniture factory supplies the teak and beech offcuts which fuel the pizza oven. However, so delicious are the pizzas, which come sizzling to your table, that perhaps there's a mystery ingredient as well! Terrific value for money. You could easily walk past this restaurant with scarcely a second glance, which goes to show that appearances can be deceptive. Not just a pizza parlour, Bully's also serves fresh pasta made daily by a band of Italians upstairs and more expensive dishes besides. Small and popular, so you'll have to jostle for a table.

Cork — Clifford's

18 Dyke Parade, Cork, Co Cork
Telephone: (021) 275333 £55
Open: lunch Tue-Fri, dinner Mon-Sat (closed Bank Holidays, 2 wks Aug)
Meals served: lunch 12.30-2.30, dinner 7.30-10.30

Once Cork's county library, this Georgian house is now rather more of an art gallery what with Michael and Deirdre Clifford's collection of contemporary Irish art lining the walls. Spend a few minutes browsing while you sip an aperitif in the first floor bar. Michael's cooking maintains a careful balance of the orthodox and the experimental on the fixed price menu. Clonakilty black pudding and tripe comes 'Clifford's style' and the wild salmon starter would do justice as a main course. All the fish and vegetables are fresh daily. The fairly priced wine list includes some 10 half bottles.

Cork — Huguenot

French Church Street, Cork, Co Cork
Telephone: (021) 273357 £30
Open: lunch Mon-Fri, dinner Sun-Fri, all day Sat (closed 25+26 Dec)
Meals served: lunch 10.30-2.30, dinner 6-10.30 (Sun 6-10), Sat 12.30-11
Welcome new French restaurant in Cork.

Cork — Isaacs

48, McCurtain Street, Cork, Co Cork
Telephone: (021) 503805 £35
Open: lunch Mon-Fri, dinner daily, (closed 3 days Xmas)
Meals served: lunch 12-2.30, dinner 6.30-10.30 (Sun 6.30-9.00)

The Ryan family of Arbutus Lodge have got together with chef Canice Sharkey to create this refreshingly relaxed middle-market restaurant in a converted 18th-century warehouse. Softly aged brickwork, terracotta paintwork and vibrant modern paintings provide a clue to what to expect of the menu: an eclectic mixture of styles and influences, all brought together in cheerful harmony under Sharkey's watchful eye. Quality and value are the aim: try the fish soup served with a gutsy rouille and garlic croutons, or a few slices of char-grilled monkfish with a punchy niçoise sauce followed, perhaps, by a luscious summer fruit compote, a shimmering palette of barely-warmed soft fruit, with home-made vanilla ice-cream.

CORK   Jacques

9 Phoenix Street, Cork, Co Cork
Telephone: (021) 277387   £50
Open: lunch Mon-Sat, dinner Tue-Sat (closed Bank Holidays, 10 days Xmas)
Meals served: lunch 12-4, dinner 6-10.30

You'll find Jacques in a small side street just behind the Imperial Hotel. Come here at mid-day for a serve-yourself lunch or in the evening for more serious fare. Specialities include locally reared guineafowl and duck, fresh fish and seafood. Whenever possible organic vegetables are used. Examples from the menu include the rather trendy (but delicious) roast monkfish with fresh beetroot and chives and rack of lamb with garlic and olive breadcrumbs in a mint-flavoured jus. Good home-made ice cream is served with shortcakes sprinkled with berries. Farmhouse cheeses are kept in excellent condition. The hand-written wine list is fairly priced.

CORK   Morrisons Island Hotel

Morrisons Quay, Cork, Co Cork
Telephone: (021) 275858   £50
Fax: (021) 275833
Open: lunch & dinner daily
Meals served: lunch 12.30-2, dinner 6-9.30

Designed and run on the same lines as Stephen's Hall in Dublin, Cork's first all-suites hotel is very central and right on the river bank so you can watch the fish from your window. Well-equipped suites include a lobby and kitchenette in addition to the usual accommodation and this compact, thoughtfully designed hotel has style, especially in the foyer with its oriental rugs and rich colours and the restaurant, which features locally-made hand-painted furniture.

CORK   O'Keeffe's

23 Washington Street West, Cork, Co Cork
Telephone: (021) 275645   £60
Open: dinner Mon-Sat (closed Bank Holidays, 1 wk Xmas)
Meals served: dinner 6.30-10.30

Marie O'Keefe is in the kitchen while husband Tony is at front of house. Decor is in shades of sweet pea colours and grey. Dishes include lamb's sweetbreads in a garlic croustade and baked aubergines with tomatoes and mozzarella as starters. Main courses feature roast monkfish or a medley of that day's seafood. Puds are good – some nice home-made ice cream. Only a year or so on, things seem to be going well!

Cork	Rochestown Park Hotel

Rochestown Road, Cork, Co Cork
Telephone: (021) 892233 £50
Fax: (021) 892178
Open: lunch & dinner daily
Meals served: lunch 12.30-2.30, dinner 7-10

Set in lovely gardens and convenient to the airport, the original part of this hotel is a former home of the Lord Mayors of Cork and features well-proportioned, gracious public rooms. Modern bedrooms are functional and comfortable with full amenities.

Dalkey	Il Ristorante

108 Coliemore Road, Dalkey, Co Dublin
Telephone: (01) 284 0800 £55
Open: dinner Tue-Sun (closed Bank Holidays except Good Friday, mid Jan-mid Feb)
Meals served: dinner 7.30-10.30

You could walk up and down Coliemore Road for years without realising that there's a restaurant up above the Club pub. Roberto and Celine Pons aren't going out of their way to proclaim the fact to one and all. But then why should they? A tiny place with just 6 tables, its subdued lighting and candles make for cosy romantic rendezvous. Although diners might be eating each other up with their eyes, there's lots of good northern Italian food besides. Zuppe pavese or gnocchi al burro e parmiggiano to start, and for main courses agnello alla creme di aglio or the old favourite saltimbocca alla Romana. All Italian wine list. Avanti!

Dingle	Doyle's Seafood Bar & Townhouse

4 John Street, Dingle, Co Kerry
Telephone: (066) 51174 £50
Fax: (066) 51816
Open: dinner Mon-Sat (closed mid Nov-mid Mar)
Meals served: dinner 6-9

The lobsters are plucked from the tank and the fish comes straight off the fishing boats in the harbour. John and Stella Doyle have been running their restaurant with rooms since 1973 and it remains as busy as ever. Start with clams and mussels in a tomato and garlic sauce with pasta, and follow with grilled turbot fillets in a champagne sauce. A bottle of Pouilly Fumé from the wine list and you're set for an enjoyable evening's eating. The 8 bedrooms are nicely furnished and will save you the trouble of booking a hotel.

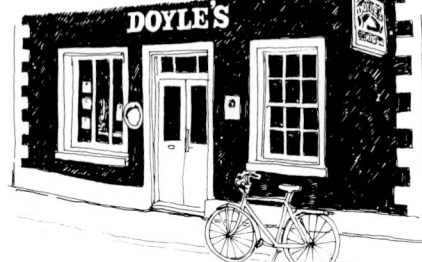

DINGLE
John Street, Dingle, Co Kerry
Telephone: (066) 51600
Open: lunch + dinner daily (closed all Tue in winter, Jan-17 Mar)
Meals served: lunch 12.30-2.30, dinner 6-10
Under new ownership, another Dingle restaurant specialising in seafood.

Half Door
£35

DUBLIN
Anglesea Street, Dublin, Co Dublin
Telephone: (01) 715622
Fax: (01) 715997
Open: lunch Mon-Fri, dinner daily (closed 25+26 Dec)
Meals served: lunch 12.30-2, dinner 5-9.45
Popular addition to Dublin's hotel scene. Eighty-six bedrooms.

Blooms Hotel
£40

DUBLIN
47 South William Street, Dublin, Co Dublin 2
Telephone: (01) 770708
Open: lunch Mon-Fri, dinner Mon-Sat
Meals served: lunch 12-2.30, dinner 6.30-12.30
Recently opened Dublin establishment, informal, modern menu.

Café Caruso
£35

DUBLIN   Le Coq Hardi

35 Pembroke Road, Ballsbridge, Dublin 4, Co Dublin
Telephone: (01) 689070   **£80**
Fax: (01) 689887
Open: lunch Mon-Fri, dinner Mon-Sat (closed Bank Holidays, 1 wk Xmas, 2 wks Aug)
Meals served: lunch 12-2.30, dinner 7-11

Le Coq Hardi is something of a Dublin institution – John and Catherine Howard run this classic restaurant with charm and enthusiasm, an elegant setting for John's excellent cooking. An tasting menu affords the opportunity to try some of Le Coq Hardi's specialities, which make good use of Irish produce. If available, try the Irish wild salmon which is served on a bed of fresh spinach leaves with a watercress butter sauce, or from the starters Le Coq Hardi smokies. A comprehensive and top-end-of-the-market wine list offers a huge choice.

DUBLIN
15 St Stephen's Lane, Dublin, Co Dublin
Telephone: (01) 764679
Open: lunch Mon-Fri, dinner Tue-Sat
Meals served: lunch 12.30-2.30, dinner 8-11.30
Popular and lively bistro, sawdust on the floors, though not cheap!

Dobbins Wine Bistro
£65

DUBLIN
41 Lower Camden Street, Dublin, Co Dublin
Telephone: (01) 753109
Open: dinner Wed-Sun (closed Bank Holidays, 1 wk Xmas)
Meals served: dinner 7-11 (snacks Mon-Fri 8am-4pm)
Under the same ownership as the former Shay Beano – unpretentious surroundings, international menu.

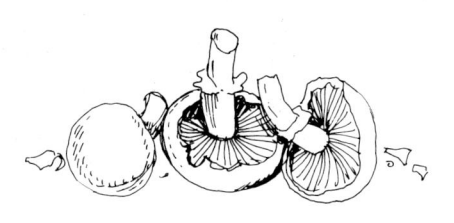

La Fiesta
£40

DUBLIN	Grey Door

22 Upper Pembroke Street, Dublin, Co Dublin
Telephone: (01) 763286 £55
Fax: (01) 763287
Open: lunch Mon-Fri, dinner Mon-Sat (closed Bank Holidays, 1 wk Xmas)
Meals served: lunch 12.30-2.15, dinner 7-11

The Grey Door restaurant offers a choice of dining in either the Grey Door restaurant or the more informal Blushes as well as a selection of private dining rooms. Choose from either the set price menu or select from the à la carte dishes, such as a shoal of fresh mussels steamed with basil and white wine or, more unusually, enquire about the forsmack – a Finnish peasant speciality. To follow, new season guineafowl boned and roasted then served with a sauce of morels. There are 7 well-equipped bedrooms to enable you to enjoy dinner and stay the night.

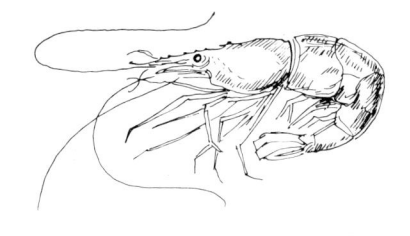

DUBLIN	Kapriol

45 Lower Camden Street, Dublin 2, Co Dublin
Telephone: (01) 751235 £60
Open: dinner Mon-Sat (closed Bank Holidays, 3 wks Aug)
Meals served: dinner 7.30-12

Giuseppe and Egidia Peruzzi run this small 9-table restaurant offering traditional Italian cooking with concessions to the Irish palate. They have no intention of expanding since that way they can still find time for their vegetable garden. Given their steady stream of customers who can blame them? Mainly Italian wine list, reasonably-priced.

DUBLIN	Longfields Hotel

Fitzwilliam Street Lower, Dublin 2, Co Dublin
Telephone: (01) 761367 £50
Fax: 761542
Open: lunch Mon-Fri, dinner daily
Meals served: lunch 12.30-2.30, dinner 6.30-10 (Fri 6.30-11, Sat 7-11, Sun 7-9)

Converted from two Georgian houses, public rooms in this small, characterful hotel are furnished like a private house with period furniture, good pictures and fresh flowers – and there is corresponding emphasis on friendly personal service. Rooms get smaller as you go up; the best on the first floor are quite spacious with bathrooms, smaller ones rather cramped with shower only, but all are individually furnished with style.

DUBLIN — Mont Clare Hotel

Merrion Square, Dublin, Co Dublin
Telephone: (01) 616799
Fax: (01) 615663
Open: lunch + dinner daily
Meals served: lunch 12-2, dinner 7-9

£50

Refurbished business hotel, characterful Dublinesque bar.

DUBLIN — Pasta Fresca

3-4 Chatham Street, Dublin 2, Co Dublin
Telephone: (01) 679 2402
Open: all day Mon-Sat (closed Bank Holidays, 1 wk Xmas)
Meals served: Mon-Thurs 8-11, Fri+Sat 8-11.30

£20

Offers just what it says in a bistro-cum-delicatessen setting.

DUBLIN — Patrick Guilbaud

46 James Place, Off Lower Baggot Street, Dublin 2, Co Dublin
Telephone: (01) 764192
Fax: (01) 601546
Open: lunch + dinner Tue-Sat (closed Bank Holidays)
Meals served: lunch 12.30-2, dinner 7.30-10.15

£75

A lighter touch is in evidence here at Patrick Guilbaud, as chef Guillaume Lebrun goes to work in the kitchen. Amuse-gueules – in both senses of the word – might include quail's eggs jokily presented as fried eggs. Ravioli de queue de langoustines au beurre de tomates is a delicious Christmas present of a dish, 3 little parcels stuffed full of perfectly cooked prawns in a rich red sauce. A couple of minutes into the blanc de turbot poêlé, and word went round that this was the best fish one seasoned diner had sunk his teeth into – ever. A lighter touch, yes, but seriously good cooking nonetheless. An excellent roast squab pigeon then followed, served on a thin potato cake with spinach and garlic juice. If you find it difficult to choose from this excellent menu, the chef will choose for you to present a well-balanced meal. This remains a comprehensive and reasonably-priced menu. Restaurant Patrick Guilbaud is elegant in its decor, food and service and remains one of my favourite Dublin restaurants.

DUBLIN — Shelbourne Hotel

St Stephen's Green, Dublin 2, Co Dublin
Telephone: (01) 766471
Fax: (01) 616006
Open: lunch + dinner daily
Meals served: lunch 12.30-2.30, dinner 6-10.30 (Sun 6-10)

£55

For the writer Elizabeth Brown the Shelbourne was the hotel to which all others were to be compared. She even went so far as to immortalize the place in a book – so now you know what to take as reading matter when you go and stay. A truly splendid establishment, it has included many famous people among its guests down through the years. It boasts no fewer than 164 bedrooms each with bathroom and many extras. Enjoy the distinguished yet friendly atmosphere of one of Dublin's finest hotels. The grills and roasts offer the best value on the restaurant menu.

DUBLIN	Stephens Hall Hotel

14/17 Lower Leeson Street, Dublin 2, Co Dublin
Telephone: (01) 610585 £55
Fax: (01) 610606
Open: lunch & dinner daily (closed 2 days Xmas)
Meals served: lunch 12-2.30, dinner 6.15-10.30

Just off St. Stephen's Green, a discreet entrance leads into this restful, understated all-suites hotel. Although especially popular with business visitors, the exceptional facilities – each suite has its own lobby, sitting/dining room with kitchenette, at least one bathroom and one or two bedrooms – make it a useful alternative for a wide range of discerning travellers, including families or groups who find ordinary hotel accommodation too restricted.

DUBLIN	Whites on the Green

119 St Stephen's Green, Dublin, Co Dublin
Telephone: (01) 751975 £55
Open: lunch Mon-Fri, dinner Mon-Sat (closed Bank Holidays, Xmas/New Year)
Meals served: lunch 12-2.30, dinner 7-10.45 (Sat 7-11)
Set menus of French cooking in this traditional Dublin restaurant.

DUN LAOGHAIRE	De Selby's

17/18 Patrick Street, Dun Laoghaire, Co Dublin
Telephone: (01) 2841761 £25
Fax: (01) 2841762
Open: dinner daily, all day Sat+Sun (closed Good Friday, 24-26 Dec)
Meals served: dinner 5.30-11, Sat 12-11, Sun 12-10
Restaurant and art gallery popular with families.

DUNDALK	Cellars

Backhouse Centre, Clanbrassil Street, Dundalk, Co Louth
Telephone: (042) 33745 £20
Open: lunch Mon-Fri
Meals served: lunch 12.30-2
Friendly small restaurant serving wholesome home-cooked food.

DUNDERRY	Dunderry Lodge Restaurant

Dunderry, Navan, Co Meath
Telephone: (046) 31671 £65
Open: lunch Sun (+ Sat May-Aug), dinner Tue-Sat (closed Bank Holidays)
Meals served: lunch 1-2, dinner 7-9.30
Popular local restaurant.

DUNWORLEY	Dunworley Cottage

Butlerstown, Clonakilty, Dunworley, Co Cork
Telephone: (023) 40314 £35
Open: lunch + dinner Wed-Sun (closed 6 Jan-early Mar)
Meals served: lunch 1-3 (by arrangement Jun-Aug) dinner 6.30-10

As Swedish owner and chef Katherine Noren says, 'I see my business as a great pleasure giving me 18 hours of work a day. It is my hobby, my living – all I ever wished for.' Who could deny it after sampling her cooking and noticing quite how seriously she takes her craft. Ingredients are organically grown, the meat reared locally, and the menu indicates gluten free, low cholesterol and vegan dishes. The home-made salami comes from her own pigs and she makes all the bread herself. The remote stone cottage with its bare floor boards and roaring fire captures that blend of Scandinavian rigour and human warmth which is to be found in Katherine herself. She's not interested in pampering her guests, but in making them enjoy their meal – there *is* a difference. Children are welcome and a special menu is available with no chips or junk food in sight. 'If we want them as customers later on',explains Katherine, 'they will have to learn to enjoy real food.'

DURRUS	Blairs Cove House

Blairs Cove, Durrus, Nr Bantry, Co Cork
Telephone: (027) 61127 £55
Open: dinner Tue-Sat (closed Nov-Feb)
Meals served: dinner 7.30-9.30

Blairs Cove House is itself a Georgian manor overlooking Dunmanus Bay. You can stay in any one of the 5 apartments in the outbuildings, one of which is a converted smokery. Sabine and Philippe de Mey are a husband and wife team who combine to ensure informal yet concerned service. Sabine supervises the kitchen using fresh ingredients, organically grown where possible. Her cooking is straightforward aiming at preserving the natural flavours. Appetizers are selected from an extensive buffet, while steaks and fish are grilled on an open wood fire. The grand piano doubles as a table for the attractive looking desserts. Good range of Irish farmhouse cheeses.

ENNIS	Auburn Lodge

Galway Road, Ennis, Co Clare
Telephone: (065) 21427 £45
Fax: (065) 21202
Open: lunch + dinner daily
Meals served: 12.30-2.30 (Sat+ Sun 12.30-3), dinner 5.30-9.30 (Sat+ Sun 6.30-9)
Modern hotel with leisure facilities. 100 bedrooms.

ENNISKERRY	Enniscree Lodge Inn

Cloon, Enniskerry, Co Wicklow
Telephone: (01) 286 3542 £50
Fax: (01) 286 6037
Open: lunch + dinner daily (closed Xmas, 3 Jan-14 Feb, also Mon+Tue in winter)
Meals served: lunch 12.30-2.30, dinner 7.30-9.30 (Sat 7.30-10, Sun 7.30-9)

Chalet-type hunting lodge which looks out over Glencree Valley to the mountains beyond – a truly astonishing prospect. Real old Irish cooking is given a modern twist which results in some tasty dishes. Brother and sister Paul Johnson and Lynda Fox have put their hearts into making a go of this place – they deserve to do well!

FURBO	Connemara Coast Hotel

Furbo, Nr Galway, Co Galway
Telephone: (091) 92108 £45
Fax: (091) 92065
Open: dinner daily
Meals served: dinner 6.30-9.30 (Sat 7-10, Sun 6.30-9)
Modern hotel with 120 bedrooms.

GALWAY	Blue Raincoat

Spanish Arch, Long Walk, Galway, Co Galway
Telephone: (091) 64642
Open: lunch + dinner Tue-Sat (closed 3 wks Jan, 25 Dec) £40
Meals served: lunch 12.30-2.30, dinner 6.30-12
Michael Ryan uses organic and wild produce whenever possible at his popular recently-opened restaurant.

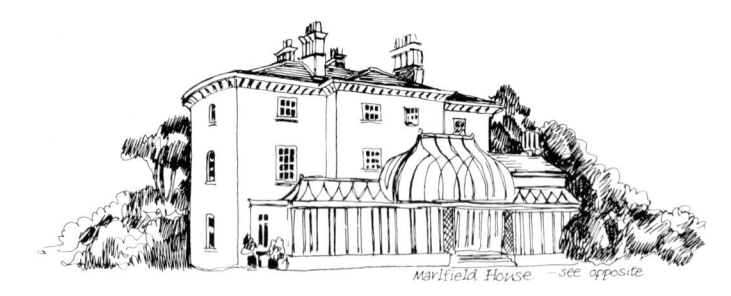

Marlfield House – see opposite

Gorey — Marlfield House

Gorey, Co Wexford
Telephone: (055) 21124
Fax: (055) 21572
Open: lunch + dinner daily (closed Dec + Jan)
Meals served: lunch 12.30-2, dinner 7-9.30

£65

Mary Bowe, owner of Marlfield House, has to her name a string of awards as long as your arm. She supervises every aspect of this renowned establishment, thereby ensuring the very highest standards in care and attention. Chef Rose Brannock has now been given time to settle down in the kitchen and she conjures up some fine food, combining country house and modern styles. In the leafy surroundings of the dining room and conservatory, enjoy dishes such as pan-fried noisettes of lamb, medallions of beef with glazed shallots and roast breast of duck on a bed of cabbage and smoked bacon. Herbs are used to great effect and come straight from the hotel's garden. Smoking is strongly discouraged. Marlfield House itself is a Regency-style mansion constructed in 1820 and was originally the home of the Earl of Courton. The house is set amidst landscaped gardens and its restful interior contains many fine period pieces. A luxurious country house hotel.

Greystones — The Hungry Monk

Greystones, Co Wicklow
Telephone: (01) 287 5759
Open: lunch Sun, dinner Tue-Sun
Meals served: lunch 12.30-3, dinner 7-11

£45

This restaurant is quite a find, above the Irish Permanent Building Society in the main street. Candles lit even at lunchtime lend a suitably monastic feel to the place. However, there's no room for self-denial on the wide-ranging menu. Hors d'oeuvres include crab claws beurre d'ail and lambs kidneys turbigo. Main courses feature poulet Mombasa and carré d'agneau – and there's much more besides. No holier than thou attitudes either towards the puddings. One notable offering is Death by Chocolate – a white chocolate terrine on a fresh fruit coulis. The wine list will cause some surprises with its 187 items – the pride and joy of owner Pat Keown.

Howth — King Sitric

East Pier, Harbour Road, Howth, Co Dublin
Telephone: (01) 326729
Fax: (01) 392442
Open: dinner Mon-Sat (closed Bank Holidays, 10 days Easter)
Meals served: dinner 6.30-11

£60

Chef/proprietor Aidan MacManus offers a wide range of excellent seafood at this fish restaurant including delicious Howth crab, either served with a Mornay sauce or cold with mayonnaise. Salmon, turbot, monkfish, brill and lobster all feature on the menu with sirloin steak for carnivores. Good home-made brown bread, Irish cheeses and puds. Relaxed friendly atmosphere in the dining room.

KANTURK	Assolas Country House

Kanturk, Co Cork
Telephone: (029) 50015 £60
Fax: (029) 50795
Open: dinner daily (closed Nov-Mar)
Meals served: dinner 7-8.30 (Sun 7-8)

Run by the Bourke family for a quarter of a century now, the Assolas Country House is a beautifully situated hotel with just 9 bedrooms. Hazel Bourke is the chef and provides some first-class food doing justice to the ingredients, many of which are home produced. Marinated lamb's kidneys, roast duck with raspberry sauce and a vegetarian special of five different types of nuts baked with cheese and apple are typical dishes on her menus. Reasonably priced wine list and friendly relaxed atmosphere.

KENMARE	Lime Tree

Shelbourne Street, Kenmare, Co Kerry
Telephone: (064) 41225 £45
Open: dinner Mon-Sat (closed Nov-Easter)
Meals served: dinner 6-9.30
Informal restaurant, chef/proprietor Maura Foley, good use of local fish.

KENMARE	Park Hotel

Kenmare, Co Kerry
Telephone: (064) 41200 £80
Fax: (064) 41402
Open: lunch + dinner daily (closed mid Nov-Xmas, 4 Jan-Easter)
Meals served: lunch 1-1.45, dinner 7-8.45

A place to reckon with, the Park Hotel at Kenmare maintains high standards both in terms of accommodation and food. Executive Chef Matthew Darcy heads a team of well-drilled chefs in the kitchen and their combined efforts lead to some impressive dishes. A la carte and table d'hote menus are offered with much to tempt the palate. Typical main courses might include truite de l'atlantique au four, sauce pomme à l'indienne, sur lit de nouilles au fumet de concombre and suprême de poulet farcie au saumon à la sauce homard. Flavours are carefully balanced and the sauces deftly constructed. An impressive all-round performance. The hotel itself has some 50 bedrooms and lovely views. Francis Brennan has worked hard to create this friendly but professionally-run hotel.

KILKENNY	Lacken House

Dublin Road, Kilkenny, Co Kilkenny
Telephone: (056) 61085 £50
Open: dinner Tue-Sat (closed 25 Dec)
Meals served: dinner 7-10
Small friendly local restaurant, simple modern cooking.

KILLARNEY	Aghadoe Heights Hotel

Aghadoe, Killarney, Co Kerry
Telephone: (064) 31766 £75
Fax: (064) 31345
Open: lunch + dinner daily (closed none)
Meals served: lunch 12.15-2, dinner 7-9.30

Lovely views of the mist-shrouded mountains from this superbly located hotel. Gleaming new interiors after recent refurbishment by owner Fredrick Losel. Further improvements, including leisure facilities, are under way. Choose from 10 starters, all at one price of £9.50, ranging from tartare of wild salmon with Beluga caviar to a more humble but tasty terrine of monkfish and brill served in a saffron jelly. From the main courses priced at £18.50, try an unusual cassoulet of calves' sweetbreads and scallops or a more straightforward smoked loin of lamb with spring onions. Good desserts. Middle-priced wine list.

KILLARNEY	Gaby's Seafood Restaurant

27 High Street, Killarney, Co Kerry
Telephone: (064) 32519 £45
Fax: (064) 32747
Open: lunch Tue-Sat, dinner Mon-Sat (also closed dinner Sun Oct-Apr, closed Feb)
Meals served: lunch 12.30-2.30, dinner 6-10

The menu is in the hands of the Kerry fishing fleet, for what they don't catch is struck off the list for that day, Gert Maes handles his raw materials with the respect they deserve, cooking the fish as simply as possible to retain their wonderful natural flavours. Kerry shellfish platter contains lobster, crab claws, oysters and other shellfish. Otherwise, fillet of brill is served in a light tomato and pernod cream sauce. Reasonably priced red and white wines from Italy, Germany and France with a smattering from the New World.

KINSALE	Max's Wine Bar

Main Street, Kinsale, Co Cork
Telephone: (021) 772443 £40
Open: lunch & dinner daily (closed Nov-Feb)
Meals served: lunch 1-3, dinner 7-10.30

Named after a dog, long since departed, who used to lie across the doorway, this delightful little restaurant has charmed visitors to Kinsale for 17 years and despite improvements, including a conservatory, remains reassuringly unchanged. Plants and fresh flowers are reflected in the highly varnished table tops and the light, creative menus are always tempting, with an emphasis on starters and salads such as hot baked crab and asparagus, served attractively on a shell-shaped dish, or just-melting warm baked goat's cheese scattered with toasted almonds on a bed of lettuce. Fresh fish is handled simply and with confidence and the home-made bread is irresistible.

KINSALE — Old Presbytery

Cork Street, Kinsale, Co Cork
Telephone: (021) 772027 £25
Open: dinner Mon-Sat (closed Xmas)
Meals served: dinner 7.30-8.30

In their quaint little brochure they mention that 'the big beds and Irish linen give you a real old sleep'. I thought that was a lovely way to put it! Downstairs the old kitchen has been converted into a dining room and offers a fixed price dinner menu with a choice of 4 starters, 3 main courses and several puddings.

LETTERFRACK — Rosleague Manor

Letterfrack, Connemara, Co Galway
Telephone: (095) 41101 £50
Fax: (095) 41168
Open: lunch + dinner daily (closed Nov-Easter)
Meals served: lunch 1-2.30, dinner 8-9.30 (Sun 8-9)

Rosleague Manor is run by brother and sister partnership Patrick and Ann Foyle. This Regency house has been carefully restored and is situated within its own gardens. The dining room with its period-style furniture and wooden floors offers some well-cooked dishes including baked devilled crab as a starter, poached wild salmon served with hollandaise or perhaps a straightforward rack of Connemara lamb cooked with fresh herbs and served with mint jelly. For pudding, chocolate and strawberry roulade or the Rosleague bread and butter pudding. Simple but reasonably-priced wine list. The new bedrooms added recently are well-furnished and bring the total to 20.

MALAHIDE — Bon Appetit

9 St James Terrace, Malahide, Dublin, Co Dublin
Telephone: (01) 845 0314 £45
Open: lunch Mon-Fri, dinner Mon-Sat (closed Bank Holidays, 1 wk Xmas)
Meals served: lunch 12.30-2, dinner 7-11
A welcome addition to the area after being transplanted from the centre of Dublin. Tables are at a premium on Saturday evenings.

MALAHIDE — Roches Bistro

12 New Street, Malahide, Co Dublin
Telephone: (01) 845 2777 £45
Open: lunch Mon-Sat, dinner Thu-Sat (closed Bank Holiday, 2 wks Jan)
Meals served: lunch 12-2.30, dinner 7-10.30

Historically correct or not, there certainly seems to be some deep-felt sympathy between the Irish and the French if their cooking is anything to go by. How else do you explain the similarity of so many dishes and why a place like Roches Bistro establishes itself in this picturesque coastal town with such ease? Come here for an eclectic menu typifying French country cooking à l'Irlandais. Bon appetit, begorrah!

Mallow — Longueville House

Mallow, Co Cork
Telephone: (022) 47156
Fax: (022) 47459
Open: lunch + dinner daily (closed 20 Dec-28 Feb)
Meals served: lunch 12.30-2, dinner 7-9

£55

The O'Callaghans ensure that Longueville House remains in good hands. Its 16 bedrooms are well kept and the old beds are charming and comfortable. Irish presidents look sternly from the paintings on the restaurant walls. The O'Callaghan's son William is the chef: particularly good are the breast of farmyard duck served with the leg confit and a ginger and coriander sauce and the Longueville lamb baked in a potato crust. Should you be dining as a party, a 'Surprise Menu' is available which allows a selection of special dishes.

Midleton — Farm Gate

The Coolbawn, Midleton, Co Cork
Telephone: (021) 632771
Open: lunch Tue-Sun, dinner Tue-Sat (closed 25+26 Dec, Good Friday)
Meals served: lunch 12-3.30, dinner 7-9.45
Delicatessen and café, lots of home baking.

£40

Moycullen — Drimcong House Restaurant

Moycullen, Co Galway
Telephone: (091) 85115
Open: dinner Tue-Sat (closed Xmas-Mar)
Meals served: dinner 7-10.30

£45

This white Georgian house provides a happy environment in which to eat some good food prepared by chef and owner Gerry Galvin. Gerry likes to keep his menus short but this doesn't mean to say that they lack interest. His regional Irish cooking has its roots firmly in the French tradition and only the best local produce is used. Game terrine, roast rack of mutton with its gravy, a confit of duck in a chutney and port flavoured sauce, and baked free-range chicken are dishes that have featured in the past. Vegetarians are well catered for with a separate menu and the organically grown vegetables lend added flavour. Friendly service and a relaxed atmosphere with the food served on polished oak tables. There are roaring fires in winter. If you feel like a weekend away from it all, try one of the Drimcong Food and Wine Experiences. An immediate choice when you're in the county.

NAVAN	Ardboyne Hotel

Dublin Road, Navan, Co Meath
Telephone: (046) 23119 £45
Fax: (046) 22155
Open: lunch + dinner daily (closed 24-27 Dec)
Meals served: lunch 12.30-2.30 (Sun 12.30-3), dinner 5-10 (Sat 5-10.30, Sun 5.30-9)
Modern 27-bedroomed hotel.

NEWMARKET-ON-FERGUS	Dromoland Castle

Newmarket-on-Fergus, Co Clare
Telephone: (061) 368 144 £85
Fax: (061) 363 355
Open: lunch + dinner daily
Meals served: lunch 12.20-2, dinner 7.30-10
Imposing hotel standing on the edge of its own lake. Award winning restaurant.

NEWPORT Newport House

Newport, Co Mayo
Telephone: (098) 41222 **£60**
Fax: (098) 41613
Open: dinner daily (closed 7 Oct-18 Mar)
Meals served: dinner 7.30-9.30

You'll enjoy charmingly old-fashioned Irish hospitality here at Newport House where the days pass quietly and without any hurry. The building is an architectural delight and the 20 bedrooms are individually furnished with antiques. In the dining room, chef John Gavin turns out some eminently respectable cooking which allows the intrinsic flavours to speak for themselves. With such good quality Irish produce why try to interfere? Medallions of venison with fresh chanterelles, poached turbot with lobster sauce and sautéed pigeon breast with peaches are characteristic dishes and home-smoked salmon is a house speciality. The wine list is impressively wide-ranging and covers a similarly broad spectrum of prices.

OUGHTERARD Currarevagh House

Oughterard, Connemara, Co Galway
Telephone: (091) 82313 **£40**
Open: dinner daily (closed Nov-Mar)
Meals served: dinner at 8

This family-run hotel is a Victorian manor set in its own 150 acres of park and woodland which guards its privacy, ensuring that guest can relax and unwind. Wander in the beautiful gardens with lawns overlooking Currarevagh Bay, take tea in the drawing room and generally get to know the place at your leisure. If you stay overnight, look out for the superb Edwardian-style breakfasts which are laid out on the dining-room sideboard. Expect good, straightforward cooking in the dining room with a traditional roast often forming the centrepiece of the menus.

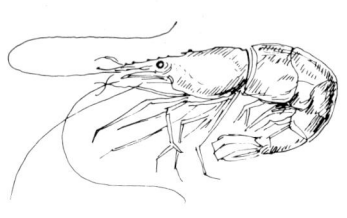

Oysterhaven	The Oystercatcher

Oysterhaven, Co Cork
Telephone: 021-770822 £65
Open: dinner daily (closed Jan)
Meals served: dinner 7.30-9.30

Down beside a creek just outside Kinsale, a flower-clad cottage has been converted and filled with pictures and antiques to make this olde-worlde restaurant. But the extensive set menu is modern and owner-chef Bill Patterson presents fashionable dishes such as wild mushrooms in a brioche, or pressed duck confit with morels and port, followed by braised pigs trotter stuffed with sweetbreads or steamed breast of guinea fowl with green grapes. Prettily presented desserts include a good crème brûlée.

Rathmullan	Rathmullan House

Rathmullan, Nr Letterkenny, Co Donegal
Telephone: (074) 58188 £45
Fax: (074) 58200
Open: lunch Sun, dinner daily (closed Nov-mid Mar)
Meals served: lunch 1-2, dinner 7.30-8.45
Georgian house overlooking Lough Swilly, in peaceful countryside. Twenty-three bedrooms.

Rathnew	Tinakilly House

Rathnew, Wicklow, Co Wicklow
Telephone: (0404) 69274 £65
Fax: (0404) 67806
Open: lunch + dinner daily
Meals served: lunch 12.30-2, dinner 7.30-9
Beautiful gardens with a glimpse of the Irish sea beyond. Amongst the amenities here they list 'peace and quiet' – sounds wonderful!

Roundwood	Roundwood Inn

Roundwood, Co Wicklow
Telephone: (01) 281 8107 £55
Open: lunch Tue-Sun, dinner Tue-Sat (closed 25 Dec, Good Friday)
Meals served: lunch 1-2.30, dinner 7.30-9.30 (Sat 7.30-10)

Chef Paul Taube cooks intuitively at the Roundwood Inn. Formerly renowned for bar food, things have shifted up a gear and now there are more sophisticated options on offer. Roast rack of Wicklow lamb, fresh lobster, fresh grilled salmon, venison ragout or sautéed half pheasant with port wine sauce.

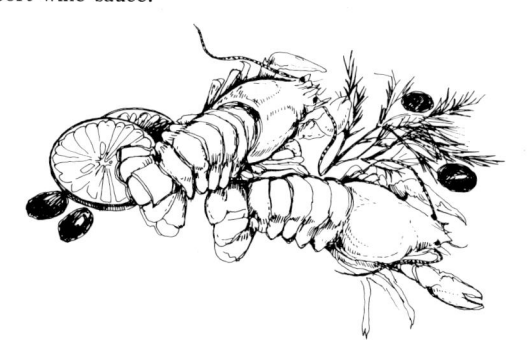

SHANAGARRY — Ballymaloe House

Shanagarry, Co Cork
Telephone: (021) 652531 £70
Fax: (021) 652021
Open: lunch Sun, dinner daily (buffet only on Sun) (closed 24-26 Dec)
Meals served: lunch at 1, dinner 7-9.30 (Sun only at 7.30)

Self-taught chef Myrtle Allen started off with just a few formica tables and ideas garnered from articles by Robert Carrier. Reading and endless experimentation, adapting French methods to Irish raw materials, and a lot of hard work have brought her a long way. For now Ballymaloe has an undisputed international reputation and many awards to its name. The dining room is the centre of interest with many paintings on the walls, including several by Jack B. Yeats. His confident handling of texture and colour has more than a little in common with Myrtle's cooking. Fish comes from Ballycotton, sea urchins and shellfish from Kenmare, meat from the local farmers and herbs, vegetables and fruit from Myrtle's own kitchen garden. Choose a starter from the huge hors d'oeuvres buffet which includes a range of seafood, pâtés, terrines and whatever else is top of Myrtle Allen's list for the day. Perhaps a roast duck with sage and onion stuffing or turbot served with sea kale and hollandaise sauce. Excellent vegetables. Leave room for the wonderful puddings, sometimes simple but always full of flavour. Good home-made ice cream. Wine list with some reasonably-priced and well-chosen wines. The 29 bedrooms have views out across the fields and it is impossible not to feel absorbed into the rural life of southern Ireland. Book well in advance for an experience not to be missed. *See also p280 – our Clover Awards section.*

SPIDDAL — Boluisce Seafood Bar

Spiddal Village, Connemara, Co Galway
Telephone: (091) 83286 £35
Open: all day Mon-Sat, dinner Sun (closed 24-26 Dec, Good Friday)
Meals served: 12-10 (Sun 4-10)
Just as it says, fresh seafood and the beautiful Connemara countryside, good value for money.

Straffan	Kildare Hotel & Country Club

Straffan, Co Kildare
Telephone: (01) 6273333 £80
Fax: (01) 6273312
Open: lunch Sun-Fri
Meals served: lunch 12.30-2, dinner 7.30-10

Set in lush countryside and overlooking its own 18-hole Arnold Palmer-designed golf course, this hotel (formerly Straffan House) holds a unique position of unrivalled opulence and a sense of other-worldliness which is heightened by a distinctly French atmosphere, a legacy from the Barton wine family who lived here in the 19th century. The interior is magnificent in concept, with superb furnishings and a wonderful collection of original paintings by well-known artists, including William Orpen and Jack B. Yeats, who has a room devoted to his work. All rooms and bathrooms are individually designed in the grand style, with great attention to detail.

Although the Byerley Turk restaurant is in a new wing, the impressively draped tall windows, marble columns and rich decor in tones of deep terracotta, cream and green harmonise perfectly with the style of the original house and it takes a sharp eye to detect the differences. The room is cleverly shaped to create semi-private areas and make the most of window tables, laid with crested china, monogrammed white linen, gleaming modern crystal and silver. Chef Michel Flamme's leanings towards classical French cuisine are tempered by traditional Irish influences – in dishes such as 'champ' potatoes served with grilled black and white pudding with apple sauce, or roast tail of monkfish with a smoked bacon and red peppercorn sauce – and, especially now that his new kitchen garden is coming on stream, by local home-grown seasonal produce, as in a simple fool of summer fruits.

Thomastown	Mount Juliet Hotel

Mount Juliet, Thomastown, Co Kilkenny
Telephone: (056) 24455 £65
Fax: (056) 24522
Open: lunch + dinner daily
Meals served: lunch 12.30-2 (Sun 1-2.30), dinner 7-9.30

A high percentage of guests are from the Continent, drawn here by the superb surroundings, the many outdoor pursuits available and the fine 18th-century building itself. There are 32 delightfully-styled suites and bedrooms. The interior of the house reflects its beautiful location with some original intricate plasterwork in the lofty Georgian dining room and some other beautifully-proportioned rooms. An extensive wine list at the top end of the range. The 18-hole Jack Nicklaus Signature Golf Course and 3-hole Golf Academy should be opened by the time you read this. The menu offers some interesting sounding choices which might include a lettuce and herb soup, a rack of lamb served in its own juice but basted with tanzy and garlic, a tranche of steamed wild salmon in a pastry trellis served on a little seaweed and accompanied by a fresh tarragon sauce.

WATERFORD	Dwyers
8 Mary Street, Waterford, Co Waterford	
Telephone: (051) 77478	£40
Open: dinner Mon-Sat (closed 3 days Xmas, 5 days Nov)	
Meals served: dinner 6-10	
Popular restaurant, modern European cooking.	

WATERFORD — Waterford Castle

The Island, Ballinakill, Waterford, Co Waterford
Telephone: (051) 78203 £65
Fax: (051) 79316
Open: lunch + dinner daily
Meals served: lunch 12.30-2 (Sun 11.30-2), dinner 7-10 (Sun 7-9)

There's always something magical about being on an island and staying at Waterford Castle is no exception to the rule. This 18th-century castle, with its gargoyles, towers and studded oak doors gives a hint of Medieval times and has plenty of what the guide books call 'character', but the dining room and lounges are comfortably light and airy with panelled walls and Regency-style furnishings. The 19 bedrooms are fittingly grand with their 4-posters and polished wood furnishings. You can dine in style here as well and chef Paul McCluskey delivers some impressive food which is both tasty and wholesome. Fillets of black sole with wild mushrooms, duckling sautéed with ginger and pears and fillet of lamb with two mint sauces are typical of what's on offer. In addition, there is a separate vegetarian menu available. Wine list is in keeping with what you would expect to find in a castle. The 300-acre island also boasts its own 18-hole golf course and facilities for other sporting pursuits.

WICKLOW — Old Rectory

Wicklow, Co Wicklow
Telephone: (0404) 67048 £50
Fax: (0404) 69181
Open: dinner daily (closed Nov-Easter)
Meals served: dinner at 8

Linda and Paul Saunders go out of their way to provide every convenience and nothing seems too much trouble – whether a booking for the next stage of your holiday or a particular food fad. In the dining room there is a friendly atmosphere, 12 people being the absolute maximum. Linda's cooking is a combination of old and new styles using organically grown produce – even edible flowers. Such emphasis upon purity of ingredients means that her canvas is small but exquisite and dishes can take a while to arrive at the table. But then this is in keeping with the general tempo of things. Reasonably-priced wine list.

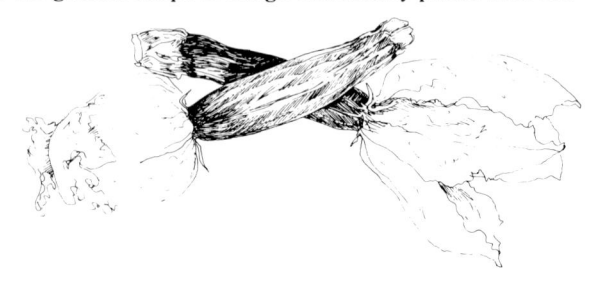

YOUGHAL	Aherne's Seafood Restaurant

163 North Main Street, Youghal, Co Cork
Telephone: (0404) 67048 £50
Fax: (024) 92424
Open: lunch + dinner daily (closed 4 days Xmas)
Meals served: lunch 12.30-2 (Sun 12.30-1.45), dinner 6.30-9.30

Now a third generation family enterprise, come here for wonderful fresh fish and sea food -pan-fried salmon with a light white wine sauce; poached sole with prawns in a beurre blanc sauce; prawns, crab, mussels, clams and oysters cooked in olive oil and their own juices. The all-day bar menu is inherited from the days when the building was a pub. Well worth a visit. There are now 10 en-suite bedrooms allowing you to stay overnight and indulge yourself in yet more delicious seafood for lunch the following day.

A Picture Round-up

CAFÉ FLO

the successful Café Flo group of Russell Joffe, offers some interesting food in attractive surroundings with a relaxed atmosphere.
These can be found at:-

205 Haverstock Hill
London NW3 4QG
071 435 6744

51 St Martin's Lane
London WC2N 4EA
071 836 8289

149 Kew Road
Richmond
Surrey TW9 2PN
081 940 8298

334 Upper Street
Islington
London N1 8EA
071 226 7916

127-129 Kensington Church Street
London W8 7LP
071 727 8142

676 Fulham Road
London SW6 5SA
071 371 9673

CAFÉ FLO

— " SPECIALITES " —

SALADE FLO 3.95
our house salad of avocado, roquefort, gruyere with salad leaves and vegetables with a basil dressing

MOULES MARINIÈRE 4.75
mussels with white wine, parsley, shallots & cream

SALADE ORIENTALE 4.75
stir fried marinated chicken salad with soya, ginger & sesame oil on a crisp salad

PÂTES AU PISTOU 3.95
Pasta with a creamy garlic, basil & parmesan sauce

PAIN A L'AIL 1.25
crusty garlic & herb bread

— " L'IDEE FLO " • 6.95 — — " PRIX FIXE " — 12.95

L'IDEE FLO	PRIX FIXE
SOUPE DU JOUR	SOUPE DE POISSONS
SALADE MIXTE	BRANDADE MAROCAINE
— " —	— " —
STEAK FRITES	SALADE FRISEE AUX LARDONS
POISSON FRITES	— " —
OMELETTE AU CHOIX	POISSON SELON LE MARCHÉ
CAFÉ FILTRE	STEAK D'AGNEAU GRILLÉE AU PISTOU ROUGE
	POULET GRILLÉ À L'HUILE DE PROVENCE
	— " —
	CAFÉ FILTRE

A few extracts from Flo's menu

One of a delightful series of postcards with which Café Flo advertises their regional food 'festivals'

BRETAGNE ARRIVÉ À 1992 **CAFÉ FLO**

St. Malo ~ Flo en Vacances — from a postcard by Ken Thompson

An extract from the afternoon menu at Café Rouge

Branches below:—

LE MENU de L'APRES MIDI

AVAILABLE from 3pm - 6pm

SOUPE de JOUR – Soup of the Day	1.95
TERRINE MAISON	2.95
Paté of Chicken Livers flavoured with Madeira	
ASSIETTE de CRUDITÉS	3.95
Selection of Crudités with Sour Cream Dip	
ASSIETTE de CHARCUTERIE	3.95
A Selection of Charcuterie and Pork Rillettes	
ASSIETTE de SAUMON FUMÉ	4.65
A Plate of Scottish Oak-Smoked Salmon	
CAMEMBERT FRIT	2.95
Deep-fried Camembert with a Fresh Fruit Coulis	
SALADE NIÇOISE	3.95
Traditional French Salad of Egg, Anchovies, Black Olives, Green Beans & Tuna	
SALADE TIÈDE de POULET, SAUCE MOUTARDE à l'ANCIENNE	3.75
Warm Chicken Salad with a Light Mustard Dressing	
SALADE d'ÉPINARDS aux FOIES de VOLAILLE	3.95
Salad of Fresh Spinach Leaves and Sauteed Chicken Livers	
SALADE de CHÈVRE TIÈDE aux OLIVES	4.50
Grilled Goats Cheese on Croutons with Salad and Black Olives	
CROQUE MONSIEUR PANACHÉ	3.95
Grilled Ham and Gruyère Cheese Sandwich served with a Small Tossed Salad	
CROQUE au THON, SALADE NIÇOISE	3.95
Grilled Tuna and Gruyère Cheese Sandwich garnished with Salad Niçoise	
BAGUETTE du CAFÉ ROUGE	4.65
Char-grilled Steak sliced into a Warm Baguette with Salad and Dijon Mayonnaise	
POMMES FRITES	.95p
CORBEILLE de PAIN	.95p
Basket of Fresh Bread and Butter	

PLEASE SEE OVERLEAF FOR OUR WINES AND BEERS

LES COUPES GLACÉES

AVAILABLE from 3pm - 6pm

CAFÉ LIEGEOIS	2.95
Coffee Ice Cream Marbled with Coffee, Chantilly Cream	
CHOCOLAT LIEGEOIS	2.95
Chocolate Ice Cream, Chocolate Sauce, Chantilly Cream	
POIRE BELLE HÉLÈNE	2.95
Vanilla Ice Cream, Pear, topped with Chocolate Sauce	
LA COUPE du ROUGE	3.15
Vanilla Ice Cream, Mango Sorbet, Fresh Seasonal Fruits with a Fresh Fruit Coulis and Chantilly Cream	

CAFE ROUGE

19 High Street
Hampstead
London NW3 1PX
071-433 3404

31 Kensington Park Road
Portobello
London W11 2EU
071-221 4449

3a Petersham Road
Richmond
Surrey TW10 5HA
081 332 2423

200 Putney Bridge Road
Putney
London SW15 2NA
081 788 4257

855 Fulham Road
Fulham
London SW6 5HJ
071 371 7600

390 Kings Road
Chelsea London SW3 5UZ   071 352 2226

6-7 South Grove
Highgate
London N6 6BP
081-342 9797

46-48 James Street
London
W1N 5HS
071 487 4847

2 Lancer Square
Kensington Church St
London W8
071 938 4200

26 High Street
Wimbledon
London SW19 2JE
081 944 5131

Hays Galleria
Tooley Street
London SE1
071 378 0097

A PICTURE ROUND-UP 555

The Café Rouge in Kensington Church St — very untypical design

The Café Rouge formula has judged the market spot on, affordable prices in an interesting decor that people recognise & whilst some say derivative in style — I say they are giving the customers what they want.
— deservedly busy bistros.

'DOWNSTAIRS AT ONE NINETY'

Cocktail tomatoes, Bocconcini & basil Bruschetta

Bright red & yellow tomatoes with vivid green basil leaves & golden bread

Lobster & chips

dipped in beer batter
chunky real chips

Poached red wine pear served with creamy Gorgonzola & rocket leaves

Good ice creams — try the cinnamon

'Downstairs at One Ninety'
190, Queen's Gate, London SW7 5EU   071-581-5666

A PICTURE ROUND-UP

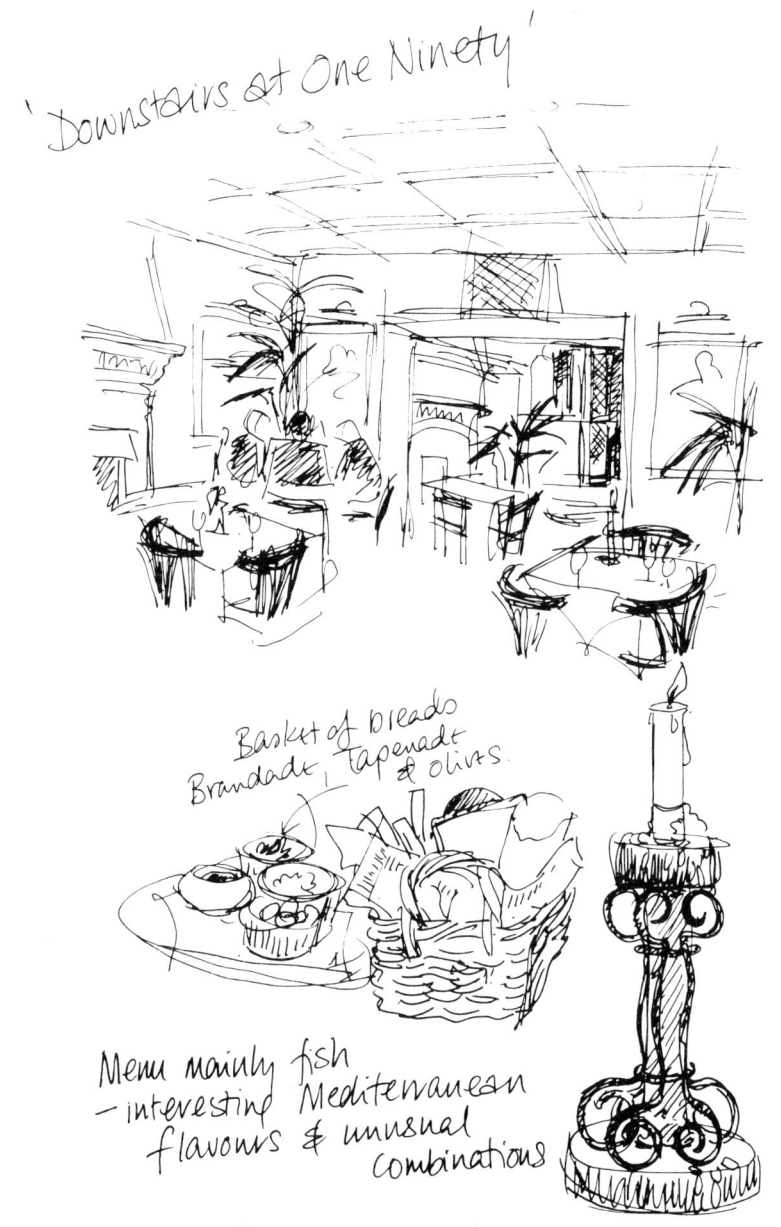

'Downstairs at One Ninety'

Basket of breads, Brandade, Tapenade & olives.

Menu mainly fish — interesting Mediterranean flavours & unusual combinations

Bourride of Salt Cod & Monkfish with Aioli   6.50
Mussel, Ginger & Saffron Chowder   4.95
Turbot Steak, Sea Asparagus & Pesto Potatoes   13.95
Saffron & Mussel Risotto with Scallop & Nori Tempura   7.50
Char-grilled Tuna Balsamico with Niçoise Salad   11.50
Fish & Chips :- Cod   Lobster   Scallop or Fritto Misto
Specials included :- Grouse, Venison   Also the AWT Seafood Pizza with truffled Leeks & Capers at 8.95

558 THE ACKERMAN CHARLES HEIDSIECK GUIDE 1993

Sketches of Scotland

'Ardsheal House Hotel' with beautiful views over Loch Linnhe

The imposing stone entrance to the Gean House in Alloa — a luxury hotel with imposing grounds & woodlands. Log fires and good food will welcome you.

The Gean House, Al

Kilberry Inn, Kilberry
Scotland PA29 6YD
(08803) 223

Tiny white cottage that delivers very good food of the home-made 'old fashioned country' sort. Bread, jams chutneys as well. Very much a dining pub.

A PICTURE ROUND-UP 559

Bishopstrow House
Nr. Warminster.

The Royal Crescent Hotel, Bath.

Three hotels within a 20 mile radius of each other & all offer a degree of comfort & luxury above the average.
All are distinguished by their attention to detail & beautiful furnishings. SEE ENTRIES.

Lucknam Park, Colerne, Nr. Bath.

CERCLE DES AMBASSADEURS DE L'EXCELLENCE

The Cercle des Ambassadeurs de l'Excellence was created by Champagne Charles Heidsieck to celebrate the 140th anniversary of this 'grande marque' champagne. This unique circle has – appropriately – 140 founder members who represent the very best of gastronomic excellence in this country. Listed below are the members (and the host restaurant/hotel, applicable at the time of the award) of the Cercle des Ambassadeurs de L'Excellence. Those who are featured in The Ackerman Charles Heidsieck Guide 1993 are in bold and throughout this guide these members are also identified by a champagne bottle symbol next to their entry.

LONDON

Member	Host restaurant/hotel
Mr Roy Ackerman, OBE	(Leading Guides)
Paul Gayler	The Lanesborough Hotel
Mr Raymond André	Le Meridien
Mr George Goring	Goring Hotel
Frances Bissell	(Food Writer)
Mr Patrick Gwynn-Jones	**Pomegranates**
Mr Neville Blech	**Mijanou**
Sonia Blech	**Mijanou**
Mr Eduard Hari	Grosvenor House Hotel
Mr Vaughan Archer	**London Hilton Hotel**
Mr Gary Hollihead	Sutherlands
Mr Don Hewitson	**Cork & Bottle**
Mr Simon Hopkinson	**Bibendum**
Mr Philip Britten	**The Capital Hotel**
Mr Lazlo Holecz	**Gay Hussar**
Mr Michael Broadbent	(Christie's)
Mr Terry Holmes	**The Ritz**
Mr Antonio Carluccio	**Neal Street Restaurant**
Mr Ronald Jones, OBE	**Claridges**
Susan Cavalier	Cavaliers
Mr Kevin Kennedy	**Boulestin**
Mr David Chambers	**Le Meridien Hotel**
Mr John King	Les Ambassadeurs
Mr Malcolm Broadbent	Cadogan Hotel
Mr Peter Kromberg	**Inter-Continental Hotel**
Mr Stephen Bull	**Stephen Bull Restaurant Ltd**
Mr David Cavalier	Cavaliers
Mr Robin Lees, CB, MBE	**(British Rest. & Caterers Ass.)**
Mr Gian Chiandetti	Forte plc
Mr David Levin	**The Capital Hotel**
Miss Prudence Leith	**Leith's Restaurant**
Mr Michael Coaker	**May Fair Inter-Continental Hotel**
Mr Brian Cotterill	(Chefs & Cooks Circle)
Mr Eddie Khoo	Le Menage à Trois
Mr Peter Davies	**Le Gavroche**
Mr Pierre Koffman	**La Tante Claire**
Mr Nico Ladenis	**Chez Nico**
Mr Rowley Leigh	**Kensington Place**
Marjan Lesnik	Claridge's
Mr Alastair Little	**Alastair Little Restaurant**
Mr Pierre Martin	**Le Suquet**
Mr Christian Delteil	**L'Arlequin**
Mr Robert Mey	**Hyatt Carlton Tower**
Sally Clarke	Clarke's
Monsieur Bruno Loubet	**Inn on the Park**
Mr Philip Corrick	RAC Club
Mr Eric Deblonde	Four Seasons Hotel
Mr Eoin Dillon	Copthorne Tara Hotel
Mr Anton Mosimann	**Mosimann's**
Mr David Dorricott	**Portman Inter-Continental**
Mr Michael Nadell	Nadell Patisserie
Mr Anton Edelmann	**The Savoy**
Mr Ricci Obertelli	**The Dorchester**
Lord Forte	Forte plc
Mr David Foskett	(Ealing College)
Mr Nicholas Picolet	**Au Jardin des Gourmets**
Mr Bernard Gaume	**Hyatt Carlton Tower**
Mr Keith Podmore	Boodles
Monsieur Jean Quéro	**Hyatt Carlton Tower**
Silvano Giraldin	**Le Gavroche**
Simone Green	**Odette's**
Mr Ramon Pajares	**The Inn on the Park**
Mr Jean-Pierre Durantet	**La Tante Claire**
Mr Bev Puxley	(Westminster College)
Mr Gary Rhodes	**The Greenhouse**
Jancis Robinson	(Writer/Broadcaster)
The Hon. Rocco Forte	Forte plc
Mr Richard Shepherd	**Langan's Brasserie**
Mr Egon Ronay	(Consultant)
Monsieur Albert Roux	**Le Gavroche**
Mr Duncan Rutter	(HCTC)
Mr Giles Shepard	The Savoy Group of Hotels
Me Herbert Striessnig	The Savoy
Mr Brian Turner	**Turner's**
Mr Bryan Webb	**Hilaire**
Mr Marco-Pierre White	**Harveys**
Carla Tomasi	Frith's
Mr Peter Webber	My Kinda Town
Sir Hugh Wontner	**The Savoy Group**
Dagmar Woodward	The May Fair
Mr Paolo Zago	**The Connaught**
Mr Antony Worrall Thompson, MOGB	**dell'Ugo**

ENGLAND

Member	Host restaurant/hotel
Mr Douglas Barrington, OBE	The Lygon Arms
Doreen Boulding	**Danesfield House**
Mr David Adlard	**Adlard's Restaurant**
Mr Willy Bauer	Wentworth Club
Mr Raymond Blanc	**Le Manoir Aux Quat'Saisons**
Mr Mauro Bregoli	**Old Manor House Restaurant**
Mr John Burton-Race	**L'Ortolan Restaurant**
Mr Kit Chapman, MBE	**The Castle Hotel**
Mr Kevin Cape	**The Bell Inn**
Mr Victor Ceserani	(Consultant)
Mr Peter Chandler	**Paris House**
Mr Pierre Chevillard	**Chewton Glen**
Mr John Dicken	**Dicken's Restaurant**
Mr Christopher Cole	**Lucknam Park**
Mr Francis Coulson	**Sharrow Bay Country House Hotel**
Mr Alain Desenclos	**Le Manoir aux Quat'Saisons**
Mr Clive Fretwell	**Le Manoir aux Quat'Saisons**
Mr Peter Herbert	**Gravetye Manor Hotel**
Mr Hugh Johnson	(Writer/Broadcaster)
Mr Tim Hart	**Hambleton Hall**
Mr Shaun Hill	**Gidleigh Park Hotel**
Mr John Huber	(Thames Valley College)
Mr Murdo MacSween	**Oakley Court Hotel**
Kathryn McWhirter	Bramlands
Joyce Molyneux	**The Carved Angel**
Mr Guy Mouilleron	(Chef/Consultant)
Sir Colin Marshall	(British Airways)
Mr Gerald Milsom, OBE	**Le Talbooth Restaurant**
Mr Harry Murray	The Imperial Hotel
Mr Bob Payton	**Stapleford Park**
Mr Martyn Pearn	**Buckland Manor**
Monsieur Michel Perraud, MOGB	**Les Alouettes**
Mr David Pitchford	**Read's Restaurant**
Monsieur Michel Roux	**The Waterside Inn**
Mr Brian Sack	**Sharrow Bay Country House Hotel**
Mr Martin Skan	**Chewton Glen**
Mr Peter Smedley	**Ston Easton Park**
The Hon John Sinclair	Cliveden
Mr Jonathan W Slater	**The Chester Grosvenor**
Kate Smith	The Beetle & Wedge Hotel
Mr Richard Smith	**The Beetle & Wedge Hotel**
Mr C A Jonathan Thompson	Hartwell House
Mr Michael Womersley	**Lucknam Park Hotel**
Mr Rick Stein	**The Seafood Restaurant**
Mr Auberon Waugh	(Writer)

SCOTLAND

Member	Host restaurant/hotel
Mr Alan Hill	**The Gleneagles Hotel**
Mrs Grete Hobbs	**Inverlochy Castle**
Mr Peter J Lederer, MI, FHCIMA	**The Gleneagles Hotel**
Mr David Wilson	The Peat Inn

WALES

Member	Host restaurant/hotel
Mr Franco Taruschio	**Walnut Tree Inn**

ALL CHAMPAGNE CHARLES HEIDSIECK IS WELL-AGED, IN A CELLAR THAT IS ABSOLUTELY ANCIENT

We have the ancient Romans (or rather their slaves) to thank for digging the deep chalk cellars in which every bottle of Champagne Charles Heidsieck spends at least three years.

The cellars are over 2,000 years old (double 'millénaires') and house many of our greatest treasures, including examples of our pure Chardonnay vintage, Charles Heidsieck Blanc des Millénaires.

Blanc des Millénaires

Charles Heidsieck
CHAMPAGNE
FOR THE RARELY IMPRESSED

Nico at Ninety & Grosvenor House Hotel

The smart polished entrance plaque reflects the standard of service that awaits you.

Grillade de coquilles St Jacques aux pochettes et aux nouilles fraîches.

NICO AT NINETY 563

Moments of intense concentration in the kitchen contrast with the unhurried serenity of the dining room.

The brigade get their heads down to produce tempting dishes such as pintade aux abricots à la farce de boudin blanc.

The hard work ethic is instilled into Nico's staff who prove that many hands do, indeed, make light work.

below: *Nico, in pursuit of perfection, requires the undivided attention of Paul Flynn, Head Chef.*

below: *Tartine briochée de foie gras chaud et d'orange caramelisée.*

The delicate furnishings of the elegant dining room.

Deft preparation.

Honey-coloured panelling, well-spaced tables with crisp, white linen on a sea-green carpet create a formal dining room with a relaxed ambience.

above: *Nico allowing time for discussion with his brigade.*

below: *Pastel-coloured, deep-cushioned settees replace the well-upholstered chairs at a few of the tables.*

EXTRA PERFECTION
DE
RÉMY MARTIN

Fine Champagne Cognac comes exclusively from grapes grown in the two best areas of the Cognac district of France - at least 50% from the Grande Champagne and the rest from the Petite Champagne.

Rémy Martin Extra Perfection is a blend of older Fine Champagne *eaux-de-vie* of particular distinction, creating an extraordinarily complex balance of rich and delicate flavours.

RÉMY MARTIN

Beautiful floral displays and clever lighting are part of the major refurbishments recently carried out at Grosvenor House.

above: *Unusual but elegant decor make the perfect setting for a refreshing drink.*

below: *Italian cuisine in stylish surroundings at the Pasta Vino Restaurant.*

above: *Sip afternoon tea whilst admiring the views over Hyde Park.*

below: *Another of the well-furnished areas for a relaxed drink.*

GROSVENOR HOUSE HOTEL 575

above: *Round-the-clock room service in the refurbished and updated suites.*

below: *Solid chairs with strong colours maintain a balance with the pastel-coloured settees creating a delicate match in the lounge.*

The intricate carvings of this table epitomise the relentless care and attention to detail paid by the Grosvenor House management and staff.

THE ACKERMAN CHARLES HEIDSIECK GUIDE 1993 **577**

1. SOUTH-WEST ENGLAND & WALES

The maps show only those villages, towns and cities where recommended hotels and restaurants may be found.

578 THE ACKERMAN CHARLES HEIDSIECK GUIDE 1993

THE ACKERMAN CHARLES HEIDSIECK GUIDE 1993

2. SOUTH & CENTRAL ENGLAND

Berwick-on-Tweed
Powburn
Alnwick
Longhorsley
NORTHUMBERLAND
Morpeth
Wylam
Hexham
Kiln Pit Hill
Brampton
Crosby-on-Eden
Wetheral
TYNE AND WEAR
Newcastle-upon-Tyne
East Boldon
Gateshead
Durham
DURHAM
West Auckland
Cotherstone
Darlington
CLEVELAND
Stokesley
Crathorne
Moulton
Richmond
Reeth
Staddlebridge
Goathland
Whitby
Helmsley
Whitwell-on-the-Hill
Kilburn
Masham
NORTH YORKSHIRE
Pateley Bridge
Markington
Knaresborough
York
Bilbrough
Harrogate
Pool-in-Wharfedale
Wath-in-Nidderdale
Hetton
Settle
Ilkley
Bolton Abbey
Haworth
WEST YORKSHIRE
Bradford
Leeds
Huddersfield
Ripponden
Delph
Barnsley
SOUTH
HUMBERSIDE
Walkington
Hull
Winteringham
Melmerby
Appleby-in-Westmorland
CUMBRIA
Bassenthwaite
Cockermouth
Applethwaite
Keswick
Ullswater
Easedale
Grasmere
Ambleside
Windermere
Bowness-on-Windermere
Kendal
Underbarrow
Lupton
Kirkby Lonsdale
Witherslack
Spark Bridge
Cartmel
Ulverston
Austwick
Clitheroe
Longridge
Langho
Garstang
Thornton-le-Fylde
Broughton
Thornton Cleveleys
Blackpool
LANCASHIRE
Ramsbottom
Bury
GREATER MANCHESTER
Isle of Man

THE ACKERMAN CHARLES HEIDSIECK GUIDE 1993 581

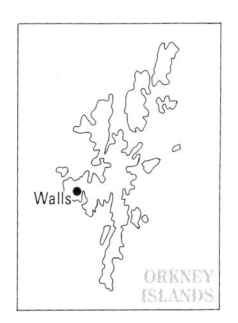

4. SCOTLAND

5. IRELAND

Index

A
Abbey Court, London W2, 65
Abbey Hotel, Penzance, 411
Abingworth Hall, Storrington, 433
Absolute End, Guernsey, 361
L'Accento Italiano, London W2, 65
Adam's Café, London W12, 66
Adare Manor, Adare, 525
Adlard's, Norwich, 404
Aghadoe Heights Hotel, Killarney, 543
Aherne's Seafood Restaurant, Youghal, 551
Airds Hotel, Port Appin, 497
Al Bustan, London SW1, 66
Al San Vincenzo, London W2, 66
Alastair Little, London W1, 67
Alba, London EC1, 68
Alderley Edge Hotel, Alderley Edge, 289
Alistair Greig's Grill, London W1, 68
Allt Yr Ynys Hotel, Walterstone, 452
Allt-Nan-Ros Hotel, Onich, 495
Les Alouettes, Claygate, 334
Alp-Horn, Edinburgh, 478
Alston Hall, Holbeton, 369
Altnaharrie Inn, Ullapool, 501
L'Altro, London W11, 69
Alverton Manor, Truro, 446
Amberley Castle, Amberley, 291
Angel Hotel, Bury St Edmunds, 322
Angel Inn, Hetton, 367
Angel Inn, Stoke-by-Nayland, 431
Ann Fitzgerald's Farmhouse Kitchen, Mathry, 513
Anna's Place, London N1, 70
Annie's, Ballydehob, 527
Annie's, Moreton-in-Marsh, 397
Annie's, Swansea, 516
Antico, Eton, 348
Arbutus Lodge, Cork, 531
Ard-Na-Coille Hotel, Newtonmore, 494
Ardanaiseig, Kilchrenan, 489
Ardboyne Hotel, Navan, 546
Ardsheal House, Kentallen Of Appin, 489
The Argyll, London SW3, 71
Arisaig House, Arisaig, 468

Ark, Erpingham, 348
L'Arlequin, London SW8, 72
Armadillo, Liverpool, 385
Armathwaite Hall, Bassenthwaite Lake, 298
Armless Dragon, Cardiff, 505
Armstrong's, Barnsley, 296
Artillery Tower, Plymouth, 412
L'Artiste Assoiffé, London W11, 72
Arts Theatre Café, London WC2, 73
Arundell Arms, Lifton, 384
Ashford Castle, Cong, 531
Ashwick House, Dulverton, 343
Assolas Country House, Kanturk, 542
At The Sign of The Angel, Lacock, 379
The Athenaeum, London W1, 73
Au Bois St Jean, London NW8, 74
Au Bon Accueil, London SW3, 74
Au Jardin Des Gourmets, London W1, 74
L'auberge, Edinburgh, 478
Auburn Lodge, Ennis, 540
Auchendean Lodge, Dulnain Bridge, 477
Audleys Wood, Basingstoke, 297
Aval du Creux, Sark, 422
L'Aventure, London NW8, 75

B
Bacco, London NW7, 75
Bahn Thai, London W1, 75
Baile-Na-Cille, Uig, 501
Balbirnie House, Markinch, 493
Balgonie House, Ballater, 470
Ballathie House, Kinclaven By Stanley, 491
Ballylickey Manor House, Ballylickey, 528
Ballymaloe House, Shanagarry, 548
La Barbe, Reigate, 416
Barnard's, Cosham, 338
Barrett's Restaurant, Glemsford, 355
Basil Street Hotel, London SW3, 76
Bath Place Hotel & Restaurant, Oxford, 407
Bath Spa Hotel, Bath, 299
Baumann's Brasserie, Coggeshall, 335
Bay Horse Inn & Bistro, Ulverston, 449
Bay Tree, Sheffield, 423
Bear Hotel, Crickhowell, 507

Bear Hotel, Woodstock, 460
Beckfords, Chepstow, 506
Beechfield House, Beanacre, 301
Beetle & Wedge, Moulsford-on-Thames, 398
Bel Alp House, Haytor, 365
Belfast Castle, Belfast, 519
Bell Inn, Aston Clinton, 294
La Belle Alliance, Blandford Forum, 307
La Belle Epoque, Knutsford, 378
La Belle Epoque, Belfast, 519
Belton Woods Hotel, Belton, 302
Belvedere In Holland Park, London W8, 76
Benedicts, Altrincham, 290
Le Berger, Bramley, 311
The Berkeley, London SW1, 77
Berkshire Hotel, London W1, 77
Bertorelli's, London WC2, 78
Bettys Café & Tea Rooms, Harrogate, 363
Bibendum Oyster Bar, London SW3, 79
Bibendum, London SW3, 78
Bibi's Italian Restaurant, Leeds, 382
Bilbrough Manor, Bilbrough, 303
Billboard Café, London NW6, 79
Billesley Manor, Stratford-upon-Avon, 435
Bishopstrow House, Warminster, 452
Bistro Montparnasse, Southsea, 427
Bistro Twenty One, Bristol, 315
Le Bistro, Hull, 370
Bistrot 190, London SW7, 80
Black Bull, Moulton, 398
Black House, Hexham, 368
Black Swan, Beckingham, 301
Blackgate Restaurant, Newcastle-upon-Tyne, 401
Blackheath House & MacDuff's Restaurant, Garvagh, 522
Blairs Cove House, Durrus, 539
Blakes Hotel, London SW7, 81
Bloom's, London E1, 82
Bloom's, London NW11, 81
Blooms Hotel, Dublin, 535
Blostin's Restaurant, Shepton Mallet, 424
Blue Anchor Inn, East Aberthaw, 507

Blue Elephant, London SW6, 82
Blue Goose, Bristol, 315
Blue Goose, Settle, 422
Blue Raincoat, Galway, 540
Blueprint Café, London SE1, 83
Bodysgallen Hall, Llandudno, 510
Boluisce Seafood Bar, Spiddal, 548
Bombay Brasserie, London SW7, 83
Bon Appetit, Malahide, 544
Boncompte's, Douglas, 343
Bond's Hotel & Restaurant, Castle Cary, 325
La Bonne Auberge, South Godstone, 426
La Bonne Franquette, Egham, 347
Restaurant Bonnet, Cranleigh, 338
Borthwick Castle, North Middleton, 495
Boscundle Manor, St Austell, 420
Restaurant Bosquet, Kenilworth, 377
Boulestin, London WC2, 84
Box Tree, Ilkley, 372
Boyd's, London W8, 85
The Brackenbury, London W6, 85
Le Braconnier, London SW14, 86
Bradfield House, Bradfield Combust, 310
Braeval Old Mill, Aberfoyle, 466
Branigans Restaurant, Belfast, 519
La Braseria, Swansea, 516
Brasserie Du Marche Aux Puces, London W10, 86
Brasserie Forty Four, Leeds, 383
Brasserie on West Regent Street, Glasgow, 483
La Brasserie, Cardiff, 505
La Brasserie, London SW3, 86
Breamish House, Powburn, 414
Bridgefield House, Spark Bridge, 428
Brockencote Hall, Chaddesley Corbett, 325
Brookdale House, North Huish, 402
Broughton Park, Broughton, 320
Brown's Hotel, London W1, 87
Browns Bistro, Clitheroe, 334
Browns Restaurant, Ipswich, 372
Browns, Cambridge, 323
Browns, Oxford, 407
Brown's, Worcester, 461
Brundholme Country House Hotel, Keswick, 377
Bryan's of Headingley, Leeds, 383
Bubb's, London EC1, 87
Buckland Manor, Buckland, 321
The Bull at Charlbury, Charlbury, 327
Bully's, Cork, 532
Bunbury's, Barry, 504
Bunchrew House, Inverness, 488
Burgh Island Hotel, Bigbury-on-Sea, 302
Burgoyne Hotel, Reeth, 416
Burts Hotel, Melrose, 493
Butley-Orford Oysterage, Orford, 406
Buttery, Glasgow, 484

C
Le Cadre, London N8, 88
Caer Beris Manor, Builth Wells, 505
Café Anjou, London N13, 88
Café Caruso, Dublin, 535
Café Cezanne, Twickenham, 447
Café Delancey, London NW1, 88
Café Delancey, London WC1, 89
Café Des Amis Du Vin, London WC2, 89
Café Du Marché, London EC1, 90
Café Fish, London SW1, 91
Café Fleur, Harrogate, 363
Café Flo, London NW3, 91
Café Flo, London WC2, 91
Café Nicoise, Colwyn Bay, 506
Café Pelican, London WC2, 92
Café Procope, Newcastle-upon-Tyne, 401
Café Royal Grill Room, London W1, 92
Calcot Manor, Tetbury, 442
Caledonian Hotel, Edinburgh, 478
Callow Hall, Ashbourne, 293
Camden Brasserie, London NW1, 93
Canal Brasserie, London W10, 93
Cannizaro House, London SW19, 94
The Capital, London SW3, 95
Le Caprice, London SW1, 96
Captain's Table, Woodbridge, 460
Le Carapace, London SW1, 96
Caravan Serai, London W1, 96
Carraro's, London SW8, 97
Carved Angel, Dartmouth, 340
Casa Cominetti, London SE6, 98
Casale Franco, London N1, 98
Cashel House, Cashel, 529
Cashel Palace, Cashel, 529
Le Cassoulet, Cardiff, 505
Castle Hotel, Taunton, 441
Castle Inn, Castle Combe, 325
Castleton House, Glamis, 483
Cavendish Hotel, Baslow, 297
Cefn Goleu Park, Gowerton, 508
Ceilidh Place, Ullapool, 501
Cellar, Anstruther, 468
Cellars, Dundalk, 538
Celtic Manor, Newport, 514
The Cemlyn, Harlech, 509
Ceruttis, Hull, 370
Champany Inn Chop & Ale House, Linlithgow, 492
Champany Inn, Linlithgow, 492
Le Champenois Restaurant, West Mersea, 454
Champers, Cardiff, 505
Le Champignon Sauvage, Cheltenham, 328
Channings Hotel, Edinburgh, 479
Chapeltoun House, Stewarton, 500
Chapter 11, London SW10, 99
Chapters, Stokesley, 431
Charingworth Manor, Charingworth, 327
Charlotte's Place, London W5, 99
Charnwood Hotel, Sheffield, 423
Château la Chaire, Jersey, 373
Chedington Court, Chedington, 328
Cheevers, Tunbridge Wells, 446
Chelsea Hotel, London SW1, 100
Cherwell Boathouse, Oxford, 408
Chester Grosvenor, Chester, 330
Chesterfield Hotel, London W1, 101
Chewton Glen, New Milton, 400
Chez Hans, Cashel, 530
Chez Liline, London N4, 101
Chez Max, Surbiton, 439
Chez Moi, London W11, 102
Chez Nous, Plymouth, 412
Chilston Park, Lenham, 384
Chilvester Hill House, Calne, 322
Chimneys, Long Melford, 386
Chinon, London W14, 103
La Chouette, Dinton, 342
Christian's, London W4, 103
Christopher's, London WC2, 104
Chung Ying Garden, Birmingham, 304

INDEX 585

Chung Ying, Birmingham, 304
Chutney Mary, London SW10, 105
Ciao, London SW6, 106
Cibo, London W14, 107
Circle East, London SE1, 107
Circus Restaurant, Bath, 299
Claire de Lune Brasserie, Bruton, 320
Clarets Restaurant, St Austell, 421
Claridge's, London W1, 108
Clarke's, Easton, 346
Clarke's, London W8, 109
Clifford's, Cork, 532
Clifton Hotel, Nairn, 494
Cliveden, Taplow, 440
The Close, Tetbury, 442
Cnapan Country House, Newport, 514
Cobbett's, Botley, 308
Cobwebs, Cowan Bridge, 338
Cockle Warren Cottage, Hayling Island, 365
Coed-y-Mwstwr Hotel, Coychurch, 507
Coffee Gallery, London WC1, 109
Collaven Manor, Sourton, 426
Collin House, Broadway, 318
Collin House, Castle Douglas, 473
Combe Grove Manor Hotel, Monkton Combe, 396
Combe House, Gittisham, 355
Comme Ca, Chichester, 332
Congham Hall, Grimston, 360
The Connaught, London W1, 110
Connemara Coast Hotel, Furbo, 540
Hotel Conrad, London SW10, 111
Conrah Country Hotel, Aberystwyth, 504
Copper Inn, Pangbourne, 409
Copperfields Restaurant, Corsham, 337
Le Coq Hardi, Dublin, 535
Cork & Bottle, London WC2, 111
Cormorant Hotel, Golant, 355
Corney & Barrow, London EC2, 112
Corney & Barrow, London EC2, 112
Corney & Barrow, London EC4, 113
Corse Lawn House, Corse Lawn, 337
Cotswold House, Chipping Camden, 332
Cottage in the Wood, Malvern, 391

The Cottage, Shanklin Old Village, 423
Cottons Hotel, Knutsford, 379
Coul House, Contin, 473
Country Friends, Dorrington, 343
County Hotel, Canterbury, 324
Courtney's Restaurant, Newcastle-upon-Tyne, 401
Crabwall Manor, Chester, 331
Craigendarroch Hotel, Ballater, 470
Crannog Seafood Restaurant, Fort William, 482
Crathorne Hall, Crathorne, 339
Creag Mor, Gairloch, 483
Creggans Inn, Strachur, 500
Crinan Hotel, Crinan, 474
Cringletie House, Peebles, 496
La Croisette, London SW10, 113
Cromlix House, Dunblane, 477
Croque-en-Bouche, Malvern, 391
Crosby Lodge, Crosby-on-Eden, 339
The Cross, Kingussie, 491
Crown Liquor Saloon, Belfast, 519
Crown at Whitebrook, Whitebrook, 518
The Crown, Southwold, 428
Crowthers, London SW14, 114
Culloden Hotel, Holywood, 523
Culloden House, Inverness, 488
Currarevagh House, Oughterard, 546
Cwrt Bleddyn Hotel, Llangybi, 511
Czech Club, London NW6, 114

D

Dalmahoy Hotel, Kirknewton, 491
Dan's, London SW3, 114
Danescombe Valley Hotel, Calstock, 322
Danesfield House, Medmenham, 394
Danieli, London W4, 114
Daphne, London NW1, 114
D'Arcy's, Glasgow, 484
De Selby's, Dun Laoghaire, 538
Deals West Restaurant Diner, London W1, 114
Dell'arte, London SW1, 115
Dell'ugo, London W1, 115
Depot, London SW14, 116
Devonshire Arms, Bolton Abbey, 307
Dew Pond, Old Burghclere, 406

Dicken's, Wethersfield, 454
Dinham Hall, Ludlow, 388
Dobbins Wine Bistro, Dublin, 535
Dolmelynllyn Hall, Dolgellau, 507
Don Pepe, London NW8, 116
The Dorchester, London W1, 117
La Dordogne, London W4, 118
Doric Tavern Wine Bar & Bistro, Edinburgh, 479
Dormy House, Broadway, 318
Dower House, Muir-of-Ord, 493
Down Hall, Hatfield Heath, 365
Downtown Sulemans, London SE1, 118
Doyle's School House, Castledermot, 530
Doyle's Seafood Bar & Townhouse, Dingle, 534
Dragon Inn, London W1, 118
Dragon's Nest, London W1, 118
Drimcong House Restaurant, Moycullen, 545
Dromoland Castle, Newmarket-on-Fergus, 546
Drum & Monkey, Harrogate, 363
Drumnacree House, Alyth, 467
Dryburgh Abbey, Dryburgh, 477
Dukes Hotel, Belfast, 519
Dukes Hotel, London SW1, 119
Dunadry Inn, Dunadry, 522
Dunain Park, Inverness, 488
Dundas Arms, Kintbury, 378
Dunderry Lodge Restaurant, Dunderry, 538
Dundonnell Hotel, Dundonnell, 478
Dunraven Arms, Adare, 525
Dunworley Cottage, Dunworley, 539
The Dusty Miller Restaurant, Pateley Bridge, 410
Dwyers, Waterford, 550
Dylanwad Da, Dolgellau, 507

E

The Eagle, London EC1, 119
Eastbury Hotel, Sherborne, 424
Eastington Grange Hotel, Stonehouse, 431
Eastwell Manor, Ashford, 293

Edwinn's Restaurant, Shepperton, 424
Egerton Grey, Porthkerry, 515
Eglantine, Tunbridge Wells, 446
El Nido, Garstang, 354
Elcot Park Resort Hotel, Elcot, 347
Eleven Park Walk, London SW10, 120
Restaurant Elizabeth, Oxford, 408
Elms Hotel, Abberley, 289
Embleton Hall, Morpeth, 397
English Garden, London SW3, 120
English House, London SW3, 121
Enniscree Lodge Inn, Enniskerry, 540
Enoteca, London SW15, 121
Epicurean & On The Park, Cheltenham, 329
Epicurean Bistro, Stow-on-the-Wold, 434
Equities, London EC2, 121
L'escargot, Herne Bay, 367
Esseborne Manor, Hurstbourne Tarrant, 372
Est, London W1, 122
L'Estaminet, London WC2, 122
Ettington Park, Stratford-upon-Avon, 435

F
The Factor's House, Fort William, 482
Fairyhill, Reynoldston, 516
Falcon Hotel, Stratford-upon-Avon, 436
La Famiglia, London SW10, 122
Fantails, Wetheral, 454
Faraday's, Aberdeen, 465
Farlam Hall, Brampton, 312
Farleyer House, Aberfeldy, 466
Farm Gate, Midleton, 545
Farmhouse Hotel & Restaurant, Lew, 384
Feathers Hotel, Woodstock, 461
Feathers Hotel, Ludlow, 388
Feldon House, Lower Brailes, 387
Fen House Restaurant, Ely, 347
The Fenja, London SW3, 123
Fern Grove, Kilmun, 490
Ferns, Louth, 387
La Fiesta, Dublin, 535
Fifehead Manor, Middle Wallop, 396
15 North Parade, Oxford, 408
La Fin De La Chasse, London N16, 123
First Floor, London W11, 123

Fischer's Baslow Hall, Baslow, 298
Fisherman's Lodge, Newcastle-upon-Tyne, 402
La Fleur de Lys, Shaftesbury, 422
Flitwick Manor, Flitwick, 352
Floodlite Restaurant, Masham, 393
Florians, London N8, 123
Food for Thought, Fowey, 353
Foresters Arms Hotel, Kilburn, 377
Forsters, East Boldon, 344
42 The Calls, Leeds, 382
Restaurant 44, Belfast, 520
Fountain House & Dedham Hall, Dedham, 341
Four Park Place, Knaresborough, 378
Fouters Bistro, Ayr, 469
Fox and Goose, Fressingfield, 354
Franc's, Altrincham, 290
Franc's, Chester, 331
Frederick's, London N1, 124
Fredrick's, Maidenhead, 390
French Brasserie, Altrincham, 290
French Partridge, Horton, 370
La Frégate, Guernsey, 361
Fung Shing, London WC2, 124
Funnywayt'mekalivin, Berwick-on-Tweed, 302

G
G & T's Village Bistro, Porth, 515
Gaby's Seafood Restaurant, Killarney, 543
Galley, Swanage, 439
Gannets Bistrot, Newark, 400
La Gaulette, London W1, 124
Gavin's, London SW15, 124
Le Gavroche, London W1, 125
Gavver's, London SW1, 126
Gay Hussar, London W1, 126
Gaylord, Manchester, 392
Geale's, London W8, 127
Gean House, Alloa, 467
Gee's, Oxford, 409
George & Dragon, Rowde, 419
George's Brasserie, Canterbury, 324
Ghyll Manor, Rusper, 419
Gidleigh Park, Chagford, 326
Gilbert's, London SW7, 127
Gilpin Lodge, Bowness-on-Windermere, 309
Glaister's, London SW10, 127
Glazebrook House, South Brent, 426

Gleneagles Hotel, Auchterarder, 469
Glenfeochan House, Kilmore, 490
Gliffaes Country House Hotel, Crickhowell, 507
Gopal's Of Soho, London W1, 127
Gordleton Mill & Provence, Lymington, 389
The Goring, London SW1, 128
Grafton Français, London SW4, 128
Grafton Manor, Bromsgrove, 319
Grahame's Seafare, London W1, 128
Gran Paradiso, London SW1, 128
Le Grandgousier, Brighton, 314
Grand Hotel, Brighton, 313
Grand Hotel, Eastbourne, 346
Grange Hotel, York, 463
Granite Corner, Jersey, 373
Grapevine Hotel, Stow-on-the-Wold, 434
Gravetye Manor, East Grinstead, 345
Graviers, Norbiton, 402
Great House, Lavenham, 380
Green Cottage, London NW3, 128
Green's, London SW1, 129
Green's Restaurant & Oyster Bar, London SW1, 130
Greenhead House, Chapeltown, 326
Greenhouse, London W1, 129
Greens Seafood Restaurant, Norwich, 404
Greenway, Cheltenham, 329
Gregans Castle, Ballyvaughan, 528
Grey Door, Dublin, 536
Greywalls Hotel, Gullane, 486
Griffin Inn, Fletching, 352
Grill St Quentin, London SW3, 130
La Grillade, Leeds, 383
Gritti, London WC2, 131
Grosvenor House, London W1, 131
Grove House, Ledbury, 381
Guernica, London W1, 131

H
The Halcyon, London W11, 132
Half Door, Dingle, 535
Halkin Hotel, London SW1, 133
Halmpstone Manor, Bishop's Tawton, 305
Hambleton Hall, Oakham, 405
Hamiltons, Twickenham, 447

INDEX

Hampshire Hotel, London WC2, 133
Hanbury Manor, Thundridge, 444
Hanchurch Manor, Hanchurch, 362
Harbour Bistro, Ramsey, 416
Harding's Restaurant, North Berwick, 495
Harley, The Restaurant & Hotel, Sheffield, 424
Harry's Place, Great Gonerby, 358
Hartwell House, Aylesbury, 295
Harveys, London SW17, 134
Harveys Café, London SW10, 135
Haven Hotel, Poole, 413
Haycock Hotel, Wansford-in-England, 452
Hayward's, Brighton, 314
Heathcote's, Longridge, 386
Henry Wong, Birmingham, 304
Highgrove House, Troon, 501
Hilaire, London SW7, 136
Hill House, Horndon On The Hill, 369
Hilton Park, Clones, 530
Hindle Wakes, Midhurst, 396
Hintlesham Hall, Hintlesham, 368
Hinton Grange, Hinton, 368
L'Hippocampe, London W1, 137
Hive on the Quay, Aberaeron, 503
Hoar Cross Hall, Hoar Cross, 369
Hob Green, Markington, 393
Hodge Hill, Cartmel, 324
Holly Tree, Kentallen Of Appin, 489
Holne Chase, Ashburton, 293
Homewood Park, Bath, 299
Honfleur, Delph, 342
Honours Mill Restaurant, Edenbridge, 347
Hooke Hall, Uckfield, 448
Hope End, Ledbury, 382
Hotel l'Horizon, Jersey, 374
Horn of Plenty, Gulworthy, 362
Horsted Place, Uckfield, 448
Hospitality Inn, Brighton, 314
L'Hotel, London SW3, 137
Howard Hotel, Edinburgh, 479
Howard's, Bristol, 316
Howe Villa, Richmond, 416
Howie's Restaurant, Edinburgh, 479
Hubble & Co, London EC1, 138
Hughenden, Goudhurst, 356

Huguenot, Cork, 532
Hungry Monk Restaurant, Jevington, 376
The Hungry Monk, Greystones, 541
Hunstrete House, Hunstrete, 371
Hunt's, Bristol, 316
Hunters Lodge, Broadway, 318
Hunters, New Alresford, 399
Hunters, Ruthin, 516
Hunts Tor House, Drewsteignton, 343
Huntsham Court, Huntsham, 371
Hyatt Carlton Tower, London SW1, 138
Hyde Park Hotel, London SW1, 139
Hyn's, Ascot, 293

I

Idle Rocks Hotel, St Mawes, 421
Inchalla Hotel, Alderney, 289
L'Incontro, London SW1, 140
Indian Cavalry Club, Edinburgh, 479
Inn On The Park Hotel, London W1, 140
Inter-Continental Hotel, London W1, 141
Invercreran Hotel, Appin, 468
Inverlochy Castle, Fort William, 483
Invery House, Banchory, 471
Isaacs, Cork, 532
Isle of Eriska, Eriska, 481
The Ivy, London WC2, 142

J

Jack Fuller's, Brightling, 313
Jacques, Cork, 533
Jade Garden, London W1, 142
Jason Court Restaurant, London W1, 142
Jenny's Seafood Restaurant, Liverpool, 385
Jeremy's at The King's Head, Cuckfield, 339
Jersey Pottery, Jersey, 374
Joe Allen, London WC2, 143
Joe's Café, London SW3, 144
John Blackmore's Restaurant, Alnwick, 289
John Howard Hotel, London SW7, 144
Jules Café, Weobley, 454
Julie's, London W11, 144

K

Kalamaras, London W2, 145
Kapriol, Dublin, 536
Kaspia, London W1, 145
Kenny's, London NW3, 146

Kenny's, London SW3, 145
Kensington Place, London W8, 146
Kildare Hotel & Country Club, Straffan, 549
Kildrummy Castle, Kildrummy, 490
Kilfinan Hotel, Kilfinan, 490
Killiecrankie Hotel, Killiecrankie, 490
King Sitric, Howth, 541
Kings Head, Richmond, 416
Kingshead House, Birdlip, 303
Kinloch House, Blairgowrie, 472
Kinloch Lodge, Sleat, 499
Kinnaird, Dalguise, 476
Kinsella's, Ipswich, 372
Kipling's, Bridge Of Allan, 472
Kitchen at Polperro, Polperro, 412
Knipoch Hotel, Oban, 495
Knockie Lodge, Whitebridge, 501
Knockinaam Lodge, Portpatrick, 497
Krug's, Farnham, 351

L

Laburnum House, Wylam, 462
Lacken House, Kilkenny, 542
Lainston House, Winchester, 456
Lake Country House, Llangammarch Wells, 511
The Lake Isle, Uppingham, 451
Lake Vyrnwy Hotel, Lake Vyrnwy, 509
Lal Qila, London W1, 147
Lancrigg Vegetarian Country House, Easedale, 344
Landgate Bistro, Rye, 419
The Lanesborough, London SW1, 147
Langan's Bistro, Brighton, 314
Langan's Bistro, London W1, 148
Langan's Brasserie, London W1, 148
Langar Hall, Langar, 379
The Langham, London W1, 149
Langley House, Wiveliscombe, 459
Lathones Manor, St Andrews, 498
Launceston Place, London W8, 50
Laurent, London NW2, 150
The Leatherne Bottel, Goring-on-Thames, 356
Leeming House, Ullswater, 449
Leigh Park Hotel, Bradford-on-Avon, 310
Leith's, London W11, 151
Lettonie, Bristol, 316

Lewtrenchard Manor, Lewdown, 384
Lido, London W1, 151
Lilly's, London W11, 151
Lime Tree, Kenmare, 542
Linden Hall, Longhorsley, 386
Lindsay House, London W1, 152
Linthwaite House, Bowness-on-Windermere, 309
Linton Springs, Linton Springs, 385
The Little Angel, Remenham, 416
Little Barwick House, Yeovil, 462
Little Byres, Dallington, 339
Little Grove, Jersey, 374
Little Thakeham, Storrington, 433
Llangoed Hall, Llyswen, 513
Llechwen Hall, Abercynon, 503
Llew Glas, Harlech, 509
Llyndir Hall, Rossett, 516
Lobster Pot, Strangford, 524
Loch Fyne Oyster Bar, Cairndow, 472
Loch Fyne Oyster Bar, Nottingham, 405
London Hilton On Park Lane, London W1, 152
Long's, Blackwater, 306
Longfields Hotel, Dublin, 536
Longueville House, Mallow, 545
Longueville Manor, Jersey, 375
Lords of the Manor, Upper Slaughter, 451
Los Remos, London W2, 177
Lou Pescadou, London SW5, 152
Louisiana, Guernsey, 361
Low Hall, Leeds, 383
Lower Pitt, East Buckland, 345
Lower Slaughter Manor, Lower Slaughter, 388
Lowman Restaurant, Tiverton, 445
Luc's Restaurant & Brasserie, London EC3, 153
Lucknam Park, Colerne, 336
Lugleys, Wootton Common, 461
Lupton Tower, Lupton, 389
Lygon Arms, Broadway, 318
Lynton House, Holdenby, 369
Lynwood House, Barnstaple, 297

M
Mabey's Brasserie, Sudbury, 438
MacCloskey's, Bunratty, 529
Maes-y-Neuadd, Talsarnau, 517
Magno's Brasserie, London WC2, 153
Magpie Café, Whitby, 455
Magpies Restaurant, Horncastle, 369
Maiden Newton House, Maiden Newton, 390
Maison Talbooth, Dedham, 341
Malletts, Maulden, 393
Mallory Court, Leamington Spa, 381
Mallyan Spout, Goathland, 355
La Malmaison, Hersham, 367
Manley's, Storrington, 433
Le Manoir aux Quat'Saisons, Great Milton, 359
Manor House Inn, Kiln Pit Hill, 377
Manor House, Castle Combe, 325
Manor House, Walkington, 452
Manor Restaurant & Hotel, Leicester, 384
The Manor, Chadlington, 326
Mansion House, Poole, 413
Manzara, London W11, 153
Manzi's, London WC2, 154
Manzi's, London E14, 154
Le Marché Noir, Edinburgh, 479
Marco's, Norwich, 404
La Marinade, Brighton, 314
Marine Ices, London NW3, 154
Market Restaurant, Manchester, 392
Markwick's, Bristol, 317
Marlfield House, Gorey, 541
Marsh Country Hotel, Eyton, 350
Marsh Goose, Moreton-in-Marsh, 397
Martha's Vineyard, Nayland, 399
Martin's Bistro & Bar, London NW1, 154
Martin's, Edinburgh, 480
Maryculter House, Maryculter, 493
Mauro's, Bollington, 307
Max's Wine Bar, Kinsale, 543
Maxine's, Midhurst, 396
May Fair Inter-Continental, London W1, 154
McClements, Twickenham, 447
McCoy's, Staddle Bridge, 429
Meadowsweet, Llanrwst, 512

Mélange, London WC2, 154
Melton's, York, 463
Le Meridien, London W1, 155
Mermaid Inn, Rye, 420
Meson Don Felipe, London SE1, 156
Meson Doña Ana, London W11, 156
Meudon Hotel, Mawnan Smith, 394
Michael's Nook, Grasmere, 356
Michel's, Ripley, 417
Middlethorpe Hall, York, 464
Le Midi, London SW6, 156
Midsummer House, Cambridge, 323
Mijanou, London SW1, 156
Milk House, Montacute, 397
Mill Arms Inn, Dunbridge, 344
Mill House, Kingham, 377
The Mill, Harvington, 364
Millburns Restaurant, London W1, 157
Miller Howe, Windermere, 457
Miller's, Harrogate, 364
Millwaters, Newbury, 400
Mimmo D'Ischia, London SW1, 157
Mirabelle, London W1, 157
Miskin Manor, Miskin, 513
Miyama, London EC4, 158
Miyama, London W1, 158
Mon Petit Plaisir, London WC2, 158
Mon Plaisir, London WC2, 158
Le Monde, Cardiff, 505
Monet's, Helmsley, 366
Monkeys, London SW3, 159
Mont Clare Hotel, Dublin, 537
Montagu Arms, Beaulieu, 301
Moon, Kendal, 376
Moore Place, Aspley Guise, 294
The Moorings, Wells-next-the-Sea, 454
Morel's, Haslemere, 364
Morrisons Island Hotel, Cork, 533
Morteyne Manor, Marston Morteyne, 393
Mortimer's Seafood Restaurant, Bury St Edmunds, 322
Mortimer's on the Quay, Ipswich, 373
Mortons House Hotel, Corfe Castle, 336
Mosimann's, London SW1, 159
Moss Nook, Manchester, 392
Motcomb's, London SW1, 160
Mottram Hall, Mottram St Andrew, 397

Mount Falcon Castle, Ballina, 527
Mount Juliet Hotel, Thomastown, 549
Mr Underhill's, Stonham, 432
Mulberry House, Torquay, 445
Mulligan's Of Mayfair, London W1, 161
Murrayshall House, Scone, 499
Le Muscadet, London W1, 161
Muset, Bristol, 317
Museum Street Café, London WC1, 162
Mustard Seed, Adare, 526

N
Nakano, London SW1, 162
Nansidwell, Mawnan Smith, 394
National Gallery Brasserie & Café, London WC2, 162
Le Nautique, Guernsey, 361
Neal Street Restaurant, London WC2, 163
Nellie Gray's Restaurant, Alderney, 289
Neshiko, London N1, 164
New Hall, Sutton Coldfield, 439
New House Country Hotel, Cardiff, 506
New Mill Restaurant, Eversley, 349
Newport House, Newport, 546
Newtons, London SW4, 164
Nick's Warehouse, Belfast, 520
Nico At Ninety, London W1, 165
Nico Central, London W1, 165
Nightingales, Taunton, 441
Nikita's, London SW10, 166
Restaurant 19, Bradford, 310
19 Grape Lane, York, 463
Norma's Café, London W4, 166
Normandie Hotel & Restaurant, Bury, 321
North & South, London SW19, 166
North West Castle, Stranraer, 500
Northcote Manor, Langho, 380
Norton House, Ingliston, 488
Norton Place, Birmingham, 304
Now & Zen, London WC2, 166
Glastonbury, 355
Number One, Swansea, 517
Number Thirty Three, Perth, 496
No. 3 Restaurant & Hotel, No. 28, Standon, 430

Number Twenty Four, Wymondham, 462
Nunsmere Hall, Sandiway, 421
Nuthurst Grange, Hockley Heath, 369

O
O'Grady's, Clifden, 530
O'Keeffe's, Cork, 533
Oakes, Stroud, 437
Oakhill House, Oakhill, 406
Oakley Court, Windsor, 458
Oaks Hotel, Porlock, 413
Ockenden Manor, Cuckfield, 339
October Café, Glasgow, 484
October Restaurant, Bearsden, 471
Odette's, London NW1, 167
Odin's Restaurant, London W1, 168
Old Bakehouse Restaurant, Little Walsingham, 385
Old Beams, Waterhouses, 452
Old Bell Hotel, Malmesbury, 391
Old Bridge Hotel, Huntingdon, 371
Old Church Hotel, Ullswater, 449
Old Coach House, Barham, 296
Old Coffee Shop, Aberdovey, 503
Old Court House Inn, Jersey, 375
Old Fire Engine House, Ely, 347
Old Forge Restaurant, Newmill-on-Teviot, 494
Old Forge, Storrington, 434
Old Government House, Guernsey, 361
Old House Hotel, Wickham, 455
Old Inn, Crawfordsburn, 522
Old Manor House, Romsey, 418
Old Manor House, West Auckland, 454
Old Mansion House, Auchterhouse, 469
Old Monastery Restaurant, Drybridge, 477
The Old Plow Inn at Speen, Speen, 429
Old Post Office, Clun, 335
Old Presbytery, Kinsale, 544
Old Rectory, Campsea Ashe, 323
Old Rectory, Llansanffraid Glan Conwy, 512
Old Rectory, Wicklow, 550
Old Station Coffee Shop, Dinas Mawddwy, 507
Old Swan, Minster Lovell, 396
Old Vicarage, Ridgeway, 417
Old Vicarage, Witherslack, 459

Old Woolhouse, Northleach, 403
Olde Stocks Restaurant, Melton Mowbray, 395
Olivers, Staplecross, 430
Olivo, London SW1, 168
One Devonshire Gardens, Glasgow, 485
190 Queen's Gate, London SW7, 168
Orso, London WC2, 169
L'Ortolan, Shinfield, 425
Osteria Antica Bologna, London SW11, 170
Ostlers Close, Cupar, 475
Over the Bridge Restaurant, Ripponden, 417
The Oystercatcher, Oysterhaven, 547

P
P.A.'s Winebar, Mumbles, 513
La Paesana, London W8, 171
Painswick Hotel, Painswick, 409
Paris House, Woburn, 460
Paris II, Huddersfield, 370
Park Hotel, Kenmare, 542
Partners Brasserie, Sutton, 439
Partners West Street, Dorking, 342
Pasta Fresca, Dublin, 537
Pâtisserie Bliss, London EC1, 171
Patrick Guilbaud, Dublin, 537
Paul's, Folkestone, 353
Restaurant Peano, Barnsley, 296
Pear Tree, Purton, 415
Peat Inn, Peat Inn, 495
Pelham Hotel, London SW7, 171
Pennyhill Park, Bagshot, 295
Pennypots, Blackwater, 306
Penrhos Court, Kington, 378
Perkins Bar Bistro, Plumtree, 411
Perry's, Weymouth, 454
Le Petit Canard, Maiden Newton, 390
La Petite Auberge, Great Missenden, 360
Pheasant Inn, Bassenthwaite Lake, 298
Pied à Terre, London W1, 171
Pierre Victoire, Edinburgh, 480
Pink Geranium, Melbourn, 395
Pinocchio's, London NW1, 171
Pizzeria Castello, London SE1, 172
Pizzeria Condotti, London W1, 172
Pj's Bar & Grill, London SW10, 172

Pj's Bar & Grill, London WC2, 172
Plas Bodegroes, Pwllheli, 516
The Plough at Clanfield, Clanfield, 333
Plumber Manor, Sturminster Newton, 438
Poissonnerie De L'Avenue, London SW3, 172
Pollyanna's, London SW11, 173
Polmaily House, Drumnadrochit, 476
Pomegranates, London SW1, 173
Le Pont De La Tour, London SE1, 174
Pool Court, Pool-in-Wharfedale, 412
Pophams Café, Winkleigh, 458
Popjoy's, Bath, 300
Poppies Restaurant, Brimfield, 315
Port-An-Eilean Hotel, Strathtummel, 500
Portaferry Hotel, Portaferry, 523
Porters, Taunton, 441
Porters English Restaurant, London WC2, 174
Porth Tocyn Hotel, Abersoch, 504
Hotel Portmeirion, Portmeirion, 515
Portobello Dining Rooms, London W11, 174
La Potinière, Gullane, 486
Le Poulbot, London EC2, 175
Le Poussin, Brockenhurst, 319
Priory Hotel, Bath, 300
Le P'Tit Normand, London SW18, 175
Puckrup Hall, Puckrup, 414

Q
Le Quai St Pierre, London W8, 175
Quality Chop House, London EC1, 176
Quayles, Cardiff, 506
Queen's Head, Glanwydden, 508
Queensberry Hotel, Bath, 300
Quince & Medlar, Cockermouth, 335
Quincy's, London NW2, 176
Quincy's, Seaford, 422

R
Ram Jam Inn, Stretton, 436
Ramore, Portrush, 524
Rampsbeck Country House Hotel, Ullswater, 449
Ramside Hall, Durham, 344
Randalls, Bollington, 307
Rankins, Sissinghurst, 425
Rathmullan House, Rathmullan, 547
Read's, Faversham, 351
Rebato's, London SW8, 177
Red Fort, London W1, 177

Redmond's, Cheltenham, 330
Regency Park Hotel, Newbury, 401
Remy's, Torquay, 445
Hotel Renouf & Renouf's Restaurant, Rochford, 418
The Restaurant, London SW7, 177
Rhinefield House, Brockenhurst, 319
Riber Hall, Matlock, 393
Richard at Lanterns, Llandudno, 510
Ristorante Bari, York, 464
Ristorante Caprese, Glasgow, 485
Il Ristorante, Dalkey, 534
Ritcher's, Wells, 454
The Ritz, London W1, 177
Riva, London SW13, 178
River Café, London W6, 179
River House, Lympstone, 389
River House, Thornton-le-Fylde, 444
Riverside, Helford, 366
Riverside Hotel, Abersoch, 504
Riverside Hotel, Ashford-in-the-Water, 294
Riverside Inn, Canonbie, 473
Riverside Hotel, Evesham, 350
Riverside Restaurant, Bridport, 313
Roadhouse, Roade, 418
Rocher's, Milford-on-Sea, 396
Roches Bistro, Malahide, 544
Rochestown Park Hotel, Cork, 534
Rococo, Kings Lynn, 377
Rogano, Glasgow, 485
Restaurant Roger Burdell, Loughborough, 387
Roger's Restaurant, Windermere, 457
Roman Camp, Callander, 472
Rombalds Hotel, Ilkley, 372
Rookery Hall, Nantwich, 399
Roscoff, Belfast, 520
Röser's, Hastings, 364
Rose's, London NW3, 179
La Rosette, Ballasalla, 296
Rosleague Manor, Letterfrack, 544
Rothay Manor, Ambleside, 291
Round Table, Edinburgh, 480
Roundwood Inn, Roundwood, 547
Royal Bath Hotel, Bournemouth, 309
Royal Berkshire, Ascot, 293
Royal Crescent Hotel, Bath, 301

Royal George, Tintern Abbey, 517
Royal Lancaster Hotel, London W2, 179
Royal Oak, Sevenoaks, 422
Royal Oak, Yattendon, 462
RSJ, London SE1, 180
Rudloe Park, Corsham, 337
Rules Restaurant, London WC2, 180
Rumbles Cottage, Felsted, 352

S
St Andrews Old Course Hotel, St Andrews, 498
St Benedict's Grill, Norwich, 405
St David's Park Hotel, Ewloe, 508
St James Court Hotel, London SW1, 181
St Margaret's Lodge, Guernsey, 361
St Olaves Court, Exeter, 350
St Pierre Park Hotel, Guernsey, 361
St Quentin, London SW3, 182
St Tudno Hotel, Llandudno, 511
Salford Hall, Abbot's Salford, 289
Sambuca, London SW3, 183
San Frediano, London SW3, 183
San Lorenzo, London SW3, 183
San Martino, London SW3, 184
Sandrini, London SW3, 184
Santini, London SW1, 184
Sardis, Darlington, 340
SAS Portman Hotel, London W1, 185
Saverys Restaurant, Frampton-on-Severn, 353
Les Saveurs, London W1, 185
The Savoy, London WC2, 186
Scott's Restaurant, London W1, 186
Sea Crest, Jersey, 375
Seafood Bar, Falmouth, 351
Seafood Restaurant, Great Yarmouth, 360
Seafood Restaurant, Padstow, 409
Seaview Hotel, Seaview, 422
Sebastian, Oswestry, 407
Seiont Manor, Llanrug, 512
La Sémillante, London W1, 187
September Brasserie, Blackpool, 306
Serpentine Restaurant, London W2, 187
Seymour House, Chipping Campden, 333
Shakespeare Hotel, Stratford-upon-Avon, 436
Sharrow Bay, Ullswater, 450

INDEX 591

Sheekey's Restaurant, London WC2, 188
Sheelin, Bellanaleck, 521
Sheila's Cottage, Ambleside, 291
Shelbourne Hotel, Dublin, 537
Sheraton Hotel, Edinburgh, 480
Sheraton Park Tower, London SW1, 188
Shieldhill, Quothquan, 498
Shiro, Ahakista, 526
Shoes Restaurant, High Ongar, 368
The Shore, Edinburgh, 481
Signor Sassi, London SW1, 189
Silver Darling, Aberdeen, 465
Silver Plough, Pitton, 411
Simply Nico, London SW1, 189
Simpson's-in-the-Strand, London WC2, 190
Singapore Garden, London NW6, 190
Singing Chef, Ipswich, 373
Slassor's, Southend-on-Sea, 427
Sloans, Birmingham, 305
Snows On The Green, London W6, 191
Soanes, Petworth, 411
Soho Soho, London W1, 192
Somewhere Else, Bury St Edmunds, 322
Sonny's, London SW13, 192
Sonny's, Nottingham, 405
Soughton Hall, Northop, 514
Soulard Restaurant, London N1, 193
Sous le Nez en Ville, Leeds, 383
Sous le Nez, Ilkley, 372
South Lodge, Lower Beeding, 387
Spaghetti Junction, Teddington, 441
Spinnakers, Salcombe, 421
Splinters Restaurant, Christchurch, 333
Sportsman's Arms, Wath-in-Nidderdale, 453
Spread Eagle, Thame, 443
The Square, London SW1, 194
Sri Siam, London W1, 194
The Stables, Ayr, 470
The Stafford, London SW1, 195
Staithes, Cheltenham, 330
Stakis St Ermin's, London SW1, 195
Stane Street Hollow, Pulborough, 415
The Stannary, Mary Tavy, 393
Stanneylands, Wilmslow, 456
Stanwell House, Lymington, 389

Stapleford Park, Stapleford, 430
Starlings Castle, Oswestry, 407
The Starr, Great Dunmow, 358
State House, Land's End, 379
Stephen Bull Bistro, London EC1, 196
Stephen Bull, London W1, 196
Stephens Hall Hotel, Dublin, 538
Steppes Country House Hotel, Hereford, 366
Stock Hill House, Gillingham, 354
Ston Easton Park, Ston Easton, 431
Stone Hall, Welsh Hook, 518
Stone House, Rushlake Green, 419
Stonehouse Court, Stonehouse, 431
Stones, Avebury, 295
Stonor Arms, Stonor, 432
Stour Bay Café, Colchester, 335
Strand Restaurant, Belfast, 521
Stratford House, Stratford-upon-Avon, 436
Studley Priory, Horton Cum Studley, 370
Summer Isles, Achiltibuie, 467
Summer Lodge, Evershot, 349
Sundial Restaurant, Herstmonceux, 367
Le Suquet, London SW3, 197
Swallow Hotel, Birmingham, 305
The Swan, Bibury, 302
The Swan, Lavenham, 381
The Swan, Southwold, 428
Sweetings, London EC4, 197
Swinton House, Stow Bridge, 434
Swynford Paddocks, Six Mile Bottom, 426
Sychnant Pass Hotel, Conwy, 506
Sydney Brasserie, London SW11, 197
Sydney Street, London SW3, 198
Sykes House, Halford, 362
Symposio, London NW1, 198
Szechuan House, Edinburgh, 481

T

Table Restaurant, Torquay, 445
Le Talbooth, Dedham, 341
Tall House Restaurant, London SE1, 198
Tandoori Lane, London SW6, 198

La Tante Claire, London SW3, 199
Tanyard Hotel, Boughton Monchelsea, 308
Taychreggan Hotel, Kilchrenan, 489
Taynuilt Hotel, Taynuilt, 500
Templeton Hotel, Templepatrick, 524
Thackeray's House, Tunbridge Wells, 447
Thailand Restaurant, London SE14, 199
Thame Lane House, Abingdon, 289
Thara's, Colchester, 335
Theobalds, Ixworth, 373
Thierry's, London SW3, 200
34 Surrey Street Restaurant, Croydon, 339
36 On The Quay, Emsworth, 348
Thistells, London SW22, 200
Thistles, Cromarty, 474
Thomas Luny House, Teignmouth, 442
Thompson's, Chichester, 332
Thornbury Castle, Thornbury, 443
Three Chimneys Restaurant, Colbost, 473
The Three Lions, Stuckton, 437
Three Main Street, Fishguard, 508
Tinakilly House, Rathnew, 547
Tiramisu, London NW6, 201
Le Tire Bouchon, London W1, 201
Tiroran House, Tiroran, 500
Tobermory Hotel, Tobermory, 501
Tollbridge, Guist, 362
Tonlegee House, Athy, 527
Topps Hotel, Brighton, 315
Tottington Manor, Edburton, 346
The Tower, Sway, 440
The Traddock, Austwick, 294
Trattoria Lucca, London NW1, 201
Tre-Ysgawen Hall, Llangefni, 511
Trenchers, Whitby, 455
Trinity House Hotel, Coventry, 338
La Truffe Noire, London SE1, 201
Truffles Restaurant, Bruton, 320
Tufton Arms, Appleby-in-Westmorland, 292
Tullich Lodge, Ballater, 470
Tullythwaite House, Underbarrow, 451
Turner's, London SW3, 202

21 Queen Street, Newcastle-upon-Tyne, 401
Twenty Trinity Gardens, London SW9, 202
Restaurant Twenty Two, Cambridge, 323
Two Fat Ladies, Glasgow, 485
Tyddyn Llan, Llandrillo, 510
Tylney Hall, Rotherwick, 418

U
Ubiquitous Chip, Glasgow, 486
Underscar Manor, Applethwaite, 292
Uplands, Cartmel, 324

V
Le Vagabond, London SW18, 202
Veronica's, London W2, 203
Victor's Restaurant, Darlington, 340
Victoria Park, Wolverhampton, 460
Victorian House, Thornton Cleveleys, 444
Village Bakery, Melmerby, 395
Village Green, Trellech, 518
Village Restaurant, Ramsbottom, 415
Village Taverna, London SW10, 203
Villandry Dining Room, London W1, 203
Vine House, Paulerspury, 410
Vintners Room, The Vaults, Edinburgh, 481

W
Wakaba, London NW3, 203
The Waldorf, London WC2, 204
Wallett's Court, Dover, 343
Walnut Tree Inn, Abergavenny, 503
Walton Park, Clevedon, 334
Walton's, London SW3, 204
Wateredge Hotel, Ambleside, 292
Waterford Castle, Waterford, 550
The Waterside Inn, Bray-on-Thames, 312
Weavers, Diss, 342
Weavers, Haworth, 365
Welcome Restaurant, Belfast, 521
Welford Place, Leicester, 384
The Well House, Liskeard, 385
Well House, Watlington, 453
Well View Hotel, Moffat, 493
The Westbury, London W1, 204
Westerwood Hotel, Cumbernauld, 475
Weston Park, Shifnal, 425
Whatley Manor, Easton Grey, 346
Whipper-In Hotel, Oakham, 406
White Hart, Coggeshall, 335
White Hart, Exeter, 350
White Horse Inn, Chilgrove, 332
The White House, Herm, 366
White House, Williton, 456
White Moss House, Grasmere, 357
The White Tower, London W1, 205
Whitechapel Manor, South Molton, 427
Whitehall, Broxted, 320
Whites on the Green, Dublin, 538
Whittington's, London EC4, 205
Whitwell Hall, Whitwell-on-the-Hill, 455
Wickens, Northleach, 403
Wig & Mitre, Lincoln, 384
The Wilds, London SW10, 205
Will's, Bridport, 313
William Harding's House, Penkridge, 410
Wilton's, London SW1, 206
Windmill, Burgh Le Marsh, 321
Wine Bar, Woodbridge, 460
Winterbourne Hotel, Bonchurch, 308
Winteringham Fields, Winteringham, 458
Wodka, London W8, 206
Woodhayes Hotel, Whimple, 455
Woods Place, Grayshott, 358
Woods, Bath, 300
Woolley Grange, Bradford-on-Avon, 311
Wordsworth Hotel, Grasmere, 357
Wyck Hill House, Stow-on-the-Wold, 435

Y
Y Bistro, Llanberis, 509
Yang Sing, Manchester, 392
Ye Olde Bell, Hurley, 371
Ye Olde Bulls Head Inn, Beaumaris, 504
Yetman's, Holt, 369
Ynyshir Hall, Eglwysfach, 508
York House, Leamington Spa, 381

Z
Zen Cargo, London W1, 207
Zen Central, London W1, 207
Zen, London SW3, 206
Zenw3, London NW3, 207
Ziani, London SW3, 207